1965–1975

ESTHER GABARA

POP AMÉRICA

PUBLISHED BY NASHER MUSEUM OF ART AT DUKE UNIVERSITY

Published on the occasion of the exhibition *Pop América, 1965–1975*, co-organized by the Nasher Museum of Art at Duke University, Durham, North Carolina, and the McNay Art Museum, San Antonio, Texas. Guest curated by Esther Gabara, E. Blake Byrne Associate Professor of Romance Studies and associate professor of Art, Art History & Visual Studies at Duke University.

EXHIBITION ITINERARY

McNay Art Museum
October 4, 2018–January 13, 2019

Nasher Museum of Art at Duke University
February 21–July 21, 2019

Block Museum of Art, Northwestern University
September 21–December 8, 2019

Nasher Museum of Art at Duke University
2001 Campus Drive
Durham, North Carolina 27705
(919) 684–5135
www.nasher.duke.edu

Cataloging information for this title is available from the Library of Congress.
Library of Congress Control Number: 2018946497
ISBN 978-0-938989-42-4

Distributed by Duke University Press

Edited by Esther Gabara

Copyedited by María Eugenia Hidalgo (Spanish) and Lisa Kahan (English)

Translated by María Eugenia Hidalgo and Clara Marín

Proofread by Molly Boarati (English), Reneé Cagnina Haynes (English), and Natalia de la Rosa (Spanish)

Design, production, and typesetting by Reneé Cagnina Haynes

Set in Plaak (by Damien Gauthier of 205TF), Archer (Hoefler & Frere-Jones), and Helvetica LT Std.

Color separations and printing by Puritan Capital, Hollis, New Hampshire

Binding by HF Group-AcmeBinding

If, despite our best efforts, we have not correctly identified all copyrights, holders are asked to contact the Nasher Museum of Art at Duke University.

Pop América, 1965–1975 is a recipient of the inaugural Sotheby's Prize. The Sotheby's Prize is an annual award to support and encourage museums to break new ground. The grant aims to recognize curatorial excellence and to facilitate exhibitions that explore overlooked or underrepresented areas of art history.

This project is supported in part by an award from the National Endowment for the Arts.

Pop América, 1965–1975 is also supported by the Andy Warhol Foundation for the Visual Arts, the Nancy A. Nasher and David J. Haemisegger Family Fund for Exhibitions, Fox Family Foundation, Ann Chanler and Andrew Scheman, Lisa Lowenthal Pruzan and Jonathan Pruzan, Kelly Braddy Van Winkle and Lance Van Winkle, Parker & Otis, and Karen M. Rabenau and David H. Harpole.

Additional thanks to the Institute for Studies on Latin American Art (ISLAA) and to its president and founder, Ariel Aisiks.

At the McNay Art Museum, this exhibition is made possible by The Brown Foundation, Inc., and the Elizabeth Huth Coates Charitable Foundation of 1992.

Nasher Museum of Art exhibitions and programs are generously supported by the Mary Duke Biddle Foundation, the late Mary D. B. T. Semans and James H. Semans, the late Frank E. Hanscom III, the Duke Endowment, the Nancy Hanks Endowment, the Courtney Shives Art Museum Fund, the James Hustead Semans Memorial Fund, the Janine and J. Tomilson Hill Family Fund, the Trent A. Carmichael Fund for Community Education, the Neely Family Fund, the E. T. Rollins Jr. and Frances P. Rollins Fund for the Nasher Museum of Art at Duke University, the Marilyn M. Arthur Fund, the Sarah Schroth Fund, the George W. and Viola Mitchell Fearnside Endowment Fund, the Gibby and Michael B. Waitzkin Fund, the K. Brantley and Maxine E. Watson Endowment Fund, the Victor and Lenore Behar Endowment Fund, the Margaret Elizabeth Collett Fund, the Nasher Museum of Art General Endowment, the Friends of the Nasher Museum of Art, and the Office of the President and the Office of the Provost, Duke University.

THE
SOTHEBY'S
PRIZE

TO BREAK NEW GROUND

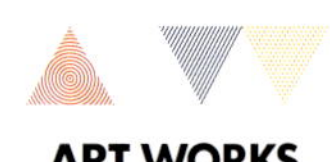

FRONT COVER
Pl. 77. Felipe Ehrenberg, *Caja no. 25495* (Box no. 25495)(detail), 1968. Acrylic on wooden box with marbles, 39.37 x 31.49 x 4.33 inches (100 x 80 x 11 cm). Collection of the Museo Universitario Arte Contemporáneo (MUAC) de la Universidad Nacional Autónoma de México (UNAM), Mexico City. Courtesy of Reina María de Lourdes Hernández Fuentes.

OPPOSITE
Pl. 26. Juan José Gurrola, *Familia Sandwich* (Sandwich Family) from the series *Dom-Art*, 1966–1967 (fabricated 2018). Photographic slide, 2 x 2 inches (5.08 x 5.08 cm). Courtesy of the Fundación Gurrola A.C. and House of Gaga, Mexico City, Mexico, and Los Angeles, California. Photo by Nattan Guzmán.

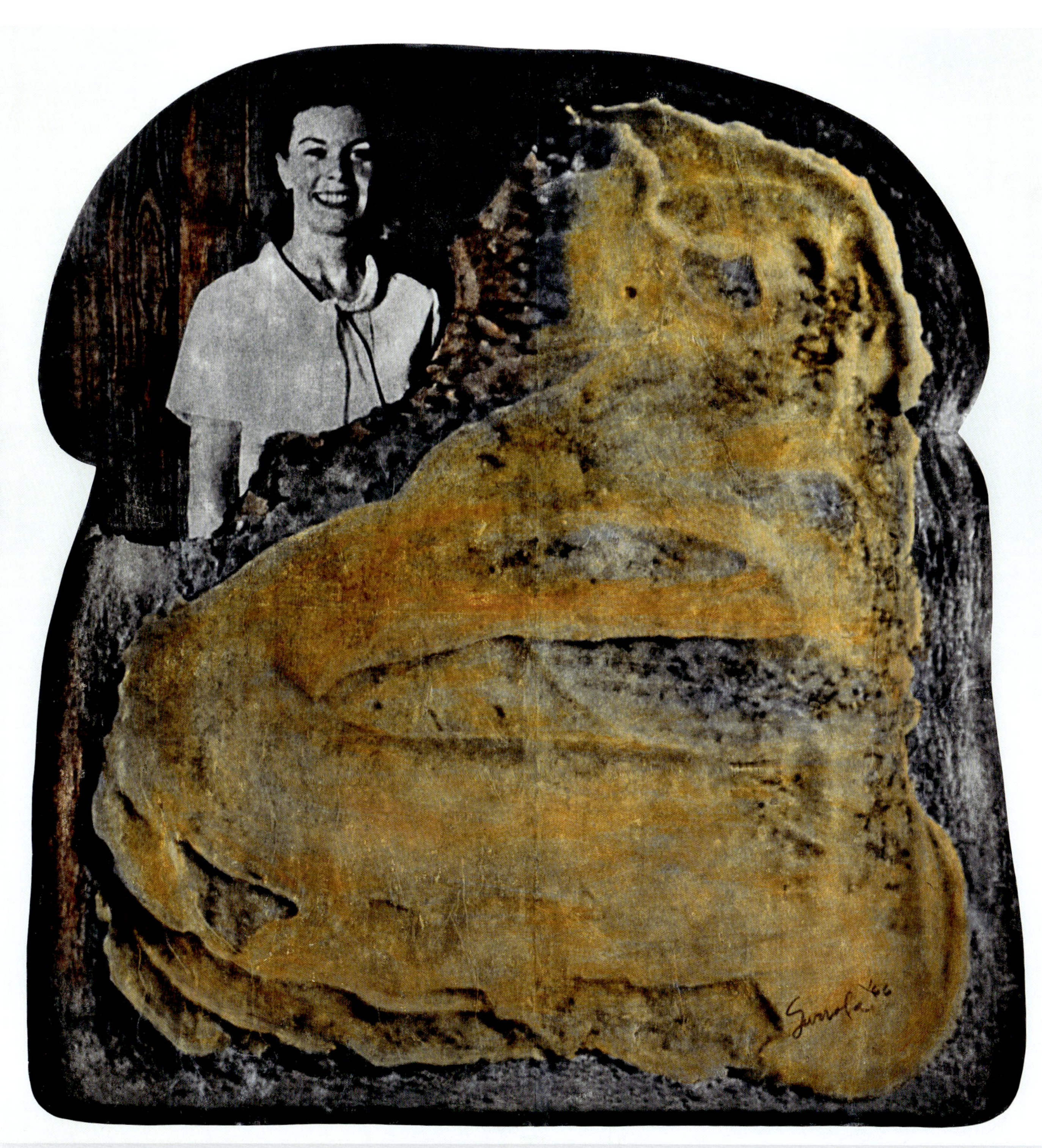

CONTENTS

DIRECTORS' FOREWORD

It is with great enthusiasm that the Nasher Museum of Art at Duke University and the McNay Art Museum partner to present *Pop América, 1965–1975*. This groundbreaking exhibition is the first to focus on Pop art in the Americas. Its original concept approaches "America" as a single continent or hemisphere, introducing new historical frameworks that reshape our very understanding of Pop. The question of Pop's placement within the art historical canon has recently been investigated in global terms, but *Pop América* opens our eyes specifically to the artistic production and critical dialogues that emerged from and around Latin America during this stirring decade. The exhibition's rigorous lines of inquiry provide the opportunity to engage in a deeper understanding of art, visual culture, and modern life in the Americas during the 1960s and 1970s. Through the study of the vibrant art included in this exhibition and bilingual catalogue, we can begin to reconsider traditional perceptions of Pop art—its definition, origins, hidden meanings, and influence—a reevaluation that is long overdue.

This close examination reveals a version of Pop that includes a variety of mediums, such as fashion, graphic design, installation, painting, prints, sculpture, and video, as well as numerous subjects that range from social justice to the media, from the environment to race and gender. Colorful dresses are considered alongside iconic printed graphics from the 1968 Olympics in Mexico. Bright Brazilian woodcuts echo Cuban political posters. Significantly, the familiar serial imagery of Andy Warhol and Roy Lichtenstein that so often defines our vision of Pop here gains historical and cultural context through the work of artistic counterparts Hugo Rivera-Scott (Chile) and Marcos Dimas (Puerto Rico). During a time of significant socio-political change in the Americas, the myriad materials of these works reflect the many pressing messages their appealing forms contain. Both the exhibition and catalogue offer inspiring ways of investigating these messages and reassessing Pop's placement in both the history of art and the hemisphere as a whole.

For the past thirteen years, the Nasher Museum has worked closely with faculty and students to create and share original research through groundbreaking exhibitions. We are proud to present another scholarly exhibition guest-curated by one of Duke University's multi-talented professors, Esther Gabara, E. Blake Byrne Associate Professor of Romance Studies and associate professor in the Department of Art, Art History & Visual Studies. Professor Gabara's commitment to restoring the role of Latino, Latin American, and Chicano artists within the Pop movement is unwavering. Her enthusiasm for the project has

inspired countless students and collaborators over many years. We are grateful for Professor Gabara's dedication to *Pop América* and look forward to sharing this exciting exhibition with students and visitors from across the region, country, and, with this catalogue, the American continent as a whole.

The McNay Art Museum has been committed to defining artistic excellence through a global lens since it opened its doors in 1954 as the first modern art museum in Texas. The museum's core collection was built by its visionary founder, Marion Koogler McNay, who acquired iconic works by artists from the United States, Mexico, and Europe, with particular emphasis on the Hispanic world through masterpieces by El Greco, Pablo Picasso, and Diego Rivera. Mrs. McNay's transhistorical approach to modern art was echoed in the decade of *Pop América* at San Antonio's 1968 HemisFair. There, McNay Trustee Robert L. B. Tobin was instrumental in fusing contemporary art with the fair's theme: the Confluence of Civilizations in the Americas. Tobin commissioned Pop artist Robert Indiana to produce a poster for HemisFair, which featured an exhibition of Spanish art masterpieces from the Prado Museum in Madrid as well as over 100 newly commissioned artworks for the fair's buildings and grounds by, among others, the Guatemalan-born Carlos Mérida and the Mexican architect and artist Juan O'Gorman. *Pop América* reflects the McNay's broad yet inclusive approach to modern art history as well as San Antonio's proud history of promoting the visual arts from across Latin America.

In order to rewrite the history of Pop art, the work of many artists whose contributions to the period have commonly been omitted is presented in the exhibition and catalogue alongside more familiar names. Almost fifty artists and artist groups from Argentina, Brazil, Chile, Colombia, Cuba, Mexico, Peru, Puerto Rico, and the United States challenge us to expand the very definition of Pop. We are grateful to each and every one of them for their inspiring work.

The scholarly contributions to this catalogue provide extensive insight into hemispheric art of the decade and set forth a new paradigm for thinking about Pop and its role in the Americas. We extend our immense gratitude to the authors: Rodrigo Alonso, independent curator; Sergio Delgado Moya, associate professor of romance languages and literatures at Harvard University; Pilar García, curator of the artistic collection, University Museum of Contemporary Art (MUAC) at the National Autonomous University of Mexico; Jennifer Josten, assistant professor of modern and contemporary art in the Department of History of Art and Architecture at the University of Pittsburgh; Camila Maroja, assistant professor of Contemporary Art in the Global World at McGill University; Natalia de la Rosa, postdoctoral associate in the Franklin Humanities Institute at Duke University (2016–2018); Roberto Tejada, Hugh Roy and Lillie Cranz Cullen Distinguished Professor at the University of Houston; and Lyle W. Williams, curator of prints and drawings at the McNay Art Museum.

We would also like to thank Natalia de la Rosa, who deserves special recognition for her many contributions to this project, including extensive research and curatorial expertise. Also, Valéria Piccoli, chief curator at the Pinacoteca do Estado de São Paulo; Mary Schneider Enriquez, Houghton Associate Curator of Modern and Contemporary Art at the Harvard Art Museums; and Edward J. Sullivan, deputy director and Helen Gould Sheppard Professor in the History of Art at the Institute of Fine Arts and College of Arts and Sciences at New York University, provided critical consultation for and early support of the exhibition.

Pop América would not have been possible without the largesse of numerous public and private lenders from throughout the Americas, listed on page 214, who kindly agreed to share their art for many months. We extend our deepest gratitude to them, as well as to numerous collaborators who facilitated the loans.

A major exhibition with international loans and its accompanying catalogue would not be possible without the financial assistance of many generous donors. We express sincere appreciation for the support of the Sotheby's Prize; the Andy Warhol Foundation for the Visual Arts; the National Endowment for the Arts; the Nancy A. Nasher and David J. Haemisegger Family Fund for Exhibitions; Fox Family Foundation; Ann Chanler and Andrew Scheman; Lisa Lowenthal Pruzan and Jonathan Pruzan; Kelly Braddy Van Winkle and Lance Van Winkle; Parker & Otis; Karen M. Rabenau and David H. Harpole; Ariel Aisiks and the Institute for Studies on Latin American Art (ISLAA); The Brown Foundation, Inc.; and the Elizabeth Huth Coates Charitable Foundation of 1992.

We are thrilled the exhibition will travel to the Block Museum of Art at Northwestern University in Evanston, Illinois. We graciously thank our colleagues there for their enthusiastic support from the project's early stages, especially Lisa Corrin, Ellen Philips Katz Director, and Corinne Granof, curator of academic programs. The exhibition's venues in the Southeast, Southwest, and Midwest assure its reach to many different populations of the United States, while the catalogue, in both English and Spanish, amplifies and extends its contents beyond museum walls and to a vast present and future readership.

For their creation of this handsome catalogue, we thank Molly Boarati, Reneé Cagnina Haynes, María Eugenia Hidalgo, Lisa Kahan, and Clara Marín for their attention to detail and exceptional design and translations.

By the time the *Pop América* exhibition closes, five years will have passed since Professor Gabara approached the Nasher Museum with the idea to present an alternate history of Pop art. The continued dedication of those working behind the scenes has been remarkable. We extend our gratitude to the entire Nasher Museum staff, with special thanks to Molly Boarati, assistant curator; Reneé Cagnina Haynes, exhibitions and publications manager; Melissa Gwynn, curatorial assistant; Wendy Hower, director of engagement and marketing; Brad Johnson, exhibition designer; Amanda Kuruc, assistant director of development; Marshall N. Price, Nancy Hanks Curator of Modern and Contemporary Art; Jessica Ruhle, director of education and public programs; Trevor Schoonmaker, chief curator and Patsy R. and Raymond D. Nasher Curator of Contemporary Art; Stephanie Wheatley, director of development; and Kelly Woolbright, registrar. We'd also like to thank the Nasher Museum Board of Advisors, listed on page 215, for their support and enthusiasm.

Finally, we owe many thanks to the staff at the McNay including René Paul Barilleaux, head of curatorial affairs; Katharine E. Carey, head of education; Rebecca Dankert, registrar for exhibitions; Jackie Edwards, assistant curator; Heather Lammers, curator of collections and senior exhibitions manager; and Ruben Luna, lead preparator and exhibitions designer. Special gratitude goes to every member of the museum's Board of Trustees, listed on page 215, including Toby Calvert, president, and Tom Frost, chairman, whose confidence and support made this vital contribution to modern art history possible.

Sarah Schroth
Mary D. B. T. and James H. Semans Director
Nasher Museum of Art at Duke University

Richard Aste
Director
McNay Art Museum

CURATOR'S ACKNOWLEDGMENTS

My first thanks are due to the artists in the exhibition, a generation whose contributions to the way we think about art today are still beginning to be understood and presented. If any of the images, language, and spirit of the decade are present in this show, it is thanks to them and especially to the generosity of conversations with Delia Cancela, Antonio Caro, Eduardo Costa, Luis Cruz Azaceta, Antonio Dias, Rupert García, Anna Maria Maiolino, Marta Minujín, Dalila Puzzovio, Hugo Rivera-Scott, and Lance Wyman. Sadly, this appreciation also serves as a memorial to Felipe Ehrenberg and Nicolás García Uriburu, two great artists whom I had the honor of interviewing prior to their deaths in 2017 and 2016, respectively.

Sarah Schroth, Mary D. B. T. and James H. Semans Director of the Nasher Museum of Art at Duke University, provided unflagging support for *Pop América, 1965–1975* from its inception, and Richard Aste, director of the McNay Art Museum, came in as an enthusiastic and insightful partner at a crucial moment. I join them in thanking the lenders and supporters of this ambitious undertaking. This exhibition would never have been possible without the fundamental contributions of Molly Boarati, assistant curator, and Melissa Gwynn, curatorial assistant, at the Nasher Museum. My thanks also to Marshall N. Price, Nancy Hanks Curator of Modern and Contemporary Art, and Trevor Schoonmaker, chief curator and Patsy R. and Raymond D. Nasher Curator of Contemporary Art, for their advice and to Wendy Hower, director of engagement and marketing; Brad Johnson, exhibition designer; Stephanie Wheatley and Amanda Kuruc in development; and Kelly Woolbright, registrar. Thanks to Reneé Cagnina Haynes, exhibitions and publications manager, for shepherding this wonderful catalogue into being. Collaborating with René Paul Barilleaux, head of curatorial affairs, and the entire staff at the McNay has been a real pleasure.

Natalia de la Rosa was more than a postdoctoral fellow; she was a crucial collaborator on all aspects of research, selection of works, and preparation of the catalogue. I would have been lost without her serious scholarship, keen eye, calm presence, and sense of humor. Camila Maroja played a crucial role in the early genesis of the project, enthusiastically connecting Duke University with Brazil and *Pop América* with her expansive knowledge of global contemporary art.

The authors of the catalogue essays provided invaluable insights into the trans-American circuits at the heart of the exhibition. A marvelous workshop hosted by the Nasher Museum and attended by Sergio Delgado Moya, Jennifer Josten, Camila Maroja, Natalia de la Rosa, Roberto Tejada, and valued advisor, Mary Schneider Enriquez, helped to clarify the central contributions of the exhibition and thus this catalogue. Our vision of *Pop América* was brought further into focus thanks to precise contributions from Buenos Aires, Mexico City, and San Antonio by Rodrigo Alonso, Pilar García, and Lyle W. Williams.

Over years of research and across the continent, brilliant scholars, keen curators and gallerists, and those who care for the archives of this generation generously shared their expertise as much as their sense of América. I cannot begin to express my deep appreciation and heartfelt *cariño* in these few words. I can say only that they made *Pop América* possible. I must thank in particular: Beverly Adams, Rocío Aranda-Alvarado, Claudia Calirman, Jasmine Cobb, Roberto Conduru, Analivia Cordeiro, Chris Dunn, Daniel Escoto, Henrique Faria, Cristina Freire, Alexandra García Waldman, Soledad García Saavedra, Clara and Stela Gerchman, Zanna Gilbert, Emiliano Gironella Parra, Pablo Helguera, Sol Henaro, Anna Indych-López, Lynda Klitch, Abigail Lapin Dardashti, Les Levine, Sandra Levinson, Florencia Malbrán, Corina Matamoros, Marli Matsumoto, Cuauhtémoc Medina, Isabela Muci, Chon Noriega, Jay Oles, Claudia Ramírez, Carmen E. Ramos,

Sara Reisman, Daniel Roesler, Gabriela Salgado, Juanita Solano, Eugenia Sucre, Joan Weinstein, Mariana Valdrighi Amaral, Claudia Zaldívar, and Adriana Zavala. Luiz Camillo Osorio has been an ongoing interlocutor and much-valued advisor. Tadeu Chiarelli and Valéria Piccoli offered a true collaboration with the amazing Pinacoteca do Estado de São Paulo. Ariel Aisiks and Estrellita S. Brodsky provided deep insights as well as critical works from their collections. There are no words to describe Edward Sullivan's unflagging mentorship in all aspects of Latin American art.

At Duke University, I wish to express appreciation to the vice provost for the arts, Scott Lindroth, and dean of humanities, Gennifer Weisenfeld. The Franklin Humanities Institute (FHI) was the home to our research team for three years, thanks to two directors: Srinivas Aravamudan, whose presence is sorely missed, and Deborah Jenson. My co-directors of the FHI Global Brazil Lab (supported by the Mellon Foundation), Christine Folch and John French, exemplified collegial collaboration. My gratitude also to Christine Chia, Laura Eastwood, and Joseph McNicholas at FHI. The Duke Brazil Initiative (DBI) provided crucial support, thanks to the vision of Provost Sally Kornbluth, Vice Provost Michael Merson, and Assistant Vice Provost Eve Duffy in the Office of Global Affairs, and Associate Director Natalie Hartman and Antonio Arce of the Center for Latin American and Caribbean Studies (CLACS). Miguel Rojas-Sotelo at CLACS offered his expertise in Latin American art and cinema. My home departments of Romance Studies and Art, Art History & Visual Studies provided additional support, and graduate students contributed their research skills, especially Marcelo Noah, Rosalía Romero, and Candela Marini; the undergraduates in my *Pop América* seminars shared their enthusiasm. It was a pleasure to collaborate with my former undergraduate student, Kristen France, now associate vice president of Latin American art at Christie's.

This exhibition has benefited from cherished collaboration with a fantastic group of scholars of Latin American art and visual culture: Beatriz Balanta, Natalia Brizuela, Mary Coffey, Claire F. Fox, Adriana Johnson, China Medel, Adele Nelson, Suzanne Li Puma, Fernando Rosenberg, Roberto Tejada, Camilo Trumper, and Alejandra Uslenghi.

My family has been my greatest source of inspiration and support, sharing laughter and tears as necessary. My parents, Vlodek and Uliana Gabara, arrived as stateless refugees in the United States in 1968, so *Pop América* also celebrates a personal fifty-year anniversary. My understanding of América is indebted to their vision of the promise of their arrival, and my sister Rachel helps me with the challenges of hewing to that promise. My husband and partner in everything, Pedro Lasch, continued this story in a sense, becoming a US citizen as the exhibition took shape. Our life together is full—of art, ideas, and debates—and I thank him for always encouraging me to take the next step. Mostly our life is full of laughter and joy thanks to our daughter, Eva. I dedicate this book to her, *por ser tan valiente, y por ser la promesa de un mejor futuro para nuestra América.*

Esther Gabara
E. Blake Byrne Associate Professor of Romance Studies and associate professor of Art, Art History & Visual Studies at Duke University

ESTHER GABARA

CONTESTING FREEDOM

Chilean artist Hugo Rivera-Scott, whose collage *Pop América* (1968, plate 3) provides the title for this exhibition, recalls: "we always thought about it as . . . 'explode America, blow up America, in that sense: Pop as an onomatopoeia' . . . ."[1] In Rivera-Scott's brief remembrance, Pop is an action. If we were to diagram the grammar of Pop, it would be a verb rather than a noun or adjective, a kind of "Popping" that emphatically produces America as its direct object.[2] "Popping" América was enacted through a fascinating range of aesthetic experiments: the familiar media of rectangular paintings and sculptures on pedestals, as well as ramshackle assemblages, unscripted performances, and language-based conceptual interventions. Indeed, Rivera-Scott emphasizes that Pop joins the language of images with the language of linguistic signs, the sense of sight with the sense of sound. The works in *Pop América, 1965–1975* feature lively exchanges: between fine arts and graphic, industrial, and fashion design; between varied returns to figuration and modernist abstraction; and between viewers, works, and artists in a radical reframing of art as dialogue. More than a style, not limited to the historical period defined by familiar anglophone examples, Pop in this exhibition does not represent a delimited movement, but rather a broad range of artistic activities. No small feat, that these actions reclaim the name of a continent that stretches from southern Chile, north to the United States and beyond, and proclaim it to be simultaneously unitary and diverse. The simple stroke of a written accent over the letter *e* declares independence from the United States' long presumption of ownership of the word, as well as from the troubled history of the idea of Latin America.[3] This exhibition welcomes viewers to this América, and invites them to participate in its making.

Opening on the fiftieth anniversary of 1968, a landmark year of social unrest, and on the 150th anniversary of the Fourteenth Amendment to the US Constitution, which guaranteed equal protection under the law, *Pop América* defies art historical commonplaces about Pop's political neutrality. Rather than a simple opposition between political art from Latin America and disinterested anglophone artists, the exhibition sets out a hotly contested and contradictory debate in and over Pop. During increasingly dictatorial regimes in Brazil and Argentina, Pop artists engaged in political resistance even as they enjoyed fashion, sexual licentiousness, and expressed a desire to drop out of modern life. In Cuba, as Jennifer Josten elaborates in her essay in this catalogue, they explicitly drew on corporate advertising and design to envision the utopia of the socialist Cuban Revolution during the consolidation of the Communist Party. When the Mexican government employed Pop and Op aesthetics in its promotion of the 1968 Olympics, those same images were used by students and workers who protested the government's repressive tactics. Similar contradictions hold true in Peru, where a leftist military regime fused Pop and agrarian utopianism, and in Colombia, where Pop emerged in the midst of what Beatriz González called "the vibration of a violent and silent ideological revolution. These contradictions hid behind apparently frivolous signs: the Beatles and fashion."[4] Latino artists in the United States, at the heart of the grandest hemispheric claim to

"America," employed Pop to reach across national borders and ethnic divides. Américan Pop combined soccer and social movements, dresses and protest posters, and performance, protest, and party. It involved the viewer in Pop as a verb, in actions that were equal parts pleasure and struggle.

These sundry Pop experiments envisioned a single continent, an América perceived from south to north as it entered a new era in hemispheric relations, one centered on ideals of freedom beset by bewildering contradictions. On the political front, left definitions of American freedom linked international socialism, Third World liberation movements, and demands for rights for women and communities of color. Right-leaning pan-Americanists promoted experiments in economic liberalization. They envisioned a hemisphere unconstrained by borders to commerce, open to free markets, and emancipated from national control over natural resources.[5] *Pop América* reveals Pop's unique capacity to embody the contradictions in these concepts of freedom, featuring art and design from both sides of this political divide that laid claim to the idea of "America."

The exhibition invites visitors into galleries organized not by themes, but by diverse actions of "Popping" América: facing América, fashioning América, mediating América, consuming América, and finally liberating América. Each gerund bids the viewers to make and remake America as they encounter the Pop objects, images, and idioms within. Ultimately, the exhibition involves viewers in the pursuit of artistic and political freedom, and encourages them to invent other names for freedom; it offers an invitation not to a single, undifferentiated America, but rather to a singular and diverse América whose residents are empowered to act.

A Pop icon since Jasper Johns produced his first *Flag* (1954–1955), a series of flags draw the viewer through the galleries. Rivera-Scott's bright collage adds text to the basic design of Roy Lichtenstein's iconic print *Explosion* (1967, plate 2). Stripping it of yellow, the Chilean bomb reproduces the pure red, white, and blue of both the Chilean and United States flags. Side by side with *Pop América*, Lichtenstein's reference to the Cuban missile crisis of 1962 comes to the fore, drawing the canonical US Pop artist closer to his South American neighbors. Chicano artist Rupert García's haunting *Black Man and Flag* (1967, plate 6), Mexican Felipe Ehrenberg's *No podemos ponerla* (We Cannot Raise It) (1969, plate 78), Rubens Gerchman's green and yellow of Brazil's soccer team *Os superhomens* (The Supermen) (1965, plate 83), and Carlos Irizarry's Puerto Rican *Moratorium* (1969, plate 66), echo Johns's Pop reprisals of flags as a mode of thinking about signs and painting.[6] Unlike Johns's painting, not one of these flags represents a country. They symbolize the dream of "*América, un continente no un país*" (America, a continent not a country) proclaimed by a Chicano movement newspaper in García's own archive.[7] Caetano Veloso's *Soy loco por ti, América* (I'm Crazy for You, America)—included on the landmark compilation album *Tropicália ou Panis et Circencis* (Tropicalia or Bread and Circuses), for which Gerchman designed the album cover (1968, plate 82)—can be understood as the anthem for this idea of América.[8] As the lyrics shift fluidly between Spanish and Portuguese, the Brazilian icon declares "*el cielo como una bandera*"

(the sky as a flag) for the continent, offering new life and a renewed ecological dimension to José Marti's famous declaration of the shared history and future promise of "Our America."[9]

PRODUCING CONSUMERS

The Americanity of Pop is associated most with the global image of US consumer culture. The artists of *Pop América* reveal that consumer culture adheres not only to this place of abundance, but also extends to the places that provide its necessary natural resources and experience corresponding extremes of scarcity and wealth. In 1967, Mário Pedrosa called these artists "'Popistas' of underdevelopment."[10] Marta Minujín's *Frac-asado* (Grilled-Tuxedo) (1975, plate 37) and *Academia del fracaso* (Academy of Failure) (1975) set out the clearest challenge to increasing competition and the valorization of material signs of success, including a singed cloak of elegance and a diploma of failure rather than achievement. Crumbs cling to carceral fork tines in Antônio Henrique Amaral's *Battlefield 31* (1974, plate 32), painted in exile during the Brazilian military dictatorship that lasted from 1964 to 1985. Boxes of ravaged flesh threaten Cuban-born Luis Cruz Azaceta's gory investigations into the New York subway as a "*laboratorio de cuestiones sociales*" (laboratory of social questions) (1974–1975, plate 31), especially of race and class. Azaceta's self-described "Apocalyptic Pop" graphically presents the impact of consumer society on the everyday lives and emotional well-being of individuals across América.[11]

As Pop consumes América, consumerism appears as part and parcel of new oppressive regimes as much as a form of individual freedom. In the vibrant and declaredly Pop scene in Buenos Aires, the Instituto Torcuato Di Tella played a central role (see Rodrigo Alonso's essay on page 196). Funded by the Argentine corporation Siam Di Tella and by grants from the Ford and Rockefeller Foundations in the United States, the institute sponsored radical experiments with the material of consumer culture.[12] Viewers of Marta Minujín and Rubén Santantonín's landmark *La Menesunda* (Mayhem) (1965, plate 98) explored the intimate and wild side of middle-class normativity as they wandered through a house-sized installation. Dalila Puzzovio won second place in the Di Tella's International Prize for her *Dalila doble plataforma* (Dalila Double Platform) (1967, plates 44, 45), platform shoes made of brightly colored Italian leather displayed in an illuminated acrylic box, first shown in a shoe store on the staunchly bourgeois Florida Street. Eduardo Costa's gold body parts in his *Fashion Fiction* series (1966–1970, plate 94) were born of his participation in the Di Tella mix, where critics Oscar Masotta and Jorge Romero Brest presented their interpretations of Pop as a new artistic phenomenon. These exuberant works embedded both the attraction and repulsion of all forms of desire in their engagement with the materials of an emergent consumer culture.

In June of 1969, though, artists featured in the Instituto Torcuato Di Tella, including León Ferrari and Antonio Berni, participated in a poster exhibition quickly shuttered by the Onganía military dictatorship then in power. *Malvenido Mister Rockefeller* (Unwelcome Mr. Rockefeller)

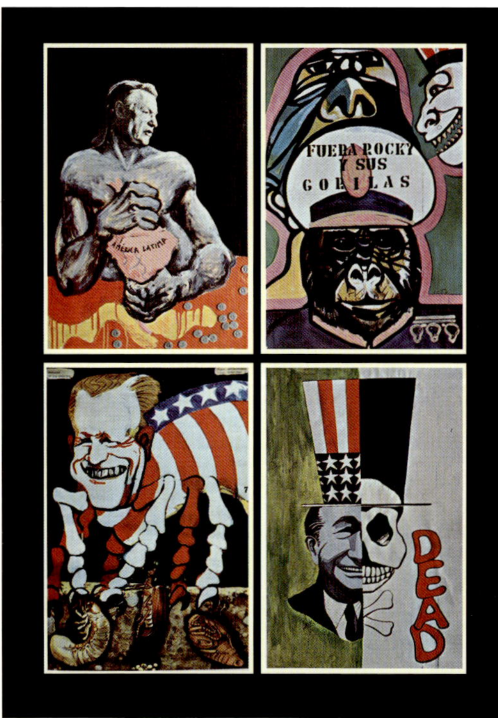
Fig. 1.1. *Ramparts* magazine (February 1970) 20.

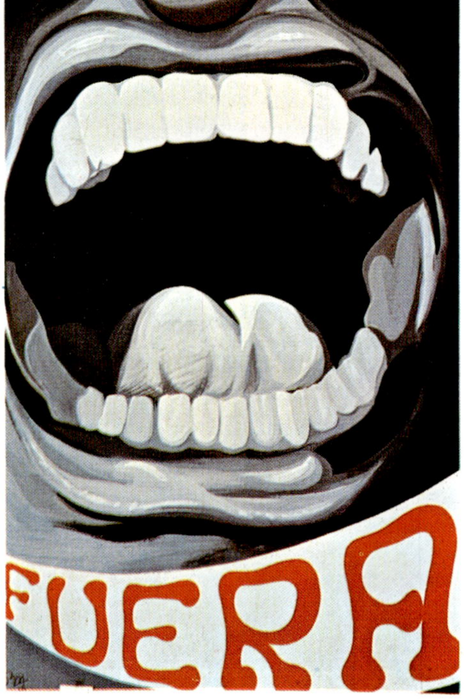
Fig. 1.2. Martha Peluffo, Untitled from the exhibition *Malvenido Mister Rockefeller* organized by the Argentinean Society of Plastic Artists on June 30, 1969. Paint on cardboard. Courtesy of the Martha Peluffo Estate and Verónica Llinás.

protested the visit of Nelson Rockefeller, New York governor and special emissary to Latin America for Richard Nixon, who leant public support to the repressive regimes that facilitated his own commercial ventures across the continent. Color reproductions of the destroyed posters in *Ramparts* magazine reveal a strong Pop presence, though a darker palette hangs over its stars, flags, and graphic lines (figure 1.1). In the span of a few years, Pop enjoyed the sponsorship of the Rockefeller Foundation and vigorously protested the pan-American tour of its scion.[13]

Martha Peluffo's contribution to *Malvenido Mister Rockefeller* features a gaping mouth (figure 1.2), a theme that appears in Jorge de la Vega's *Go, Go, Go* (1967, plate 103), Anna Maria Maiolino's print (1967, plate 22) and soft relief titled *Glu... Glu... Glu...* (Gulp... Gulp... Gulp...) (figure 1.3), Cruz Azaceta's subway paintings, and Cildo Meireles's series of pastel drawings (figure 1.4). Sensual, almost scatological, images of consumption reflect the new relationship between commerce, governance, and art in the hemisphere, which Claire F. Fox traces from the Di Tella north to San Antonio's World Fair, the HemisFair, and on to Mexico City's Olympic celebrations in 1968.[14] Rafael Squirru, brother of Di Tella Pop artist Charlie Squirru, was the director of cultural affairs for HemisFair and favored Pop and Conceptualism over the abstract painting of his predecessors. Fox notes the strange collaborations that resulted: Frito Lay and PepsiCo presented the indigenous Mexican acrobats Los Voladores de Papantla and an unrealized proposal that Minujín stage a happening. HemisFair proclaimed itself the "Gateway to Latin America" and promoted the image of a "singular continent . . . the event planners' vision of a borderless continent achieved through trade liberalization."[15] Robert Indiana's poster design for HemisFair (1967, plate 5) featured the Spanish cry, "*VIVA*" (LONG LIVE) as its structural motif, with a large "V" pointing southward to Mexico, even as arrows target the outline of Texas. Mexican leaders invited HemisFair to establish its Latin American branch office in the capital city to promote the upcoming Olympic Games. As in Buenos Aires, Pop became the visual language for debate over new economic policies and the consumer society they promoted as harbingers of freedom and democracy. The Pop and Op art inspired designs of the Olympic Organizing Committee proclaimed Mexico's readiness to host an international tourist community, and the government promoted the project of economic liberalization (1967, plates 50, 56).[16] In protest, the student movement took up the immense, brilliantly designed publicity campaign that linked Mexico's democratic face with these new economic policies to reveal their repressive nature (1968, plates 57–60). The short essays in this catalogue by Rodrigo Alonso, Pilar García, and Lyle W. Williams on Buenos Aires, Mexico City, and San Antonio provide windows into the sites along this trajectory, just one of many pan-American circuits constituted by Pop.

Artists responded to this hemispheric social experiment in consumerism by experimenting with the Pop object as just another "thing."[17] In 1970 in Buenos Aires, Marta Minujín, Jorge Romero Brest, Raquel Edelman, and Edgardo Giménez founded Fuera de Caja, Centro de Arte para Consumir (Out of the Box, Art Center for Consuming) in the Promenade Alvear Gallery. Andrea Giunta explains that they "embraced an aesthetic of kitsch and everyday consumption" in a store featuring Giménez's design of a rabbit (1970, plate 47) in its advertising, as well as his ceramics, wood, glass, and paper designs. Gerchman, the self-pro-

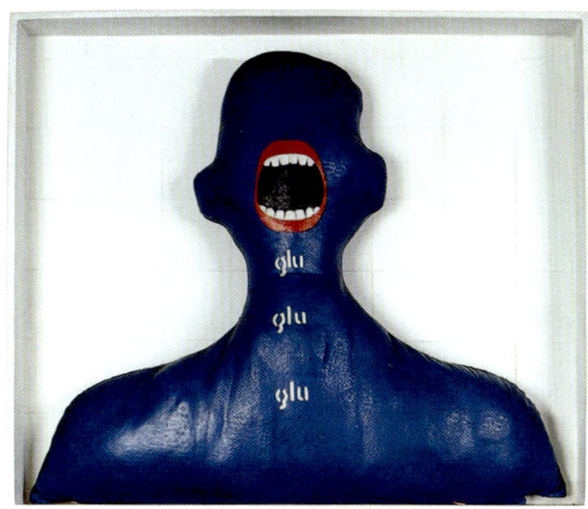
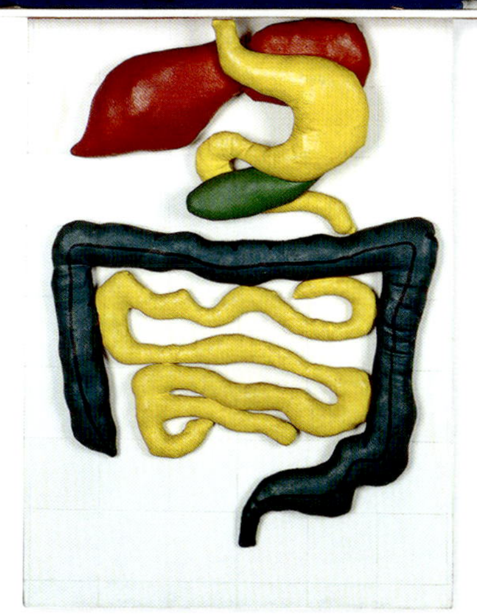

Fig. 1.3. Anna Maria Maiolino, *Glu… Glu… Glu…* (Gulp… Gulp… Gulp…), 1966. Acrylic ink and paint on wood, 42.9 x 23.4 x 4.87 inches (110 x 60 x 12.5 cm). Gilberto Chateaubriand Collection, Museu de Arte Moderna, Rio de Janeiro, Brazil. © Anna Maria Maiolino. Photo by Vicente de Mello.

Brazilian critic and curator Frederico Morais brilliantly posits the centrality of this Pop object in a manifesto accompanying his landmark exhibit *Do corpo à terra* (From Body to Earth) (1970). For Morais, these Pop objects made possible two important modes of contemporary art: Performance (or Body) art, and Earth (or Environmental) art:

> *"Pop" is the reification of common objects, fetishization of the obvious and the quotidian . . . With "Pop" the playacting has ended. It is the kingdom of the object, which is presented and does not represent. Object modified, serialized, transformed, accumulated, prepared, augmented, terrorized, mummified, destroyed, compressed, reused, combined, divided, multiplied. Enigmatic object. The entrails and the blood of the object—abject, objectum, to object, to contest, to counter. Locating itself face to face with man, obliging him to its initiatives. Object amplified to the limits of gigantism—for that reason situated outside the museum. The found object. The ludic object—piece of a toy, ritual, or game . . . . Man as merchandise in a mercantile society. The object is his shell, his image, his packaging . . . . Industrial trash—and the peripheral country lives from the surplus, as from the remnants, frequently, does the artist.*[22]

claimed "king of bad taste" in Rio de Janeiro, made flattened *caixas* (boxes) (1966, plate 106) of simple wood and cheap decorative elements, often with painted portraits of urban working class people.[18] Mexican Felipe Ehrenberg painted similar wooden boxes with left and right arrows, bright colors, and multiple media images. Ehrenberg's *cajas* (boxes) (1968, plate 77), like Gerchman's *caixas*, convert the art object into a literal and empty container of an image.[19] Titled with numbers as if off an assembly line, the works' disorienting perspectives instill a sense of precariousness in the viewer. Gerchman's *Abrigos: Caixas de morar* (Shelters: Boxes for Living) were featured in the São Paulo "Pop Biennial" (1967) (see Camila Maroja's essay on page 42) and later in the "Fashion Show Poetry Event" at the Center for Inter-American Relations in New York in January 1969 (see page 14, figure 1.5). Organized by Eduardo Costa, John Perreault, and Hannah Weiner, Gerchman's box homes were one of the wearable artworks featured by Pop icons including Andy Warhol, Allan D'Arcangelo, Marisol, Claes Oldenburg, and James Rosenquist.[20] Artists incorporated diverse aesthetic values in these objects, and foregrounded the debate over the free market as freedom, even as their apparent frivolity evaded the censorship of repressive regimes and embellished movements for civil rights.[21]

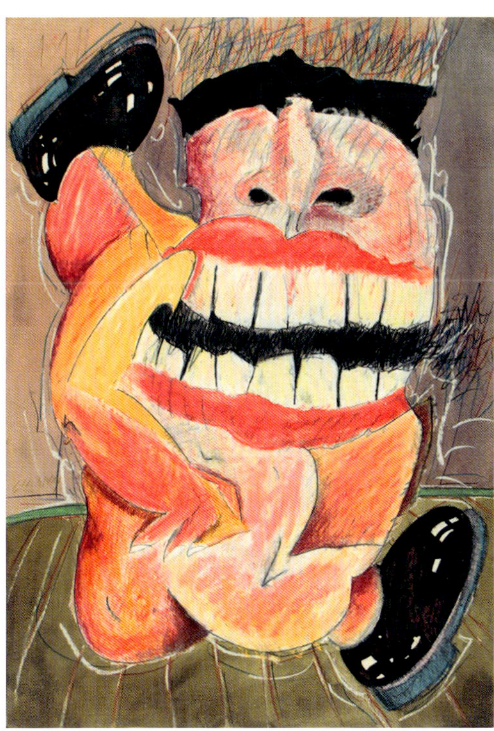

Fig. 1.4. Cildo Meireles, Untitled, 1976. Oil pastel, acrylic, and crayon on paper; 27 x 19.5 inches (70 x 50 cm). Courtesy of the artist and Galerie Lelong & Co, New York, New York.

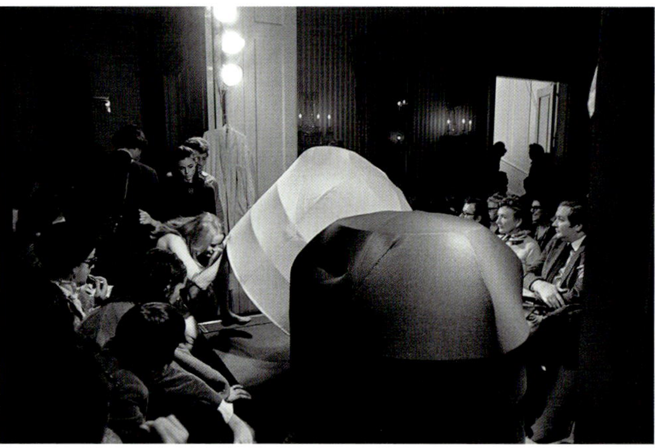

Fig. 1.5. Robert R. McElroy, *Poetry and Fashion, New York, January 14, 1969,* from the series *I.C. Happenings: New York, 1958–1963,* 1969. Photographic negative. Collection of the Getty Research Institute, Los Angeles, California; 2014.M.7. © J. Paul Getty Trust.

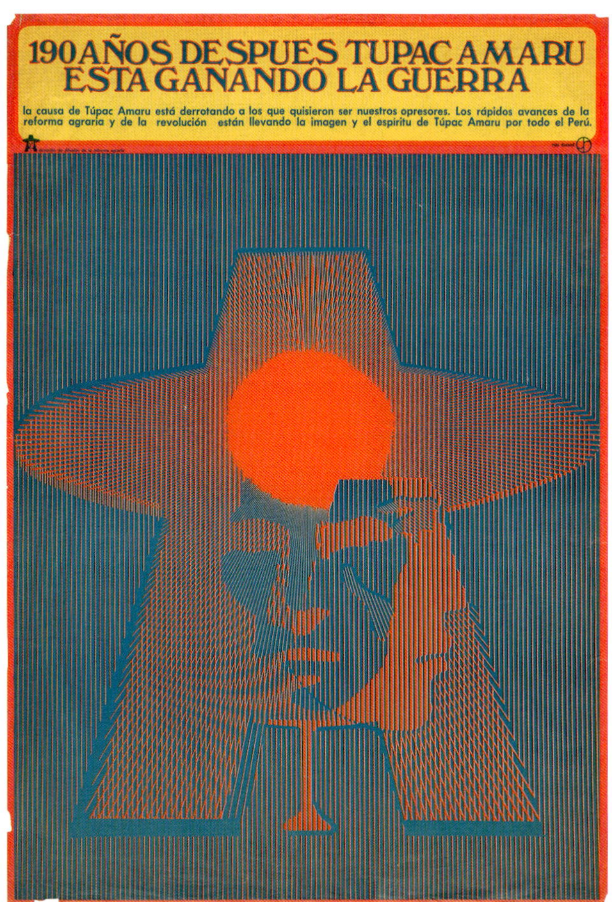

Fig. 1.6. Jesús Ruiz Duránd, *190 años después Túpac Amaru II está ganando la guerra* (190 Years After Tupac Amaru II Is Winning the War), 1968–1970. Offset-lithographic print on paper, 39 x 27.3 inches (100 x 70 cm). Sam L. Slick Collection of Latin American and Iberian Posters, Center for Southwest Research, University Libraries, University of New Mexico, Albuquerque; PICT000–674–3362.

Though other terms for new kinds of figuration also circulated throughout the continent, Pop represented a particularly fertile cross-section of experiments with form, site, medium, and concept (see Camila Maroja and Natalia de la Rosa's essays on pages 42 and 158). Far from Brazil, Pop served as such a bridge in a performance by Chicana artist Judith F. Baca in the Woman's Building in Los Angeles in 1976, in which she transformed herself into a 1940s *pachuca.*[23] The performance, emblematic of Chicana feminist engagements of style as radical art and politics, was the source of her mixed-media sculpture *Las tres Marías* (The Three Marías) (1976, plate 1), which features a mirror that reflects the viewer as an active participant in the work. Viewers of *Pop América* find themselves in what Morais called the "object-situation and not object-category," facing works that range from Meireles's small dollar bills (1974–1978) to Gerchman's gigantic *LUTE* (FIGHT) (1967, plate 73). In these situations, Pop as a verb invites them to seek the free exchange of ideas, things, and images.

POPULAR ART IN THE PUBLIC SPHERE

Mass media is a key component of the bad taste and disputed situations of these attractive and enigmatic objects. Colombian Beatriz González's graphic paintings—which she called "under-painting for under-developed countries"—embrace the flatness, poor cropping and framing, and low-quality printing of press photographs (see Sergio Delgado Moya's essay on page 172).[24] Like Gerchman and González, Waldemar Cordeiro, Eduardo Costa, Antonio Dias, Antonio Manuel, Raúl Martínez, and Emilio Hernández Saavedra incorporated media images in their work. These artists also escaped the confines of the museum by inserting art into existing circuits of commerce, media, and politics. Ana Longoni and Fernando Davis name this "inscription" into media circuits as a defining element of Argentine art of the 1960s—Conceptual and Pop art alike—crediting Minujín and Santantonín with "the popularization and 'mass-mediatization' of Pop."[25] The artists featured in *Pop América* investigated media theory in order to spark what Jesús Martín Barbero later would call active "mediation," as opposed to the passive consumption of mass media.[26] The extensive personal archive of Rupert García, whose graphic art production reflected a deep awareness of the political struggles and print traditions and techniques of Mexico, Cuba, Chile, and the African-American civil rights movement, reflects this continental phenomenon. In García's copy of the September 1975 issue of *Artes Visuales,* published by the Museum of Modern Art in Mexico City, essays by Peruvian critic Juan Acha and Argentine Jorge Romero Brest accompany a translation of Marshall McLuhan's "Structural Analysis of Mass Media," a media work by Minujín, and a video still of Jorge Luis Borges being interviewed by art critic Jorge Glusberg.[27]

Pop artists relinquished the privileges of mastery and originality in order to create "open" media works and inspire active viewers. Costa celebrated the "*millones de espectadores*" (millions of spectators) of his media masterpiece *Fashion Fiction,* the readers of *Vogue* who did not realize it was a work of art.[28] Acha echoed that Pop artists demanded "open works, cool, so that before [them] we sharpen our vision and imagine with total freedom that which the artist wishes

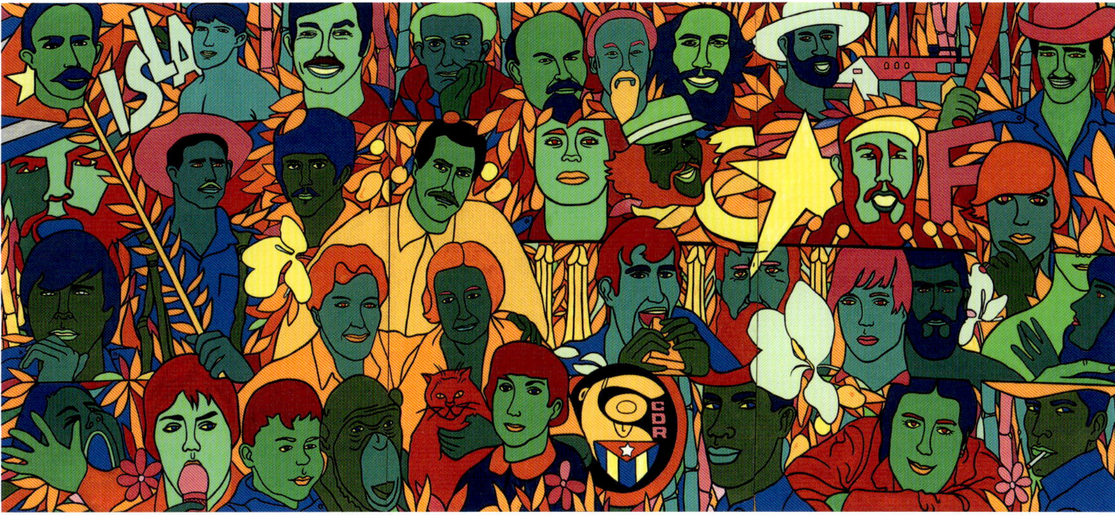

Fig. 1.7. Raúl Martínez, *Isla 70* (Island 70), 1970. Oil on canvas, 78 x 175.89 inches (200 x 451 cm). Collection of the Museo Nacional de Bellas Artes de La Habana, Cuba.

to say, since he does not say anything explicitly in the work. That is to say, the contemplator should give meaning to the work."[29] When Pop artists in Lima were accused of plagiarizing their US and British peers, rather than deny the presumption that Latin American art was derivative, Acha defended Lichtenstein and Warhol from similar claims that they reproduced the mass media image in its repressive totality. Hernández Saavedra responded to this "Affaire Pop Art" with a letter and a reproduction of his painting *Bang Bang* (1967, plate 35), making an ironic public confession of plagiarizing an English advertising photograph and his total failure to be "authentic."[30] For these critics and artists, the open and unoriginal Pop image made space for involved, amateur viewers across the continent.

Acha further argues in favor of Pop in the Peruvian context by comparing urban Lima's relationship to the Andes with the distance between New York and rural areas of the United States. If Pop could be US American despite its immense rural terrain, it could also be South American. At the time, a poster campaign by Peru's leftist military dictatorship (1968–1973) featured Pop prints by Jesús Ruiz Durand, which combined computer-generated and hand-drawn comic book techniques to celebrate agrarian reform and indigenous resistance figures such as Túpac Amaru II (figure 1.6).[31] Rupert García's graphic oeuvre also features a surprising range of heroic portraits, from Frida Kahlo and Pablo Picasso to Angela Davis and an unnamed Maya man (1970, plate 100). Raúl Martínez's portraits present José Martí alongside throngs of anonymous Cubans from the city and the countryside. He combined photography with painting and drawing in a years-long project, including the intimate *El vaquero* (Cowboy) (c. 1969, plate 104), culminating in the massive painting *Isla 70* (Island 70) (figure 1.7). Martínez grounded his Pop art in exchanges between trained and untrained artists, between visual practices of "the people" and graphic design, and between academic painting and posters.

Martínez concluded that, in contrast to Andy Warhol, "my art is Pop in the sense of being *popular*."[32] *Cultura popular* is best translated as folk art, and includes aesthetic traditions and political histories of peoples of indigenous and African descent.[33] More than just the representation of indigenous populations in the Pop idiom, the artists in *Pop América* highlighted the diversity of popular aesthetic traditions that they drew upon. Anna Maria Maiolino's *Glu... Glu... Glu...* (Gulp... Gulp... Gulp...) and Antônio Henrique Amaral's print portfolio *O meu e o seu: impressões de nosso tempo* (Mine and Yours: Impressions of Our Time) (1967, plates 86–93) make use of woodcut print techniques from the heavily Afro-Brazilian Northeast (see Roberto Tejada's essay on page 124). Gaping bodily orifices face texts that query the relationship—social and grammatical—between you and me, mine and yours, self and other. The design team of the Mexico City Olympics referenced *cultura popular* as well as mass culture, even inviting Huichol weavers from the Sierra Madre to their Mexico City office to demonstrate the compositions that worked their way into the pulsing circles of *MEXICO '68* (1967, plate 50).[34] Carla Stellweg wrote that Gerchman too "confronted issues of importance to Brazil's 'black' society . . . . Gerchman moved to New York in 1968, where he found his work had few connections with Pop art, but did have affinities with certain popular expressions, such as the murals of Chicano and Puerto Rican artists."[35] *Pop América* reveals that those "affinities" embedded social and political engagement within the aesthetics of Pop across the continent. The popular expressions named by Martínez reside at the heart of Pop's open objects, things, and situations.

IMAGE—WORD—WORLD

Pop's embrace of openness and inauthenticity set the stage for radical forms of contemporary art without abandoning the accessibility of figurative images. Argentine critic Oscar Masotta wrote that Pop's use of familiar consumer objects and mass media counterintuitively made possible a "radical critique of any realism." Masotta distinguishes Pop figuration from earlier schools of realism, much as Morais proclaimed its "end of playacting." Pop performs this critique by operating as a "meta-language" rather than as a metaphor; by "representing the represented," it invites viewers to see works as images of an image rather than as representations of real objects in the world.[36] Masotta calls Pop an "art of semiotics," drawing on analyses from a field that studied signs and symbols—visual and linguistic—and that assailed realism for its re-inscription of class hierarchies.[37]

Pop América reveals that Pop's foundation in semiotics was widespread, and crucial to its role in the emergence of Conceptual art. Ehrenberg even titled one of his wooden box structures, painted with iconic Pop arrows and repeating silkscreened portraits, *Arte Conceptual* (Conceptual Art) (figure 1.8). Throughout the exhibition, early Conceptual works hang alongside Pop works from the same years. For example, the bright green plants of García Uriburu's painting *La pantera roja* (The Red Panther) (1969, plate 14) are shown with the silkscreen manifesto for his famous "coloration" series— begun in Venice in 1968 and continued throughout his life—in which he dyed major urban waterways green as an environmental protest (1968–1973, plates 8–13). Hernández Saavedra's mod painting *Bang Bang* shares an empty, white center with his *El museo de arte borrado* (The Erased Museum of Art) (1970, plate 41), both inviting a reflection on the character of contemporary art circuits in Peru.

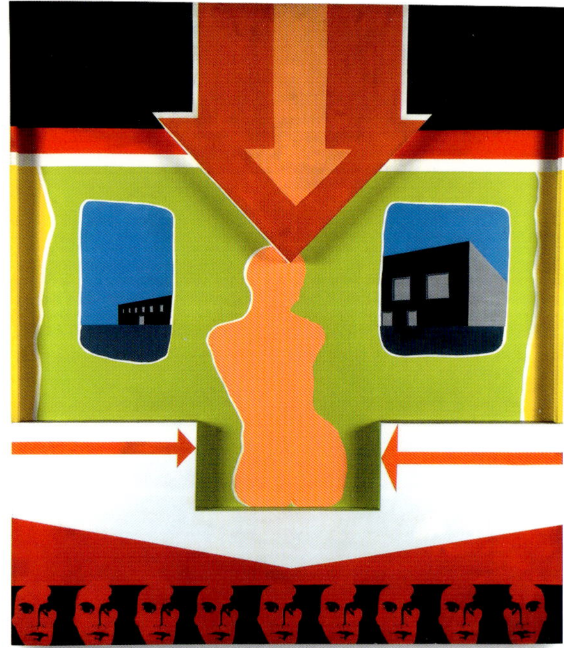

Fig. 1.8. Felipe Ehrenberg, *Arte Conceptual* (Conceptual Art), 1968. Acrylic on wooden box, 78.74 x 70.86 x 2.16 inches (200 x 180 x 5.5 cm). Courtesy of Reina María de Lourdes Hernández Fuentes.

The proximity of these works in the exhibition reveals that Pop shared Conceptual art's radical emphasis on the idea, and restores the image to the typical emphasis on text in Conceptual art. Hélio Oiticica, a key figure in contemporary Latin American art, expressed his admiration for Gerchman precisely for his "effort to create an imagetical [sic] world that could stand up with international Pop-Op images." He declares Gerchman "the first synthesis of imagetical [sic] imagination in Tropical lands . . . *the image-word-world*, the invention of the Brazilian image, in itself different to [sic] American Pop . . . where image, word, poetic, or conceptual points are all equivalent in making a total image."[38] Oiticica encounters Pop's defining openness in Gerchman's series *Cartilha no superlativo* (Primer in the Superlative), which placed the words *AR* (AIR) (c. 1972, plate 74), *LUTE* (FIGHT) (1967, plate 73), and *TERRA* (EARTH) in different sites, media, and scales. These words take shape as images and objects, which gain meaning from the site they occupy. This reading primer for Brazil's large illiterate population had a profound impact on Gerchman's concept of "total images," as he sought to include popular art and diverse populations at the crossroads of Pop, Conceptualism, and even Concrete poetry.[39]

Pop as an art of semiotics also makes sense of abstract elements seen within the generally figurative artworks in *Pop América*. Signs are geometric shapes that, through repetition, communicate concrete information in daily life, such as "no right turn," or "STOP." In Pop art, signs appear simultaneously as abstract form and figurative illustration. Yellow and black diagonal lines that warn of danger on a roadway fill Gerchman's canvases and *caixas*, and operate both as accurate representations of street signs, and as abstract geometric shapes and lines (1966, plate 106). In Antonio Berni's *Mediodía* (Noontime) (1976, plate 21), those same yellow and black signs frame a contrast between shiny cars and a black and white image of workers hunched over a poor meal, directing their warning of danger at the perils of consumerism. Nelson Leirner humorously addresses the same commercial circuit in two works that engaged fashion, which French semiotician Roland Barthes analyzed for its complex deployment of signs in *The Fashion System* that very year (1967).[40] *Stripencores* (Stripincolors) (1968, plate 62) features four dresses composed of color panels and zippers, made in different lengths for four seasons of the year that do not exist in São Paulo. Leirner's *Homage to Fontana II* (see page 44, figure 2.2) fuses geometric abstraction with Pop colors in an edition of four stretched canvases held together by the same zippers. Leirner's works join the human figure with pure abstraction, and zip close the cut that Italo-Argentine artist Lucio Fontana famously made in his canvases. The striptease of the title warns that the suture is only temporary, and promises that the cut will reopen to expose a naked and vulnerable body. Indeed, Cuban artist Raúl Martínez and US art historian Shifra Goldman conclude that the interplay between abstraction, Pop figuration, and graphic design as types of signs is common to "our continent"—which they name as "América"—and ascribe this interchange to its long struggle for liberation.[41]

POP AS PASSAGEWAY

The heterogeneity of Pop led Antonio Dias to name it a "passageway" toward radical new forms of contemporary art.[42] His series

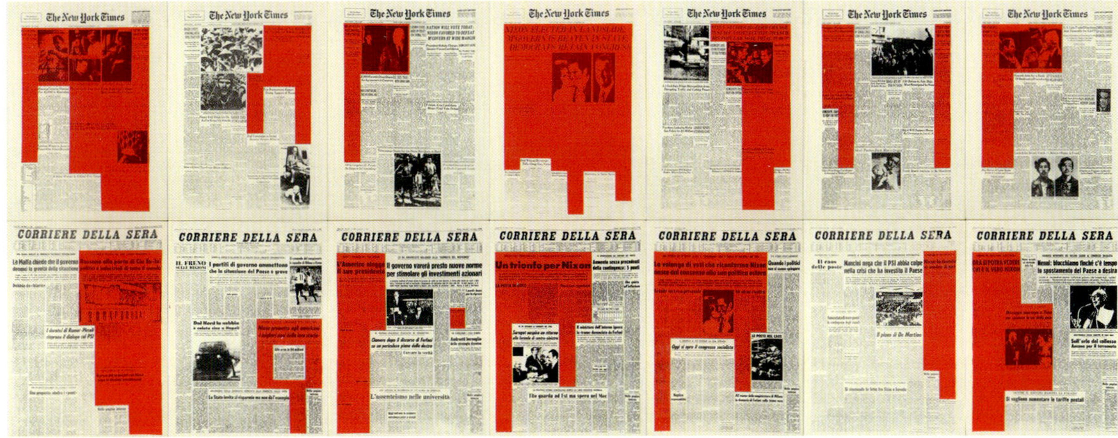

Fig. 1.9. Antonio Dias, *The Illustration of Art/Dazibao/ The Shape of Power*, 1972. Acrylic and screenprints on canvas, 47.6 x 124.8 inches (121 x 137 cm). Courtesy of the artist and Galeria Nara Roesler, New York, New York, and Rio de Janeiro, Brazil. © Antonio Dias.

The Illustration of Art (1971–1978)—represented by two works in the exhibition—exemplifies this itinerary and the intimate bonds between North and South America. The title plays on Pop's association with figuration as the visual representation of an event or a person—as illustration—but Spanish and Portuguese speakers also hear an echo of *Ilustração* and *Ilustración*, the words for the eighteenth-century Enlightenment philosophy centered on ideals of the individual, freedom, and scientific reason. Including videos, installations, intervened mass-media images, performance, and abstract and figurative painting, the series passes through Pop to explode the logic of "illustration" in art. The diptych *Uncovering the Cover-Up* (1973, plate 80) from the series whites out the eyes, nose, and mouth of international *Newsweek*'s May 28, 1973, cover image of North Carolina Senator Sam Ervin, and attaches it to a flat red canvas by means of abstract rectangles of black and red. The silkscreened image of "Senator Sam" was used for masks in a disturbing performance confronting racist stereotypes, *Score for Dangerous Performers* (1973), and the same red rectangles haunt his conversion of newspaper coverage of Nixon's war in Vietnam into geometric forms (figure 1.9).

Dias's selection of Ervin as a two-faced figure who obscured as much as he revealed crystalizes the intense and circuitous relationship between Pop, politics, and the idea of América. The year the Brazilian artist made *Uncovering the Cover-Up*, Ervin was chairman of the Senate Select Committee to Investigate Campaign Practices, which revealed Richard Nixon's role in the Watergate break-in. Before that, Ervin signed the infamous Southern Manifesto (1956), opposing the desegregation of public schools. Dias's Senator Sam embodies a continental American debate: Ervin's role in the downfall of Nixon was welcomed in South America, where the US president's extension of the war in Vietnam was viewed as an expansion of its hemispheric, colonial regime. Yet the senator's promotion of the anti-black racism that plagued Brazil and the rest of América was toxic. If for Ervin these contradictions across left and right politics were resolved by an absolute adherence to the Enlightenment ideal of individual freedoms, Dias's *The Illustration of Art* demands a confrontation with the paradox of the very idea of freedom.

In the face of this paradox, the artists of *Pop América* deployed Pop as a verb in their search for forms of liberation from the aesthetic constraints of art schools and museums, from the stresses of urban life and demands of new economies, for people of color oppressed by colonial and neo-colonial regimes across the continent, and even the liberation of nature itself. Rupert García's *Unfinished Man* (1968, plate 101) provides a portrait of that liberation in a truncated figure embodying the artistic, political, and emotional anxieties of the watershed year of 1968. Black outlines reinterpret painterly and political strategies of Mexican muralism; a gaping mouth portrays the psychological pain of Ralph Ellison's *Invisible Man* (1952), the pioneering novel of Black subjectivity published a decade prior; and, a pale blue sky echoes atmospheres by Los Angeles Pop artist Ed Ruscha.[43] Like Gerchman's blue *AR*, Uriburu's green waters, and Judith F. Baca's *Great Wall of Los Angeles* (see page 18, figure 1.10)—which sited a history of América featuring Black, Latino, and Asian peoples in the Los Angeles river basin— García's blue sky participated in what Morais called Pop's "returning to the problem of nature."[44] The Pop liberation of América involved its air, land, and water as much as its people, natural formations that unite a continent in defiance of the political borders that divide them.[45]

Not at all a comprehensive survey of the vast number of artists active during this decade across the continent, the galleries of *Pop América* feature open works that welcome viewers to América and to participate in Consuming América, Fashioning América, Liberating América, Mediating América, and Facing América. These gerunds motivate the repetition and redundancy of Pop, as well as its play of sign and image, body and thing, and fine and popular arts. They draw viewers toward freedom's potential for liberation and confront them with its broken promises, in this decade and our own.

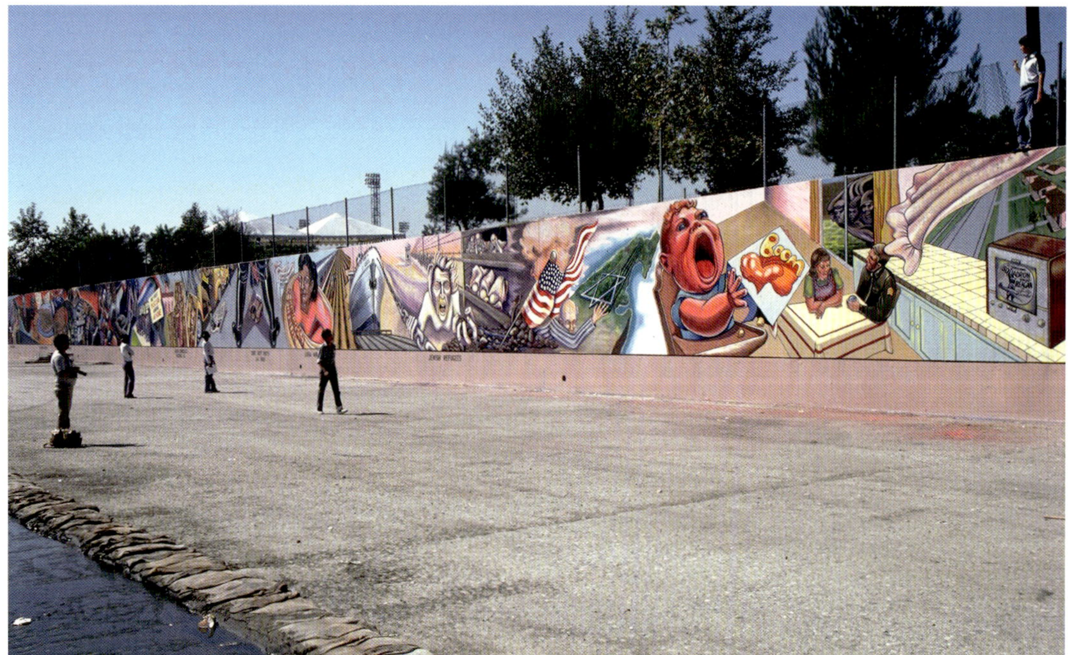

Fig. 1.10. Judith F. Baca, *The Great Wall of Los Angeles*, 1950s section "Baby Boom," 1976–1983. Acrylic on cast concrete, 13 x 2,400 feet (4 x 731.52 m). ©1976 Image courtesy of the artist and the Social and Public Art Resource Center Archives, Venice, California.

NOTES

1   Hugo Rivera-Scott, Skype interview by Esther Gabara and Natalia de la Rosa, November 2, 2016.

2   *Pop América* follows the proposal made by the exhibition *Home—So Different, So Appealing* curated by Chon Noriega, Mari Carmen Ramírez, and Pilar Tompkins Rivas for LACMA (2017), which suggested that Latin American and Latino art could elaborate a "universal concept." Here, however, that universal concept is America. Aníbal Quijano and Immanuel Wallerstein defined "Americanity" as the character of the continent that served as the testing ground of experiments with capitalism, from its sixteenth-century colonial formulation to the present. If Pop circulated worldwide in manifestations that have enjoyed increasing visibility in exhibitions such as the Walker Art Center's *International Pop* (2015) and the Tate Modern's *The World Goes Pop* (2015), *Pop América* presents the Americanity that adhered to it during its travels. See Aníbal Quijano and Immanuel Wallerstein, "Americanity as a Concept, or the Americas in the Modern World-System," *International Social Science Journal* 44:4 (1992): 549–557.

3   Alfredo Jaar, interview by Esther Gabara, October 4, 2007. The accent over the *é* also avoids the *s* of the "Americas." There is no Americas plural, Chilean artist Alfredo Jaar insists, for that *s* is only necessary if one accepts that its singular form belongs to the United States. The substantial bibliography on the troubled history of "Latin America" includes historical landmarks such as Edmundo O'Gorman, *La invención de América: El universalismo de la cultura occidental* (Mexico: UNAM, 1958); more recent manifestos such as Walter D. Mignolo, *The Idea of Latin America* (Oxford: Blackwell Publishing, 2005); and debates in art history departments and museums as much as auction houses over whether to display

Latin American modern and contemporary artists separately from their European and US counterparts.

4   Beatriz González, "Actitudes transgresoras de una década," in *Sin título 1966-1968. Luis Caballero* (Bogotá: Museo Nacional de Bogotá, 1997), 29.

5   See Claire F. Fox, *Making Art Pan-American: Cultural Policy and the Cold War* (Minneapolis: University of Minnesota Press, 2013). The chapter, "The Last Party," sets out that new experiments with economic liberalization invited the participation of US corporations and enjoyed the support of Washington, and yet were spearheaded by military dictatorships and repressive regimes.

6   On Johns's flag as sign, see Brian M. Reed, "Hand in Hand: Jasper Johns and Hart Crane," *Modernism/Modernity* 1:1 (2010): 21–45.

7   *Sin Fronteras: El periódico de la raza de bronce*, vol. 1, no. 2 (March 1974). The Chicano Movement, known as *El Movimiento*, was the civil rights-era movement of Mexican Americans.

8   *Tropicália* is a word coined by visual artist Hélio Oiticica for his installation in the landmark *New Brazilian Objectivity* exhibit in the Museum of Modern Art in Rio de Janeiro in 1967. See Carlos Basualdo, *Tropicália: A Revolution in Brazil Culture* (São Paulo: Cosac Naify, 2005), 12–13. The *Tropicália* movement exploded onto the Brazilian scene in 1967-1968 with musicians Caetano Veloso and Gilberto Gil.

9   Cuban national hero José Martí published his famous essay celebrating "native" Spanish American nature in contrast to imported "false erudition" in 1891 in *Revista Ilustrada*, a Spanish language periodical in New York, and soon thereafter in *El Partido Liberal* in Mexico City.

10 See Sofia Gotti, "Popau, Pop, or an 'American Way of Living?' An Introduction to Aracy Amaral's 'From the Stamps to the Bubble,'" *ArtMargins* 5:2 (2016): 109.

11 Luis Cruz Azaceta, interview by Esther Gabara, February 14, 2017. Cruz Azaceta recently attributed the characterization of his painting as Apocalyptic Pop to *New York Times* art critic Grace Glueck. While she did describe the painting *The City Painter of Hearts* as an "apocalyptic canvas," Glueck did not use this exact phrase. "Art View; Of Beasts and Humans: Some Contemporary Views," *New York Times*, November 14, 1982. In a 1989 interview by Bob Loescher, the artist claimed the phrase as his own. "Luis Cruz Azaceta: An Interview," Video Data Bank, 1989, http://www.vdb.org/titles/luis-cruz-azaceta-interview, accessed September 22, 2017.

12 These foundations were established following the breakup of Standard Oil into multiple companies, and used to maintain some control over them and to avoid a large tax burden. Sylvia Sigal highlights that the Di Tella "is distinct for its explicit vocation as a public but not a state institution." See Jorgelina Corbatta, "Oscar Masotta: divergencias y convergencias," *The Colorado Review of Hispanic Studies* 6 (2008): 98.

13 See Rodrigo Alonso, *El Espíritu Pop* (Mar del Plata, Argentina: MAR/Museo de Arte Contemporáneo, 2013), 136; and David Horowitz, "*Malvenido Rockefeller!* A Special Exhibition from Argentina," *Ramparts*, February 1970, 20. Ferrari's landmark sculpture *La Civilización Occidental y Cristiana* (1965) was removed from the Di Tella before his exhibition opened in 1965, but Antonio Berni's *La voracidad o la pesadilla de Ramona* (1964) was exhibited there in the same year. See also the 2012 exhibit on *Malvenido Rockefeller!* at the Centro Cultural de la Cooperación Floreal Gorini,

which presented Ferrari's archival photographs of the 1970 exhibit, http://www.arsomnibus.com/web/muestra/malvenido-rockefeller.

14   Fox's *Making Art Pan-American* provides extensive archival research and analysis that guides me here.

15   Fox, *Making Art Pan-American*, 182, 185.

16   See Marta Ramos-Yzquierdo, *Felipe Ehrenberg 67//15: Siempre en el medio* (exhibition catalogue Galería Freijó, Madrid, Spain, 2015). Led by PRI loyalist and architect Pedro Ramírez Vázquez, a year-long Cultural Olympiad was planned by members of the Department of Artistic and Cultural Activities, including Eduardo Terrazas, Beatrice Trueblood, Manuel Villazón, and Lance Wyman.

17   See Romero Brest in Alonso, *El Espíritu Pop*, 218. Brest also cites Rafael Squirru's "prophetic and inspired" vision of Marta Minujín's work as a new departure that had nothing to do with Surrealism. It is crucial to note here that for Oscar Masotta as well, Pop's redundancy and reproduction enjoys a fundamental difference from Surrealism's psychoanalytic bent founded in metaphor. Masotta, *El "Pop-Art"* (Buenos Aires: Columba, 1967), 10. As Alonso suggests, Mexican Alberto Gironella's assemblages made of the detritus of contemporary life can be read in similar terms, his deep fascination with Robert Rauschenberg contributing to his creation of "things" that break with prior forms of Realism and Surrealism in art. Alonso, *El Espíritu Pop*, 44.

18   See *Rubens Gerchman: O Rei do Mau Gosto*, ed. Clara Gerchman (Rio de Janeiro: J.J. Carol, 2016).

19   Los Angeles gallerist Virginia Dwan's 1964 exhibit, *Boxes*, famously foregrounded Pop art's relationship to this object. See James Meyer, *Dwan Gallery: Los Angeles to New York, 1959-1971* (Chicago: University of Chicago Press, 2016).

20   Costa, Perreault, and Weiner wrote that the "Fashion Show Poetry Event" "is not only fashion, poetry, and art, it is where these arbitrary categories overlap and as categories dissolve and become irrelevant. The 'Fashion Show Poetry Event' is a new kind of theater." See *Hannah Weiner's Open House*, ed. Patrick Durgin (Berkeley: Kenning Editions, 2006), 58. See also Eugenio Valdés Figueroa, *Rubens Gerchman: With the Resignation Letter in the Pocket* (Rio de Janeiro: Casa Daros, 2015). Thanks to Jennifer Josten for her help at the Getty Research Institute.

21   Elena Shromberg emphasizes that the years of the so-called "economic miracle" of economic liberalization were also the *anos de chumbo* (years of lead), the period of heaviest political repression by the military dictatorship. Shromberg, *Art Systems: Brazil and the 1970s* (Austin: University of Texas, 2016), 7, 12.

22   Frederico de Morais, *Manifesto Do Corpo à Terra*, April 18, 1970. ICAA-Museum of Fine Arts Houston, digital archives, record no. 1110794 (author's translation).

23   *Pachucos* and *pachucas* were Mexican-Americans whose highly stylized zoot suits and dresses came to represent cultural and political resistance to racism in Los Angeles and the US Southwest in the 1940s. On Baca's *Las tres Marías* (The Three Marías) and other works, see Anna Indych-López, *Judith F. Baca* (Minneapolis: University of Minnesota Press, 2018). Thanks to Anna Indych-López for her generous insight into these works.

24   See Carolina Ponce de León, *Beatriz González: What an Honor to be with You* (New York: El Museo del Barrio, 1998), 34.

25   They reference the billboard *¿Por qué son tan geniales?* (Why Are They So Groovy?), 1965 by Dalila Puzzovio, Carlos Squirru, and Edgardo Giménez, and the anti-happenings of the Grupo Arte de los Medios, made-up of Roberto Jacoby, Eduardo Costa, and Raúl Escari. See Ana Longoni and Fernando Davis, "Cuidado con la pintura" (ensayo preliminar), in *Doscientos años de pintura argentina, tomo III* (Buenos Aires: Banco Hipotecario, 2014), 20.

26   Jesús Martín Barbero, *Communication, Culture and Hegemony: From the Media to Mediations*, trans. Elizabeth Fox and Robert A. White (London: Newbury Park: SAGE Publications, 1993).

27   Marshall McLuhan, "Análisis estructural de los medios de comunicación," *Artes Visuales* 7 (July/September, 1975): 2–3; Box 14 in the Rupert and Sammi Madison García Collection at the University of California, Santa Barbara Library. Thanks to Rosalía Romero for her research in the Madison García archive.

28   Eduardo Costa, interview by Esther Gabara, July 15, 2015.

29   Juan Acha, "Arte Pop: Procedimientos y finalidades," *El Comercio*, May 25, 1969, 38.

30   Emilio Hernández Saavedra, "A propósito del plagio," *El Comercio*, May 23, 1969, 19. Pop's embrace of inauthenticity and its continental rather than nationalist emphasis established clear differences from the avant-garde movements in the first decades of the twentieth century.

31   See Anna Cant, "Land for Those Who Work It: A Visual Analysis of Agrarian Reform Posters in Velasco's Peru," *Journal of Latin American Studies* 44 (2012): 19.

32   Shifra E. Goldman, *Dimensions of the Americas: Art and Social Change in Latin America and the United States* (Chicago: The University of Chicago Press, 1994), 149 (emphasis added).

33   Jesús Martín Barbero argues that these forms of popular culture and folk art production are crucial to the public's active mediation. Thomas E. Crow's *The Long March of Pop* traces elements of rural "folk" art, providing a longer "march," but one that still narrowly defines American Pop as belonging to the United States. See Crow, *The Long March of Pop: Art, Music, and Design, 1930-1995* (New Haven: Yale University Press, 2014).

34   Lance Wyman, interview by Esther Gabara, July 20, 2017.

35   Carla Stellweg, "Magnet—New York: Conceptual, Performance, and Installation Art by Latin American Artists in New York," in *The Latin American Spirit: Art and Artists in the United States, 1920-1970* (New York: Bronx Museum of the Arts, 1988), 308. In a separate essay, Stellweg notes that the landmark Whitney Museum exhibition *Handpainted Pop: An American Tradition, 1955-1962* (1993) was indeed very traditional for its continued exclusion of Chicano painters; "Rupert García: Chicaneidad, Art and Cultural Politics," in *Rupert García: Aspects of Resistance* (New York: Alternative Museum, 1993).

36   Masotta, *El "Pop-Art,"* 15. In Roberto Tejada's contribution to this catalogue, he suggests that metaphor and this meta-language are not as mutually exclusive as Masotta suggests.

37   Semiotics, the social science of how language communicates meaning, played a formative role in Brazilian thought. Structural linguistics and anthropology were leading schools of thought in literature, art, and the social sciences in Brazil, in large part due to the residence of French anthropologist Claude Lévi-Strauss in the country in the late 1930s. On Lévi-Strauss in Brazil, see Esther Gabara, *Errant Modernism: The Ethos of Photography in Mexico and Brazil, 1920-1940* (Durham: Duke University Press, 2008). For an overview of structuralist and poststructuralist critiques of realism, see Robert Anchor, "Realism and Ideology: The Question of Order," *History and Theory* 22: 2 (1983): 107–119. On the importance of Italian semiotician Umberto Eco for Gerchman and his group of artists and critics, see Cristina Mura, *Rubens Gerchman: E o Brasil dos Anos 60 e 70* (São Paulo: Alameda, 2016).

38   Typewritten manuscript, April 1969, The Museum of Modern Art, New York, artist file, Rubens Gerchman.

39   Gerchman translates "Cartilha no superlativo" somewhat awkwardly as "Primer in the Superlative." He writes that being from "Below the Equator" inspired him to make a series of projects around language; the enormous, sculptural words, which were part of a major shift in his work whose "start was in the necessity to create a special kind of object and size that would teach people how to read. Since 1965 I was worried with that problem and as you all know ¾ of the population below the Equator is illiterate. I never accomplished this project to the very end." Dated New York Oct. 1970, see *Rubens Gerchman: O Rei do Mau Gosto*, 104–115. Brazilian Concrete poetry, led by major figures including Haroldo and Augusto de Campos, Décio Pignatari, and Wlademir Dias-Pino, emerged in the mid-1950s and emphasized the visual structure of poetry.

40   The Fashion Show Poetry Event also focused on the "total phenomenon of fashion as a language." Costa, Perreault, and Weiner wrote in 1968: "Fashion language is a complicated code....There are various verbal (written and oral) to visual and visual to verbal translations that take place in the 'Fashion Show Poetry Event.'" See *Hannah Weiner's Open House*, 57.

41   Goldman, *Dimensions of the Americas*, 165, 147.

42   Antonio Dias, interview by Esther Gabara, November 9, 2016.

43   Rupert García, interview by Esther Gabara, September 25, 2015. García spent hours staring at the California sky in order to achieve the precise color of blue in this work.

44   Anna Katherine Brodbeck, "The Salão da Bússola (1969) and Do Corpo à Terra (1970): Parallel Developments in Brazilian and International Art," *RACAR* 382 (2013): 119.

45   On the environmental basis of this social art work, see the documentary film: *The Great Wall of Los Angeles*, artist: Judith F. Baca, video editing: Ernesto Quintero and Farhad Akhmetov, script consultants: Danny Haro and Dianna M. Perez, SPARC Productions, 2007.

ESTHER GABARA

AMÉRICA REPLICA:
NO REPLICA LA LIBERTAD

El artista chileno Hugo Rivera-Scott, cuyo collage *Pop América* (1968, lámina 3) da título a esta exposición, recuerda que: "lo pensamos siempre como [...] 'explota América, revienta América', en ese sentido: el pop como una onomatopeya".[1] En el breve comentario de Rivera-Scott, el pop es una acción: hacer explotar o reventar a América. Si hiciéramos un diagrama de la gramática del pop, éste sería un verbo en lugar de un sustantivo o adjetivo, una especie de "popizar" que enfáticamente produce América como objeto directo.[2] Ese "popizar" de América se materializó en una variedad fascinante de experimentos estéticos: desde los ya conocidos medios de pinturas rectangulares y esculturas sobre pedestales hasta ensamblajes precarios, performances improvisados e intervenciones conceptuales de base lingüística. En efecto, Rivera-Scott enfatiza que el pop une el lenguaje de las imágenes con el de los signos lingüísticos, el aspecto de la vista con el del sonido. Las obras presentadas en *Pop América, 1965–1975* plasman animados intercambios: entre las bellas artes y el diseño gráfico, industrial y de modas; entre diversos regresos a la figuración y a la abstracción moderna; y entre los espectadores, las obras y los artistas en un reencuadre radical del arte como diálogo. Más que un estilo, sin limitarse al período histórico definido por los familiares ejemplos anglófonos, el pop en esta exposición representa una amplia gama de actividades artísticas, y no un movimiento delimitado. Y no es poca cosa que estas actividades reclamen el nombre de un continente que se extiende desde Chile en el sur hasta más allá de Estados Unidos en el norte, y lo proclamen unitario y diverso al mismo tiempo. El simple gesto de una tilde sobre la "e" declara que América se independiza de la larga presunción de Estados Unidos de

que ese nombre le pertenece en exclusivo, y que también se independiza de la conflictiva historia de la idea de América Latina.[3]

Pop América —que se inaugura al cumplirse cincuenta años desde el 1968, momento histórico de agitación social, y ciento cincuenta desde la Decimocuarta Enmienda de la Constitución de Estados Unidos de América, que garantiza la igual protección de sus ciudadanos ante la ley— desafía los lugares comunes de la historia del arte respecto a la neutralidad política del pop. En vez de plantear una simple oposición entre el arte político de América Latina y los indiferentes artistas anglófonos, la exposición plantea un debate contradictorio y muy controversial acerca del pop y dentro del pop mismo. Bajo regímenes cada vez más dictatoriales en Brasil y Argentina, los artistas pop se involucraron en la resistencia política a la vez que disfrutaban la moda y el libertinaje sexual y expresaban su deseo de alejarse de la vida moderna. En Cuba, como lo describe Jennifer Josten en su ensayo para este catálogo, se inspiraron de manera explícita en la publicidad y el diseño corporativo para visualizar la utopía socialista de la Revolución Cubana durante el período de consolidación del Partido Comunista. Cuando el gobierno mexicano empleó estéticas pop y op para promocionar los Juegos Olímpicos de 1968, los estudiantes y trabajadores utilizaron esas mismas imágenes para protestar contra las tácticas represivas gubernamentales. Contradicciones similares surgieron en Perú, donde un régimen militar de izquierda fusionó el pop con el utopismo agrario, y también en Colombia, donde el pop surgió en medio de lo que Beatriz González llamó "la vibración de una revolución ideológica, violenta y silenciosa. Tales contradicciones se escondían tras signos en apariencia frívolos: los Beatles y la moda".[4] Los artistas latinos en Estados Unidos, el lugar del hemisferio que se adjudicaba más que nadie ser "América", emplearon el pop para rebasar fronteras nacionales y divisiones étnicas. El pop de América combinó el fútbol con los movimientos sociales, los vestidos con los carteles de protesta, el performance con activismo y fiesta. Involucró al espectador en el pop como verbo, en acciones que eran tanto de placer como de lucha.

Estos variopintos experimentos pop visualizaban un solo continente, una América percibida de sur a norte en el comienzo de una nueva era de relaciones hemisféricas, una era centrada en ideales de libertad plagados de contradicciones desconcertantes. En el frente político, las definiciones izquierdistas de la libertad americana vinculaban al socialismo internacional con los movimientos tercermundistas de liberación y los reclamos de derechos para las mujeres y las comunidades de color. Por su parte, los panamericanistas de tendencias derechistas promovían experimentos de liberalización económica; visualizaban un hemisferio sin fronteras comerciales, abierto a los mercados libres y emancipado del control nacional sobre los recursos naturales.[5] *Pop América, 1965-1975* revela la capacidad única que tuvo el pop de plasmar las contradicciones inherentes a estos conceptos de libertad, presentando arte y diseño de ambos lados de esa línea política que dividía dos espacios que reclamaban para sí la idea de América.

Esta exposición propone al espectador un recorrido por galerías que no están organizadas por temas, sino por las diversas acciones en que se "popiza" América: encarando América, modelando América, mediando América, consumiendo América y finalmente liberando América. Cada gerundio pide al espectador que haga y rehaga a América a medida que va encontrándose con los objetos, imágenes y lenguajes pop. Al final, la exposición incluye a los espectadores en la lucha por la libertad artística y política, exhortándolos a inventar otros nombres para la libertad. Se extiende una invitación, no a una sola América, sin diferencias, sino a una América singular y diversa cuyos residentes están empoderados para actuar.

Una serie de banderas —íconos del pop desde que Jasper Johns produjo su primera *Flag* (Bandera) (1954-1955)— llevan al visitante por las galerías. El vívido collage de Rivera-Scott añade texto al diseño básico de la icónica litografía de Roy Lichtenstein titulada *Explosion* (Explosión) (1967, lámina 2). Despojada del amarillo, la bomba chilena reproduce el rojo, blanco y azul de las banderas tanto de Chile como de Estados Unidos. Al lado de *Pop América*, la alusión de Lichtenstein a la crisis cubana de los misiles en 1962 pasa a primer plano, acercando al canónico artista del pop estadounidense a sus vecinos sudamericanos. La evocadora obra del chicano Rupert García, *Black Man and Flag* (Hombre negro y bandera) (1967, lámina 6), junto a *No podemos ponerla* (1969, lámina 78) del mexicano Felipe Ehrenberg, el verde y amarillo del equipo de fútbol brasileño en *Os superhomens* (Los superhombres) (1965, lámina 83) de Rubens Gerchman y *Moratorium* (Moratoria) (1969, lámina 66) del puertorriqueño Carlos Irizarry, hacen eco de Jasper Johns y sus banderas como reflexiones acerca de los símbolos y la pintura.[6] Pero a diferencia de la obra de Johns, ninguna de estas otras banderas representa a un país. Simbolizan el sueño de "América, un continente no un país" proclamado por un periódico del Movimiento Chicano que se conserva en el archivo de Rupert García.[7] La canción *Soy loco por ti, América*, de Caetano Veloso —incluida en el histórico álbum compilatorio *Tropicália ou panis et circencis* (Tropicalia, o pan y circo), cuya portada diseñó Gerchman (1968, lámina 82)— podría considerarse el himno de esta idea de América.[8] Con letra que fluye entre el español y el portugués, el ícono brasileño declara que "el cielo es como una bandera" para el continente, dando nueva vida y una renovada dimensión ecológica a la famosa declaración de José Martí sobre la historia compartida y la proyección de futuro de "Nuestra América".[9]

LA PRODUCCIÓN DE CONSUMIDORES, Y LOS CONSUMIDORES QUE PRODUCEN

La americanidad del pop se asocia ante todo con la imagen global de la cultura del consumo en Estados Unidos. Los artistas de *Pop América* revelan que la cultura del consumo no concierne solo a esa tierra de la abundancia, sino que se extiende a los países que le proporcionan los recursos naturales necesarios y que experimentan extremos correlativos de escasez y de riqueza. En 1967, Mário Pedrosa denominó a estos artistas como los "popistas del subdesarrollo".[10] Las obras *Frac-asado* (1975, lámina 37) y *Academia del fracaso* de Marta Minujín presentan el reto más claro a la creciente competencia y a la valorización de los símbolos materiales del éxito empleando una elegante prenda de vestir chamuscada y un diploma de fracaso en vez de logro. En *Battlefield 31* (Campo de batalla 31) (1974, lámina 32), pintada por Antônio Henrique Amaral en el exilio durante la dictadura militar brasileña que se extendió desde 1964 hasta 1985, se distinguen unas migajas en tenedores con dientes que parecen barrotes de cárcel. Cajas de carne deteriorada aparecen amenazantes en las morbosas exploraciones que hace el cubano americano Luis Cruz Azaceta del subterráneo de Nueva York como "laboratorio de cuestiones sociales" (1974–1975, lámina 31), cuestiones sobre todo de raza y clase. Lo que el propio Azaceta denominó su "pop apocalíptico" presenta de manera explícita el impacto de la sociedad consumista en la vida cotidiana y el bienestar emocional de las personas en toda América.[11]

Mientras el pop consume a América, el consumismo se convierte en parte integral de los nuevos regímenes opresores y a la vez en manifestación de la libertad individual. En la escena vibrante y manifiestamente pop de Buenos Aires, el Instituto Torcuato Di Tella tuvo un papel central (ver el ensayo de Rodrigo Alonso en la página 196). Con fondos de la corporación argentina Siam Di Tella y subsidios de las fundaciones estadounidenses Ford y Rockefeller, el instituto patrocinó experimentos radicales con el material de la cultura del consumo.[12] Uno de ellos fue *La Menesunda* (1965, lámina 98), histórica obra de Marta Minujín y Rubén Santantonín donde los espectadores podían explorar el lado íntimo y extravagante de la normatividad burguesa a medida que recorrían una instalación del tamaño de una casa. Dalila Puzzovio obtuvo el segundo lugar del Premio Internacional Di Tella por su *Dalila doble plataforma* (1967, láminas 44, 45), unos zapatos de plataforma hechos de cuero italiano en colores brillantes, presentados en una caja de acrílico iluminada, que se expusieron por primera vez en una zapatería de la calle Florida, área tenazmente burguesa. Asimismo, la idea de incluir partes del cuerpo doradas en su serie *Fashion Fiction* (Ficción de moda) (1966–1970, lámina 94) nació cuando Eduardo Costa formaba parte del grupo del Instituto Torcuato Di Tella, donde también los críticos Oscar Masotta y Jorge Romero Brest presentaron sus interpretaciones del pop como un fenómeno artístico nuevo. En su tratamiento de materiales propios de la incipiente cultura del consumo, estas obras exuberantes encarnan la atracción y la repulsión de todas las formas del deseo.

Sin embargo, en junio de 1969, los artistas asociados con Di Tella, incluidos León Ferrari y Antonio Berni, participaron en una exposición de carteles que rápidamente fue clausurada por el régimen de Onganía. *Malvenido Mister Rockefeller* fue una protesta contra la visita de Nelson Rockefeller, gobernador de Nueva York y emisario especial de Richard Nixon en América Latina, quien públicamente apoyaba a los regímenes represivos que facilitaban sus negocios privados en todo el continente. Las reproducciones a color de los carteles destruidos que publicó la revista *Ramparts* revelan una fuerte presencia pop, aunque una paleta más oscura envuelve las estrellas, banderas y líneas gráficas (ver página 12, figura 1.1). En el lapso de unos pocos años, el pop gozó del patrocinio de la Fundación Rockefeller y protagonizó una enérgica protesta contra la gira panamericana de su adalid.[13]

La obra de Martha Peluffo para *Malvenido Mister Rockefeller* es una gran boca abierta (ver página 12, figura 1.2), tema que aparece en *Go, Go, Go* (Ve, ve, ve) (1967, lámina 103) de Jorge de la Vega, así como en los grabados y relieves suaves de Anna Maria Maiolino titulados *Glu... Glu... Glu...* (1967, lámina 22; ver página 13, figura 1.3), en las pinturas del subterráneo de Cruz Azaceta y en la serie de dibujos al pastel de Cildo Meireles (ver página 13, figura 1.4). Imágenes sensuales, casi escatológicas del consumismo reflejan la nueva relación entre el comercio, la gobernanza y el arte en el hemisferio, relación que Claire Fox traza desde Di Tella hacia el norte hasta la Feria Mundial de San Antonio, la HemisFair, y pasando por los Juegos Olímpicos de Ciudad de México en 1968.[14] Rafael Squirru, hermano del artista pop Charlie Squirru, también relacionado con Di Tella, fue director de asuntos culturales de HemisFair, quien favoreció el pop y el conceptualismo, a diferencia de sus predecesores que favorecían la pintura abstracta. Fox observa que esto resultó en colaboraciones extrañas: Frito Lay y PepsiCo presentaron a los acróbatas indígenas mexicanos Los Voladores de Papantla, así como una propuesta de un happening de Minujín que al final no se llevó a cabo. HemisFair se autoproclamó "Gateway to Latin America" (Puerta hacia Latinoamérica) y promovió la imagen de un "continente singular [...] la visión de sus organizadores de un continente sin fronteras logrado mediante la liberalización del comercio".[15] El diseño de Robert Indiana para el cartel de HemisFair (1967, lámina 5) tiene como motivo estructural el grito de "VIVA", con una gran "V" que apunta en dirección al sur, hacia México, al mismo tiempo que unas flechas señalan la silueta del estado de Texas. Los líderes mexicanos invitaron a HemisFair a establecer su oficina latinoamericana en Ciudad de México a fin de promover los juegos olímpicos que se iban a celebrar allí. Al igual que en Buenos Aires, el pop se convirtió en el lenguaje visual para el debate acerca de las nuevas políticas económicas y la sociedad consumista que éstas promovían como heraldos de la libertad y la democracia. Los diseños de vertiente pop y op del Comité Organizador de los Juegos Olímpicos proclamaban que México estaba listo para recibir a una

comunidad de turistas internacionales, y el gobierno promovía el proyecto de liberalización económica (1967, láminas 50, 56).[16] En protesta contra esta posición, el movimiento estudiantil se apoderó de la inmensa y brillantemente diseñada campaña publicitaria, que vinculaba la cara democrática del país con estas nuevas políticas económicas, para revelar su aspecto represivo (1968, láminas 57–60). Los ensayos breves de este catálogo escrito por Rodrigo Alonso, Pilar García y Lyle W. Williams sobre Buenos Aires, Ciudad de México y San Antonio arrojan luz a lo largo de esta trayectoria, tan solo uno de los muchos circuitos panamericanos constituidos por el pop.

Los artistas reaccionaron a este experimento social hemisférico de consumismo experimentando a su vez con el objeto pop como simplemente otra "cosa".[17] En 1970 en Buenos Aires, Marta Minujín, Jorge Romero Brest, Raquel Edelman y Edgardo Giménez fundaron Fuera de Caja, Centro de Arte para Consumir, en la Galería Promenade Alvear. Andrea Giunta explica que "adoptaron una estética del kitsch y el consumo cotidiano" en una tienda que exhibía en su publicidad el diseño de un conejo (1970, lámina 47) hecho por Giménez junto con diseños del mismo artista en cerámica, madera, vidrio y papel. Gerchman, quien se autoproclamó el "rey del mal gusto" en Río de Janeiro, producía *caixas* (cajas) (1966, lámina 106) aplanadas de madera sencilla con elementos decorativos baratos, a menudo con retratos pintados de gente de la clase obrera urbana.[18] El mexicano Felipe Ehrenberg pintó cajas similares de madera con flechas en distintas direcciones, colores brillantes y múltiples imágenes de los medios masivos. Las cajas (1968, lámina 77) de Ehrenberg, así como las *caixas* de Gerchman, convierten al objeto de arte en recipiente literal, y vacío, de una imagen.[19] Tituladas con números, como si salieran de una línea de ensamblaje, las obras ostentan perspectivas desorientadoras que provocan en el espectador una sensación de precariedad. Los *Abrigos: Caixas de morar* (Refugios: Cajas de habitar) de Gerchman se exhibieron en la Bienal "pop" de São Paulo (1967) y luego en el "Fashion Show Poetry Event" (Evento de moda y poesía) en el Centro de Relaciones Interamericanas de Nueva York en enero de 1969, organizado por Eduardo Costa, John Perreault y Hannah Weiner (ver página 14, figura 1.5) (ver el ensayo de Camila Maroja en la página 52). Las cajas de habitar de Gerchman fueron una de las "obras de arte para usar" que produjeron íconos del pop como Andy Warhol, Allan D'Arcangelo, Marisol, Claes Oldenburg y James Rosenquist.[20] Estos artistas incorporaron diversos valores estéticos en el objeto de arte y a la vez dieron relieve al debate sobre el mercado libre como forma de libertad, si bien su aparente frivolidad logró evadir la censura de las regímenes represivos y adornaron los movimientos de derechos civiles.[21]

El crítico y curador de arte brasileño Frederico Morais plantea brillantemente la centralidad de este objeto pop en un manifiesto que acompañó su histórica exposición *Do corpo à terra* (Del cuerpo a la tierra) (1970). Según Morais, estos objetos pop posibilitaron dos importantes modalidades del arte contemporáneo: el arte del performance (o del cuerpo) y el arte de la tierra (o ambiental):

El "pop" es la reificación de los objetos comunes, la fetichización de lo obvio y lo cotidiano. [...] Con el "pop" se acabó la simulación. Es el reino del objeto, que es presentado y no representado. Objeto modificado, seriado, transformado,

acumulado, preparado, aumentado, aterrorizado, momifi-
cado, destruido, comprimido, reaprovechado, combinado,
dividido, multiplicado. Objeto enigmático. Las entrañas y
la sangre del objeto —abyecto, objectum, objetar, contestar,
contrariar. Confrontando al hombre, obligándolo a tomar
iniciativas. Objeto amplificado al límite del gigantismo— y
por ello mismo situado fuera del museo. El objeto encontra-
do. El objeto lúdico —pedazo de un juguete, ritual o juego.
[...] El hombre como mercancía en la sociedad mercantil. El
objeto es la cáscara, su imagen, el empaque. [...] Desecho
industrial— y es de las sobras que viven los países periféri-
cos, así como de los restos, con frecuencia, vive el artista.[22]

Aunque por el continente circularon otros términos para las nuevas
formas de figuración, el pop reunió un muestrario particularmente
fértil de experimentos con la forma, la ubicación, el medio y el concepto de las obras de arte (ver el ensayo de Camila Maroja y Natalia
de la Rosa en las páginas 52 y 166). Lejos de Brasil, el pop extendió su
puente a un performance de Judith F. Baca en el Woman's Building
de Los Ángeles, en 1976, donde la artista chicana se transformó en
una pachuca de los años cuarenta.[23] Este performance, emblema del
acercamiento feminista chicano al estilo como arte y política radical,
fue la base para la escultura de técnica mixta *Las tres Marías* (The
Three Marías) (1976, lámina 1), donde Baca incluye un espejo que refleja al espectador y lo convierte en participante activo de la obra. Los
espectadores de *Pop América* se encuentran en lo que Morais llamaba
el "objeto-situación y no objeto-categoría", enfrentándose a obras que
van desde los pequeños billetes de dólares de Meireles (1974–1978)
hasta el gigantesco *LUTE* (LUCHA) (1967, lámina 73) de Gerchman.
En estas situaciones, el pop como verbo los invita a buscar el libre
intercambio de ideas, cosas e imágenes.

EL ARTE POPULAR EN LA ESFERA PÚBLICA

Los medios masivos de información son un componente clave del mal
gusto y las controvertidas situaciones de estos objetos atractivos y
enigmáticos. Las pinturas gráficas de la colombiana Beatriz González
—que ella llamó "subpinturas para países subdesarrollados"— adoptan
la planitud, el mal encuadre o recorte, y la impresión de baja calidad de
las fotografías de prensa (ver el ensayo de Sergio Delgado Moya en la
página 172).[24] Al igual que Gerchman y González, Waldemar Cordeiro,
Eduardo Costa, Antonio Dias, Antonio Manuel, Raúl Martínez y Emilio
Hernández Saavedra incorporaron imágenes de los medios masivos en
sus obras. Y también estos artistas escaparon de las restricciones de
los museos al insertar su arte en los circuitos existentes del comercio,
los medios masivos y la política. Ana Longoni y Fernando Davis señalan esta "inscripción" en los circuitos mediáticos como un elemento
que definió al arte argentino de la década de 1960 —tanto el arte pop
como el conceptual— atribuyendo "la popularización y 'massmediati-
zación' del pop" a Minujín y Santantonín.[25] Los artistas presentados en
Pop América investigaron la teoría de los medios masivos para incitar
lo que Jesús Martín Barbero luego denominaría "mediación" activa, a
diferencia del consumo pasivo de los medios masivos.[26] El extenso
archivo personal de Rupert García, cuya producción de arte gráfico

refleja una profunda conciencia de las luchas políticas y las tradiciones y técnicas de la estampa en México, Cuba, Chile y el movimiento
afroamericano de derechos civiles, refleja este fenómeno continental. En dicho archivo se encuentra el número de septiembre de 1975
de *Artes Visuales*, revista publicada por el Museo de Arte Moderno
en Ciudad de México, donde aparecen ensayos del crítico peruano
Juan Acha y de Jorge Romero Brest acompañando una traducción
de "Structural Analysis of Mass Media" (Análisis estructural de los
medios de comunicación) de Marshall McLuhan, una obra mediática
de Minujín y un fotograma del video de una entrevista que el crítico
de arte Jorge Glusberg hizo a Jorge Luis Borges.[27]

Los artistas pop renunciaron a los privilegios del dominio técnico y la
originalidad para poder crear obras mediáticas "abiertas" e inspirar y
activar al espectador. Costa celebró a los "millones de espectadores" de
su obra maestra mediática *Fashion Fiction*, los millones de lectores de
Vogue que no se dieron cuenta de que se trataba de una obra de arte.[28]
Asimismo, Acha declaró que los artistas pop exigían "'obras abiertas',
frías, para que ante [ellas] agudicemos la visión e imaginemos con
toda libertad lo que quiere decir el artista, ya que éste no dice nada
explícito en la obra. Es decir, el contemplador debe dar significaciones
a la obra".[29] Cuando en Lima algunos artistas pop fueron acusados de
plagiar a sus colegas estadounidenses y británicos, en vez de refutar el
supuesto de que el arte latinoamericano era derivativo, Acha defendió
a Lichtenstein y a Warhol, quienes también fueron acusados de reproducir las imágenes de los medios masivos en su represiva totalidad.
Hernández Saavedra respondió a este "affaire del arte pop" con una
carta y una reproducción de su pintura *Bang Bang* (1967, lámina 35),
haciendo confesión pública, en vena irónica, de haber plagiado una
fotografía publicitaria inglesa y de su total falta de "autenticidad".[30]
Para estos críticos y artistas, el carácter abierto y "no original" de la
imagen pop abrió espacio para implicar a los espectadores aficiona-
dos en todo el continente.

Acha continúa su argumento a favor del pop en el contexto peruano
al comparar la relación entre la zona urbana de Lima y la zona de los
Andes con la distancia entre Nueva York y las áreas rurales de Estados
Unidos. Si el pop podía ser norteamericano a pesar del enorme territorio rural de Estados Unidos, también podía ser sudamericano. Hacia
esa época, en una campaña de carteles propulsada por la dictadura
militar izquierdista del Perú (1968–1973) aparecieron imágenes pop
creadas por Jesús Ruiz Durand combinando técnicas de dibujo estilo
cómic a mano y por computadora para homenajear a figuras de la
reforma agraria y de la resistencia indígena como Túpac Amaru II
(ver página 14, figura 1.6).[31] La producción gráfica de Rupert García
también incluye una sorprendente gama de retratos heroicos, desde
Frida Kahlo y Pablo Picasso hasta Angela Davis y un hombre maya
anónimo (1970, lámina 100). Los retratos de Raúl Martínez presentan
a José Martí junto a multitudes de cubanos anónimos, tanto de la ciudad como del campo. Martínez combinó fotografía con pintura y dibujo en un proyecto de varios años que incluye la obra de tono íntimo
El vaquero (c. 1969, lámina 104) y culmina con la pintura de grandes
dimensiones titulada *Isla 70* (ver página 15, figura 1.7). Martínez ancló
su arte pop en el intercambio entre artistas con formación y sin ella,
entre las prácticas visuales "del pueblo" y el diseño gráfico, y entre la
pintura académica y el cartel.

Martínez concluye que, a diferencia de Andy Warhol, "mi arte es pop en el sentido de que es *popular*".[32] El cubano enfatiza la presencia de una cultura popular que abarca las tradiciones estéticas e historias políticas de los pueblos de ascendencia indígena y africana.[33] Pero más que representar a los pueblos indígenas en el lenguaje pop, los artistas de *Pop América* resaltan la diversidad de las tradiciones estéticas populares que los inspiraban. *Glu... Glu... Glu...*, de Anna Maria Maiolino, y el portafolio de grabados de Antônio Henrique Amaral *O meu e o seu: impressões de nosso tempo* (Mío y tuyo: Impresiones de nuestros tiempos) (1967, láminas 86–93) emplean las técnicas de xilografía del noreste de su país, región mayoritariamente afrobrasileña (ver el ensayo de Roberto Tejada en la página 132). En estos trabajos vemos orificios corporales abiertos frente a textos que cuestionan la relación —social y gramática— entre tú y yo, mío y tuyo, el sujeto y el otro. El equipo de diseño de los Juegos Olímpicos de México utilizó referencias a la cultura popular y la cultura de masas, incluso invitaron a tejedores huicholes de la Sierra Madre a su oficina en Ciudad de México para que les mostraran sus diseños y los incorporaron en los pulsantes círculos del logotipo de *MÉXICO '68* (1967, lámina 50).[34] Carla Stellweg escribió que Gerchman también "abordó temas relevantes a la sociedad 'negra' brasileña. [...] Gerchman se mudó en 1968 a Nueva York, donde encontró que su obra tenía pocos vínculos con el arte pop, pero sí afinidades con ciertas expresiones populares, tales como los murales de los artistas chicanos y puertorriqueños".[35] *Pop América* revela que esas "afinidades" insertaban el compromiso social y político dentro de la estética pop en todo el continente. Las expresiones populares que menciona Martínez están en el corazón de las situaciones, las cosas y los objetos de carácter abierto del arte pop.

IMAGEN—PALABRA—MUNDO

El hecho de que el pop acogiera la apertura y la inautenticidad preparó el terreno para vertientes radicales del arte contemporáneo sin abandonar la accesibilidad de las imágenes figurativas. El crítico argentino Oscar Masotta escribió que esta práctica pop de utilizar los objetos de consumo cotidianos y los medios masivos de información hizo posible, contradictoriamente, una "crítica radical a todo realismo". Masotta distingue la figuración pop de las escuelas anteriores de realismo, del mismo modo que Morais declaró que con el pop "se acabó la simulación". El pop opera esta crítica al funcionar como metalenguaje en vez de metáfora; al "representar lo representado", invita al espectador a ver las obras como imágenes de imágenes y no como representaciones de objetos reales en el mundo.[36] Masotta llama al pop un "arte semiótico", basado en los análisis de una disciplina que estudia los signos y los símbolos —visuales y lingüísticos— y que atacó al realismo por su reinscripción de las jerarquías de clase.[37]

Pop América revela que esa base en la semiótica fue un fenómeno generalizado y crucial al papel del pop en el surgimiento del arte conceptual. Ehrenberg incluso tituló una de sus cajas de madera, pintada con icónicas flechas pop y retratos serigráficos que se repiten, *Arte Conceptual* (ver página 16, figura 1.8). En el transcurso de esta exposición pueden verse obras conceptuales tempranas junto a obras pop de los mismos años. Por ejemplo, las plantas verde vivo de *La pantera roja* (1969, lámina 14) de García Uriburu están contiguas a

la serigrafía del manifiesto para su famosa serie de "coloraciones" (comenzada en Venecia en 1968 y continuada a lo largo de su vida), que consistía en teñir de verde importantes cuerpos de agua urbanos a manera de protesta ambiental (1968–1973, láminas 8–13). La obra *mod* de Hernández Saavedra titulada *Bang Bang* comparte un centro blanco vacío con su otra obra *El museo de arte borrado* (1970, lámina 41), con lo cual ambas invitan a reflexionar sobre el carácter de los circuitos del arte contemporáneo en el Perú.

La proximidad de estas obras en la exposición revela que el pop compartía con el arte conceptual su énfasis radical en la idea, y restaura la imagen al típico énfasis del texto en el arte conceptual. Hélio Oiticica, figura clave del arte contemporáneo latinoamericano, expresó su admiración por Gerchman precisamente por su "tentativa de crear un lenguaje nuestro, característico, que hiciera frente a la imagética [sic] pop y op internacional". Declara que Gerchman representa la "primera síntesis de la imaginación imagética [sic] en tierras tropicales. [...] *la imagen-palabra-mundo*, la invención de la imagen brasileña, diferente del pop americano. [...] donde la imagen, la palabra y los propósitos poéticos o conceptuales son equivalentes entre sí en la construcción de la imagen total".[38] Oiticica encuentra la apertura que define al pop en la serie de Gerchman titulada *Cartilha no superlativo* (Cartilla en superlativo), donde las palabras *AR* (AIRE) (c. 1972, lámina 74), *LUTE* (LUCHA) (1967, lámina 73) y *TERRA* (TIERRA) aparecen ubicadas en diversos lugares, medios y escalas. Estas palabras cobran forma como imágenes y objetos que adquieren significación del sitio donde se ubican. Esta cartilla de lectura para la extensa población analfabeta de Brasil tuvo un profundo impacto en el concepto de la "imagen total" de Gerchman, dada su aspiración de incluir el arte popular y una diversidad de poblaciones en la confluencia del pop con el conceptualismo e incluso la poesía concreta.[39]

El pop como arte semiótico también ayuda a comprender los elementos abstractos que aparecen dentro de las obras generalmente figurativas que se incluyen en *Pop América*. Los signos son formas geométricas que, por repetición, comunican información concreta en la vida cotidiana, como "no vire a la derecha" o "PARE". En el arte pop, los signos aparecen simultáneamente como forma abstracta e ilustración figurativa. Los lienzos y *caixas* de Gerchman están llenos de líneas diagonales negras y amarillas, como las que señalan peligro en una vía pública, y en estas obras funcionan a la vez como representaciones fieles de señales viales y como formas geométricas abstractas (1966, lámina 106). En *Mediodía* (1976, lámina 21), de Antonio Berni, esos mismos signos amarillos y negros enmarcan el contraste entre un lustroso auto y la imagen en blanco y negro de dos trabajadores inclinados en torno a unos pobres alimentos, en este caso para señalar los peligros del consumismo. Nelson Leirner aborda con humor el mismo circuito comercial en dos obras que conectan con la moda, cuyo complejo despliegue de códigos fue analizado por el semiólogo francés Roland Barthes ese mismo año (1967) en el texto *El sistema de la moda*.[40] *Stripencores* (Stripencolores) (1968, lámina 62) presenta cuatro vestidos compuestos de paneles de colores y zíperes en largos diferentes para las cuatro estaciones del año que no existen en São Paulo. Por su parte, *Homenagem a Fontana II* (Homenaje a Fontana) (ver página 44, figura 2.2) fusiona la abstracción geométrica con los colores pop en una edición de cuatro lienzos en bastidor sujetos entre

sí por los mismos zíperes. Las obras de Leirner unen la figura humana
con la abstracción pura y cierran con zíper el famoso corte que el
artista italo-argentino Lucio Fontana hacía en sus lienzos. El *striptease* del título nos advierte que la sutura es meramente temporal y
promete que el corte se reabrirá para exponer un cuerpo desnudo y
vulnerable. En efecto, el artista cubano Raúl Martínez y la historiadora de arte estadounidense Shifra Goldman concluyen que la interacción entre la abstracción, la figuración pop y el diseño gráfico como
tipologías de signos es algo común a "nuestro continente" —que
llaman "América"— y adjudican este intercambio a su larga lucha por
la liberación.[41]

EL POP COMO PASAJE

Considerando su heterogeneidad, Antonio Dias denomina al pop como
un "pasaje", un corredor hacia nuevas formas radicales de arte contemporáneo.[42] Su serie *The Illustration of Art* (La ilustración del arte) (1971–
1978) —representada en esta exposición con dos obras— ejemplifica ese
itinerario y los íntimos vínculos que existen entre América del Norte
y del Sur. El título juega con la asociación entre el pop y la figuración
como representación visual de un suceso o una persona —una ilustración—, pero también podemos pensar en Ilustración con mayúscula: la
filosofía dieciochesca centrada en las ideas del individuo, la libertad
y la razón científica. Compuesta de videos, instalaciones, imágenes
mediáticas intervenidas, performance y pintura abstracta y figurativa,
esta serie pasa por el conducto del pop para explosionar la lógica
de la "ilustración" en el arte. En el díptico *Uncovering the Cover-Up*
(Descubriendo el encubrimiento) (1973, lámina 80), parte de esta serie,
el artista tapa con blanco los ojos, la nariz y la boca de una imagen de
Sam Ervin, senador por Carolina del Norte, publicada en la portada de
la edición internacional de *Newsweek* el 28 de mayo de 1973; utilizando
rectángulos negros y rojos, hace un enlace entre el retrato del senador
y un lienzo rojo plano. La imagen del "Senador Sam", reproducida en
serigrafía, se utilizó a manera de máscaras en un perturbador performance que abordaba los estereotipos racistas, *Score for Dangerous
Performers* (Partitura para intérpretes peligrosos, 1973). En otra obra,
los mismos rectángulos rojos invaden la cobertura periodística de la
guerra de Nixon en Vietnam, convirtiéndola en formas geométricas
(ver página 17, figura 1.9).

El hecho de que Dias haya seleccionado a Ervin como prototipo del
personaje de dos caras, que esconde tanto como revela, cristaliza la
relación intensa y sinuosa entre el pop, la política y la idea de América.
El año en que el artista brasileño produjo *Uncovering the Cover-Up*,
Ervin era presidente del comité especial del Senado para investigar
prácticas de campaña, el cual descubrió el papel de Richard Nixon en
el caso de Watergate. Antes de esto, Ervin había firmado el tristemente
célebre Southern Manifesto (Manifiesto de Sur) (1956), que se oponía
a eliminar la segregación racial en las escuelas públicas. El "Senador
Sam" de Dias encarna un debate continental americano. Por un lado, el
papel que jugó Ervin en la caída de Nixon fue celebrado en América
del Sur, donde la extensión de la guerra de Vietnam promovida por el
presidente se veía como una expansión del régimen colonial estadounidense en el hemisferio. Por otro lado, estaba el hecho virulento de
que el senador promoviera el racismo contra los negros que aquejaba

también a Brasil y al resto de América. Si para Ervin estas contradicciones entre políticas de izquierda y derecha se resolvían mediante
la total fidelidad a los ideales de la Ilustración y las libertades del
individuo, con *The Illustration of Art* Dias exige que confrontemos la
paradoja inscrita en la idea misma de libertad.

Los artistas de *Pop América* utilizaron el pop como verbo para
explorar opciones de liberación ante esta paradoja: liberación de las
restricciones estéticas de las escuelas de arte y los museos, del estrés
de la vida urbana y las exigencias de las nuevas economías, para las
personas de color oprimidas por regímenes coloniales y neocolo-
niales en todo el continente, e incluso la liberación de la naturaleza
misma. *Unfinished Man* (Hombre inacabado) (1968, lámina 101) de
Rupert García hace un retrato de esa liberación en una figura trunca-
da que encarna las ansiedades artísticas, políticas y emocionales de
un año que constituyó un punto de inflexión, el 1968. Los contornos
negros reinterpretan las estrategias políticas y pictóricas de los
muralistas mexicanos; una boca abierta representa el dolor psicoló-
gico del *Hombre invisible* (1952) de Ralph Ellison, novela pionera por
su investigación de la subjetividad afroamericana, publicada en la
década previa; y un cielo azul pálido recuerda las atmósferas de Ed
Ruscha, artista pop de Los Ángeles.[43] Como el *AR* azul de Gerchman,
como las aguas verdes de Uriburu y como *Great Wall of Los Angeles*
(Gran muralla de Los Ángeles) (ver página 18, figura 1.10) de Judith F.
Baca —que sitúa una historia de América con pueblos negros, latinos
y asiáticos en la cuenca del río Los Ángeles—, el cielo azul de García
participó en lo que Morais llamó el "regreso al problema de la naturaleza".[44] La liberación pop de América incluía su aire, tierra y agua
tanto como su gente, formaciones naturales que unen a un continente desafiando las fronteras políticas que lo dividen.[45]

Sin pretender ofrecer un panorama exhaustivo del enorme número
de artistas activos durante esta década a lo largo del continente, *Pop
América 1965–1975* presenta a través de sus galerías obras abiertas que
dan la bienvenida al espectador a participar consumiendo, modelando,
liberando, mediando y encarando América. Estos gerundios motivan la
repetición y redundancia del pop, así como sus juegos de signos e imágenes, cuerpo y cosa, bellas artes y artes populares. A la vez, acercan al
espectador al potencial emancipador de la libertad y lo confrontan con
sus promesas rotas, en esa década y en la nuestra.

NOTAS

1   Hugo Rivera-Scott en entrevista por Skype con Esther Gabara y Natalia de la Rosa, 2 de noviembre de 2016.

2   *Pop América* sigue la propuesta presentada por la exposición *Home —So Different, So Appealing*, comisariada por Chon Noriega, Mari Carmen Ramírez y Pilar Tompkins Rivas para LACMA (2017), que sugiere que el arte latinoamericano y latino pueden conformar un "concepto universal". Aquí, sin embargo, ese concepto universal es América. Aníbal Quijano e Immanuel Wallerstein definieron "la americanidad" como el carácter del continente que sirvió como terreno de experimentación con el capitalismo desde su formulación colonial en el siglo XVI hasta el presente. Si el pop viajó por el mundo en manifestaciones que han gozado de creciente visibilidad en exposiciones como *International Pop* (2015) en el Walker Art Center y *The World Goes Pop* (2015) en el Tate Modern, *Pop América* presenta la americanidad que se adhirió al pop en sus viajes. Ver Aníbal Quijano e Immanuel Wallerstein, "Americanity as a Concept, or the Americas in the Modern World-System", *International Social Science Journal* 44:4 (1992): 549–557.

3   Alfredo Jaar en entrevista con Esther Gabara, 4 de octubre de 2007. El acento en la palabra "América" en un título de idioma inglés permite evitar la "s" de "the Americas". No existen las Américas en plural, insiste el artista chileno Alfredo Jaar, porque esa "s" solo es necesaria si uno acepta que el singular le pertenece a Estados Unidos. La copiosa bibliografía sobre la accidentada historia de "América Latina" incluye hitos como Edmundo O'Gorman, *La invención de América: El universalismo de la cultura occidental* (México: UNAM, 1958); manifiestos más recientes como Walter D. Mignolo, *The Idea of Latin America* (Massachusetts, Oxford: Blackwell Publishing, 2005); y debates en los museos y facultades de historia del arte así como en las casas de subasta acerca de si exponer a los artistas latinoamericanos modernos y contemporáneos en secciones separadas de sus contrapartes europeos y estadounidenses.

4   Beatriz González, "Actitudes transgresoras de una década", en *Sin título 1966-1968. Luis Caballero* (Bogotá: Museo Nacional de Bogotá, 1997), 29.

5   Ver Claire F. Fox, *Making Art Pan-American: Cultural Policy and the Cold War* (Minneapolis: University of Minnesota Press, 2013). El capítulo "The Last Party" (La última fiesta) propone que los nuevos experimentos de liberalización económica acogieron la participación de las corporaciones estadounidenses y recibieron el apoyo de Washington, aunque estaban encabezados por dictaduras militares y regímenes represivos.

6   Ver más información sobre la bandera de Johns como signo en Brian M. Reed, "Hand in Hand: Jasper Johns and Hart Crane", *Modernism/Modernity* 1:1 (2010): 21–45.

7   *Sin Fronteras: El periódico de la raza de bronce* vol. 1 no. 2, marzo de 1974. El Chicano Movement, conocido como *El Movimiento*, fue un movimiento de mexicano-americanos en la época de las luchas por los derechos civiles en Estados Unidos.

8   Tropicália fue una palabra acuñada por el artista visual Hélio Oiticica para su instalación en la histórica exposición *Una nueva objetividad brasileña* en el Museo de Arte Moderno de Río de Janeiro en 1967, y para 1968 había sido adoptada por los músicos Caetano Veloso y Gilberto Gil. El movimiento Tropicália irrumpió en la escena brasileña en 1967-1968 con los músicos Caetano Veloso y Gilberto Gil. Ver Carlos Basualdo, *Tropicália: A Revolution in Brazil Culture* (São Paulo, Brasil: Cosac Naify, 2005), 12–13.

9   El héroe nacional cubano José Martí publicó su famoso ensayo que celebraba la naturaleza "nativa" hispanoamericana en contraste con la "falsa erudición" importada en 1891 en *La Revista Ilustrada*, publicación periódica de Nueva York en idioma español, y al poco tiempo en *El Partido Liberal* en Ciudad de México.

10 Ver Sofia Gotti, "Popau, Pop, or an 'American Way of Living?' Introducción a Aracy Amaral 'From the Stamps to the Bubble,'" *ArtMargins* 5:2 (2016): 109.

11 Luis Cruz Azaceta en entrevista con Esther Gabara, 14 de febrero de 2017. Cruz Azaceta recientemente atribuyó la caracterización de sus pinturas como pop apocalíptico a la crítica de arte del *New York Times* Grace Glueck (entrevista con Esther Gabara, 14 de febrero de 2017). Aunque Glueck en efecto describió la obra *The City Painter of Hearts* como un "lienzo apocalíptico", no utilizó la frase exacta. "Art View; Of Beasts and Humans: Some Contemporary Views", *New York Times*, 14 de noviembre de 1982. En una entrevista de 1989 con Bob Loescher, el artista declaró que la frase era suya. "Luis Cruz Azaceta: An Interview", Video Data Bank, 1989, http://www.vdb.org/titles/luis-cruz-azaceta-interview, consultado el 22 de septiembre de 2017.

12 Estas fundaciones fueron establecidas tras la desintegración de Standard Oil en múltiples compañías y se utilizaban para mantener control sobre ellas y para evitar pagar altos impuestos. Sylvia Sigal destaca que Di Tella, "se distingue por su vocación explícita, *de institución pública pero no estatal*". Ver Jorgelina Corbatta, "Oscar Masotta: divergencias y convergencias", *The Colorado Review of Hispanic Studies* 6 (2008): 98.

13 Ver Rodrigo Alonso, *El Espíritu Pop* (Mar del Plata, Argentina: MAR/Museo de Arte Contemporáneo, 2013), 136; y David Horowitz, "Malvenido Rockefeller! A Special Exhibition from Argentina", *Ramparts*, febrero de 1970, 20. La histórica escultura de Ferrari *La Civilización Occidental y Cristiana* (1965) fue retirada del Instituto Torcuato Di Tella antes de que se inaugurara la exposición del artista en 1965, pero la obra *La voracidad o la pesadilla de Ramona* (1964) de Antonio Berni sí se expuso allí ese mismo año. Ver también la exposición de 2012 sobre *Malvenido Rockefeller!* en el Centro Cultural de la Cooperación Floreal Gorini, que presentó fotografías del archivo de Ferrari de la exposición de 1970, http://www.arsomnibus.com/web/muestra/malvenido-rockefeller.

14 El libro *Making Art Pan-American* de Fox contiene la investigación exhaustiva y análisis documental que me guía en este caso.

15 Fox, *Making Art Pan-American*, 182, 185.

16 Ver el catálogo de la exposición *Felipe Ehrenberg 67//15*, comisariada por Marta Ramos-Yzquierdo, Galería Freijo, s.p. Liderados por el arquitecto y fiel partidario del PRI Pedro Ramírez Vázquez, miembros del Departamento de Actividades Culturales y Artísticas, entre ellos Eduardo Terrazas, Beatrice Trueblood, Manuel Villazón y Lance Wyman, planearon una Olimpiada Cultural de un año de duración.

17 Ver Romero Brest en Alonso, *El Espíritu Pop*, 218. Romero Brest también cita la visión "profética e inspirada" de Rafael Squirru sobre la obra de Marta Minujín en términos de ser una nueva propuesta que no tenía nada que ver con el surrealismo. Es esencial observar aquí que también para Oscar Masotta la redundancia y reproducción del pop difiere fundamental del giro psicoanalítico del surrealismo, que se basa en la metáfora. Masotta, *El "Pop-Art"* (Buenos Aires: Columba, 1967), 10. Como lo sugiere Alonso, los ensamblajes del mexicano Alberto Gironella, construidos con deshechos de la vida contemporánea, pueden interpretarse en términos similares, dado que su gran fascinación por Robert Rauschenberg contribuyó a que creara "cosas" que rompían con formas anteriores de realismo y surrealismo en el arte. Alonso, *El Espíritu Pop*, 44.

18 Ver *Rubens Gerchman: O Rei do Mau Gosto*, ed. Clara Gerchman (Río de Janeiro: J.J. Carol, 2016).

19 Virginia Dwan, galerista de Los Ángeles, organizó en 1964 la exposición titulada *Boxes*, famosa por haber puesto de relieve la relación del arte pop con este objeto. Ver James Meyer, *Dwan Gallery: Los Angeles to New York, 1959-1971* (Chicago: University of Chicago Press, 2016).

20 Costa, Perreault y Weiner escribieron que el "Fashion Show Poetry Event" "no solo es moda, poesía y arte, es donde estas categorías arbitrarias se traslapaban, se disuelven y se vuelven irrelevantes". El "Fashion Show Poetry Event" es una nueva forma de teatro"; ver *Hannah Weiner's Open House*, ed. Patrick Durgin (Berkeley: Kenning Editions, 2006), 58. Ver también Eugenio Valdés Figueroa, *Rubens Gerchman: With the Resignation Letter in the Pocket* (Río de Janeiro: Casa Daros, 2015). Quisiera agradecer a Jennifer Josten su ayuda en el Getty Research Institute.

21 Elena Shromberg enfatiza que los años del supuesto "milagro económico" de la liberalización económica también fueron "años de chumbo" (años de plomo), la época de las peores represiones políticas impuestas por la dictadura militar. Ver Shromberg, *Art Systems: Brazil and the 1970s* (Austin: University of Texas, 2016), 7, 12. Quisiera agradecer a Jennifer Josten su ayuda a la Getty Research Institute.

22 Frederico de Morais, *Manifesto do Corpo à Terra*, 18 de abril de 1970. Archivo digital ICAA-MFAH, registro no. 1110794. Traducción del original portugués.

23 Los pachucos y pachucas eran mexicano-americanos cuya vestimenta —trajes tipo zoot suit y vestidos elegantes, un tanto extravagantes— se convirtió en un

símbolo de resistencia cultural y política al racismo en Los Ángeles y el suroeste de Estados Unidos en la década de 1940. Para obtener mayor información acerca de *Las tres Marías* y otras obras de Baca, ver Anna Indych-López, *Judith F. Baca* (Minneapolis: University of Minnesota Press, 2018). Agradezco a Indych-López sus generosas aclaraciones sobre estas obras.

24   Ver Carolina Ponce de León, *Beatriz González: What an Honor to Be with You* (Nueva York: El Museo del Barrio, 1998), 34.

25   Se refieren a la valla publicitaria *¿Por qué son tan geniales?* (1965) de Dalila Puzzovio, Carlos Squirru y Edgardo Giménez, y a los anti-happenings del Grupo Arte de los Medios, compuesto de Roberto Jacoby, Eduardo Costa y Raúl Escari. Ver Ana Longoni y Fernando Davis, "Cuidado con la pintura" (ensayo preliminar), en *Doscientos años de pintura argentina*, tomo III (Buenos Aires: Banco Hipotecario, 2014), 20.

26   Ver Jesús Martín Barbero, *De los medios a las mediaciones. Comunicación, cultura y hegemonía* (Barcelona: Editorial Gustavo Gili, 1987).

27   Marshall McLuhan, "Análisis estructural de los medios de comunicación", *Artes Visuales*, 7 (julio/septiembre, 1975): 2–3; Caja 14 en la Rupert and Sammi Madison García Collection en la biblioteca de la Universidad de California, Santa Barbara. Agradezco a Rosalía Romero su investigación en el archivo Madison García.

28   Eduardo Costa en entrevista de Esther Gabara, 15 de julio de 2015.

29   Juan Acha, "Arte Pop: Procedimientos y finalidades", *El Comercio*, 25 de mayo de 1969, 38.

30   Hernández Saavedra, "A propósito del plagio", *El Comercio*, 23 de mayo de 1969, 19. El hecho de que el pop acogiera la inautenticidad y enfatizara lo continental en vez de la identidad nacional estableció diferencias claras con los movimientos de vanguardia nacionalistas anteriores en el siglo XX.

31   Ver Anna Cant, "Land for Those Who Work It: A Visual Analysis of Agrarian Reform Posters in Velasco's Peru", *Journal of Latin American Studies* 44 (2012): 19.

32   Énfasis añadido; visto en Shifra E. Goldman, *Dimensions of the Americas: Art and Social Change in Latin America and the United States* (Chicago: The University of Chicago Press, 1994), 149.

33   Jesús Martín Barbero argumenta que estas formas de cultura popular y producción de arte popular son esenciales a la meditación activa del público. *The Long March of Pop*, de Thomas Crow, traza los elementos del arte popular rural, describiendo una "marcha" más larga pero que aún define al pop americano como propio de Estados Unidos. Ver Crow, *The Long March of Pop: Art, Music, and Design, 1930–1995* (New Haven: Yale University Press, 2014).

34   Lance Wyman en entrevista con Esther Gabara, 20 de julio de 2017.

35   Carla Stellweg, "Magnet–New York: Conceptual, Performance, Environmental, and Installation Art by Latin American Artists in New York", en *The Latin American Spirit: Art and Artists in the United States, 1920-1970* (Nueva York: Bronx Museum of the Arts, 1988), 308. En dos ensayos separados, Stellweg observa que la histórica exposición del Whitney Museum titulada *Handpainted Pop: An American Tradition, 1955-1962* (1993) en efecto fue muy tradicional, dado que siguió excluyendo a pintores chicanos; "Rupert García: Chicaneidad, Art and Cultural Politics", en *Rupert García: Aspects of Resistance* (Nueva York: Alternative Museum, 1993).

36   Oscar Masotta, *El "Pop-Art"*, 15. En su contribución a este catálogo, Roberto Tejada sugiere que la metáfora y este metalenguaje no son tan mutuamente excluyentes como sugiere Masotta.

37   La semiótica, la ciencia social que estudia la forma en que el lenguaje comunica significados, jugó un papel formativo en el pensamiento brasileño. La antropología y la lingüística estructural eran escuelas de pensamiento importantes en la literatura, el arte y las ciencias sociales de Brasil, en gran parte debido a que el antropólogo francés Claude Lévi-Strauss residió en el país a finales de la década de 1930. Para obtener más información acerca de Lévi-Strauss en Brasil, ver Esther Gabara, *Errant Modernism: The Ethos of Photography in Mexico and Brazil, 1920-1940* (Durham: Duke University Press, 2008). Ver ejemplos de críticas estructuralistas y posestructuralistas del realismo en Robert Anchor, "Realism and Ideology: The Question of Order", *History and Theory* 22: 2 (1983): 107–119. Sobre la importancia del semiólogo italiano Umberto Eco para Gerchman y su grupo de artistas y críticos, ver Cristina Mura, *Rubens Gerchman e o Brasil dos Anos 60 e 70* (São Paulo: Alameda, 2016).

38   Manuscrito mecanografiado [original en inglés], abril de 1969, The Museum of Modern Art, Nueva York, archivo del artista Rubens Gerchman.

39   Gerchman traduce de manera un tanto torpe "Cartilha no superlativo" como "Primary in the Superlative" (Cartilla en superlativo). Escribe que el hecho de venir de "debajo del ecuador" lo inspiró a hacer una serie de proyectos en torno al lenguaje; las enormes palabras escultóricas fueron parte de ese importante cambio de rumbo en su trabajo que nació "por la necesidad de hacer un tipo de objeto de tamaño especial que le enseñara a la gente a leer. Este asunto me preocupa desde 1965 y, como saben, ¾ de la población que vive debajo del ecuador es analfabeta. Nunca llevé este proyecto a su fin". Fechado octubre de 1970, Nueva York. Ver *Rubens Gerchman: O Rei do Mau Gosto*, 104–115. La poesía concreta brasileña, liderada por figuras importantes como Haroldo y Augusto de Campos, Décio Pignatari y Wlademir Dias-Pino, surgió a mediados de los años cincuenta y enfatizaba la estructura visual de la poesía.

40   El "Fashion Show Poetry Event" arriba mencionado también se centraba en el "fenómeno total de la moda como lenguaje"; Costa, Perreault y Hannah Weiner escribieron en 1968 que: "El lenguaje de la moda es un código complicado. [...] En el 'Fashion Show Poetry Event' se llevan a cabo varias traducciones de lo verbal (escrito y oral) a lo visual y de lo visual a lo verbal". Ver *Hannah Weiner's Open House*, 57.

41   Goldman, *Dimensions of the Americas*, 165, 147.

42   Antonio Dias en entrevista con Esther Gabara, 9 de noviembre de 2016.

43   Rupert García en entrevista con Esther Gabara, 25 de septiembre de 2015. Rupert García pasó horas mirando el cielo californiano para lograr ese tono preciso de azul en esta obra.

44   Anna Katherine Brodbeck, "The Salão da Bússola (1969) and Do Corpo à Terra (1970): Parallel Developments in Brazilian and International Art", *RACAR* 382 (2013): 119.

45   Para obtener más información sobre la base ambiental de esta obra de arte social, ver el documental *The Great Wall of Los Angeles*; artista: Judith F. Baca, edición: Ernesto Quintero y Farhad Akhmetov, consultores de guion: Danny Haro y Dianna M. Pérez, SPARC Productions, 2007.

WELCOME TO AMÉRICA

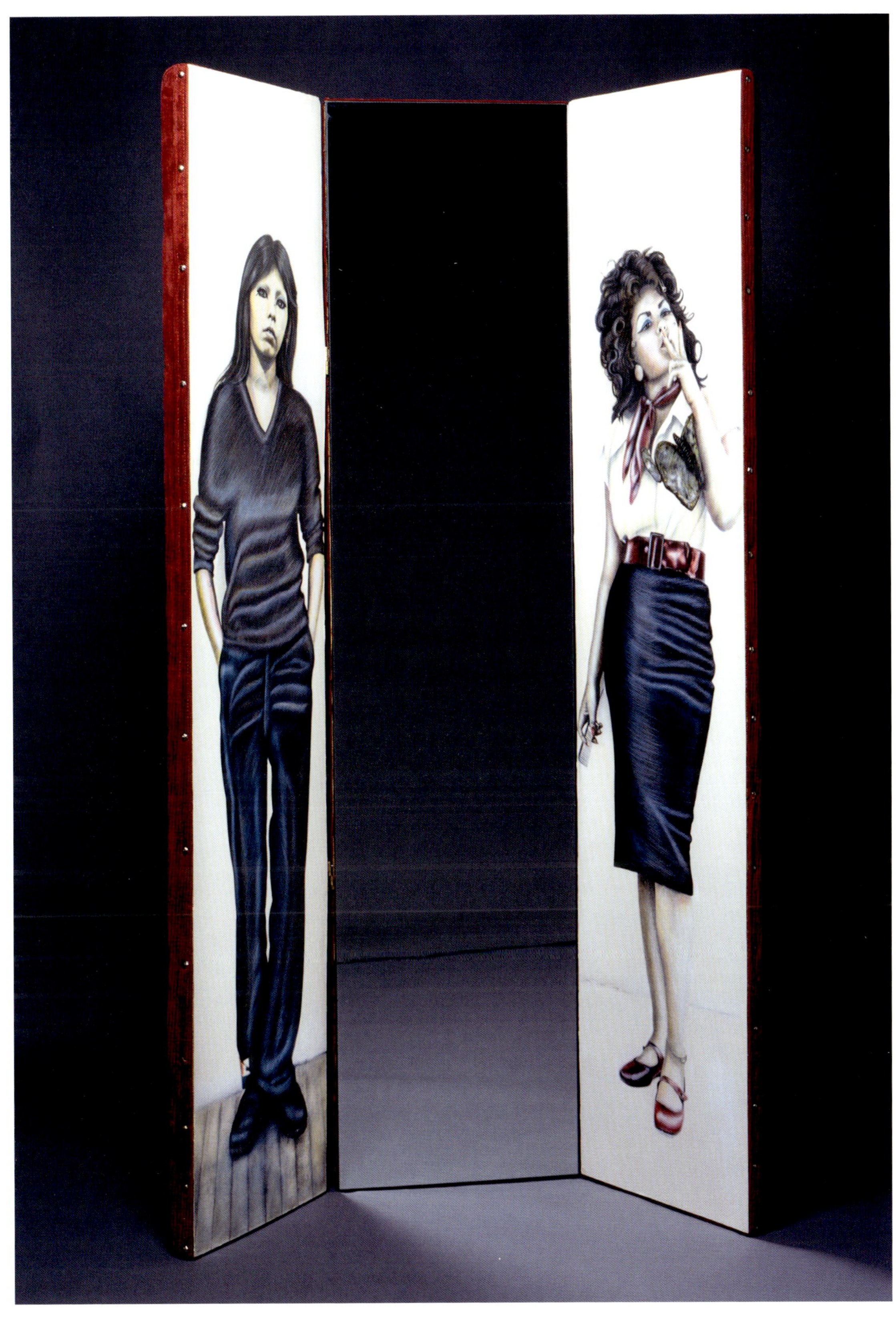

Pl. 1. Judith F. Baca, *Las tres Marías* (The Three Marías), 1976. Colored pencil on paper mounted on panel with upholstery backing and mirror, 68.25 x 50.25 x 2.25 inches (173.36 x 127.64 x 5.72 cm), overall. Collection of the Smithsonian American Art Museum, Washington, DC. Museum purchase made possible by William T. Evans. © Judith F. Baca. Image courtesy of Smithsonian American Art Museum, Washington, DC/Art Resource, New York, New York.

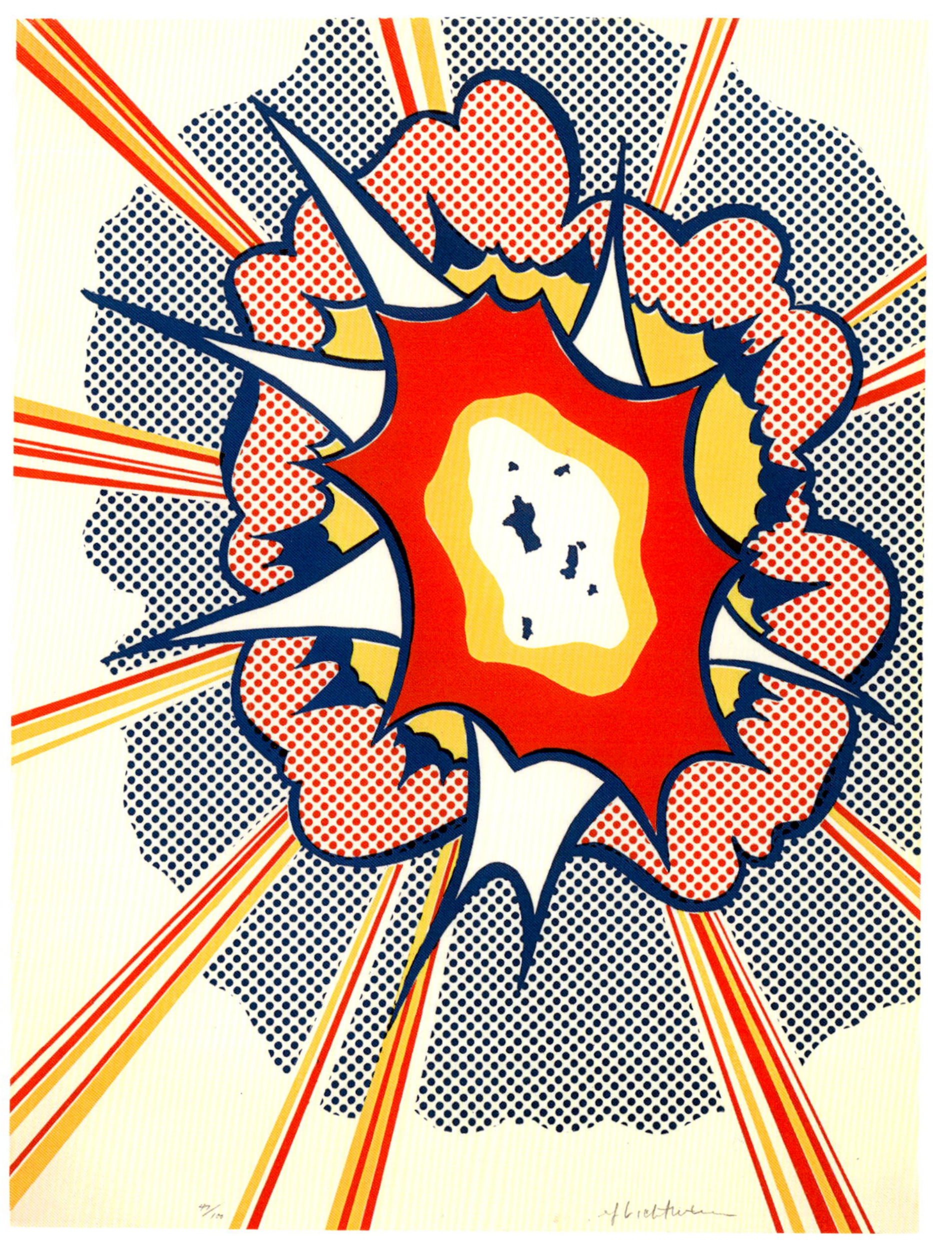

Pl. 2. Roy Lichtenstein, *Explosion* from *Portfolio 9*, 1967. Lithograph on Rives paper, 22.15 x 17.12 inches (56.2 x 43.5 cm). Collection of Jonathan J. Prinz. Image courtesy of Albright-Knox Art Gallery, Buffalo, New York. Licensed by Art Resource, New York, New York.

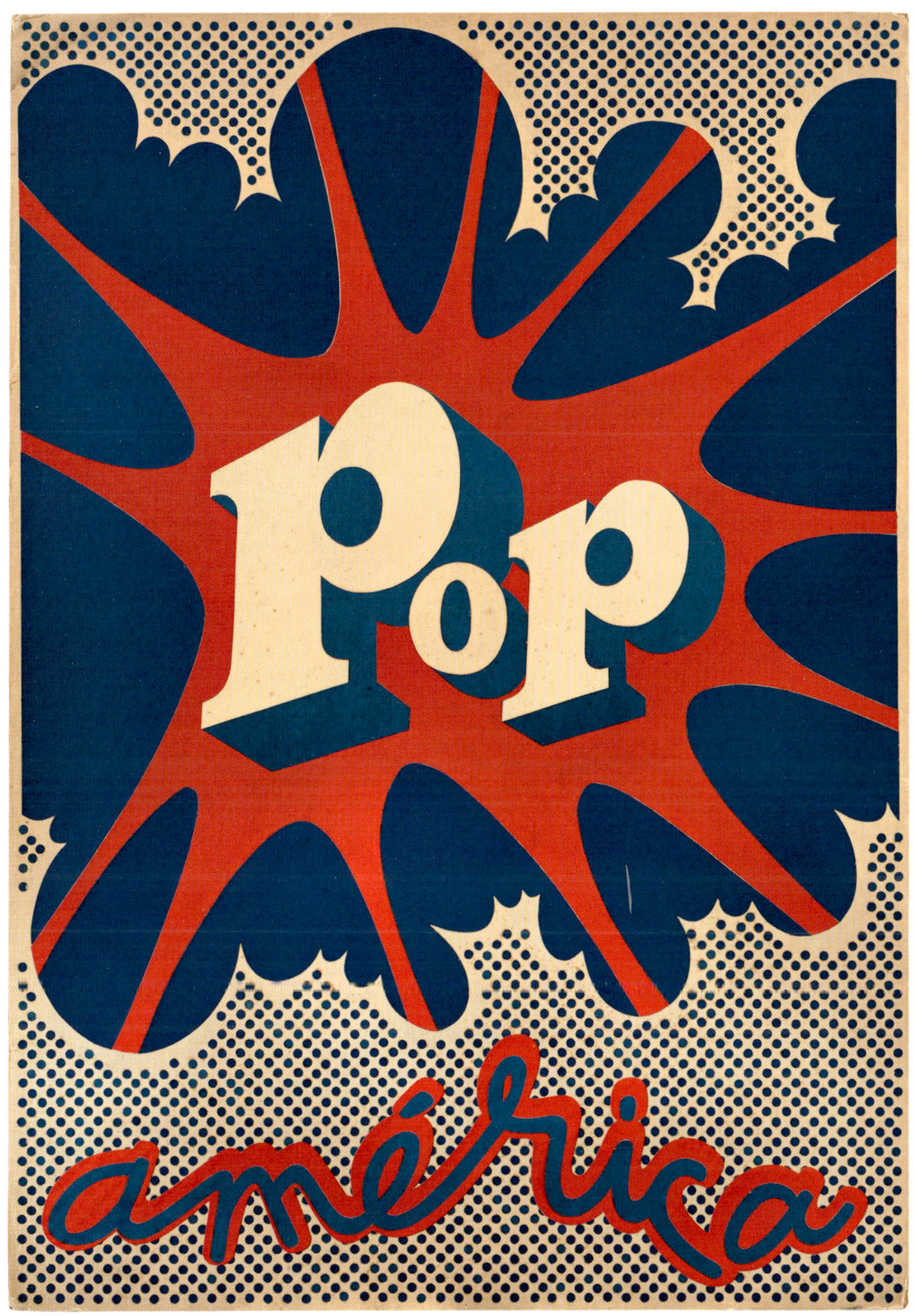

Pl. 3. Hugo Rivera-Scott, *Pop América*, 1968. Collage on cardboard, 30 x 21.5 inches (76.5 x 54.5 cm). Courtesy of the artist. © Hugo Rivera-Scott. Photo by Jorge Brantmayer.

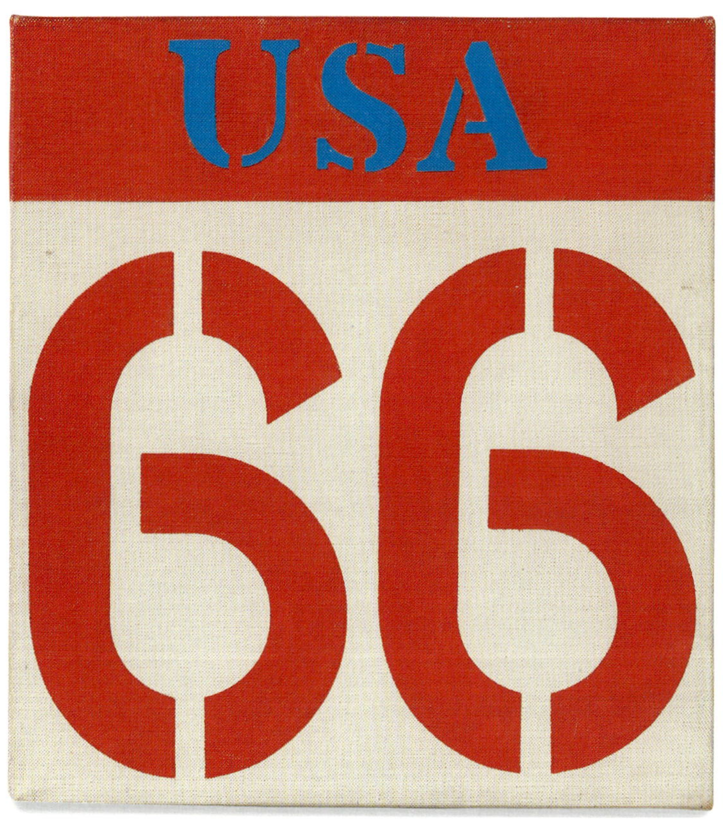

Pl. 4. Robert Indiana, *Route 66*, 1962. Oil on canvas, 12.25 x 11.5 inches (31.11 x 29.21 cm). Collection of the Weatherspoon Art Museum, the University of North Carolina at Greensboro. Museum purchase with funds from the Benefactors Fund. © 2018 Morgan Art Foundation Ltd. Licensed by Artists Rights Society (ARS), New York, New York.

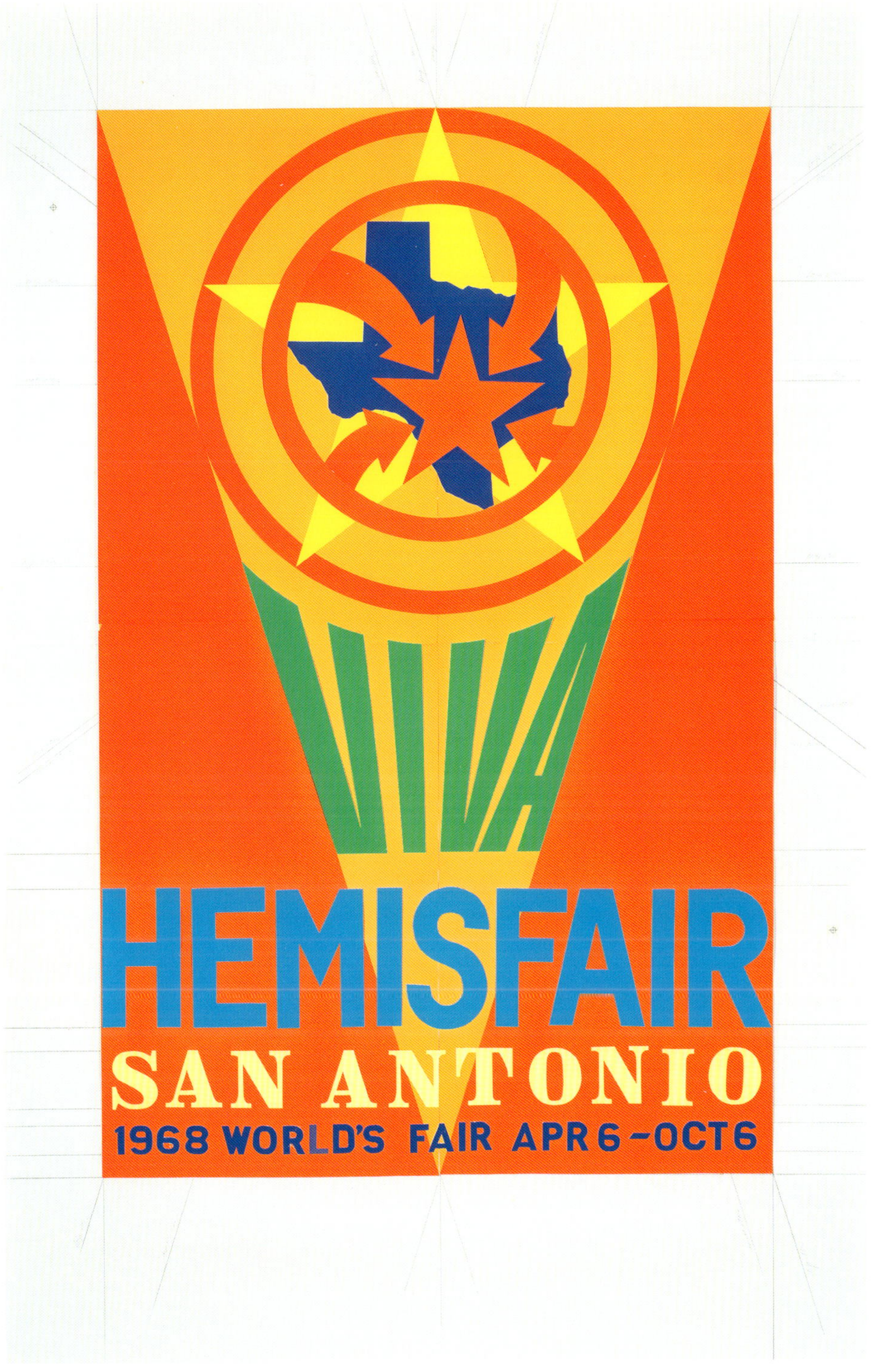

Pl. 5. Robert Indiana, Study for *Viva HemisFair* poster, 1967. Collage and graphite on board, 60 x 40 inches (152.4 x 101.6 cm). Collection of the Tobin Theatre Arts Fund, San Antonio, Texas. Courtesy of the McNay Art Museum, San Antonio, Texas. © 2018 Morgan Art Foundation Ltd. Licensed by Artists Rights Society (ARS), New York, New York.

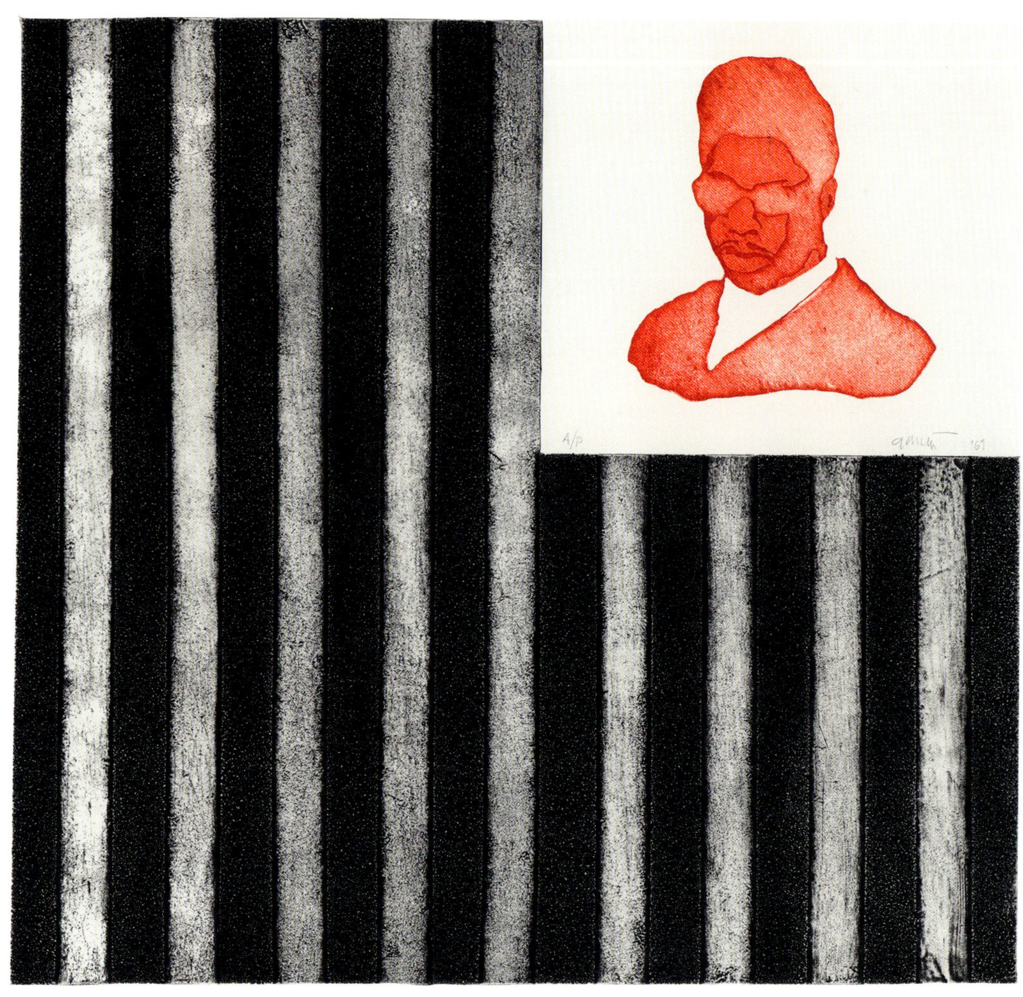

Pl. 6. Rupert García, *Black Man and Flag*, 1967. Etching and collagraph on paper, 21.65 x 23.18 inches (55.4 x 58.9 cm). Collection of the Fine Arts Museums of San Francisco, De Young, Legion of Honor Museum, California. Gift of Mr. and Mrs. Robert Marcus. © Rupert García. Courtesy of the artist and Rena Bransten Gallery, San Francisco, California.

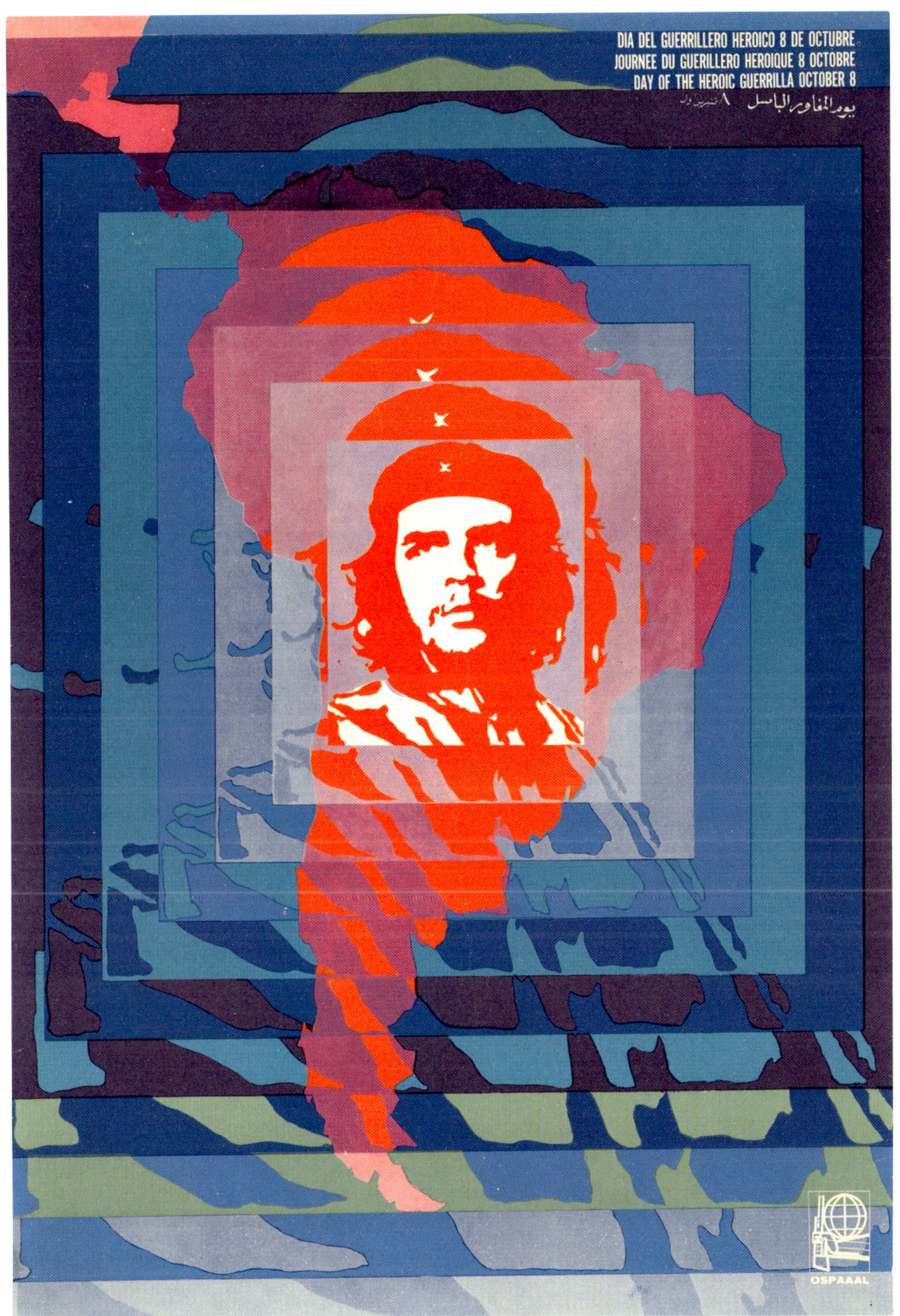

Pl. 7. Elena Serrano (artist) and OSPAAAL (publisher), *Día del guerrillero heroico* (Day of the Heroic Guerrilla), 1968. Offset lithograph on paper, 19.5 x 13.56 inches (49.4 x 34.5 cm). Collection of the Prints & Photographs Division, Library of Congress, Washington DC. Gift of Gary Yanker, 1975–1983.

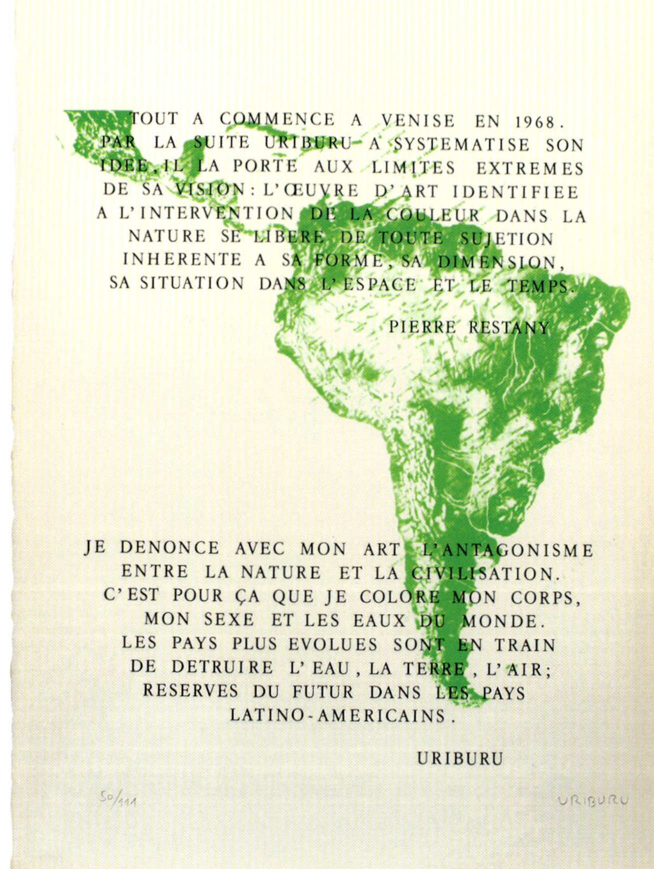

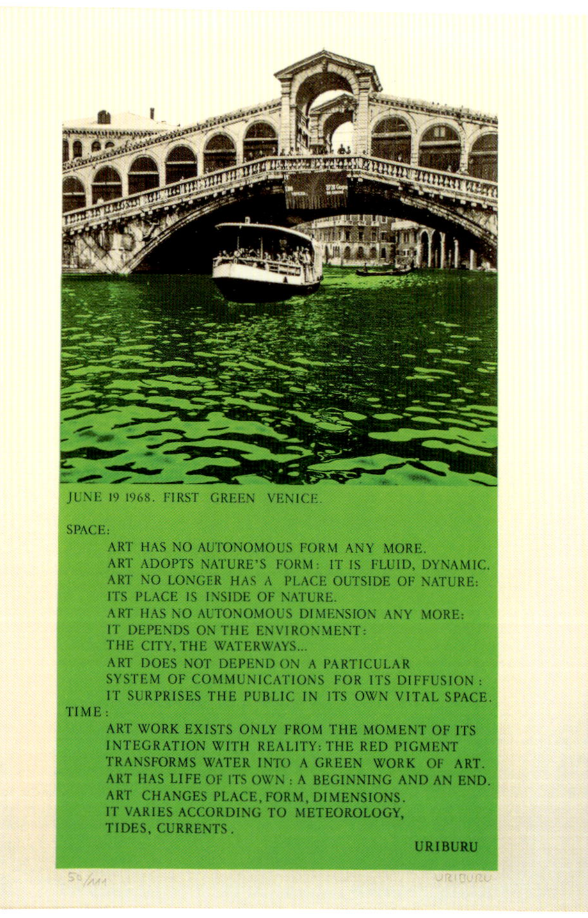

LEFT TO RIGHT, Pls. 8, 9. Nicolás García Uriburu, Artist's Statement and *June 19, 1968, First Green Venice* from the portfolio *Manifiesto* (Manifesto), 1973. **OPPOSITE (TOP TO BOTTOM), Pls. 10–13.** Nicolás García Uriburu, *1970: Intercontinental Environment of the Waters*; *Sex Coloration, New York, October 1971*; *Vertical Project: Green Coloration, Iguazú Falls, Argentina*; and *Latinoamérica: Reservas naturales del futuro, unida o sometida* (Latin America: Natural Resources of the Future, United or Repressed) from the portfolio *Manifiesto* (Manifesto), 1973. Portfolio of six screenprints on paper, 30 x 22.25 inches (76.2 x 56.5 cm), each. Collection of El Museo del Barrio, New York, New York. Gift of Margarita J. Aguilar. © Nicolás García Uriburu.

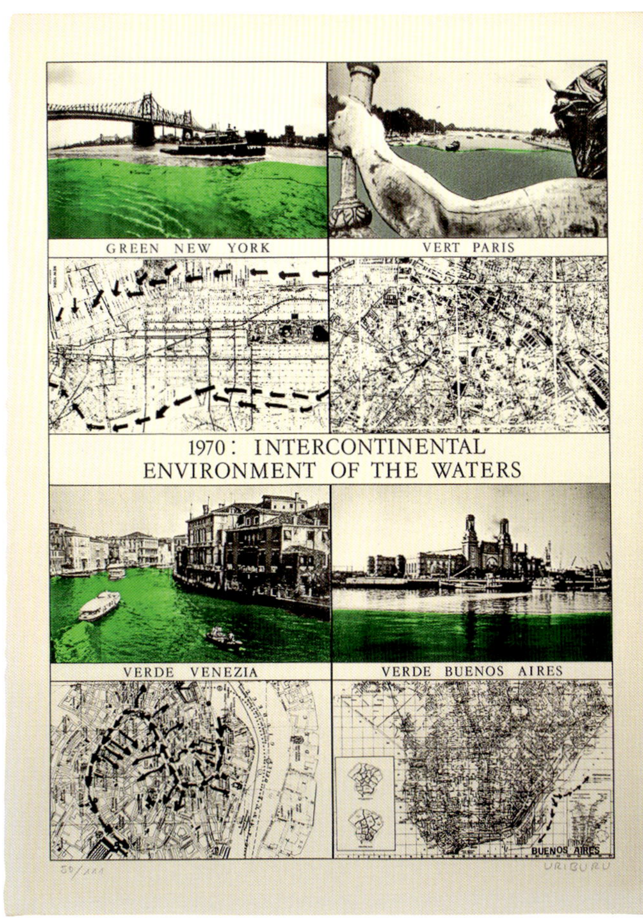

GREEN NEW YORK
VERT PARIS
1970 : INTERCONTINENTAL
ENVIRONMENT OF THE WATERS
VERDE VENEZIA
VERDE BUENOS AIRES
BUENOS AIRES
URIBURU

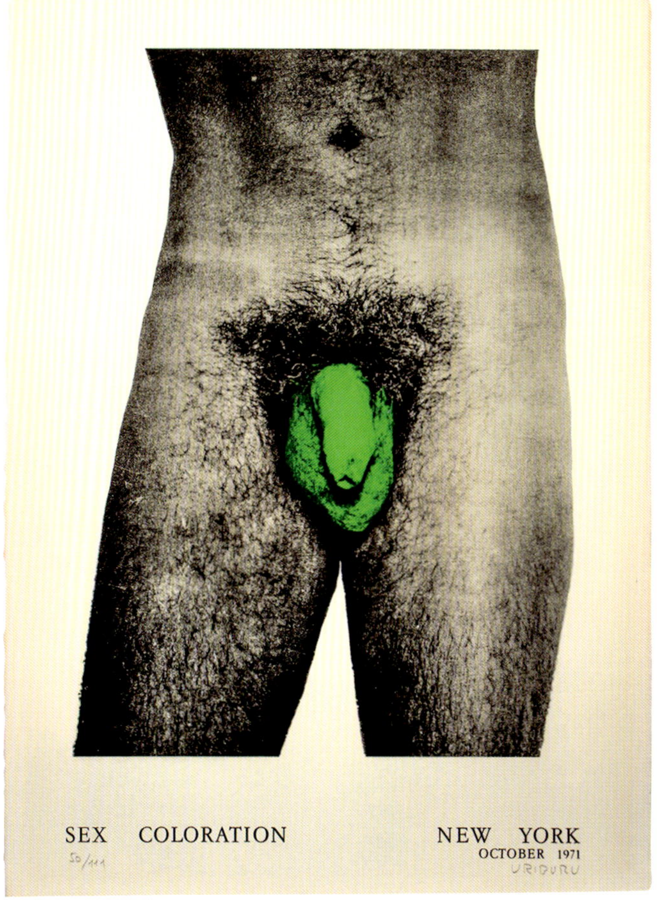

SEX COLORATION
NEW YORK
OCTOBER 1971
URIBURU

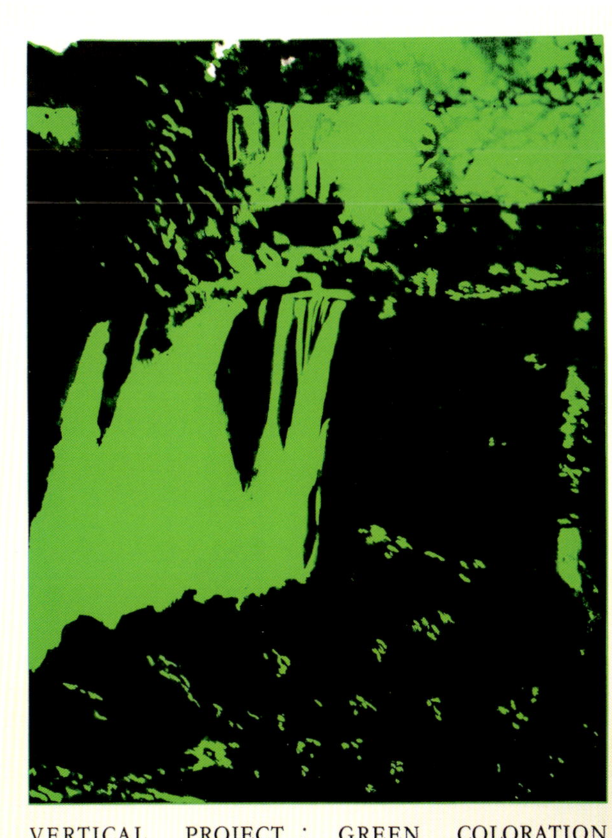

VERTICAL PROJECT : GREEN COLORATION
IGUAZÚ FALLS ARGENTINA
URIBURU

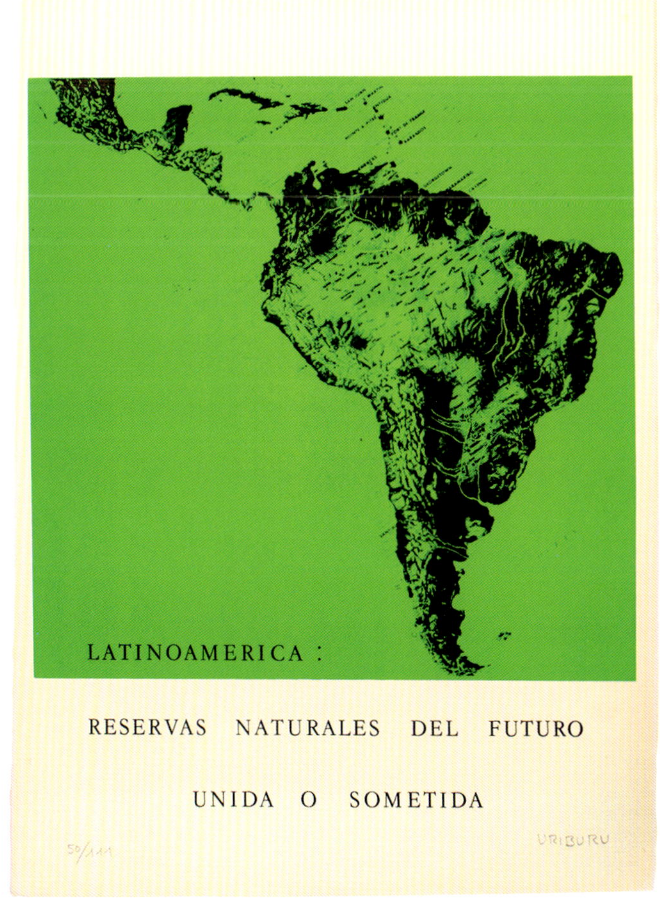

LATINOAMERICA :
RESERVAS NATURALES DEL FUTURO
UNIDA O SOMETIDA
URIBURU

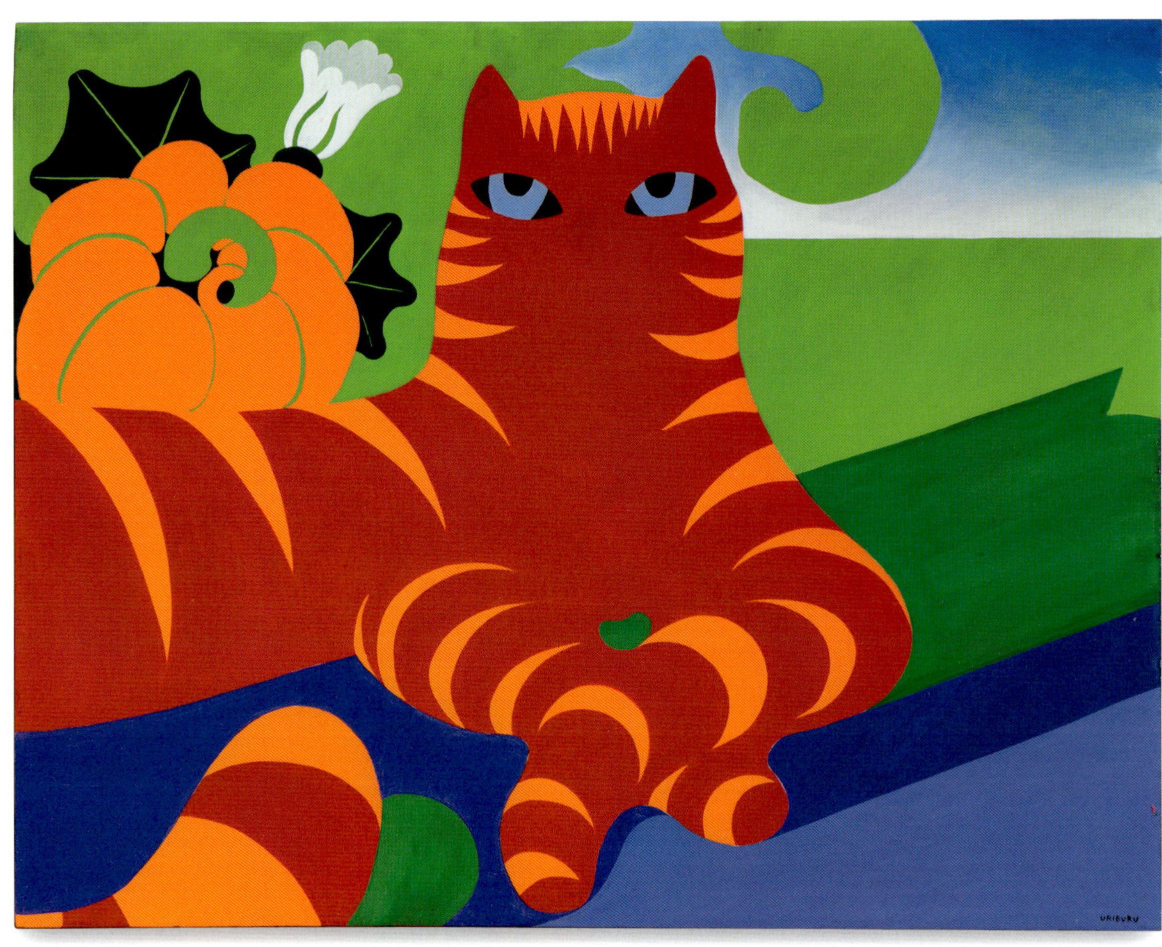

Pl. 14. Nicolás García Uriburu, *La pantera roja* (The Red Panther), 1969. Oil on canvas, 39.5 x 50.75 inches (100 x 129 cm). Private collection. Art © Nicolás García Uriburu. Digital image © Christie's Images Limited, 2018.

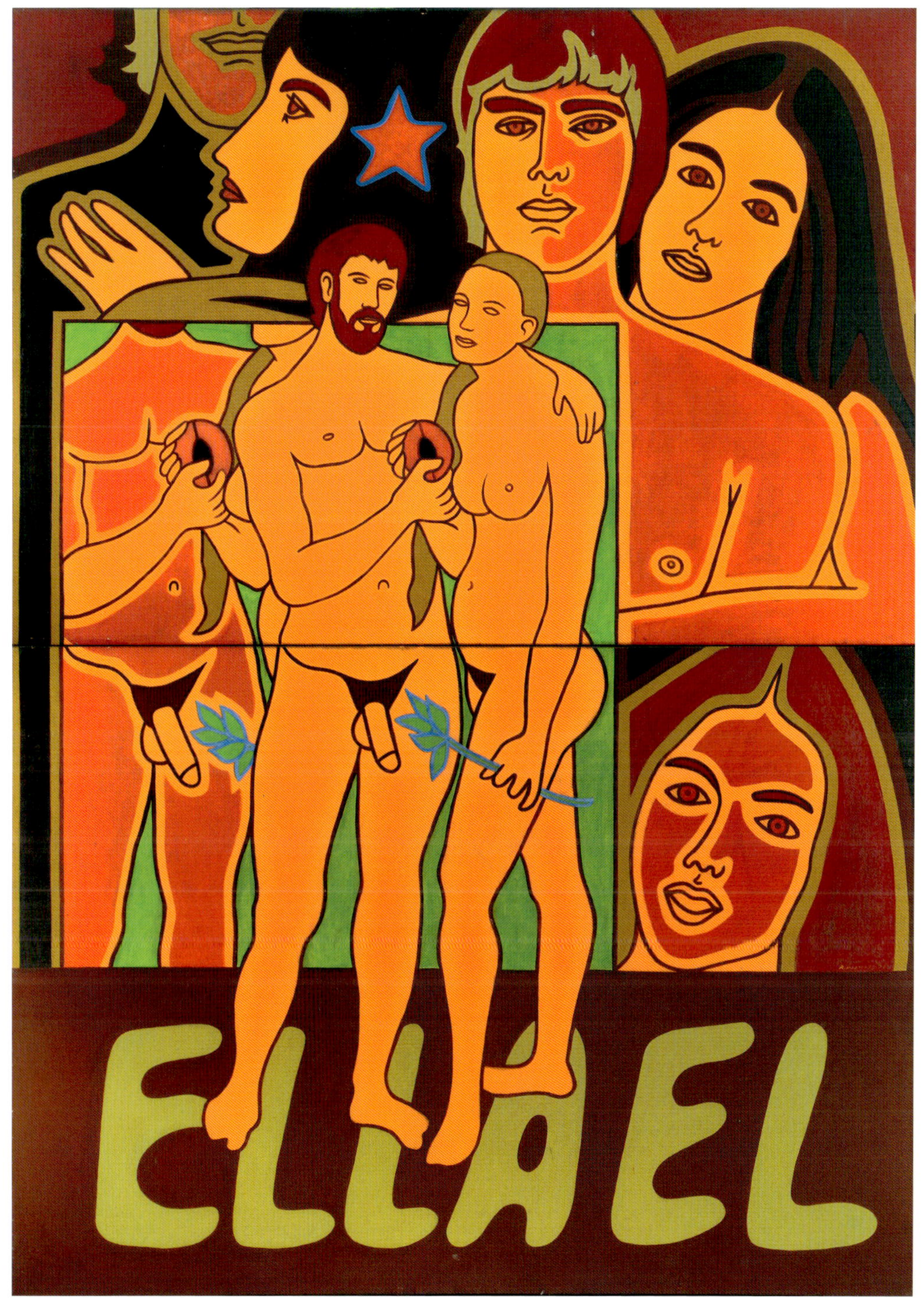

Pl. 15. Raúl Martínez, *Adán y Julieta* (Adam and Juliet), 1973. Acrylic on canvas, 84.37 x 60.25 inches (214.32 x 153.03 cm), overall. Pizzuti Collection, Columbus, Ohio. © Raúl Martínez Estate, Ciego de Ávila, Cuba. Image courtesy of the Raúl Martínez Estate and Corina Matamoros.

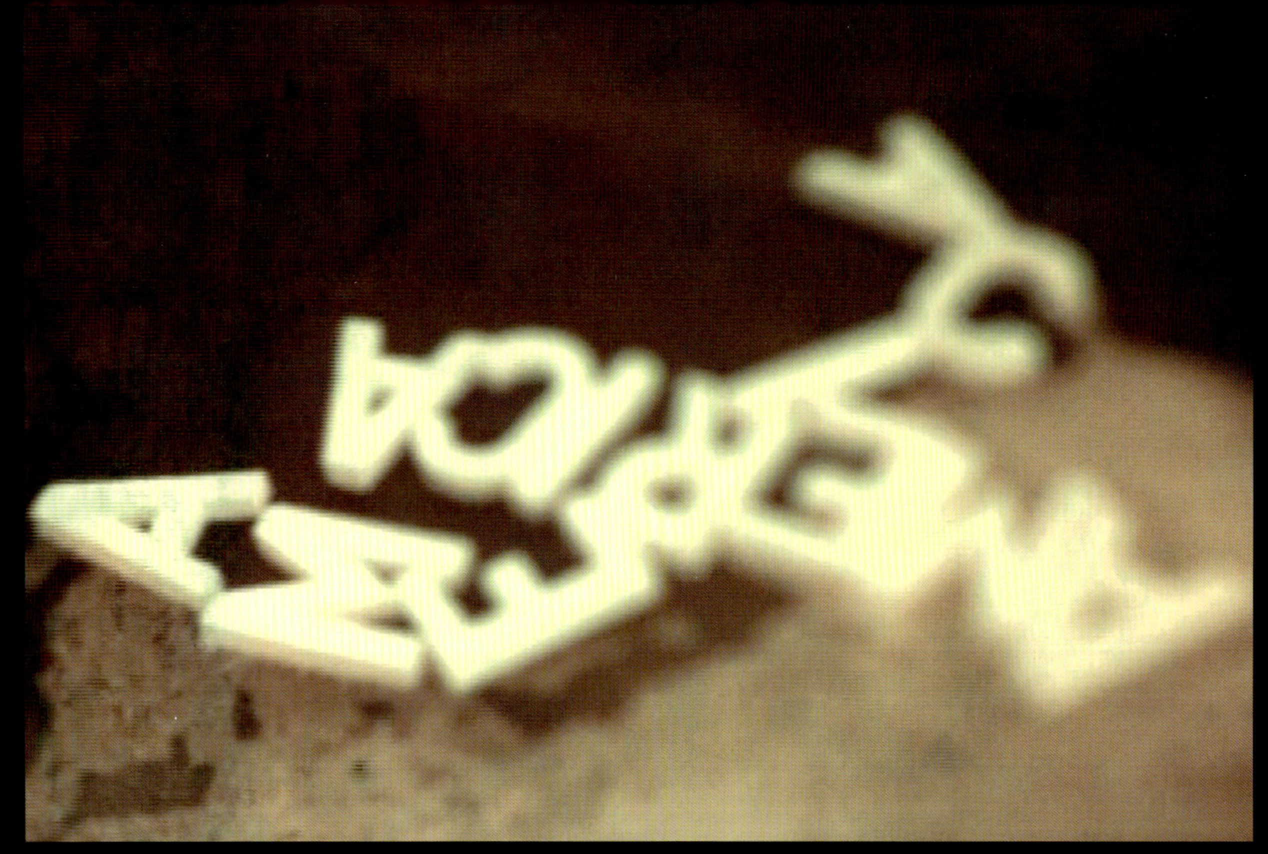

Pl. 16. Rubens Gerchman, *Triunfo hermético* (Hermetic Triumph) (stills), 1972. 35mm film transferred to video (color, sound), 12:00 minutes. Courtesy of the Rubens Gerchman Institute. © Rubens Gerchman Institute, Rio de Janeiro, Brazil.

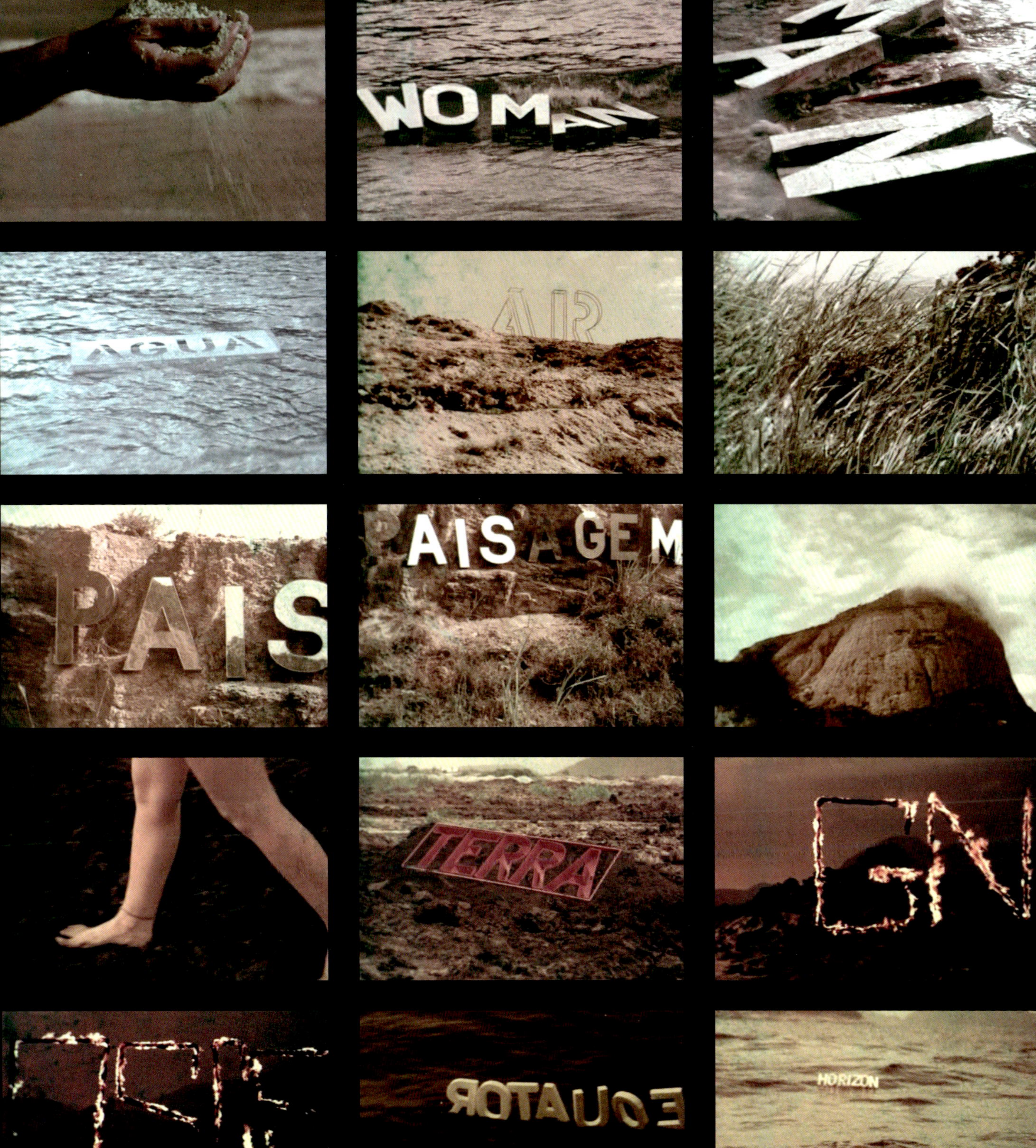

WOMAN
MAN
AGUA
AIR
PAIS
PAISAGEM
TERRA
HORIZON
EQUATOR

CAMILA MAROJA

POP GOES CONCEPTUAL: VISUAL LANGUAGE IN AMÉRICA

The IX Bienal de São Paulo in 1967 immediately became known as the "Bienal do Pop" (Pop Biennial). This nomenclature reflected not only one of the exhibition's most prominent national representations—*Ambiente USA: 1957–1967* (Environment USA: 1957–1967), which featured iconic works by Andy Warhol and Robert Indiana, among others—but also referred to a shared tendency among many of the artists to seek the direct appropriation of reality in their work.[1] By uniting artworks as diverse as Julio Le Parc's kinetic objects and Nelson Leirner's "paintings" with polyester and zippers under the Pop label (see page 44; figures 2.1, 2.2), the biennial's Pop rubric generated a false impression of artistic homogeneity. Indeed, by amassing a range of local terminologies that were operative in the late 1960s, including popular and Environmental art, *objetos* (objects), *nouveau réalisme* (New Realism), and *nova objetividade* (New Objectivity), the exhibit appeared to contradict the very idea of Pop as a global art movement.[2] Mexican art critic Ida Rodríguez Prampolini argued as much in a letter written to the exhibition committee urging them to scrap the outdated biennial criteria, as reflected in its offering a "grand prize for painting," and to establish new artistic categories such as *arte integrado* (integrated art). She even challenged the organizers to stop displaying artworks according to country, because "art has no political borders."[3]

Rodríguez Prampolini's vision of an integrated global village as imagined by media guru Marshall McLuhan proved to be overly optimistic, however, and contrasted vividly with the passionate public reaction to the show. Indeed, the IX Bienal became the first São Paulo biennial to be vandalized when one leftist demonstrator, taking advantage of a half-hour blackout, inscribed "*Viva Guevara. Fora USA!*" (Long Live Guevara. USA Out!) next to James Gill's *Marilyn* (see page 45, figure 2.3). Only a few months later, during the IV Salão de Arte Moderna do Distrito Federal, extreme-right militants used axes to hack off the wall Claudio Tozzi's panel *GUEVARA VIVO OU MORTO... (GUEVARA, ALIVE OR DEAD...)* (see page 46, figure 2.4), a Pop depiction of Cuban revolutionary icon Che Guevara.[4] As these attacks demonstrate, Pop art's appropriation of reality could not be separated from politics during the heyday of the Cold War and, contrary to Rodríguez Prampolini's belief, art did have political boundaries. Even more importantly, these acts of violence against Pop artworks—one from the left and one from the right—threaten the supposedly univocal category of Pop and compel us to rethink the canonization of Latin American Conceptual art, or Conceptualism, a movement that became known in the region for its leftist political inflection.[5] These actions demonstrate that the shared visual vocabulary of Pop and Conceptual art could code-switch, communicating radically different meanings depending on its agent and audience.

This exhibition invites viewers to rethink Pop in América, to view it as an action, a verb, and not just as an art movement or collection of objects. Pop actions, like Hugo Rivera-Scott's insertion of an accent in his *Pop América* collage (1968, plate 3), root aesthetic production in specific visual and verbal languages. In what follows, I examine artists who engaged Pop as a verb, and so decenter the globality assigned—then and now—to artistic movements that originated in traditional art centers. Appropriating and subverting a vocabulary that circulated in the upper part of the continent, these vernacular Pop productions challenge key parameters of art history, including the dyad of original and copy. Several of the Latin American artists featured in *Pop América* employ, for example, the iconic image of Coca-Cola advertisements and products—commercial icons whose history in the southern part of the hemisphere is inseparable from imperialist and neoliberal political interventions. They transform the vocabulary of Pop by making the ubiquitous Coca-Cola sign mutable, while transporting it to new sites.

The art historical opposition between Andy Warhol's *Green Coca-Cola Bottles* (see page 47, figure 2.5) and Cildo Meireles's *Inserções em circuitos ideológicos* (Insertions into Ideological Circuits) from

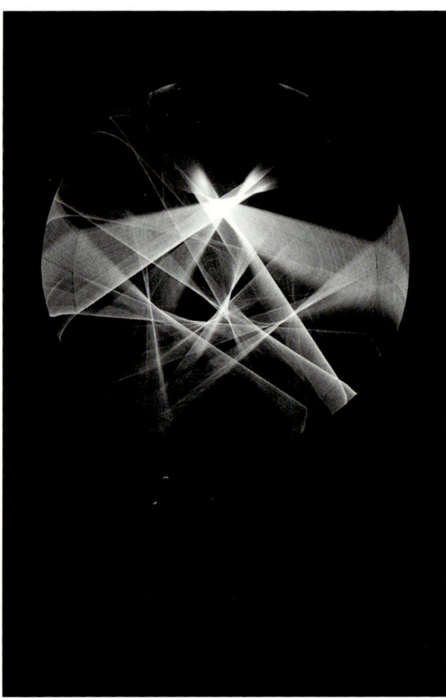

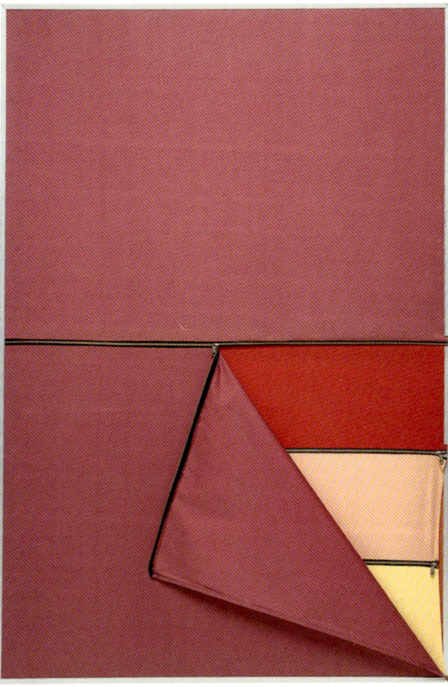

the *Projeto Coca-Cola* (Coca-Cola Project) (1970, plate 17) exemplifies the field's reductive framing of related artistic innovations as distinct art movements. Canonical interpretations of Pop art have narrowly defined it by an interest in popular culture and mass media, particularly in the United States. Conversely, Conceptual art is simplistically characterized by a leftist political agenda, especially in Latin America, which was then undergoing a series of political upheavals.[6] These definitions, however, blur when considering artworks that mobilized Pop language in the 1960s and 1970s. Take, for instance, two artworks that displayed the image of Che Guevara: Tozzi's hacked-off panel *GUEVARA VIVO OU MORTO…* and Roberto Jacoby's "anti-poster," *Un guerrillero no muere para que se lo cuelgue en la pared* (A Guerrilla Doesn't Die to Be Hung on a Wall) (1968, plate 65). Tozzi's work, which epitomizes Brazilian Pop art, makes a clear leftist political statement even as it enlists imagery drawn from mass media and popular imagery. Jacoby's artwork was created following the celebrated Conceptual event, *Tucumán Arde* (Tucuman Is Burning), but employed an unmistakably Pop visual vocabulary by reproducing the recognizable image of Che Guevara's portrait in flat, striking colors.[7]

In 1967, the same year that Tozzi's panel was hacked, the artist Hélio Oiticica called attention to the hybridity of Latin American artworks, declaring in his landmark installation *Tropicália* (see page 48, figure 2.7) that "purity is a myth." A reconsideration of Pop in América is thus necessary in order to take account of this collective interest in hybridity, a key component in Pop's artistic system of signs, which explored reproduction technologies and valorized the copy. Pop as an action can circulate in different geopolitical contexts, while undergoing constant transformation. Different agents can use, therefore, the iconic Pop Coca-Cola imagery to communicate varied messages to their intended recipients.[8]

In Warhol's serialized 1962 representation, the iconic Coke bottle is carefully arranged above its logo and materializes the artist's aphorism, "Pop art is liking things."[9] But if "a Coke is a Coke" in the United States—where it is "consumed by the President, Liz Taylor, and you," as Warhol explained—the same Coke reifies different connotations in works by Latin American artists that are often described as Conceptual.[10] In Meireles's 1970 insertion, he famously used the same silk-screening techniques that made Warhol's early 1960s factory production possible in order to appropriate Coca-Cola's distribution system to spread political messages. He printed slogans such as "Yankees Go Home!" on empty bottles that were returned, refilled, and distributed. Meireles displayed three of these "appropriated" bottles, each containing different quantities of the black liquid, to reveal both the written message and the artist's strategy in the groundbreaking exhibition at the Museum of Modern Art in New York, *Information* (1970), which has come to be known as the first Conceptual art exhibition in the United States.

A few months after the opening of the MoMA show, in the exhibition *Nova Crítica* (1970), art critic and curator Frederico Morais displayed the real challenges facing Meireles's attempt to democratize art and protest. He filled the floor of the Petite Galerie, an avant-garde venue in Rio de Janeiro, with fifteen thousand bottles of Coca-Cola, only a few of which contained the artist's silk-screened texts (see page 47,

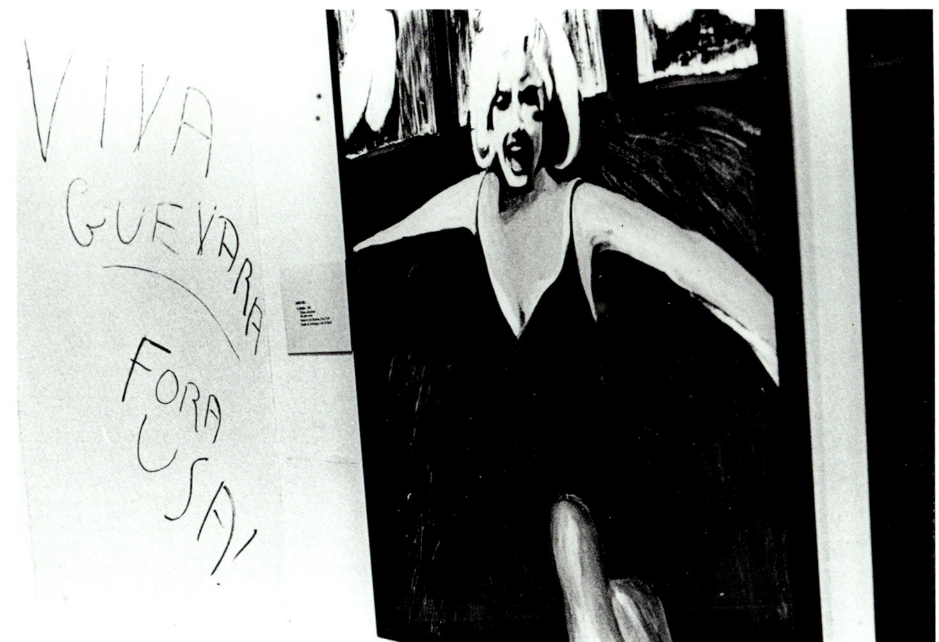

Fig. 2.3. Photo of *Ambiente USA: 1957–1967* during the IX Bienal de São Paulo, Brazil; right *Marilyn* (1962) by James Gill, left, interventon by the public confronting the political context of the period.

figure 2.6).[11] Morais's installation lasted only for one night, becoming simultaneously a Pop happening and an interactive environment. It invited viewers to appreciate the minute scale of the protest actions and artworks in comparison to the vast power of the multinational corporation. The installation also blurred the distinction between artistic theory and practice, an early example of the work Morais would produce in the 1970s as both art critic and artist. In this ephemeral event, the materiality, iconicity, and serialized display of the bottles served as a diaphanous but solid ground and highlighted the importance of Pop materiality in Meireles's iconic Conceptual work.

Coca-Cola marketing materials rather than the characteristic bottle offer the substance of Hélio Oiticica and Neville D'Almeida's environmental work, *CC5 Hendrixwar/Cosmococa Programa-in-Progress* (see page 48, figure 2.8). Conceived when the two Brazilians were living in New York, the work consists of hammocks, slide projections, a soundtrack, and photographs of drawings made with cocaine on the album cover of Jimi Hendrix's *War Heroes* (1971). A promotional matchbox with the Coca-Cola logo punctuates a sequence of slides that feature Hendrix's face embellished with lines of white powder. As the branded matchbox is placed over his mouth and nose, it conflates the company's trademark with addictive consumerism. *Cosmococa* cannibalizes commodity culture in the service of a countercultural message, however, its cultural politics remain ambivalent. *Cosmococa* thus escapes being easily categorized within canonical Pop or Conceptual frameworks. Furthermore, Oiticica and D'Almeida's incorporation of *cultura popular* (largely associated with rural and folk expressions),

in the form of the gently swaying hammocks as unlikely beds for the viewer's enjoyment of the loud rock music and cocaine of New York, suggests that, in a period of rapid modernization in Latin America, mass consumerism, Pop culture, and *cultura popular* necessarily inhabited the same space and mutually contaminated each other.[12]

The wordplay between Coca-Cola and cocaine extends to Antonio Caro's *Colombia Coca-Cola* (1976 [fabricated 2010], plate 19), a work that has become emblematic of Colombian Conceptual art. Playing upon Colombia and Coca-Cola's eight letters, Caro uses the calligraphy of the logo to paint the country's name on tin, in the style of the hand-painted signs advertising the drink on small stores and restaurants found across Latin America. The artwork eventually became a trademark of the Colombian artist himself, who has continuously remade and marketed the work. Like Warhol, Caro had worked in an advertising agency, a formative experience that familiarized him with elements of design and gave him an artistic education that made up for his lack of academic art training.[13] And yet the visible presence of the artist's hand in the crudeness of Caro's handmade banners and posters inserts this serialized production into the artisanal tradition of Latin America's folklore, further demonstrating the entanglement between Pop culture and *cultura popular* in the region.[14]

Caro, Meireles, and Oiticica engage multiple meanings and uses of Coca-Cola and its accompanying commercial apparatus in América, and so reveal that popular culture during the 1960s and 1970s included an urban commodity culture advanced by the presence of transna-

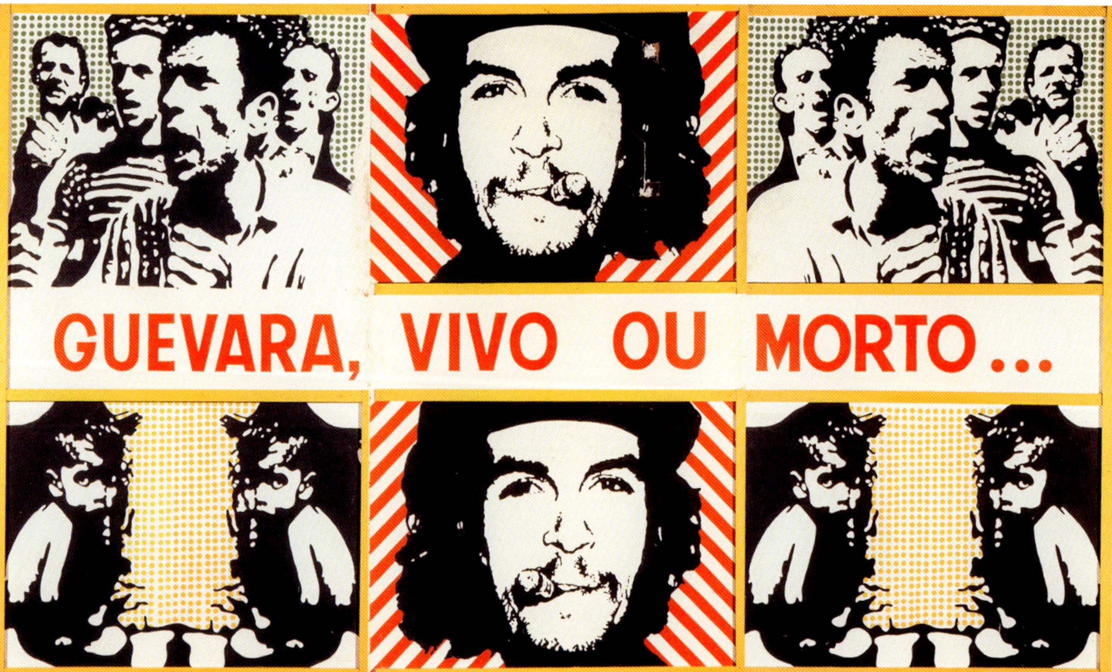

Fig. 2.4. Claudio Tozzi, *GUEVARA VIVO OU MORTO...* (GUEVARA, ALIVE OR DEAD...), 1967. Acrylic on particle board, 68.25 x 117 inches (175 × 300 cm). © Agência Estado. Image courtesy of the Arquivo Histórico Wanda Svevo and the Fundação Bienal de São Paulo, Brazil.

tional capitalism (as evinced by the presence of Coca-Cola), and an indigenous *cultura popular* insinuated in artworks such as *Colombia Coca-Cola*. The image of Coca-Cola becomes a sign that can speak to different geopolitical contexts and inhabit what literary critic Silviano Santiago has termed the "*entre-lugar*," or the in-between spaces of Latin America.[15] The tensions between canonical forms of Pop epitomized by Warhol's "egalitarian" Coke, and appropriations of Pop iconography deemed Conceptual like Caro's *Colombia Coca-Cola* vitalize this shared visual language uttered from América. They displace any easy binary between an essentially commercial US Pop art and a strictly political Conceptual art from Latin America. As such, these artworks urge us to review both the neutrality of a global conception of Pop art and the centrality of Conceptualism in Latin America, and to think hemispherically about American art.

Oscar Masotta, a widely influential Argentine intellectual in this decade, promoted an understanding of Pop as visual language in his landmark book, *El "Pop-Art."*[16] Drawing on writings on semiotics by Ferdinand de Saussure and Roland Barthes, Masotta concluded that Pop art is a movement that problematizes the relationship between images and their physical referents. Pop images, he argued, rather than being subject to the arbitrariness of the semiological sign, operate as codes that can be cracked in multiple ways, undermining the security of the stable referent and making it subject to local cultures.[17]

Brazilian artist Rubens Gerchman similarly explored this ability of the Pop sign to perform as an open code in the 1967–1972 series *Cartilha no superlativo* (Primer in the Superlative), which he began in his native Rio de Janeiro and continued during the four years he spent in New York on a Guggenheim Fellowship. In this series, the artist produced what Hélio Oiticica described as "a total image" by fusing "image, word, poetic, or conceptual points."[18] When displayed in Gerchman's home city, Rio de Janeiro, these artworks fleshed out words in the lush scenery such as *AR* (AIR) (c. 1972, plate 74), spelled in large open letters breathing in the tropical landscape; *LUTE* (FIGHT) (1967, plate 73), with its giant red Formica letters standing side-by-side as a call to arms against the backdrop of asphalt; and *TERRA* (EARTH), its letters buried in the rich earthy soil, surrounded by and serving as a vessel for the material they spell. In these works, the signifier (the image of the word) and the signified (the meaning) become equally expressive, presenting Portuguese both as language and object. Embodying air, land, and urban guerrilla fighting, these signs were deeply embedded in the local realities of a contradictory Brazil, which at the time was being widely hailed as a tropical paradise undergoing an economic miracle under a military dictatorship. This national inflection, however, took on a different meaning when presented in Manhattan, where Gerchman, like many other Latin American intellectuals, was in voluntary exile. There, this production could be "read" as an emblem of the regional struggle of Latin America, plagued by totalitarian governments and united against North American imperialism. Gerchman included some of this series in the film *Triunfo hermético* (Hermetic Triumph), which blends the word structures into Rio's sultry landscape, presenting a tropical synthesis even when the works are spelled out in English, as

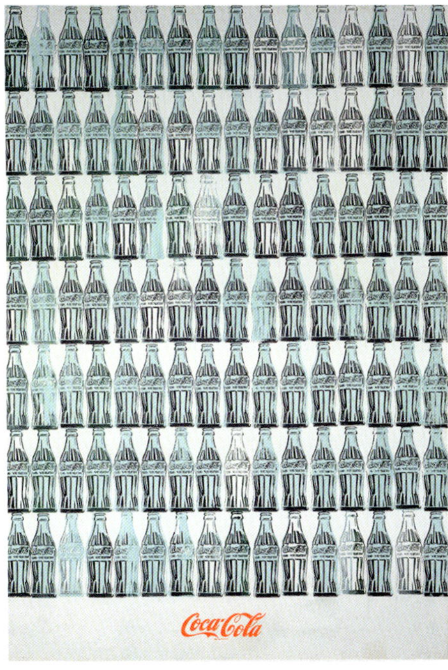

Fig. 2.5. Andy Warhol, *Green Coca-Cola Bottles*, 1962. Silkscreen ink, acrylic, and pencil on linen; 82.5 x 57 inches (209.55 x 144.78 cm). © 2018 The Andy Warhol Foundation for the Visual Arts, Inc. Licensed by Artists Rights Society (ARS), New York, New York.

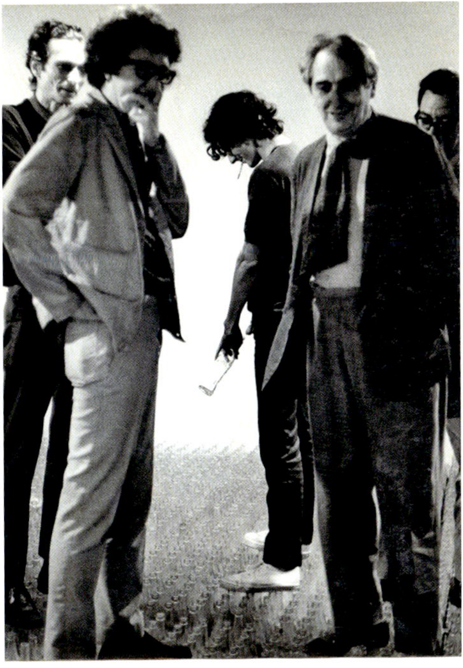

Fig. 2.6. Frederico Morais (left), Mário Pedrosa (right), and Antonio Manuel (center) in the exhibition *Nova Crítica* at the Petite Galerie, Rio de Janeiro, Brazil, 1970. Black-and-white photograph. © Frederico Morais. Image courtesy of the Arquivo Aracy Amaral, Folder: Frederico Morais.

in "MAN-WOMAN" floating on the Atlantic Ocean (1972, plate 16). These works share the immediacy of Pop art and present text as in Conceptual art, performing linguistically as well as pictorially.

As Oiticica argued, Gerchman's work, while forming an image-laden world similar to Masotta's conception of Pop as semiotics, was striking enough to resist being subsumed into "the international Pop-Op images."[19] Oiticica thus distinguished Gerchman's production from US Pop art by emphasizing its local aesthetic genealogy. As Gerchman himself wrote in a 1970 letter to MoMA curator Kynaston McShine, who at the time was preparing the exhibition *Information*, "language has been a major preoccupation in Brazilian visual arts since the foundation of the Concrete poetry movement," which later expanded into the "'Neoconcrete Manifesto' (with the participation of poet Ferreira Gullar) in 1959."[20] Unlike the elitist avant-garde Concrete experiments of the previous decades, Gerchman's *Cartilha no superlativo*—in its Pop inflection—collapsed high and low culture. It proved artist Waldemar Cordeiro's 1965 claim that "visual language experimentations are no longer incompatible with mass culture. Or rather, they are only possible within this framework."[21] At that time, Cordeiro, the former leader of the Concrete Ruptura movement, himself was working on what Augusto de Campos termed *Popcretos*, or tridimensional paintings that transformed the purely constructivist propositions of the 1950s into semantic structures that integrated political images with the aim of making them accessible to a wider public.

Oiticica's effort to distinguish Gerchman's production from the Pop art movement as it was practiced in the United States was motivated by his desire to define a distinctly local Pop idiom. To do so, he coined the name *nova objetividade brasileira* (new Brazilian objectivity).[22] Oiticica had used this term as the title of an exhibition he curated at the Museu de Arte Moderna in Rio in April 1967.[23] Featuring works by Gerchman, Antonio Dias, Lygia Clark, and others similar to those included under the Pop rubric in the IX São Paulo Biennial, the exhibition's catalogue carefully separated *nova objetividade* from US Pop art.[24]

Oiticica's argument was embodied in his own work included in McShine's *Information. Barracão Experiment 2* was a "leisure proposition" Oiticica composed of private compartments containing mattresses separated by curtains and connected by ladders, an arrangement that created intimate spaces within the museum where participants could lounge.[25] By inviting viewers to inhabit the museum, the installation bridged art and life, not only by appropriating reality, as critics had pinpointed as the shared tendency of the IX São Paulo Biennial, but also through a desire to transform the sensorial world by performing aesthetic and ethical acts. In the accompanying catalogue, Oiticica wrote that these environments were intended to enable participants to contemplate their own actions, leading to "open" or "unconditioned" behavior (see page 49, figure 2.9). Oiticica had already elaborated on the importance of the viewer's participation during a symposium organized by the 1967 IV Salão de Arte Moderna do Distrito Federal, the same venue where Tozzi's Pop *Guevara* was attacked by extreme right-wing militants, and that opened a few months after the exhibitions *Nova Objetividade Brasileira* and the IX Bienal de São Paulo.[26] The IV Salão, under the directorship of Morais, was the first official venue

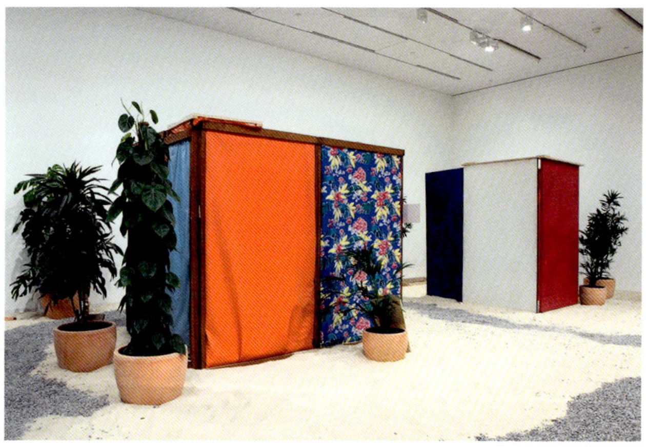

Fig. 2.7. Hélio Oiticica, *Tropicália, Penetrables PN 2 'Purity is a myth'* and *PN 3 'Imagetical,'* 1966–1967. Wooden frames, cotton fabric, plastic sheets, carpet, nylon fabric, patchouli root, cinnamon sticks, sand, plants, metal, terracotta, brick, and other materials; 96.72 x 590.46 x 247.65 inches (248 x 1,514 x 635 cm). Collection of the Tate Gallery, London, Great Britain. Purchased with assistance from the American Fund for the Tate Gallery, the Latin American Acquisitions Committee, Tate Members, and the Art Fund 2007; T12414. © Projeto Hélio Oiticica, Rio de Janeiro, Brazil. Digital image © Tate, London, Great Britain/Art Resource, New York, New York.

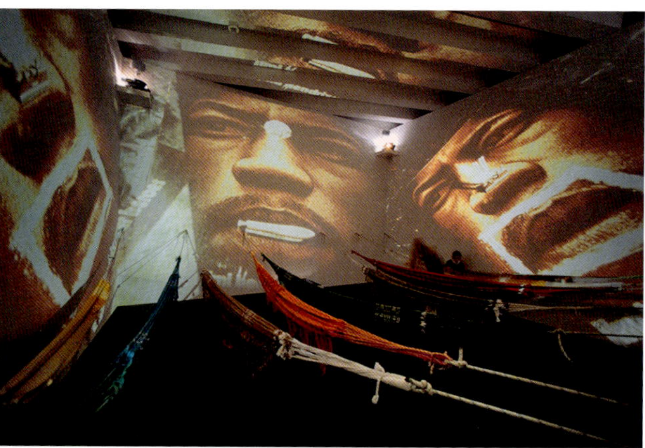

Fig. 2.8. Hélio Oiticica and Neville D'Almeida, *CC5 Hendrixwar/Cosmococa Programa-in-Progress*, 1973. Colored hammocks, 35mm slides, and audio by Jimi Hendrix; 196.87 x 236.25 x 236.25 inches (541.41 x 600.08 x 600.08 cm), minimum room dimension. Collection of the Walker Art Center, Minneapolis, Minnesota. T. B. Walker Acquisition Fund, in honor of Katy Halbreich, 2007; 2007.9.1–192. © 2010 Neville D'Almeida and Projeto Hélio Oiticica. Courtesy of Galerie Lelong & Co, New York, New York.

to adopt the term "object" in its call for artists, which it defined as "the ensemble of artistic manifestations such as relief, kinetic art, environmental art, appropriations (natural materials, industrial materials, and commodities), *objets trouvés*, art sensory-participant, etc."[27] Broadly described and encompassing a myriad of terms, the "object" was intended not as another artistic category but as an "anti-category," a way to shatter traditional artistic divisions according to medium. The last of these terms, "art sensory-participant," was directly inspired by Oiticica's proposition that, by eliciting direct participation, Brazilian *nova objetividade* would lead the public to an "experimental exercise of freedom."[28]

Following the Concrete and Neoconcrete abstract movements of the 1950s, in which Oiticica himself had participated, the aim of this new generation of the local avant-garde was to create popular objects and environments working with the Pop idiom that Oiticica referred to as *nova objetividade brasileira*. Here Oiticica understood "objectivity" both in reference to objective reality and to the new concept of the object as a way to let go of traditional art history. For Oiticica, *nova objetividade* was not an art movement but a "state" or an "arrival, made of multiple tendencies."[29] By refusing to see Brazilian vernacular Pop as an art movement, Oiticica echoed Mário Pedrosa's argument in the article *Arte ambiental, arte pós-moderna, Hélio Oiticica* (Environmental Art, Postmodern Art, Hélio Oiticica) (1966), in which the leading Brazilian critic claimed that the immediacy of Pop artworks marked the end of modernism and the advent of a new cultural cycle concerned not with the future, like the avant-gardes of the early twentieth century, but with the present. Pedrosa, describing Oiticica's

environmental work as marking the transition from the visual to a "total source of sensoriality," affirmed that "by now we have entered another cycle, one that is no longer purely artistic, but cultural, radically different from the preceding one and begun (shall we say?) by Pop art. I would call this new cycle of antiart 'postmodern art.'"[30] To Pedrosa, in other words, Pop did not connote the existence of an art world armed with a theoretical apparatus that allowed Warhol's Brillo boxes to be recognized as art inside a fully formed gallery system.[31] Instead, Pop marked the entrance of art into the larger sphere of culture, ending art's autonomy and fulfilling its promise of overturning hierarchical definitions between high and low art forms with an inclusive alternative—one that could blend rock music and hammocks.[32]

Marta Minujín, who in 1966 had been declared by art historian Jacqueline Barnitz as the "Latin American answer to Pop," shared Oiticica's interest in sensory participation, as demonstrated by two of her works, *Minuphone* (1967) and *Minucode* (1968), which were included in the *Information* exhibition catalogue (figure 2.10).[33] *Minuphone* was an interactive telephone booth intended to expand the participant's auditory and visual faculties. After dialing a number, the user, rather than reaching a person on the other side of the line, communicated with various sensory experiences such as smoke, wind, lights, and voice deformations, effectively holding a conversation with multiple mediums. Images of the dialers were transmitted live by a closed-circuit TV camera onto a monitor placed in the booth's floor, imbricating users into the artwork and immersing them

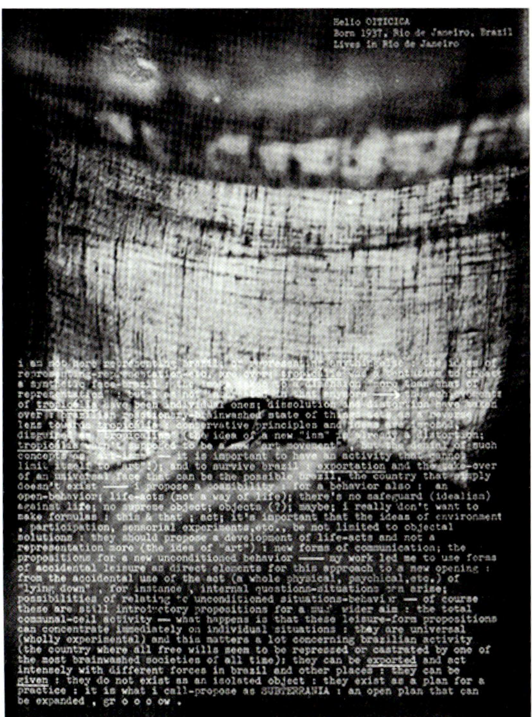

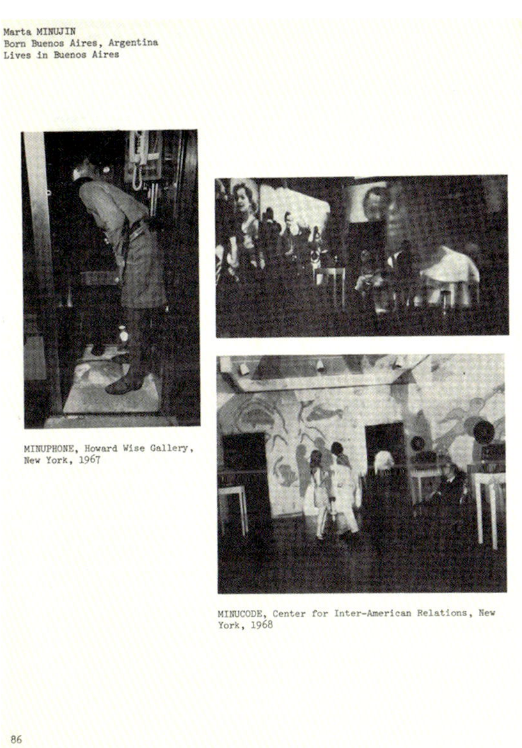

MINUPHONE, Howard Wise Gallery,
New York, 1967

MINUCODE, Center for Inter-American Relations, New
York, 1968

86

TOP TO BOTTOM, Figs. 2.9, 2.10. *Information* exhibition catalogue
edited by Kynaston L. McShine and published by the Museum of
Modern Art, New York, New York, 1970; 10.75 x 8.25 inches (27.30 x
20.95 cm). Courtesy of the artist and Galerie Lelong & Co, New York,
New York. Digital Image © The Museum of Modern Art, New York,
New York. Licensed by SCALA/Art Resource, New York, New York.

in an all-encompassing experience that comes close to meeting
Marshall McLuhan's definition of "technology."[34]

Writing from Buenos Aires, Masotta described Minujín's work not as
the "Latin American answer to Pop," but as dematerialized art—a term
that would become synonymous with Conceptual art in the United
States following the publication of Lucy R. Lippard's *Six Years: The
Dematerialization of the Art Object* in 1973.[35] In 1967, soon after having defined Pop as language, Masotta gave a talk titled "*Después del
Pop: nosotros desmaterializamos*" ("After Pop, We Dematerialize") in
which he argued that the "anti-happening" was the Argentine contribution to the international avant-garde.[36] He anchored this emerging dematerialized artistic activity in *arte de los medios* (media art).
Masotta, differentiating between the medium out of which the object is
created and its artistic content, explained that in the case of new media production, "[t]he 'material' ('immaterial,' 'invisible') with which
informational works of this type are made is none other than the
processes, the results, the facts, and/or the phenomena of information
set off by the mass information media."[37] In other words, television,
radio, and printed media (or a telephone booth) are the mere vehicles
through which the artwork's true content (information) is communicated—hence the dematerialization of the artwork. Masotta's concept
of dematerialization is indeed an apt description for *Minuphone* and
offered a local vernacular for Conceptual art. The notion of dematerialization equally commences the definition of Conceptualism in Latin
America and emphasizes its entanglement with Pop.[38]

Despite his own contribution to the widespread canonization of
Conceptual art in Latin America as eminently political, Luis Camnitzer
writes that upon seeing its presumably apolitical Pop counterpart in
New York during the 1960s, his first response was a vexing feeling "that
it was a movement that should have sprung up on the periphery and not
in the center." Latin Americans, he believed, should have been the ones
spearheading this attack on the imperialism of the consumer object.[39]
Within an understanding of Pop as an art movement rather than a
verb that could be appropriated, Camnitzer reluctantly concluded that
"attempts to produce vernacular Pop in Argentina, Brazil, and Colombia
brought only facile and folklorized versions of the formal solutions
developed in New York." He thus dismissed Pop art in Latin America
as "symptomatic of incomplete derivation," even when the content
was grounded in local politics.[40] Here Camnitzer, like most critics,
overlooked the way in which the telling use of the prefix "anti-" in so
many Latin American artworks (as in Pedrosa's antiart and Masotta's
anti-happening) disturbs the premise that Pop is a US art movement.
Both the prefix "anti-" and the anti-category "object," as described for
the IV Salão, subvert standard hegemonic methods of artistic classifi-
cation, just as the Pop action of blurring "high" and "low" boundaries
and its democratization of the copy challenges an art history structured
by concepts of influence that condemn these works as "derivative." As
the appropriated Coca-Cola imagery that popped up in the continent
demonstrates, thinking about Pop in América as a verb makes a stark
distinction between Pop and Conceptual art movements no longer
necessary, or even possible. These artworks mobilize a shared visual
language whose final meaning is defined by their insertion in a given
culture, whether Pop culture, *cultura popular*, or the space in between.

NOTES

1   "*Cada movimento tem a sua moda*," *O Estado de São Paulo* (São Paulo), September 13, 1967, 8. The United States brought two exhibitions to the IX Bienal de São Paulo: *Ambiente USA: 1957-1967*, containing the work of twenty-one artists, and a solo show by Edward Hopper, which the curator William Seitz described as "a certain way to portray American reality." See Esther Gabara's Introduction on Juan Acha's dismissal of the concepts of copy and influence.

2   This myriad of local terms did not go unnoticed. Trying to help the public to keep up with art, journalists published pedagogical articles such as "Learn the Right Name of the Things Featured in This Biennial" that included terms such as Kinetic art, Op art, Pop art, and *Nova Objectividade*. *Jornal da Tarde*, November 30, 1967, Folder: clippings, Archive Wanda Svevo, Fundação Bienal de São Paulo.

3   Ida Rodríguez Prampolini, Letter to the São Paulo Biennial Foundation, October 5, 1967, Archive Wanda Svevo, Fundação Bienal de São Paulo.

4   The IV Salão ran between December 1967 and February 1968. For more on the Tozzi episode, see Claudia Calirman, "Pop and Politics in Brazilian Art," in *International Pop*, eds., Darsie Alexander et al. (Minneapolis: Walker Art Center, 2015), 119-130.

5   The canonization of Latin American Conceptualism in the 1990s by agents like Mari Carmen Ramírez and Luis Camnitzer can be attributed to the efforts of Latin American art professionals to eschew the "fantastic" designation promoted by exhibitions such as *Art of the Fantastic: Latin America, 1920–1987*, Indianapolis Museum of Art (1987).

6   Scholars including Thomas Crow and Hal Foster have argued that Warhol's production should be viewed beyond the canonical interpretation that was promoted mainly by the artist himself. See, for instance, Crow, "Saturday Disasters: Trace and Reference in Early Warhol," *Art in America* 75 (May 1987): 128–136. The canonization of Latin American Conceptual art as political was inaugurated in the United States by Mari Carmen Ramírez in her 1993 article, "Blue Print Circuits: Conceptual Art and Politics in Latin America," in *Latin American Artists of the Twentieth Century*, ed. Waldo Rasmussen (New York: The Museum of Modern Art, 1993), 156–169. This rigid narrative has been challenged by critics such as Miguel A. López and Josephine Watson, "How Do We Know What Latin American Conceptualism Looks Like?," *Afterall: A Journal of Art, Context, and Enquiry*, no. 23 (Spring 2010): 5–21.

7   Mari Carmen Ramírez, "Tactics for Thriving on Adversity: Conceptualism in Latin America, 1960–1980," in *Global Conceptualisms: Points of Origin 1950s–1980s*, eds., Luis Camnitzer et al. (New York: Queens Museum of Art, 1999), 53–68. Ramírez pinpointed *Tucumán arde*, a multi-part collective exhibition held in Buenos Aires and Rosario, Argentina, as emblematic of Latin American Conceptual art.

8   Marta Traba, "El diseño Pop. Sus cuatro soluciones más destacadas: A) Beatriz González, B) Sonia Gutiérrez y Ana Mercedes Hoyos, C) Santiago Cárdenas, D) Bernardo Salcedo," in *Historia abierta del arte colombiano* (Bogotá: Colcultura y Museo La Tertulia, 1984). Calling attention to the underdeveloped situation of Colombia and Brazil, respectively, Marta Traba used the term *pop ubicado* (located pop) and Mário Pedrosa spoke of *popistas do subdesenvolvimento* (Popists of underdevelopment) to refer to artists that worked in the Pop idiom from within the periphery. Mário Pedrosa, "From American Pop to Dias, the Sertanejo," in *Mário Pedrosa, Primary Documents*, eds., Glória Ferreira and Paulo Herkenhoff (New York: The Museum of Modern Art, 2015), 321.

9   Andy Warhol, "What is Pop Art? Part I," interview by G. R. Swenson, *ARTnews* 62, no. 7 (1963): 25–27, 60–64.

10   Andy Warhol, *The Philosophy of Andy Warhol: From A to B and Back Again* (London: Cassell, 1975).

11   Morais conceived *Nova Crítica* as a way to engage in a new artistic criticism in which the role of the critic, the artist, and the public would blur. Indeed, the event also included other works such as a blank canvas that had been left in public bathrooms for the public to write on and photographs of Meireles's work *Tiradentes: Totem-Monumento para o Prisioneiro Político* juxtaposed with biblical passages. *Nova Crítica* was a critical commentary on the work of Tereza Simões, Guilherme Magalhães, and Meireles, displayed at the Petite Galerie in the exhibition *Agnus Dei* (1970). See Francisco Bittencourt, "Dez anos de experimentação," in *Crítica de arte no brasil: Temáticas contemporâneas*, ed. Glória Ferreira (Rio de Janeiro: Funarte, 2006), 179.

12   For an analysis of Oiticica's work beyond his involvement with the Concrete and Neoconcrete movements in the 1950s, see the catalogue, Lynn Zelevansky et al., *Hélio Oiticica: To Organize Delirium* (Pittsburgh: Carnegie Museum of Art and Munich: DelMonico Books/Prestel, 2016).

13   Brandon Holmquest, Antonio Caro, and Víctor Manuel Rodríguez, *BOMB*, n. 110, *The Americas Issue: Colombia and Venezuela* (Winter 2010): 22.

14   Caro rose to prominence in 1970, when journalist Alegre Levy covered his participation in the XXI Salón Nacional de Artistas at the Museo Nacional in Bogotá's major daily newspaper. In the exhibition, the artist presented a bust of the former president, Carlos Lleras Restrepo (1966–70), which was made roughly out of salt, outfitted with a pair of black glasses, and enclosed in a glass case. On the opening night, Caro poured water over the bust, purposely destroying the work and accidentally creating a puddle, as he had not tested the waterproofness of the glass case containing it. The scandal transformed the opening into a Pop happening and generated instantaneous publicity for the young artist. The choice of salt, a material associated in Colombia with folk practices of carving in salt rock endangered by the installation of modern refineries, enabled the disappearance of the piece and the work's political critique of the cycle of modernization promoted by Lleras at the expense of the rural population. More importantly, the use of salt highlighted the ongoing negotiations between mass consumerism and *cultura popular* as part of Colombia's daily reality in the 1970s. For a discussion of Caro's negotiations with Colombian politics and the international art world, see Gina McDaniel Tarver, "Art Does Not Fit Here: Colombian Conceptual Art between the International 'New Avant-Garde' and Colombian Politics," *Third Text*, v. 26, no. 6 (November, 2012): 729–744.

15   Santiago coined the term "entre-lugar" to describe literary production coming from European ex-colonies such as Brazil, which he argued generates new parameters that avoid habitual assumptions of European derivation or jingoistic, nationalist expressions. Similarly, Pop art circulating in the continent defied uncritical visions of the nation state, even as they dialogued directly with local productions and traditions. Silviano Santiago, *The Space in Between: Essays on Latin American Culture* (Durham: Duke University Press, 2001).

16   Oscar Masotta, *El "Pop-Art"* (Buenos Aires: Ed. Columba, 1967).

17   Masotta built on Roland Barthes's *Mythologies* (1957) to construct his understanding of images as signs that can be interpreted. See Ana Longoni and Mariano Mestman, "After Pop, We Dematerialize: Oscar Masotta, Happenings, and Media Art at the Beginnings of Conceptualism," in *Listen, Here, Now! Argentine Art of the 1960s: Writings of the Avant-Garde*, ed. Inéz Katzenstein (New York: The Museum of Modern Art, 2004), 165.

18   Hélio Oiticica, "Tropicália Time Series 1," *Information* exhibition papers, the Museum of Modern Art Archives, April 1969. Gerchman sent Oiticica's text to curator Kynaston McShine together with some photographs of his works, in an (unsuccessful) attempt to be included in the show.

19   Ibid. See Esther Gabara's "Image–Word–World" in the Introduction to this catalogue.

20   Rubens Gerchman, letter to Kynaston McShine, *Information* exhibition papers, the Museum of Modern Art Archives, April 3, 1970. Just as the 1967 biennial became known as the first major Pop exhibition, *Information*, originally conceptualized as a survey of experimental art, became known in art history as the first US Conceptual art show, due much to the presence of artworks considered foundational for US Conceptual art, such as Joseph Kosuth's *One and Three Chairs* (1965). MoMA has made the original press releases, as well as the catalogue, available online at: https://www. moma.org/calendar/exhibitions/2686.

21   Waldemar Cordeiro, "*Realismo ao nível da cultura de massa*," *Propostas 65* (São Paulo: Fundação Armando Álvares Penteado, 1965). Unless noted, all translations are Camila Maroja's.

22   Hélio Oiticica, "Esquema geral da nova objetividade,"
      in *Nova Objetividade Brasileira* (Rio de Janeiro:
      MAM, 1967), n.p. The essay has been translated into
      English and published in Alexander Alberro and Blake
      Stimson, eds., *Conceptual Art: A Critical Anthology*
      (Cambridge: MIT Press, 2000), 40–42.

23   The exhibition *Nova Objetividade Brasileira* opened at
      the Museum of Modern Art in Rio de Janeiro in April
      1967. In it, Oiticica presented his celebrated installation
      Tropicália, cited in the beginning of this essay.

24   In creating a local genealogy for *nova objetividade*,
      Oiticica is not promoting a nationalist reading of Pop
      as representative of Brazil, but indeed saw Pop as
      marking the end of representations. In the catalogue
      of the exhibition *Information*, he wrote, "i am not here
      representing brazil; or representing anythingelse [sic]:
      the ideas of representing-representation are over."

25   The work's description in the exhibition's checklist
      associates it with Oiticica's experiments at Essex
      University and his design of "nests." The checklist
      is available at: https://www.moma.org/documents/
      moma_master-checklist_326690.pdf.

26   The notion of a Brazilian idiom organized around the
      concept of "objectivity" delineated in the preface of
      Nova Objetividade Brasileira and expanded in IV Salão
      was presented first in an event parallel to the collective
      exhibition *Propostas 66* (November, 1966), in which
      Oiticica delivered the paper "The Situation of the
      Avant-Garde in Brazil." See Hélio Oiticica, "Situação
      da Vanguarda no Brasil," in *Crítica de arte no brasil:
      Temáticas contemporâneas*, ed. Glória Ferreira (Rio de
      Janeiro: Funarte, 2006), 147–148.

27   Morais defined the concept of the object. He also
      coordinated the exhibition and the parallel events
      "Simpósio de Escultura Brasileira—retrospectiva e
      atualização" and Festival de Filmes de arte.

28   Hélio Oiticica, "O aparecimento do suprasensorial," in
      *Hélio Oiticica, Aspiro ao grande labirinto: Textos de
      Hélio Oiticica (1954-1969)*, eds., Luciano Figueiredo,
      Lygia Pape, and Waly Salomão (Rio de Janeiro:
      Rocco, 1986), 102–105. Originally presented during
      the *Simpósio de Escultura Brasileira—retrospectiva e
      atualização*. Oiticica cites Mário Pedrosa's celebrated
      expression "experimental exercise of freedom."

29   Oiticica, "Esquema geral da nova objetividade," n.p.
      Analyzing Oiticica's text, curator Darsie Alexander
      notes that "the impulse to create a first-this-then-that
      chronology for Pop has elided the work of numerous
      artists operating within aesthetic structures and
      timelines that resisted a selective historical approach."
      See Alexander, "Introduction: The Edge of Pop," in
      International Pop, 77–84.

30   Mário Pedrosa, "Arte ambiental, arte pós-moderna,
      Hélio Oiticica," in *Mário Pedrosa, Primary Documents*,
      eds., Glória Ferreira and Paulo Herkenhoff (New York:
      The Museum of Modern Art, 2015), 314–316. Published
      originally as "Arte ambiental, arte pós-moderna, Hélio
      Oiticica," in *Correio da Manhã* (Rio de Janeiro: 1966), n.p.

31   I am referring here to Arthur Danto's celebrated work
      about Pop art as marking the end of art by abandoning
      a mimetic approach to aesthetics. See Arthur C. Danto,
      *After the End of Art: Contemporary Art and the Pale of
      History* (Princeton: Princeton University Press, 2014).

32   Sônia Salzstein, writing about Brazilian artist Antonio
      Dias, elaborates on Pop as a strategy to re-examine
      modernity and Western (art) history in the 1980s by
      critically examining postmodernism and multicul-
      turalism. See Sônia Salzstein, "Pop as a Crisis in the
      Public Sphere," in *Pop Art and Vernacular Cultures*, ed.
      Kobena Mercer (Cambridge: MIT Press, 2007), 88–109.

33   Jacqueline Barnitz, "A Latin Answer to Pop," *Arts
      Magazine*, June 1966, 36–39. For a keen examination
      of Marta Minujín's elusive engagement with Pop, see
      Catherine Spencer, "Performing Pop: Marta Minujín
      and the 'Argentine Image-Makers,'" *Tate Papers* n.
      24 (Autumn 2015), http://www.tate.org.uk/research/
      publications/tate-papers/24.

34   McLuhan's 1960s theories foreground media's capac-
      ity to generate new structures of consciousness by
      reshaping our sensory perceptions: "Most technology
      produces an amplification that is quite explicit in its
      separation of the senses. Radio is an extension of the
      aural, high-fidelity photography of the visual. But
      TV is above all, an extension of the sense of touch,
      which involves maximal interplay of all the senses."
      See Marshall McLuhan, *Understanding Media: The
      Extensions of Man* (Cambridge: MIT Press, [1964]
      1994), 333.

35   Cf. Lucy R. Lippard, *Six Years of Dematerialization of
      the Art Object from 1966 to 1972* (New York: Praeger,
      1973). The term was first proposed together with
      John Chandler. See Lippard and Chandler, "The
      Dematerialization of Art" (1967), first published in *Art
      International* 12.2 (February 1968): 31–36.

36   Written and delivered as a lecture in 1967. Later
      published in Oscar Masotta, *Conciencia y estructura*
      (Buenos Aires: Editorial Jorge Álvarez, 1969).

37   English translation available: http://post.at.moma.org/
      sources/8/publications/138.

38   On her website, Minujín places the *Minuphone* under
      the designation of *arte efímero*, or ephemeral art.
      Artist's website: http://www.marta-minujin.com.

39   Luis Camnitzer, "Political Pop," in *Luis Camnitzer:
      On Art, Artists, Latin America, and Other Utopias*, ed.
      Rachel Weiss (Austin: University of Texas Press, 2009),
      31. Camnitzer has been, together with Ramírez, one of
      the main promoters of Latin American Conceptual art,
      or *conceptualismo*, his favorite term. See Camnitzer,
      *Conceptualism in Latin American Art: Didactics of
      Liberation* (Austin: University of Texas Press, 2007).

40   Camnitzer, "Political Pop," 32.

CAMILA MAROJA

EL POP SE HACE CONCEPTUAL: LENGUAJE VISUAL EN AMÉRICA

La IX Bienal de São Paulo, en 1967, de inmediato se dio a conocer como la "Bienal do Pop" (Bienal del Pop). Esta denominación aludía no solo a una de las representaciones nacionales más destacadas de la muestra —*Ambiente USA: 1957-1967*, que incluyó obras icónicas de Andy Warhol y Robert Indiana, entre otros—, sino también a la tendencia que compartían muchos artistas de apropiarse directamente de la realidad en su trabajo.[1] Al unir bajo la etiqueta del pop obras tan diversas como los objetos cinéticos de Julio Le Parc y las "pinturas" de Nelson Leirner con poliéster y zípers, la rúbrica "pop" de la bienal generó una falsa impresión de homogeneidad artística global (ver página 44; figuras 2.1, 2.2). De hecho, la exposición reunió una variedad de terminologías locales operantes a finales de los años sesenta, tales como arte popular y ambiental, objetos, nuevo realismo y nueva objetividad, lo cual parece contradecir la idea misma del pop como un movimiento artístico.[2] La crítica de arte mexicana Ida Rodríguez Prampolini sostiene lo anterior en una carta que escribió al comité de la bienal para exhortarlos a eliminar los criterios obsoletos de ésta, como por ejemplo la otorgación de un "gran premio de pintura", y a establecer nuevas categorías artísticas tales como el arte integrado. La carta incluso retaba a los organizadores a dejar de exponer las obras por países, ya que el "arte no tiene fronteras políticas".[3]

Sin embargo, la visión de Rodríguez Prampolini de una aldea global integrada, como la imaginó el gurú de los medios masivos Marshall McLuhan, resultó demasiado optimista, y contrastó vivamente con la reacción apasionada del público a la exposición. En efecto, la IX Bienal fue la primera bienal de São Paulo que sufrió un acto de vandalismo cuando un manifestante izquierdista, aprovechando un apagón de media hora, escribió *"Viva Guevara. Fora USA!"* (Viva Guevara. ¡Fuera Estados Unidos!) junto a la obra *Marilyn* de James Gill (ver página 45, figura 2.3). Apenas unos meses más tarde, en el IV Salão de Arte Moderna do Distrito Federal, militantes de extrema derecha arrancaron de la pared, a golpe de hacha, el panel de Claudio Tozzi titulado *GUEVARA VIVO OU MORTO...* (GUEVARA VIVO O MUERTO...) (ver página 46, figura 2.4), una representación del ícono de la revolución cubana.[4] Como lo demuestran estos ataques, la apropiación de la realidad que efectúa el arte pop no podía separarse de la política en el apogeo de la Guerra Fría y, a diferencia de lo que creía Rodríguez Prampolini, el arte sí tenía fronteras políticas. Pero incluso más importante resulta el hecho de que estos actos de violencia contra obras pop —uno del izquierdismo y otro del derechismo— comprometen la supuesta categoría unívoca del pop y nos obligan a reconsiderar la canonización del arte conceptual (o conceptualismo) latinoamericano, movimiento que se dio a conocer en la región por sus inflexiones políticas.[5] Estos actos demuestran que el vocabulario visual compartido del pop y el arte conceptual podía hacer alternancias de código, comunicar significados radicalmente diferentes dependiendo de sus agentes y sus públicos.

Esta exposición invita al espectador a repensar el pop en América, a verlo como una acción, un verbo, y no solo como un movimiento artístico o una colección de objetos. Las acciones pop, como la tilde que agregó Hugo Rivera-Scott en su collage *Pop América* (1968, lámina 3), arraigan la producción estética en lenguajes visuales y verbales específicos. A continuación examino la obra de artistas que abordaron el pop como verbo, con lo cual descentraron la universalidad atribuida —entonces y ahora— a los movimientos artísticos originados en los centros de arte tradicionales. Apropiándose y subvirtiendo un vocabulario que circulaba en la parte superior del continente, estas producciones pop vernáculas cuestionan parámetros clave de la historia del arte, incluido el binomio de original y copia. Varios de los artistas latinoamericanos presentados en *Pop América* utilizan, por ejemplo, la icónica imagen de los productos y anuncios de Coca-Cola, símbolos comerciales cuya trayectoria en la parte sur del hemisferio resulta inseparable de las intervenciones políticas imperialistas y neoliberales. Estas obras transforman el vocabulario del pop efectuando mutaciones en el ubicuo signo de la Coca-Cola y transportándolo a nuevos emplazamientos.

En la historia del arte, la oposición entre *Green Coca-Cola Bottles* (Botellas verdes de Coca-Cola) de Andy Warhol (ver página 47, figura 2.5) e *Inserções em circuitos ideológicos: Projeto Coca-Cola* (Inserciones en circuitos ideológicos: Proyecto Coca-Cola) de Cildo Meireles (1970, lámina 17) ejemplifica el enfoque reduccionista con que la disciplina académica tiende a enmarcar innovaciones artísticas afines como movimientos artísticos distintos. Las interpretaciones canónicas del arte pop lo han definido estrictamente como un interés en la cultura de masas y los medios masivos de comunicación, sobre todo en Estados Unidos. Por su parte, el arte conceptual es caracterizado de forma simplista como un arte de agenda política izquierdista, sobre todo en América Latina, para aquel entonces escenario de una serie de turbulencias políticas.[6] Sin embargo, estas definiciones se desdibujan si tomamos en cuenta las obras de arte que movilizaron el lenguaje pop en las décadas de 1960 y 1970. Consideremos, por ejemplo, dos obras que contenían la imagen del Che Guevara: el panel de Tozzi que sufrió los hachazos, *Guevara vivo ou morto*, y el "antiafiche" de Roberto Jacoby, *Un guerrillero no muere para que se lo cuelgue en la pared* (1968, lámina 65). La obra de Tozzi, epítome del arte pop brasileño, hace una contundente declaración política de izquierda al tiempo que se vale visualmente de la imaginería popular y mediática. La obra de Jacoby fue creada después del célebre evento conceptual *Tucumán arde*, pero emplea un vocabulario visual inequívocamente pop al reproducir la reconocible imagen del Che Guevara en colores planos y llamativos.[7]

En 1967, el mismo año del hachazo al panel de Tozzi, el artista Hélio Oiticica llamó la atención sobre la hibridez de las obras de arte latinoamericanas, declarando en su histórica instalación *Tropicália* (ver página 48, figura 2.7) que la "pureza es un mito". Resulta entonces necesario repensar el pop en América para dar cuenta de este interés colectivo en la hibridez, componente clave del sistema de signos del pop, que exploró las tecnologías de reproducción y valorizó la copia. El pop como acción puede circular en contextos geopolíticos diferentes, transformándose constantemente. Por lo tanto, diferentes agentes pueden usar las icónicas imágenes pop de la Coca-Cola para comunicar mensajes de diversa naturaleza a sus públicos particulares.[8]

En la representación seriada que hizo Warhol en 1962, la botella de Coca-Cola aparece repetida con esmero encima de su logo, materializando el aforismo del artista: "el pop consiste en que te gusten las cosas".[9] Pero si "una Coca-Cola es una Coca-Cola" en Estados Unidos —donde la "beben el Presidente, Liz Taylor y tú", como explicó Warhol[10]— esa misma Coca-Cola reifica diferentes connotaciones en las obras de artistas latinoamericanos que suelen categorizarse como conceptuales. En su famosa "inserción" de 1970, Meireles se apropió del sistema de distribución de Coca-Cola para diseminar mensajes políticos empleando las mismas técnicas serigráficas que viabilizaron la producción estilo fábrica de Warhol a principios de los años sesenta. Meireles imprimió eslóganes como "Yankees Go Home!" (¡Qué se vayan los gringos!) en botellas vacías retornables que luego se rellenaron y redistribuyeron. Tres de estas botellas "apropiadas" —cada una con diferente cantidad del oscuro líquido para que podamos apreciar el mensaje escrito y la estrategia del artista— fueron mostradas en la pionera exposición del Museum of Modern Art de Nueva York titulada *Information* (Información) (1970), hoy considerada la primera exposición de arte conceptual en Estados Unidos.

Unos meses después de inaugurada la muestra del MoMA tuvo lugar la exposición *Nova crítica* (1970), donde el crítico y curador Frederico Morais demostró a lo que realmente se enfrentó Meireles en su acto de protesta y democratización del arte. Morais llenó el piso de la Petite Galerie, un espacio vanguardista en Río de Janeiro, con quince mil botellas de Coca-Cola, de las cuales solo unas pocas contenían los textos serigrafiados del artista (ver página 47, figura 2.6).[11] La instalación de Morais duró solo una noche, con lo cual, además de ambiente interactivo, fue un happening pop. Su propósito era que el espectador lograra apreciar la escala mínima de los actos de protesta y las obras de arte en comparación con el enorme poder de la empresa multinacional. La instalación también borraba la distinción entre teoría y práctica artística, tal como continuaría haciéndolo Morais a lo largo de los años setenta en su arte y en su crítica. En este evento efímero, la materialidad, la iconicidad y el despliegue seriado de las botellas daba a la obra un soporte diáfano pero sólido, que a la vez recalcaba la importancia de la materialidad pop en la icónica obra conceptual de Meireles.

Más que la característica botella, son los materiales de mercadeo de Coca-Cola los que dan sustancia a la obra ambiental de Hélio Oiticica y Neville D'Almeida, *CC5 Hendrixwar/Cosmococa Programa-in-Progress* (ver página 48, figura 2.8). Concebida cuando ambos brasileños residían en Nueva York, la obra consiste de hamacas, proyecciones de diapositivas, una banda sonora y fotografías de dibujos hechos con cocaína sobre la portada del disco *War Heroes* (1971) de Jimi Hendrix. Una caja de fósforos promocional con el logo de Coca-Cola irrumpe en una secuencia de diapositivas del rostro de Hendrix adornado con rayas de polvo blanco. La caja de fósforos va apareciendo sobre su boca o su nariz, asociando la marca de la compañía con el consumismo adictivo. Dado que *Cosmococa* canibaliza la cultura de los bienes de consumo para transmitir un mensaje de la contracultura, su política cultural es ambivalente y, por consiguiente, rehúye ser categorizada fácilmente dentro de los marcos canónicos pop o conceptual. Asimismo, el hecho de que Oiticica y D'Almeida incorporaran la cultura popular incluyendo hamacas de suave vaivén —que servirían de improbables camas para que los espectadores disfrutaran la música rock a todo volumen y la cocaína de Nueva York— sugiere que, en una época de rápida modernización en América Latina, el consumo masivo, la cultura pop y la cultura popular inevitablemente ocupaban el mismo espacio y se contaminaban mutuamente.[12]

El juego semántico entre Coca-Cola y cocaína se extiende a *Colombia Coca-Cola* (1976 [fabricado en 2010], lámina 19), de Antonio Caro, obra emblemática del arte conceptual colombiano. Jugando con las ocho letras de Colombia y de Coca-Cola, Caro utiliza la caligrafía del logo para pintar el nombre del país en latón, al estilo de los letreros pintados a mano que anuncian la bebida en tiendas pequeñas y restaurantes en toda América Latina. La obra se convirtió con el tiempo en sello distintivo del artista, quien no ha dejado de rehacerla y comercializarla. Al igual que Warhol, Caro había trabajado en una agencia publicitaria, experiencia formativa que lo familiarizó con los elementos del diseño y le dio una educación artística que compensó su falta de formación académica.[13] Sin embargo, la presencia visible de la mano del artista en la tosquedad de las pancartas y los carteles en efecto hechos a mano por Caro inserta esta producción seriada en la tradición artesanal del folclor latinoamericano, demostrando una vez más cuán entrelazadas están la cultura pop y la cultura popular en esta región.[14]

Caro, Meireles, y Oiticica abordan múltiples significados y usos de la Coca-Cola y su sistema comercial en Estados Unidos, revelando que la cultura de masas en las décadas de 1960 y 1970 abarcaba una cultura urbana de bienes de consumo fomentada por la presencia del capitalismo trasnacional (como lo demuestra la presencia de Coca-Cola), y también una cultura popular local insinuada en obras de arte como *Colombia Coca-Cola*. La imagen de la Coca-Cola se convierte en signo que se articula en a contextos geopolíticos diferentes, y habita lo que el crítico literario Silviano Santiago ha llamado el "entre-lugar" de América Latina.[15] Las tensiones entre las formas canónicas del pop, encarnadas por las Coca-Colas "igualitarias" de Warhol, y las apropiaciones de la iconografía pop consideradas conceptuales, como la *Colombia Coca-Cola* de Caro, vigorizan este lenguaje visual compartido que habló América. Es así que desplazan cualquier binomio fácil de un arte pop estadounidense esencialmente comercial y un arte conceptual latinoamericano estrictamente político. Como tal, estas obras nos instan a reexaminar tanto la neutralidad de un concepto global del pop como la centralidad del conceptualismo en América Latina y a pensar en el arte americano en términos hemisféricos.

El intelectual argentino Oscar Masotta, muy influyente en esa década, promovió un entendimiento del pop como lenguaje visual en su seminal libro *El "Pop-Art"*.[16] Basándose en los escritos semióticos de Ferdinand de Saussure y Roland Barthes, Masotta concluye que el pop es un movimiento que problematiza la relación entre las imágenes y sus referentes físicos. Sostiene que las imágenes pop, más que estar sujetas a la arbitrariedad del signo semiológico, operan como códigos que pueden ser descifrados de múltiples maneras, socavando así la seguridad del referente estable y supeditándolo a las culturas locales.[17]

El artista brasileño Rubens Gerchman también exploró este potencial del signo pop como código abierto en su serie de 1967–1972 titulada *Cartilha no superlativo* (Cartilla en superlativo), comenzada en su Río de Janeiro natal y continuada durante los cuatro años que pasó en Nueva York con una Beca Guggenheim. En esta serie el artista produjo lo que Hélio Oiticica describió como "una imagen total" al fusionar los aspectos de "la imagen, la palabra, los conceptos y las poéticas".[18]

Al exponerlas en el exuberante escenario de Río de Janeiro, estas obras daban cuerpo a palabras como *AR* (AIRE) (c. 1972, lámina 74), escrita en grandes letras abiertas que respiraban el paisaje tropical; *LUTE* (LUCHA) (1967, lámina 73), con sus enormes letras de Formica roja colocadas hombro a hombro, como un llamado a las armas contra un fondo de asfalto; y *TERRA* (TIERRA), con sus letras enterradas en la tierra fértil, rodeadas y a la vez recipientes del material que deletreaban. En estas obras, el significante (la imagen de la palabra) y el significado son igualmente expresivos, presentan al portugués como idioma y como objeto. Encarnando al aire, la tierra y la lucha de la guerrilla urbana, estos signos estaban arraigados en las realidades locales de un Brasil contradictorio, que en esa época era celebrado por muchos como un paraíso tropical en pleno milagro económico bajo una dictadura militar. Sin embargo, esta inflexión nacional adquirió un sentido diferente cuando la obra se presentó en Manhattan, donde Gerchman, como muchos otros intelectuales latinoamericanos, se encontraba en exilio voluntario. Allí, se podía "leer" esta producción como un emblema de la lucha regional de América Latina, plagada por gobiernos totalitarios y unida contra el imperialismo norteamericano. Gerchman incluyó parte de esta serie en la película *Triunfo hermético*, que mezcla las estructuras de las palabras con el paisaje sensual de Río, presentando una síntesis tropical aun cuando hay palabras en idioma inglés, como la "MAN-WOMAN" que flota en el océano Atlántico (1972, lámina 16). Estas obras comparten la inmediatez del arte pop y presentan el texto como en el arte conceptual, operando de manera lingüística y pictórica a la vez.

Como sostiene Oiticica, la obra de Gerchman, si bien crea un mundo cargado de imágenes que lo vinculan a la noción de Masotta sobre el pop como semiótica, es lo suficientemente impactante como para no quedar subsumida en "la imagética [sic] pop y op internacional".[19] Es decir, Oiticica hace la diferencia entre la producción de Gerchman y el arte pop estadounidense al enfatizar la genealogía estética local de la primera. Como Gerchman mismo escribió en una carta de 1970 al curador del MoMA Kynaston McShine, quien en ese momento preparaba la exposición *Information*, "el lenguaje ha sido una importante inquietud en las artes visuales brasileñas desde la fundación del movimiento de poesía concreta", expandido luego con el "'manifiesto neoconcreto' (con la participación del poeta Ferreira Gullar) en 1959".[20] A diferencia del elitismo de los experimentos concretos vanguardistas de las décadas anteriores, la *Cartilha no superlativo* (Cartilla en superlativo) de Gerchman —con su inflexión pop— fusionó las llamadas alta y baja culturas. Fue la prueba de lo argumentado en 1965 por Waldemar Cordeiro: "las exploraciones del lenguaje visual dejaron de ser incompatibles con la cultura de masas. O más bien, únicamente son posibles dentro de ese ámbito".[21] En ese entonces, Cordeiro, antiguo líder del movimiento de arte concreto Ruptura, estaba trabajando en lo que Augusto de Campos llamó *Popcretos*, pinturas tridimensionales que transformaron las propuestas puramente constructivistas de los años cincuenta en estructuras semánticas que incorporaban imágenes políticas con el fin de hacerlas accesibles a un público más amplio.

El interés de Oiticica en hacer la diferencia entre la producción de Gerchman y el movimiento pop estadounidense estaba motivado por su deseo de definir un lenguaje pop claramente local. Para lograrlo, acuñó el término *nova objetividade brasileira* (nueva objetividad brasileña).[22] Oiticica había usado este término como título de una exposición que había comisariado en el Museu de Arte Moderna en Río de Janeiro en abril de 1967.[23] Con obras de Gerchman, Antonio Dias, Lygia Clark y otras similares a las que se expusieron bajo la rúbrica del pop en la IX Bienal de São Paulo, el catálogo de la exposición hacía una cuidadosa separación entre la *nova objetividade* y el arte pop estadounidense.[24]

El argumento de Oiticica quedó plasmado en su obra includa en la exposición *Information*, comisariada por McShine. *Barracão Experiment 2* era una "propuesta de esparcimiento" que constaba de compartimientos privados con colchones separados por cortinas y conectados por escaleras, creando así espacios íntimos dentro del museo donde los participantes podían descansar.[25] Al invitar a los espectadores a habitar el museo, la instalación tendía un puente entre el arte y la vida, no solo porque se apropiaba de la realidad —cosa que los críticos habían señalado como tendencia común en la IX Bienal de São Paulo— sino también por una voluntad de transformar el mundo sensorial a través de actos estéticos y éticos. En el catálogo de la exposición, Oiticica escribió que la intención de estos ambientes era propiciar que los participantes contemplaran sus propios actos, lo cual generaría un comportamiento "abierto" o "incondicionado" (ver página 49, figura 2.9). Oiticica ya había examinado la importancia de la participación del público en un simposio organizado en 1967 por el IV Salão de Arte Moderna do Distrito Federal (el mismo lugar donde la obra pop *Guevara* de Tozzi fue atacada por individuos de extrema derecha), el cual se inauguró pocos meses después de la exposición *Nova objetividade brasileira* y la IX Bienal de São Paulo.[26] El IV Salão, bajo la dirección de Frederico Morais, fue el primer espacio oficial que adoptó el término "objeto" en su convocatoria para los artistas, definiéndolo como "el conjunto de manifestaciones artísticas tales como relieve, arte cinético, arte ambiental, apropiaciones (materiales naturales, industriales y bienes de consumo), *objets trouvés*, arte sensorial-participativo, etc.".[27] Descrito de una manera amplia que abarcaba multitud de términos, el "objeto" no tenía como fin crear otra categoría artística, sino ser una "anticategoría", una manera de romper con las divisiones tradicionales basadas en las técnicas artísticas. El último de esos términos, "arte sensorial-participativo", provenía directamente de la propuesta de Oiticica de que, al provocar la participación directa del público, la *nova objetividade* brasileña lo conduciría a un "ejercicio experimental de libertad".[28]

Tras los movimientos abstractos concreto y neoconcreto de los años cincuenta, en los que Oiticica había participado, el propósito de esta nueva generación de la vanguardia local era crear objetos y ambientes populares usando el lenguaje pop que Oiticica denominó la *nova objetividade brasileira*. En este caso, Oiticica entendía por "objetividad" no solo la realidad objetiva sino también el nuevo concepto del objeto como recurso para liberarse de la historia del arte tradicional. Para Oiticica, la *nova objetividade* no era un movimiento artístico sino un "estado" o una "llegada, construida de múltiples tendencias".[29] Al rehusarse a considerar el pop vernáculo brasileño como un movimiento artístico, Oiticica se hacía eco del argumento de Mário Pedrosa en el artículo titulado "Arte ambiental, arte pós-moderna, Hélio Oiticica" (Arte ambiental, arte posmoderno, Hélio Oiticica), donde el notable crítico de arte brasileño sostenía que la inmediatez de las obras de

arte pop marcó el fin del arte moderno y la llegada de un nuevo ciclo cultural que no se interesaba por el futuro, como las vanguardias de principios del siglo XX, sino que se interesaba en el presente. Pedrosa afirma que el arte ambiental de Oiticica marca la transición de lo visual hacia una "fuente total de sensorialidad", y que "estamos ahora en otro ciclo, que ya no es puramente artístico, sino cultural, radicalmente diferente del anterior e iniciado, digamos, por el arte pop. A este nuevo ciclo de vocación antiarte yo lo llamaría 'arte posmoderno'".[30] Es decir que para Pedrosa el pop no connotaba la existencia de un mundo del arte con el tipo de aparato teórico que permitió que las cajas de Brillo de Warhol fueran reconocidas como arte dentro de un sistema de galerías plenamente establecido.[31] Más bien, el pop marcó el ingreso del arte a una esfera cultural más amplia, con lo cual puso fin a su autonomía y cumplió la promesa de echar abajo las definiciones jerarquizantes de "alta" y "baja" cultura proponiendo una alternativa incluyente, que podía combinar música rock con hamacas.[32]

Marta Minujín, quien en 1966 fue declarada la "repuesta latinoamericana al pop"[33] por la historiadora de arte Jacqueline Barnitz, compartía el interés de Oiticica por la participación sensorial, como puede apreciarse en dos de sus obras, *Minuphone* (1967) y *Minucode* (1968), ambas incluidas en el catálogo de la exposición *Information* (ver página 49, figura 2.10). *Minuphone* era una cabina telefónica interactiva concebida para expandir las facultades auditivas y visuales del participante. Después de marcar el número, en vez de contactar a una persona, el usuario se comunicaba con varias experiencias sensoriales, tales como humo, viento, luces y voces distorsionadas, teniendo, a todos los efectos, una conversación con múltiples medios. Las imágenes de los participantes se transmitían en directo mediante una cámara de televisión circuito cerrado a un monitor colocado en el piso de la cabina, imbricando a los usuarios en la obra de arte, sumergiéndolos en una experiencia integral que se acerca a lo que Marshall McLuhan definió como "tecnología".[34]

Escribiendo desde Buenos Aires, Masotta describió la obra de Minujín no como la "respuesta latinoamericana al pop", sino como un "arte desmaterializado", término que se convertiría en sinónimo de arte conceptual en Estados Unidos tras la publicación de *Six Years: The Dematerialization of the Art Object* de Lucy R. Lippard en 1973.[35] En 1967, al poco tiempo de haber definido al pop como un lenguaje, Masotta dictó una conferencia titulada "Después del Pop, nosotros desmaterializamos",[36] en la cual sostuvo que el "anti-happening" era la contribución argentina a la vanguardia internacional. Masotta anclaba esta emergente actividad artística desmaterializada en el "arte de los medios de comunicación en masa". Haciendo la diferencia entre la materia de la cual se construye el objeto y su contenido artístico, Masotta explicaba que, en el caso de la nueva producción de los medios, "la 'materia' ('inmaterial', 'invisible') con la que se construyen obras informacionales de tal tipo no es otra que los procesos, los resultados, los hechos y/o los fenómenos de la información desencadenada por los medios de información masiva".[37] Dicho de otra forma, la televisión, la radio y los medios impresos (o una cabina telefónica) son meros vehículos mediante los cuales se comunica el verdadero contenido (la información) de la obra de arte —de ahí la desmaterialización de la obra de arte—. El concepto de desmaterialización que propone Masotta es en efecto una apta descripción de *Minuphone* y ofrece un vernáculo local para el arte conceptual. Asimismo, la noción de desmaterialización inicia la definición del conceptualismo en América Latina y destaca su empalme con el pop.[38]

A pesar de que él mismo contribuyó a difundir la canonización del conceptualismo en América Latina como un arte eminentemente político, Luis Camnitzer escribe que al ver la contraparte pop, presuntamente apolítica, en Nueva York en los años sesenta su primera reacción fue de irritación "porque era un movimiento que tendría que haber surgido en la periferia y no en el centro". Pensaba que los latinoamericanos tendrían que haber sido los que encabezaran el ataque contra el imperialismo del objeto de consumo.[39] Entendiendo el pop como movimiento artístico y no como verbo que podía apropiarse, Camnitzer concluía con reticencia que "los intentos de producir un pop vernáculo en Argentina, Brasil y Colombia solo produjeron versiones simplistas y folclorizadas de las soluciones formales desarrolladas en Nueva York". De este modo el artista desestima al arte pop en América Latina por ser "sintomático de una derivación incompleta", aun cuando el contenido estaba anclado en las situaciones políticas locales.[40] En este caso, y como la mayoría de los críticos, Camnitzer pasó por alto el hecho de que el revelador prefijo "anti" en tantas obras latinoamerica-

nas (como el antiarte de Pedrosa y el anti-happening de Masotta) logra socavar la premisa de que el pop es un movimiento artístico estadounidense. Tanto el prefijo "anti" como la anticategoría "objeto", según se describió para el IV Salão, subvierten los métodos hegemónicos convencionales de clasificación artística, justamente como el acto pop de desdibujar los límites entre lo "alto" y lo "bajo" y democratizar la copia cuestiona una historia del arte estructurada por nociones de influencia que descartan estas obras por "derivativas". Como lo demuestra la apropiación de la imaginería de Coca-Cola, cuando se piensa al pop en América como verbo ya no es innecesario, o incluso posible, hacer una distinción rigurosa entre los movimientos de arte pop y arte conceptual. Estas obras movilizaron un lenguaje visual compartido cuyo significado final está definido por su inserción en una cultura determinada, ya sea la cultura pop, la cultura popular o el "entre-lugar".

NOTAS

1   "Cada movimiento tem a sua moda", *O Estado de São Paulo* (São Paulo), 13 de septiembre de 1967. Estados Unidos llevó dos exposiciones a la IX Bienal de São Paulo: *Ambiente USA: 1957-1967*, con obras de veintiún artistas, y una exposición individual de Edward Hopper, que el curador William Seitz describió como "una manera particular de retratar la realidad estadounidense". Consultar lo que escribe Gabara en su introducción sobre el rechazo de Juan Acha a los conceptos de copia e influencia.

2   Esta multitud de términos locales no pasó desapercibida. Para ayudar al público a mantenerse al día con el arte, los periodistas publicaban artículos didácticos tales como "*Aprenda a chamar pelo nome certo as coisas desta bienal*" (Aprenda a llamar por su nombre correcto las cosas incluidas en esta bienal), explicando términos como arte cinético, arte op, arte pop y nueva objetividad. *Jornal da Tarde*, 30 de noviembre de 1967, Archive Wanda Svevo, Fundação Bienal de São Paulo.

3   Ida Rodríguez Prampolini, carta a la Fundación de la Bienal de São Paulo, 5 de octubre de 1967, Archivo Wanda Svevo, Fundação Bienal de São Paulo.

4   El IV Salão se llevó a cabo de diciembre de 1967 hasta febrero de 1968. Para obtener mayor información sobre el incidente con Tozzi, ver Claudia Calirman, "Pop and Politics in Brazilian Art", en *International Pop*, eds., Darsie Alexander et al. (Minneapolis: Walker Art Center, 2015), 119–130.

5   La canonización del conceptualismo latinoamericano en la década de 1990 por personas como Mari Carmen Ramírez y Luis Camnitzer puede atribuirse a los esfuerzos de los profesionales del arte en América Latina por romper con la designación de "fantástico" que promovieron exposiciones como *Art of the Fantastic: Latin America, 1920–1987*, Indianapolis Museum of Art (1987).

6   Académicos como Thomas Crow y Hal Foster han argumentado que la producción de Warhol debería ser considerada más allá de la interpretación canónica promovida principalmente por el artista mismo. Ver, por ejemplo, Crow, "Saturday Disasters: Trace and Reference in Early Warhol", *Art in America* 75 (mayo de 1987): 128–136. La canonización del arte conceptual latinoamericano como arte político empezó en Estados Unidos con Mari Carmen Ramírez y su artículo de 1993 titulado "Blue Print Circuits: Conceptual Art and Politics in Latin America", en *Latin American Artists of the Twentieth Century*, ed. Waldo Rasmussen (Nueva York: MoMA, 1993), 156–169. Esta narrativa rígida ha sido cuestionada por críticos tales como Miguel A. López y Josephine Watson, "How Do We Know What Latin American Conceptualism Looks Like?," *Afterall: A Journal of Art, Context, and Enquiry*, no. 23 (primavera 2010): 5–21.

7   Mari Carmen Ramírez, "Tactics for Thriving on Adversity: Conceptualism in Latin America, 1960–1980", en *Global Conceptualisms: Points of Origin 1950s–1980s*, eds., Luis Camnitzer et al. (Nueva York: Queens Museum of Art, 1999), 53–68. Ramírez señaló en específico a *Tucumán arde*, una exposición colectiva de múltiples componentes que se realizó en Buenos Aires y Rosario, como emblemática del arte conceptual latinoamericano.

8   Marta Traba, "El diseño Pop. Sus cuatro soluciones más destacadas: A) Beatriz González, B) Sonia Gutiérrez y Ana Mercedes Hoyos, C) Santiago Cárdenas, D) Bernardo Salcedo", en *Historia abierta del arte colombiano* (Bogotá: Colcultura y Museo La Tertulia, 1984). Llamando la atención sobre la situación de subdesarro-

llo en Colombia y Brasil, respectivamente, Marta Traba utilizó el término "pop ubicado" y Mário Pedrosa habló de "popistas do subdesenvolvimento" para referirse a los artistas que trabajaban el lenguaje pop desde dentro de la periferia. Mário Pedrosa, "From American Pop to Dias, the Sertanejo", en *Mário Pedrosa, Primary Documents*, eds., Glória Ferreira y Paulo Herkenhoff (Nueva York: The Museum of Modern Art, 2015), 321.

9   Andy Warhol, "What is Pop Art? Part I", entrevistado por G. R. Swenson, *ARTnews* 62, no. 7 (1963): 25–27, 60–64.

10 Andy Warhol, *The Philosophy of Andy Warhol: From A to B and Back Again* (Londres: Cassell, 1975).

11 Morais concibió *Nova Crítica* como vehículo para abordar una nueva forma de crítica de arte que desdibujara los límites entre papel del crítico, del artista y del público. En efecto, el evento también incluyó obras como un lienzo en blanco que se colocó en el baño público para que el público escribiera en él y fotografías de la obra *Tiradentes: Totem-monumento para o prisionero político* de Meireles, yuxtapuestas a textos bíblicos. *Nova Crítica* hacía un comentario crítico de las obras de Tereza Simões, Guilherme Magalhães y Meireles expuestas en la Petite Galerie en la exposición *Agnus Dei* (1970). Ver Francisco Bittencourt, "Dez anos de experimentação", en *Crítica de arte no Brasil: Temáticas contemporâneas*, ed. Glória Ferreira (Río de Janeiro: Funarte, 2006), 179.

12 Para ver un análisis de la obra de Oiticica más allá de su participación en los movimientos concreto y neoconcreto en la década de 1950, consultar el catálogo Lynn Zelevansky et al., *Hélio Oiticica: To Organize Delirium* (Pittsburgh: Carnegie Museum of Art y Múnich: DelMonico Books/Prestel, 2016).

13   Brandon Holmquest, Antonio Caro y Víctor Manuel Rodríguez, *BOMB*, no. 110, *The Americas Issue: Colombia and Venezuela* (invierno 2010): 22.

14   Caro se hizo notar en 1970, cuando el periodista Alegre Levy publicó un artículo en el diario principal de Bogotá sobre su participación en el XXI Salón Nacional de Artistas en el Museo Nacional. En la exposición, el artista presentó un busto del expresidente Carlos Lleras Restrepo (1966–70) hecho burdamente con sal, ataviado con lentes negros y colocado en una caja de vidrio. La noche de la inauguración, Caro vertió agua sobre el busto, destruyendo la obra intencionalmente, aunque sin quererlo creó un charco, ya que no había comprobado si la caja de vidrio que contenía el busto era a prueba de agua. El escándalo transformó la inauguración en un happening pop, generándole publicidad instantánea al joven artista. La decisión de usar sal —material asociado en Colombia con la práctica folclórica de esculpir en sal de roca y puesto en peligro por la instalación de las refinerías modernas— permitió hacer desaparecer la obra, logrando una crítica política del ciclo de modernización que Lleras había promovido a expensas de la población rural. Pero sobre todo, el uso de la sal ponía de relieve las constantes negociaciones entre el consumo masivo y la cultura popular que eran parte de la realidad cotidiana de Colombia en los años setenta. Puede verse una discusión sobre las negociaciones de Caro con la política colombiana y el mundo internacional del arte en Gina McDaniel Tarver, "Art Does Not Fit Here: Colombian Conceptual Art between the International 'New Avant-Garde' and Colombian Politics", *Third Text*, v. 26, no. 6 (noviembre de 2012): 729–744.

15   Santiago acuñó el término "entre-lugar" para describir la producción literaria proveniente de las antiguas colonias europeas como Brasil, que según él genera nuevos parámetros que esquivan los supuestos habituales de origen europeo o expresiones patrioteras y nacionalistas. De manera similar, el arte pop que circuló en el continente desafiaba las visiones no críticas del estado-nación, al tiempo que dialogaba directamente con las producciones y tradiciones locales. Silviano Santiago, *The Space in Between. Essays on Latin American Culture* (Durham: Duke University Press, 2001).

16   Oscar Masotta, *El "Pop-Art"* (Buenos Aires: Ed. Columba, 1967).

17   Masotta se basó en el texto *Mythologies* (1957) de Roland Barthes para desarrollar su concepto de las imágenes como signos que pueden ser interpretados. Ver Ana Longoni y Mariano Mestman, "After Pop, We Dematerialize: Oscar Masotta, Happenings, and Media Art at the Beginnings of Conceptualism", en *Listen, Here, Now! Argentine Art of the 1960s: Writings of the Avant-Garde*, ed. Inéz Katzenstein (Nueva York: The Museum of Modern Art, 2004), 165.

18   Hélio Oiticica, "Tropicália Time Series 1", documentos de la exposición *Information*, manuscrito en los archivos del Museum of Modern Art, abril de 1969. Gerchman envió el texto de Oiticica al curador Kynaston McShine junto con fotografías de su obra, intentando (sin éxito) lograr que lo incluyeran en la exposición.

19   Ibíd. Ver "Imagen–Palabra–Mundo" en la introducción de Esther Gabara a este catálogo.

20   Rubens Gerchman, carta a Kynaston McShine, documentos de la exposición *Information*, archivos del Museum of Modern Art, 3 de abril de 1970. Así como la bienal de 1967 se conocería como la primera exposición importante de pop, *Information*, ideada en su origen como una muestra panorámica de arte experimental, se conocería en la historia del arte como la primera exposición de arte conceptual en Estados Unidos, en gran parte debido a la presencia de obras basadas en estructuas linguísticas como *One and Three Chairs* de Joseph Kosuth (1965). El MoMA tiene disponibles los comunicados de prensa originales y el catálogo en la página: https://www.moma.org/calendar/exhibitions/2686.

21   Waldemar Cordeiro, "Realismo ao nível da cultura de massa", *Propostas 65* (São Paulo: Fundação Armando Álvares Penteado, 1965). Todas las traducciones son de Camila Maroja, a menos que se señale.

22   Hélio Oiticica, "Esquema geral da nova objetividade", en *Nova objetividade brasileira* (Río de Janeiro: MAM, 1967), s.p. El ensayo fue traducido al inglés y publicado en Alexander Alberro y Blake Stimson, eds., *Conceptual Art: A Critical Anthology* (Cambridge: MIT Press, 2000), 40–42.

23   La exposición *Nova objetividade brasileira* se inauguró en el Museo de Arte Moderno en Río de Janeiro en abril de 1967. Allí presentó Oiticica su célebre instalación *Tropicália*, citada al comienzo de este ensayo.

24   Al crear una genealogía local para *nova objetividade*, Oiticica no promovía una lectura nacionalista del pop como representativo de Brasil, pero en efecto él percibía el pop como el fin de la representación. En el catálogo de la exposición *Information*, escribió: "no estoy aquí representando a Brasil; ni representando a nada: se terminaron las ideas de representar-representación".

25   La descripción de la obra en la lista de la exposición la relaciona con los experimentos realizados por Oiticica en Essex University y su diseño de "nidos". La lista de obras está disponible en: https://www.moma.org/documents/moma_master-checklist_326690.pdf.

26   La noción de un lenguaje brasileño organizado en torno al concepto de la "objetividad", descrita en el prefacio de *Nova objetividade brasileira* y desarrollada en el IV Salão, fue presentada primero en un evento paralelo a la exposición colectiva *Propostas 66* (noviembre de 1966), donde Oiticica leyó su texto "Situação da Vanguarda no Brasil" (Situación de la vanguardia en Brasil). Ver Hélio Oiticica, "Situação da Vanguarda no Brasil", en *Crítica de arte no Brasil: Temáticas contemporâneas*, ed. Glória Ferreira (Río de Janeiro: Funarte, 2006), 147–148.

27   Morais definió el concepto del objeto. También coordinó la exposición y los eventos paralelos "Simpósio de Escultura Brasileira —retrospectiva e atualização" y Festival de Filmes de Arte.

28   Oiticica, "O aparecimento do suprasensorial", en *Hélio Oiticica, Aspiro ao grande labirinto: Textos de Hélio Oiticica* (1954–1969), eds., Luciano Figueiredo, Lygia Pape y Waly Salomão (Río de Janeiro: Rocco, 1986), 102–105. Presentado originalmente en el *Simpósio de Escultura Brasileira —retrospectiva e atualização*. Se publicó más tarde en el texto, Oiticica cita la famosa expresión de Mário Pedrosa "ejercicio experimental de libertad".

29   Oiticica, "Esquema geral da nova objetividade", s.p. Al analizar el texto de Oiticica, la curadora Darsie Alexander observa que "el impulso de crear una cronología del pop tipo "primero esto y luego lo otro" ha hecho que se omita la obra de muchos artistas que trabajaron dentro de estructuras estéticas y cronológicas que se resisten a enfoques históricos selectivos". Ver Alexander, "Introduction: The Edge of Pop", *International Pop*, 77–84.

30   Mário Pedrosa, "Arte ambiental, arte pós-moderna, Hélio Oiticica", *Mário Pedrosa, Primary Documents*, eds., Glória Ferreira y Paulo Herkenhoff (Nueva York: The Museum of Modern Art, 2015), 314–316. Publicado en su origen con el título "Arte ambiental, arte pós-moderna, Hélio Oiticica", en *Correio da Manhã* (Río de Janeiro: 1966), s.p.

31   Me refiero a la celebrada obra de Arthur Danto en que afirma que el arte pop marca el fin del arte al abandonar el acercamiento mimético a la estética. Ver Arthur C. Danto, *After the End of Art: Contemporary Art and the Pale of History* (Princeton: Princeton University Press, 2014).

32   Sônia Salzstein, aludiendo al artista Antonio Dias, profundiza en el pop como estrategia para reexaminar la modernidad y la historia (del arte) occidental en la década de 1980, haciendo un análisis crítico de la posmodernidad y el multiculturalismo. Ver Sônia Salzstein, "Pop as a Crisis in the Public Sphere", en *Pop Art and Vernacular Cultures*, ed. Kobena Mercer (Cambridge: MIT Press, 2007), 88–109.

33   Jacqueline Barnitz, "A Latin Answer to Pop", *Arts Magazine*, junio de 1966, 36–39. Ver un análisis incisivo del elusivo trabajo pop de Marta Minujín en Catherine Spencer, "Performing Pop: Marta Minujín and the 'Argentine Image-Makers'", *Tate Papers*, no. 24 (otoño 2015), http://www.tate.org.uk/research/publications/tate-papers/24

34   Las teorías de McLuhan en los años sesenta ponen de relieve la capacidad que tienen los medios masivos de generar nuevas estructuras de consciencia transformando nuestra percepción sensorial: "La mayoría de las tecnologías produce una amplificación muy explícita en su separación de los sentidos. La radio es una extensión de lo aural, y la fotografía de alta fidelidad lo es de lo visual. Pero la televisión es sobre todo una extensión del sentido del tacto, lo cual implica la interacción máxima de todos los sentidos". Ver Marshall McLuhan, *Understanding Media: The Extensions of Man* (Cambridge: MIT Press, [1964] 1994), 333.

35   Ver Lucy R. Lippard, *Six Years of Dematerialization of the Art Object from 1966 to 1972* (Nueva York: Praeger, 1973). El término fue propuesto por primera vez junto con John Chandler. Ver Lippard y Chandler, "The Dematerialization of Art" (1967), publicado originalmente en *Art International* 12.2 (febrero de 1968): 31–36.

36   Escrito y leído como ponencia en 1967. Más tarde publicado en *Oscar Masotta: Conciencia y estructura* (Buenos Aires: Editorial Jorge Álvarez, 1969).

37   La traducción al inglés: http://70.32.114.117/gsdl/collect/revista/index/assoc/HASH0151/2678704a.dir/r9y10_24nota.pdf.

38   En su página de internet, Minujín ubica la obra *Minuphone* bajo el rubro de arte efímero. Ver la página de la artista: http://www.marta-minujin.com.

39   Luis Camnitzer, "Political Pop", en *Luis Camnitzer: On Art, Artists, Latin America, and Other Utopias*, ed. Rachel Weiss (Austin: University of Texas Press, 2009), 31. Camnitzer ha sido, junto con Ramírez, uno de los principales promotores del arte conceptual latinoamericano, o conceptualismo, como prefiere llamarlo. Ver Luis Camnitzer, *Conceptualism in Latin American Art: Didactics of Liberation* (Austin: University of Texas Press, 2007).

40   Camnitzer, "Political Pop", 32.

CONSUMING

AMÉRICA

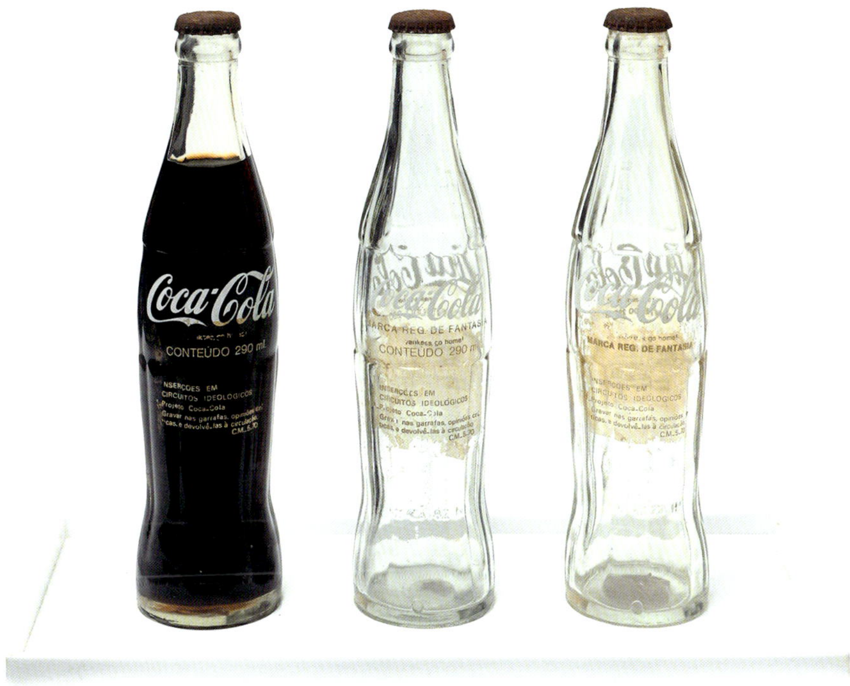

Pl. 17. Cildo Meireles, *Inserções em circuitos ideológicos* (Insertions into Ideological Circuits) from *Projeto Coca-Cola* (Coca-Cola Project), 1970. Three glass Coca-Cola bottles, three metal caps, liquid, and vinyl-transfer text; 9.25 x 2.33 x 2.33 inches (23.49 x 5.92 x 5.92 cm), each bottle. Private collection.

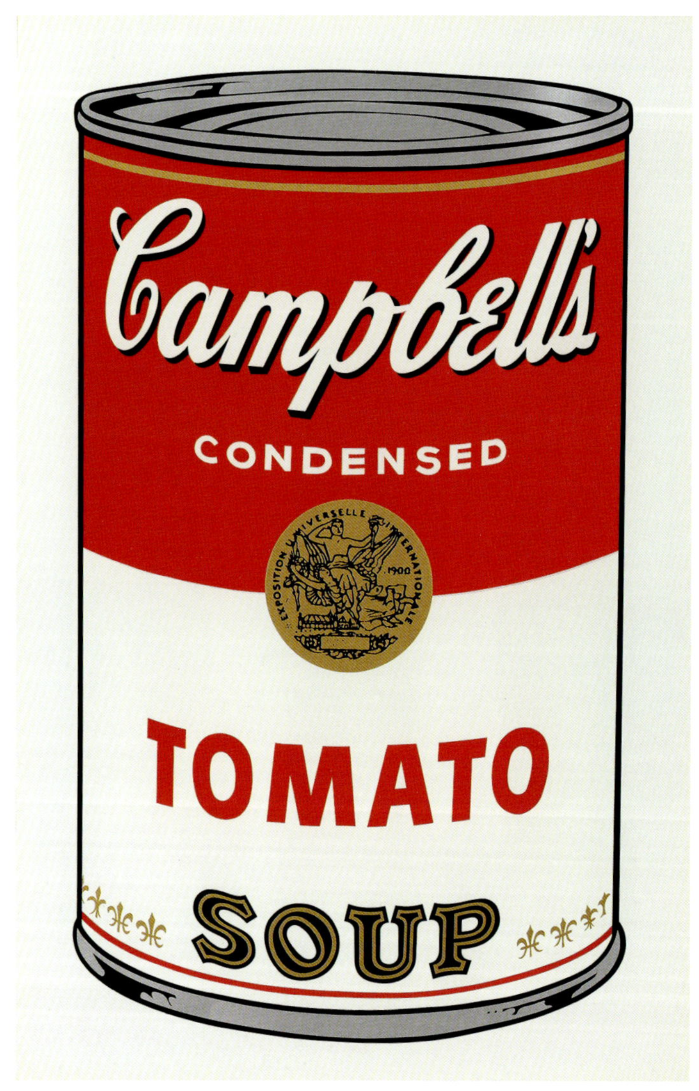

Pl. 18. Andy Warhol, *Campbell's Soup I (Tomato)*, 1968. Screenprint on paper, 35.06 x 23.18 inches (89.1 x 58.9 cm). Collection of the Nasher Museum of Art at Duke University, Durham, North Carolina. Gift of the Andy Warhol Foundation for the Visual Arts, Inc. © 2018 The Andy Warhol Foundation for the Visual Arts, Inc. Licensed by Artists Rights Society (ARS), New York, New York.

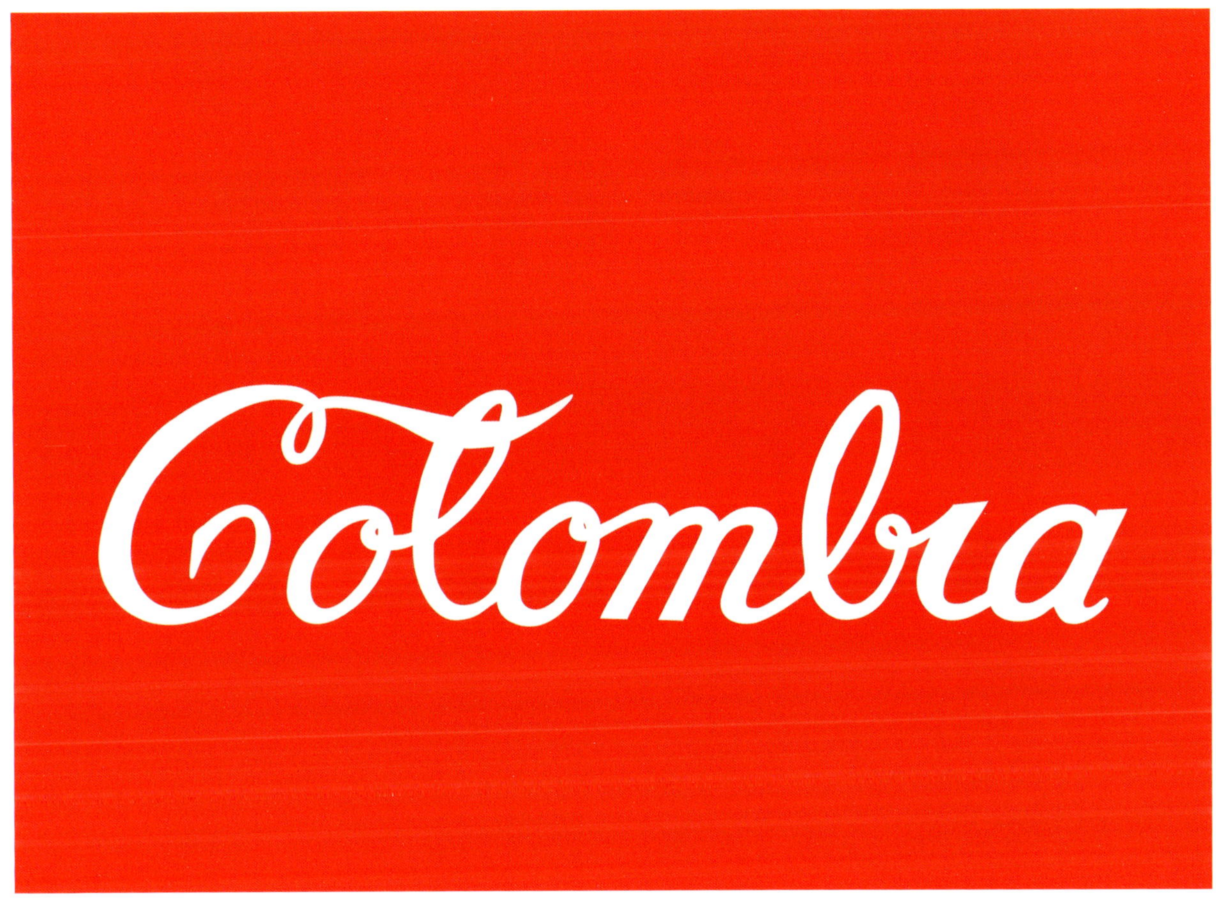

Pl. 19. Antonio Caro, *Colombia Coca-Cola*, 1976 (fabricated 2010). Enamel on sheet metal, edition 11/25, 19.5 x 27.5 inches (49.53 x 69.85 cm). Collection of the MIT List Visual Arts Center, Cambridge, Massachusetts. Purchased with funds from the Alan May Endowment. © Antonio Caro. Image courtesy of the artist and Casas Riegner, Bogotá, Colombia.

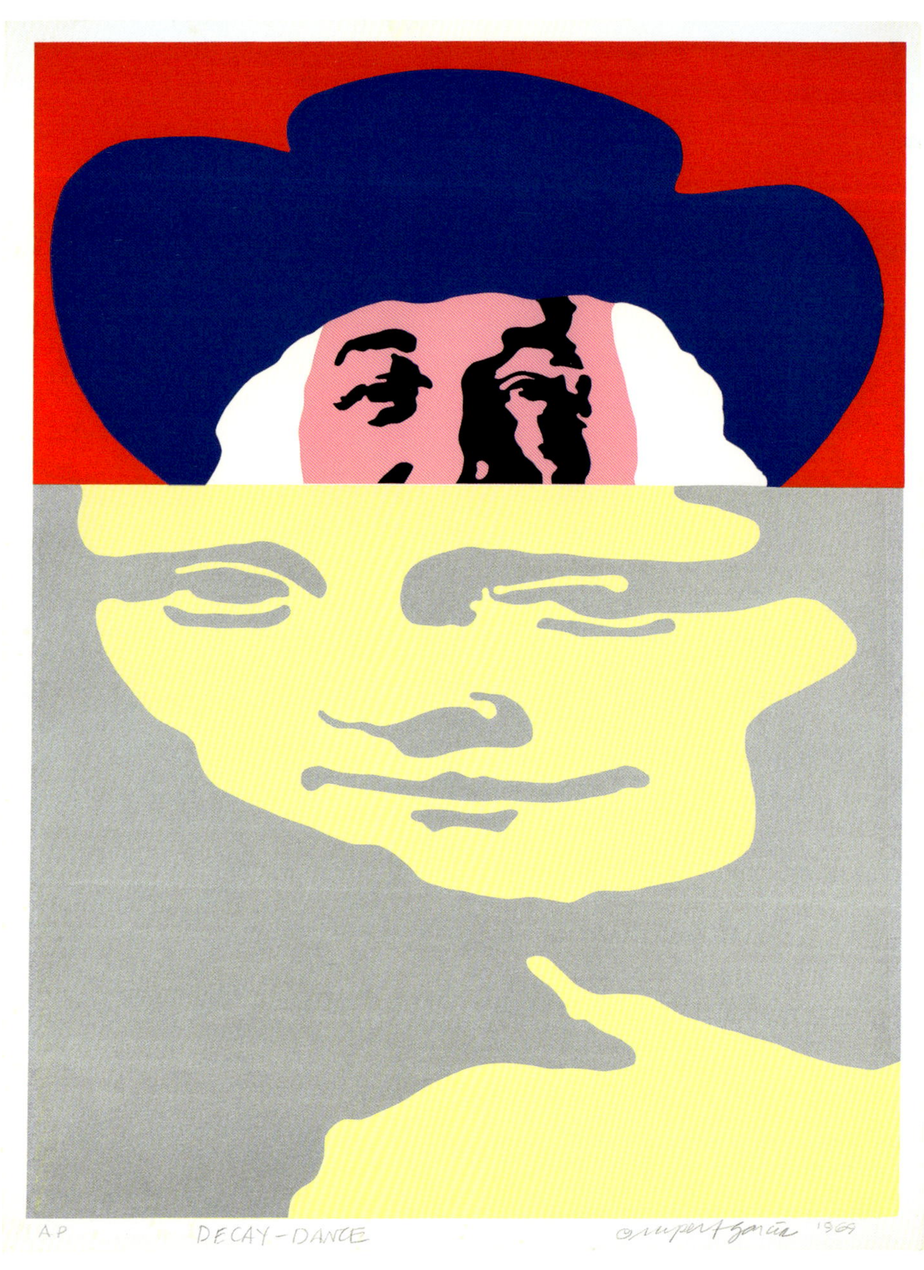

Pl. 20. Rupert García, *Decay Dance*, 1969. Screenprint on paper, artist's print, 26.12 x 20.87 inches (66.4 x 50.9 cm). Collection of the Fine Arts Museums of San Francisco, De Young, Legion of Honor Museum, California. Gift of Mr. and Mrs. Robert Marcus. © Rupert García. Courtesy of the artist and Rena Bransten Gallery, San Francisco, California.

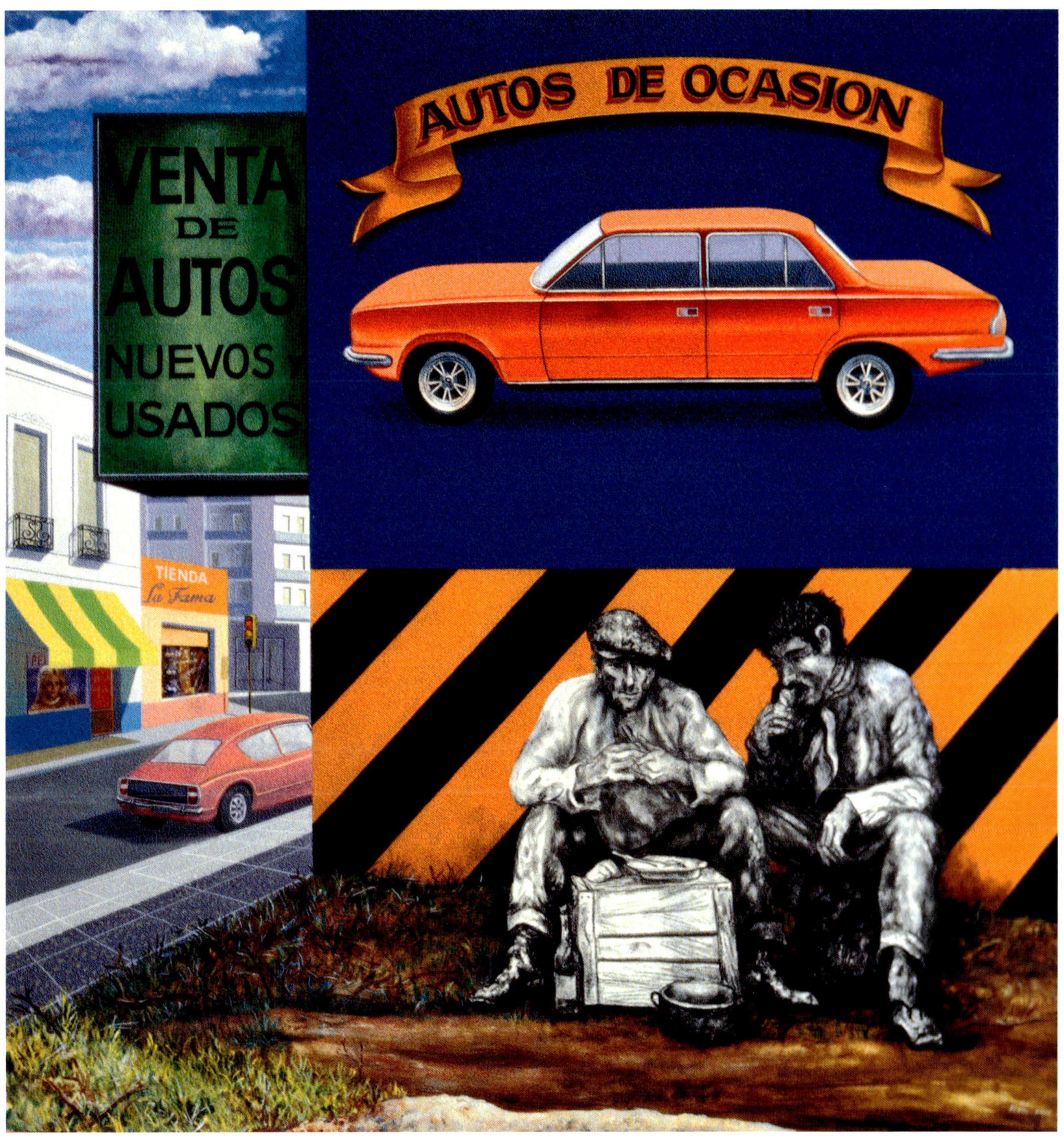

Pl. 21. Antonio Berni, *Mediodía* (Noontime), 1976. Acrylic and collage on canvas, 78.22 x 78.34 inches (198.7 x 199 cm). Collection of the Blanton Museum of Art, the University of Texas at Austin. Barbara Duncan Fund. © José Antonio Berni.

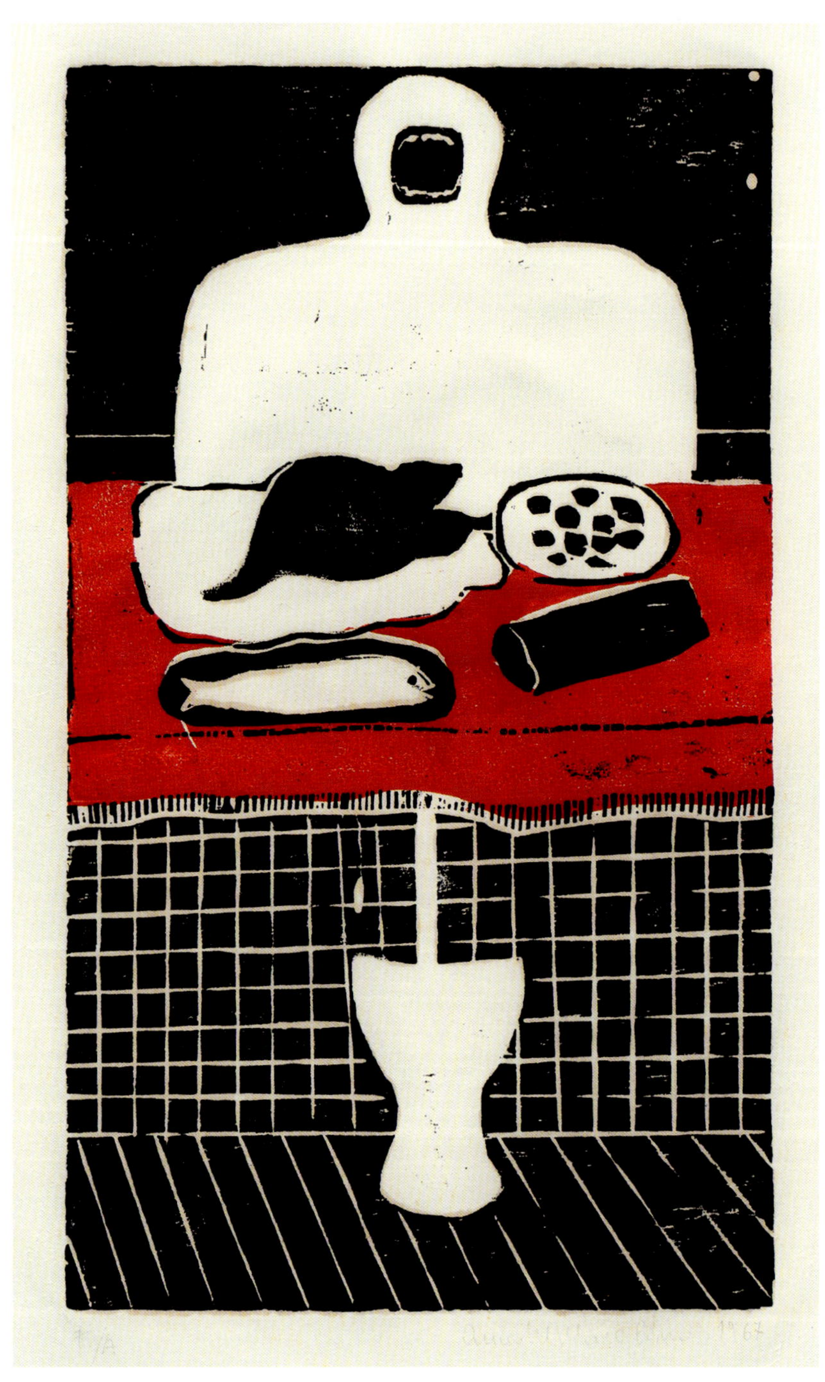

Pl. 22. Anna Maria Maiolino, *Glu... Glu... Glu...* (Gulp... Gulp... Gulp...), 1967. Woodcut on paper, 24.48 x 16.88 inches (62.2 x 42.9 cm). Collection of the Pinacoteca do Estado de São Paulo, Brazil. Donated by the artist, 2007. Image courtesy of the Pinacoteca do Estado de São Paulo, Brazil. Photo by Edouard Fraipont.

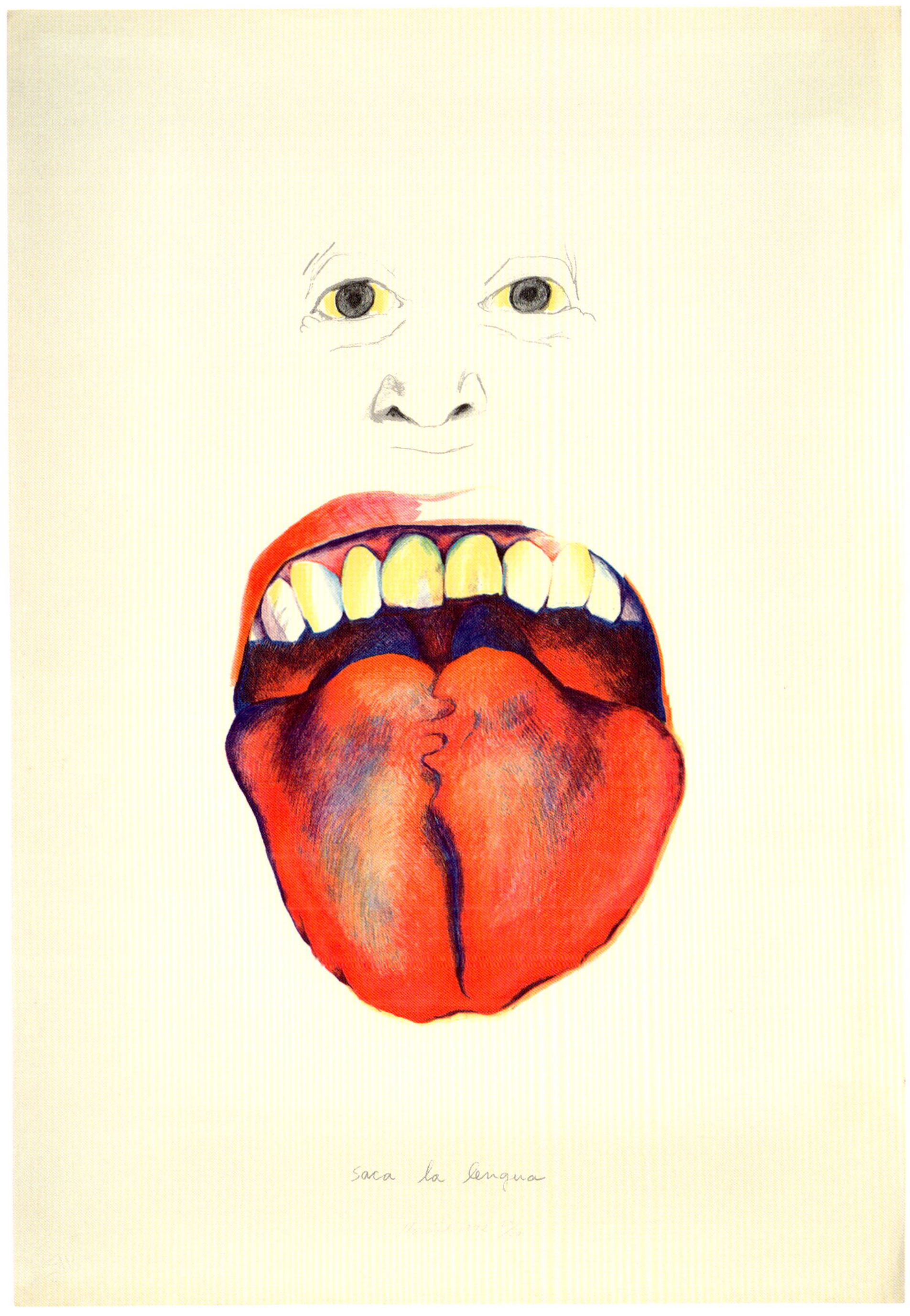

Pl. 23. Marisol Escobar (known as Marisol), *Saca la lengua* (Stick Out Your Tongue) from the portfolio *La paz* (Peace), 1972. Lithograph on paper, edition 24/150, 41.25 x 29.25 inches (104.77 x 74.29 cm). Collection of the McNay Art Museum, San Antonio, Texas. Gift of Don and Lynn Watt. © 2018 Estate of Marisol. Licensed by Artists Rights Society (ARS), New York, New York.

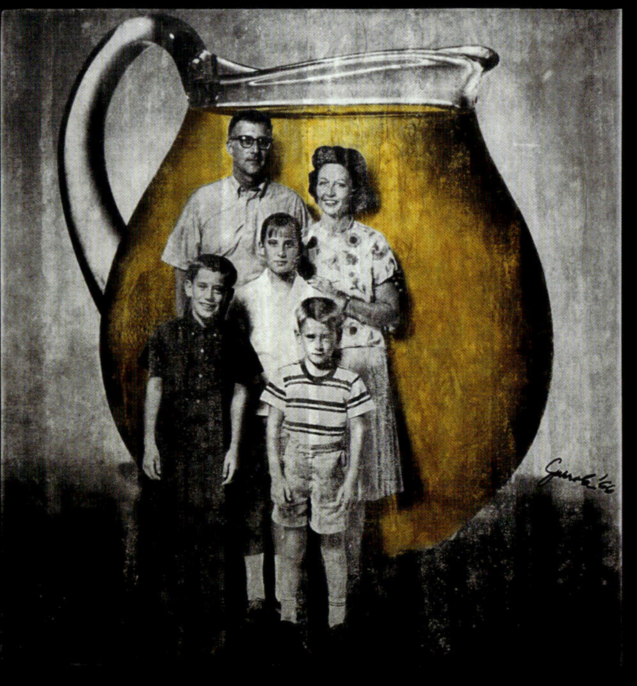
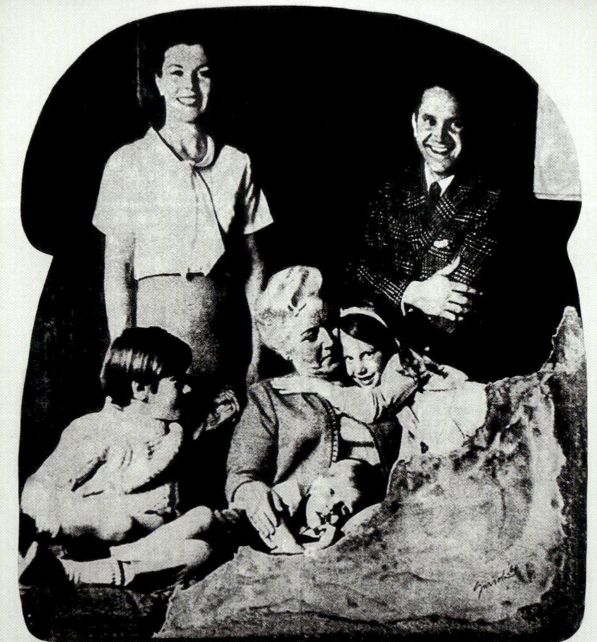
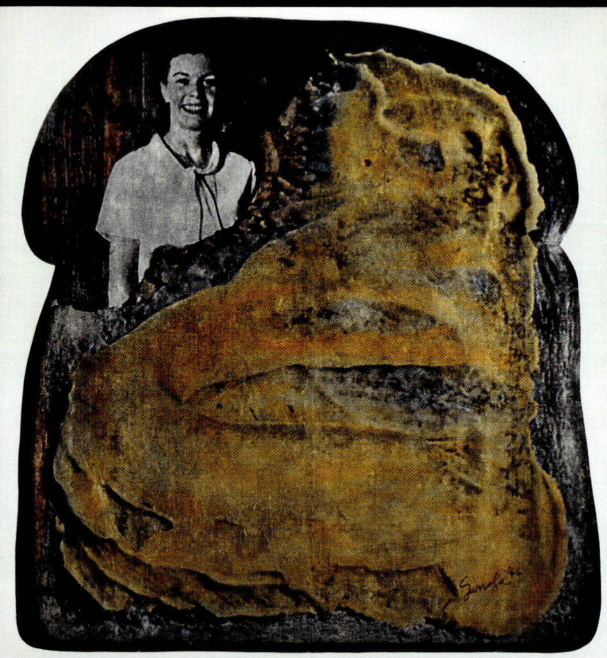

CLOCKWISE, Pls. 24–26. Juan José Gurrola, *Familia Kool Aid* (Kool Aid Family), *Familia Sandwich* (Sandwich Family), and *Familia Sandwich* (Sandwich Family) from the series *Dom-Art*, 1966–1967 (fabricated 2018). Photographic slides, 2 x 2 inches (5.08 x 5.08 cm), each. Courtesy of the Fundación Gurrola A.C. and House of Gaga, Mexico City, Mexico, and Los Angeles, California. Photo by Nattan Guzmán.

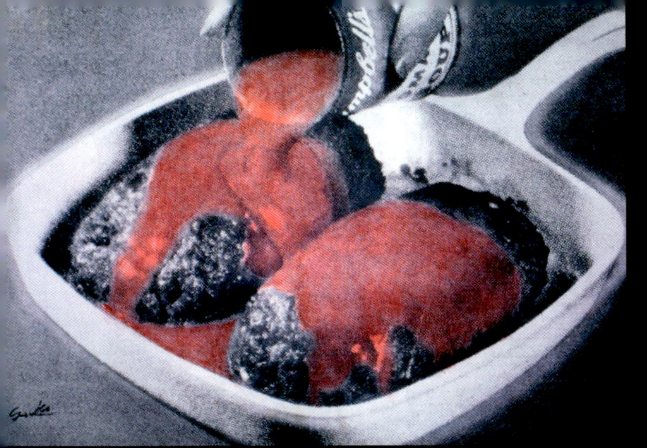
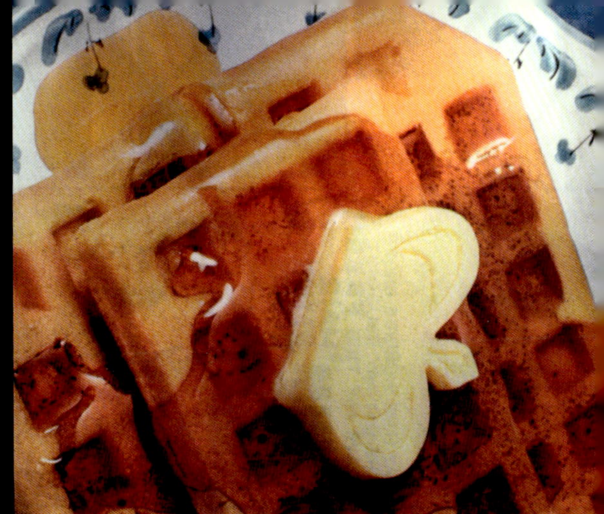
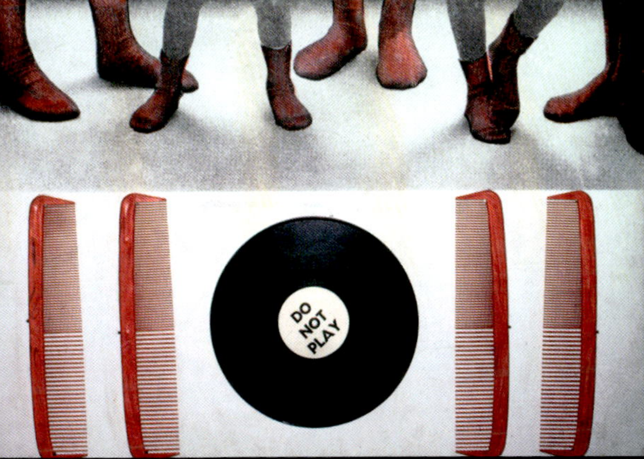
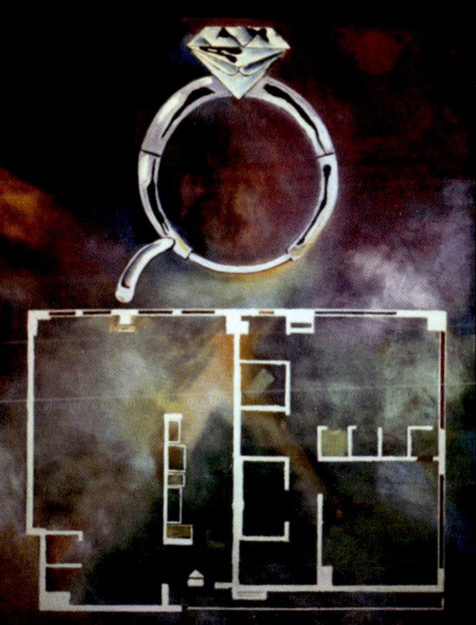

CLOCKWISE, Pls. 27, 28. Juan José Gurrola, Sin título (Untitled) and Sin título (Untitled) from the series *Dom-Art*, 1966–1967 (fabricated 2018). **Pls. 29, 30.** *Plano y anillo* (Plan and Ring) and *No tocar* (Do Not Play) from the series *Dom-Art*, 1966–1967 (fabricated 2018). Photographic slides, 2 x 2 inches (5.08 x 5.08 cm), each. Courtesy of the Fundación Gurrola A.C. and House of Gaga, Mexico City, Mexico, and Los Angeles, California. Photo by Nattan Guzmán.

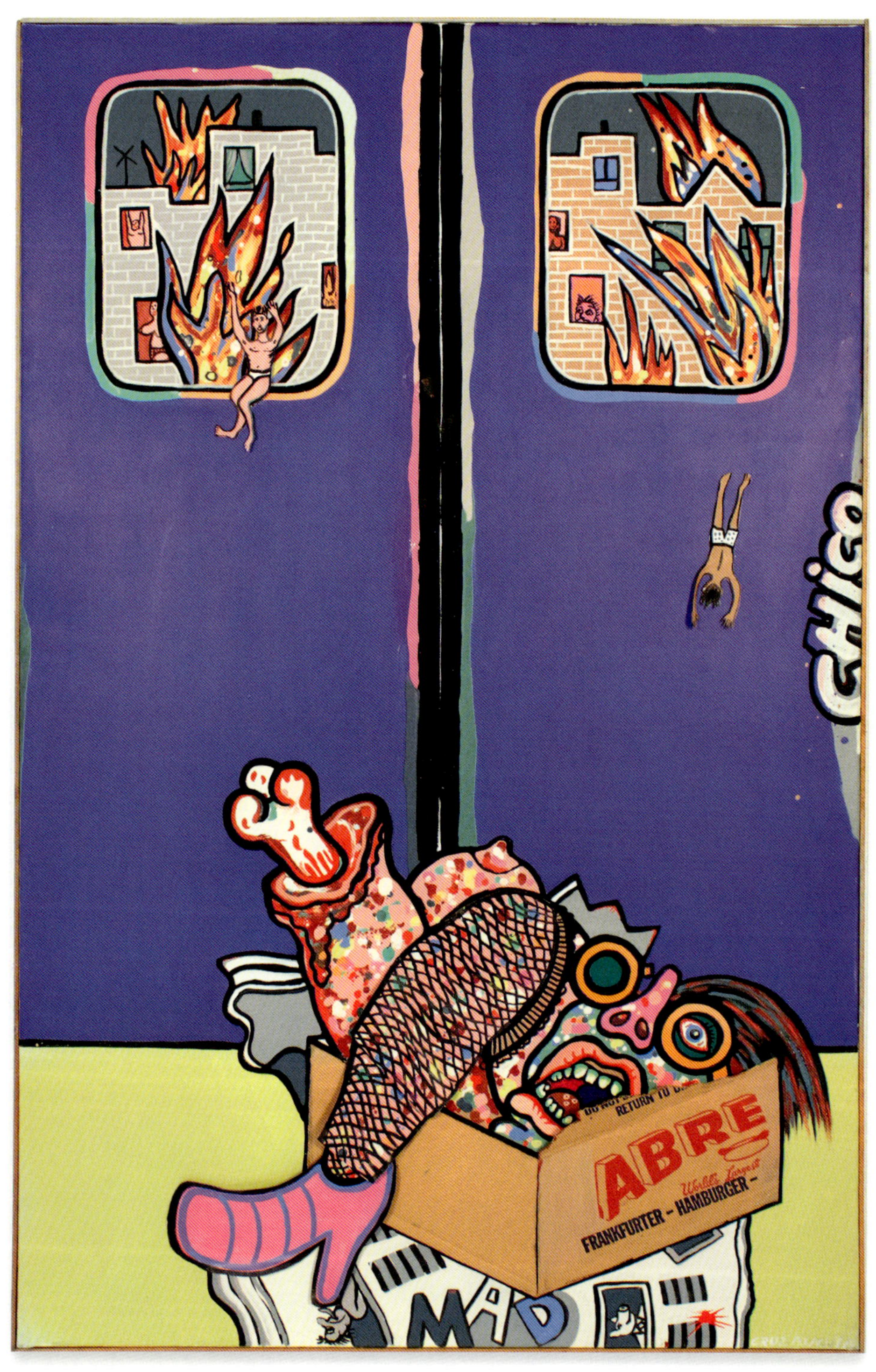

Pl. 31. Luis Cruz Azaceta, *Ji Ji Ji Express*, 1974–1975. Oil, canvas cutouts, and cardboard on canvas; 70 x 45 inches (177.8 x 114.3 cm). Courtesy of the artist and Arthur Rogers Gallery, New Orleans, Louisiana. Photo by Dylan Cruz Azaceta.

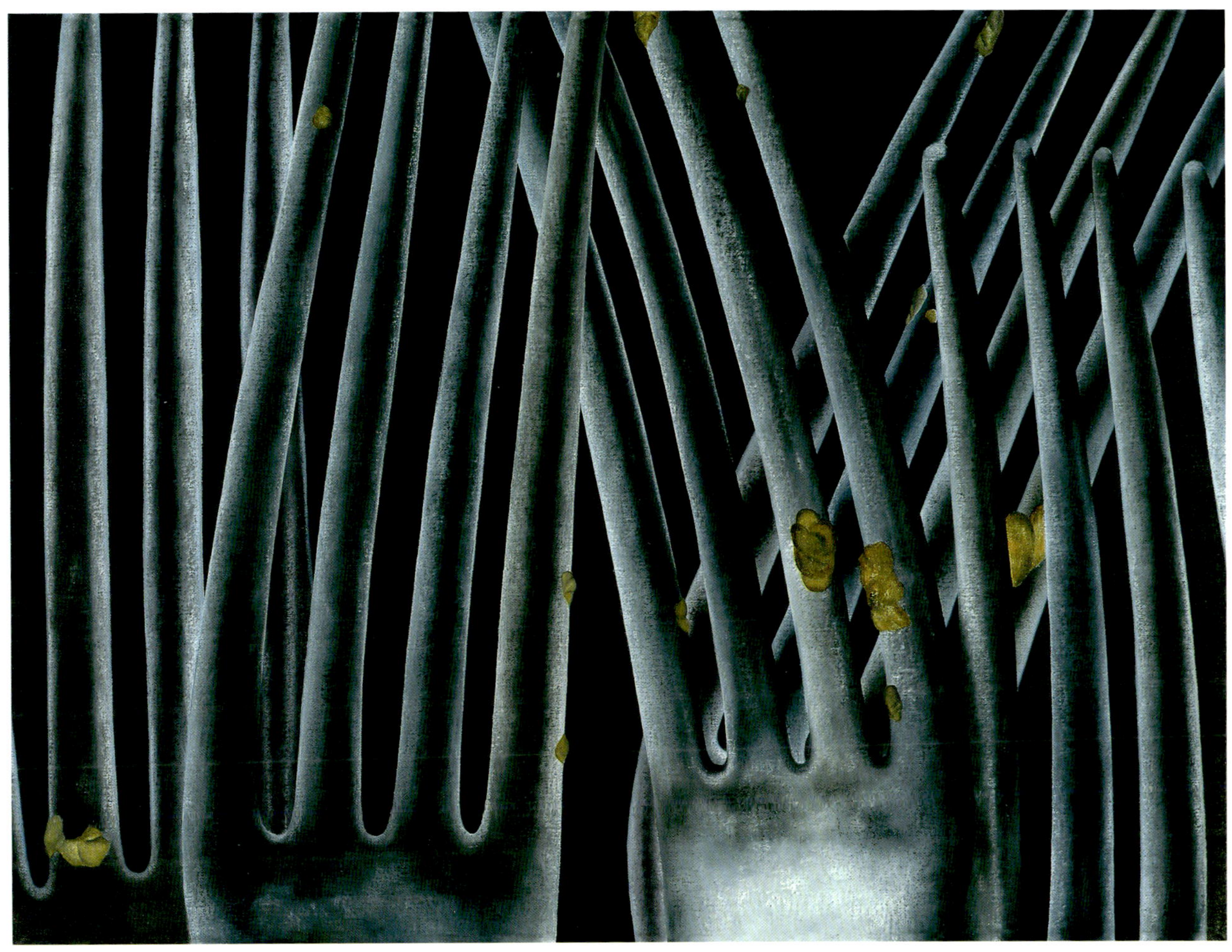

Pl. 32. Antônio Henrique Amaral, *Battlefield 31*, 1974. Oil on canvas, 36.02 x 48.03 inches (91.5 cm x 122 cm). Collection of the Blanton Museum of Art, the University of Texas at Austin. Archer M. Huntington Museum Fund. Licensed by Artists Rights Society (ARS), New York, New York/AUTVIS, São Paulo, Brazil.

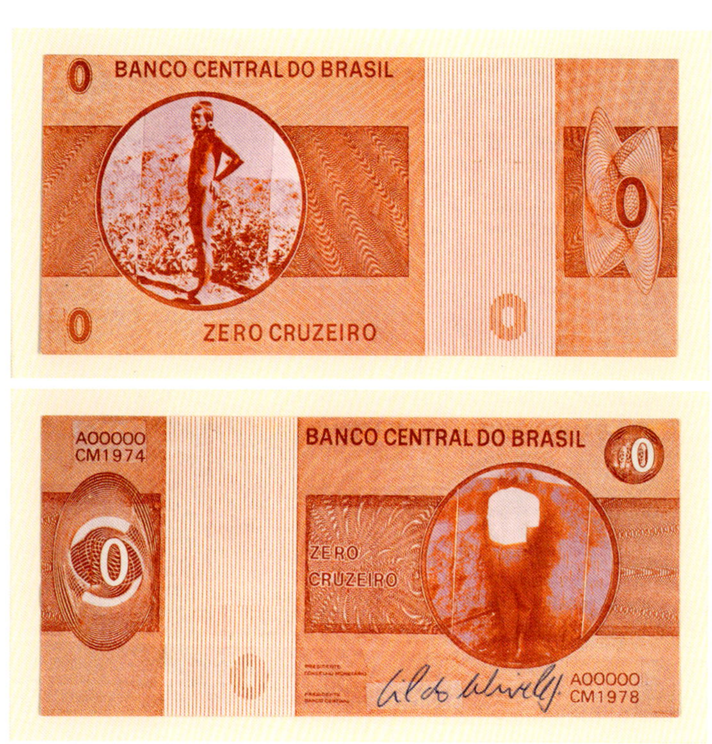

Pl. 33. Cildo Meireles, *Zero cruzeiro* (Cero cruceiro), 1974–1978. Photolithograph on paper, 2.79 x 6.1 inches (7.1 x 15.5 cm). Collection of the Blanton Museum of Art, the University of Texas at Austin. Gift of Paulo Figueiredo.

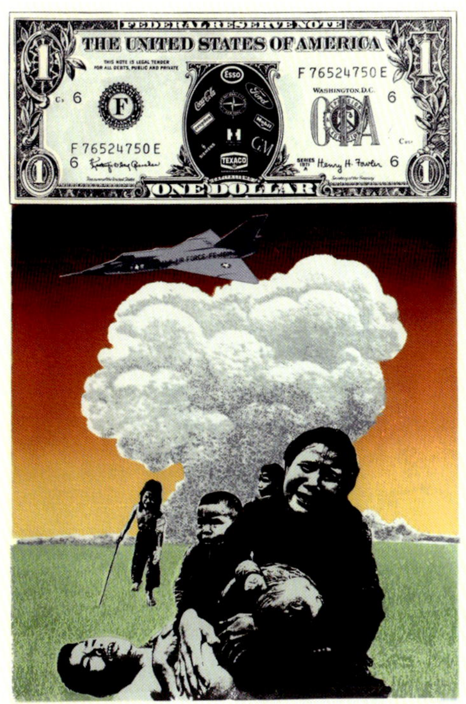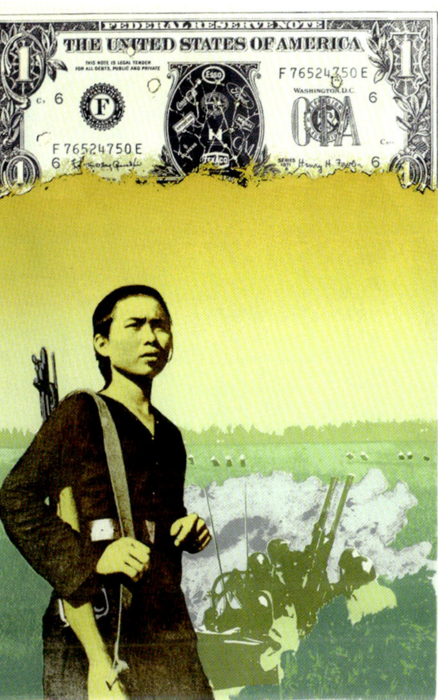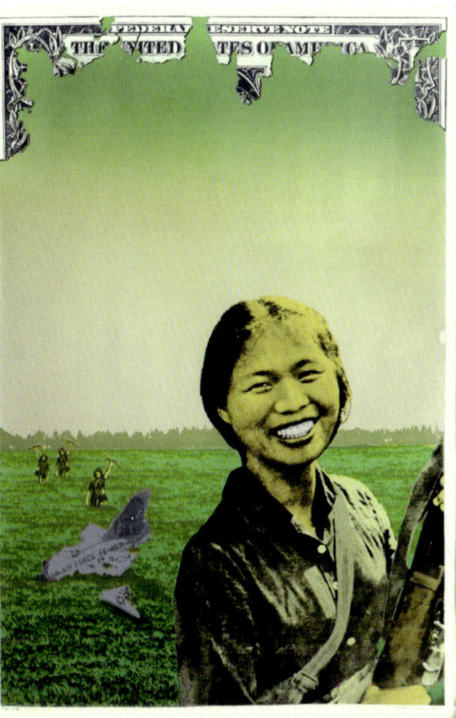

Pl. 34. Taller 4 Rojo (Diego Arango and Nirma Zárate, founding members), *Agresión del imperialismo* (Aggression of Imperialism), 1972. Screenprints on photographic paper, 39.76 x 28.15 inches (101 x 71.5 cm), each panel. Collection of the Museo de Arte de la Universidad Nacional de Colombia, Bogotá.

JENNIFER JOSTEN

REVOLUTIONARY CURRENTS: POP DESIGN BETWEEN CUBA, MEXICO, AND CALIFORNIA

In the 1960s, artists and graphic designers working in Havana, Mexico City, and the San Francisco Bay Area took hold of visual strategies associated with Pop art to articulate political messages on a public scale. While Andy Warhol, Roy Lichtenstein, and others adapted the language of mass consumer culture to paintings for the New York art market, artists allied with progressive Cuban, Mexican, African American, and Chicano social movements deployed similar devices—particularly the serially repeated, high-contrast photographic image and the heavily outlined cartoon figure—in mass-produced posters that demanded an end to neo-imperialist policies and practices throughout the world. These easel paintings and ephemeral posters share a flat, mechanically reproduced aesthetic, the result of pushing paint across cut-away forms or mesh screens printed with photomechanically transferred designs. Whereas Warhol and Lichtenstein employed stencils and silkscreens as distancing maneuvers that generated critical, cold, or ironic stances, revolutionary designers in Cuba, Mexico, and the United States deployed them to articulate messages of affirmation and international solidarity. Meanwhile, official organizations in all three countries co-opted Pop and Op styles for graphic and urban design, which effectively sold new images of the nation or region to local and international publics alike.

Though peoples across the geographic region encompassing Cuba and greater Mexico (including modern-day California and the Southwest United States) have long been closely connected in political and cultural terms, this was arguably never more apparent than in the Pop-derived designs that circulated widely among these areas in the late 1960s and early 1970s. Within these images, however, a crucial difference must be noted: though designers in Cuba and those employed by the Organizing Committee of Mexico City's 1968 Olympic Games and San Antonio's 1968 HemisFair worked to promote state-sponsored agendas (albeit of opposing political ideologies), their peers among Mexico's '68 Movement, the US Chicano Movement, and the Black Panther Party seized Pop strategies to subvert official discourses. Pop, then, was an equal-opportunity language—available to official and subversive, conservative and progressive causes alike.

A POP REVOLUTION

Andy Warhol is often credited with popularizing silkscreen (also known as serigraphy) as an artistic medium when Marilyn Monroe's tragic death in 1962 led to his first serial reproductions based on a 1953 publicity still of the actress. But the technique had already been pressed into use by 1961 for the posters that the Instituto Cubano del Arte e Industria Cinematográficos (Cuban Institute of Cinematic Art and Industry, hereafter ICAIC) produced to accompany each of the films it released or distributed. They did so, in part, because the technology was readily available; prior to the revolution, the island had been a hub for printing commercial materials and disseminating them throughout América due to its key location between the United States, the Caribbean, and the Gulf of Mexico.[1] The fact that posters could be printed in relatively large numbers and transported easily and cheaply made them a key export of Cuba's revolution, fueling their embrace and emulation in Mexico, the Bay Area, and beyond by the later 1960s.

ICAIC was the first cultural organization to be founded in the months following Cuba's January 1959 revolution, when the guerrilla movement led by Fidel Castro succeeded in toppling the dictatorship of Fulgencio Batista. In the years that followed, Castro pursued a nonconformist path to socialism and communism, emphasizing moral rather than material incentives and promoting anti-imperialist causes throughout Latin America and the world. Crucial to this nonconformist stance was an embrace of eclectic cultural forms. Though evident across the arts and architecture, Cuba's avant-garde internationalism was arguably most visible in its graphic design, from ephemeral fliers to urban-scaled political billboards. The seeds of this phenomenon were planted at ICAIC.

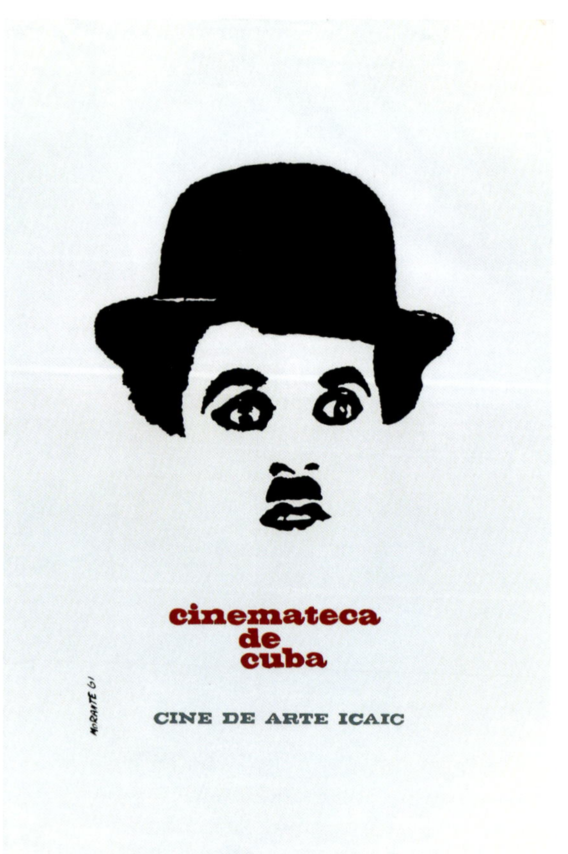

Fig. 3.1. Rafael Morante (designer) and Instituto Cubano del Arte e Industria Cinematográficos (ICAIC, publisher), *Cinemateca de Cuba*, 1961. Screenprint on paper, 29.93 x 20.06 inches (76 x 51 cm). Collection of the Center for the Study of Political Graphics, Culver City, California; 2011–096. Image courtesy of the designer and Instituto Cubano del Arte e Industria Cinematográficos (ICAIC), Cinemateca de Cuba, Havana.

Though Cuba's box office sales were among the highest per capita in the world at the time of the revolution (1.5 million tickets sold a week, to a population of less than seven million), it had no national film industry; most screenings had been of B-grade Hollywood productions.[2] Cuba's existing theater network offered a prime opportunity for ICAIC's founding director, filmmaker, and guerrilla fighter Alfredo Guevara, to replace US cultural imperialism with a new national cinematic tradition.[3] It was decided that, as with avant-garde Soviet and Polish cinema, each film shown in Cuba would be accompanied by an original poster. In contrast to their splashy capitalist antecedents, these did not seek to generate ticket sales (a non-issue when films were among few available forms of entertainment). Instead, they were aesthetic complements to the films themselves, commemorating screenings, while also enhancing the urban environment as artworks in their own right, replacing the commercial advertising that had saturated the capital under Batista.[4]

ICAIC produced its first film posters in a recently nationalized offset printshop. When the US economic embargo led to a reorganization of industrial resources in March 1961, the institute's poster designers took up silkscreen, which, beyond its aesthetic appeal, was more sustainable as a manual process that required few parts. Due to the high cost of importing paper and ink from Europe or China, the first posters were restricted to black and one other color (typically red), and no more than half the surface area of each design could be covered with ink.[5] These material limitations led Rafael Morante, ICAIC's head poster designer, to conceive what could be considered a Pop approach for an early poster for the Cinemateca de Cuba, the new national

film archive (figure 3.1). Flat black shapes float on a bare white field, suggesting the telltale bowler hat, expressive eyes, and moustache of the Tramp, Charlie Chaplin's famous silent film character of the 1920s and 1930s. Morante's economical design communicates the ICAIC's mission on multiple levels. Cognoscenti would recognize the Tramp as a symbol of the origins of international film history, and of committed leftist politics. For a broader public, he symbolized the clean slate from which the ICAIC built a revolutionary national film culture, by sending *cines móviles* (moving cinemas)—projectors strapped to trucks and carts—throughout the underdeveloped countryside where Chaplin's silent films were screened for illiterate audiences who had never before seen a moving image.

Just as Warhol did for his first Pop paintings, Morante likely used an opaque or Grant projector to enlarge and establish the outlines of the Tramp's features from a photograph, converting a series of gradual values into clearly defined solid forms. This act of conversion for the purposes of mass-reproduction was key to a fundamental function of Pop: transforming individuals into icons. In 1967, following Morante's death, it would give rise to the ultimate Pop icon: the Argentine-born guerrilla leader Ernesto "Che" Guevara. By then, Cuba had established a veritable army of designers and photographers whose works, characterized by a high degree of visual and textual sophistication, united aesthetic and political aims. Crucially, it had also developed mechanisms for disseminating this output to its allies abroad.

Josten

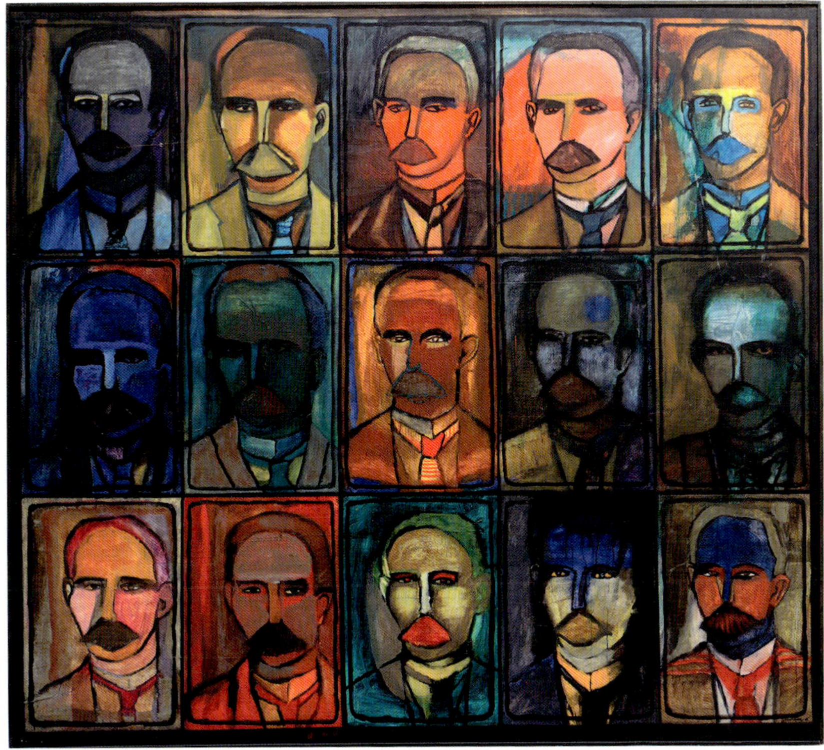

Fig. 3.2. Raúl Martínez, *15 repeticiones de Martí* (15 Repetitions of Martí), 1966. Oil on canvas, 77 x 88 inches (198.5 x 225.5 cm). Collection of the Museo Nacional de Bellas Artes de La Habana, Cuba.

In the first years of the revolution, however, Cuban cultural and political posters developed on parallel tracks and with limited international diffusion. Designers for the ICAIC, the Casa de las Américas (House of the Americas), and the Consejo Nacional de Cultura (National Council of Culture), the island's three main cultural organizations, followed Morante's lead in producing innovative posters that engaged a wide range of internationalist themes and styles. Those working for political organizations, meanwhile, gravitated to the tropes of commercial advertising for literacy and public health campaigns, and to social realism for military mobilizations such as the 1961 Playa Girón (Bay of Pigs) invasion and the 1962 missile crisis. The year 1965 brought a new moment of radicalization, with the formation of the Partido Comunista de Cuba (Communist Party of Cuba) and Castro's assertions of autonomy from the Soviet Union, which were enacted in Che's campaigns to incite anti-imperialist revolutions in other parts of the world—first in Africa and subsequently in South America. If the rejection of Soviet policies was integral to the development of Cuba's unique revolutionary character, so too was the rejection of Soviet socialist realism integral to the development of its unique revolutionary posters. As Che asked in an open letter that year, "Why endeavor to seek in the frozen forms of socialist realism the only valid recipe?"[6]

Beyond the hegemonic global political forces at work, the course of Cuba's poster movement shifted toward Pop as a result of the innovations of certain individual designers. One of these was Raúl Martínez, who, like Warhol, began his career as a commercial artist, working as a sign painter and studying at Chicago's Institute of Design. Returning to Havana in 1954, he led a split life, producing Abstract Expressionist paintings for anti-Batista exhibitions, while simultaneously pursuing a lucrative career as a designer for a commercial agency. When nationalization programs shuttered the agency in 1960, Martínez began working for the state designing public service announcements and *Lunes de Revolución* (Monday of Revolution), a progressive cultural supplement. While censorship was not an issue, his abstract paintings found little traction in the new climate. He soon turned to photography, and began adding words (a holdover from his sign-painting days) and collaging photographs onto the all-over painted surfaces of his canvases, in consonance with the "new realisms" then being pursued by many in the West including fellow Cuban Antonia Eiriz.[7]

In a 1982 interview, Martínez suggested that once he realized that the mass-produced, public-facing poster was revolutionary Cuba's truest art form, he began applying its theory to his painting. "I began with the subject of [José] Martí, and the style of popular painting one could see in the plazas and the headquarters of the Committees in Defense of the Revolution . . . . I had lost my ability as a draftsman, so that the faces emerged with a certain torpidness that I liked."[8] Martínez's "torpid" faces are quintessentially Pop; flat and cartoon-like with thick black outlines, they are instantly recognizable and well-suited to mechanical reproduction. By 1966, he had transmuted the grids of his magazine layouts and book covers onto his canvases, filling them with the rounded, heavily outlined faces of heroes and public figures. Whereas Warhol applied silkscreen to canvas, Martínez made slight variations to his repeated figures by hand; in *15 repeticiones de Martí*

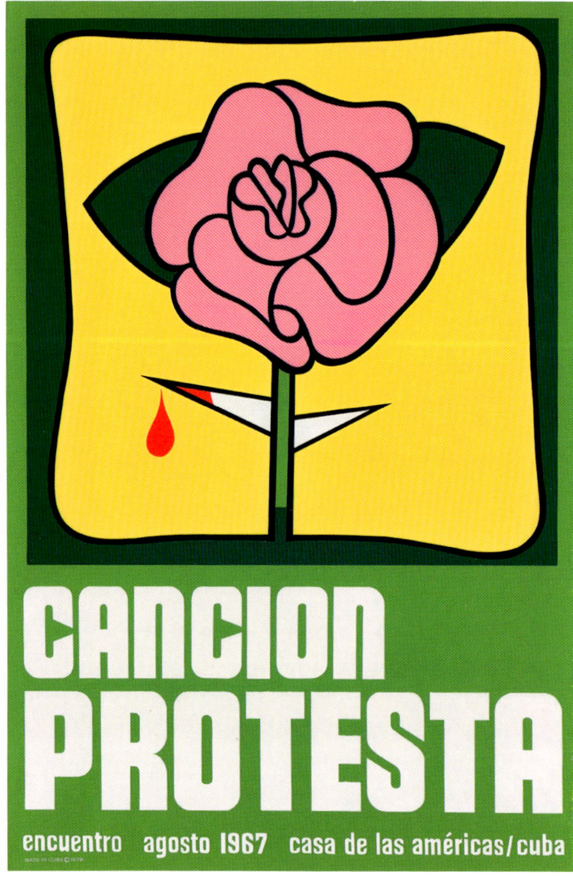

Fig. 3.3. Alfredo Rostgaard, *Canción protesta* (Protest Song), 1967. Screenprint on paper, 44.25 x 29.87 inches (112.4 x 75.9 cm). Collection of the Museum of Modern Art, New York, New York. Gift of the International Council and Library, Latin American Archive of the Museum of Modern Art, 678.1980. Digital Image © The Museum of Modern Art. Licensed by SCALA/Art Resource, New York, New York.

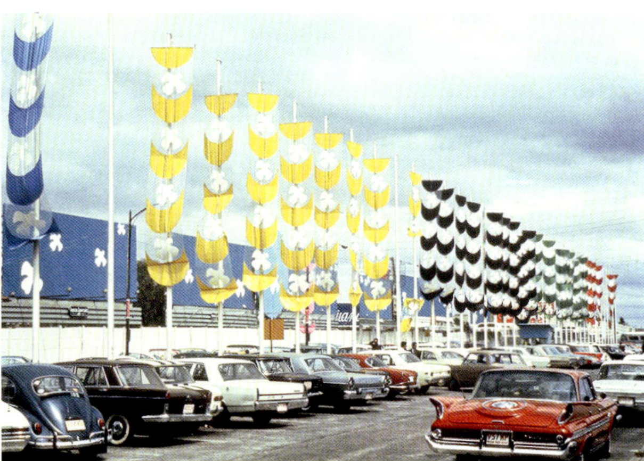

Fig. 3.4. Throughout Mexico City, brightly colored banners heralded the coming Olympics while underscoring the country's self-proclaimed role as international "peacemaker," 1968. Photo by Pedro Ramírez Vázquez. Courtesy of the Archivo del Arquitecto Pedro Ramírez Vázquez, Mexico City, Mexico.

(15 Repetitions of Martí) (see page 75, figure 3.2), broad washes of paint evoke Warhol's overlapping silkscreen layers.

By 1968, Martínez had returned his Pop figures and grids to the political and cultural posters that initially inspired them. In one of the best-known ICAIC posters, for Humberto Solás's film *Lucía*, three flattened, cartoonish faces of the same woman, each different in color and attire, communicate the film's subject: the experiences of three women named Lucía living in three eras of the Cuban republic (1968, plate 46). With this and his other poster designs, the Pop ethos of Martínez's paintings—which remained relatively inaccessible to most Cubans, in terms of their display and their prices—found wider exposure in the streets.

While Martínez's oscillations between graphic design, photography, and painting deeply impacted post-revolutionary aesthetics on the island, designer Alfredo Rostgaard had a transformative effect not only on Cuba's poster movement, but also on the graphics of the era writ large. From his first ICAIC posters for Santiago Álvarez's anti-imperialist documentaries in the mid-1960s, designed when he was in his early twenties, Rostgaard led the way in synthesizing contemporary visual forms with trenchant political messages. A hallmark of this was his 1967 *Canción protesta* (Protest Song) (figure 3.3), a poster for a musical symposium at the Casa de las Américas whose Pop-inflected design proved particularly resonant for the hemispheric left in the sixties. On a bold green background overlaid with yellow, Rostgaard placed a flat, abstracted pink rose whose contours are outlined in black. A single drop of bright red blood hangs from one of its two thorns, symbolizing the intertwined beauty, pain, and poignancy of protest music. This was the moment, the designer later recalled, that the distinction between political and cultural organizations and their corresponding posters dissolved; designing posters in Cuba was acknowledged as an inherently political act, regardless of the specific motivation behind each design.[9]

CIRCULATING SOLIDARITY

Rostgaard's bleeding rose was soon adapted to other committed cultural forms outside Cuba, including the covers of the April 1968 issue of *El Corno Emplumado* (The Plumed Horn) (plate 68), a Mexico City-based bilingual poetry journal, and Dugald Stermer's book *The Art of Revolution: Castro's Cuba, 1959–1970* (1970, plate 69). The latter, a collection of ninety-six large-format, high-quality color reproductions of Cuban posters of the 1960s accompanied by an essay by Susan Sontag, did much to bring Cuba's quintessential revolutionary art—particularly its Pop manifestations—into the hands of an international intelligentsia in the late 1960s and early 1970s.[10] These adaptations of Rostgaard's design exemplify David Joselit's definition of Pop as an "international style," "a shared vocabulary . . . that can accommodate context-specific statements from diverse locations that nonetheless remain intelligible as they travel."[11]

This shared Pop vocabulary was prominent in 1968 Mexico, in both official and countercultural forms. If the flattened pink rose symbolized culture, the flattened white dove—drawn by Picasso, taken up by

Fig. 3.5. Jesús Martinez, *"Paloma de la paz" atravesada por una bayoneta* ("Dove of Peace" pierced by a bayonet), 1968. Ink and gouache on paper, 27.49 x 18.91 inches (70.5 x 48.5 cm). Collection of El Museo Universitario Arte Contemporáneo (MUAC) de la Universidad Nacional Autónoma de México, Mexico City; 08–780102.

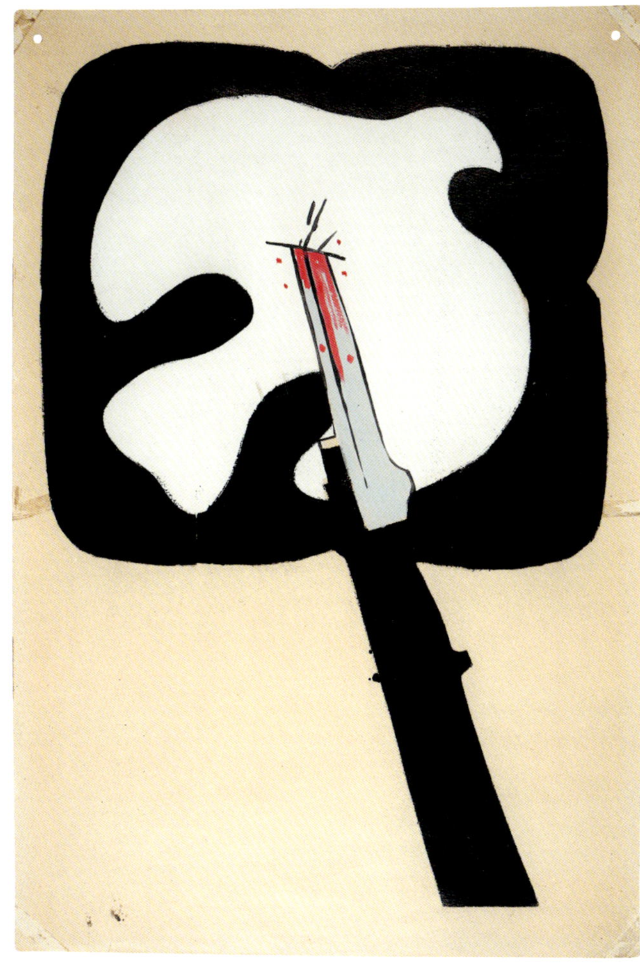

French Communists in 1949, and "Pop-ified" by US designer Lance Wyman for Mexico City's 1968 Olympic Games—symbolized peace (figure 3.4).[12] Mexico was the only nation in América to maintain diplomatic relations with Castro's Cuba after 1961. This strategic Cold War non-alignment on the part of the ruling Partido Revolucionario Institucional (Institutional Revolutionary Party, hereafter PRI) earned it the Olympic bid. During the two weeks of the games, the PRI furthered its association with revolutionary Cuba (and Havana in particular) by papering over commercial billboards with Wyman's Pop doves, as well as cartoons, photographs, and artworks—creating a colorful, eclectic anti-capitalist environment for the benefit of international visitors and color television viewers.[13] These adornments provided a temporary progressive façade for a repressive state that had opened fire on a peaceful meeting of Mexico's pro-democracy student and worker movement at Tlatelolco ten days before the opening ceremony, killing, jailing, and driving hundreds underground. Though lacking in arms, artists associated with the '68 Movement had equal recourse to the vocabulary of Pop for the ephemeral posters they surreptitiously printed and disseminated (plates 57–60). In a silkscreen poster by

Jesus Martínez that is one of the movement's most poignant symbols, Wyman's peace dove pictogram has been pierced with a bayonet that draws blood like the thorn of Rostgaard's rose (figure 3.5).[14] Its reduced palette, of black with red accents, further aligns this iconic Mexican design with its Cuban parallels.

Susan Sontag wrote that "the revolutionary élan of Cuba is profoundly rooted in its *not* settling for the achievements of a national revolution, but being passionately committed to the cause of revolution on a global scale. Thus Cuba is probably the only communist country in the world where people really care about Vietnam."[15] This internationalism, spearheaded by Che in his words and actions, was part and parcel of Cuba's resistance to Soviet orthodoxy and search for more culturally, historically, and geographically similar partners in trade and defense.[16] Following the first Tricontinental Conference, composed of Communist party delegates from Latin America, Asia, and Africa in 1966, the Organización de Solidaridad con los Pueblos de Asia, Africa, y América Latina (Organization for Solidarity with the Peoples of Asia, Africa, and Latin America; hereafter OSPAAAL)

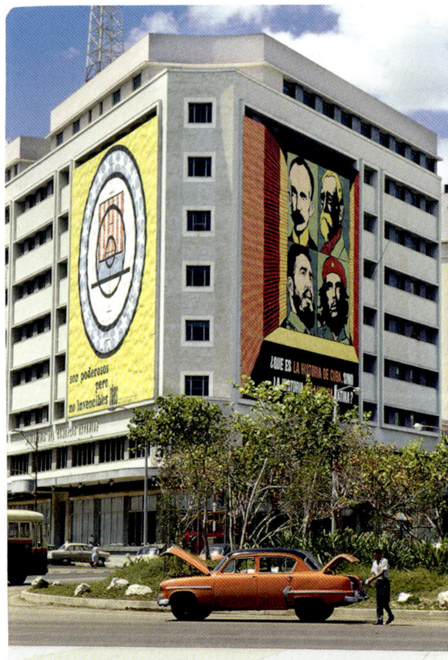

Fig. 3.6. Lee Lockwood, Havana Comercio (Foreign Trade) building exterior, former headquarters of CMQ radio station, 1967. Color photograph. © Lee Lockwood. Image courtesy of the Lee Lockwood Estate and TASCHEN, www.taschen.com.

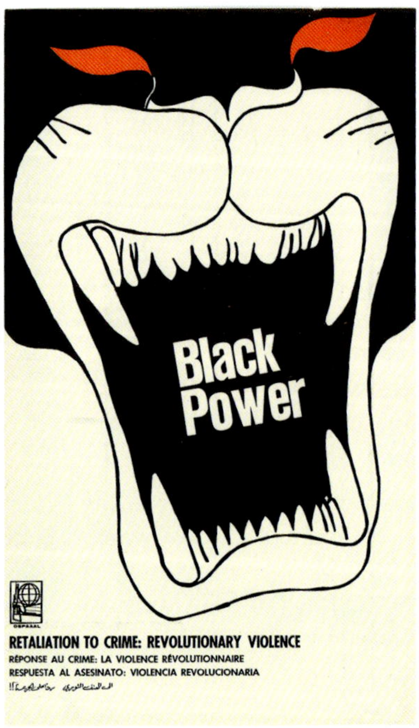

Fig. 3.7. Alfredo Rostgaard (designer) and OSPAAAL publisher), *Black Power*, 1968. Offset lithograph on paper, 22 x 13 inches (55.9 x 33 cm). Collection of the Smithsonian National Museum of African American History and Culture, Washington, DC; 2012.46.17.1.

and the Organización Latinoamerica de Solidaridad (Latin American Solidarity Organization, hereafter OLAS) were established. Designing and disseminating posters, billboards, and magazines were crucial functions of these organizations, which focused on providing ideological support rather than military or humanitarian aid.

On a 1967 visit to Havana, photographer Lee Lockwood captured two monumental poster-murals that powerfully illustrate the brightly colored, conceptually rigorous Pop ethos that then dominated Cuban graphics (figure 3.6). Each of the six-story vertical designs, formed from several large sheets of paper, were attached to the side of the Trade Ministry. The poster on the left, sponsored by OLAS, figured an abstracted US flag on a monochromatic yellow field, viewed as if through the sight of a rifle. Underneath was written, in lowercase serif letters, "they are powerful but not invincible." On the other side, colorful photo-derived images of José Martí and Máximo Gómez, heroes of Cuba's War of Independence, were paired with Fidel Castro and Che Guevara in a grid reminiscent of Martínez's (and Warhol's) compositional strategies. Irregular lines in red, black, and yellow radiate out, bringing a sense of depth to the flattened images; below, in block letters, appeared the question "What is the history of Cuba, if not the history of Latin America?"

Similar sentiments—and images—were disseminated far afield of Havana in the pages of *Tricontinental*, a bimonthly magazine published by OSPAAAL in English, Spanish, French, and Arabic editions and distributed by the tens of thousands to progressive organizations around the world to generate solidarity among anti-imperialist struggles in Asia, Africa, and Latin America. Rostgaard was its designer; beyond boldly designed covers and features, each issue included a folded poster by him and other Cuban designers, commemorating a day of solidarity with a particular nation, ethnic group, or continent. Following Che's principles, the majority of these depicted arms, explicitly advocating armed insurrection.[17]

Thomas Crow has noted that "the communication network among graphic designers is wide and quick in its circulation of ideas."[18] This network—which is inherently international, and extends across the spectrum from commercial to protest design—explains the close relationship that developed between *Tricontinental*'s designers in Havana and Emory Douglas, minister of culture and lead designer of the newspaper of the Black Panther Party. Founded in Oakland, California, in 1966, the Panthers' militant, anti-imperialist agenda aligned closely with that of OSPAAAL, including their shared emphasis on the dissemination of potent, Pop-inflected graphic design. Following Martin Luther King, Jr.'s assassination in April 1968, Rostgaard designed an OSPAAAL poster in which the words "Black Power" appear in the cavernous mouth of a cartoon-like, white fanged, and red-eyed black panther (figure 3.7). Soon thereafter, Douglas appropriated Rostgaard's design, adapting it to protest the incarceration of leader Huey Long by montaging his photograph into the panther's mouth.[19] In August of the same year, OSPAAAL designer Lázaro Abreu Padrón adapted one of Douglas's cartoon-like drawings, of a group of armed African Americans in black berets, for a poster expressing solidarity with them (1968, plate 72). As Douglas later explained, these exchanges were informal: "they would see art that I'd done in the paper and

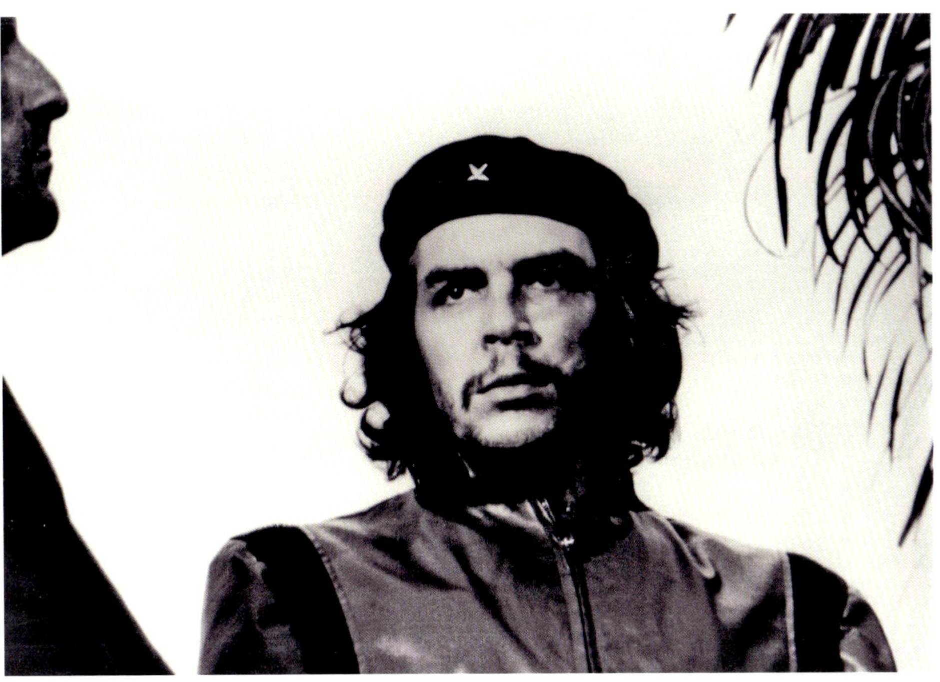

Fig. 3.8. Korda (Alberto Díaz Gutiérrez), *Guerrillero Heroico* (Che Guevara), 1960. Black-and-white photograph. Image courtesy of Banque d'Images, ADAGP/Art Resource, New York, New York. Licensed by Artists Rights Society (ARS), New York, New York.

they would remix them into posters and redesign them and send them out to the world . . . . It wasn't like plagiarizing because it was solidarity in the context of the struggle."[20] Strikingly, as Carol A. Wells has noted, no such two-way exchanges occurred with designers associated with the Chicano Movement, despite their enthusiastic reception of OSPAAAL graphics.[21]

Among the many icons of the late sixties, none could compare in impact to the image of Che. Physically absent from Cuba after 1965—first on an unsuccessful attempt to foment guerrilla insurrection in the Congo, and later in the Andes—his image soon came to dominate public spaces; this tendency only increased following his October 1967 assassination by CIA-sponsored military forces in highland Bolivia. By then, according to K.S. Karol, "Cuba was living quite literally under Che's sign. Everywhere his giant portraits stared down, and immense billboards proclaimed his slogan in black on red: We must create two, three, many Vietnams—a call to launch other anti-imperialist struggles.[22] Though photographer Alberto Díaz Gutiérrez (known as Korda) captured his famous shot of Che looking off into the distance at a mass funeral in 1960, the image was not widely disseminated until after the guerrilla's death (figure 3.8). Monumental enlargements of the photograph were erected in Cuba, and flattened, high-contrast, brightly colored iterations began appearing in the mass media and on the streets throughout América in the service of progressive and radical social causes.[23] Its appeal lies in Che's upturned face and faraway gaze, which evoke the internationally inclined "new man" he called forth in his writings.

In Havana, Elena Serrano designed a poster for *Tricontinental* that, while printed in offset, relies on the flat color aesthetics of silkscreen to figure Korda's Che not as a man but as an icon, issuing revolutionary sentiment throughout the continent from the heart of the Andes (1968, plate 7). Meanwhile, in Buenos Aires, artist Roberto Jacoby placed a high-contrast black-and-white version of the image above a declaration that the guerrilla fighter doesn't die to be hung on the wall (1968, plate 65). That Korda's image was not adapted by designers before 1967 may be ascribed to its limited distribution on the part of the photographer, and to the revolutionary government's resistance to idolizing living leaders. Importantly, though, and as had been the case with Warhol's Marilyns, Che's transformation into an icon required both his death under tragic circumstances and a source image distanced from that tragedy in both its date and its content.[24]

Within months, Pop-derived versions of Korda's image appeared in progressive contexts around the world. One of the first in the United States was a 1968 silkscreen poster by Rupert García. As in Morante's *Cinemateca de Cuba* design, the flat shaded features of an individual (now Che, not Chaplin) emerge from a white ground, in black shapes likely drawn using a Grant projector. Below them, stencil-form letters declare "RIGHT ON!," a well-known Black Panther slogan. Raised in agricultural Stockton, California, García served in the US Army in Thailand before returning to the Bay Area and enrolling in the art department of San Francisco State College (SFSC) on the GI Bill in 1966. His first prints, such as *Black Man and Flag* (1967, plate 6),

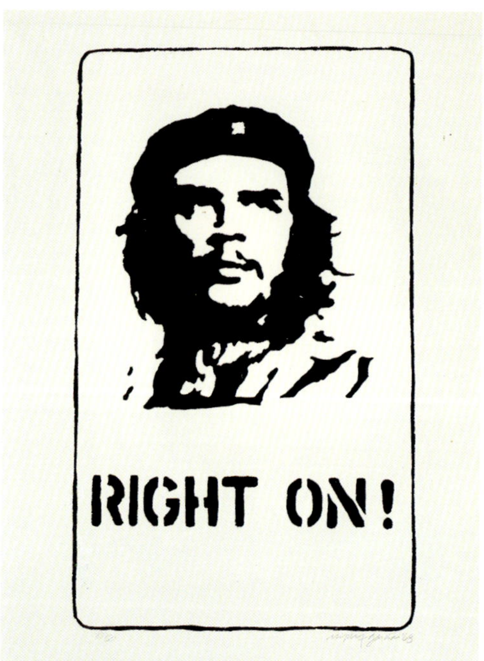

Fig. 3.9. Rupert García, *RIGHT ON!*, 1968. Lithograph on paper, 25.98 x 19.96 (66 x 50.7 cm). Collection of the Fine Arts Museums of San Francisco, De Young, Legion of Honor Museum, California. Gift of Mr. and Mrs. Robert Marcus, 1990.1.61. © Rupert García. Image courtesy of the artist and the Fine Arts Museums of San Francisco, De Young, Legion of Honor Museum, California.

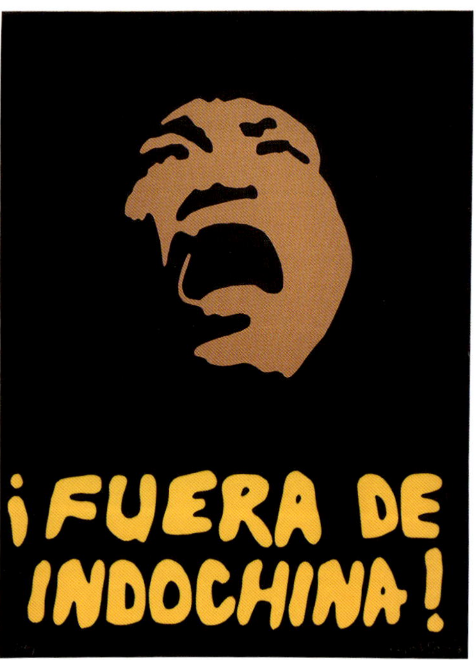

Fig. 3.10. Rupert García, *¡Fuera de Indochina!*, 1970. Screenprint on paper, 23.67 x 17.78 inches (60.7 x 45.6 cm). Collection of the Fine Arts Museums of San Francisco, De Young, Legion of Honor Museum, California. Gift of Mr. and Mrs. Robert Marcus, 1990.1.83. © Rupert García. Image courtesy of the artist and the Fine Arts Museums of San Francisco, De Young, Legion of Honor Museum, California.

reveal his engagement with the visual vocabularies of both Pop and civil rights. García soon became involved in SFSC's historic 1968 student strike, and began making silkscreen posters—including *RIGHT ON!*—to support the student bail fund (figure 3.9).[25] These early designs adroitly synthesize the graphic conventions of the local and international print materials he was avidly consuming in venues such as San Francisco's Modern Times bookstore, which carried *Black Panther* and *Tricontinental* as well as reprints of Mexico '68 posters.[26] By 1970, García's command of Pop vocabulary and silkscreen technique facilitated such powerful works as *¡Fuera de Indochina!* (Out of Indochina!) (figure 3.10), in which the contours of an anguished, open-mouthed face erupt from a stark black ground, punctuated by loose yellow letters. Produced for the 1970 Chicano Moratorium in East Los Angeles, its imagery, like that of Berkeley-based Chicano artist Malaquias Montoya's *Vietnam Aztlan*, would have been equally at home in the pages of *Tricontinental*, if only they had reached Rostgaard's hands. Not only do these posters articulate the deeply internationalist ethos of the Chicano Movement, they represent the culmination of a decade of efforts across América to, in García's words, subvert mass-media images "to moral purposes for which they were not designed; the art of social protest."[27]

In the final analysis, designers operating within the transnational circuit that encompassed Cuba, Mexico, and parts of the United States in the 1960s and 1970s took recourse in Pop-derived images and styles not only to subvert, but also to affirm official discourses. What most unites their proposals is their boldness—both in terms of color, contrast, and scale, and their succinct, conceptually potent visual messages. From Havana to Mexico City to the San Francisco Bay and back, poster makers embraced internationalism while bucking social norms and socialist realism, generating revolutionary currents that radiated from América to the world.

NOTES

1   Reynaldo González, "When Posters Decide to Come Home," in *¡Mira Cuba!: Manifesti cinematografici, politici e sociali = Carteles de cine, políticos y sociales = Movie, Political and Social Posters*, ed. Luigino Bardellotto (Cinisello Balsamo, Milano: Silvana, 2013), 31. Edmundo Desnoes offered the first analysis of Cuba's revolutionary poster movement, "Los carteles de la Revolución cubana," *Casa de las Américas*, no. 51–52 (November 1968): 223–231. The first English-language study appeared two years later: Dugald Stermer, *The Art of Revolution* (New York: McGraw-Hill, 1970). More recent overviews include Lincoln Cushing, *Revolución!: Cuban Poster Art* (San Francisco: Chronicle Books, 2003). The prevalence of silkscreen printing in Cuba prior to 1968 marks a difference from Paris, where the technique was not widely used prior to its introduction to the Ateliers Populaires during the general strike that May. See Victoria HF Scott, "Silk-Screens and Television Screens: Maoism and the Posters of May and June 1968 in Paris" (PhD diss., State University of New York at Binghamton, 2010); Liam Considine, "Screen Politics: Pop Art and the Atelier Populaire," *Tate Papers*, no. 24 (Autumn 2015), http://www.tate.org.uk, accessed August 18, 2017.

2   David Craven, "Cuban Art and Culture," in *Cuba, A Different America*, eds., Wilber A. Chaffee and Gary Prevost (Totowa, NJ: Rowman & Littlefield, 1992), 133.

3   Alfredo Guevara, "Realidades y perspectivas de un nuevo cine," *Cine Cubano* 1, no. 1 (1960): 4.

4   Susan Sontag, "Posters: Advertisement, Art, Political Artifact, Commodity," in *The Art of Revolution*, xiv.

5   María Eulalia Douglas, *La tienda negra: el cine en Cuba, 1897–1990* (La Habana: Cinemateca de Cuba, 1996), 159. Posters were issued in print runs of 250–500 and rarely seen outside Havana.

6   Ernesto "Che" Guevara, "Socialism and Man in Cuba (1965)," in *Contemporary Latin American Social and Political Thought: An Anthology*, ed. Iván Márquez (Lanham: Rowman & Littlefield, 2008), http://ebookcentral.proquest.com.

7   For a detailed biography and incisive analysis of the development of Martínez's artistic practice, see Corina Matamoros Tuma, *Raúl Martínez, la gran familia* (Havana: Ediciones Vanguardia Cubana, 2012). On the prevalence of collage and object-based strategies in Western Europe and New York c. 1960, see Julia Robinson, ed., *New Realisms, 1957–1962: Object Strategies between Readymade and Spectacle* (Madrid: Museo Nacional Centro de Arte Reina Sofía; Cambridge: MIT Press, 2010).

8   Raúl Martínez, quoted in Shifra M. Goldman, "Painters into Poster Makers: A Conversation with Two Cuban Artists," in *Dimensions of the Americas: Art and Social Change in Latin America and the United States* (Chicago: University of Chicago Press, 1994), 148–149.

9   Alfredo Rostgaard, interview by Jennifer Josten, January 20, 2000. See Jennifer Josten, "A Shout from the Wall: The Development of the Cuban Revolutionary Poster, 1959–1970" (BA thesis, Wellesley College, 2000), 88. In a 1982 interview with Shifra Goldman, Rostgaard noted his high regard for the film posters and other works of US designer Saul Bass. Goldman, "Painters into Poster Makers," 151.

10   Stermer, *The Art of Revolution*. On the history and aims of *El Corno Emplumado*, see Margaret Randall, "Remembering *El Corno Emplumado*," Open Door Archive, January 16, 2015, http://opendoor.northwestern.edu/.

11   David Joselit, "'International Pop' and 'The World Goes Pop,'" *Artforum International* 54:5 (January 2016): 231.

12   On political uses of Picasso's white dove, see Gertje Utley, *Picasso: The Communist Years* (New Haven: Yale University Press, 2000), chap. 7. In the 1950s, Diego Rivera incorporated it into his mosaic designs for the National Autonomous University of Mexico's new University Olympic Stadium. Natalia de la Rosa in conversation with Jennifer Josten, October 2017.

13   Helen Escobedo, "An Artist's Eye View of Mexico," *The Art Gallery* XIX, no. 1 (1975): 129, 131.

14   On this image in the broader context of '68 Movement graphics, see George F. Flaherty, *Hotel Mexico: Dwelling on the '68 Movement* (Oakland: University of California Press, 2016), 168–169.

15   Sontag, "Posters," xviii.

16   Ernesto F. Betancourt, "Exporting the Revolution to Latin America," in *Revolutionary Change in Cuba*, ed. Carmelo Mesa-Lago (Pittsburgh: University of Pittsburgh Press, 1971).

17   For a richly illustrated history of these posters, see Richard Frick, *Das Trikontinentale Solidaritätsplakat = El cartel Tricontinental de solidaridad = The Tricontinental Solidarity Poster = L'affiche Tricontinentale de la solidarité* (Bern: Commedia-Verlag, 2003).

18   Thomas Crow, *The Long March of Pop: Art, Music, and Design, 1930–1995* (New Haven: Yale University Press, 2015), 326.

19   Tom Wilson, "Paper Walls: Political Posters in an Age of Mass Media," in *West of Center: Art and the Counterculture Experiment in America, 1965–1977*, eds., Elissa Auther and Adam Lerner (Minneapolis: University of Minnesota Press, 2012), 173–175.

20   Dhruv Shah, "Interview with Revolutionary Artist Emory Douglas," *I Am Hip-Hop Magazine*, January 20, 2015, http://www.iamhiphopmagazine.com/interview-revolutionary-artist-emory-douglas/.

21   Carol A. Wells, "La Lucha Sigue: From East Los Angeles to the Middle East," in *Just Another Poster?: Chicano Graphic Arts in California*, ed. Chon A. Noriega (Santa Barbara: University Art Museum, University of California, Santa Barbara, 2001), 178.

22   K. S. Karol, *Guerrillas in Power: The Course of the Cuban Revolution* (New York: Hill & Wang, 1970), 291–292.

23   Korda's photograph and its afterlives have been the subject of three book-length studies: David Kunzle, *Che Guevara: Icon, Myth, and Message* (Los Angeles: UCLA Fowler Museum of Cultural History in collaboration with the Center for the Study of Political Graphics, 1997); Trisha Ziff, ed., *Che Guevara: Revolutionary & Icon* (New York: Abrams Image, 2006); Michael Casey, *Che's Afterlife: The Legacy of an Image* (New York: Vintage, 2009). The first recorded publication of Korda's photograph was in *Paris Match* in August 1967. Its adaptation for the poster-mural and Paris-based designer Roman Cieślewicz's orange and purple Pop version, *Che sí*, for the cover of the October 1967 issue of *Opus International* represent early adaptations; on the latter, see Crow, *The Long March of Pop*, 326–327. Korda's image began circulating more widely just as another mechanically-reproduced image of Che was hitting newsstands in October: Freddy Alborta's photograph of his dead body, laid out in a Christ-like manner on a wash basin in a Bolivian village, surrounded by the CIA-sponsored military personnel who brought an end to his campaign to export Cuba-style guerrilla revolution to South America. In contrast to Korda's, this image was the basis of only one set of notable artworks: the silkscreen paintings Warhol's collaborator Gerard Malanga attempted, unsuccessfully, to sell under the more famous artist's name in 1968. See Casey, *Che's Afterlife*, 118–119.

24   Thomas Crow has argued that in adapting Korda's image to posters and billboards in and after 1967, Cuban designers were influenced by Warhol's Marilyns and other celebrity photo-based works. In contrast, I argue that—as demonstrated by Morante's 1961 Cinemateca de Cuba poster—they had already engaged with the conceptual and formal strategies that made it possible to transform images into icons via silkscreen before Warhol. Crow, *The Long March of Pop*, 336–337.

25   Ramón Favela, *The Art of Rupert García: A Survey Exhibition* (San Francisco: Chronicle Books: Mexican Museum, 1986), 19.

26   Lincoln Cushing, "One Struggle, Two Communities," interview by Rupert García, September 19, 2003, accessed August 9, 2017, http://www.docspopuli.org/articles/Cuba/BACshow.html. The Rupert García and Sammi Madison García Collection at the University of California, Santa Barbara, includes several issues of *Tricontinental* and *Black Panther*, as well as *Mexico 1968: A Study of Domination and Repression* (New York: North American Congress on Latin America, November 1968). Thanks to Rosalía Romero for her research assistance with this material.

27   Rupert García, "Media Supplement, 1969–1970" (MA thesis, San Francisco State College, 1970), 1. Also quoted in Favela, *The Art of Rupert García*, 19. On internationalism in Chicano posters, see Wells, "La Lucha Sigue," and George Lipsitz, "Not Just Another Social Movement: Poster Art and the Movimiento Chicano," in *Just Another Poster?*, 78.

JENNIFER JOSTEN

CORRIENTES REVOLUCIONARIAS: EL DISEÑO POP ENTRE CUBA, MÉXICO Y CALIFORNIA

En la década de 1960, muchos artistas y diseñadores gráficos en La Habana, Ciudad de México y el área de la Bahía de San Francisco se apoderaron de las estrategias visuales asociadas con el arte pop para transmitir mensajes políticos al público amplio. Mientras que Andy Warhol, Roy Lichtenstein y otros adaptaron el lenguaje de la cultura del consumo masivo a sus pinturas para el mercado del arte de Nueva York, los artistas vinculados con los movimientos sociales progresistas cubanos, mexicanos, afroamericanos y chicanos utilizaron métodos similares (sobre todo las imágenes fotográficas de alto contraste repetidas serialmente, así como las figuras de contornos gruesos típicas de las caricaturas y los dibujos animados) en carteles producidos en masa para abogar por el fin de políticas y prácticas neoimperialistas alrededor del mundo. En ambos casos, las pinturas de caballete y los carteles efímeros comparten una estética plana, reproducida de manera mecánica, haciendo pasar pintura a través de formas recortadas o de una malla tensada a la cual se han transferido diseños fotomecánicamente. Pero si bien Warhol y Lichtenstein usaron el estíncil y la serigrafía como herramientas de distanciamiento para generar posturas críticas, frías o irónicas, los diseñadores revolucionarios en Cuba, México y Estados

Unidos emplearon estas mismas técnicas para comunicar mensajes de afirmación y solidaridad internacional. Al mismo tiempo, diversas organizaciones oficiales en los tres países se apropiaron de los estilos pop y op y los aplicaron a programas de diseño gráfico y urbano que lograron vender con eficacia nuevas imágenes de la nación o región al público local e internacional.

Aunque desde hace mucho tiempo los pueblos de la región que abarca Cuba y la zona mexicana (incluyendo lo que hoy en día es California y el suroeste de Estados Unidos) han estado muy vinculados en términos políticos y culturales, podría decirse que este fenómeno nunca fue tan evidente como en los diseños de vertiente pop que se difundieron ampliamente en esas áreas entre finales de los años sesenta y principios de los setenta del siglo XX. Sin embargo, existe en estas imágenes una diferencia crucial que debe mencionarse: aunque tanto los diseñadores de Cuba como los que trabajaron en 1968 para el Comité Organizador de los Juegos Olímpicos en México y el HemisFair de San Antonio promovían agendas patrocinadas por sus respectivos gobiernos (si bien con ideologías políticas opuestas), sus colegas del movimiento estudiantil mexicano de 1968, el movimiento chicano en

Estados Unidos y el Partido Panteras Negras utilizaron las estrategias pop para subvertir los discursos oficiales. El pop, por lo tanto, era un lenguaje con "igualdad de oportunidades", a disposición de las causas oficiales y las subversivas, de las con señadoras y las progresistas.

UNA REVOLUCIÓN POP

A Andy Warhol con frecuencia se le atribuye el haber popularizado la serigrafía como medio artístico cuando, tras la trágica muerte de Marilyn Monroe en 1962, creó sus primeras reproducciones seriadas basándose en una foto publicitaria tomada a la actriz en 1953. Sin embargo, la técnica ya había sido empleada en 1961 en los carteles producidos por el Instituto Cubano del Arte e Industria Cinematográfica (ICAIC) para acompañar las películas que estrenaba o distribuía. Esto sucedió en parte porque ya los cubanos tenían acceso a dicha tecnología. Antes de la revolución, la isla había sido un gran centro para la impresión de materiales comerciales y su diseminación en todas las Américas debido a su posición estratégica entre Estados Unidos, el Caribe y el Golfo de México.[1] El hecho de que los carteles podían imprimirse en cantidades relativamente grandes y transportarse de manera fácil y económica los convirtió en uno de los principales productos de exportación de la revolución cubana, fomentando que fuesen adoptados y emulados en México, el área de la Bahía de San Francisco y otros lugares a fines de la década de 1960.

El ICAIC fue la primera organización cultural que se estableció en Cuba tras la revolución de enero de 1959, cuando el movimiento guerrillero encabezado por Fidel Castro logró derrocar la dictadura de Fulgencio Batista. En los años siguientes, Castro siguió un camino contestatario hacia el socialismo y el comunismo, enfatizando los incentivos morales en vez de materiales y promoviendo las causas antiimperialistas en Latinoamérica y el mundo. La aceptación de formas culturales eclécticas fue parte crucial de esta postura inconforme. Ese internacionalismo vanguardista cubano era evidente en las artes y la arquitectura, pero ciertamente fue más notorio en su diseño gráfico, desde panfletos efímeros hasta vallas de tema político insertadas en el entorno urbano. Las semillas de este fenómeno fueron sembradas en el ICAIC. Aunque en la época de la revolución las ventas de taquilla en Cuba eran de las más altas per cápita en el mundo (1.5 millones de boletos vendidos por semana a una población de menos de siete millones), no existía industria cinematográfica nacional; la mayoría de las películas que se exhibían eran producciones de segunda hechas en Hollywood.[2] La red de teatros existente proporcionó una excelente oportunidad al fundador y director del ICAIC, el cineasta y guerrillero Alfredo Guevara, para remplazar el imperialismo cultural estadounidense con una nueva tradición cinematográfica.[3] También decidieron, al igual que en el cine vanguardista soviético y polaco, que cada película proyectada en Cuba iría acompañada de un cartel original. A diferencia de sus llamativos antecedentes capitalistas, estos carteles no tendrían el propósito de generar venta de boletos (no era necesario, dado que el cine era de las pocas formas de entretenimiento disponibles). Más bien serían complementos estéticos para conmemorar la exhibición de las películas y de paso embellecer el

entorno urbano a manera de obras de arte, remplazando la publicidad que había saturado la capital durante el mandato de Batista.[4]

El ICAIC produjo sus primeros carteles de cine en un taller de offset recién nacionalizado. Cuando el embargo económico de Estados Unidos llevó a una reorganización de los recursos industriales en marzo de 1961, los diseñadores de carteles del instituto comenzaron a emplear la serigrafía, la cual, además de su atractivo estético, resultaba más sostenible por ser un proceso manual que requiere pocos componentes. Dado que importar papel y tinta de Europa o China era muy costoso, los primeros carteles estuvieron limitados al negro y algún otro color (por lo general el rojo), y no podía cubrirse de tinta más de la mitad de la superficie de cada diseño.[5] Estas limitaciones materiales llevaron a Rafael Morante, jefe de diseñadores del ICAIC, a concebir lo que podría considerarse una propuesta pop para uno de los primeros carteles de la Cinemateca de Cuba, el nuevo archivo cinematográfico nacional (ver página 74, figura 3.1). Sobre un campo blanco flotan formas planas negras que sugieren el reconocible bombín, los ojos expresivos y el bigote de Charlot, el famoso personaje de las películas silentes de Charlie Chaplin en las décadas de 1920 y 1930. El diseño económico de Morante comunica a varios niveles la misión del ICAIC. Los iniciados reconocerían a Charlot como símbolo de los orígenes de la historia internacional del cine y de posturas izquierdistas comprometidas. Para el público en general, Charlot simbolizaba un nuevo comienzo a partir del cual el ICAIC crearía una cultura de cine nacional revolucionaria, enviando cines móviles (proyectores montados en camionetas y carretas) a las subdesarrolladas áreas rurales, donde se proyectaban las películas mudas de Chaplin para un público analfabeto que nunca había visto imágenes en movimiento.

Al igual que lo hizo Warhol para su primer cuadro pop, es posible que Morante usara un proyector opaco o "Grant" para ampliar y establecer el contorno de los rasgos de Charlot a partir de una fotografía, convirtiendo una serie de valores graduales en formas sólidas claramente definidas. Este acto de conversión para fines de reproducción en masa también fue clave para una de las funciones fundamentales del pop: transformar al individuo en ícono. En 1967, ya muerto Morante, este recurso produciría el ícono pop por excelencia: el guerrillero argentino Ernesto "Che" Guevara. Para entonces, Cuba había establecido un verdadero ejército de diseñadores y fotógrafos en cuya obra, caracterizada por un alto grado de sofisticación visual y textual, se unían los fines estéticos y políticos. Y sobre todo, Cuba también había desarrollado mecanismos para difundir esta producción a sus aliados en el extranjero.

No obstante, durante los primeros años de la revolución, los carteles culturales y políticos cubanos se desarrollaron de manera paralela y con poca difusión internacional. Los diseñadores del ICAIC, la Casa de las Américas y el Consejo Nacional de Cultura, las principales organizaciones culturales de la isla, siguieron el ejemplo de Morante y produjeron carteles innovadores que abordaban una gran variedad de temas y estilos internacionalistas. Al mismo tiempo, los que trabajaban para las organizaciones políticas se volcaron en los tropos de la publicidad comercial para sus campañas de alfabetización y salud pública, y en el realismo social para movilizaciones militares como la invasión de Playa Girón (Bahía de Cochinos) y la crisis de los misiles de 1962. El año de 1965 trajo un nuevo momento de radicalización con la formación del Partido Comunista de Cuba y las declaraciones de Castro sobre la autonomía del país respecto a la Unión Soviética, promulgada en las campañas del Che para incitar revoluciones anti-imperialistas en otras partes del mundo (primero en África y luego en Sudamérica). Así como el rechazo de las políticas soviéticas fue fundamental en el desarrollo del distintivo carácter revolucionario de Cuba, el rechazo del realismo socialista soviético fue fundamental al desarrollo de sus distintivos carteles revolucionarios. Como lo planteó el Che en una carta abierta aquel año: "¿Por qué pretender buscar en las formas congeladas del realismo socialista la única receta válida?".[6]

Más allá de las fuerzas políticas hegemónicas del momento, el movimiento cartelista cubano se acercó al pop gracias a las innovaciones de ciertos diseñadores en particular. Uno de ellos fue Raúl Martínez, quien, como Warhol, comenzó su carrera como artista comercial; trabajó como pintor de letreros y estudió en el Instituto de Diseño de Chicago. Al regresar a La Habana en 1954, inició una doble vida: hacía pinturas expresionistas abstractas para exposiciones antibatistianas a la vez que cultivaba una lucrativa carrera como diseñador para una agencia publicitaria. Cuando la agencia quedó clausurada en 1960 debido al programa de nacionalización de empresas, Martínez se fue a trabajar para el estado diseñando anuncios de servicio público y *Lunes de Revolución*, un suplemento cultural progresista. Aunque no hubo problemas de censura, sus pinturas abstractas no tuvieron mucha acogida en este nuevo clima. Al poco tiempo se inclinó hacia la fotografía y empezó a colocar palabras (vestigios de su época de rotulista) y collages fotográficos sobre las superficies pintadas de sus lienzos, en consonancia con los "nuevos realismos" que muchos artistas de Occidente abordaban entonces (incluida la cubana Antonia Eiriz).[7]

En una entrevista de 1982, Martínez comentó que al darse cuenta de que los carteles producidos en masa para un público amplio era la manifestación artística más genuina de la revolución cubana, empezó a aplicar esa teoría a sus pinturas. "Empecé con el tema de [José] Martí y el estilo de pintura popular que se veía en las plazas y las sedes de los Comités de Defensa de la Revolución [...]. Había perdido mi habilidad de dibujante, entonces los rostros surgieron con una torpeza que me gustó".[8] Los rostros "torpes" de Martínez son prototípicos del pop; planos y caricaturescos, de trazos negros gruesos, son sumamente reconocibles y perfectos para reproducción mecánica. Hacia 1966, el artista había transferido las retículas de sus diseños de revistas y portadas de libros a sus lienzos, llenándolos con rostros redondos de líneas fuertes que representaban a héroes y figuras públicas. Mientras que Warhol trasladó la serigrafía al lienzo, Martínez hacía manualmente ligeras variaciones a sus figuras repetidas. En *15 repeticiones de Martí* (ver página 75, figura 3.2), las amplias aguadas de pintura evocan las capas de color que Warhol superponía por medio de la serigrafía.

Ya en 1968 Martínez había devuelto sus figuras y retículas pop a los carteles políticos y culturales que las habían inspirado. En uno de los carteles más conocidos del ICAIC, el de la película *Lucía* de Humberto Solás, tres rostros de la misma mujer, aplanados al estilo del cómic, cada uno de color distinto y arreglado de manera diferente, comunican el tema en cuestión: las experiencias de tres mujeres llamadas Lucía que viven en tres épocas de la república cubana (1968, lámina 46). Con esté y otros carteles, el espíritu pop de las pinturas de Martínez —que seguían siendo relativamente inaccesibles para la mayoría de los cubanos en términos de precio y lugares de exposición— tuvo mayor presencia en las calles.

Si bien las oscilaciones de Martínez entre el diseño gráfico, la fotografía y la pintura tuvieron un fuerte impacto en la estética postrevolucionaria de la isla, el diseñador Alfredo Rostgaard tuvo un efecto transformador no solo en el movimiento cartelístico, sino también en la gráfica de la época en general. Desde sus primeros carteles bajo el ICAIC para los documentales antiimperialistas de Santiago Álvarez a mediados de los sesenta, cuando contaba poco más de veinte años, Rostgaard abrió brecha al sintetizar las formas visuales contemporáneas con incisivos mensajes políticos. Un ejemplo emblemático fue su *Canción protesta* de 1967 (ver página 76, figura 3.3), un cartel para un simposio musical en la Casa de las Américas cuyo diseño de inflexiones pop tuvo particular resonancia en la izquierda del hemisferio. Sobre un fondo verde donde se superpone un área amarilla, Rostgaard colocó una rosa de formas simplificadas y contornos en negro. Una única gota de sangre rojo vivo cuelga de una de sus dos espinas, simbolizando el enlace de la belleza, el dolor y la emotividad en la música de protesta. Este fue el momento, según luego recordaría el artista, en que se desvaneció la distinción entre las organizaciones políticas y las culturales, y entre sus correspondientes carteles; el cartelismo en Cuba se reconocía como un acto intrínsecamente político, independientemente de la motivación específica de cada diseño.[9]

HACER CIRCULAR LA SOLIDARIDAD

La rosa sangrante de Rostgaard pronto fue adaptada a otros esfuerzos culturales de compromiso social y político fuera de Cuba, como la portada del número de abril de *El Corno Emplumado* (lámina 68), revista bilingüe de poesía producida en México, y la portada del libro de Dugald Stermer *The Art of Revolution: Castro's Cuba, 1959–1970* (publicado luego en español como *El arte en la revolución: Cuba y Castro, 1959–1970*) (1970, lámina 69). Este último, una colección de 96 excelentes reproducciones a color en gran formato de carteles cubanos de los años sesenta, con un ensayo de Susan Sontag, facilitó la difusión del arte cubano por excelencia —sobre todo en sus manifestaciones pop— entre los intelectuales internacionales a fines de los años sesenta y principios de los setenta.[10] Estas adaptaciones del diseño de Rostgaard ejemplifican la definición que hizo David Joselit del pop como un "estilo internacional", "un vocabulario compartido [...] que se puede adaptar a propuestas de contexto específico en lugares diversos que, incluso al viajar, siguen siendo inteligibles".[11]

Este vocabulario pop compartido ganó prominencia en México en 1968, tanto en el ámbito oficial como en el contracultural. Si la rosa aplanada simbolizaba la cultura, la paloma blanca aplanada —dibujada por Picasso, adoptada por los comunistas franceses en 1949 y "popificada" por el diseñador estadounidense Lance Wyman para los Juegos Olímpicos de México en 1968— simbolizaba la paz (ver página 76, figura 3.4).[12] México era la única nación del continente americano que mantenía relaciones diplomáticas con Cuba después de 1961. Esta estrategia de no alineación seguida por el Partido Revolucionario Institucional (PRI) durante la Guerra Fría fue la razón por la cual México resultó elegido para organizar los juegos olímpicos. Durante las dos semanas de los juegos, el PRI afianzó su asociación con la Cuba revolucionaria (y con La Habana en particular) al cubrir las vallas publicitarias con las palomas pop de Wyman y con caricaturas, fotografías y obras de arte, creando un entorno colorido, ecléctico y anticapitalista para los visitantes internacionales y los espectadores con televisores a color.[13] Esta decoración dio temporalmente una fachada progresista a un estado represor que, a diez días de la ceremonia de inauguración, había abierto fuego en la Plaza de las Tres Culturas en Tlatelolco contra una manifestación pacífica del movimiento estudiantil y obrero en pro de la democracia, con un saldo de muertos, prisioneros y cientos que tuvieron que pasar a la clandestinidad. Aunque no tenían armas, los artistas asociados con el movimiento del 68 sí tuvieron acceso al vocabulario del pop para los carteles efímeros que imprimieron y diseminaron a escondidas (láminas 57–60). En un cartel serigráfico de Jesús Martínez que constituye uno de los símbolos más conmovedores del movimiento, el pictograma de la paloma blanca de la paz de Wyman ha sido atravesado por una bayoneta que lo hace sangrar, como la espina de la rosa de Rostgaard (ver página 77, figura 3.5).[14] Su paleta reducida, de negro con acentos rojos, acerca aún más este diseño icónico mexicano a sus contrapartes cubanos.

Susan Sontag escribió que "el brío revolucionario de Cuba parte de *no* contentarse con los logros de una revolución nacional, sino de estar apasionadamente comprometidos con la causa de la revolución en una escala mundial. De ese modo, Cuba es quizás el único país comunista del mundo donde el pueblo demuestra un sincero interés por Vietnam".[15] Este internacionalismo, encabezado por el Che en palabra y acción, fue parte integral de la resistencia cubana a la ortodoxia soviética y también a la hora de buscar aliados de comercio y defensa que fueran más afines cultural, histórica y geográficamente.[16] Tras la primera Conferencia Tricontinental, compuesta de delegados de partidos comunistas latinoamericanos, asiáticos y africanos en 1966, se crearon la Organización de Solidaridad con los Pueblos de Asia, África y América Latina (OSPAAAL) y la Organización Latinoamérica de Solidaridad (OLAS). Una de las funciones esenciales de estas organizaciones —dedicadas a dar apoyo ideológico más que ayuda militar o humanitaria— fue diseñar y diseminar carteles, vallas de propaganda y revistas.

En una visita a La Habana en 1967, el fotógrafo Lee Lockwood retrató dos carteles-murales monumentales que ilustran con fuerza el espíritu pop de colores brillantes y rigor conceptual que predominaba en la gráfica cubana en ese momento (ver página 78, figura 3.6). Los diseños verticales de seis pisos de alto, hechos con varias tiras grandes de papel, estaban colocados en la pared lateral del Ministerio de Comercio. El cartel del lado izquierdo, patrocinado por la OLAS, mostraba una versión abstracta de la bandera de Estados Unidos sobre un campo monocromo amarillo, vista como a través de la mira de un rifle. En la parte inferior, en letras minúsculas, aparecía el texto: "son poderosos pero no invencibles". Del otro lado, coloridas imágenes a partir de fotos de José Martí y Máximo Gómez, héroes de la Guerra de Independencia Cubana, aparecían junto a imágenes de Fidel Castro y el Che Guevara en una retícula que recuerda las estrategias compositivas de Martínez (y Warhol). Irradiaban de ella líneas irregulares rojas, negras y amarillas, dando un efecto de profundidad a las imágenes aplanadas; abajo, en letras de imprenta, aparecía la pregunta: "¿Qué es la historia de Cuba sino la historia de América Latina?".

Sentimientos —e imágenes— similares se diseminaron a zonas remotas fuera de La Habana en las páginas de *Tricontinental*, una revista bimensual publicada por la OSPAAAL en ediciones en inglés, español, francés y árabe, y distribuida por decenas de miles a organismos progresistas en todo el mundo con el fin de fomentar la solidaridad entre las luchas antiimperialistas en Asia, África y América Latina. El diseñador era Rostgaard. Además de portadas y artículos de audaz diseño, cada número incluía un cartel doblado, diseñado por el propio Rostgaard u otros diseñadores cubanos, que conmemoraba un día de solidaridad con alguna nación, etnia o continente en particular. A tono con los principios del Che, la mayoría de estos carteles mostraban armas, promoviendo de manera explícita la insurrección armada.[17]

Thomas Crow ha señalado que "la red de comunicación entre los diseñadores gráficos es amplia y las ideas circulan rápidamente".[18] Esta red —que es internacional por naturaleza y abarca desde el diseño comercial hasta el contestatario— explica la estrecha relación que se creó entre los diseñadores de *Tricontinental* en La Habana y Emory Douglas, ministro de cultura y principal diseñador del periódico del Partido Panteras Negras. Fundado en 1966 en Oakland, California, este partido tenía una agenda militante antiimperialista muy semejante a la de la OSPAAAL, incluido el énfasis en la diseminación de diseños gráficos impactantes de vertiente pop. Tras el asesinato de Martin Luther King, Jr. en abril de 1968, Rostgaard diseñó un cartel para la OSPAAAL en el que aparecen las palabras "Black Power" (Poder Negro) en la boca cavernosa de una pantera negra estilo cómic, con colmillos blancos y ojos rojos (ver página 78, figura 3.7). Al poco tiempo Douglas se apropió del diseño de Rostgaard para protestar contra la encarcelación del líder Huey Long, y montó el retrato de Long en la boca de la pantera.[19] En agosto de ese mismo año, Lázaro Abreu Padrón, diseñador de la OSPAAAL, adaptó uno de los dibujos caricaturescos de Douglas, un grupo de afroamericanos armados, con boinas negras, para un cartel de solidaridad hacia ellos (1968, lámina 72). Douglas luego explicó que estos intercambios eran informales: "Ellos veían arte que yo había creado para el periódico y lo mezclaban a su manera en carteles, lo rediseñaban y lo enviaban por el mundo […]. No era plagio porque era solidaridad en el contexto de la lucha".[20] Sorprendentemente, como lo ha señalado Carol A. Wells, no hubo intercambios de este tipo con los diseñadores asociados al movimiento chicano, a pesar de que éste acogió con entusiasmo los trabajos gráficos de la OSPAAAL.[21]

Entre los muchos íconos de finales de los años sesenta, nada se compara con la imagen del Che. Aunque físicamente ausente de Cuba a partir de 1965 —primero en un fallido intento de fomentar una insurrección guerrillera en el Congo, y más tarde en los Andes—, su imagen comenzó a dominar los espacios públicos, y esta tendencia fue aumentando tras su asesinato en octubre de 1967 por fuerzas militares patrocinadas por la Agencia Central de Inteligencia de Estados Unidos (CIA) en la sierra de Bolivia. Para entonces, según K.S. Karol, "Cuba vivía literalmente bajo el signo del Che. Sus enormes retratos miraban con fijeza por todas partes, y su eslogan aparecía en inmensas vallas propagandistas en negro sobre rojo: 'Crear dos, tres, muchos Vietnam', un llamado a poner en marcha otras luchas antiimperialistas".[22] Aunque el fotógrafo Alberto Díaz (conocido como Korda) fue quien tomó la famosa foto del Che mirando hacia lo lejos en un funeral masivo en 1960, la imagen no tuvo amplia difusión hasta la muerte del guerrillero (ver página 79, figura 3.8). En Cuba se colocaron ampliaciones monumentales, y tanto en los medios masivos como en las calles de toda América empezaron a aparecer versiones aplanadas, de colores vivos muy contrastados, en apoyo de causas sociales progresistas y radicales.[23] El atractivo de esta foto reside en el rostro del Che, la frente en alto, mirando a la distancia, evocando al "hombre nuevo" de talante internacionalista que él mismo promovía en sus escritos.

En La Habana, Elena Serrano diseñó un cartel para *Tricontinental* que, aunque impreso en offset, emplea la estética serigráfica de colores planos para representar al Che de Korda no como hombre, sino como ícono, fomentando desde el corazón de los Andes el sentimiento revolucionario en todo el continente (1968, lámina 7). Mientras tanto, en Buenos Aires, el artista Roberto Jacoby colocó una versión de la imagen en blanco y negro a alto contraste encima del texto "Un guerrillero no muere para que se lo cuelgue en la pared" (1968, lámina 65). El hecho de que la imagen de Korda no fuera utilizada por los diseñadores antes de 1967 puede deberse a que el fotógrafo restringió su distribución, además de que el gobierno revolucionario se oponía a convertir en ídolos a los líderes vivos. Es importante señalar que, como las Marilyns de Warhol, la transformación del Che en ícono requirió no solo que muriera en circunstancias trágicas, sino una imagen que estuviera distanciada de esa tragedia en fecha y contenido.[24]

A los pocos meses aparecieron versiones en vertiente pop de la imagen de Korda en contextos progresistas alrededor del mundo. Una de las primeras en Estados Unidos fue un cartel serigráfico de 1968 de Rupert García. Igual que en el diseño de Morante para la Cinemateca de Cuba, los rasgos planos de una persona (en este caso el Che en vez de Chaplin) emergen del fondo blanco como formas negras, seguramente dibujadas con ayuda de un proyector Grant. En la parte inferior se lee en letra estilo estencil "RIGHT ON!" (algo así como ¡Bien hecho! o ¡De acuerdo!), un famoso eslogan de los Panteras Negras. García creció en la zona rural de Stockton, California, y sirvió en el ejército estadounidense en Tailandia antes de regresar a la zona de San Francisco e ingresar en la facultad de artes del San Francisco State College (SFSC) en 1966, aprovechando los beneficios del GI Bill (que proporcionaba financiamiento a soldados para estudios universitarios). Sus primeras obras gráficas, como *Black Man and Flag* (Hombre negro y bandera) (1967, lámina 6), muestran su adopción de los vocabularios tanto del pop como de los derechos civiles. García se incorporó a la histórica huelga estudiantil del SFSC en 1968 y empezó a crear carteles serigráficos —como *RIGHT ON!*— en apoyo del fondo de fianza para los estudiantes (ver página 80, figura 3.9).[25] Estos pri-

meros diseños combinan hábilmente las convenciones gráficas de los impresos locales e internacionales que García asimilaba con avidez en lugares como la librería Modern Times de San Francisco, que vendía las revistas *Black Panther* y *Tricontinental* además de reimpresiones de carteles mexicanos del movimiento del 1968.[26] Para 1970, García dominaba el vocabulario pop y las técnicas de la serigrafía, produciendo impactantes obras como *¡Fuera de Indochina!* (ver página 80, figura 3.10), donde el contorno de una cara angustiada con la boca abierta emerge de un escueto fondo negro con letras amarillas. Producido en 1970 para el movimiento Chicano Moratorium en el este de Los Ángeles, su imaginería —como la de *Vietnam Aztlán*, de Malaquias Montoya, artista chicano radicado en Berkeley— habría tenido perfecta cabida en las páginas de *Tricontinental* si tan solo hubiera llegado a manos de Rostgaard. Estos carteles no solo articulan el *ethos* profundamente internacionalista del movimiento chicano, sino que representan la culminación de una década de esfuerzos en toda América para, como dijo García, subvertir las imágenes de los medios masivos "hacia fines morales para los cuales no fueron diseñados: el arte de la protesta social".[27]

En conclusión, los diseñadores activos dentro del circuito transnacional que abarcaba Cuba, México y ciertas zonas de Estados Unidos en las décadas de 1960 y 1970 se valieron de imágenes y estilos derivados del pop no solo para subvertir los discursos oficiales, sino también para afirmarlos. El elemento que más unifica sus propuestas es la audacia, tanto en términos de color, contraste y escala, como de sus mensajes visuales sucintos y conceptualmente impactantes. Desde La Habana hasta Ciudad de México y la zona de la Bahía de San Francisco, los cartelistas abrazaron el internacionalismo a la vez que rechazaban las normas sociales y el realismo social, generando corrientes revolucionarias que irradiaron desde América hacia el mundo.

1   Reynaldo González, "When Posters Decide to Come Home", en *¡Mira Cuba!: Manifesti cinematografici, politici e sociali = Carteles de cine, políticos y sociales = Movie, Political and Social Posters*, ed. Luigino Bardellotto (Cinisello Balsamo, Milano: Silvana, 2013), 31. Edmundo Desnoes ofreció un primer análisis del movimiento cubano de carteles revolucionarios, "Los carteles de la Revolución cubana", *Casa de las Américas*, no. 51–52 (noviembre de 1968): 223–231. El primer estudio en inglés apareció dos años después: Dugald Stermer, *The Art of Revolution* (Nueva York: McGraw-Hill, 1970). Entre los escritos más recientes se encuentra: Lincoln Cushing, *Revolución!: Cuban Poster Art* (San Francisco, CA: Chronicle Books, 2003). La prevalencia de la serigrafía en Cuba antes de 1968 marca una diferencia con respecto a París, donde la técnica no se había extendido antes de su introducción en los Ateliers Populaires durante la huelga general de mayo de ese año. Ver Victoria HF Scott, "Silk-Screens and Television Screens: Maoism and the Posters of May and June 1968 in Paris" (tesis de doctorado, State University of New York at Binghamton, 2010); Liam Considine, "Screen Politics: Pop Art and the Atelier Populaire", *Tate Papers*, no. 24 (otoño de 2015), http://www.tate.org.uk, consultado el 18 de agosto de 2017.

2   David Craven, "Cuban Art and Culture," en *Cuba, A Different America*, eds., Wilber A. Chaffee y Gary Prevost (Totowa: Rowman & Littlefield, 1992), 133.

3   Alfredo Guevara, "Realidades y perspectivas de un nuevo cine", *Cine Cubano* 1, no. 1 (1960): 4.

4   Susan Sontag, "Posters: Advertisement, Art, Political Artifact, Commodity", en *The Art of Revolution*, xiv.

5   María Eulalia Douglas, *La tienda negra: El cine en Cuba, 1897–1990* (La Habana: Cinemateca de Cuba, 1996), 159. Los carteles se imprimían en tiradas de 250–500 unidades y rara vez se veían fuera de La Habana.

6   Ernesto "Che" Guevara, "Socialism and Man in Cuba (1965)", en *Contemporary Latin American Social and Political Thought: An Anthology*, ed. Iván Márquez (Lanham: Rowman & Littlefield, 2008), http://ebookcentral.proquest.com.

7   Para una biografía detallada y un análisis incisivo del desarrollo de la práctica artística de Martínez, ver Corina Matamoros Tuma, *Raúl Martínez: La gran familia* (La Habana: Ediciones Vanguardia Cubana, 2012). Sobre la prevalencia del collage y las estrategias del objeto en Europa Occidental y Nueva York c. 1960, ver Julia Robinson ed., *New Realisms, 1957–1962: Object Strategies between Readymade and Spectacle* (Madrid: Museo Nacional Centro de Arte Reina Sofía; Cambridge: MIT Press, 2010).

8   Raúl Martínez, citado en Shifra M. Goldman, "Painters into Poster Makers: A Conversation with Two Cuban Artists", en *Dimensions of the Americas: Art and Social Change in Latin America and the United States* (Chicago: University of Chicago Press, 1994), 148–149.

9   Alfredo Rostgaard en entrevista con Jennifer Josten, 20 de enero de 2000. Ver Jennifer Josten, "A Shout from the Wall: The Development of the Cuban Revolutionary Poster, 1959–1970" (tesis de licenciatura en artes, Wellesley College, 2000), 88. En una entrevista de 1982 con Shifra Goldman, Rostgaard habló de su gran aprecio por los carteles de cine y otras obras del diseñador estadounidense Saul Bass. Goldman, "Painters into Poster Makers", 151.

10   Stermer, *The Art of Revolution*. Para obtener más información sobre la historia y los propósitos de *El Corno Emplumado*, ver Margaret Randall, "Remembering *El Corno Emplumado*", Open Door Archive, 16 de enero de 2015, http://opendoor.northwestern.edu/.

11   David Joselit, "'International Pop' y 'The World Goes Pop'", *Artforum International* 54:5 (enero de 2016): 231.

12   Para obtener más información sobre los usos políticos de la paloma blanca de Picasso, ver Gertje Utley, *Picasso: The Communist Years* (New Haven: Yale University Press, 2000), cap. 7. En la década de 1950, Diego Rivera la incorporó a sus diseños de mosaicos para el nuevo Estadio Olímpico de la Universidad Nacional Autónoma de México. Natalia de la Rosa en conversación con Jennifer Josten, octubre de 2017.

13   Helen Escobedo, "An Artist's Eye View of Mexico", *The Art Gallery* XIX, no. 1 (1975): 129, 131.

14   Para obtener más información sobre esta imagen en el contexto más amplio de la gráfica del movimiento del 68, ver George F. Flaherty, *Hotel Mexico: Dwelling on the '68 Movement* (Oakland: University of California Press, 2016), 168–169.

15   Sontag, "Posters", xviii.

16   Ernesto F. Betancourt, "Exporting the Revolution to Latin America", en *Revolutionary Change in Cuba*, ed. Carmelo Mesa-Lago (Pittsburgh: University of Pittsburgh Press, 1971).

17   Ver una historia ampliamente ilustrada de estos carteles en Richard Frick, *Das Trikontinentale Solidaritätsplakat = El cartel Tricontinental de solidaridad = The Tricontinental Solidarity Poster = L'affiche Tricontinentale de la solidarité* (Berna: Commedia-Verlag, 2003).

18   Thomas Crow, *The Long March of Pop: Art, Music, and Design, 1930–1995* (New Haven: Yale University Press, 2015), 326.

19   Tom Wilson, "Paper Walls: Political Posters in an Age of Mass Media", en *West of Center: Art and the Counterculture Experiment in America, 1965–1977*, eds., Elissa Auther y Adam Lerner (Minneapolis: University of Minnesota Press, 2012), 173–175.

20   Dhruv Shah, "Interview with Revolutionary Artist Emory Douglas", *I Am Hip-Hop Magazine*, 20 de enero de 2015, http://www.iamhiphopmagazine.com/interview-revolutionary-artist-emory-douglas/.

21   Carol A. Wells, "La Lucha Sigue: From East Los Angeles to the Middle East", en *Just Another Poster?: Chicano Graphic Arts in California*, ed. Chon A. Noriega (Santa Barbara: University Art Museum, University of California, Santa Barbara, 2001), 178.

22   K. S. Karol, *Guerrillas in Power: The Course of the Cuban Revolution* (Nueva York: Hill & Wang, 1970), 291–292.

23   La fotografía tomada por Korda y sus posteriores encarnaciones han sido el tema de tres libros: David Kunzle, *Che Guevara: Icon, Myth, and Message* (Los Ángeles: UCLA Fowler Museum of Cultural History en colaboración con el Center for the Study of Political Graphics, 1997); Trisha Ziff, ed., *Che Guevara: Revolutionary & Icon* (Nueva York: Abrams Image, 2006); Michael Casey, *Che's Afterlife: The Legacy of an Image* (Nueva York: Vintage, 2009). La primera publicación documentada de la foto de Korda fue en *Paris Match* en agosto de 1967. Su adaptación para el cartel-mural en la figura 3.6 y la versión pop en naranja y morado titulada *Che sí*, del diseñador radicado en París Roman Cieślewicz para la portada de octubre de 1967 de *Opus International*, son de las primeras adaptaciones; sobre esta última, ver Crow, *The Long March of Pop*, 326–327. La imagen de Korda empezó a difundirse más ampliamente al mismo tiempo que otra imagen del Che reproducida mecánicamente que aparecía publicada en octubre: la foto tomada por Freddy Alborta de su cadáver, colocado como un Cristo en un lavadero de un pueblo boliviano, rodeado de los militares patrocinados por la CIA que pusieron fin a su campaña de exportar a América del Sur la revolución de guerrilla, al estilo cubano. A diferencia de la de Korda, esta imagen se utilizó como base en un solo conjunto notable de obras: las pinturas en serigrafía que el colaborador de Warhol, Gerard Malanga, intentó sin éxito vender en 1968 bajo el nombre de Warhol. Ver Casey, *Che's Afterlife*, 118–119.

24   Thomas Crow sostiene que cuando adaptaron la imagen de Korda a carteles y vallas propagandistas a partir de 1967, los diseñadores cubanos tuvieron influencia de las Marilyns de Warhol y otras obras basadas en fotografías de celebridades. Yo sostengo más bien que, como lo demuestra el cartel *Cinemateca de Cuba*, realizado por Morante en 1961, los cubanos ya estaban empleando estrategias conceptuales y formales que les permitían transformar imágenes en íconos a través de la serigrafía, y esto antes de Warhol. Ver Crow, *The Long March of Pop*, 336–337.

25   Ramón Favela, *The Art of Rupert García: A Survey Exhibition* (San Francisco: Chronicle Books: Mexican Museum, 1986), 19.

26   Lincoln Cushing, "One Struggle, Two Communities", entrevista con Rupert García, 19 de septiembre de 2003, consultado el 9 de agosto, 2017, http://www.docspopuli.org/articles/Cuba/BACshow.html. La Rupert García and Sammi Madison García Collection de la Universidad de California, Santa Barbara, incluye varios números de *Tricontinental y Black Panther*, así como *Mexico 1968: A Study of Domination and Repression* (Nueva York: North American Congress on Latin America, noviembre de 1968). Quisiera agradecer a Rosalía Romero su ayuda en la investigación de este tema.

27   Rupert García, "Media Supplement, 1969–1970" (tesis de máster, San Francisco State College, 1970), 1. También citado en Favela, *The Art of Rupert García*, 19. Para obtener más información sobre el internacionalismo en los carteles chicanos, ver Wells, "La Lucha Sigue", and George Lipsitz, "Not Just Another Social Movement: Poster Art and the Movimiento Chicano", en *Just Another Poster?*, 78.

FASHIONING AMÉRICA

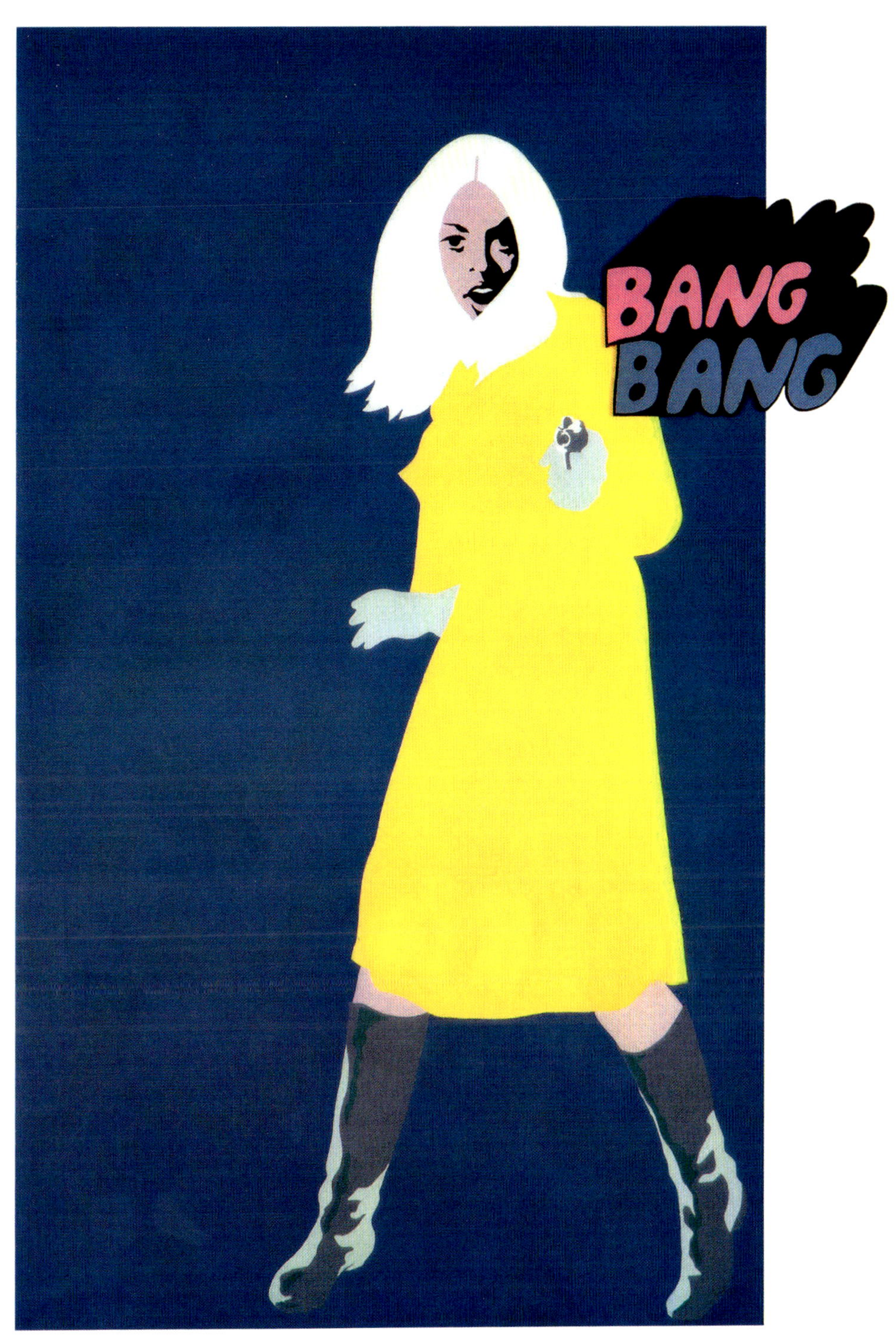

Pl. 35. Emilio Hernández Saavedra, *Bang Bang*, 1967. Latex paint on fabric, 78.62 x 55 inches (200 x 140 cm). Courtesy of the Private Archives of Emilio Hernández Saavedra, Lima, Peru, and Henrique Faria Fine Art, New York, New York, and Buenos Aires, Argentina.

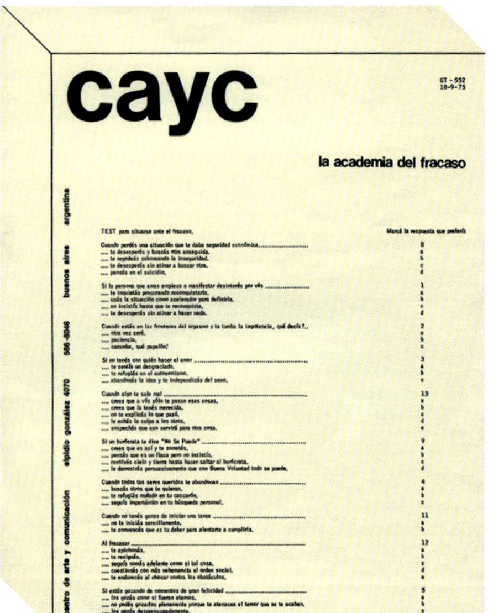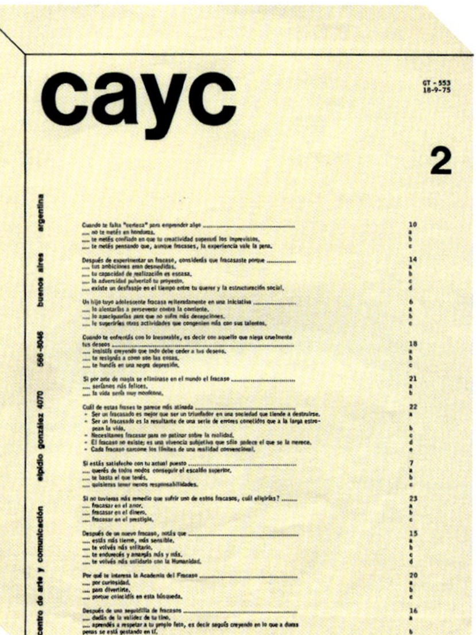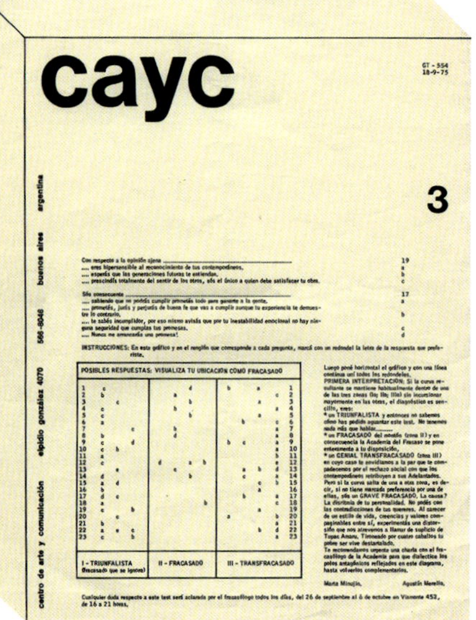

Pl. 36. Marta Minujín, *Test para situarse en el fracaso* (Test to Situate Yourself in the Face of Failure), 1975. Archival documents, 8.5 x 11 inches (21.59 x 27.94 cm). Estrellita B. Brodsky Collection.

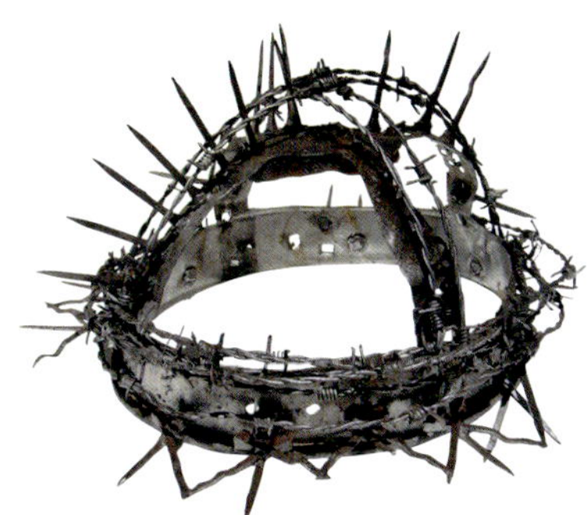

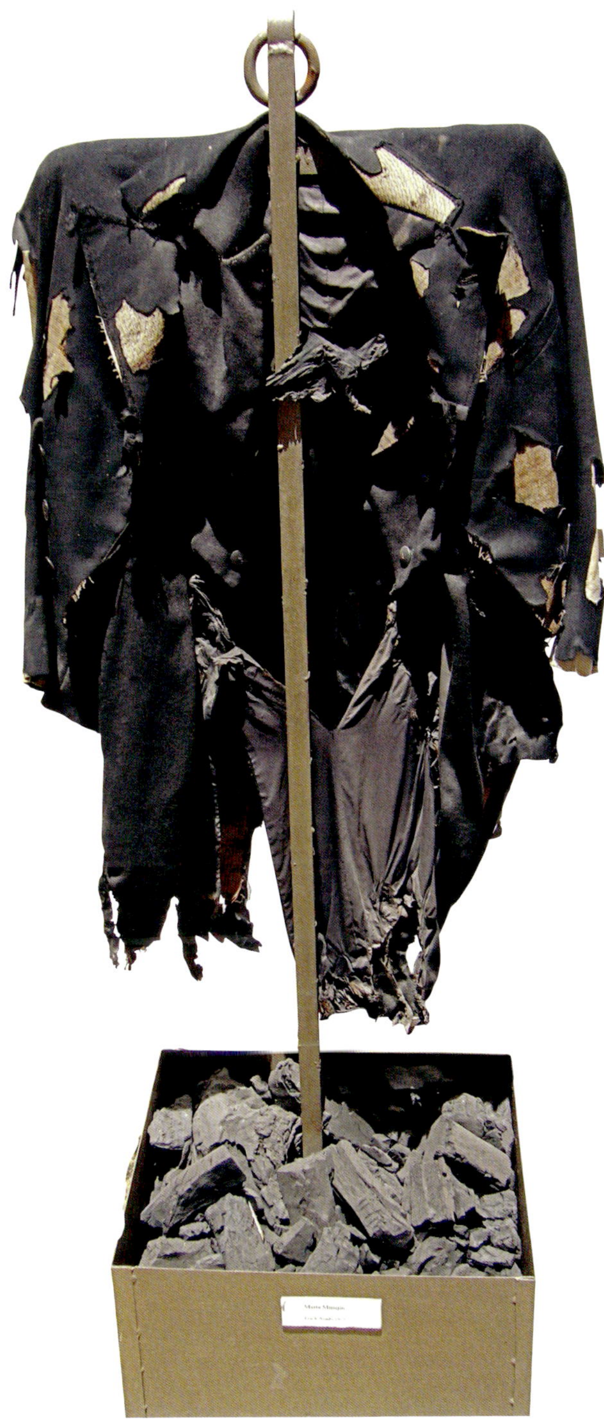

Pl. 37. Marta Minujín, *Frac-asado* (Grilled-Tuxedo), 1975. Mixed-media dress on stand and metal crown of thorns, 62.5 inches (158.75 cm), overall. Estrellita B. Brodsky Collection.

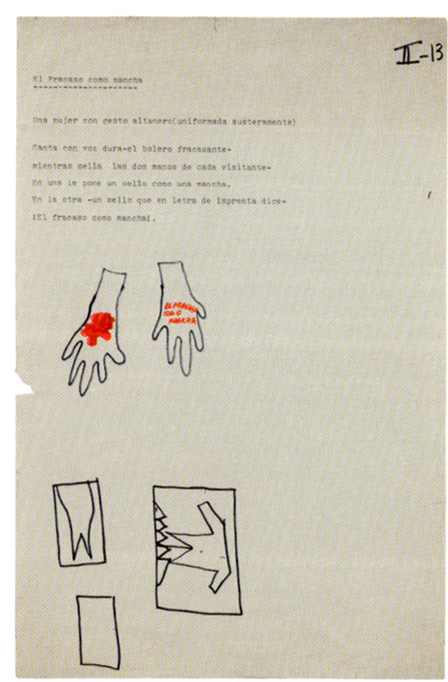

El Fracaso como mancha

Una mujer con gesto altanero(uniformada austeramente)

Canta con voz dura-el bolero fracasante-
mientras sella las dos manos de cada visitante-
En una le pone un sello como una mancha.
En la otra -un sello que en letra de imprenta dice-
¡El fracaso como mancha!.

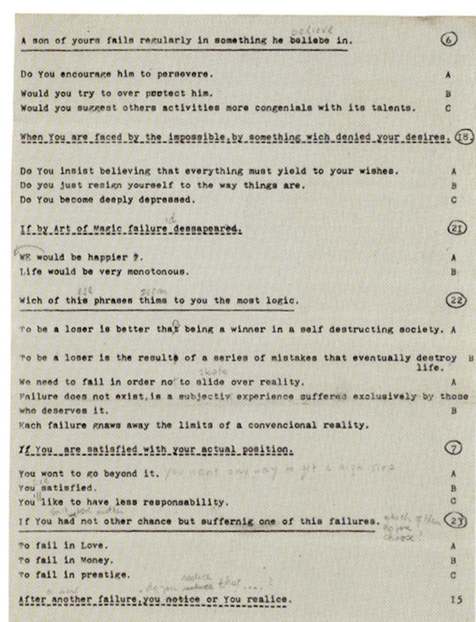

A son of yours fails regularly in something he beliebe in.   (6)

Do You encourage him to persevere.   A

Would you try to over protect him.   B
Would you suggest others activities more congenials with its talents.   C

When You are faced by the impossible,by something wich denied your desires.   (18)

Do You insist believing that everything must yield to your wishes.   A
Do you just resign yourself to the way things are.   B
Do You become deeply depressed.   C

If by Art of Magic failure dessapeared.   (21)

WE would be happier ?.   A
Life would be very monotonous.   B

Wich of this phrases thims to you the most logic.   (22)

To be a loser is better that being a winner in a self destructing society.   A

To be a loser is the results of a series of mistakes that eventually destroy B
                                                                              life.
We need to fail in order no to slide over reality.   A
Failure does not exist,is a subjectiv experience suffered exclusively by those
who deserves it.   B
Each failure gnaws away the limits of a convencional reality.

If You are satisfied with your actual position.   (7)

You wont to go beyond it.   A
You satisfied.   B
You like to have less responsability.   C
If You had not other chance but suffernig one of this failures.   (23)

To fail in Love.   A
To fail in Money.   B
To fail in prestige.   C

After another failure,you notice or You realice.   15

TOP, Pl. 38. Marta Minujín, *Máximo galardón* (Top Prize), 1975. Pencil on paper, 20 x 17.5 inches (50.8 x 44.5 cm). **BOTTOM (LEFT TO RIGHT), Pl. 39.** *El fracaso como mancha* (Failure as a Stain), 1975. Archival document, 9 x 8.7 inches (23 x 22 cm). **Pl. 40.** *Test ("A Son of Yours Fails Regularly in Something He Believe[s] In")*, 1975. Archival document, 14 x 8.5 inches (35.5 x 21.5 cm). Estrellita B. Brodsky Collection.

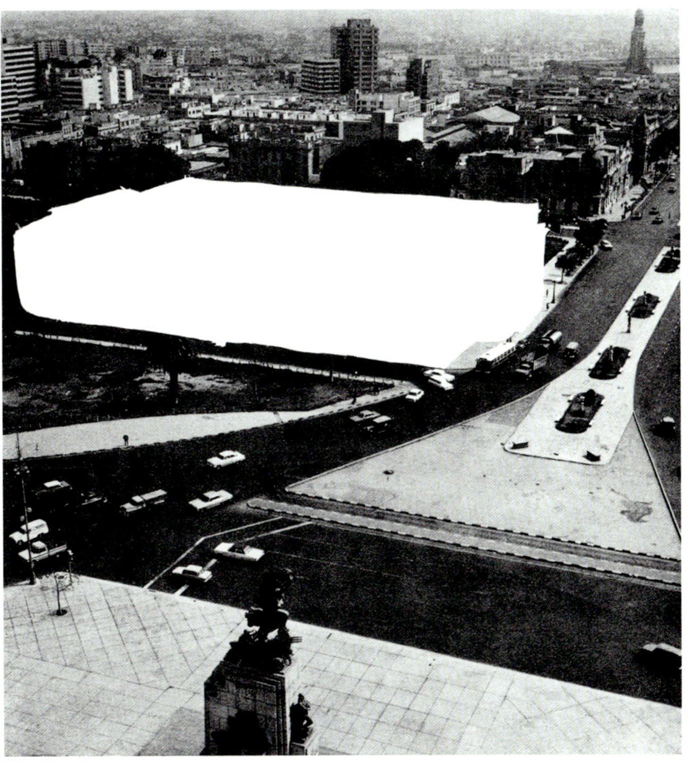

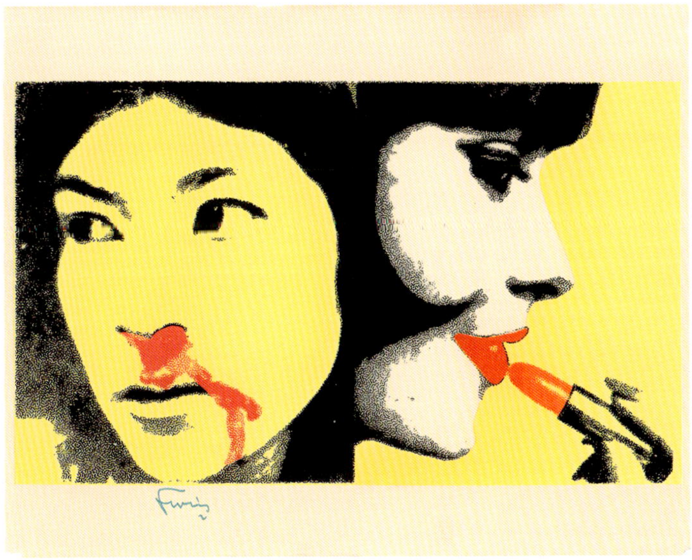

TOP, Pl. 41. Emilio Hernández Saavedra, *El museo de arte borrado* (The Erased Museum of Art), 1970 (printed 2016). Inkjet printing on cotton Hahnemühle paper (photo by Rag Baryta), 21.06 x 19.68 inches (53.5 x 50 cm). Courtesy of the Private Archives of Emilio Hernández Saavedra, Lima, Peru, and Henrique Faria Fine Art, New York, New York, and Buenos Aires, Argentina. **BOTTOM, Pl. 42.** José Gómez Fresquet (known as Frémez), *Vietnam (La modela y la vietnamita)* (Vietnam [The Model and the Vietnamese Woman]) from the series *Canción Americana* (American Song), 1969. Lithograph on paper, 18.06 x 23.37 inches (45.8 x 59.3 cm). Collection of the Center for Cuban Studies, New York, New York.

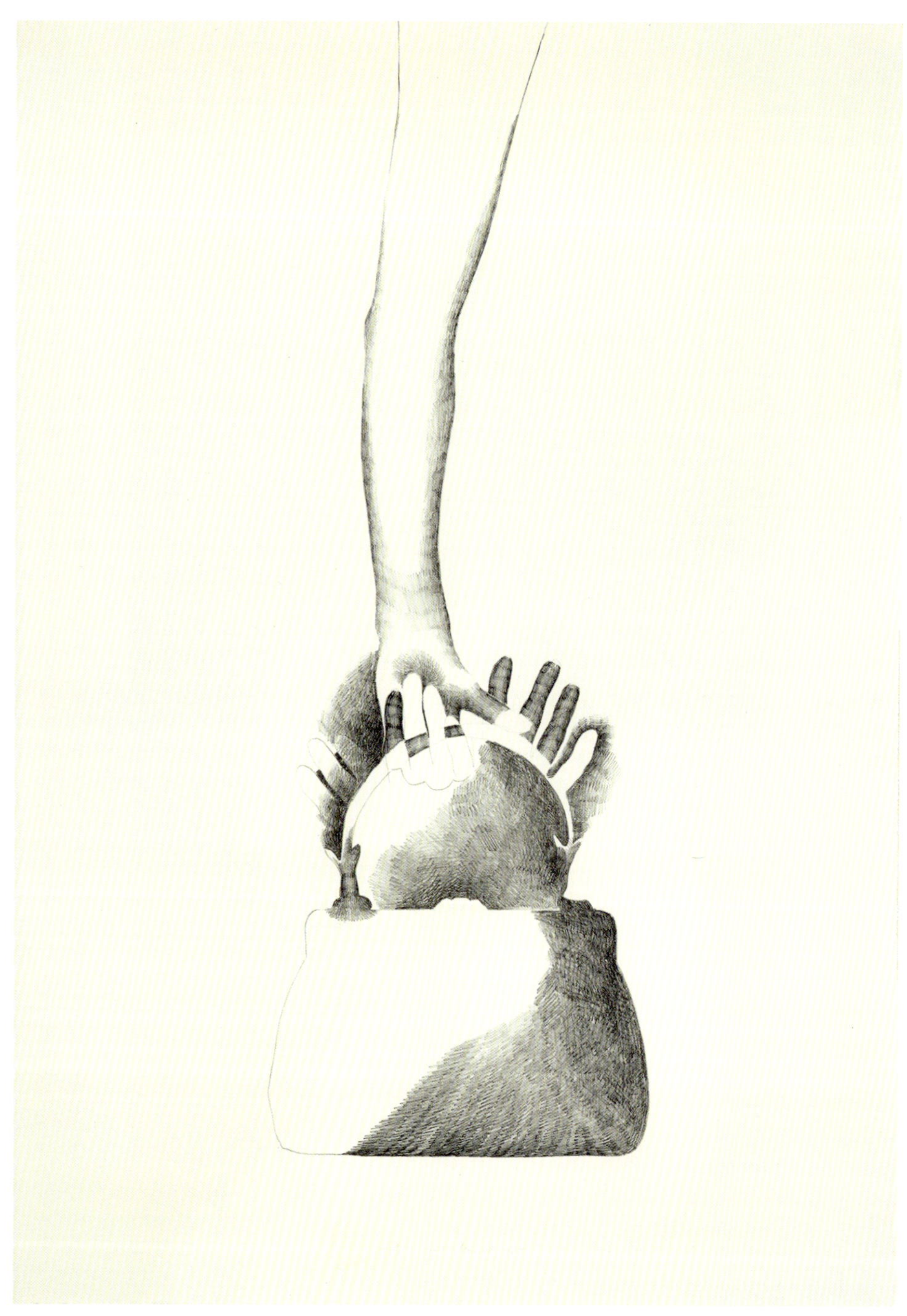

Pl. 43. Marisol Escobar (known as Marisol), *Hand and Purse*, 1965. Lithograph on paper, artist's proof, 41.5 x 29.5 inches (105.4 x 74.9 cm). Collection of the North Carolina Museum of Art, Raleigh. Purchased with funds from the National Endowment for the Arts and the North Carolina State Art Society (Robert F. Phifer Bequest). © 2018 Estate of Marisol. Licensed by Artists Rights Society (ARS), New York, New York.

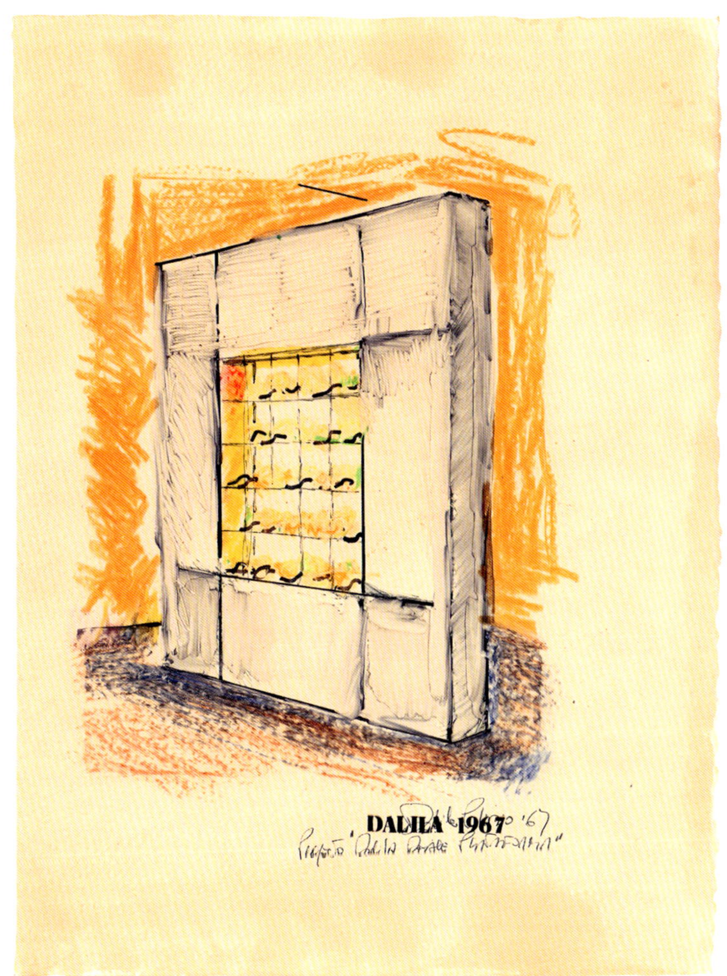

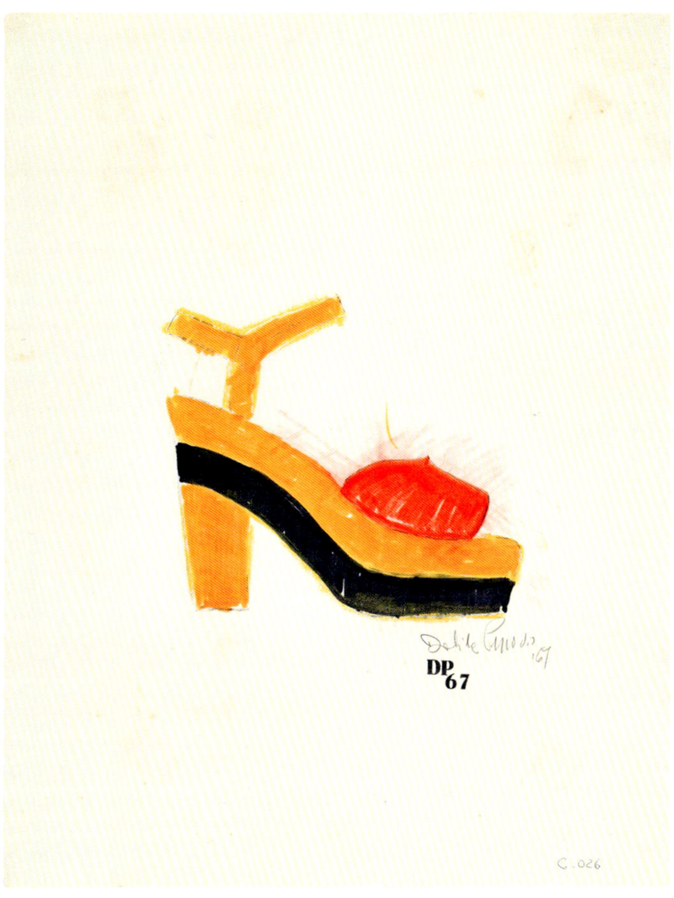

LEFT, Pl. 44. Dalila Puzzovio, *Dalila doble plataforma* (Dalila Double Platform), 1967. Ink and crayon on Fabriano paper with PVC additions and acetate paper on top, 18.25 x 12 inches (46.35 x 30.48 cm). **RIGHT, Pl. 45.** *Dalila doble plataforma* (Dalila Double Platform), 1967. Pencil and crayon on paper, 14.12 x 11.18 inches (35.87 x 28.41 cm). Private collection.

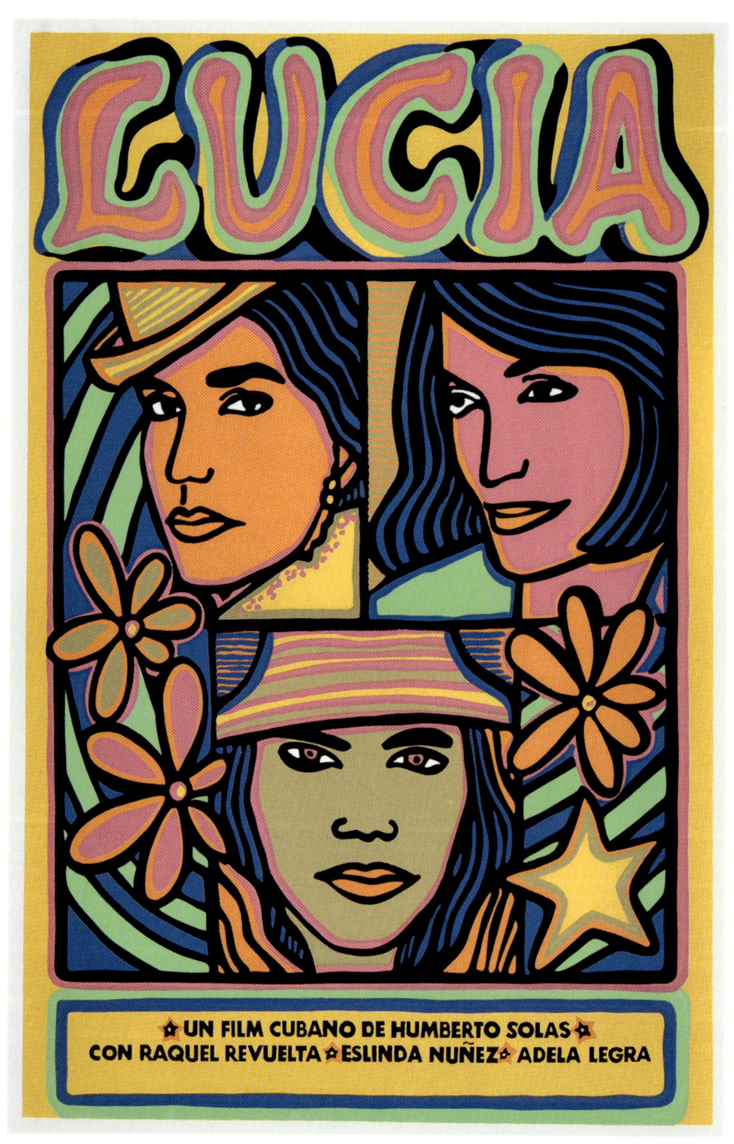

Pl. 46. Raúl Martínez, *Lucía*, 1968. Screenprint on paper, 29.87 x 20 inches (75.9 x 50.8 cm). Collection of the Ackland Art Museum, the University of North Carolina at Chapel Hill. Gift of Dr. David L. Craven. © Raúl Martínez Estate, Ciego de Ávila, Cuba. Courtesy of the Raúl Martínez Estate and Corina Matamoros.

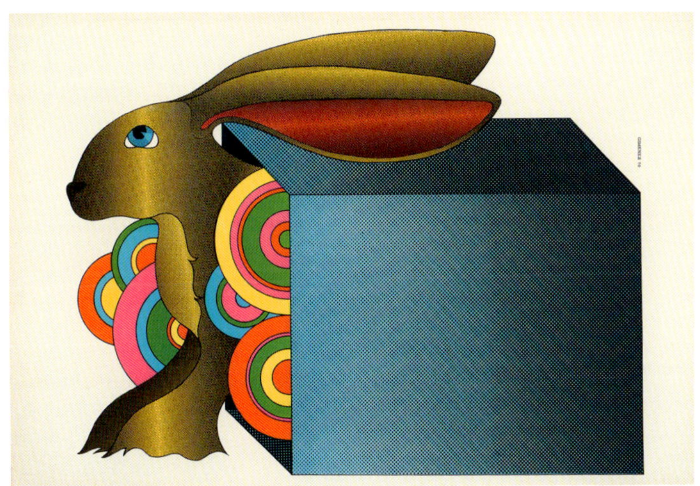

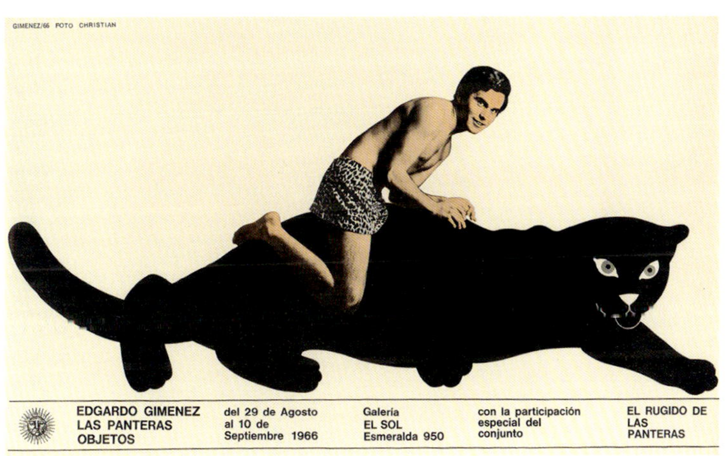

TOP, Pl. 47. Edgardo Giménez, *Sin título (Fuera de caja)* (Untitled [Out of the Box]), 1970. Offset print on paper, 14.75 x 22 inches (37.46 x 55.88 cm). **BOTTOM, Pl. 48.** Edgardo Giménez, *Las panteras, objetos* (The Panthers, Objects), 1966. Offset print on paper, 13.75 x 23 inches (34.92 x 58.42 cm). Private collection. © Edgardo Giménez.

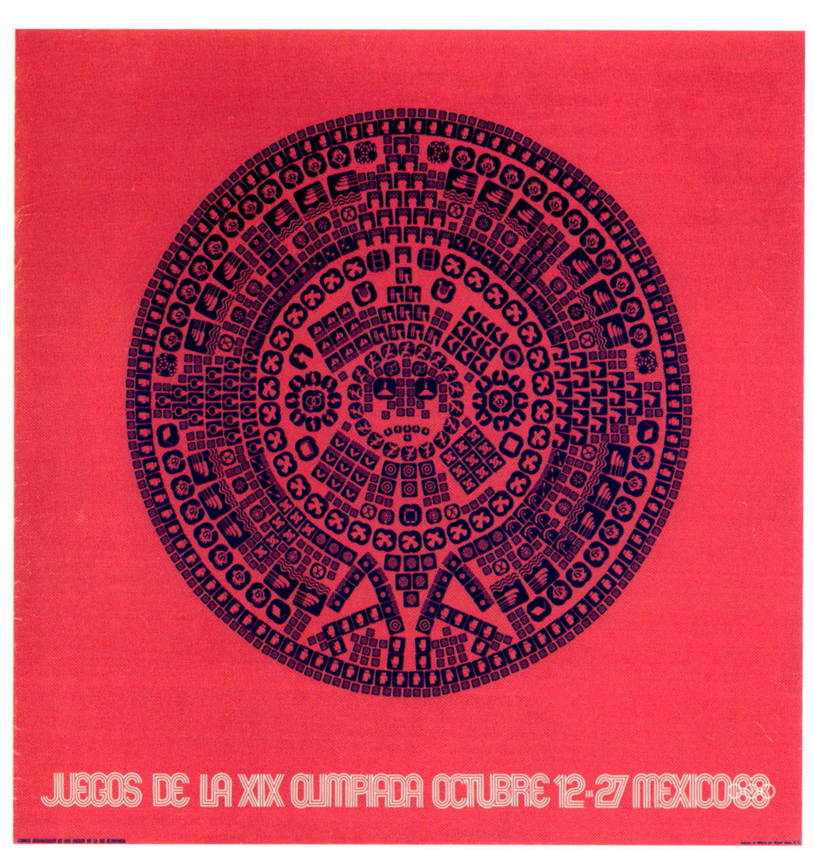

Pl. 49. Lance Wyman and Jan Stornfelt, Image of an Aztec calendar made from Olympic sport and cultural event icons, 1968. Offset lithograph on paper, 23.5 x 23.5 inches (59.69 x 59.69 cm). Courtesy of the artist.

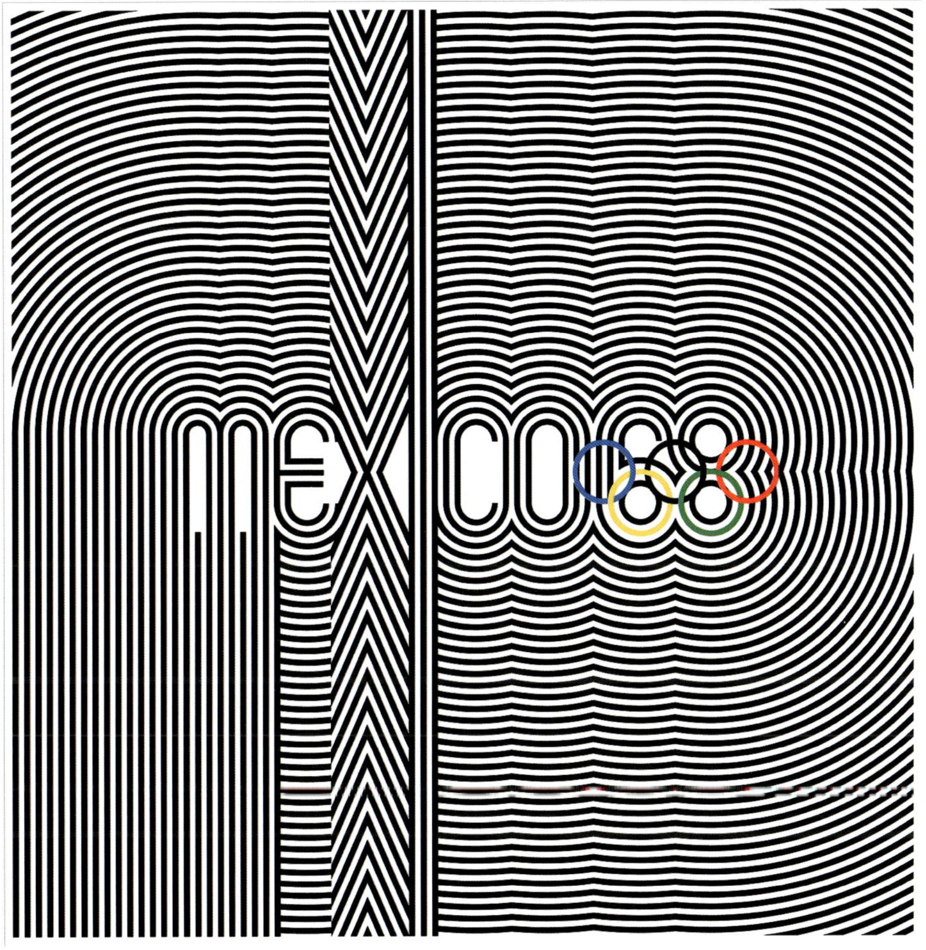

Pl. 50. Lance Wyman, Eduardo Terrazas, Pedro Ramírez Vázquez, and the Department of Publications and Urban Design of the Organizing Committee of the XIX Olympiad, *Mexico '68*, 1967. Offset lithograph on paper, 33.87 x 34.12 inches (86.04 x 86.67 cm). Private collection.

Pl. 51. Lance Wyman, Third pre-Olympic postal issue (basketball), 1967. **OPPOSITE (TOP TO BOTTOM), Pls. 52–55.** Lance Wyman, Third pre-Olympic postal issue (cycling, diving, field hockey, and rowing), 1967. Postage stamps, 10.25 x 8.68 inches (26.03 x 22.06 cm), each. Courtesy of the artist.

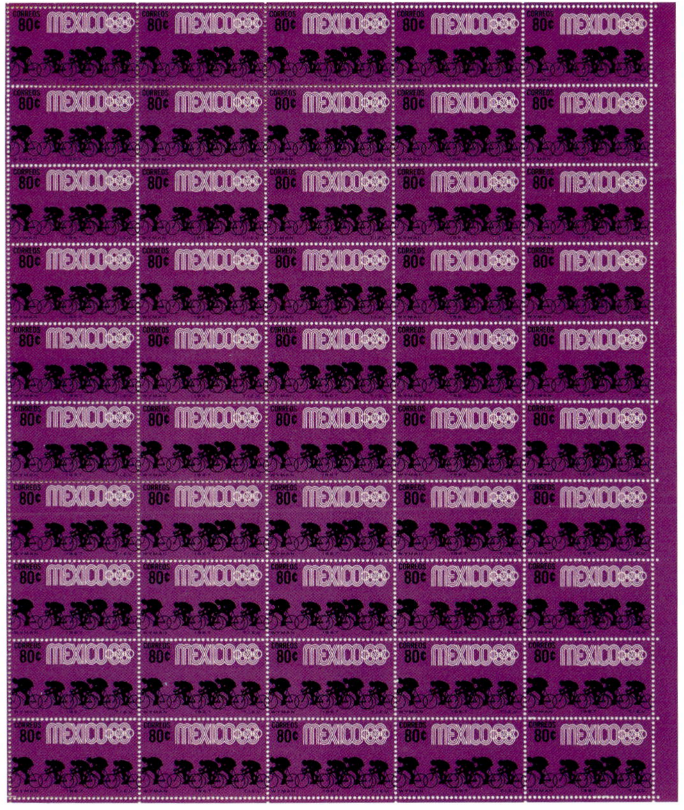

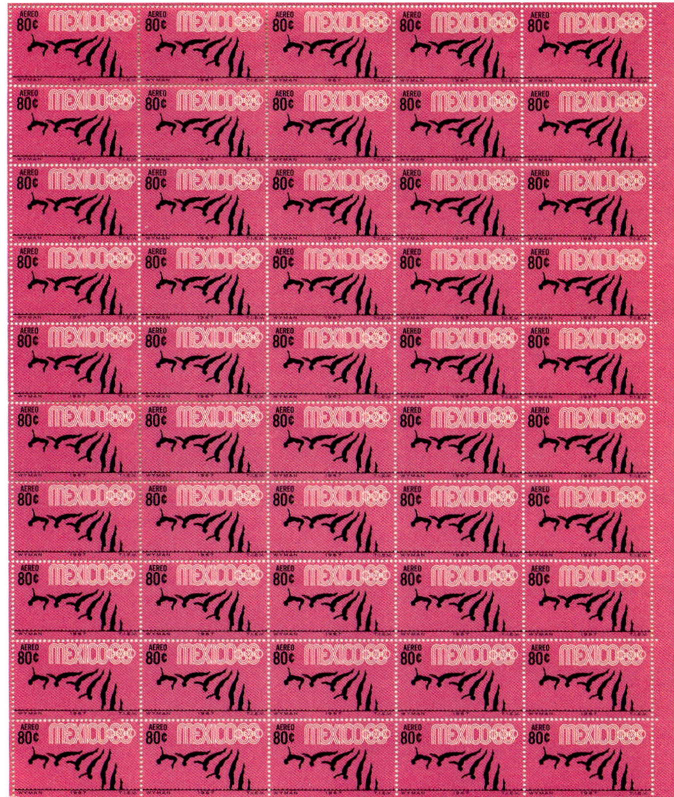

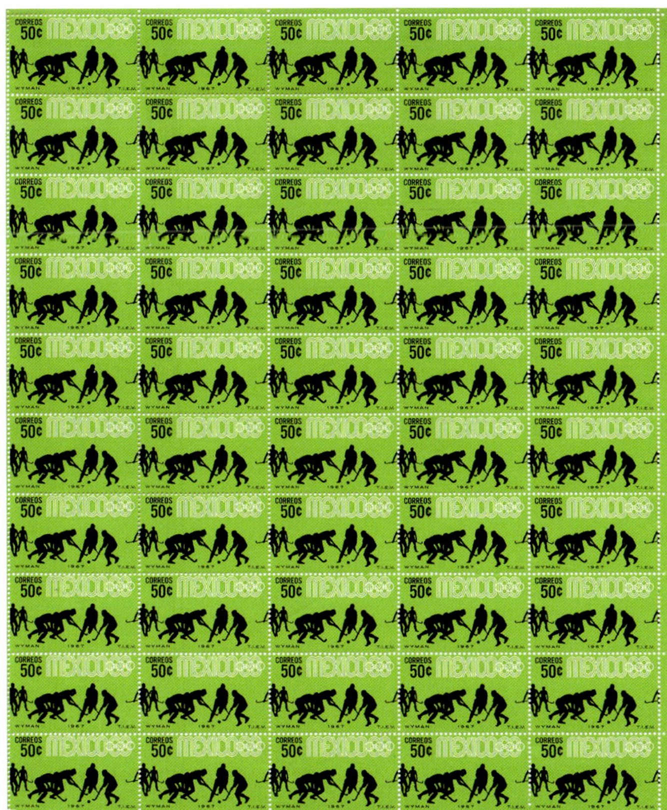

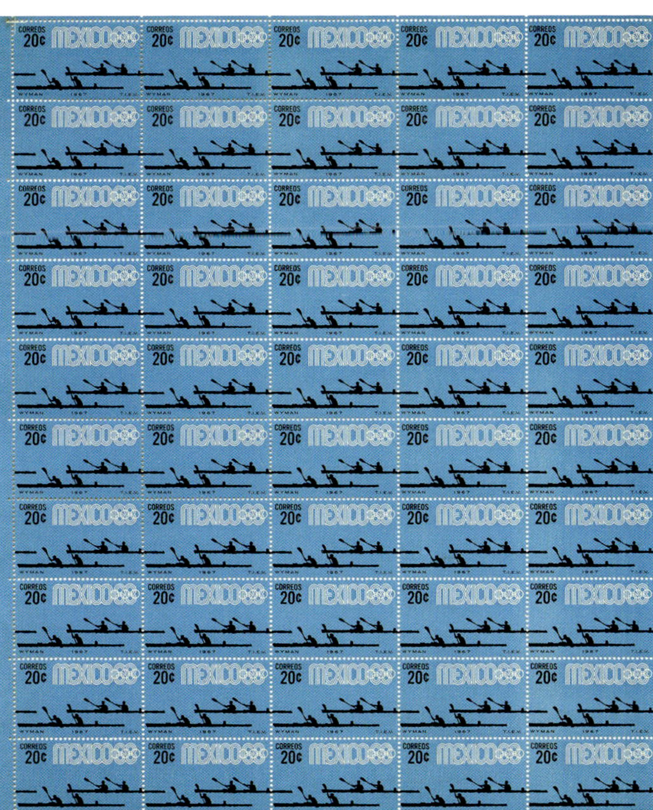

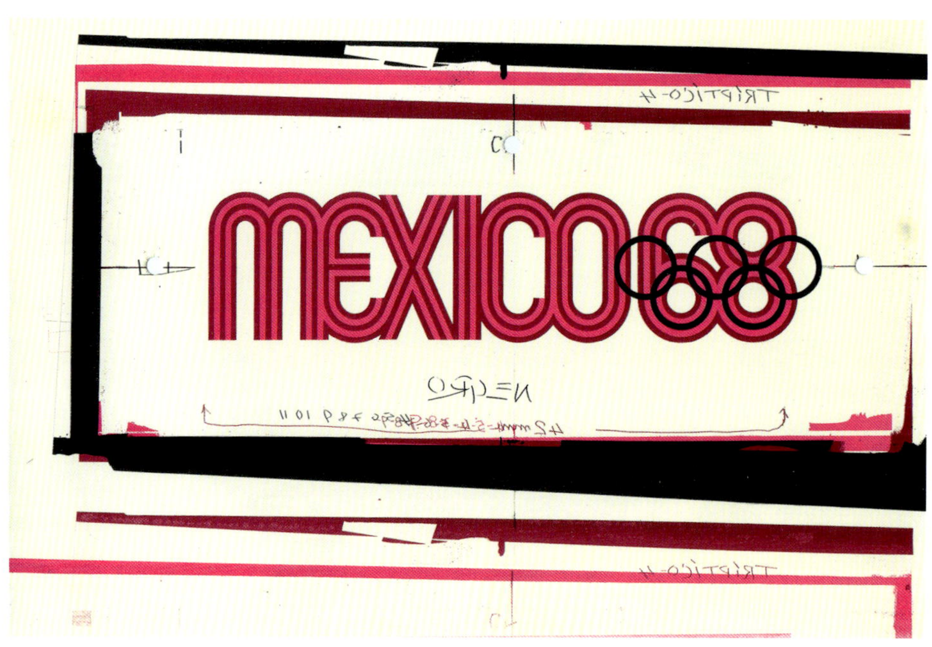

Pl. 56. Lance Wyman, Logotype color proof for Olympic newsletter masthead, 1967. Offset print on paper, 8 x 11.87 inches (20.32 x 30.16 cm). Courtesy of the artist.

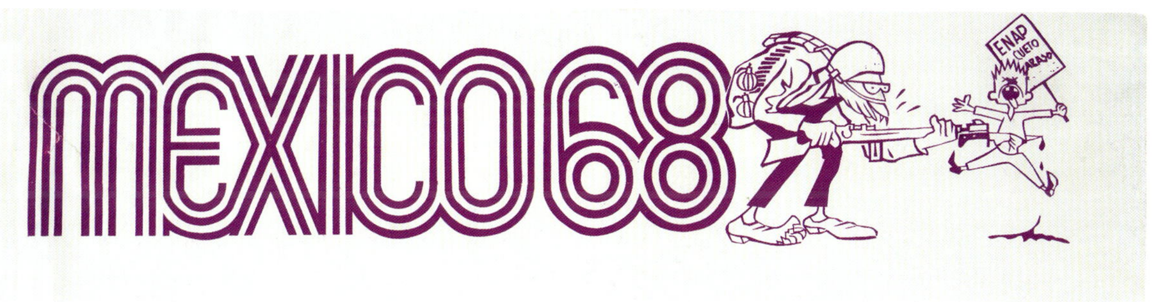

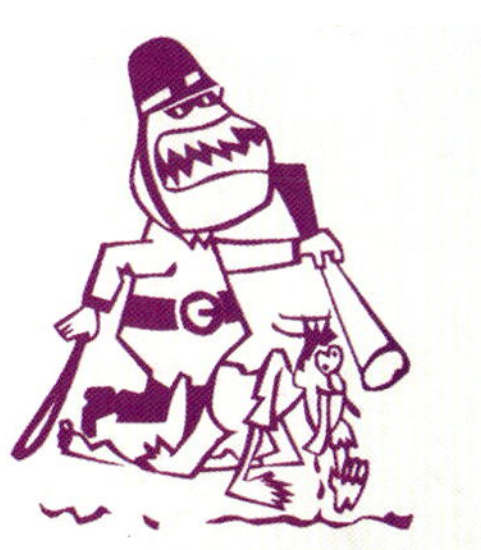

TOP, Pl. 57. Artist unknown, *México '68 (granadero)* (Mexico 68 [Grenadier]) from the series *Gráfica del '68* (Prints of '68), 1968. Linocut on paper, 4.72 x 27.55 inches (12 x 70 cm). **BOTTOM, Pl. 58.** Artist unknown, *México '68 (ENAP, Cueto abajo)* (Mexico '68 [ENAP, Down with Cueto]) from the series *Gráfica del '68* (Prints of '68), 1968. Linocut on paper, 5.11 x 27.55 inches (13 x 70 cm). Collection of the Museo Universitario Arte Contemporáneo (MUAC) de la Universidad Nacional Autónoma de México (UNAM), Mexico City. Donated by Arnulfo Aquino, 2002.

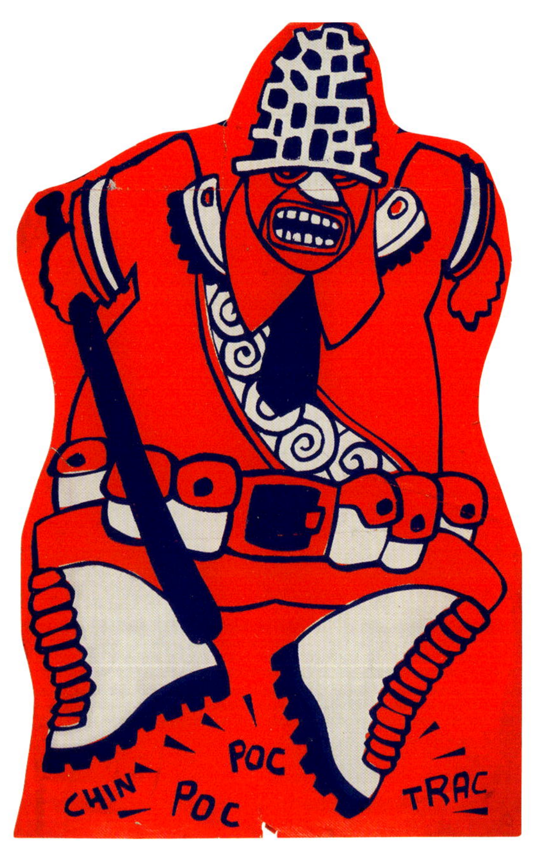

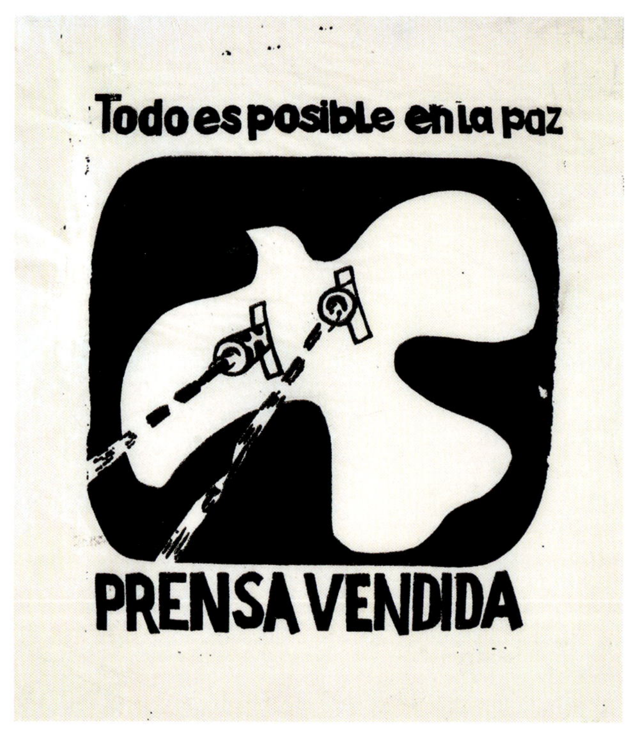

LEFT, Pl. 59. Artist unknown, *Caricatura, granadero a color* (Caricature, Grenadier in Color) from the series *Gráfica del '68* (Prints of '68), 1968. Screenprint on paper, 13.18 x 8.46 inches (33.5 x 21.5 cm). **RIGHT, Pl. 60.** Artist unknown, *Todo es posible en la paz. Prensa vendida* (Everything is Possible in Peace. Sell-Out Press) from the series *Gráfica del '68* (Prints of '68), 1968. Linocut on paper, 12 x 11.22 inches (30.5 x 28.5 cm). Collection of the Museo Universitario Arte Contemporáneo (MUAC) de la Universidad Nacional Autónoma de México (UNAM), Mexico City. Donated by Arnulfo Aquino, 2002.

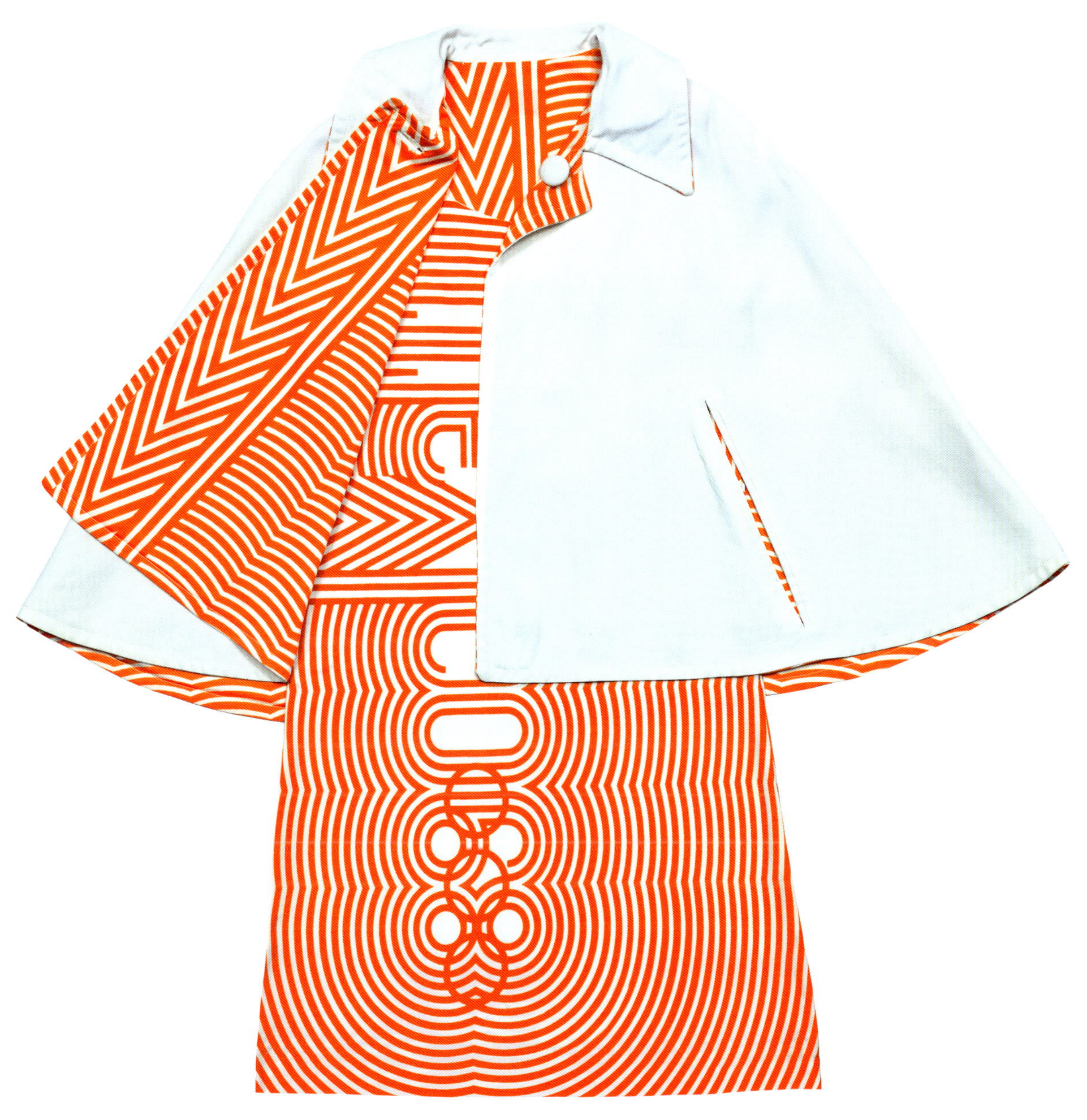

Pl. 61. Lance Wyman and Julia Johnson-Marshall, Hostess dress and cape from the XIX Olympics, 1968. Screenprinted polyester knit (jersey) and cotton twill, 31.25 inches (79.38 cm) center back length, dress; 24.5 inches (62.23 cm) center back length, cape. Collection of the Los Angeles County Museum of Art, California. Purchased with funds provided by the Bernard and Edith Lewin Deaccession Fund. © Lance Wyman. Digital Image © Museum Associates/LACMA.

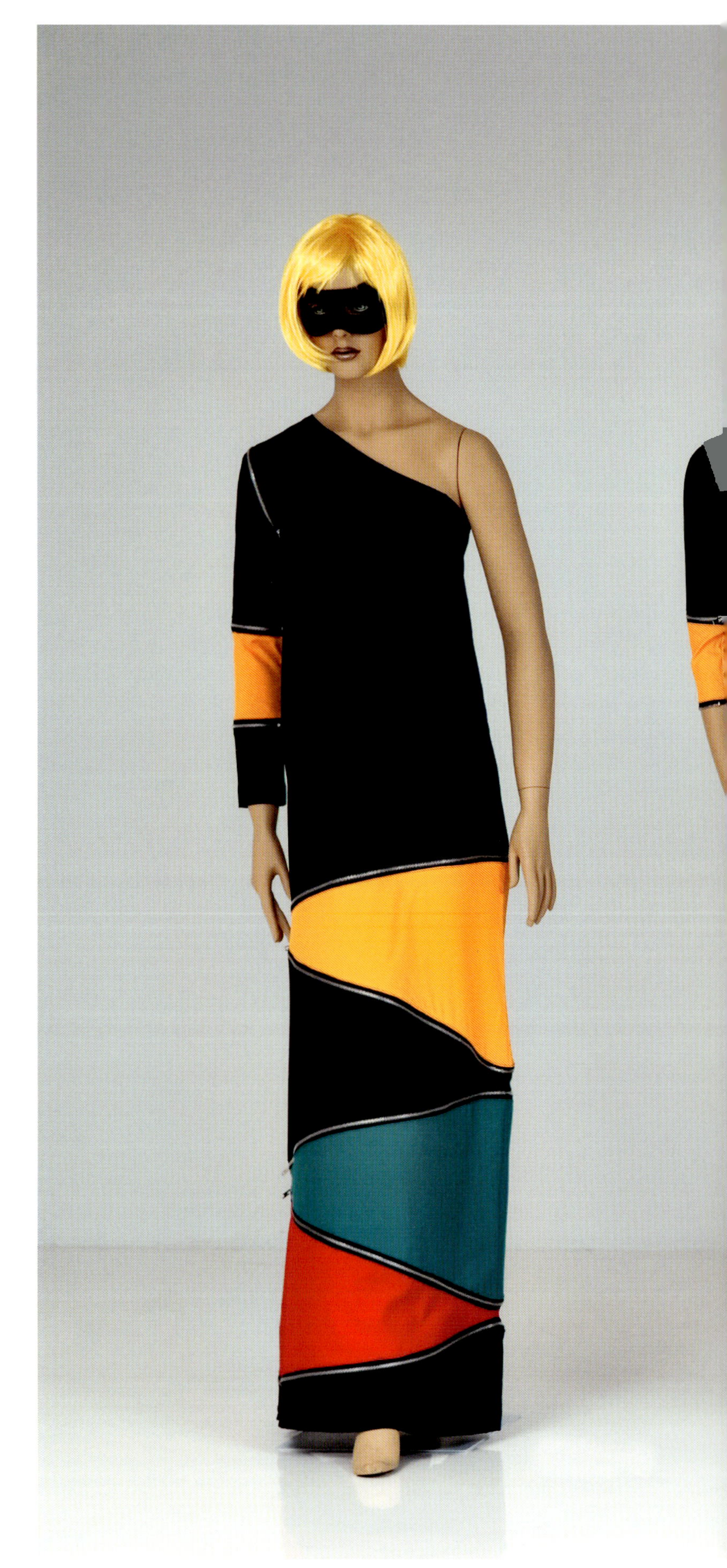

Pl. 62. Nelson Leirner, *Stripencores* (Stripincolors), 1968. Fabric and zippers; left to right, 62 x 26 inches (157 x 65 cm), 50 x 24 inches (128 x 60 cm), 39 x 21.5 inches (100 x 54 cm), and 31.5 x 20.5 inches (80 x 52 cm). Courtesy of the artist and Silvia Cintra + Box 4 Gallery, Rio de Janeiro, Brazil.

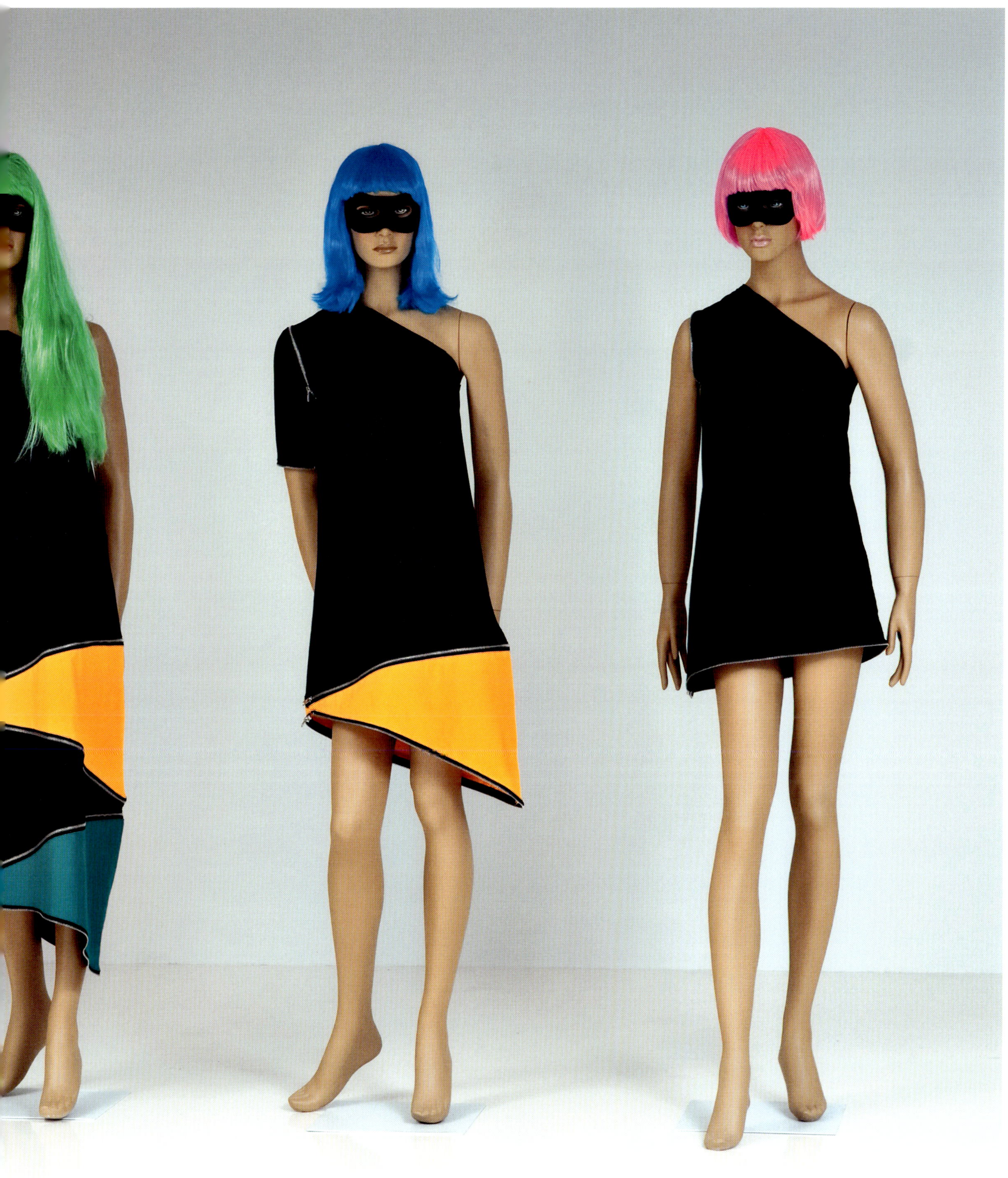

LIBERATING

AMÉRICA

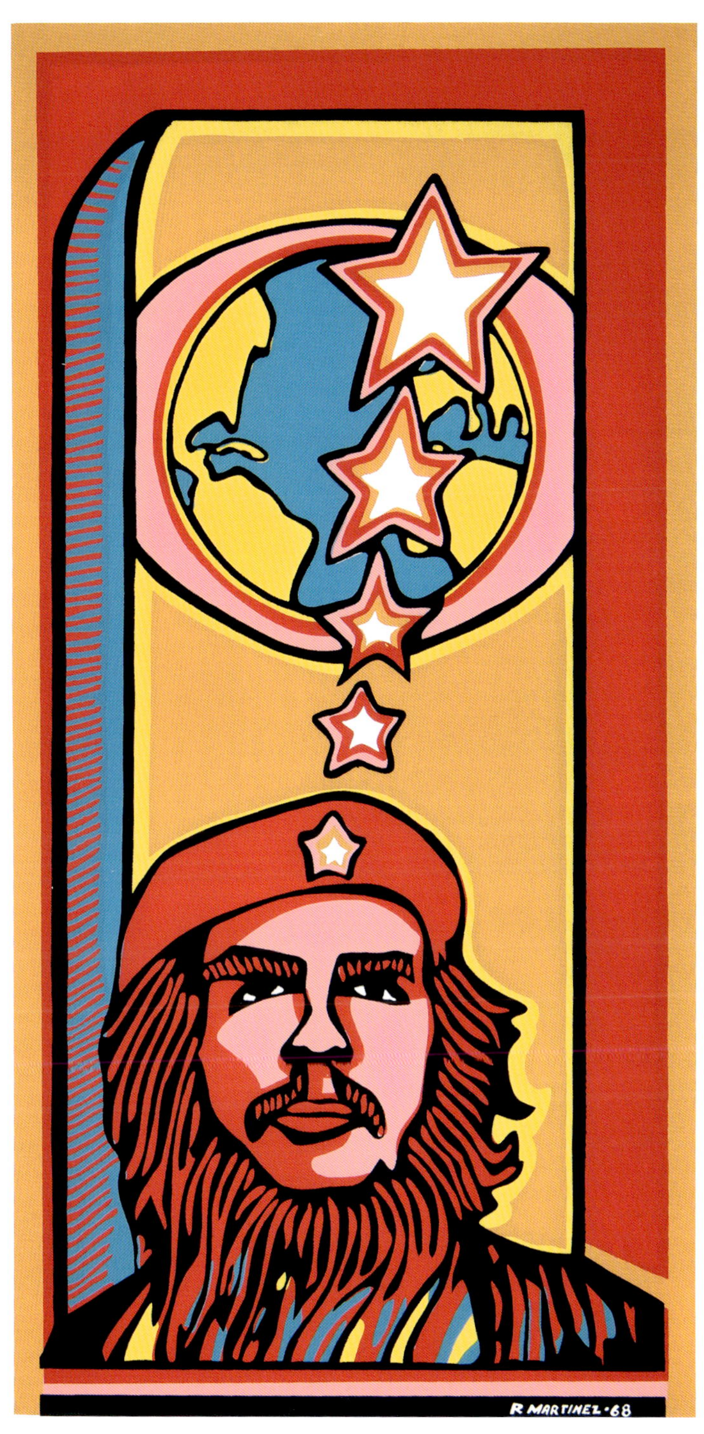

Pl. 63. Raúl Martinez, *Che*, 1968. Screenprint on paper, 29.93 x 20.06 inches (76 x 51 cm). Collection of the Ackland Art Museum, the University of North Carolina at Chapel Hill. Gift of Dr. David L. Craven. © Raúl Martínez Estate, Ciego de Ávila, Cuba. Courtesy of the Raúl Martínez Estate and Corina Matamoros.

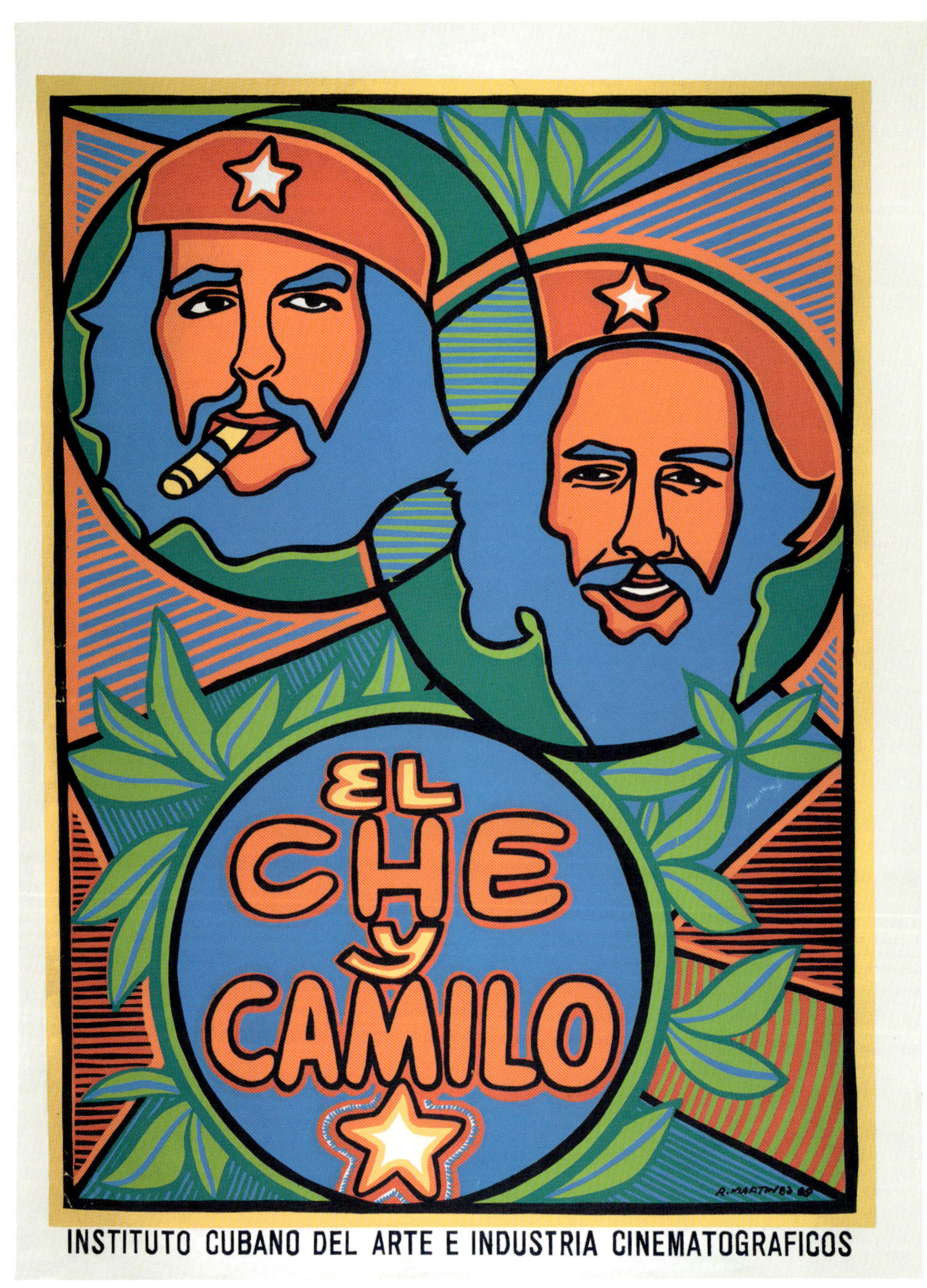

Pl. 64. Raúl Martínez, *El Che y Camilo* (Che [Guevara] and Camilo [Cienfuegos]), 1968. Screenprint on paper, 31 x 23 inches (79 x 58.5 cm). Collection of the David M. Rubenstein Rare Book & Manuscript Library, Duke University, Durham, North Carolina. Bobbye S. Ortiz Papers. © Raúl Martínez Estate, Ciego de Ávila, Cuba. Courtesy of the Raúl Martínez Estate and Corina Matamoros.

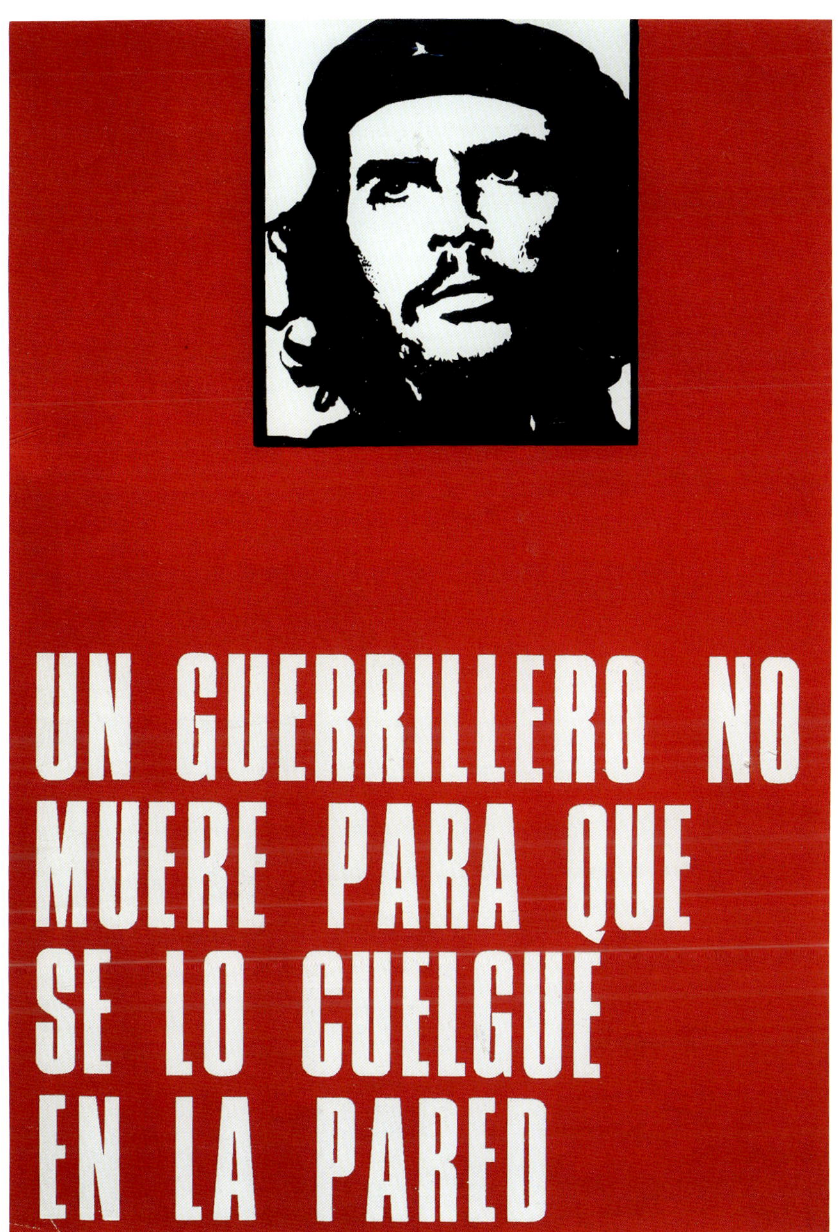

Pl. 65. Roberto Jacoby, *Un guerrillero no muere para que se lo cuelgue en la pared* (A Guerrilla Doesn't Die to Be Hung on a Wall), 1968. Screenprint on paper, 14.96 x 10.43 inches (38 x 26.5 cm). Private collection.

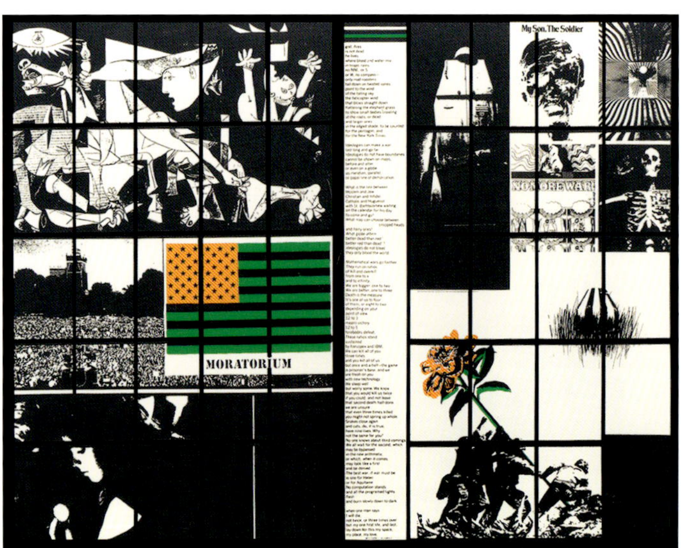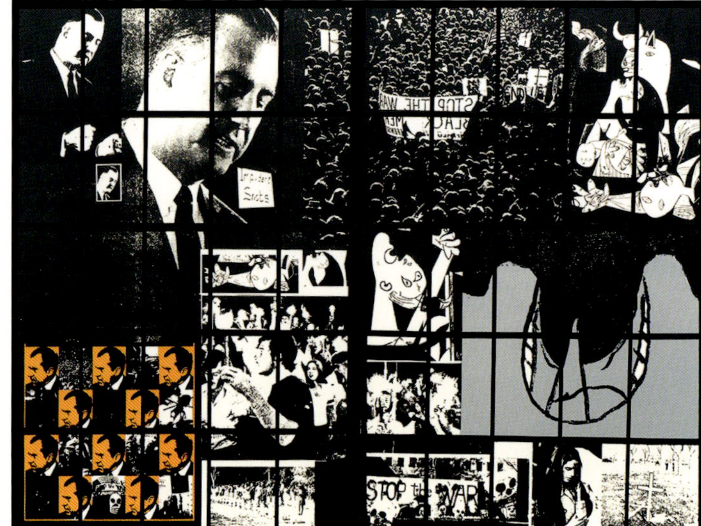

Pl. 66. Carlos Irizarry, *Moratorium*, 1969. Screenprints on paper; edition 20/100, left panel, and 18/100, right panel; 22 x 30 inches (55.9 x 76.2 cm), left panel, and 22.25 x 30 inches (56.5 x 76.2 cm), right panel. Collection of El Museo del Barrio, New York, New York.

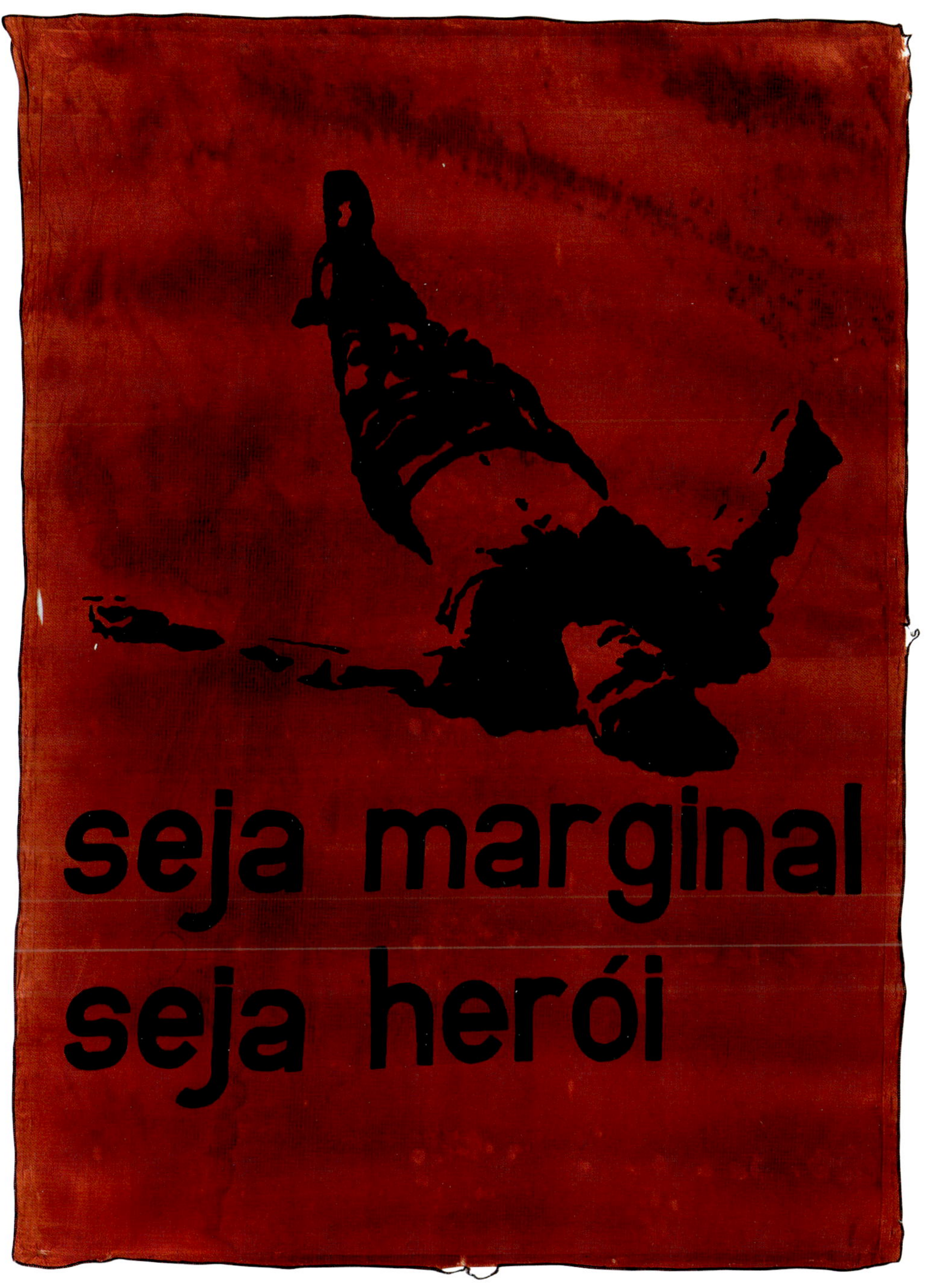

Pl. 67. Hélio Oiticica, *Bandera-poema (Seja marginal, seja herói)* (Flag Poem [Be an Outlaw, Be a Hero]), 1968. Screenprint on fabric, 44 x 32.06 inches (111.76 x 81.44 cm). Private collection. © César and Cláudio Oiticica.

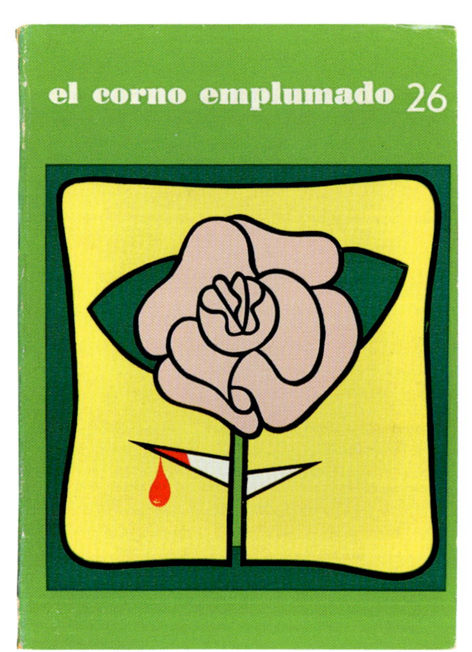

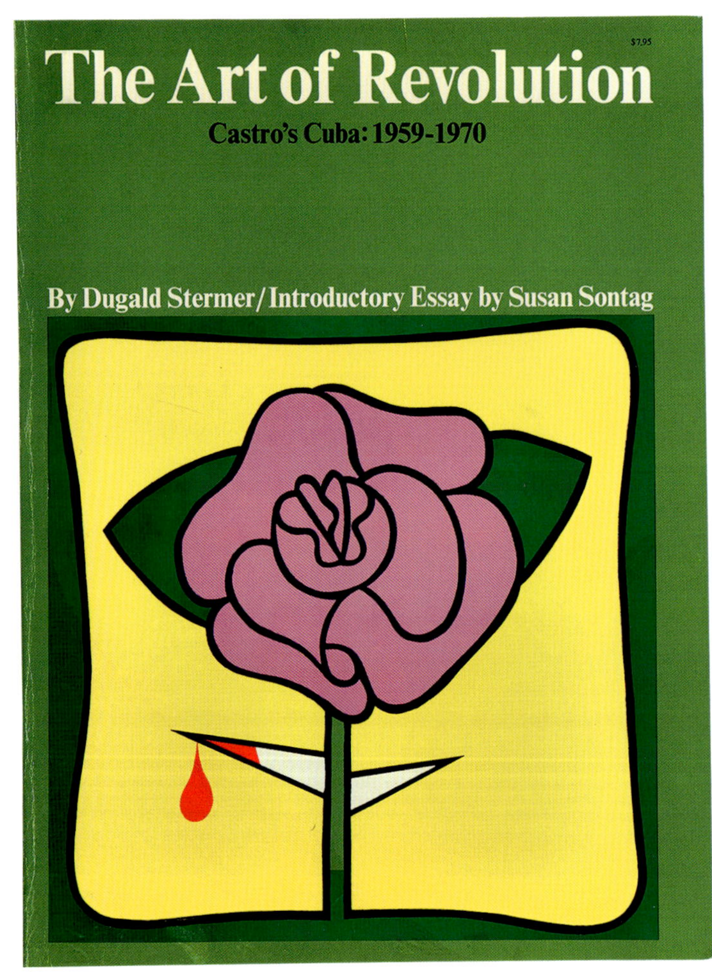

LEFT, Pl. 68. Sergio Mondragón and Margaret Randall (editors), *El Corno Emplumado* (The Plumed Horn), April 1968 (issue no. 26). Printed quarterly journal, 7.68 x 5.5 inches (19.52 x 13.97 cm). Private collection. **RIGHT, Pl. 69.** Dugald Stermer (editor) and McGraw-Hill (publisher), *The Art of Revolution: Castro's Cuba, 1959–1970*, 1970. Paperback book, 17.5 x 13.25 inches (44.45 x 33.65 cm). Collection of Duke University Libraries, Durham, North Carolina. Images courtesy of the Nasher Museum of Art at Duke University, Durham, North Carolina. Photos by Peter Paul Geoffrion.

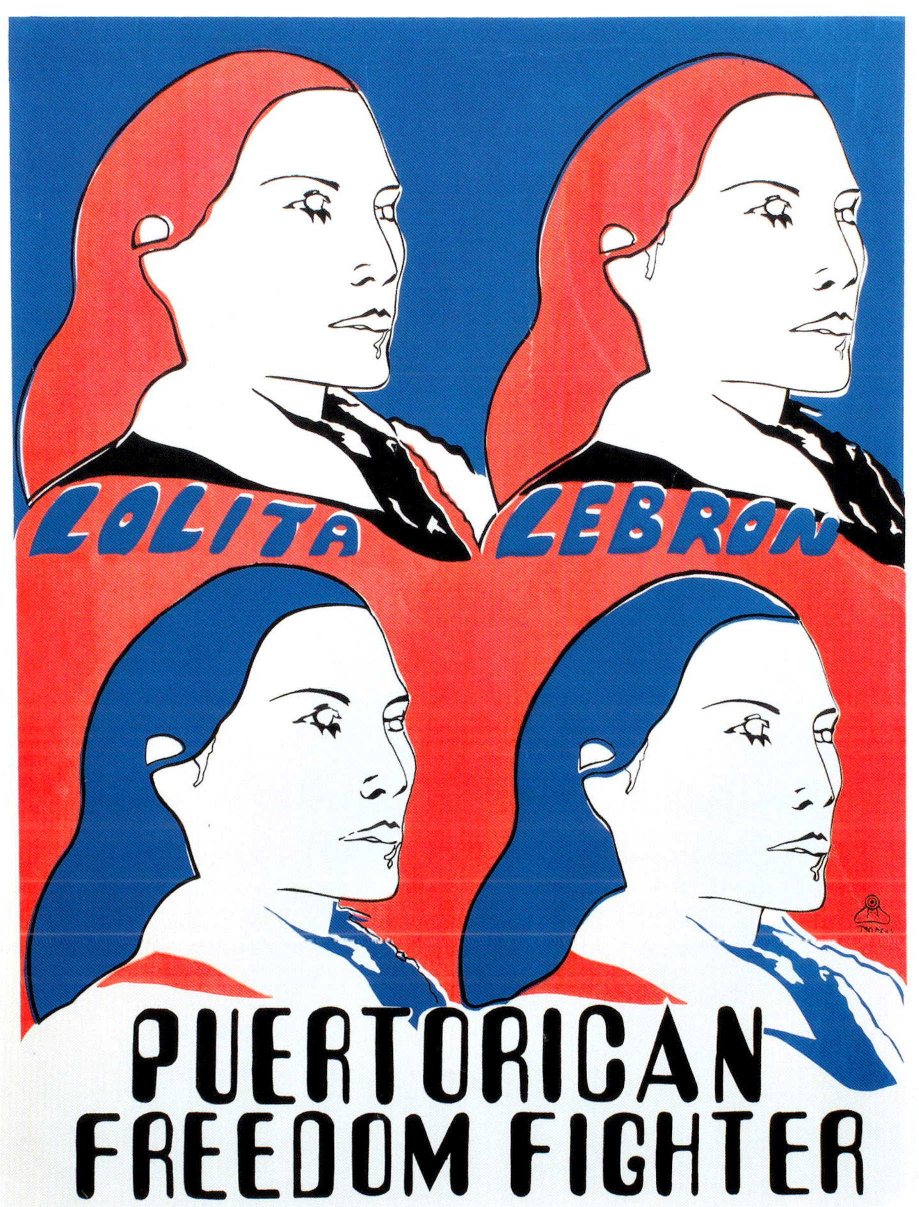

Pl. 70. Marcos Dimas, *Lolita Lebrón, Puerto Rican Freedom Fighter*, 1971. Screenprint on paper, 28.5 x 22.62 inches (72.4 x 57.46 cm). Collection of El Museo del Barrio, New York, New York.

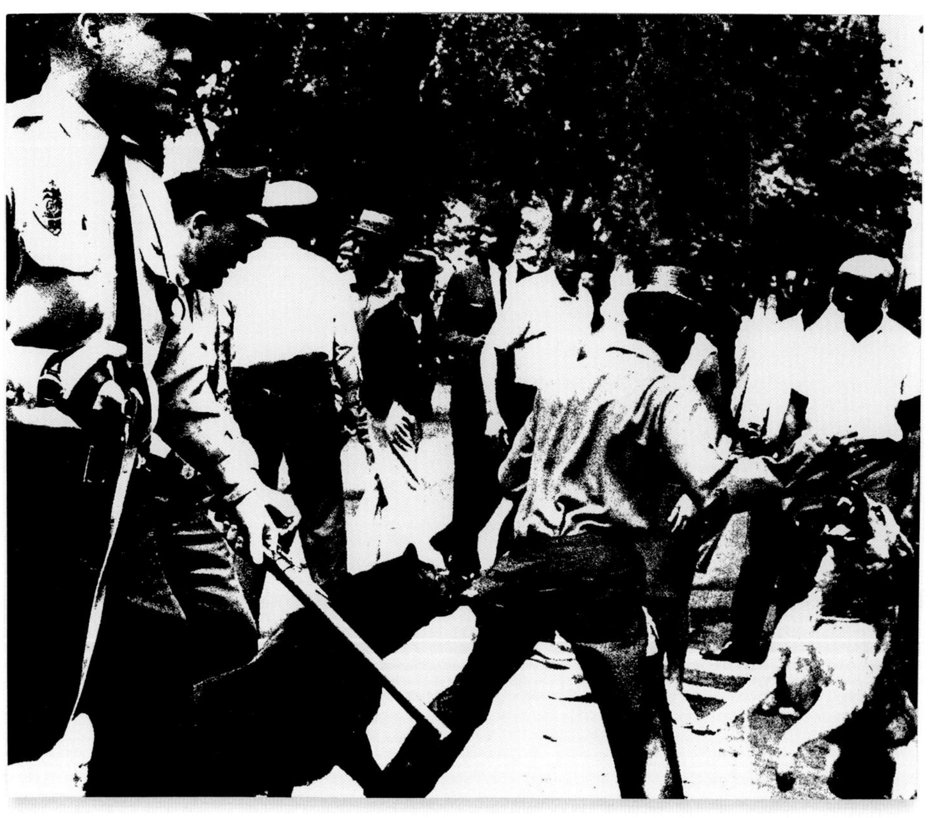

Pl. 71. Andy Warhol, *Birmingham Race Riot* from the portfolio *X+X (Ten Works by Ten Painters)*, 1964. Screenprint on wove paper, 20 x 24 inches (50.8 x 60.96 cm). Collection of the Amon Carter Museum of American Art, Fort Worth, Texas. Gift of Edith G. Halpert. © 2018 The Andy Warhol Foundation for the Visual Arts, Inc. Licensed by Artists Rights Society (ARS), New York, New York.

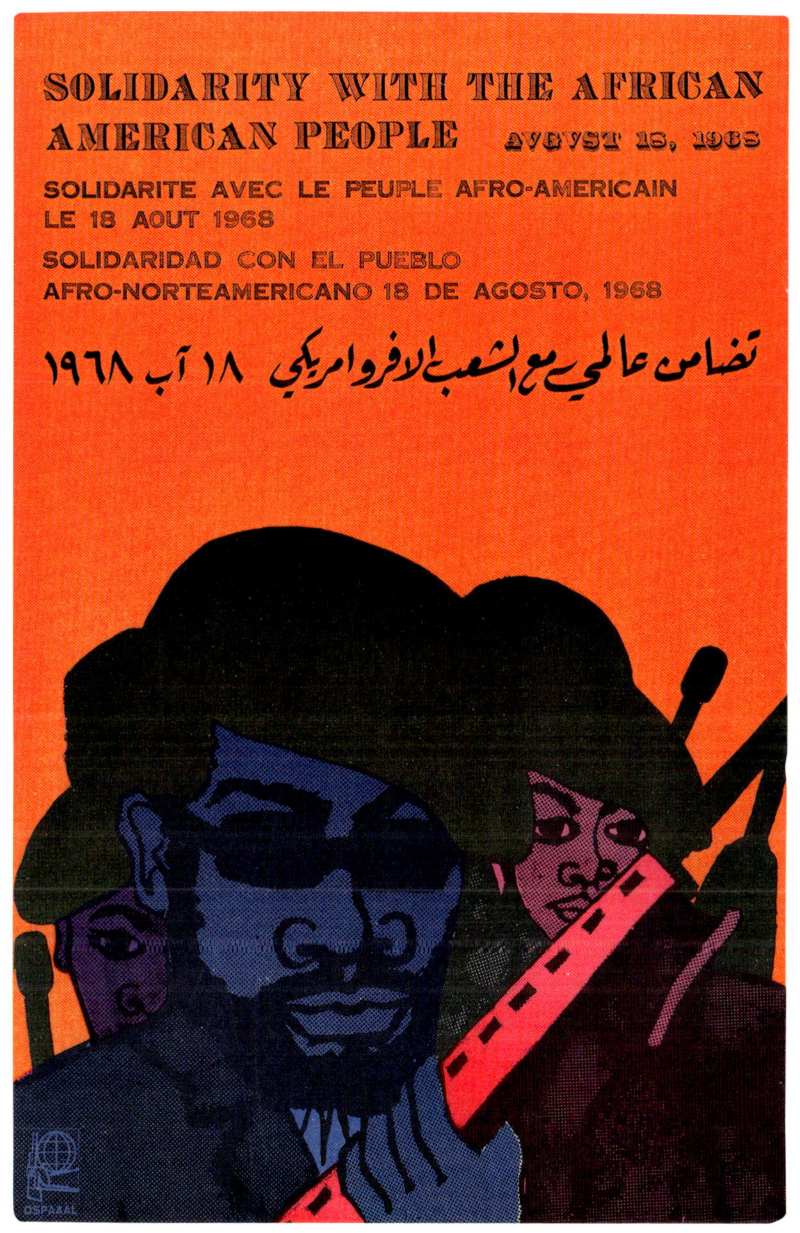

Pl. 72. Lázaro Abreu Padrón (designer), Emory Douglas (artist), and OSPAAAL (publisher), *Solidarity with the African American People*, 1968. Offset lithograph on paper, 21.31 x 14 inches (54.1 x 35.6 cm). Collection of the Prints and Photographs Division, Library of Congress, Washington, DC. Gift of Gary Yanker, 1975–1983. Image courtesy of the Prints & Photographs Division, Library of Congress, Washington, DC.

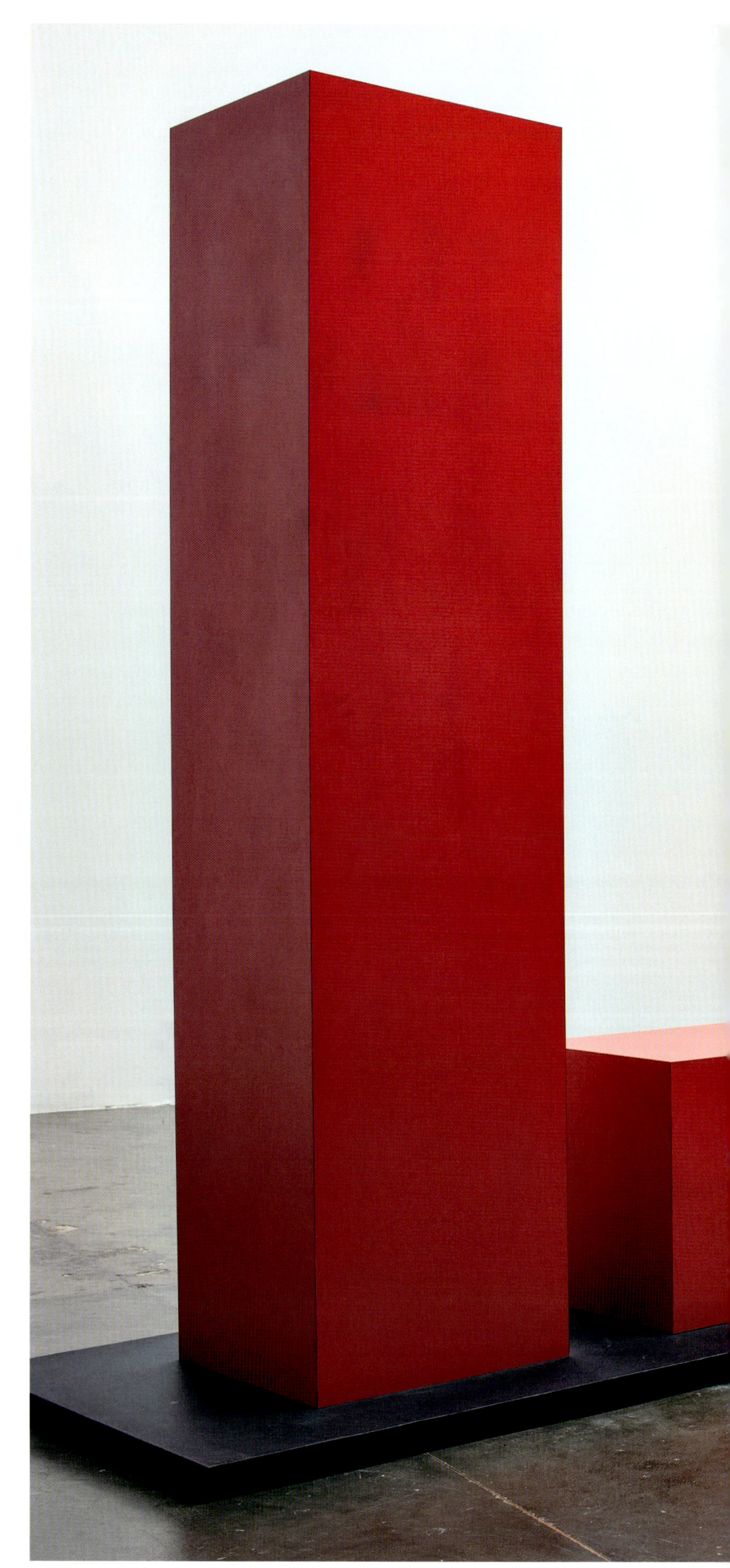

Pl. 73. Rubens Gerchman, *LUTE* (FIGHT) from the series *Cartilha no superlativo* (Primer in the Superlative), 1967 (fabricated 2018). Formica on fiberboard, 68.89 x 220.47 x 27.55 inches (175 x 560 x 70 cm). Courtesy of the Rubens Gerchman Institute. © Rubens Gerchman Institute, Rio de Janeiro, Brazil.

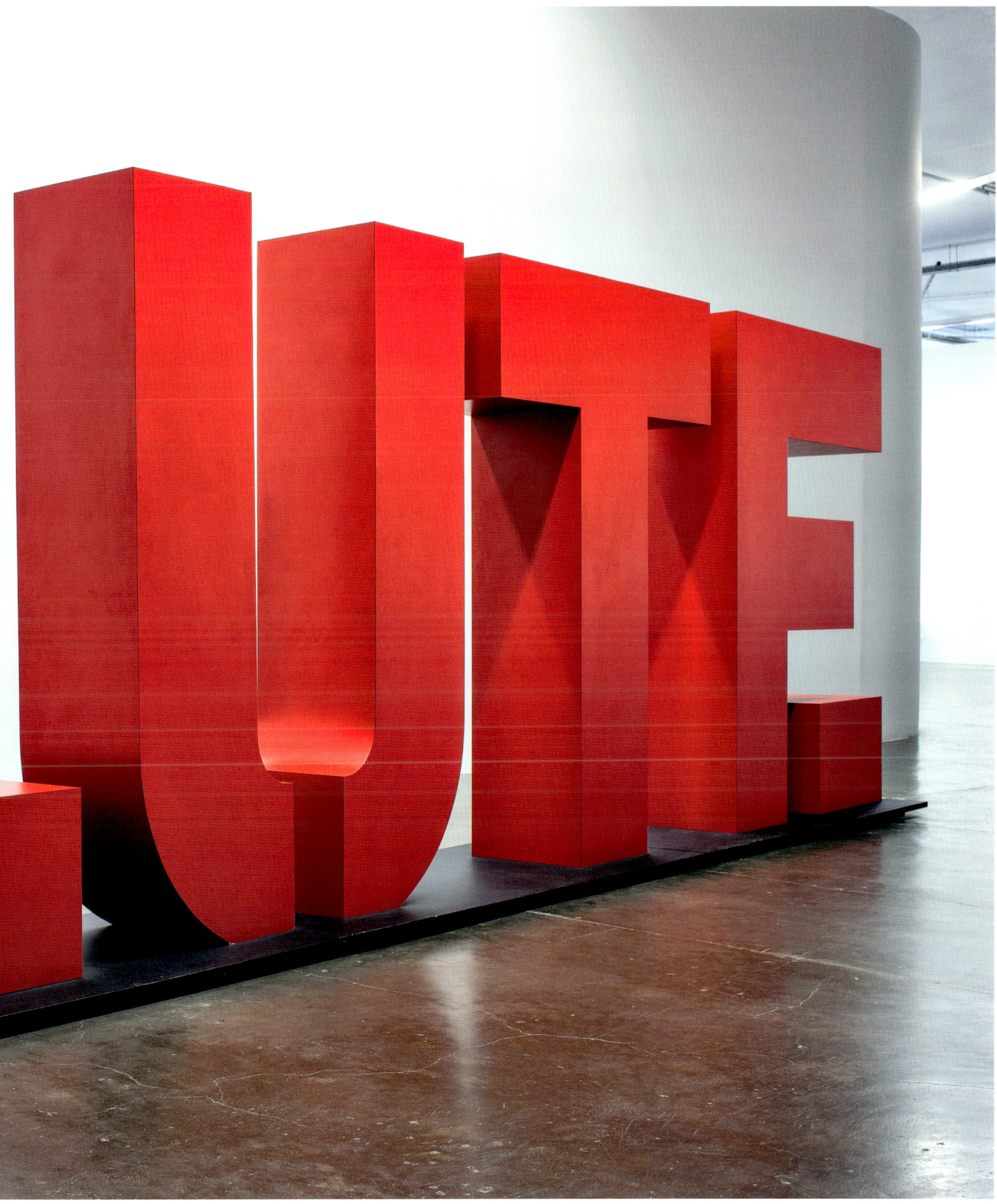

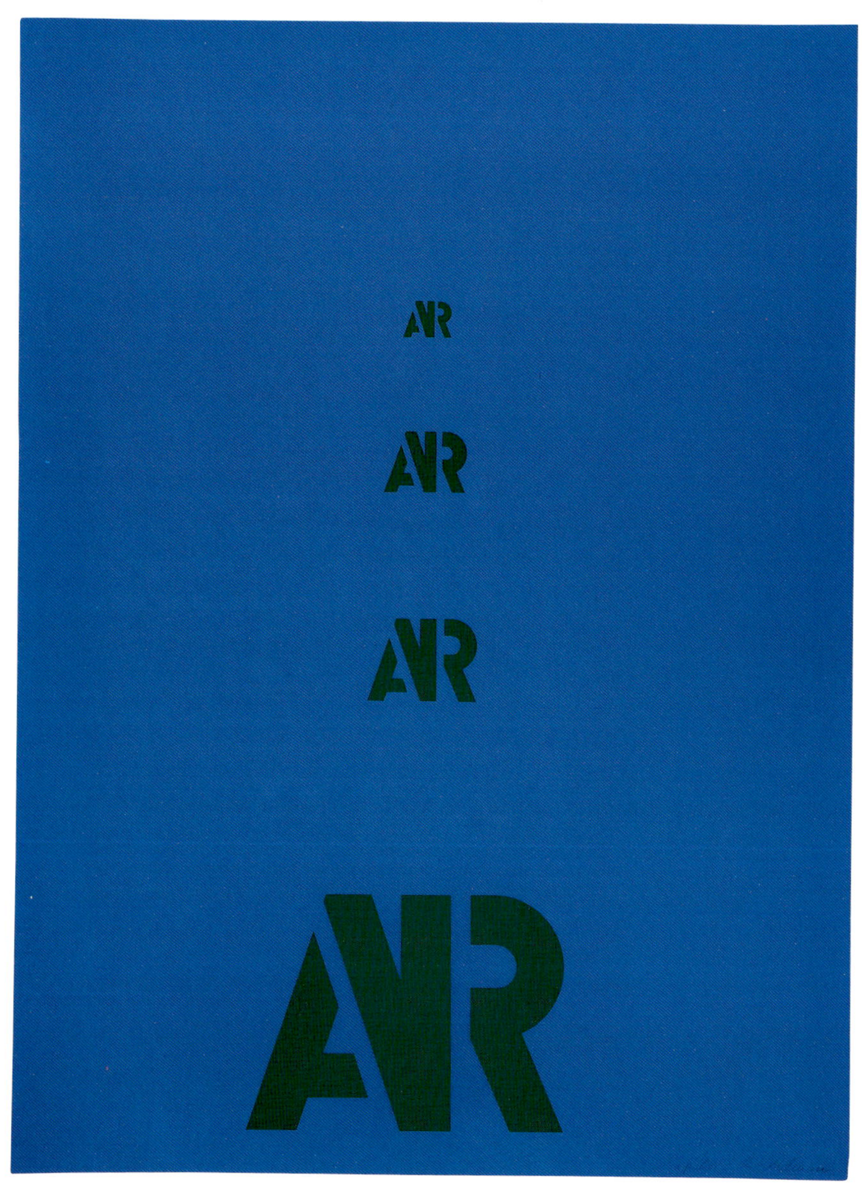

Pl. 74. Rubens Gerchman, *AR* (AIR) from the series *Cartilha no superlativo* (Primer in the Superlative), c. 1972. Screenprint on paper, edition AP/68, 24.37 x 18.25 inches (61.91 x 46.35 cm). Collection of the Weatherspoon Art Museum, the University of North Carolina at Greensboro. Museum purchase with funds from the Benefactors Fund. © Rubens Gerchman Institute, Rio de Janeiro, Brazil.

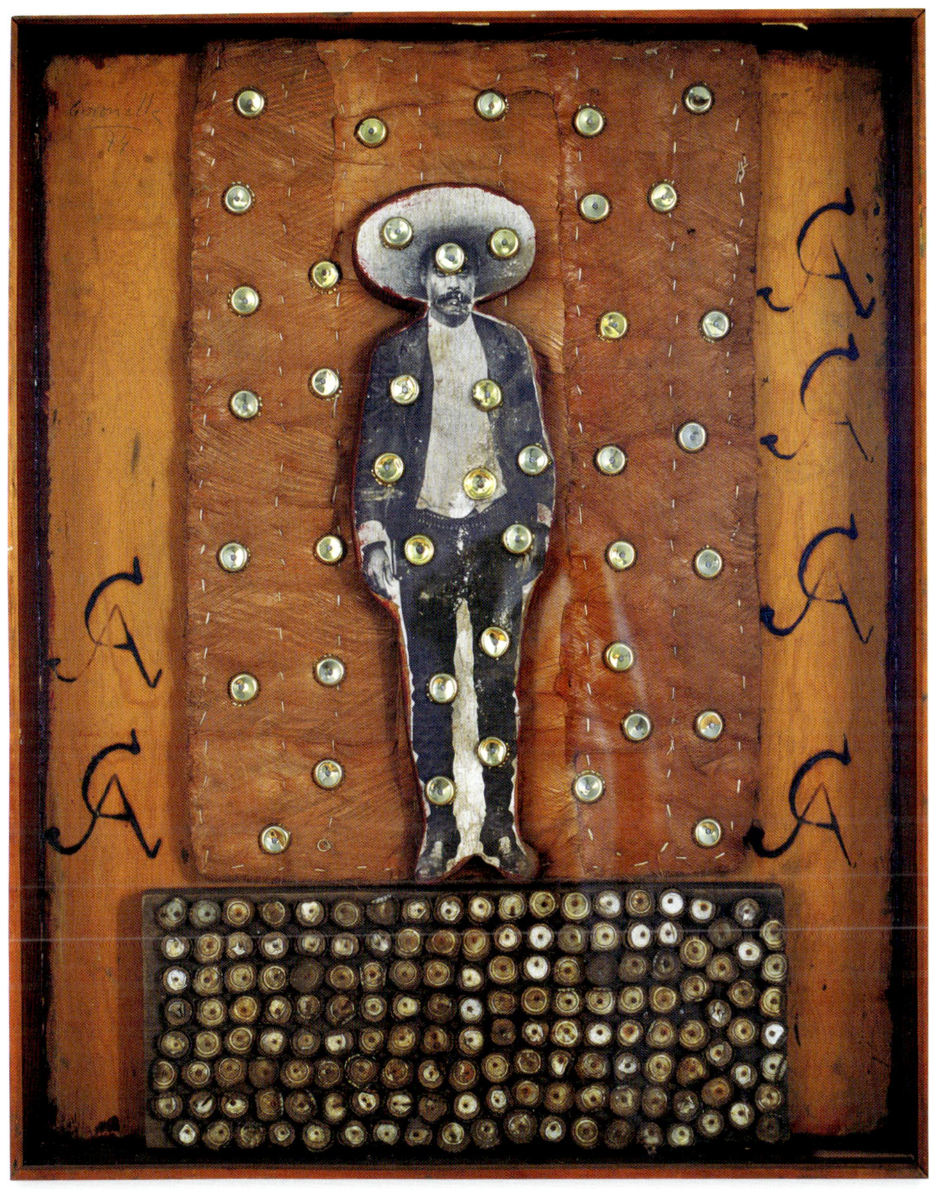

Pl. 75. Alberto Gironella, *Zapata con marca de ganado* (Zapata with Cattle Brand), 1972. Assemblage, 39.37 x 31.49 inches (100 x 80 cm). Collection of Emiliano Gironella Parra. © Fundación Parra Gironella. Photo by Bons de Swan.

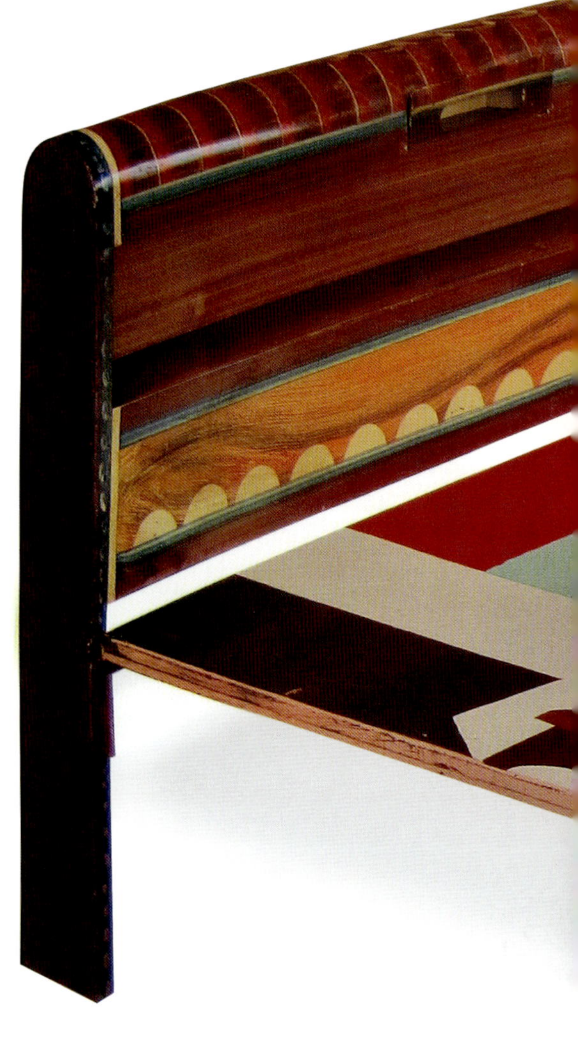

Pl. 76. Beatriz González, *La muerte del justo* (Death of the Just), 1973. Enamel on metal sheet mounted on metal furniture, 47.24 x 70.86 x 35.43 inches (120 x 180 x 90 cm). Collection of Diane and Bruce Halle. © Beatriz González. Courtesy of the artist and Casas Riegner Gallery, Bogotá, Colombia.

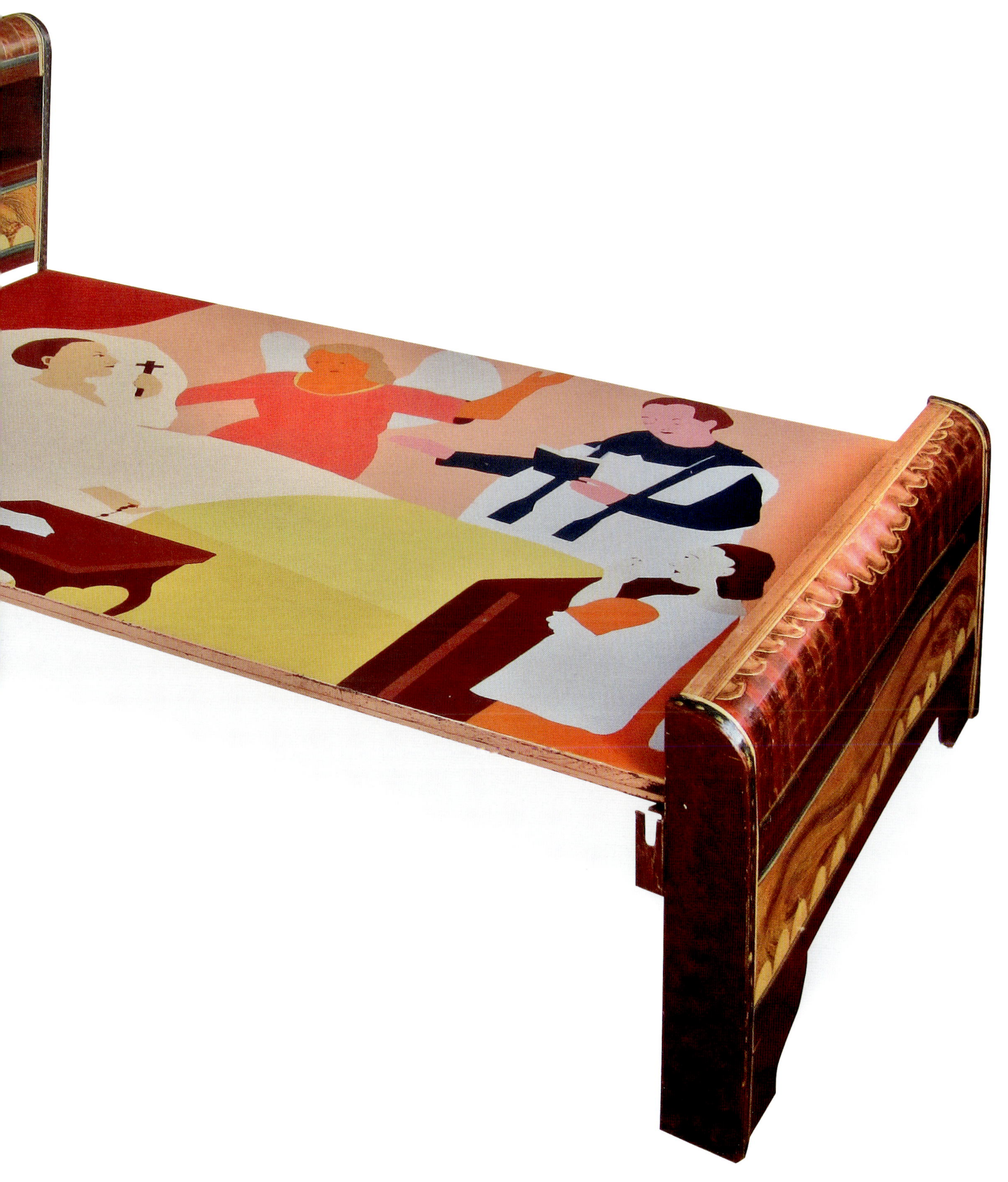

ROBERTO TEJADA

PRINTED MATTERS

From Brazilian woodcuts to Chicano visual culture, a diverse array of artistic tendencies can be found in the printed material created in América during the 1960s. Ambivalent about certain forms of avant-gardism and opposed to US political and cultural supremacy, artists from São Paulo to San Francisco turned to figuration and the anatomy of language as means for redirecting Pop art innovation. The story begins in Mexico City, where in January 1962, the poets Margaret Randall and Sergio Mondragón published the first issue of *El Corno Emplumado* (The Plumed Horn) (1968, plate 68), a bilingual literary-arts magazine.[1] By 1967, Randall and Mondragón, who founded the journal in their mid-twenties, had published twenty issues of *El Corno Emplumado* and the perfect-bound quarterly had gained a reputation as one of the most influential cultural documents of its time.

El Corno Emplumado featured avant-garde poetry and contemporary art, and was international and multimedia in scope. Original and translated poetry appeared together with line drawing illustrations and cultural and political news items. Artworks eventually featured on the cover of each issue. The aim was to capture contemporary thought by highlighting artistic experimentation: critical analyses of US foreign policy joined views of inter-American society and its politics through poetic and artistic expression. This cosmopolitan perspective tracked changes following the Cuban Revolution, and activated a network of artists and institutions in what Harris Feinsod has described as an "expression of geopolitical desire, a vision of an alternate world order."[2]

The first four issues of *El Corno Emplumado* (January–October 1962) coincided with a symposium held at the Museum of Modern Art (MoMA) in New York on the emergent attributes and values of Pop art, featuring curators and critics Peter Selz, Henry Geldzahler, Hilton Kramer, Dore Ashton, Leo Steinberg, and poet Stanley Kunitz. That roundtable, published in the April 1963 issue of *Arts Magazine*, rehearsed a public debate about Pop art's relationship to the avant-garde and mass media: the "pervasive, persistent, and compulsive" qualities of the popular press, urban billboards, and national television.[3] Some participants judged Pop art iconography to be a mere visual transposition at odds with aesthetic transformation; or rather that its style indicated the "new role of subject matter, after almost a century of formalist indoctrination."[4]

The MoMA symposium defined what would become mainstream exchanges about this influential tendency in contemporary US art in light of a mounting national and international scene of political restlessness and social dissent. In Mexico City, *El Corno Emplumado*, too, was at the center of artistic and political debates. As a small-scale enterprise that survived on both private and public patronage, it made sly references to mass media and capitalist consumer culture and made room for Pop art expressions in spaces marginal to such hegemonic institutions as MoMA. The magazine betrayed as well a particular Pop art sensibility that combined anti-imperialist outrage over US warfare in Southeast Asia and involvement in Latin America, as well as frustration with the authority of the US art world in the hemisphere.

El Corno Emplumado's unlikely contribution to an expanded history of Pop in América appears in the idiosyncratic back matter of the first issue (see page 126, figure 4.1), and includes illustrations by Latin American artists containing elements derived from comic strips, commercial window displays, and commercial design. Even as they solicited paid advertising, the editors ironized Madison Avenue aspirations, and poet Anselm Hollo recalled that Randall and Mondragón made ends meet by translating US comic strips into Spanish.[5] The back pages of the first issue included conventional midcentury magazine ads promoting Lenox dinnerware ("*Nuevas . . . Diferentes . . . Resistentes . . .*") and Gerber baby food (see page 126, figure 4.2). In the fourth issue, however, an advertisement for the Mexican chain of supermarkets, Gigante S.A., doubled as a Pop art poem lampooning the totalizing nature of alleged consumer satisfaction. It offered in cascading typography household items: ". . . • quail/• food/• cars/• turtles/• tortillas/• books/• dry cleaning/• instant keys/*in a word* EVERYTHING . . ." (see page 127, figure 4.3).[6] The poker-faced ad copy with its absurdist sequence may have been inspired by an advertisement that German-born Mexican artist Mathias Goeritz had conceived in early December 1961. With eleven other artist ringleaders (and a real-life hen) Goeritz organized an act of anti-art mischief called *Los Hartos* (The Sick and Tired). Goeritz referenced this media phenomenon in his ad in the third issue of *El Corno Emplumado*, which matched self-promoting copy with an attack on the quintessential US commodity fetish: "MATHIAS GOERITZ | is SICK & TIRED but | DRINK Coca-Cola." (see page 127, figure 4.4).[7] Disavowing Dadaism with an earnest quasi-ethical or spiritual call, Goeritz's contribution to Pop revealed deep ambivalence about innovation, which he and his weary crowd of artists were eager to call fraud.[8] *El Corno Emplumado*'s anti-imperialist standpoint was so fused with crafty derisions of capitalist consumer expectations that it made irreverence on a conceptual order compatible with action in the streets—an apt description of Pop in América.[9]

The journal also helped launch the multiform career of Mexican artist Felipe Ehrenberg (1943–2017), whose lifelong commitments blurred the categories of Pop, Fluxus, and Conceptual art. Ehrenberg's work encompassed actions and happenings with the art collective Grupo Proceso Pentágono (Pentagon Process Group); advocacy on behalf of Chicano artists from California during the early 1970s; and book arts, namely Beau Geste Press, which he founded in Devon, England, with fellow artist and spouse Martha Hellion ("Our Press is not a business, it's a way of life.").[10] His contributions to *El Corno Emplumado* included mixed media works on paper for two covers (issues 22 and 23) and a series of drawings (issues 19, 20, 22, and 23) that skewered art historical classicism with a visual economy akin to that of the political cartoon and Dada collage, and with no small dose of Pop audacity and deadpan (see page 127, figure 4.5).

Ehrenberg's interest in cliché led him to deflate the solemnity of such art historical antecedents as Diego Velázquez, El Greco, and Francisco Goya. With this Pop-inspired attitude, Ehrenberg produced a quasi-cartoon self-portrait in issue 19 (see page 127, figure 4.6). The artist's crowned head and mustachioed face appear in a drawing within the drawing as though emanating from an egg-shaped aura—a personhood reduced to the office-stamp number 857334. Below, a body double, whose head and shoulders are concealed by the overlay, sits

with hands pressed together, resting over a legend that makes Pop art reference to commercial patents and intellectual property: "I reserve the right to withhold all premiums or referrals received by my person in addition to any monies thereby obtained through sales."[11]

In Ehrenberg's sardonic self-reflexivity, such quips were not adverse to metaphor, a quality Dore Ashton lamented as crucially missing in Pop aesthetics. To Henry Geldzahler's claim—that Pop art was "instant art history, art history made so aware of itself that it leaps to get ahead of art," therefore "immediately contemporary"—Ehrenberg added an element of ambiguity. The cover image of *El Corno Emplumado* 22 (see page 128, figure 4.7) contained a vertical comic strip or jigsaw puzzle featuring a motif in probable allusion to Raphael's *Portrait of a Young Man with an Apple* (c. 1505). In Ehrenberg's rendition, however, the apple is displaced onto the lower frames in the form of a giant red disk that overwhelms the subject, signaled by an arrow and legend identifying the shape as *alba* (dawn). Above, a caption reads: "With dawn transformed/I closed my/eyes and saw/the moon."[12] The high-minded punchlines of this brand of Old Master conceptual comedy are in keeping with what Ashton identified in Pop art as an "antidote to idealism."[13] Ideological euphoria was rendered uncertain in his cover art for *El Corno Emplumado* 23, whose pages showcased a section of poetry from revolutionary Cuba (see page 129, figure 4.8). Layered onto a saturated background of blue, white, and red, comprising the chevron and stripes of the Cuban flag, are seven male heads in a pyramid formation. The insurgents, with disheveled hair and scruffy beards associated with the revolution, lack facial features, but they appear superimposed onto another shape—by turns yellow, red, white—suggesting a human heart or a deformed dove of peace.[14]

El Corno Emplumado united linotype commercial printing, the graphic arts, small-scale forms of figuration, advertisements with a Pop sensibility, and reports of art and protest in América. In 1968, two years after the above-mentioned contributions to *El Corno Emplumado*, Ehrenberg made a shadow-box work entitled *Arte Conceptual* (Conceptual Art) (see page 16, figure 1.8), where various elements combine to make axiomatic claims about the relationship of popular commercial amusements to sexed perception and estrangement, and about the status of artworks. The composition activates the viewing process with a series of red instructional arrows that point to the back view of a Venus de Milo silhouette. Her inset figure is rendered as though seated on a ledge, looking out the windows of an airplane; this scene, in turn, gives way to another, a low-rise industrial building sited on a desolate landscape. This midway aesthetic—a sideshow stand replete with visual uproar meant to beckon a male-identified drive in the form of the desire for a trophy, the art historical female nude—is further confirmed at the bottom of the frame by a row of identical faces. Patterned in high contrast red and black, the faces are unspecified regarding sex and betray a stunned expression of disbelief or disaffection.

In a similar work, *Caja no. 25495* (Box no. 25495) (1968, plate 77), Ehrenberg applies his familiar iconography of arrows and discs, now grey and black, over sober fields of solid red, yellow, and slate blue. Boxed areas and shelf formations provide surface and depth, and a stenciled figure 25495 refers back to comparable number-stamp motifs in Ehrenberg's earlier self-portrait drawings. There is a playful disjunction

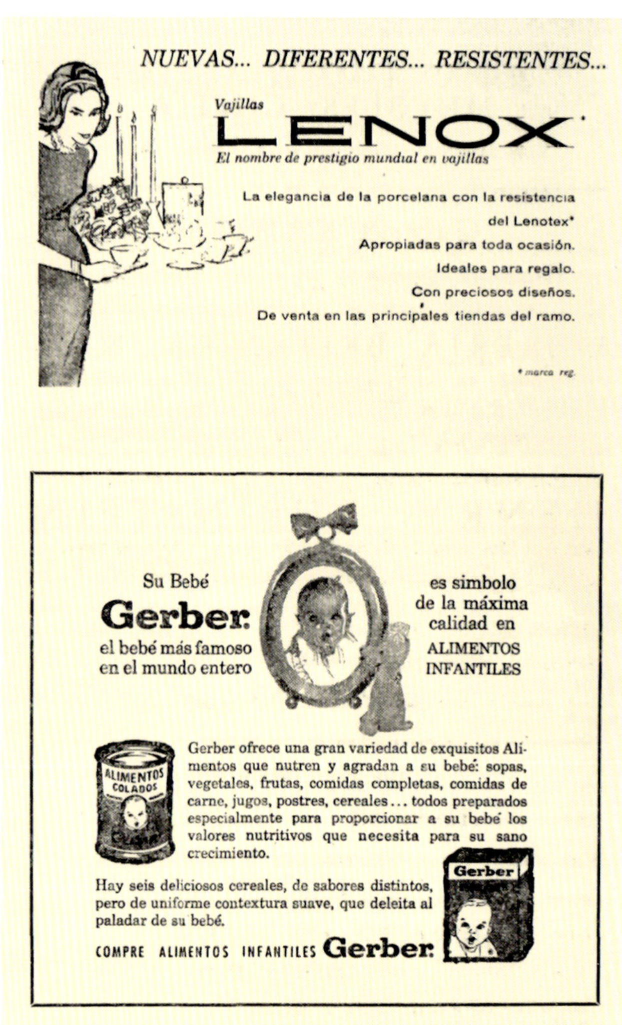

ABOVE (LEFT TO RIGHT), Figs. 4.1, 4.2. Sergio Mondragón, Margaret Randall, and Harvey Wolin (editors), Front cover and back matter, advertisements for Lenox dinnerware and Gerber baby food (*El Corno Emplumado*, issue no. 1, 1962). Bilingual and quarterly printed journal, 7.68 x 5.5 inches (19.52 x 13.97 cm), each. © Margaret Randall. Courtesy of the Open Door Archive, Northwestern University, Evanston, Illinois.

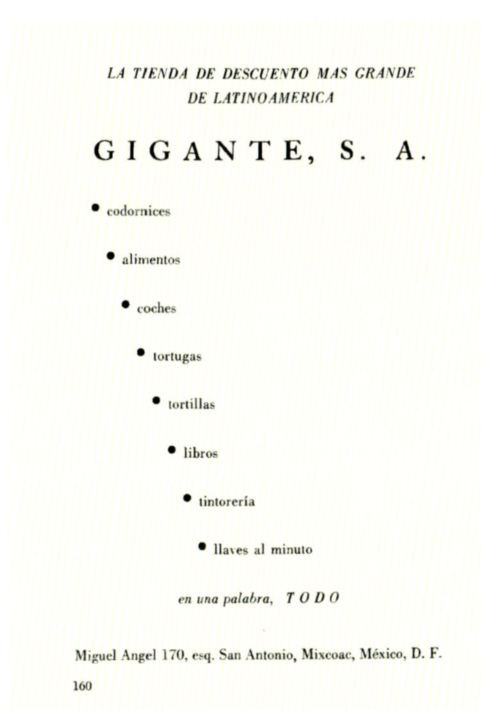

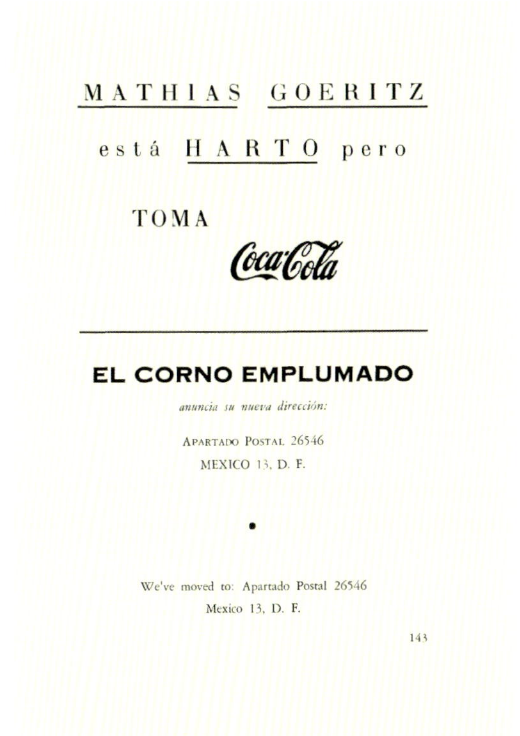

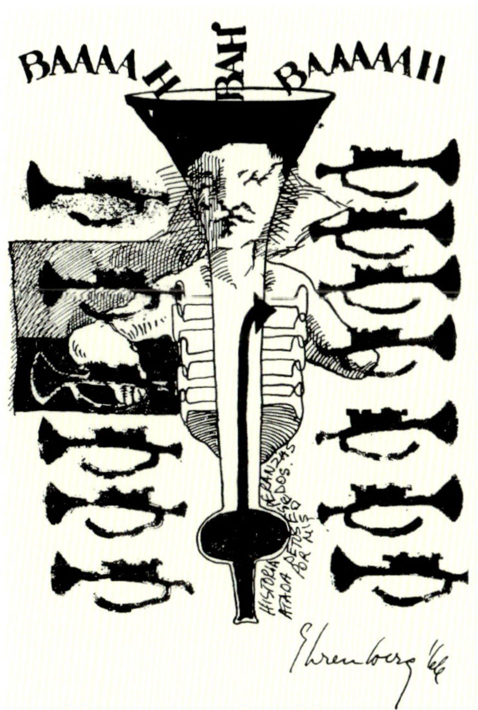

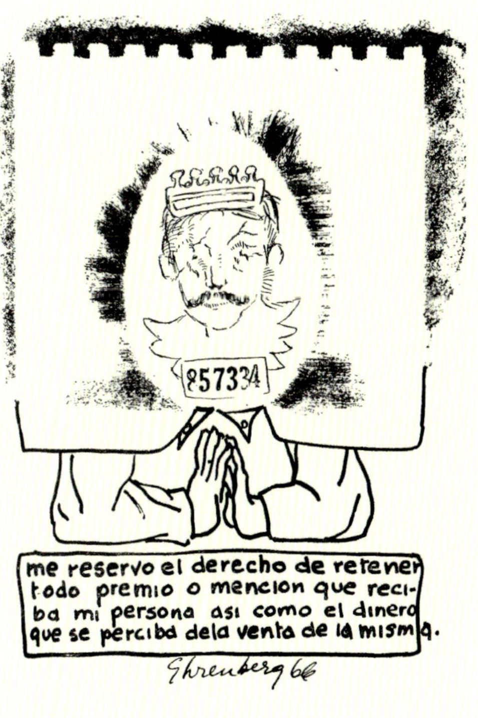

TOP (LEFT TO RIGHT), Fig. 4.3 Sergio Mondragón and Margaret Randall (editors), Back matter, advertisement for Gigante, SA (*El Corno Emplumado*, issue no. 5, 1963). **Fig. 4.4** Sergio Mondragón and Margaret Randall (editors), Back matter, advertisement for Mathias Goeritz (*El Corno Emplumado*, issue no. 3, 1962). **BOTTOM (LEFT TO RIGHT), Figs. 4.5, 4.6.** Sergio Mondragón and Margaret Randall (editors) and Felipe Ehrenberg (artist), *Untitled* (Cover illustration, *El Corno Emplumado*, issue no. 20, 1966) and *Untitled* (Cover illustration, *El Corno Emplumado*, issue no. 19, 1966). Bilingual and quarterly printed journal, 7.68 x 5.5 inches (19.52 x 13.97 cm), each. © Margaret Randall. Courtesy of the Open Door Archive, Northwestern University, Evanston, Illinois.

between the two- and three-dimensionality of this work, as well as between the diagrammatic dancers clad in leotards—placeholders for unfettered expression—and the boxed-in allusions to freight delivery and office management. The box also contained marbles that clattered hidden from view when the box was held or moved by viewers or museum handlers.[15] Ehrenberg suggests that mainstream Pop art's celebration of consumer culture is a contradiction in terms for societies where, as in Mexico, individuals are likely to be subsumed within the jumbles of bureaucracy.

These paintings further underscore the degree to which Ehrenberg's contributions to *El Corno Emplumado* presented earlier art historical periods as perverse forms of symbolic capital and conspicuous consumption—the print-culture version of Geldzahler's Pop as "instant art history." Ehrenberg's drawings and cover artwork coupled figurative expression, Conceptual art discursiveness, and popular media to confirm the primacy of printed matter. With a quarterly circulation of 3,000, *El Corno Emplumado*—a craft object by mass-produced

standards, but ambitious in international scope—was the ideal support for less monumental forms of experimentation in Latin America.

There emerged a kind of print culture Pop at the margins of the style's hegemonic domains and the lower rungs of its media hierarchies. In Brazil, Antônio Henrique Amaral's portfolio *O meu e o seu: impressões de nosso tempo* (Mine and Yours: Impressions of Our Time) (1967, plates 86–93) employed elements derived from popular printmaking and the information media, housed in a tightly fitted metal folder or cover encasing the work as though to suggest a classified institutional dossier.[16] Seven woodcut prints comprise a sequence of bold compositions critical of contemporary Brazilian society, mass-media distractions, and the violent political authoritarianism of the military dictatorship. Referencing the broadside tradition known as *literatura de cordel* (string literature), but with subject matter that speaks to sexual depravity and violence, Amaral's portfolio offers a grotesque comic-strip iconography at odds with the US monopoly on popular cultural forms.

Solid shades of aqua blue and pink, for example, lend volume to an axis that serves as the central shape of *o idolatrado* (The Idolized) (1967, plate 88).[17] A microphone monument, crowned by a quartet of hands in the act of providing applause ("*CLAC! CLAC!*"), is seen grafted onto a pair of feet firmly planted on a column sustained by an audience of onlookers. The crowd below appears overwhelmed by the elongated faces that flank the sides of the print, each face in possession of three mouths; each mouth in turn with protruding teeth and tongue. Telescoping cone-shaped megaphone speakers blare strains of a rock-n-roll anthem whose lyrics "*YÊ, YÊ, YÊ*" ("YEAH, YEAH, YEAH") are at once shorthand for the idolatry of a specific cultural import and a stand-in for stadium forms of authority.

In *Personagem contemporâneo* (Contemporary Character) (1967, plate 90), Amaral employed folklore and experimental figurative distortions that display what Frederico Morais identified as Pop art's coterminous democratization of subject matter and of resources and media.[18] In the print, mouth motifs shape the cranium of a figure surrounded by disembodied hands and feet. The female subject waves banners for *paz* (peace) and *prosperidade* (prosperity), below which the place names Korea and Vietnam are supported by feet protruding from the lower frame. The figure's visible gastric tract contains the dates 1914 and 1939, the inaugural dates of World War I and World War II, leading to the final function of her digestive system: a question mark in the form of feces meant to interrogate the related modes of consumption and waste.

Premier Brazilian art critic Mário Pedrosa associated a disaffection with US models of mass culture not only as a return of the repressed in the form of folk vernacular, but also as the most profound upheaval of the disenfranchised. In "Gewgaws and Pop Art," Pedrosa casts doubt on Roy Lichtenstein's contributions to contemporary art in Brazil, instead highlighting "an obscure 'cultural subset' emerg[ing] explosively from the urban environment of those artists who call into question the cultural whole from which—with fascinating invention—comes the North American Pop artist and exercises his activities. These are the black uprisings."[19] Pedrosa identified specific social bodies within the everyday particulars that US Pop art had aspired to present.

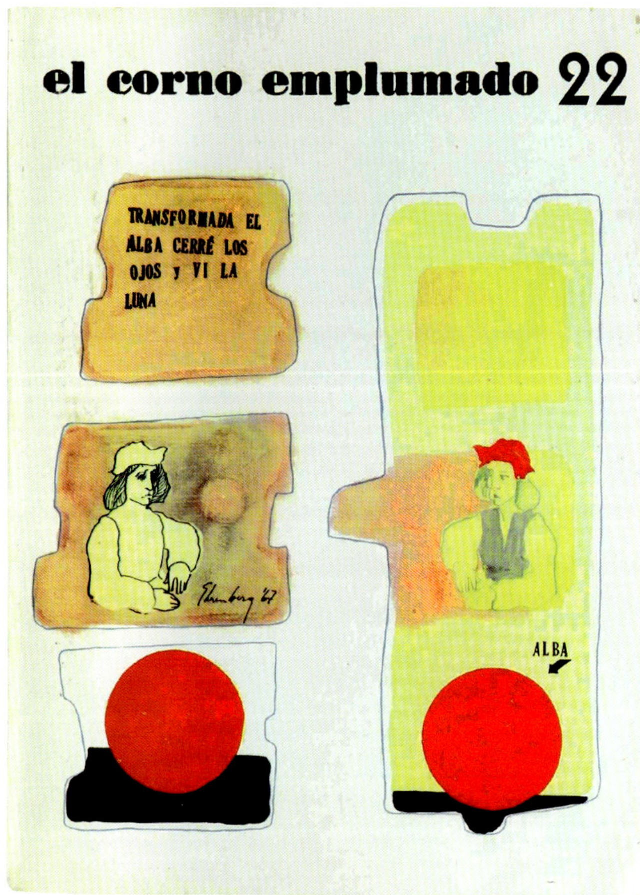

Fig. 4.7. Sergio Mondragón and Margaret Randall (editors) and Felipe Ehrenberg (artist), Front cover (*El Corno Emplumado*, issue no. 22, 1967). Bilingual and quarterly printed journal, 7.68 x 5.5 inches (19.52 x 13.97 cm). Courtesy of Reina María de Lourdes Hernández Fuentes and the Open Door Archive, Northwestern University, Evanston, Illinois. © Margaret Randall.

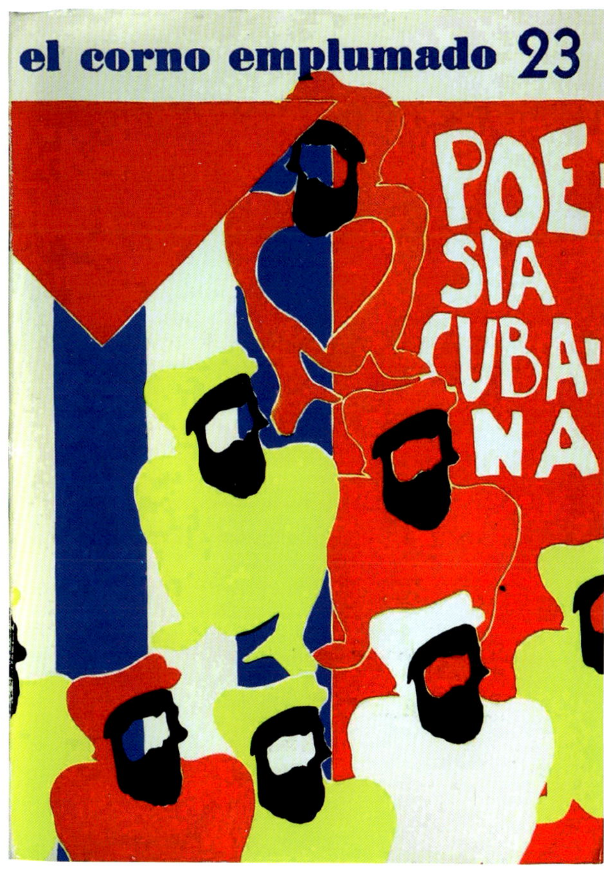

Fig. 4.8. Sergio Mondragón and Margaret Randall (editors) and Felipe Ehrenberg (artist), Front cover (*El Corno Emplumado*, issue no. 23, 1967). Bilingual and quarterly printed journal, 7.68 x 5.5 inches (19.52 x 13.97 cm). © Margaret Randall. Courtesy of Reina María de Lourdes Hernández Fuentes and the Open Door Archive, Northwestern University, Evanston, Illinois.

sensual and social life that US society had repressed as "cultural subsets." These socially and racially disenfranchised subjects organized politically to emerge "explosively from the urban environment." In an early collagraph, *Black Man and Flag* (1967, plate 6), red and black values compose a vertically suspended American flag. Added to the black and white stripes, García substituted the star field with a red-hued effigy, the bust of an unspecified civil rights or black liberation leader. The print intensified the imperative for the inclusion of blackness in the national imagination symbolically promised by the red, white, and blue. García's flag-portrait diagnosed attitudes that journalist Ruben Salazar would describe in his series of 1969–1970 articles for the *Los Angeles Times* on black and brown relations in California. García's image of a black man on the national flag speaks of a moment prior to what Salazar identified as "growing distrust" on the part of young Chicanos "to form a new coalition . . . this time with the blacks . . . until they, the Chicanos, find their own identity in their own way."[22] García's work preempts and refutes this idea. Consistent with Salazar in another article, García understood the partial view of ethno-nationalist representation and that, insomuch as Anglos had failed in coalition efforts, a "black and brown rift [could] only help those interested in slowing down the civil rights struggle."[23]

An internationalist in the turbulent period of a "worldwide Anti-Imperialist upsurge," Rupert García was reluctant to consider Chicano identity apart from either allied social struggles or the broadest cultural archive of modernism, and he imbued his poster art at once with cosmopolitan and anti-colonial perspectives.[24] In *Decay Dance* (1969, plate 20), solid areas of red, blue, and pink compose the background, buckled wide-brim hat, and the partial but unequivocal face of the Quaker Oats logo. Below, in silver ink laid over yellow paper, floats a ghostly image of the Mona Lisa, so distorted and in high contrast as to resemble the face of Marcel Duchamp's 1919 readymade *L.H.O.O.Q.* García, an avid student of Mexican history, philosophy, and culture, was also an early conversant in the Surrealist canon, the existentialism of Jean-Paul Sartre, the poetry of Octavio Paz, and the photography of Manuel Álvarez Bravo. His practice was the result of a Surrealist analogy that combined two unlikely constituents: the art ontologies laid bare by Duchamp and the "social-economic-racial dimension of protest" exemplified in the writings of Martin Luther King, Jr. The result was what García described as a "socio-aesthetic machine" that inverted the visual grammar of Pop art to contest art-historical relations in which whiteness monopolized the category of universal artist "dealing with the conditions of humanity in a post-industrialized context."[25]

Axiomatic homologies or disjunctions between visual signs and applied language informed the practice of other Chicano artists. Some, like Melesio Casas and Judith F. Baca, increased the critical level of Pop art meanings derived from mass culture commodities, fashion magazines, comic strips, or commercial design by adding cognitive dissonance of the kind generally associated with Conceptual art. In *Humanscape 62* (1970, plate 85), Casas gleefully took aim at the blatant racism in the derogatory term for Mexican-descended peoples, at the specific social capital of the Girl Scouts of America, and at the Frito-Lay company mascot known as the "Frito Bandito" depicting a Mexican bandit stereotype. He countered the Pop art photorealism of advertising and commercial packaging with folk figuration, even as

El Movimiento (the Chicano Movement) emerged concurrent to these uprisings, first within the United Farm Workers struggle led by César Chávez and Dolores Huerta in California, then in the urban barrios of the Southwest. The poet Jayne Cortez wrote of the August 1965 uprisings in Watts: "Black people were tired of the contradictions, the inequalities, the mounting violations, police brutality, unemployment, lack of opportunity, lack of respect, and the amount of sacrifices made as a consequence of white domination."[20] El Movimiento radicalized Mexican-American life and culture with startling visual styles and reached critical mass at the anti-war rally of the Chicano Moratorium in Los Angeles on August 29, 1970. For many Chicano artists of the late 1960s and early 1970s, there were no arbitrary separations between "everyday life, art, politics, history," and direct action.[21]

At the foreground of this art and activism was Rupert García, whose poster art decried anti-black racism, the war in Vietnam, and US collusion in the social terrors of Latin America. Concurrent with Amaral and Ehrenberg, Bay Area-based García addressed the questions of folkways, sexuality, and race that Mário Pedrosa had in mind when he identified the failure of mainstream Pop artists to address the human he suggested cross-cultural links between pre-Conquest iconography (Quetzalcoatl, the green "plumed serpent," the skull of Tezcatlipoca) and native peoples of the American Southwest and Mexico. By contrast, Judith Baca's mixed-media triptych, *Las tres Marías* (The Three Marías) (1976, plate 1), with its back-embossed upholstered panels, visually transforms the viewer's self-reflection in the front central mirror, therein gendered and racialized according to the terms composing the side panels, two finely rendered naturalist depictions of Chicana expression on paper. Viewer features reflected in the mirror—regardless of sex, age, or ethnicity—are equated and contrasted, on the left, with the figure of a butch Chicana homegirl, and, on the right, with the 1940s *huisa* (*güisa* or *weesa*), the high femme model of Mexican-American beauty.

Returning to the visual references in *Decay Dance*, Rupert García subverts the Quaker Oats logo's allusions to paternalism and wholesomeness with the quintessential art historical representation of femininity in the *Mona Lisa*. By mongrelizing these two Euro-ethnic icons and enacting a wordplay in the title, García satirizes gendered and racialized Cold War idealizations about the US household, which are mirrored in the market forces that drive art history. With great economy of design, he charges against a strand of modernism that had failed to recognize as avant-garde the contributions made by artists from the Latin American diaspora, while suggesting as well that—as a dominant style for certain art world elites—mainstream Pop's idiom was fated to flicker out or otherwise decline into decadence (*Decay Dance*).

Margaret Randall and Sergio Mondragón described the hemispheric and aesthetic aspirations of *El Corno Emplumado* as a "moving totality," which I've rehearsed here as well by linking Mexico City, New York, São Paulo, Los Angeles, and San Francisco in the late 1960s.[26] Mário Pedrosa encountered a "heteroclite repertory of resources and objects" that were not the "types" exemplified by the cultural supremacy of the United States or by its commercial products.[27] They were instead atypical examples that corroborate the idea that Pop art in América thrived surreptitiously, in the margins—in the footnotes and back pages, so to speak—in printed matter that encompassed literary journals, magazine advertisements, illustrations, comic-strips, woodcut-print composites, social-protest posters, and in a body of writing proper to that archive. A brand of print culture Pop subsisted in the pages of a poetry journal, in a limited-edition print sequence, and in the public promise of silkscreens conceived as though from a "socio-aesthetic machine." These examples remain at odds with the omnipresence of more mainstream media and principles of taste. They activated regional information-media references, unexpected anti-art iconographies, and alternate distribution networks, central to movements of social critique and particular to experiences of contrary consciousness in América.

1   Even as Randall and Mondragón often found they had to endure the "jealous and petty local literary scene" in Mexico that often overlooked their ambitious hemispheric efforts, they nonetheless knew the magazine was "very much a part of the world literary scene." See "Editor's Note," *El Corno Emplumado* 21 (January 1967): 6. Literary historian Harris Feinsod writes that: "Just four years later, after Ernesto Cardenal declared the young countercultural poets Randall and Mondragón to represent "la *verdadera Unión Panamericana*" (the true Pan-American Union) in the pages of their little magazine *El Corno Emplumado*, dozens of young poets flocking to Mexico City also thought they were assembling the "First Gathering of American Poets" as an alternative to the Alliance for Progress. Harris Feinsod, *The Poetry of the Americas, From Good Neighbors to Countercultures* (New York: Oxford University Press, 2017), 5. The roster of writers and artists featured in *El Corno Emplumado* is vast. They include: Ernesto Mejía Sánchez, Rochelle Owens, Homero Aridjis, Rachel Jodorowsky, Robert Kelley, Diane Wakoski, Anselm Hollo, Ernesto Cardenal, Kathleen Fraser, Paul Blackburn, Michael McClure, Thelma Nava, Ulises Carrión, Frank Lima, Lorenzo Thomas, and Jerome Rothenberg; as well as Elaine de Kooning, Leonora Carrington, Juan Soriano, Marisol, Franz Kline, and José Luis Cuevas, among others. For a brief discussion of Kurt Stavenhagen (1899, Frankfurt, Germany–1984, Mexico City), a friend and neighbor of Diego Rivera's, see Byron W. Knoblock, "Important Private Collection of Pre-Columbian Art in Mexico," *Central States Archaeological Journal*, vol. 3, no. 4 (April 1957): 143–146.

2   Feinsod, *The Poetry of the Americas, From Good Neighbors to Countercultures*, 2.

3   Dore Ashton et al., "A Symposium on Pop Art," *Arts Magazine*, vol. 37, no. 6 (April 1963): 37.

4   Ibid., 40. In advance of the Museum of Modern Art Pop symposium (1962), Peter Selz announced in the press release that the discussion "dealing primarily with American artists" would address and "analyze the esthetics of the movement and its value as a meaningful comment on contemporary life as well as the problematic relationship of art to mass culture." Peter Selz, cited in press release, the Museum of Modern Art, no. 38, December 3, 1962.

5   Anselm Hollo, cited in *El Corno Emplumado: una historia de los sesenta*, directed by Anne Mette Nielsen and Nicolenka Beltrán (Denmark: Angulos Production, 2005), DVD. *El Corno Emplumado* 21 featured a Pop-inspired cover photograph by Jean Marie Chourguoz and a Pop comic strip by Colombian artist Hálvaro Barrios (20–25). In the latter, speech bubbles violently wound the mouth and body of a female subject, while also providing meta-commentary on the comic strip speech bubble itself, emanating from a (possibly empty) glass whose speech is yet another glass, with additional caustic references to the violence in Colombia and to the use of hallucinogenic drugs ("Esta hoja continene LSD").

6   Back matter, *El Corno Emplumado* 5 (January 1963): 160.

7   Back matter, *El Corno Emplumado* 3 (July 1962): 143.

8   The roster of artists included: Consuelo Abascal de Lemionet, Benigno Alvarado, Octavio Asta, Francisco Ávalos, José Luis Cuevas, Pedro Friedeberg, Mathias

Goeritz, Kati Horna, Inocencia (the hen), Agripina Maqueda, Jesús Reyes Ferreira, and Benito Rodríguez. The manifesto read as follows: "The fed ups reject any association with any artistic group, including, of course, the neo-dadaists who ignore that DADA is eternal. The fed ups are also fed up with DADA. Its realism is of a MORAL nature.//The fact that the fed ups are exhibiting their work at the Antonio Souza Gallery does not imply identification on any of the parts. It's purely coincidental.//If by any reason this exhibition would offend the sensibility of the people related to the arts, the fed ups would like to categorically declare that their intention has never been that of hurting anybody. Their intentions are good. They're just fed up.// We are fed up with the pretentious imposition of logic and of reason, of functionalism, of decorative calculus, and of the chaotic pornography of individualism, of the glory of the day, of the fashion of the moment, of vanity and of ambition, of bluff and of the artistic joke, of conscious and subconscious egocentrism, of fatuous concepts, of the exceedingly tedious propaganda of the isms and the ists, figurative or abstract. Fed up also with the preciosity of an inverted aesthetic; fed up with the copy or stylization of a heroically vulgar reality. Fed up, above all, with the artificial and hysterical atmosphere of the so-called art world, with its adulterated pleasures, its gaudy salons and its terrifying vacuum.//We recognize the necessity of abandoning the illusory dreams of the glorification of the ego and of deflating art. We recognize that human work, at the present time, is most vigorous where the so-called artist less intervenes. We recognize, more and more, the importance of the service, or of any abnegated act based on a natural ethic, all logic aside—the cultivation of an orchard, the fulfilling of a professional duty, or the education of a child.//We try to begin anew from below in a spiritual-sociological sense. All established values will have to be rectified: Believe without asking in what! Make, or at least try to make man's work become a PRAYER." See Mauricio Marcín, ed., *Estamos hartos (otra vez)* (Mexico City: Museo Experimental el Eco, 2014), 3.

9   See, for example, the exhibition organized by Soledad García and Daniela Berger, *La emergencia del pop en Chile: Irreverencia y calle*, Museo de la Solidaridad Salvador Allende, 2016. Another advertisement in issue 20 was signed "el corno emplumado" and composed a protest list. "We Protect//· the brutal police treatment, prison, illegal trial and pending death sentence against the peruvian guerilla leader HUGO BLANCO.//· the total ideological persecution which includes current dosing of the national universities and university publishing houses in argentina.//· the wave of repression, blackmail and fear unleashed throughout the entire american continent by the state department of the united states of America." See *El Corno Emplumado* 20 (October 1966): 134.

10   Jennifer Higgie, "Beau Geste Press CAPC, Bordeaux, France," *Frieze* online, February 16, 2017. See also Donna Conwell, "Beau Geste Press," *Getty Research Journal*, no. 2 (2010): 183–192.

11   Felipe Ehrenberg, illustration, *El Corno Emplumado* 19 (July 1966): 6.

12   Ehrenberg, cover, *El Corno Emplumado* 22 (April 1967).

13   Ashton et al., "A Symposium on Pop Art," 39.

14   The cover art of *El Corno Emplumado* 26 (April 1968) "reproduced the famous Cuban Protest Song poster by Alfredo Rostgaard of the rose with a drop of blood falling from a single thorn, already an icon of the times." See Sergio Mondragón and Margaret Randall, "*El Corno Emplumado* 26," Open Door Archive, accessed June 3, 2017, http://opendoor.northwestern.edu/ archive/items/show/61.

15   Pilar García, interview by Esther Gabara, December 18, 2017.

16   Antônio Henrique Amaral, *O meu e o seu; impressões de nosso tempo: 7 gravuras originais*, with essay by Ferreira Gullar (São Paulo: Edição Mirante das Artes, 1967), n.p. The edition comprised 300 copies with an additional twenty non-commercial copies lettered from A to L; and with the design of the metal encasing suggested by Ruben de Freitas Martins (São Paulo, 1928–1968).

17   The all-lowercase font style was pervasive in Latin America in the 1960s, as echoed in the typographic design of *El Corno Emplumado*.

18   Frederico Morais, "A gravura brasileira: os anos 60/70," in *Mostra da Gravura Brasileira* (São Paulo, Brazil: Fundação Bienal de São Paulo, 1974), 44. See also Documents of 20th-Century Latin American and Latino Art, International Center for the Arts of the Americas at the Museum of Fine Arts, Houston, ICAA Record ID: 1110706, accessed June 16, 2017.

19   Mário Pedrosa, "Gewgaws and Pop Art," in *Mário Pedrosa: Primary Documents*, eds., Glória Ferreira and Paulo Herkenhoff, trans. Stephen Berg (New York: The Museum of Modern Art, 2015), 201. Originally published as Mário Pedrosa, "Quinquilharia e pop art," *Correio da Manhã*, Rio de Janeiro, August 14, 1967, sec. 4, 1.

20   Jayne Cortez, "In Her Own Words," in *Watts: Art and Social Change in Los Angeles, 1965–2002*, ed. Jerome Fortier (Milwaukee: Haggerty Museum of Art, Marquette University, 2003), 33–34.

21   Paul Karlstrom, "Oral history interview with Rupert García," Smithsonian Archives of American Art, 1995, online, accessed May 30, 2017.

22   Ruben Salazar, "Chicanos Would Find Identity Before Coalition with Blacks," *Los Angeles Times*, February 20, 1970, C7, ProQuest Historical Newspapers.

23   Ruben Salazar, "Black-Brown Friction Growing," *Los Angeles Times*, October 26, 1969, ProQuest Historical Newspapers. See also, Ruben Salazar, "Chicanos Told to Fight Like Blacks for Respect," *Los Angeles Times*, April 9, 1969, ProQuest Historical Newspapers: "'Chicanos can learn from our black brothers, we can and must learn how to fight effectively for what we want. We have to get ourselves together in high school UMAS and in the community to become strong enough in our unity that "the Man" will see and be afraid.' This was the advice given Mexican-American youths by the underground newspaper *Chicano Student Movement* in its February issue. Since then UMAS (United Mexican-American Students) has been suspended from Roosevelt High School, following a peaceful sit-in which UMAS claims it did not lead."

24   Amiri Baraka, "Emory Douglas: a 'Good Brother,' a 'Bad' Artist," in *Black Panther: The Revolutionary Art of Emory Douglas*, ed. Sam Durant (New York: Rizzoli, 2007), 169. The poster art of Emory Douglas shares both formal and social affinities with the art of Rupert García.

25   Karlstrom, interview.

26   Sergio Mondragón and Margaret Randall, "Editor's Note," *El Corno Emplumado* 19 (July, 1966): 5.

27   Pedrosa, "Gewgaws and Pop Art," 201.

ROBERTO TEJADA

LO IMPRESO Y SU PAPEL

Desde la xilografía brasileña hasta la cultura visual chicana, el material impreso creado en América durante la década de 1960 presenta una gama muy diversa de tendencias artísticas. Desde São Paulo hasta San Francisco, artistas con opiniones ambivalentes respecto a ciertas formas de vanguardismo y opuestos a la supremacía política y cultural de Estados Unidos recurrieron a la figuración y la anatomía del lenguaje como medio de reorientar la gestión innovadora del arte pop. La historia comienza en Ciudad de México, cuando en enero de 1962 los poetas Margaret Randall y Sergio Mondragón publicaron el primer número de *El Corno Emplumado* (1968, lámina 68), una revista bilingüe de arte y literatura.[1] Para 1967, Randall y Mondragón, que contaban veintitantos años cuando fundaron la revista, ya habían publicado veinte números trimestrales en formato empastado, y *El Corno Emplumado* se había establecido como uno de los documentos culturales más influyentes de su época.

De enfoque internacional y multimedia, *El Corno Emplumado* publicaba poesía vanguardista y arte contemporáneo. Se incluían poemas tanto en lengua original como traducidos, dibujos lineales a manera de ilustración y artículos de la actualidad política y cultural. Con el tiempo fueron apareciendo obras de arte en las portadas. El objetivo era captar el pensamiento contemporáneo poniendo de relieve la experimentación artística: análisis críticos de la política exterior estadounidense compartían espacio con opiniones sobre la sociedad interamericana y su política a través de la poesía y la expresión artística. Esta perspectiva cosmopolita siguió los cambios ocurridos

tras la Revolución Cubana y activó una red de artistas e instituciones en lo que Harris Feinsod describió como la "expresión de un deseo geopolítico, la visión de un orden mundial alterno".[2]

Los cuatro primeros números de *El Corno Emplumado* (enero–octubre de 1962) coincidieron con un simposio llevado a cabo en el Museum of Modern Art (MoMA) de Nueva York sobre los nacientes atributos y valores del arte pop, con la participación de los curadores y críticos Peter Selz, Henry Geldzahler, Hilton Kramer, Dore Ashton y Leo Steinberg, y el poeta Stanley Kunitz. Dicha mesa redonda, publicada en el número de abril de 1963 de *Arts Magazine*, fue el ensayo de un debate público sobre la relación del arte pop con la vanguardia y los medios masivos de comunicación: el carácter "ubicuo, persistente y compulsivo" de la prensa popular, las vallas publicitarias urbanas y la televisión nacional.[3] Algunos de los participantes consideraban que la iconografía del arte pop era simplemente una transposición visual y no una transformación estética, o más bien que su estilo mostraba "el nuevo papel del contenido, tras casi un siglo de adoctrinamiento formalista".[4]

El simposio del MoMA definió lo que se convertiría en discusión común acerca de esta influyente tendencia en el arte contemporáneo estadounidense a la luz del creciente ambiente de descontento político e inconformidad social a nivel nacional e internacional. En Ciudad de México, también *El Corno Emplumado* se encontraba en el centro de debates artísticos y políticos. Siendo una publicación a pequeña escala que sobrevivía con patrocinios tanto privados como públicos, no faltaban en ella las indirectas hacia los medios masivos y la cultura capitalista del consumo, además de que acogía expresiones del pop provenientes de espacios al margen de instituciones hegemónicas como el MoMA. Asimismo la revista revelaba una sensibilidad particular del arte pop que combinaba la indignación antiimperialista por los actos bélicos de Estados Unidos en el sureste de Asia y su intervención en América Latina con la frustración ante la autoridad que ejercía el mundo del arte estadounidense en el hemisferio.

La improbable contribución de *El Corno Emplumado* a una historia más amplia del pop en América aparece en las idiosincráticas páginas últimas del primer número (ver página 126, figura 4.1) e incluye ilustraciones de artistas latinoamericanos con elementos derivados de tiras cómicas, escaparates de tiendas y diseños comerciales. Si bien la revista vendía espacio para anuncios, los editores ironizaban las pretensiones tipo Madison Avenue, y el poeta Anselm Hollo relata que Randall y Mondragón traducían tiras cómicas estadounidenses al español para llegar a fin de mes.[5] Las últimas páginas del primer número contenían el tipo de anuncio convencional de mediados del siglo XX que promovía las vajillas Lenox ("Nuevas… Diferentes… Resistentes…") y los alimentos Gerber para bebés (ver página 126, figura 4.2). Sin embargo, ya en el cuarto número de la revista, un anuncio para la cadena mexicana de supermercados Gigante S.A. fungía de poema pop, satirizando el carácter totalizante de la supuesta satisfacción del consumidor. Ofrecía artículos domésticos en una tipografía escalonada: "· codornices/· alimentos/· coches/· tortugas/· tortillas/· libros/· tintorería/· llaves al minuto/*en una palabra, TODO*" (ver página 127, figura 4.3).[6] El texto serio del anuncio presentado en esta secuencia absurda pudo haberse inspirado en un anuncio concebido a principios de diciembre de 1961 por el artista mexicano de origen alemán Mathias Goeritz. Con once otros artistas cómplices (y una gallina viva), Goeritz organizó un irreverente acto antiarte llamado *Los Hartos*, y luego aludió a este fenómeno mediático en un anuncio que colocó en el tercer número de *El Corno Emplumado*. El anuncio combinaba un texto de autopromoción con un ataque al fetiche de consumo norteamericano por excelencia: "MATHIAS GOERITZ | está HARTO pero | TOMA Coca-Cola" (ver página 127, figura 4.4).[7] Renegando del dadaísmo en un sincero gesto cuasi ético o espiritual, la aportación de Goeritz al pop revelaba una profunda ambivalencia frente a la innovación, estando él y su grupo de hartos colegas listos para denunciarla como fraude.[8] La postura antiimperialista de *El Corno Emplumado* estaba tan ligada a la burla hacia las expectativas consumistas del capitalismo que hacía compatible la irreverencia de orden conceptual con la acción en las calles —una apta descripción del pop en América.[9]

La revista también ayudó a lanzar la multiforme carrera del artista mexicano Felipe Ehrenberg (1943–2017), en cuya práctica se desdibujaron los límites entre el pop, Fluxus y el arte conceptual. Dentro de su vasto quehacer, Ehrenberg realizó acciones y happenings con el colectivo de arte Grupo Proceso Pentágono, apoyó activamente los derechos de los artistas chicanos de California a principios de los años setenta y trabajó la producción editorial como práctica artística, concretamente con Beau Geste Press, la editorial que fundó en Devon, Inglaterra, con su esposa y colega en el arte, Martha Hellion ("Nuestra editorial no es un negocio, es un modo de vida").[10] Sus aportaciones a *El Corno Emplumado* incluyen obras en técnica mixta sobre papel para dos portadas (números 22 y 23) y una serie de dibujos (números 19, 20, 22 y 23) que satirizan a los clásicos de la historia del arte con una economía visual hermana de las caricaturas políticas y los collages dadaístas, sin carecer de la audacia y el humor irónico del pop (ver página 127, figura 4.5).

Interesado en la exploración de los clichés, Ehrenberg quiso "desinflar" la solemnidad de precedentes artísticos como Diego Velázquez, el Greco y Francisco Goya. Con esta actitud de inspiración pop produjo un autorretrato cuasicaricaturesco que apareció en el número 19 (ver página 127, figura 4.6). La cabeza del artista, con corona y un gran bigote, aparece en un dibujo dentro del dibujo como si emanara de un aura en forma de huevo —una identidad reducida a un sello con el número *857334*—. Debajo vemos un cuerpo con la cabeza y los hombros tapados por la superposición del rostro-sello; tiene las manos juntas y descansa los brazos sobre una leyenda que alude en clave pop a las patentes comerciales y la propiedad intelectual: "Me reservo el derecho de retener todo premio o mención que reciba mi persona así como el dinero que se perciba de la venta de la misma".[11]

Dentro de la autorreflexividad sardónica de Ehrenberg, este tipo de ocurrencia no desdeñaba la metáfora, cualidad de la cual, según Dore Ashton, lamentablemente carecía la estética pop. A la afirmación de Henry Geldzahler —que el arte pop era "historia del arte instantánea, historia del arte tan consciente de sí misma que se adelanta al arte" y, por ende, es "inmediatamente contemporánea"— Ehrenberg agregó un elemento de ambigüedad. La portada del número 22 de *El Corno Emplumado* (ver página 128, figura 4.7) contiene una especie de tira cómica o rompecabezas vertical con un motivo en posible alusión al *Retrato de joven con manzana* de Rafael (c. 1505). En la versión de Ehrenberg, sin embargo, la manzana se ha desplazado hacia los cuadros inferiores en forma de un enorme disco rojo que ahoga al sujeto, con una flecha apuntando hacia ella y una leyenda que la identifica con el alba. La leyenda dice: "Transformada el/alba cerré los/ojos y vi la/luna".[12] El humor pretencioso de este tipo de comedia conceptual a costa de los grandes maestros va en consonancia con lo que Ashton identificó en el arte pop como un "antídoto para el idealismo".[13] Por otra parte, la euforia ideológica se tornó incierta en la imagen de Ehrenberg para la portada del número 23 de la revista (ver página 129, figura 4.8), que incluía una sección de poesía dedicada a la Cuba revolucionaria. Siete cabezas masculinas, agrupadas en forma de pirámide, aparecen superpuestas sobre un fondo saturado de azul, blanco y rojo que lleva el triángulo y las franjas de la bandera cubana. Los insurgentes, desaliñados y con las típicas barbas descuidadas de los revolucionarios, carecen de rasgos faciales, pero aparecen colocados encima de otra figura —a veces amarilla, roja o blanca— que sugiere un corazón humano o una paloma de la paz deformada.[14]

En *El Corno Emplumado* se unían el proceso comercial de linotipia, las artes gráficas, el arte figurativo de pequeña escala, la publicidad de sensibilidad pop y otras formas de arte y protesta en América. En 1968, dos años después de sus citadas aportaciones a la revista, Ehrenberg creó una obra tipo caja (shadow box) titulada *Arte Conceptual* (ver página 16, figura 1.8) donde se combinan diversos elementos para suscitar enunciados axiomáticos sobre la relación del entretenimiento popular comercial con las percepciones sexuadas y la alienación, y también sobre el estatus de la obra de arte. La composición activa el proceso de observación con una serie de flechas instructivas rojas que apuntan a una vista trasera de la silueta de la Venus de Milo. La figura parece estar sentada en el borde de un muro, mirando por las ventanas de un avión; esta escena lleva a otra: un edificio industrial, no muy alto, en medio de un paisaje desolado. Esta estética de puesto de feria —cuyo alboroto visual está destinado a atraer el deseo visceral masculino de lograr un trofeo, en este caso el desnudo femenino proveniente de la historia del arte— se reafirma en la parte inferior del cuadro con una línea de rostros idénticos. En un patrón rojo y negro de alto contraste, los rostros son asexuales y en su atónita expresión comunican incredulidad o descontento.

En una obra similar, *Caja no. 25495* (1968, lámina 77), Ehrenberg emplea su conocida iconografía de flechas y discos, pero ahora en gris y negro sobre sobrios campos sólidos en rojo, amarillo y azul grisáceo. Las áreas encuadradas y las formaciones estilo recuadro proporcionan superficie y profundidad, y el número 25495 en esténcil remite a motivos comparables de números y sellos en los autorretratos anteriores de Ehrenberg. Hay una disyunción lúdica entre la bidimensionalidad y la tridimensionalidad de esta obra, así como entre los diagramáticos bailarines con leotardos —comodines para la expresión sin riendas— y las alusiones a la entrega de paquetes y la gestión oficinesca. Alguna vez la caja también contuvo canicas que hacían ruido, sin ser vistas, cuando los espectadores o empleados del museo la manipulaban.[15] Ehrenberg sugiere que la celebración de la cultura consumista que ocurre en el arte pop resulta paradójica en sociedades como México, donde el individuo suele quedar subsumido en la maraña burocrática.

Estas pinturas subrayan aún más hasta qué punto las obras de Ehrenberg para *El Corno Emplumado* presentaban los períodos históricos del arte como formas perversas de capital simbólico y consumo conspicuo —versión en la cultura de imprenta de lo que Geldzahler llamaba el arte pop como "la historia del arte instantánea"—. Los dibujos y diseños de portada creados por Ehrenberg unen la expresión figurativa con el discurso del arte conceptual y los medios populares para reafirmar la primacía del material impreso. Con un tiraje trimestral de 3,000 ejemplares, *El Corno Emplumado* —objeto artesanal si se mira en términos de producción masiva, pero ambicioso en su alcance internacional— fue la plataforma ideal para las formas menos monumentales de experimentación en América Latina.

Una especie de cultura pop de imprenta surgió al margen del ámbito hegemónico del estilo y los rangos inferiores de sus jerarquías mediáticas. En Brasil, Antônio Henrique Amaral empleó en su porfolio *O meu e o seu: impressões de nosso tempo* (Lo mío y lo tuyo: impresiones de nuestros tiempos) (1967, láminas 86–93) elementos derivados del grabado popular y los medios de información; las obras van colocadas dentro de una carpeta o cubierta de metal bien ajustada que las envuelve, como sugiriendo que se trata de un expediente institucional clasificado.[16] Siete grabados en madera conforman una secuencia de audaces composiciones que critican la sociedad contemporánea brasileña, las distracciones creadas por los medios masivos y el violento autoritarismo político de la dictadura militar. Haciendo referencia a la tradición de pliegos sueltos conocida como literatura de cordel, pero con temas de depravación sexual y violencia, el portafolio de Amaral nos ofrece

una grotesca iconografía tipo tira cómica que no concordaba con el monopolio estadounidense sobre las formas de la cultura de popular.

Un ejemplo es *o idolatrado* (el idolatrado) (1967, lámina 88), donde áreas sólidas aguamarina y rosa dan volumen a un eje que sirve de figura central a la obra.[17] Un monumento en forma de micrófono, coronado por un cuarteto de manos en el acto de aplaudir ("*CLAC! CLAC!*"), se encuentra injertado sobre un par de pies plantados firmemente en una columna sostenida por un grupo de espectadores. La multitud en la parte inferior del cuadro parece estar abrumada por los rostros alargados que flanquean el grabado, cada uno con tres bocas con sus correspondientes lenguas y dientes. Unos megáfonos cónicos que se extienden telescópicamente retumban con una canción de *rock and roll* cuyo texto "*YÊ, YÊ, YÊ*" es al mismo tiempo símbolo de la idolatría prodigada a una importación cultural específica y del tipo de autoridad sobre las masas que se da en los estadios.

En *Personagem contemporâneo* (Personaje contemporáneo) (1967, lámina 90), Amaral emplea el folclor y las distorsiones figurativas experimentales que evidencian lo que Frederico Morais identificó como la democratización concurrente de temas, recursos y medios en el arte pop.[18] En este grabado, varias bocas van formando el cráneo de una figura rodeada de manos y pies sin cuerpo. Esta figura femenina agita banderitas en pro de la paz y la prosperidad, debajo de las cuales se encuentran los nombres de Corea y Vietnam apoyados en unos pies que surgen del borde inferior del cuadro. El visible tracto gastrointestinal de la figura contiene las fechas 1914 y 1939, respectivamente los años de inicio de la primera y la segunda guerras mundiales, y esto conduce a la función final del sistema digestivo: un signo de interrogación en forma de heces que cuestiona por asociación los procesos de consumo y deshecho.

El notable crítico de arte brasileño Mário Pedrosa vinculó el descontento por los modelos estadounidenses de la cultura de masas no solo con el regreso de lo reprimido en forma de un vernáculo folclórico, sino también con el más contundente levantamiento de los desfavorecidos. En "Quinquilharia e pop art" (Quincallería y arte pop), Pedrosa pone en tela de juicio las aportaciones de Roy Lichtenstein al arte contemporáneo en Brasil, y más bien resalta "un oscuro 'subconjunto cultural' [que] emerge explosivamente del entorno urbano de aquellos artistas, [y] que vuelve a cuestionar el todo cultural donde, con fascinante inventiva, surge y ejerce el artista pop norteamericano. Se trata de las revueltas negras".[19] Pedrosa identifica cuerpos sociales específicos dentro de la cotidianidad estadounidense que el arte pop había aspirado a presentar.

El Movimiento Chicano surgió en paralelo a estas revueltas, primero en el contexto de la lucha de la United Farm Workers (Unión de Trabajadores Campesinos), liderada por César Chávez y Dolores Huerta en California, y luego en los barrios urbanos del suroeste del país. Sobre las revueltas de agosto de 1965 en Watts la poeta Jayne Cortez escribió: "El pueblo negro estaba cansado de las contradicciones, la desigualdad, el creciente número de violaciones de derechos, la brutalidad policiaca, el desempleo, la falta de oportunidades, la falta de respeto y la cantidad de sacrificios hechos a consecuencia de la dominación del hombre blanco".[20] El Movimiento Chicano radicalizó la vida y la cultura mexicano-americana con sorprendentes estilos visuales, alcanzando su masa crítica con la manifestación antibélica de la Moratoria Chicana en Los Ángeles el 29 de agosto de 1970. Para muchos artistas chicanos de finales de los años sesenta y principios de los setenta, no existían diferencias arbitrarias entre "la vida cotidiana, el arte, la política y la historia" o la acción directa.[21]

En un primer plano de este contexto artístico y activista estuvo Rupert García, cuyo cartelismo denunció el racismo contra los negros, la guerra de Vietnam y la participación de Estados Unidos en las terribles represiones sociales en América Latina. Desde el área de la Bahía de San Francisco y concurriendo con Amaral y Ehrenberg, García abordó las mismas cuestiones de tradiciones populares, sexualidad y raza que Mário Pedrosa tenía en mente cuando identificó el hecho de que los artistas pop del *mainstream* no abordaban el sector de vida social y sensual que la sociedad estadounidense había reprimido como "subconjuntos culturales". Estos sujetos desfavorecidos en el plano social y racial se organizaron políticamente y emergieron "explosivamente del entorno urbano". En una colografía temprana, *Black Man and Flag* (Hombre negro con bandera) (1967, lámina 6), unas franjas blancas y negras componen una bandera estadounidense suspendida en vertical. García sustituyó el campo de estrellas por una efigie rojiza, el busto no identificado de algún líder de los derechos civiles o la liberación negra. El grabado enfatiza la urgencia de incluir la negritud en el imaginario nacional prometido simbólicamente por el rojo, blanco y azul. Este retrato-bandera de García diagnostica las posturas que describiría el periodista Ruben Salazar en su serie de artículos publicados entre 1969 y 1970 en el *Los Angeles Times* respecto a las relaciones entre las comunidades de color en California. La imagen de un hombre negro que García coloca sobre la bandera nacional representa un momento anterior a lo que Salazar identificó como una "creciente desconfianza" de los jóvenes chicanos en cuanto a "formar una nueva coalición [...] esta vez con los negros [...] hasta que ellos, los chicanos, encuentren su propia identidad a su propia manera".[22] La obra de García se adelanta a esta idea y la refuta. En línea con otro artículo de Salazar, García entendía la visión parcial de la representación etno-nacionalista y el hecho de que, en la medida en que los anglos habían fracasado en sus esfuerzos por crear una coalición, un "distanciamiento entre negros y morenos no haría más que ayudar a los interesados en frenar la lucha por los derechos civiles".[23]

De ideas internacionalistas en el turbulento período de una "ola mundial antiimperialista", Rupert García se resistía a considerar la identidad chicana como algo separado de las luchas sociales relacionadas o del más amplio acervo cultural del modernismo, y es por esto que sus carteles están impregnados de perspectivas tanto cosmopolitas como anticoloniales.[24] En *Decay Dance* (Danza de la decadencia) (1969, lámina 20), el fondo está compuesto de áreas sólidas de rojo, azul y rosa, un sombrero de ala ancha y el rostro parcial pero inequívoco del logo de la avena Quaker Oats. En la parte inferior, en tinta plateada sobre papel amarillo, flota una imagen fantasmal de la Mona Lisa, tan contrastada y distorsionada que se parece al rostro del *readymade L.H.O.O.Q.*, concebido por Marcel Duchamp en 1919. García era un apasionado de la historia, la filosofía y la cultura de México, y también versado en el canon surrealista, el existencialismo de Jean-Paul Sartre, la poesía de

Octavio Paz y la fotografía de Manuel Álvarez Bravo. Su práctica era producto de una analogía surrealista que combinaba dos componentes improbables: las ontologías del arte dejadas al descubierto por Duchamp y la "dimensión socio-económico-racial de la protesta" ejemplificada en los escritos de Martin Luther King, Jr. El resultado era lo que García describió como una "máquina socio-estética", que invertía la gramática visual del arte pop para refutar las dinámicas históricas del arte en virtud de las cuales la blancura monopolizaba la categoría del artista universal "que lidia con las condiciones de la humanidad en un contexto postindustrializado".[25]

Las prácticas de otros artistas chicanos estuvieron fundadas en homologías o disyunciones axiomáticas entre los signos visuales y el lenguaje aplicado. Algunos, como Mel Casas y Judith Baca, elevaron el nivel crítico de los significados que el pop derivaba de los productos de la cultura popular, las revistas de moda, las tiras cómicas o los diseños comerciales, añadiendo una especie de disonancia cognitiva por lo general asociada con el arte conceptual. En *Humanscape 62* (Paisaje humano) (1970, lámina 85), Casas se regodea en atacar el flagrante racismo del término despectivo aplicado a las personas de ascendencia mexicana, el capital social específico de las Niñas Exploradoras de Estados Unidos y el personaje de la compañía Frito-Lay conocido como el "Frito Bandito", cuya imagen era el estereotipo de un bandido mexicano. Casas contrarresta el fotorrealismo pop de la publicidad y los empaques comerciales con la figuración folclórica, al tiempo que sugiere vínculos interculturales entre la iconografía de la época anterior a la conquista española (Quetzalcóatl, la verde "serpiente emplumada", la calavera de Tezcatlipoca) y los pueblos nativos de México y el suroeste de Estados Unidos. En contraste, el tríptico en técnica mixta de Judith Baca, *Las tres Marías* (The Three Marías) (1976, lámina 1), con sus paneles tapizados por la parte trasera, transforma visualmente el reflejo del espectador en el panel de espejo central, proyectando su género y raza de acuerdo con los términos que establecen los paneles laterales, dos detallados dibujos naturalistas de mujeres chicanas sobre papel. Los rasgos del espectador que se reflejan en el espejo —independientemente de su género, edad o etnicidad— se ven equiparados y contrastados, del lado izquierdo, con la figura de una joven de barrio chicana, de aspecto marimacho, y del lado derecho con una huisa, o güisa, el modelo de belleza femenina mexicano-americana de la década de 1940.

Volviendo a las referencias visuales en *Decay Dance*, Rupert García subvierte las alusiones del logo de Quaker Oats al paternalismo y al estilo de vida sano con la representación por excelencia de la feminidad en la historia del arte, la Mona Lisa. Al mestizar estos dos íconos euroétnicos y hacer un juego de palabras con el título, García satiriza las idealizaciones de género y raza aplicadas a los hogares estadounidenses en la época de la Guerra Fría, las cuales se ven reflejadas en las fuerzas de mercado que impulsan la historia del arte. Con gran economía de diseño, el artista se lanza en contra de una de Finición de arte moderno que no reconoció como vanguardistas las aportaciones hechas por los artistas de la diáspora latinoamericana, sugiriendo también que —como estilo dominante de ciertas élites artísticas mundiales— el lenguaje del pop en su corriente principal estaba destinado a extinguirse o caer en decadencia (*Decay Dance*).

Margaret Randall y Sergio Mondragón describieron las aspiraciones hemisféricas y estéticas de *El Corno Emplumado* como una "totalidad móvil", y es esto lo que también he intentado hacer en este texto al vincular Ciudad de México, Nueva York, São Paulo, Los Ángeles y San Francisco en el contexto de fines de los años sesenta.[26] Mário Pedrosa encontró un "repertorio heteróclito de recursos y objetos" que no eran los "tipos" ejemplificados por la supremacía cultural de Estados Unidos ni por sus productos comerciales.[27] Más bien eran ejemplos atípicos que corroboran la idea de que el arte pop en el continente americano floreció subrepticiamente, de forma marginal —en las notas a pie de página y las últimas páginas de las revistas, por así decirlo—, en el material impreso que comprendía revistas literarias, anuncios, ilustraciones, tiras cómicas, composiciones xilográficas y carteles de protesta social, y en un cuerpo de escritos propios de ese acervo. Un estilo de cultura pop de imprenta subsistió en las páginas de una revista de poesía, en una secuencia de grabados de edición limitada y en la promesa pública de serigrafías concebidas como una "máquina socio-estética". Estos ejemplos van a contrapelo con la omnipresencia de los medios y cánones del gusto más *mainstream*. Más bien activaron referencias a medios de información regionales, inesperadas iconografías antiarte y redes alternas de distribución que fueron centrales para los movimientos de crítica social y particulares al desarrollo de conciencias de oposición en América.

NOTAS

1 Aunque Randall y Mondragón tuvieron que enfrentarse a "la envidiosa, reaccionaria y pequeña escena [literaria] mexicana local", que muchas veces desdeñaba sus ambiciosos esfuerzos hemisféricos, sí sabían que la revista era "con mucho, parte de la escena literaria mundial". Ver "Nota de los editores", *El Corno Emplumado* 21 (enero de 1967): 6. El historiador literario Harris Feinsod escribe que: "Solo cuatro años más tarde, después de que Ernesto Cardenal declarara que los jóvenes poetas contraculturales Randall y Mondragón representaban "la verdadera Unión Panamericana" en las páginas de su pequeña revista *El Corno Emplumado*, docenas de jóvenes poetas que llegaban a Ciudad de México también pensaron que estaban realizando el "Primer Encuentro de Poetas de América" como alternativa a la Alianza para el Progreso. Harris Feinsod, *The Poetry of the Americas, From Good Neighbors to Countercultures* (Nueva York: Oxford University Press, 2017), 5. La lista de escritores y artistas que figuraron en *El Corno Emplumado* es enorme. Entre ellos están: Ernesto Mejía Sánchez, Rochelle Owens, Homero Aridjis, Rachel Jodorowsky, Robert Kelley, Diane Wakoski, Anselm Hollo, Ernesto Cardenal, Kathleen Fraser, Paul Blackburn, Michael McClure, Thelma Nava, Ulises Carrión, Frank Lima, Lorenzo Thomas y Jerome Rothenberg; así como Elaine de Kooning, Leonora Carrington, Juan Soriano, Marisol, Franz Kline y José Luis Cuevas. Para una breve discusión sobre Kurt Stavenhagen (1899, Frankfurt-1984, Ciudad de México), amigo y vecino de Diego Rivera, ver Byron W. Knoblock, "Important Private Collection of Pre-Columbian Art in Mexico", *Central States Archaeological Journal*, vol. 3, no. 4 (abril de 1957): 143–146.

2 Feinsod, *The Poetry of the Americas, From Good Neighbors to Countercultures*, 2.

3 Dore Ashton et al., "A Symposium on Pop Art", *Arts Magazine*, vol. 37, no. 6 (abril de 1963): 37.

4 Ibíd., 40. Antes del simposio del MoMA sobre arte pop en 1962, Peter Selz anunció en un comunicado de prensa que la discusión "primordialmente sobre artistas norteamericanos" abarcaría y "analizaría la estética del movimiento y su valor como comentario significativo sobre la vida contemporánea, así como la problemática relación del arte con la cultura de masas". Peter Selz, citado en comunicado de prensa, el Museum of Modern Art, no. 38, 3 de diciembre de 1962.

5 Anselm Hollo, citado en *El Corno Emplumado: una historia de los sesenta*, dirigida por Anne Mette Nielsen y Nicolenka Beltrán (Dinamarca: Angulos Production, 2005), DVD. En el número 21 de *El Corno Emplumado* apareció una fotografía en vertiente pop de Jean Marie Chourguoz en la portada y una tira cómica pop del artista colombiano Hálvaro Barrios (20–25). En esta última, unas burbujas de diálogo hieren violentamente la boca y el cuerpo de un personaje femenino, al mismo tiempo que ofrecen un metacomentario sobre la burbuja de diálogo misma, que emana de un vaso (posiblemente vacío) cuyo diálogo es otro vaso, además de otras referencias mordaces a la violencia en Colombia y al uso de drogas alucinógenas ("Esta hoja contiene LSD").

6 Últimas páginas, *El Corno Emplumado* 5 (enero de 1963): 160.

7 Últimas páginas, *El Corno Emplumado* 3 (julio de 1962): 143.

8 Los artistas eran: Consuelo Abascal de Lemionet, Benigno Alvarado, Octavio Asta, Francisco Ávalos,

José Luis Cuevas, Pedro Friedeberg, Mathias Goeritz, Kati Horna, Inocencia (la gallina), Agripina Maqueda, Jesús Reyes Ferreira y Benito Rodríguez. El manifiesto dice lo siguiente: "Estamos hartos de la pretenciosa imposición de la lógica y de la razón, del funcionalismo, del cálculo decorativo y, desde luego, de toda la pornografía caótica del individualismo, de la gloria del día, de la moda del momento, de la vanidad y de la ambición, del bluff y de la broma artística, del consciente y subconsciente egocentrismo, de los conceptos fatuos, de la aburridísima propaganda de los ismos y de los istas, figurativos o abstractos. Hartos también del preciosismo de una estética invertida; hartos de la copia o estilización de una realidad heroicamente vulgar. Hartos, sobre todo, de la atmósfera artificial e histérica del llamado mundo artístico, con sus placeres adulterados, sus salones cursis y su vacío escalofriante.//Reconocemos la necesidad de abandonar los sueños ilusorios de la glorificación del yo y de desinflar el arte. Reconocemos que la obra humana, en la actualidad, se presenta con más vigor donde menos interviene el llamado artista. Reconocemos, cada vez más, la importancia del servicio, o sea, de cualquier acto abnegado basado en una ética natural, fuera de toda lógica –el cultivo de una hortaliza, el cumplimiento de un deber profesional o la educación de un niño.//Tratamos de empezar otra vez y desde abajo, en un sentido sociológico espiritual. Habrá que rectificar a fondo todos los valores establecidos: ¡Creer sin preguntar en qué! Hacer o, por lo menos, intentar que la obra del hombre se convierta en una ORACIÓN.//Los hartos rechazan relación alguna con cualquier grupo artístico incluyendo, desde luego, los neo-dadaístas que ignoran que DADA es eterno. Los hartos están también hartos de DADA. Su realismo es de índole MORAL.//El hecho de que los hartos exhiban sus obras en la Galería de Antonio Souza no implica identificación de parte de ninguno de los bandos. Se trata de una mera coincidencia.//Si por alguna razón esta exposición llegara a ofender los sentimientos de las personas relacionadas con el arte, los hartos quisieran declarar categóricamente que no han querido herir a nadie. Sus intenciones son buenas. Están simplemente hartos.//. Ver Mauricio Marcín, ed., *Estamos hartos (otra vez)*, (Ciudad de México: Museo Experimental El Eco, 2014), 3.

9   Ver, por ejemplo, la exposición organizada por Soledad García y Daniela Berger, *La emergencia del pop en Chile: Irreverencia y calle*, Museo de la Solidaridad Salvador Allende, 2016. Otro anuncio en el número 20 llevaba la firma de "el corno emplumado" y era una lista de protestas: "Protestamos//• Por el tratamiento policíaco, prisión y proceso antijurídico de que es objeto el líder campesino del Perú, Hugo Blanco, […] y sobre quien pende amenaza de fusilamiento.//• Por el arbitrario cierre de las Universidades Nacionales y de la Editorial Universitaria de Buenos Aires (EUDEBA), así como por la persecución ideológica […].//[…]//• Por la ola de represiones desencadenada a todo lo largo de este Continente por el Departamento de Estado Norteamericano. Ver *El Corno Emplumado* 20 (octubre de 1966): 134.

10   Jennifer Higgie, "Beau Geste Press, CAPC, Bordeaux, France", *Frieze* online, 16 de febrero de 2017. Ver también Donna Conwell, "Beau Geste Press", *Getty Research Journal*, no. 2 (2010): 183–192.

11   Felipe Ehrenberg, ilustración, *El Corno Emplumado* 19 (julio de 1966): 6.

12   Ehrenberg, portada, *El Corno Emplumado* 22 (abril de 1967).

13   Ashton et al., "A Symposium on Pop Art", 39.

14   El arte de la portada de *El Corno Emplumado* 26 (abril de 1968) "reprodujo el famoso cartel cubano *Canción protesta* de Alfredo Rostgaard con la rosa y una gota de sangre que cae de una espina, ya un ícono de los tiempos". Ver Sergio Mondragón y Margaret Randall, "*El Corno Emplumado* 26", Open Door Archive, consultado el 3 de enero de 2017, http://opendoor. northwestern.edu/archive/items/show/61.

15   Pilar García en entrevista con Esther Gabara, el 18 de diciembre de 2017.

16   Antônio Henrique Amaral, *O meu e o seu; impressões de nosso tempo: 7 gravuras originais*, con ensayo de Ferreira Gullar (São Paulo: Edição Mirante das Artes, 1967), s.p. El tiraje fue de 300 ejemplares y otros 20 ejemplares no comerciales enumerados con letras de A a L, en una carpeta metálica cuyo diseño fue sugerido por Ruben de Freitas Martins (São Paulo, 1928-1968). El colofón dice: "Éste álbum, criado e produzido pelo artista, terminou de ser impresso aos cinco dias de Julho de mil novecentos e sessenta e sete nas oficinas de Gráfica Paulicéa, rua Casimiro de Abreu 575 em São Paulo, com a colaboração dedicada de todos os seus funcionários A capa metálica nasceu de uma sugestão feita por Ruben Martins. O papel utilizado foi Super White 250 gramas de fabricação da indústria de Papel Leon Feffer S. A. O artista expressa admiração e reconhecimento a Adriano Van Moorsel e Durval F. Andrade pelo carinho e entusiasmo que demostraram pelo álbum, possibilitando sua execução.//São Paulo, Julho de 1967".

17   La tipografía toda en minúsculas era muy común en América Latina en los años sesenta, como puede verse en el diseño tipográfico general de *El Corno Emplumado*.

18   Frederico Morais, "A gravura brasileira: os anos 60/70", en *Mostra da Gravura Brasileira* (São Paulo: Fundação Bienal de São Paulo, 1974), 44. Ver también Documents of 20th-Century Latin American and Latino Art, International Center for the Arts of the Americas at the Museum of Fine Arts, Houston, ICAA Record ID: 1110706, consultado el 16 de junio de 2017.

19   Mário Pedrosa, "Gewgaws and Pop Art", en *Mário Pedrosa: Primary Documents*, eds., Glória Ferreira y Paulo Herkenhoff, trad. Stephen Berg (Nueva York: The Museum of Modern Art, 2015), 201. Publicado originalmente como Mário Pedrosa, "Quinquilharia e pop art", *Correio da Manhã*, Río de Janeiro, 14 de agosto de 1967, sec. 4, 1.

20   Jayne Cortez, "In Her Own Words", en *Watts: Art and Social Change in Los Angeles, 1965-2002*, ed. Jerome Fortier (Milwaukee: Haggerty Museum of Art, Marquette University, 2003), 33–34.

21   Paul Karlstrom, "Oral history interview with Rupert García", Smithsonian Archives of American Art, 1995, Internet, consultado el 30 de mayo de 2017.

22   Ruben Salazar, "Chicanos Would Find Identity Before Coalition with Blacks", *Los Angeles Times*, 20 de febrero de 1970, C7, ProQuest Historical Newspapers.

23   Ruben Salazar, "Black-Brown Friction Growing", *Los Angeles Times*, 26 de octubre de 1969, ProQuest Historical Newspapers. Ver también Ruben Salazar, "Chicanos Told to Fight Like Blacks for Respect", *Los Angeles Times*, 9 de abril de 1969, ProQuest Historical Newspapers: "'Los chicanos pueden aprender de nuestros hermanos negros, podemos y debemos aprender a pelear eficazmente por lo que queremos. Tenemos que unirnos en las UMAS de escuela secundaria y en la comunidad para fortalecernos de tal modo en nuestra unión que "el Jefe" nos vea y se asuste'. Este fue el consejo que dio a la juventud mexicano-americana el periódico clandestino *Chicano Student Movement* en su tirada de febrero. Desde entonces la UMAS (United Mexican-American Students) ha quedado suspendida en la Roosevelt High School, luego de una sentada pacífica que UMAS niega haber liderado".

24   Amiri Baraka, "Emory Douglas: a 'Good Brother,' a 'Bad' Artist", en *Black Panther: The Revolutionary Art of Emory Douglas*, ed. Sam Durant (Nueva York: Rizzoli, 2007), 169. El arte cartelístico de Emory Douglas comparte afinidades tanto formales como sociales con el arte de Rupert García.

25   Karlstrom, entrevista.

26   Sergio Mondragón y Margaret Randall, "Editor's Note", *El Corno Emplumado* 19 (julio de 1966): 5.

27   Pedrosa, "Gewgaws and Pop Art", 201.

MEDIATING

AMÉRICA

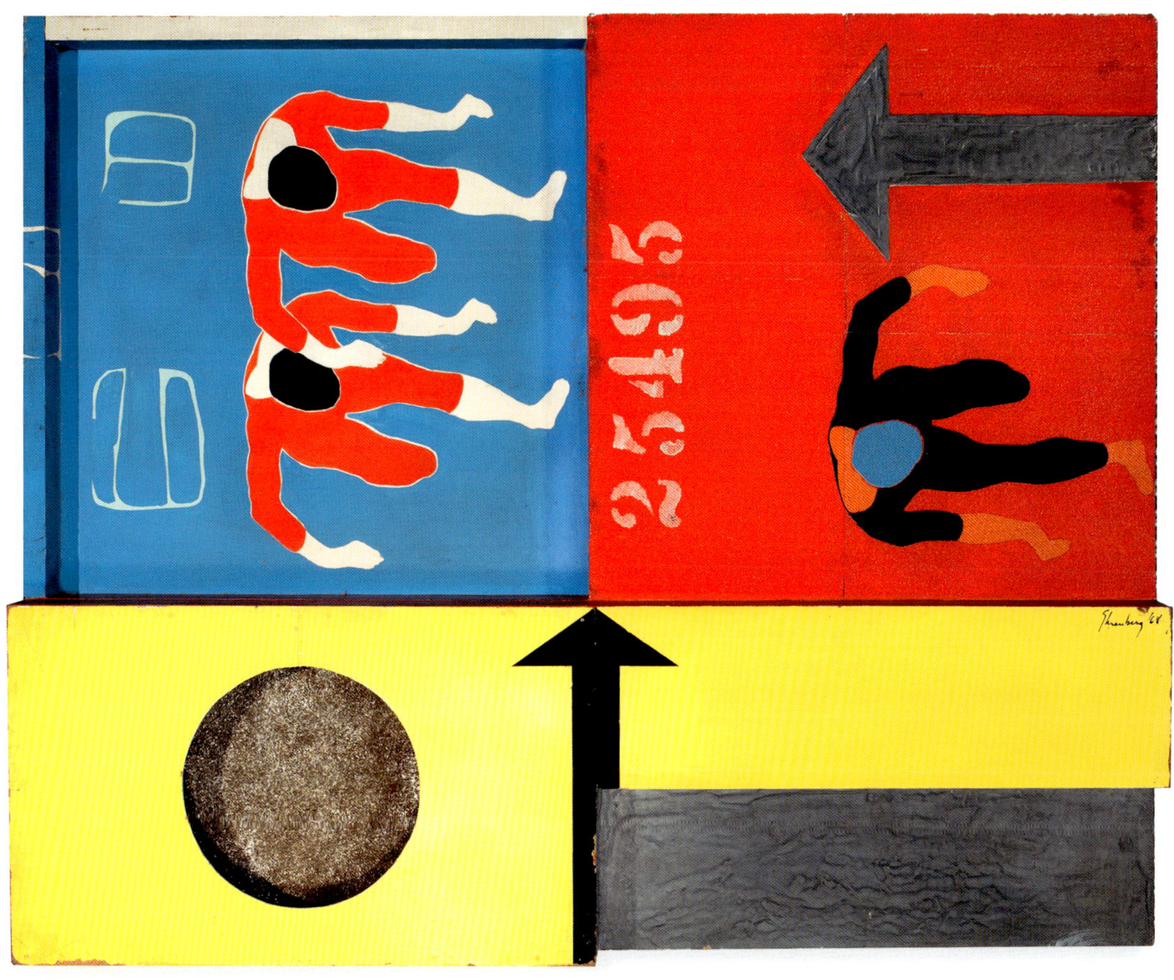

PI. 77. Felipe Ehrenberg, *Caja no. 25495* (Box no. 25495), 1968. Acrylic on wooden box with marbles, 39.37 x 31.49 x 4.33 inches (100 x 80 x 11 cm). Collection of the Museo Universitario Arte Contemporáneo (MUAC) de la Universidad Nacional Autónoma de México (UNAM), Mexico City. Courtesy of Reina María de Lourdes Hernández Fuentes.

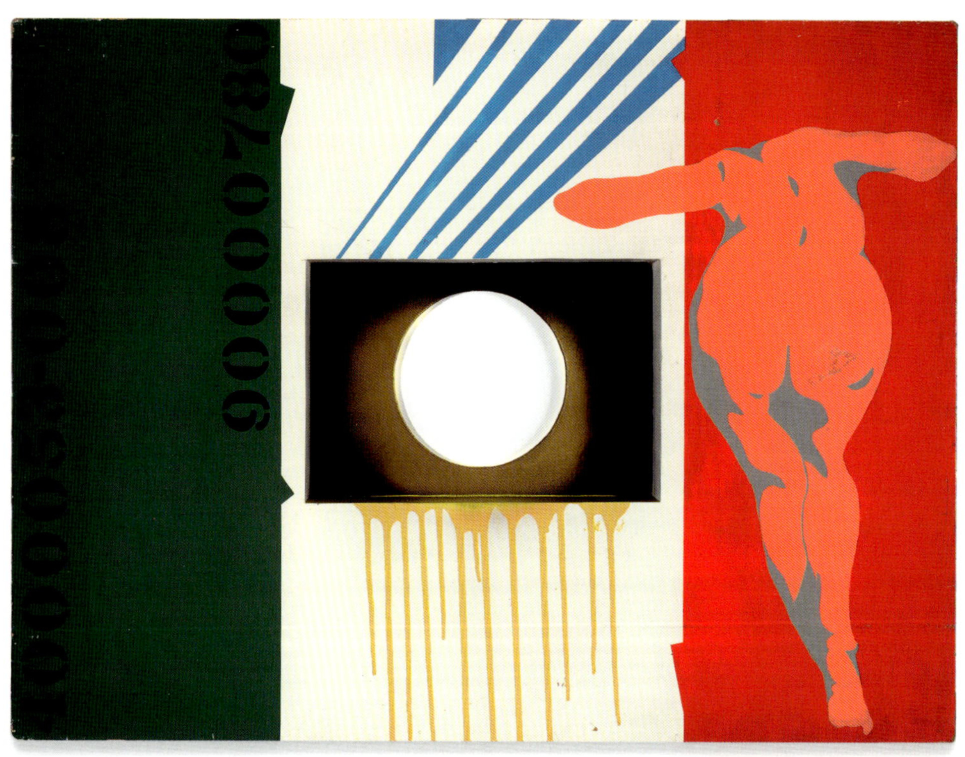

Pl. 78. Felipe Ehrenberg, *No podemos ponerla* (We Cannot Raise It), 1969. Acrylic on wooden box, 23.42 x 31.49 x 2.16 inches (59.5 x 80 x 5.5 cm). Collection of the Museo Universitario Arte Contemporáneo (MUAC) de la Universidad Nacional Autónoma de México (UNAM), Mexico City. Courtesy of Reina María de Lourdes Hernández Fuentes.

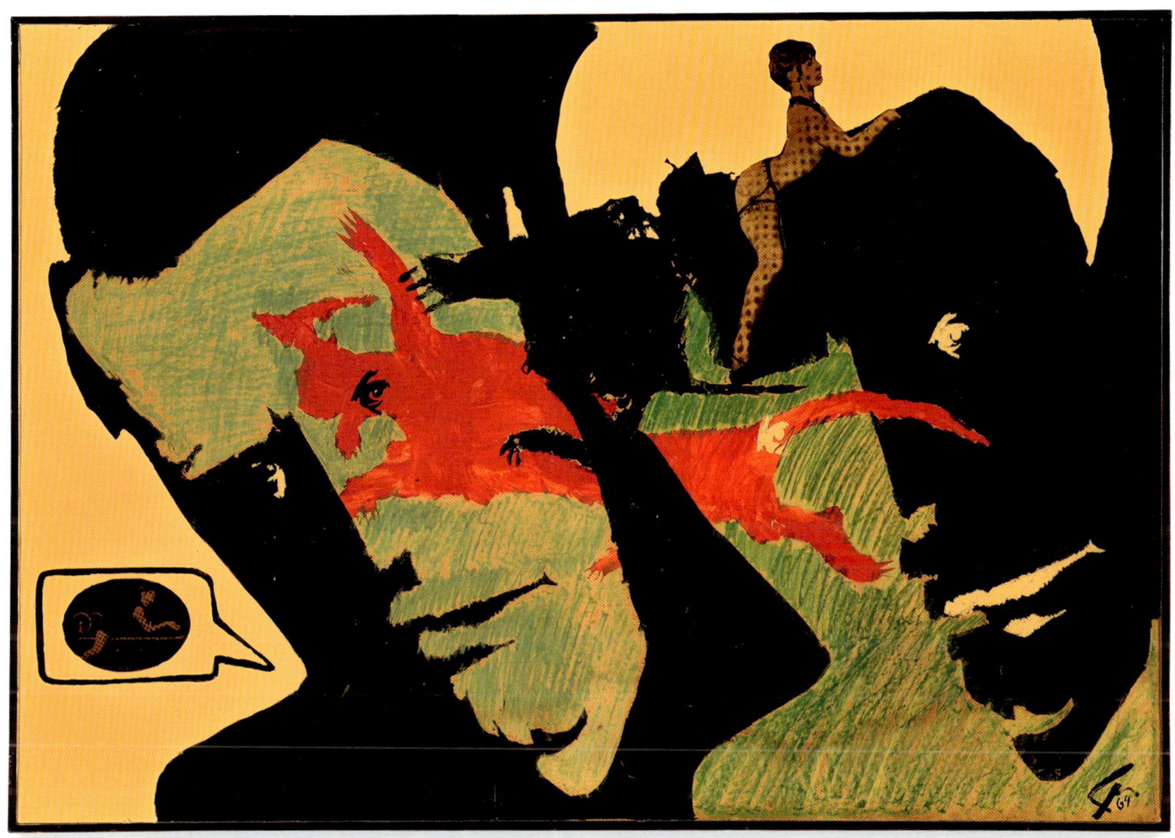

Pl. 79. Geraldo de Barros, *Diálogo* (Dialogue), 1964. Acrylic, enamel, oil pastel, oil, and newspaper on particle board; 30.9 x 45.03 inches (78.5 x 114.4 cm). Collection of Roger Wright on long-term loan to the Pinacoteca do Estado de São Paulo, Brazil. © Fabiana and Lenora de Barros. Photo by Edouard Fraipont.

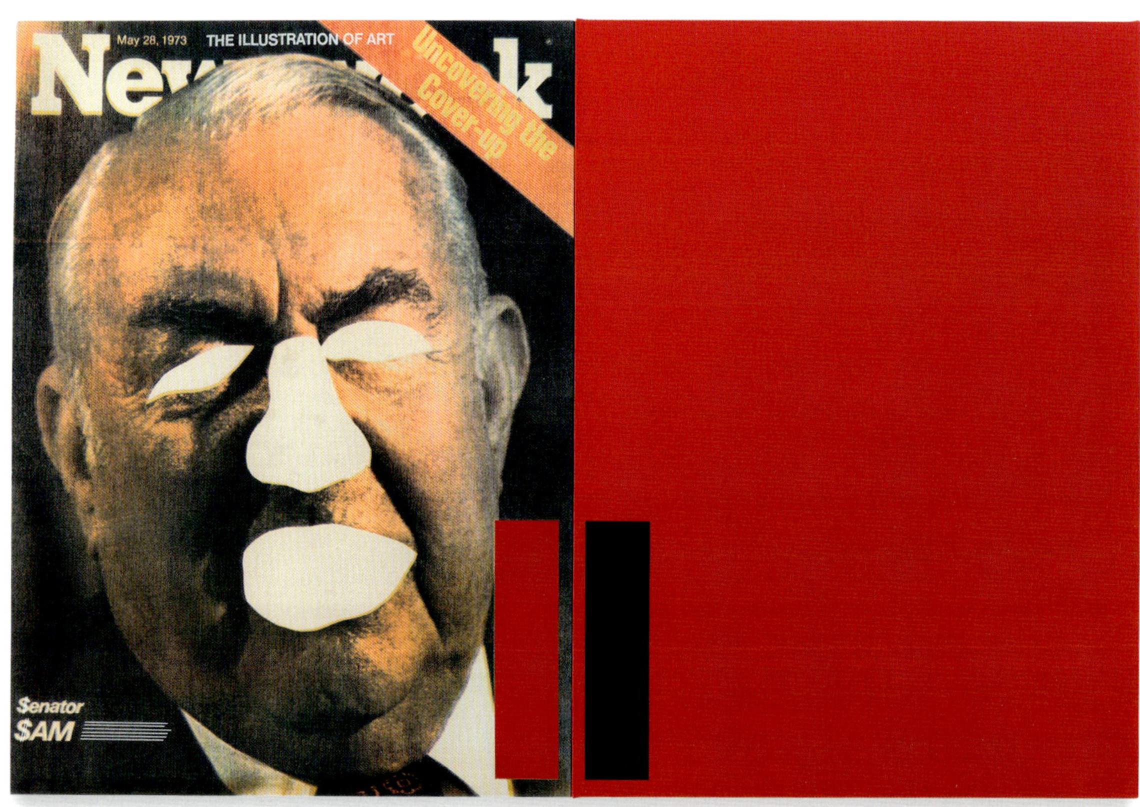

Pl. 80. Antonio Dias, *The Illustration of Art/Uncovering the Cover-Up*, 1973. Screenprint and acrylic on canvas, 35.82 x 53.54 inches (91 x 136 cm). Courtesy of the artist and Galeria Nara Roesler, New York, New York, and Rio de Janeiro, Brazil. © Antonio Dias.

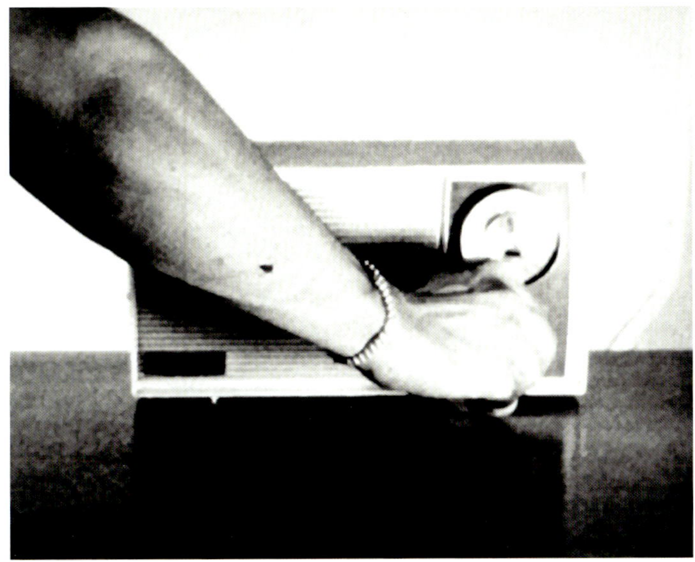
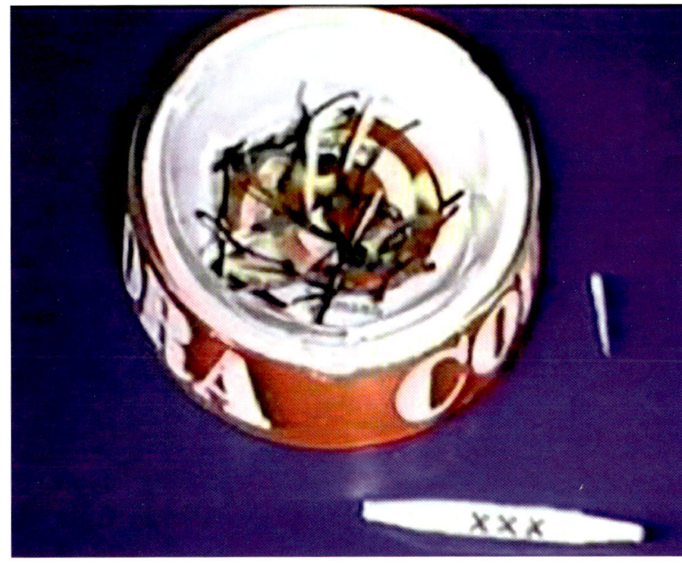
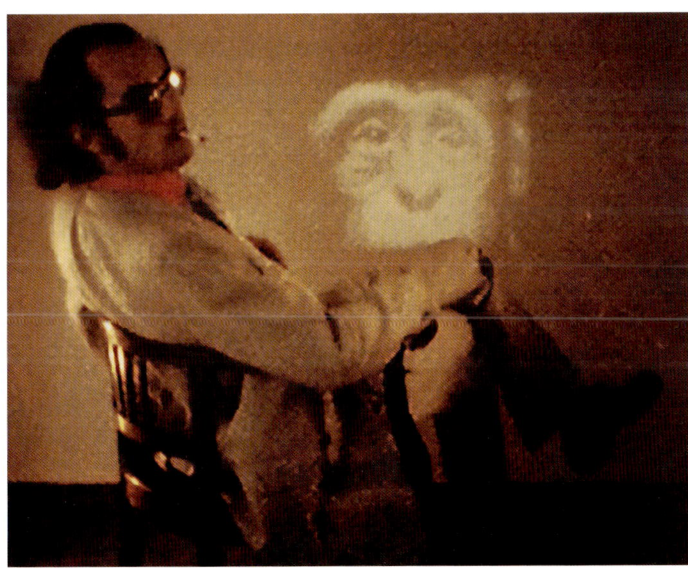
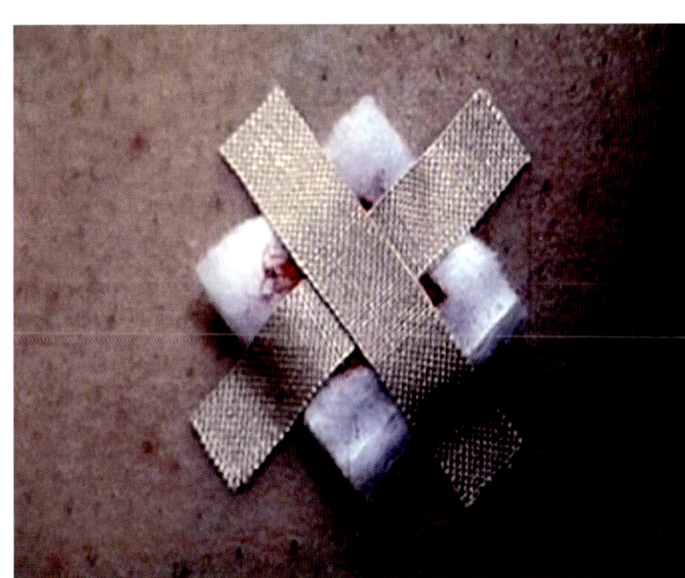

Pl. 81. Antonio Dias, *The Illustration of Art I*, 1971. Super 8mm transferred to video (color, silent), 4:12 minutes. Courtesy of the artist and Galeria Nara Roesler, New York, New York, and Rio de Janeiro, Brazil. © Antonio Dias.

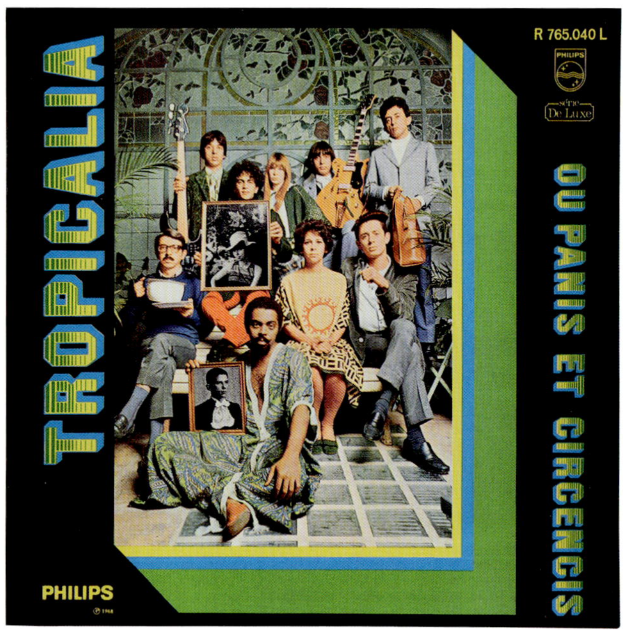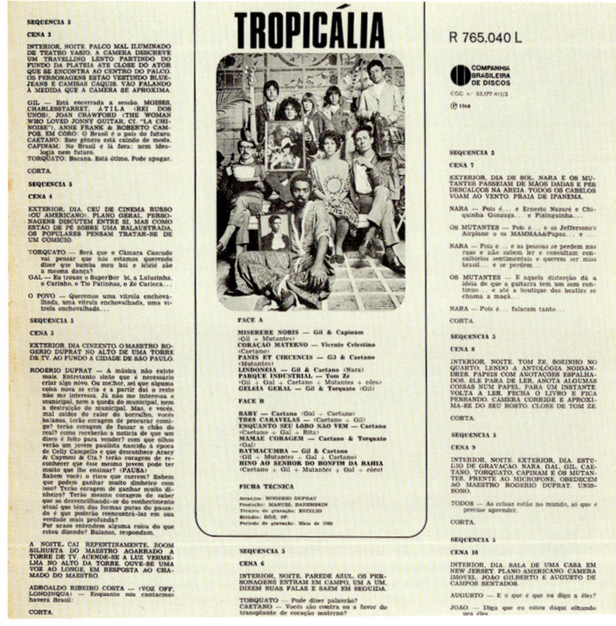

Pl. 82. Rubens Gerchman, *Tropicália ou panis et circencis* (Tropicalia or Bread and Circuses), 1968. Album cover (front and back), original pressing, 12.59 x 12.59 inches (32 x 32 cm). Collection of Marcelo Noah and Marina Bedran. © Rubens Gerchman Institute, Rio de Janeiro, Brazil. Image courtesy of the Nasher Museum of Art at Duke University, Durham, North Carolina. Photo by Peter Paul Geoffrion.

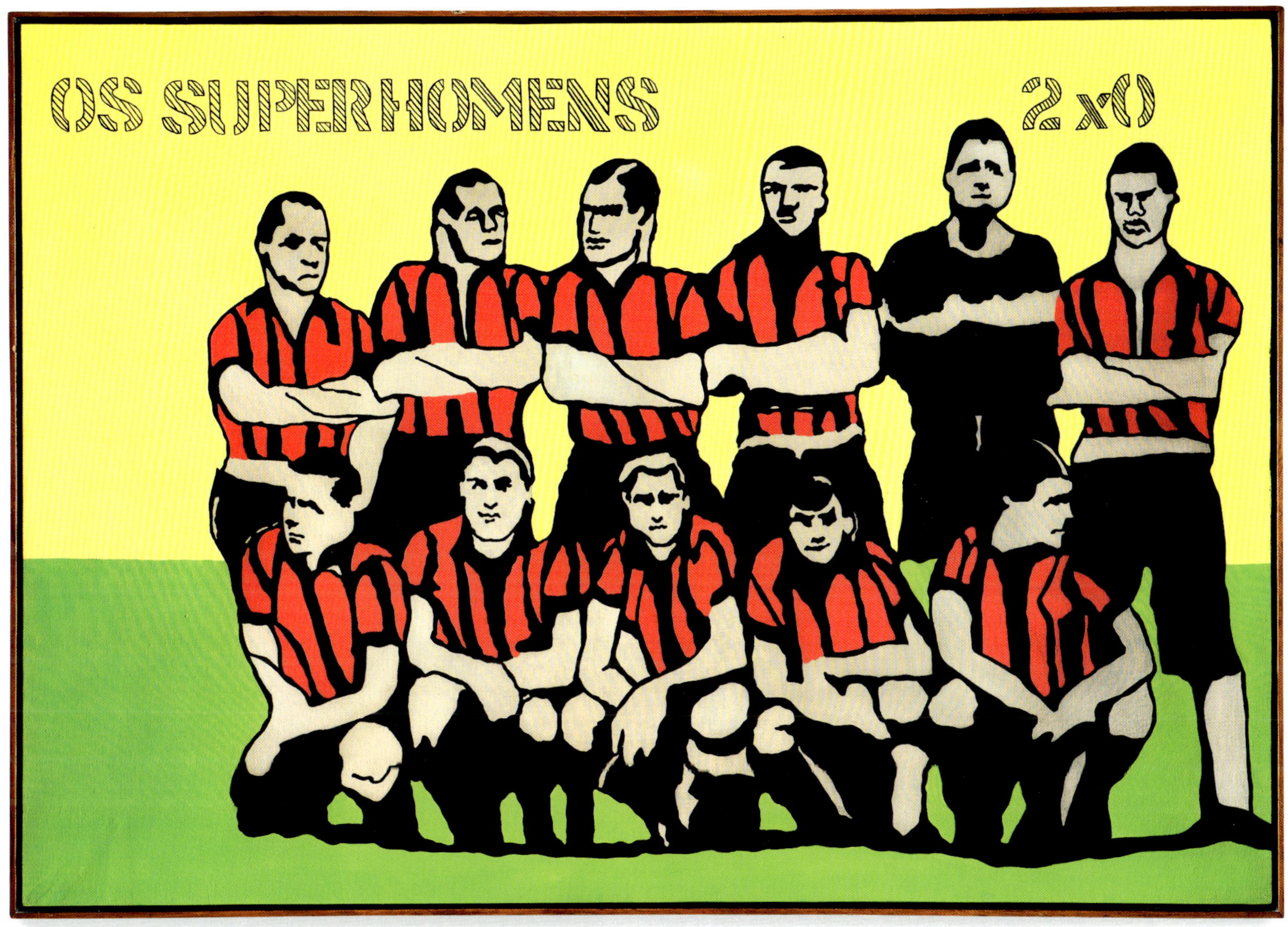

Pl. 83. Rubens Gerchman, *Os superhomens* (The Supermen/Los superhombres), 1965. Acrylic on canvas, 43.18 x 63 inches (109.7 x 160 cm). Collection of Roger Wright on long-term loan to the Pinacoteca do Estado de São Paulo, Brazil. © Rubens Gerchman Institute, Rio de Janeiro, Brazil. Photo by Edouard Fraipont.

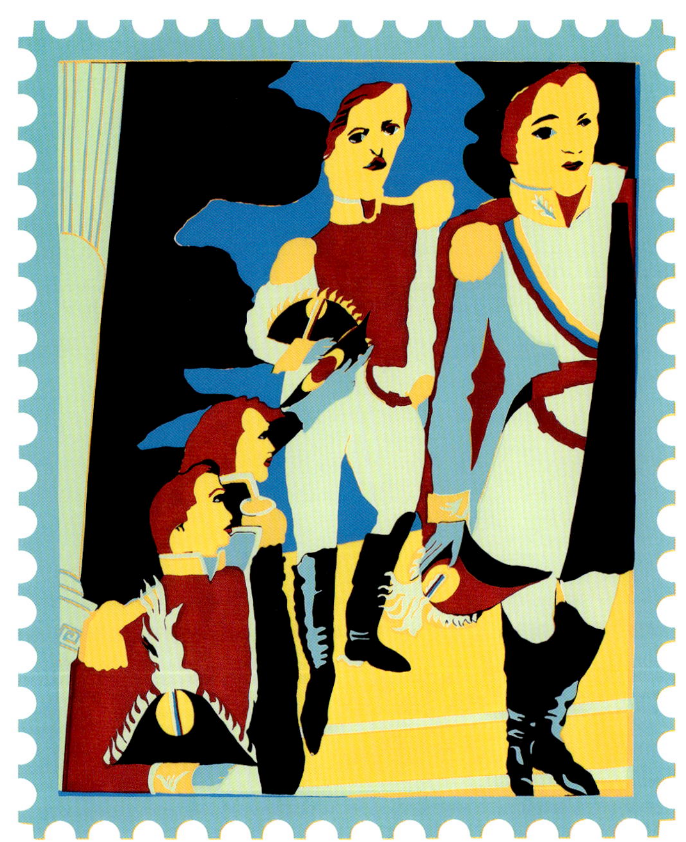

Pl. 84. Beatriz González, *Lesa majestad* (High Treason), 1974. Screenprint on BFK Rives paper, artist's proof, 30.11 x 22.24 inches (76.5 x 56.5 cm). Collection of the Blanton Museum of Art, the University of Texas at Austin. Archer M. Huntington Museum Fund. © Beatriz González. Courtesy of the artist and Casas Riegner Gallery, Bogotá, Colombia.

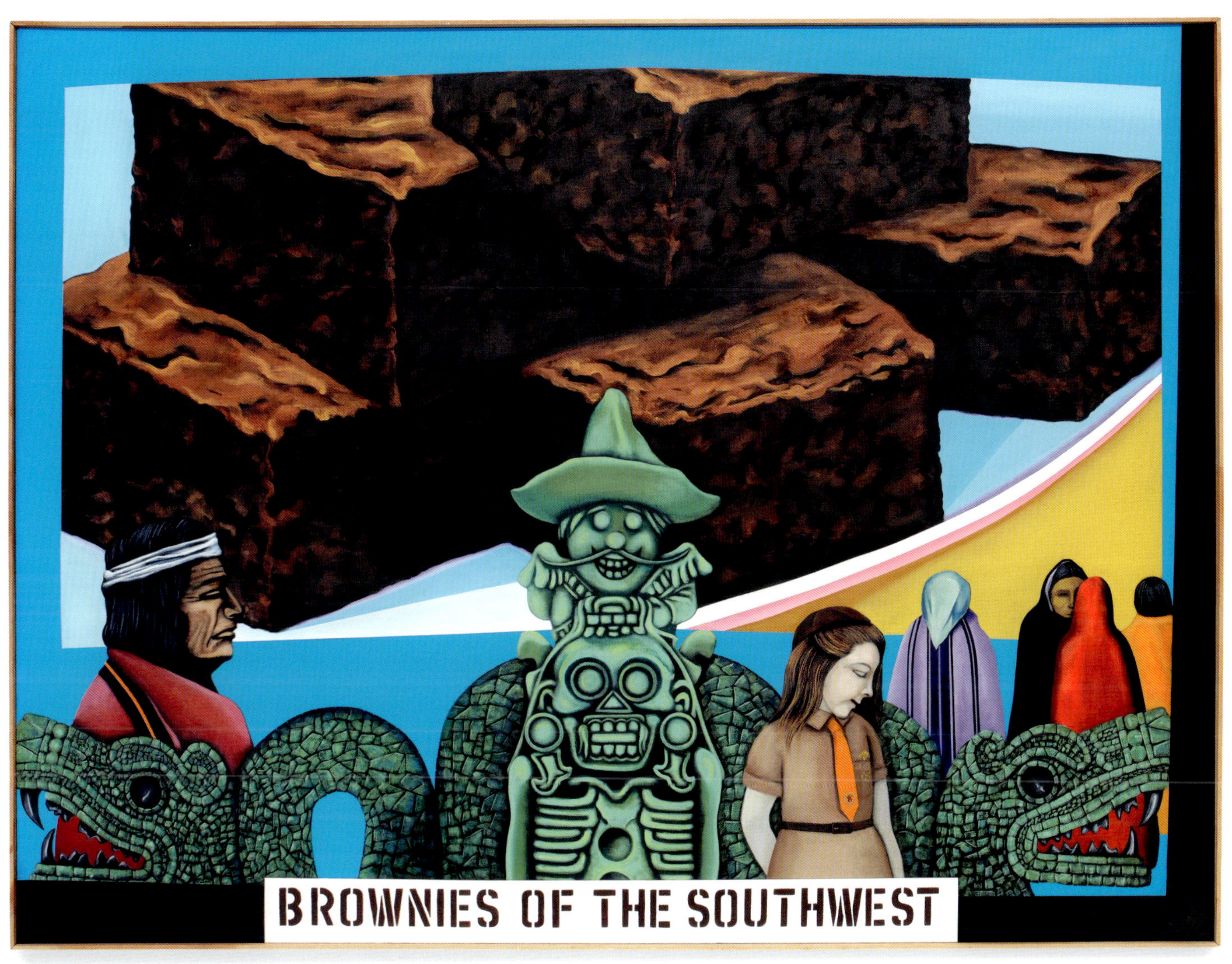

Pl. 85. Melesio Casas, *Humanscape 62*, 1970. Acrylic on canvas, 73 x 97 inches (185.42 x 246.38 cm). Collection of the Smithsonian American Art Museum, Washington, DC. Museum purchase through the Luisita L. and Franz H. Denghausen Endowment. © Mel Casas Family Trust.

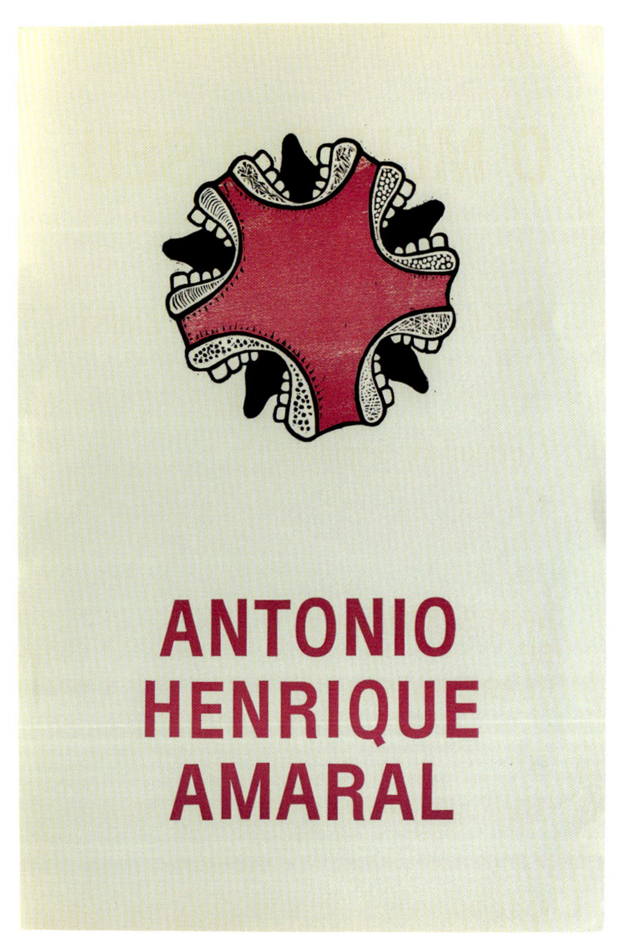

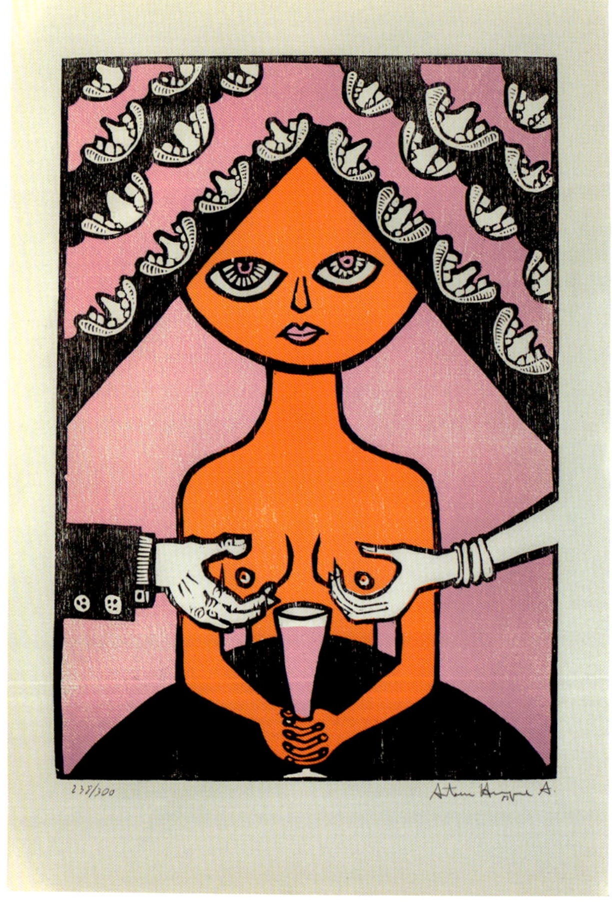

LEFT TO RIGHT, Pls. 86, 87. Antônio Henrique Amaral, *Bocas* (Mouths) and *Madona* (Madonna), from the portfolio *O meu e o seu: impressões de nosso tempo* (Mine and Yours: Impressions of Our Time), 1967. Woodcut on paper, edition 238/300, 27.56 x 23.62 inches (70 x 60 cm), each. Collection of Clayton C. Kirking and Edward J. Sullivan. Licensed by Artists Rights Society (ARS), New York, New York/AUTVIS, São Paulo, Brazil. Photo by Jeremy Lawson.

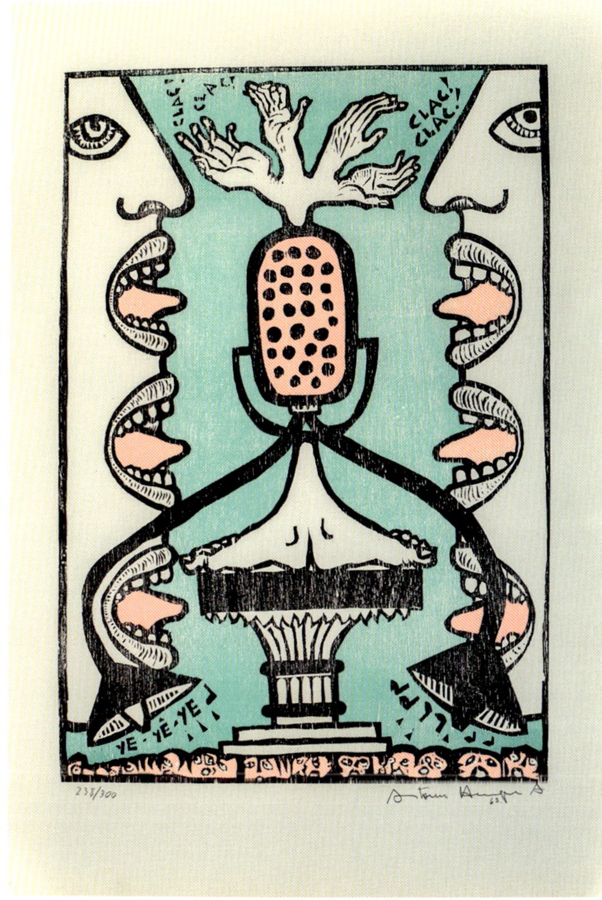
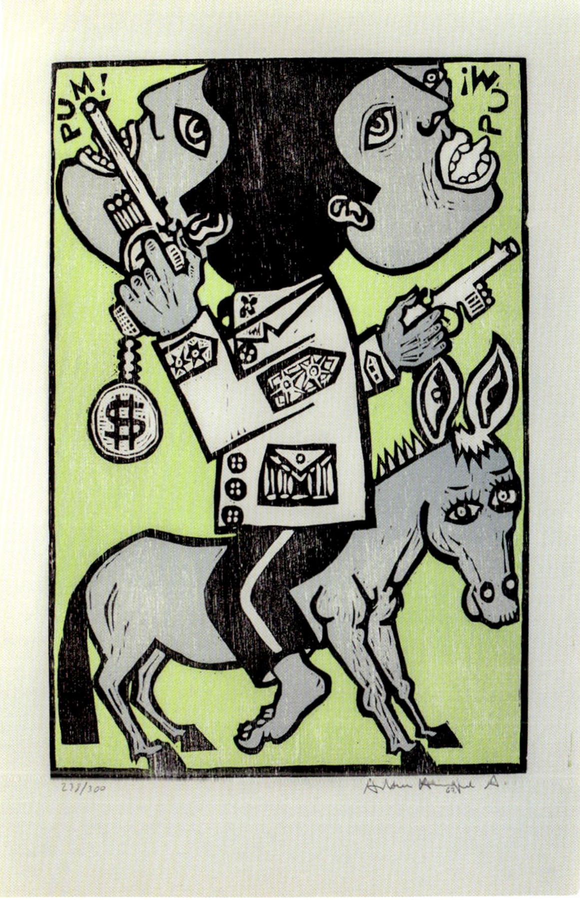

LEFT TO RIGHT, Pls. 88, 89. Antônio Henrique Amaral, *o idolatrado* (the idolized) and *Passatempo Séc. XX* (20th-Century Hobby) from the portfolio *O meu e o seu: impressões de nosso tempo* (Mine and Yours: Impressions of Our Time), 1967. Woodcut on paper, edition 238/300, 27.56 x 23.62 inches (70 x 60 cm), each. Collection of Clayton C. Kirking and Edward J. Sullivan. Licensed by Artists Rights Society (ARS), New York, New York/AUTVIS, São Paulo, Brazil. Photo by Jeremy Lawson.

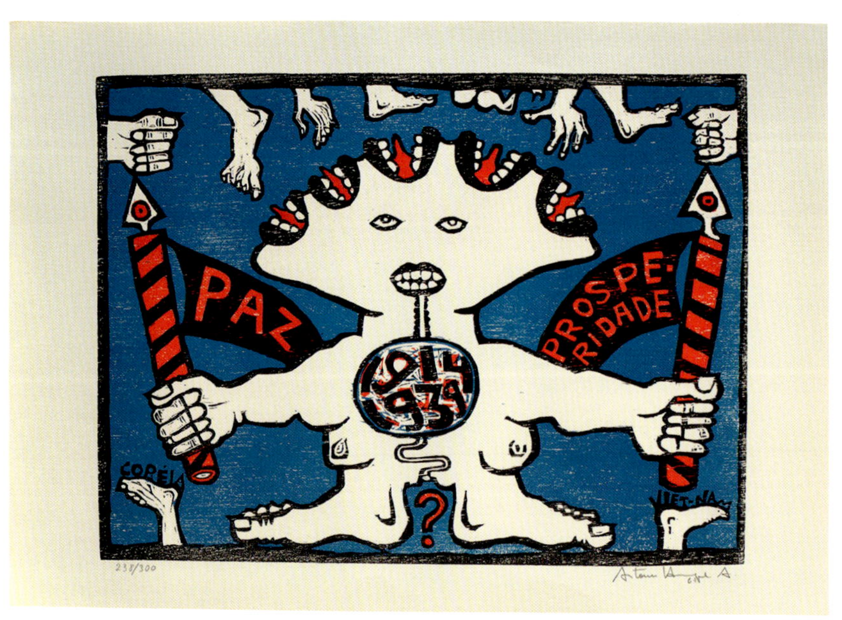

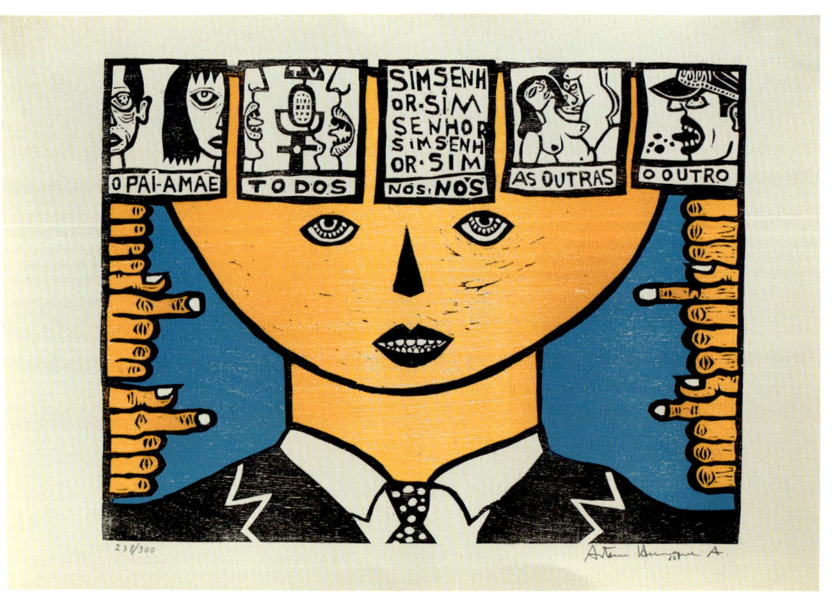

TOP TO BOTTOM, Pls. 90, 91. Antônio Henrique Amaral, *Personagem contemporâneo* (Contemporary Character) and *Realidades, culpas?* (Realities, Remorses?) from the portfolio *O meu e o seu: impressões de nosso tempo* (Mine and Yours: Impressions of Our Time), 1967. Woodcut on paper, edition 238/300, 23.62 x 27.56 inches (60 x 70 cm), each. Collection of Clayton C. Kirking and Edward J. Sullivan. Licensed by Artists Rights Society (ARS), New York, New York/ AUTVIS, São Paulo, Brazil. Photo by Jeremy Lawson.

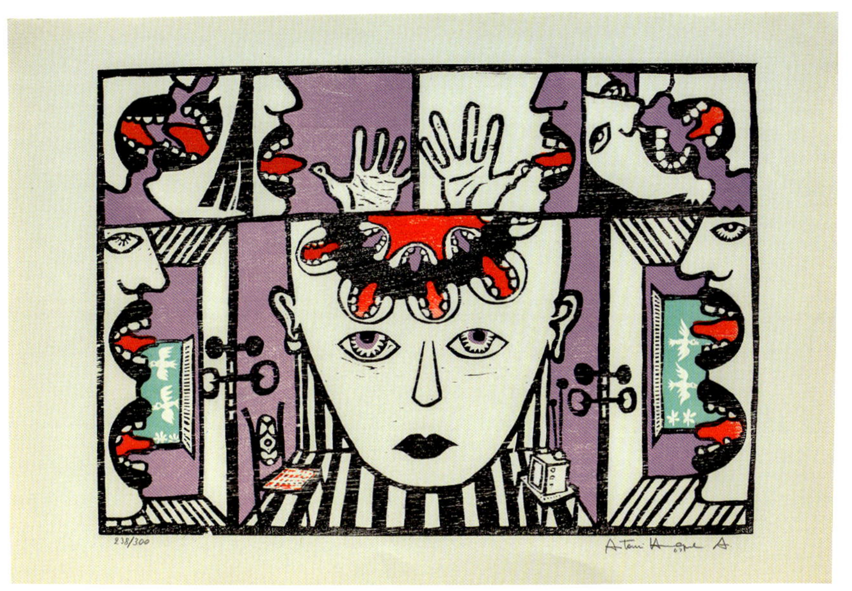

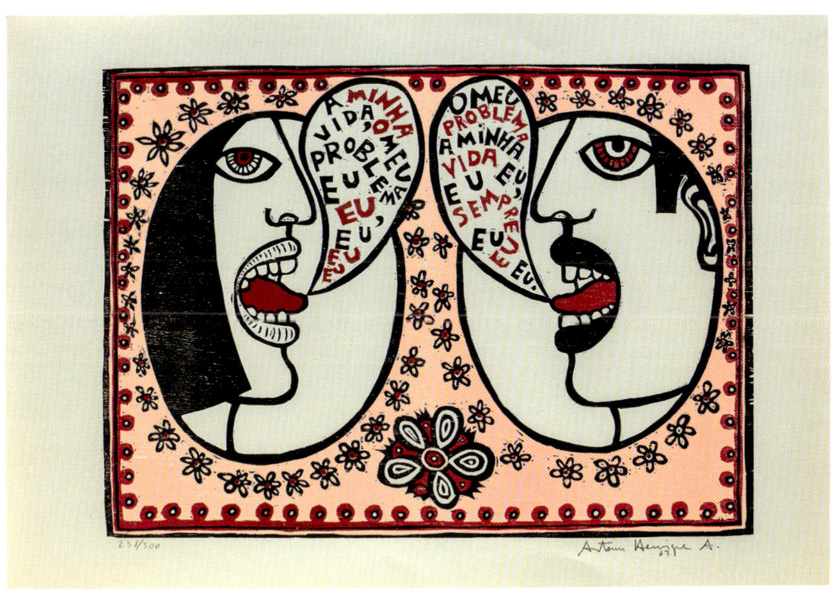

TOP TO BOTTOM, Pls. 92, 93. Antônio Henrique Amaral, *Sem saída* (No Way Out) and *Um + um = dois?* (One + One = Two?) from the portfolio *O meu e o seu: impressões de nosso tempo* (Mine and Yours: Impressions of Our Time), 1967. Woodcut on paper, edition 238/300, 23.62 x 27.56 inches (60 x 70 cm), each. Collection of Clayton C. Kirking and Edward J. Sullivan. Licensed by Artists Rights Society (ARS), New York, New York/AUTVIS, São Paulo, Brazil. Photo by Jeremy Lawson.

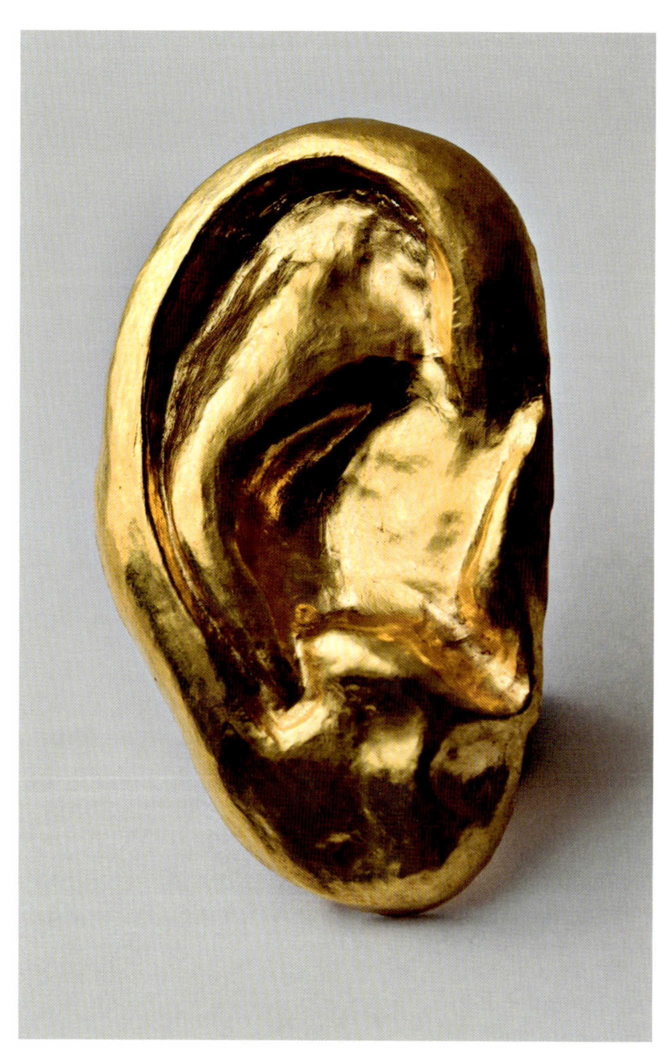

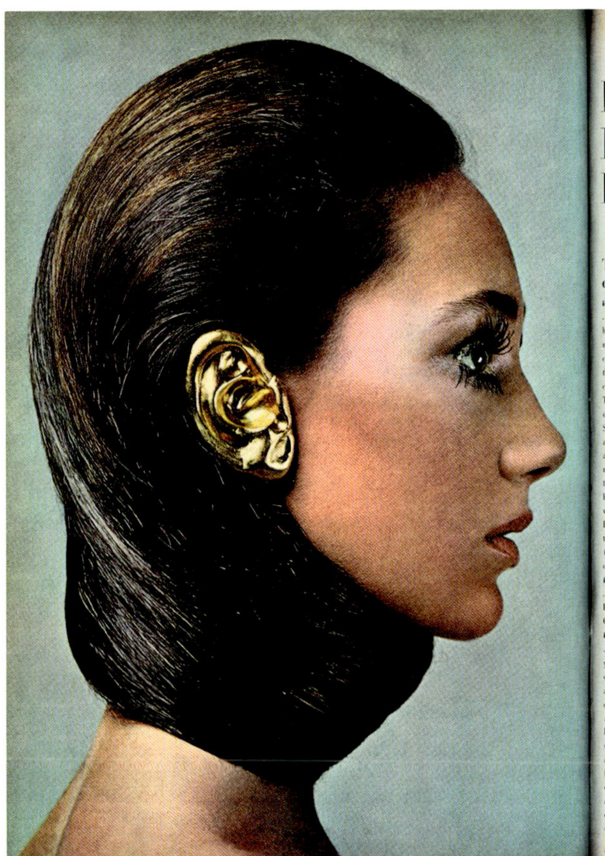

Pl. 94. Eduardo Costa, *Fashion Fiction I*, 1966–1970. 24-karat gold wearable sculpture and photograph (first published in *Vogue*, February 1, 1968; photo by Richard Avedon and modeled by Maria Berenson), 2.55 x 1.57 x 0.59 inches (6.5 x 4 x 1.5 cm), ear; 12 x 5 inches (30.5 x 24 cm), magazine. Courtesy of the artist (ear) and private collection (magazine). Sculpture © Eduardo Costa. Photograph by Richard Avedon, © The Richard Avedon Foundation.

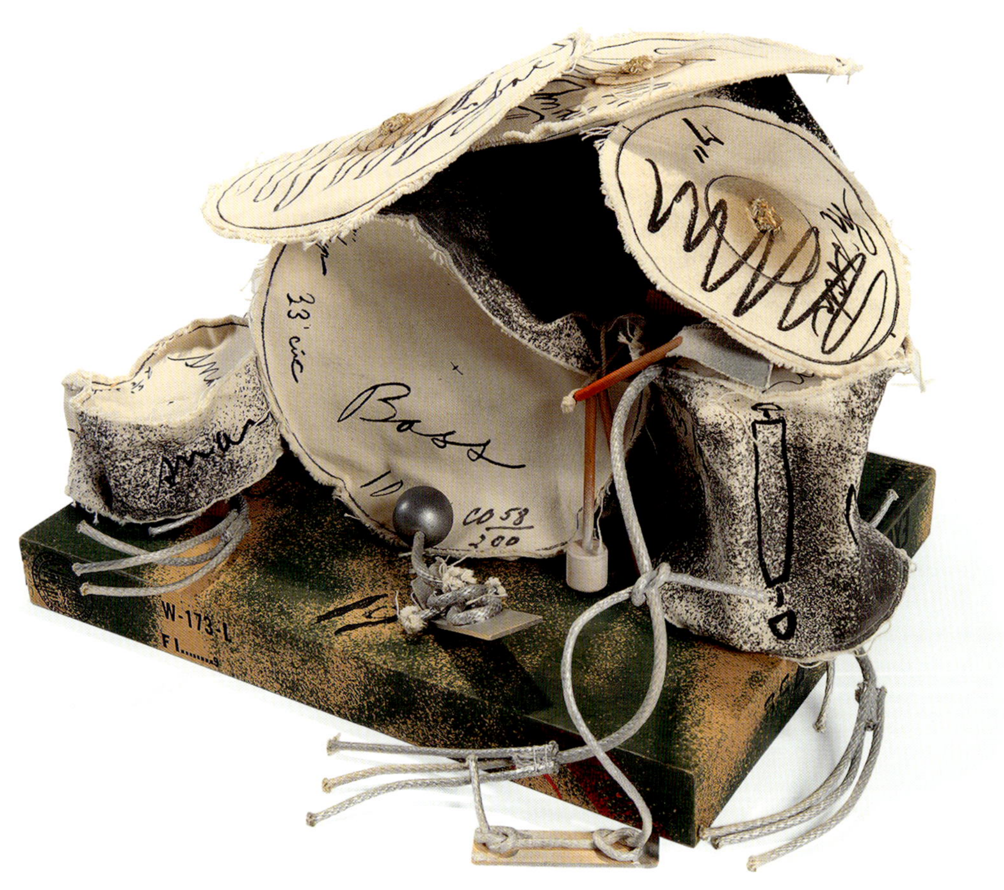

Pl. 95. Claes Oldenburg, *Miniature Soft Drum Set*, 1969 (completed 1970). Screenprints on canvas with wood and rope, edition 58/200, 9.75 x 19 x 13.75 inches (24.8 x 48.3 x 34.9 cm), dimensions variable. Collection of the McNay Art Museum, San Antonio, Texas. Gift of Robert L. B. Tobin.

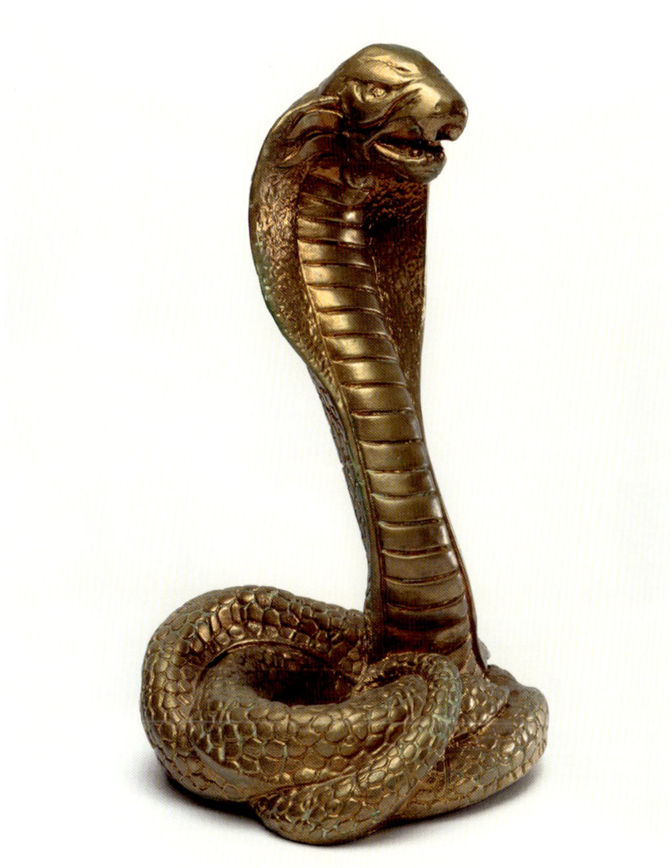

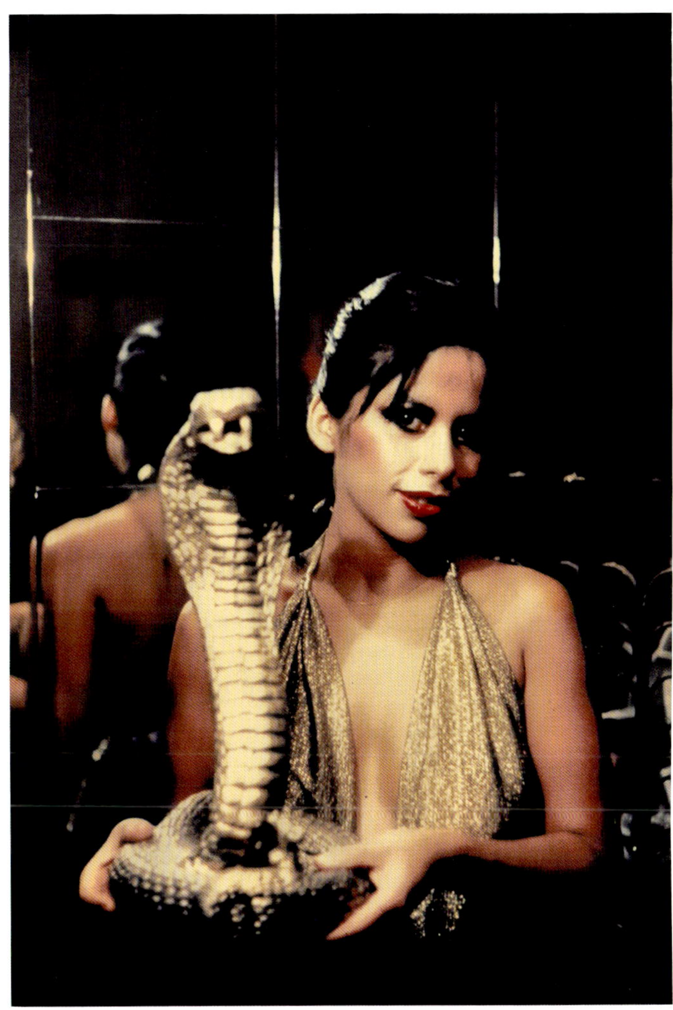

LEFT, Pl. 96. Asco (Harry Gamboa, Jr., Gronk, Willie F. Herrón III, and Patssi Valdez), *No Movie Award*, 1975. Plaster with gold spray paint, 17 x 10 x 10 inches (45.1 x 25.4 x 25.4 cm). Collection of the UCLA Chicano Studies Research Center, Los Angeles, California. The Gronk Papers. © Asco. **RIGHT, Pl. 97.** Gronk, *Patssi Valdez Receiving No Movie Award for Best Actress*, 1976. Chromogenic print, 20 x 13 inches (50.8 x 33.02 cm). Collection of the UCLA Chicano Studies Research Center, Los Angeles, California. The Gronk Papers. © Gronk. Images courtesy of the Nasher Museum of Art at Duke University, Durham, North Carolina. Photos by Robert Wedemeyer.

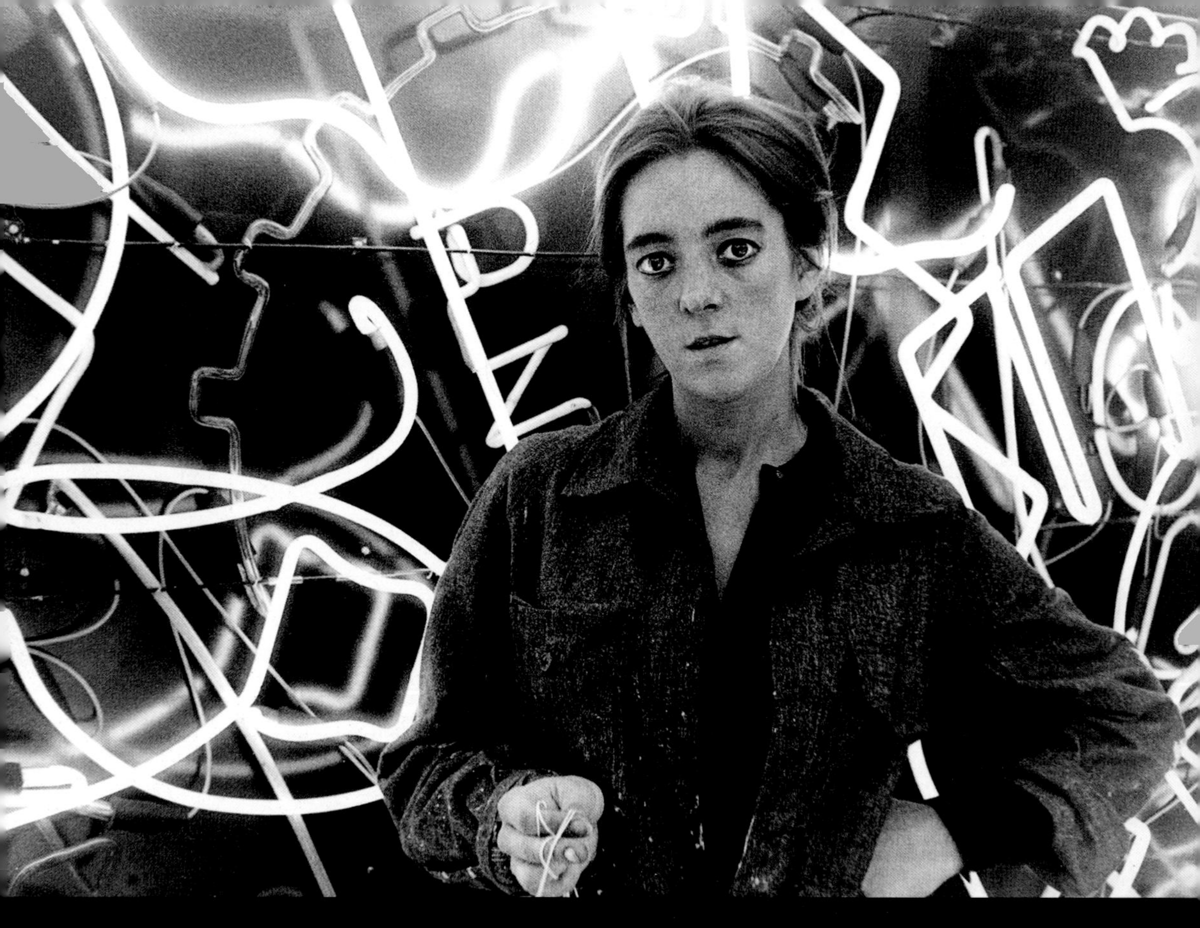

PI. 98. Marta Minujín and Rubén Santantonín, *La Menesunda* (Mayhem), 1965 (stills). 16mm film transferred to video (black and white, sound), documented by Leopoldo Maler in collaboration with David Lamelas, Floreal Amor, Rodolfo Prayon, and Pablo Suárez; 8:09 minutes. Courtesy of Marta Minujín Archives, Buenos Aires, Argentina.

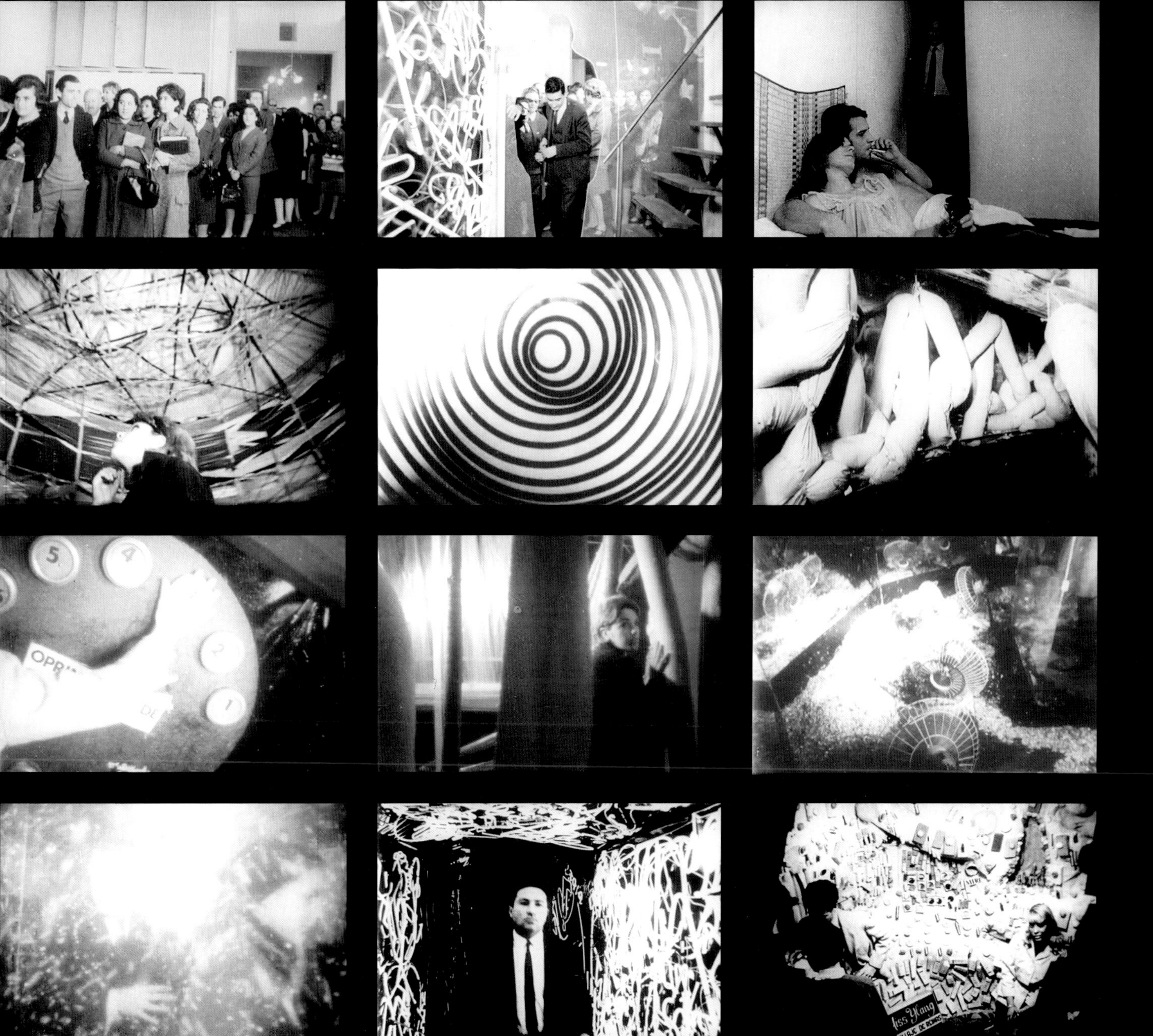

NATALIA DE LA ROSA

POP WRITING IN AMÉRICA: BETWEEN ART CRITICISM AND THEORY

In 1965, Cuban American art critic Mario Amaya raised an issue intrinsic to the movement called Pop art: the difficulty in describing it.[1] The works he analyzed had been mass-produced, used urban "folk" references, and presented a new impulse to merge life and art into a single sphere. Pop's avant-garde nature, which Amaya likened to the ready-made, emerged from assembly lines and mass media out of London and New York, media that utilized a language related to film, television, comics, newspapers, glossy magazines, fashion, billboards, and advertising.[2]

While Amaya, who lived in New York at the time, was writing this early account of Pop art and identifying the critics that were defining this new moment in art history, such as Pierre Restany, Lucy Lippard, Max Kozloff, Lawrence Alloway, Harold Rosenberg, and even Clement Greenberg, several voices in Argentina, Peru, Brazil, Colombia, and Mexico were also beginning to analyze the drastic changes taking place in the arts in each of these countries.[3] A new and unusual art movement was emerging in Latin America, as was a change in critical writing. Different postures manifested themselves in these first references to Pop art, ranging from effusive attacks to unwavering support, and in certain cases, radical reappropriation. The intention of this essay is not to establish a definition of Pop art in América, following the approach suggested by Amaya, but rather to reflect on its impact on critical writing and to study the dialogue between specific actors who were part of its conception and, in many cases, public presentation. The examples cited are from some of Pop's first exhibitions that included installations, happenings, and interdisciplinary and mediatic experiments that were fundamental to the development of contemporary art in this context.[4]

Jorge Romero Brest, Damián Bayón, Juan Acha, Marta Traba, Mário Pedrosa, Aracy Amaral, Frederico Morais, and Oscar Masotta were all critics who showed the need for political action through writing due to changes in their individual circumstances.[5] The debates over Pop emerged at a time of political turmoil that led many of these actors to change from art criticism to critical theory, along with the development of the roles of theorist-artist and artist-theorist.[6] In the context of political upheavals, the critic was no longer merely an observer of artistic production, but rather an active participant.[7]

A clear example is the case of Argentine critic Jorge Romero Brest, who confessed to momentarily setting aside his critical judgment when looking at Claes Oldenburg's "objects" in 1963. In doing so, he reconsidered classical art in relation to Pop art and was able to support expressions capable of responding to "being in the world," as was the case with *Revuélquese y viva* (Roll Around and Live) (1964) by Marta Minujín.[8] In Brazil, Mário Pedrosa tried to avoid treating Pop art as Dada, and instead analyzed the works as a reflection of the changing times.[9] Argentine critic Marta Traba, who lived and worked in Colombia, showed constant mistrust and accused these images of being imitations, soon after suggesting that Colombian artist Beatriz González had nationalized Pop art.[10] In Peru, Juan Acha, though at first skeptical, supported the first "Pop" exhibits that were accompanied by actions and happenings (see page 160, figure 5.1).[11] In

Argentina, Oscar Masotta analyzed printed images by Andy Warhol, Claes Oldenburg, and Robert Rauschenberg in order to deepen his approach to structuralism, and dedicated a text to the movement, suggesting the concepts of "*imagineros*" (image-makers) and later "dematerialization" in a subsequent text on happenings.[12] Masotta clearly reacted to a series of images, objects, and practices that, in spite of their dialogue with North American Pop art, also differed from it, as seen in an anti-happening he and Roberto Jacoby staged.[13]

It should be noted that not all writings were homogeneous; many of them expressed different stances: while Traba fall into an extremism with few nuances, Masotta kept his distance from the groups of art critics concerned with deciphering Latin American identity and instead built a theoretical alternative based on interdisciplinarity and direct relationships with artists. On the other hand, Acha adapted economic concepts based on dependency theory and found unconventional variants by translating his training as a chemical engineer into a theory akin to the physiology of vision, similar to Mário Pedrosa's views.[14] This new criticism led Brazilian Frederico Morais to a method of artistic creation and the development of an avant-garde related to collective participation and the activation of objects.[15] Beyond these individual points, this overview clarifies how Pop art was approached from a variety of perspectives that highlight the complexity of its development in a context that opened the borders of what was considered "Latin American" and redefined the concept of "American."

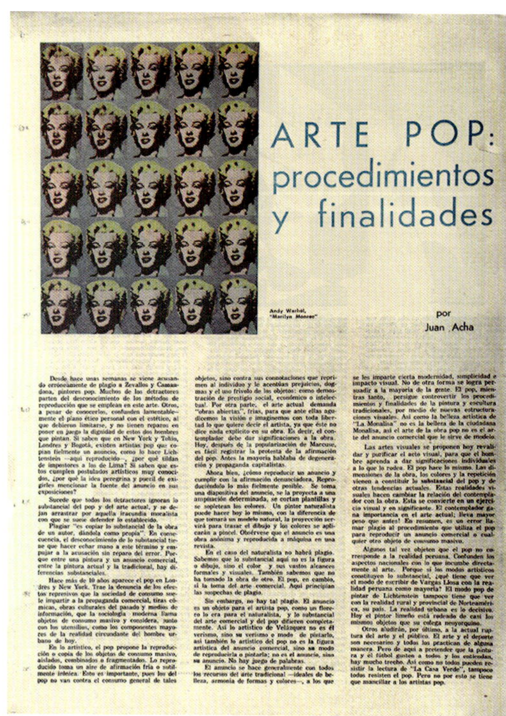

Fig. 5.1. Juan Acha (author), "Arte Pop: procedimientos y finalidades" (Pop Art: Procedures and Objectives), *El Comercio* (Lima, Peru), May 25, 1969, 38–39. Courtesy of the Archivo Mahia Biblos y Juan Acha/Proyecto Juan Acha AC, Mexico City, Mexico.

FROM ART CRITICISM TO THEORY

This essay proposes thinking of Pop art as a series of dialogues generated throughout the hemisphere. As networks created by connecting dialogues expanded, a momentum was created in various parts of the region that proposed interventions through technology and consumerism, eliciting responses from what was then called the Third World. If there is one point these authors agreed on, it is that Pop art served as a breaking point, as a new stage for avant-garde reassessment and political-aesthetic repositioning.[16] It should be noted that this "urban" artistic tendency, at least in the United States, arose from an economic program that sought to have a direct impact on various points of the American continent.[17] Therefore, Pop art cannot be considered an isolated product, but rather was born of the relation of the US with the rest of the continent.[18] In terms of the critical-theoretical response, art criticism began with an analysis of developmentalism, followed by a condemnation of dependency, and even an incipient of decolonial thought in the face of the world crisis at the beginning of 1970s, which had direct consequences across the entire continent.[19] At the same time, within the United States, social movements began to question the contradictions of global socio-economic conditions.[20] This essay, in a sense, highlights the pressure exerted by the Third World during a decade when it tried to alter a world economic order at the dawn of finance capitalism.[21] The writings that appeared during this process are proof of the dissolution of a promise of modernization and of an awareness of new forms of coloniality, and Pop art was a clear way of addressing those issues.

Beyond the taxonomy that Damián Bayón presented of the various critics in the region, it is clear that this practice began a reformulation of the active role of the intellectual, and in some cases, a response to traditional Marxist postulations, offering a leftist alternative in the form of radical and dissenting positions.[22]

In the early 1970s, several studies were published on "Latin America" that addressed the issue of what it meant to be Latin American and on Latin American art, with research based on books published on the arts of each country, magazines with a transnational perspective, exhibits, international symposiums, and institutions that underpinned the creation of a critical structure focused on these questions.[23] The network grew as the actors involved left their respective countries because of the imposition of dictatorships, coups d'état, and repression.[24] Leaving their national context allowed many of these figures to expand and radicalize their critical and theoretical proposals.

In his book *Del trance a lo transitorio* (From Trance to Transitory) (1977), Brazilian critic Frederico Morais presented a list of all the regional publications that helped "socialize art criticism."[25] Morais was responding to Juan Acha's article "*Hacia una crítica de arte como productora de teorías*" (Toward Art Criticism as a Producer of Theories) (1976), in which the Peruvian-Mexican critic called for the creation of concepts based on the local reality, such as the theory of non-objectualism he had been developing throughout those years.[26] Acha studied popular art and culture, graphic and industrial design, denouncing the fetishizing of art, that is, the commercialization and distribution of works of art and its impact on society. Non-objectual

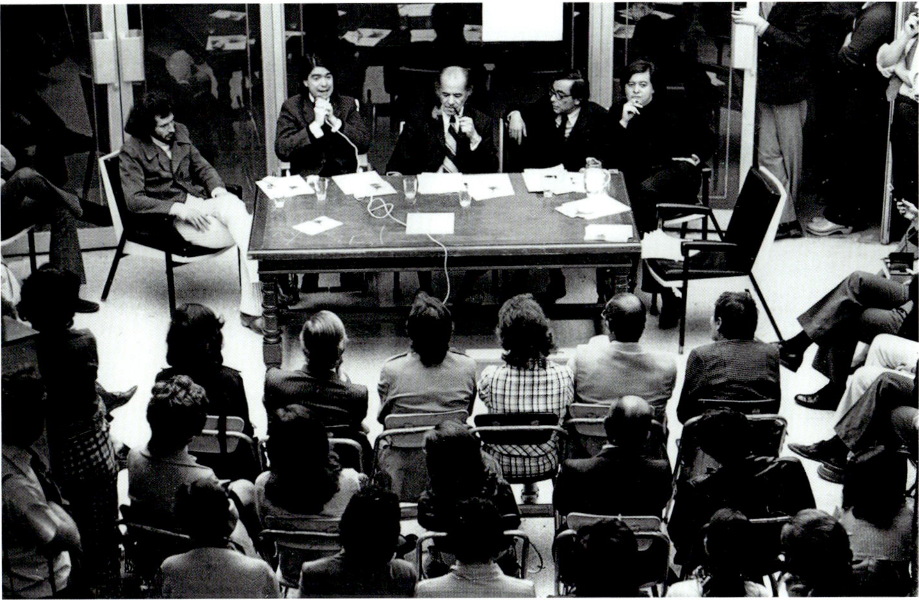

Fig. 5.2. Roundtable at the Museo de Arte Moderno, Mexico (Arnaldo Coen, Juan García Ponce, Juan Acha, Salvador Elizondo, and Juan José Gurrola), August 1973. Photo by Paulina Lavista. Courtesy of the Archivo de la Promotora Cultural Fernando Gamboa, AC, Mexico City, Mexico.

practices included the art of ideas, urban interventions, ephemeral and artisanal objects, corporeal actions, and media practices (figure 5.2).[27]

In this response, Frederico Morais presented different critical viewpoints developed between 1950 and 1970. As precedents, the critic cited the works of Jorge Romero Brest and Mário Pedrosa.[28] Regarding the following generation, he referred to Juan Acha, Marta Traba, and Damián Bayón, and went on to name the young critics who were presenting new contributions in the 1970s: Jorge Alberto Manrique, Rita Eder, Mirko Lauer, Jorge Glusberg, Néstor García Canclini, Aracy Amaral, and Morais himself. He concluded that all of these voices called for the need for cohesive critique and artistic plurality. According to him, the questions of the existence, characteristics, and needs of Latin American art should evolve into putting this theory—and art itself—into action (praxis) in view of the crisis of the avant-garde.[29] Morais felt that avant-gardism was an artistic posture and attitude that implied radical behavior, be it political or anti-artistic, and a form of direct impact on reality.[30]

Having overcome the internationalist tendency of art and faced with the danger of falling back into the nationalist rhetoric promoted by various dictatorships, artistic production and criticism developed an active response that included political transformation based on art that, instead of resisting, was meant to liberate by being designated as a "vital necessity" and a "free individual impulse."[31] In order to achieve this liberation, artistic strategies had to become radicalized. One option was to appropriate external media outlets in order to cre-

ate an alternative media that would alter the visual-sensorial conditions of the viewer—as Juan Acha stated in his text *"El arte del video tape contra la TV"* (Video Tape Art Against TV).[32] Another option was to reclaim local forms of expression, where Pop and "the popular" came together to generate a synthesis of a new image or object that revealed social and economic realities.

POP AND UNDERDEVELOPMENT: ART, DESIGN, AND CRAFT

The text *"Vanguardia y subdesarrollo"* (Avant-Garde and Underdevelopment) (1969) by poet Ferreira Gullar, written at the time the military regime in Brazil became entrenched, marked a fundamental change in theories about art. Through a study based in the revolutionary radicalism of the avant-garde, Gullar underlined the expansion of political issues and popular inclusion in art. In this text, the poet expressed the need for a radical avant-garde conscious of a game of mirrors between developed and underdeveloped countries. He analyzed postwar economies with divergent social structures, which had the underlying promise of "novelty," and generated a practically unresolvable paradox: "We need their industry and know-how, but with that industry and know-how that we need in order to be liberated, comes domination."[33] The clash of economic models of industrialized and non-industrialized countries was decisive in rethinking artistic production, for it would be deemed evidence of a new cultural and economic dependency.

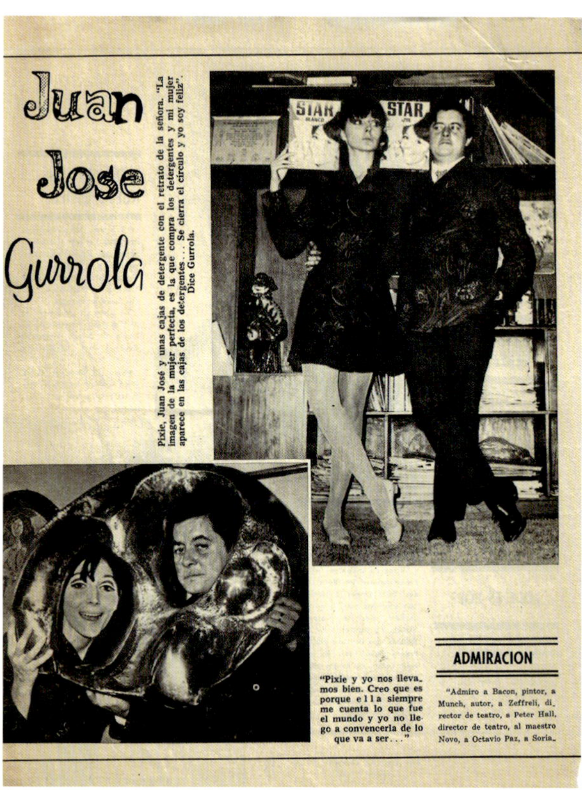

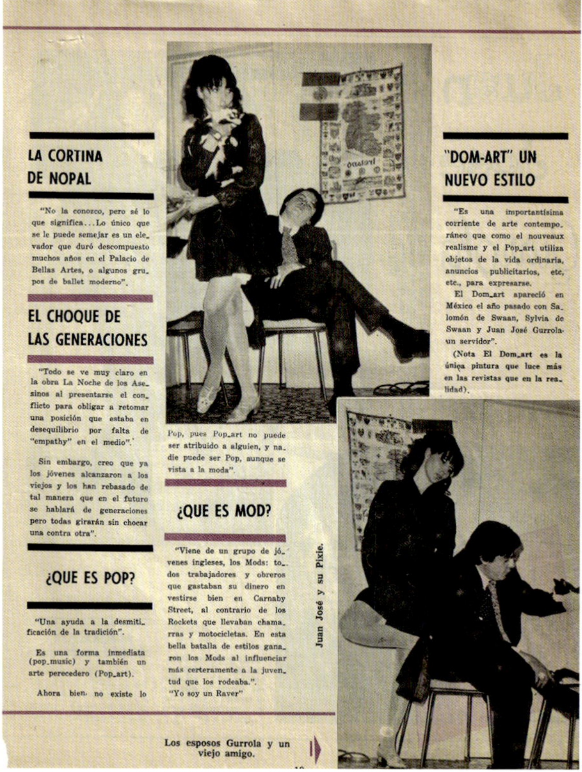

TOP TO BOTTOM, Figs. 5.3, 5.4. "Juan José Gurrola," *Onda Magazine*, no. 1, 1967. Image courtesy of the Fundación Gurrola A.C. and House of Gaga, Mexico City, Mexico, and Los Angeles, California.

In 1968, the same year of the coup d'état led by Juan Velasco Alvarado in Peru, Juan Acha presented a text with a title similar to Gullar's, in which he broke down the different developmentalist concepts confronted by the Third World.[34] In this first tentative program, Acha pointed out a middle ground that existed between underdeveloped and industrialized societies, making room for a new cultural model that could unite the two poles.

Though Pop art images had usually been accused of serving the modernizing project, by Traba for example, in truth works of art created in Latin America had maintained a certain ambivalence toward the term "popular." It seems that this urban "folk" art that Amaya described could be not only bright and cheerful, but that from the beginning, in addition to the cosmopolitan impulse of certain artists such as Delia Cancela or Emilio Hernández Saavedra in response to Bob Dylan, Twiggy, and floral shirts, there were works that put two production models into tension in satirical and violent versions.[35] One example is Chilean artist Guillermo Núñez who, in response to the Vietnam War, referred to "the death or vulnerability of soldiers."[36]

There are other divergent cases of regional Pop art. One of them is "*Pop lunfardo*" (Argentinian slang Pop), a term suggested by Pierre Restany, which emerged from Nicolás García Uriburu's series of "buses" in 1964 and the group project *La Menesunda* (Mayhem) (1965, plate 98), whose manifesto was signed by Rubén Santantonín, Marta Minujín, and Jorge Romero Brest, showing the collaboration between artists and critics.[37] Other examples are Rubens Gerchman's *caixas* (boxes) (1966, plate 106), and *Lindonéia, a Gioconda do subúrbio* (Lindonéia: The Mona Lisa of the Slum) (1966–1968, plate 105) in which he points out the spread of images by the media, while at the same time referencing the urban-popular realm. Similarly in Peru, Jesús Ruiz Durand presented a series of posters for Velasquismo (see page 14, figure 1.6) between 1968 and 1973 that combined "solarized" Op and Pop formulas with an agrarian theme, thereby launching the concept of "*pop achorado*" (rogue Pop).[38] These solutions turned imitation into appropriation, updating the definition of popular and subverting cosmopolitanism.[39] In Mexico, Juan José Gurrola presented *Dom-Art* (1966–1967, plates 24–30), or domestic art, a series of works that consisted of collage, ephemeral paintings, media-based actions, and sound happenings (figures 5.3, 5.4). As part of these exercises, he produced a collage where a can of Campbell's soup had been opened, thereby creating a dichotomy, the mirroring of the United States described by Ferreira Gullar. This strategy was compared to the Tezcatlipoca (Smoking Mirror) from pre-Hispanic cosmogony, representing the introduction of the "American Way of Life" into Mexican culture.[40] At the same time, Gurrola staged a poetic-advertising sound piece that joined interpretations of *The Moon Was Yellow* (1958) by the duo Ferrante & Teicher, opera songs in the style of American singer Mrs. Miller, and fake, humorous radio advertisements mixed with real ones from the program "*La hora nacional*" (The National Hour). This experimental approach, which also considered architecture to be a consumer good, led to the happening titled *Museo Dinámico Dom* (Dynamic Dom Museum) presented at the unveiling of a house designed by architect Manuel Larrosa for the Michel family in Mexico City in 1967.

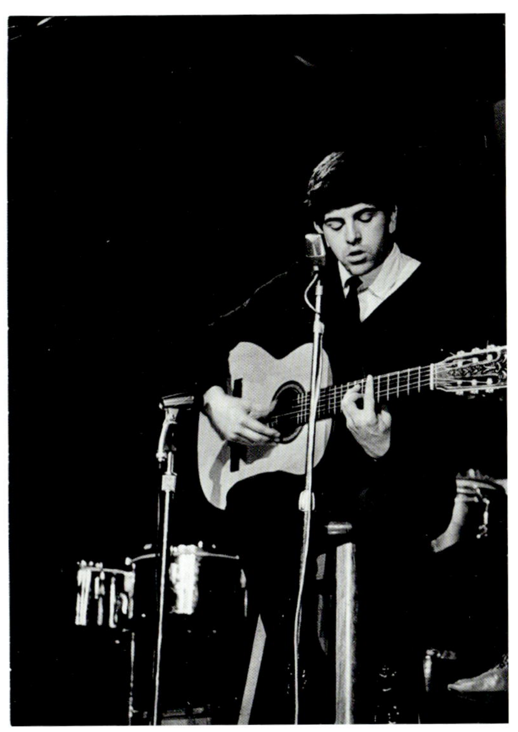

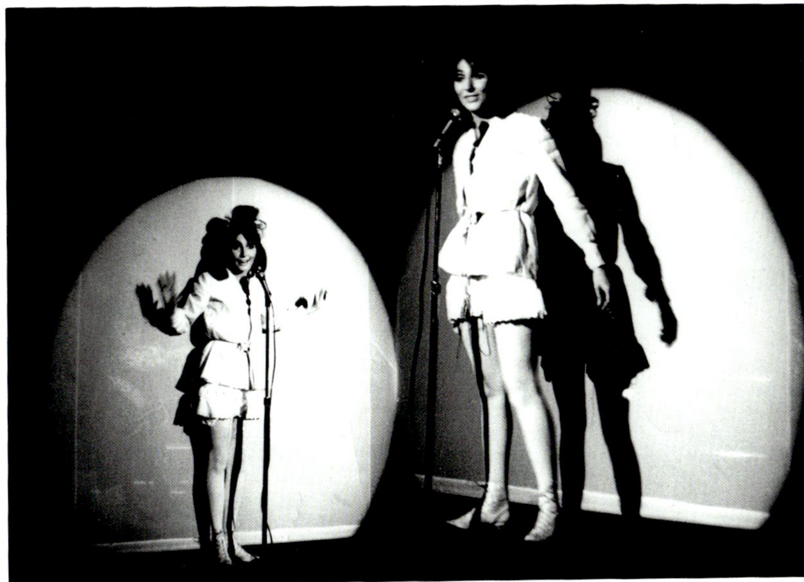

LEFT TO RIGHT, Figs. 5.5, 5.6. *2+8 en Pop* (2+8 in Pop), Music show: Pixie Hopkin and Nacho Méndez perform *Casa de la paz* (House of Peace) and *Jesús Urueta*, 1964. Image courtesy of the Fundación Gurrola A.C. and House of Gaga, Mexico City, Mexico, and Los Angeles, California.

In "*Vanguardismo y subdesarrollo*," Juan Acha also discussed the pertinence of a cultural revolution in which the artist would be able to create an alternative to the formula for consumption generated by industrialized countries.[41] It was not just a matter of unveiling the contradictions of mass culture and a fanaticism for technology described by Marshall McLuhan, but of generating efforts that would allow this intervention to go beyond the art circuit.[42] Roberto Jacoby, Eduardo Costa, and Raúl Escari had suggested these interventions in their happenings and manifesto "*Un arte de los medios de comunicación*" (An Art of Communications Media) (1966), and ended up disassociating themselves from Pop art.[43] These are moments of fusion between art and everyday life through concrete (media) interventions, as was the case with *Fashion Fiction I* for *Vogue* magazine by Eduardo Costa (1966–1970, plate 94) and the musical project *2+8 en Pop* (2+8 in Pop) by Pixie Hopkin and Nacho Méndez, produced by Juan José Gurrola in 1964 (figures 5.5, 5.6).

The avant-garde utopia presented by Acha, which became radicalized throughout the following decade, called for an awareness of how the means of production, consumption, and distribution of capitalism functioned, with the aim of "denouncing the errors of the consumer society and suggesting certain improvements through the avant-garde."[44] These works and practices that Acha called non-objectual are recorded as television images in the form of video-art, ephemeral practices, and photocopy art, but also in local crafts. These juxtapositions were made clear in the show *Chicles, chocolates y cacahuates: obras y conceptos*

(Chewing Gum, Chocolate, and Peanuts: Works and Concepts) (1973) by Felipe Ehrenberg, in which the artist, editor, and neologist combined work he produced in England with the Beau Geste Press between 1968 and 1974, with other works that were "similar to Pop."[45] The show was presented in the Peralvillo neighborhood in Mexico City: documents in progress, impossible projects, mail art, iconic-verbal condemnations, recipes, poetry, collages, slogans, even elements of Mexican popular culture and of "our everyday awareness," like *lucha libre* (wrestling).[46] There were also occasions when theory merged with practice and action was translated into an active manifesto: Masotta put on a happening in 1967 to produce ambivalent meanings in communication; Morais provoked the residents of Belo Horizonte in *Do Corpo à Terra* (From Body to Earth) (1970) by organizing a series of interventions, situations, and actions in public spaces; and Acha announced that critique, just like art, was only possible through public action (1978).[47]

In conclusion, the Pop art described by these authors, seen in this brief examination, is not an art that simply shows or fragments assembly line objects. They are works that respond and exhibit an extreme condition of capitalism by claiming an alternative where theory, like art, sought to merge with life. The goal was to modify the conditions put in place on this continent by that economic model. In addition to writings and actions, these questions remain unanswered and a part of a dialogue that is still essential to the entire hemisphere.

NOTES

1   Mario Amaya, *Pop Art ...and After* (New York: The Viking Press, 1965), 9. Amaya's exact quote is: "It is almost impossible to define Pop Art in any strict sense, the way one can define, say Cubism or Surrealism." Amaya also points out that artists themselves felt uncomfortable with the term "Pop artists" and refused to be labeled as such, not wanting to be grouped into any single movement. The term Pop art first appeared in England, coined by Lawrence Alloway. See Lawrence Alloway, "The Arts and the Mass Media," *Architectural Design & Construction*, no. 28 (February 1958): 84–85.

2   Amaya, *Pop Art ...and After*, 15.

3   Amaya refers to the following texts: Lawrence Alloway, "Pop Art since 1949," *The Listener* (London: December 27, 1962); Lucy R. Lippard, "New York Letter," *Art International* IX, no. 3 (April 1965): 48–64; Lucy R. Lippard, "New York Letter," *Art International* IX, no. 4 (May 1965): 52–59; Max Kozloff, "'Pop' Culture and the New Vulgarians," *Art International* VI, no. 2 (March 1962): 34–37; The Museum of Modern Art, "Pop Art Symposium at the Museum of Modern Art," December, 1962. Reprinted in *Arts Magazine*, vol. 37, no. 7, April 1963.

4   All of these actors wrote critical and theoretical texts on Pop production, while collaborating in specific exhibition spaces. Jorge Romero Brest and Oscar Masotta did so at the Instituto Torcuato Di Tella, until the disappearance of the Centro de Artes Visuales in 1970; Damián Bayón organized seminars and exhibitions at the University of Texas at Austin. Juan Acha, after going into exile, was assistant director of the Museo de Arte Moderno in Mexico, which went from being a museum dedicated to national art to the linchpin of regional criticism, and the collection became more focused on Latin American art. Marta Traba was director of the Museo de Arte Moderno de Bogotá, and Aracy Amaral was director of the Pinacoteca de São Paulo, where she was instrumental in including works of art from what she has called the "Pop generation."

5   It is also important to note the role of people such as Adelaida de Juan in Cuba, Ida Rodríguez Prampolini in Mexico, and Alaíde Foppa in Guatemala who were not "Latin Americanists," but represented another group that believed in critique as a form of political action.

6   One of the studies that analyzes the role of the intellectual as an active character and promoter of political transformation from the arts was carried out by Ana Longoni, based on the figure of Oscar Masotta. See Ana Longoni, ed., "Oscar Masotta: Vanguardia y revolución en los años sesenta," in *Oscar Masotta. Revolución en el arte* (Buenos Aires: Editorial Mansalva, 2017), 7–67. Artists who considered artistic practice and writing to be linked include: Roberto Jacoby, Eduardo Costa, Felipe Ehrenberg, Juan José Gurrola, Beatriz González, and Hélio Oiticica.

7   These critics analyzed authors linked to structuralism, critical theory, theory of communication, and post-structuralism. They also entered into dialogue with currents that included the philosophy of liberation, and with local theorists such as Aníbal Quijano, who was consulted by Mirko Lauer and Juan Acha, or

Paulo Freire, consulted by Frederico Morais. See Aníbal Quijano, *Dominación y cultura. Notas sobre problemas de la participación cultural* (Buenos Aires: CLACSO, 2014); Mirko Lauer, *Introducción a la pintura peruana* (Lima: Mosca Azul Editores, 1976); Juan Acha, "El geometrismo reciente en Latinoamérica," en *El geometrismo mexicano* (Mexico, IIE-UNAM, 1977), 29–50; Paulo Freire, *Pedagogy of the Oppressed*, ed. Myra Bergman (London: Penguin Books, 2017).

8   Jorge Romero Brest, "Report and Reflection on Pop Art," in *Listen, Here, Now!: Argentine Art of the 1960s. Writings of the Avant-Garde*, ed. Inés Katzenstein (New York: The Museum of Modern Art, 2004), 119–129. This passage also appears in Andrea Giunta, *Vanguardia e internacionalismo. Arte argentino de los sesenta* (Buenos Aires, Mexico, Barcelona: Paidós, 2001). Rodrigo Alonso marks the beginning of "*Pop vernáculo*" (vernacular Pop) in Argentina, which was at the tail end of existentialism and similar to the beginnings of French new realism, through exhibitions of the Braque Award and *Ver y Estimar* in 1962. In 1964, it consolidated, with the presence of the top international representatives of the movement, including Robert Rauschenberg at the Premio Di Tella, and then institutionalized in 1966, with awards given to Susana Salgado, Dalila Puzzovio, and Juan Stoppani at the Instituto Torcuato Di Tella. See Rodrigo Alonso, *El Espíritu Pop* (Mar del Plata: Museo de Arte Contemporáneo de Mar del Plata, 2014).

9   Lorenzo Mammì, "Preface" in *Mário Pedrosa. Arte e Ensaios* (São Paulo: Cosac Naify, 2015), 16.

10   Marta Traba, "Beatriz González," *Revista Eco*, no. 169 (November 1974): 65–73. See also, Marta Traba, *Dos décadas vulnerables en las artes plásticas latinoamericanas, 1950–1970* (Buenos Aires: Siglo Veintiuno Editores, 2005).

11   Juan Acha, "Arte Pop: procedimientos y finalidades," *El Comercio*, supplement, *El Dominical*, May 25, 1969, 38–39. See also Juan Acha, "Ambientes expresionistas de Teresa Burga," *El Comercio*, July 27, 1967, 23. This period is analyzed in Miguel A. López, "Cosmopolitan F(r)ictions. Aesthetics and Political Redefinitions of an Idea of the Avant-Garde in the 1960s" in *Arte contemporáneo. Colección Museo de Arte de Lima*, ed. Sharon Lerner (Lima: Museo de Arte de Lima, 2013), 17–39.

12   Oscar Masotta, "El Pop-Art and 'Happenings,'" *Oscar Masotta. Revolución en el arte*, 69–130 and 131–206.

13   Roberto Jacoby, "Against the Happening," *Listen, Here, Now!*, 229.

14   Dependency theory is an economic model that was popular in the 1960s and 1970s. It appeared in response to the Economic Commission for Latin America's development program and suggested a dialectical analysis of the region with other centers. The authors who developed this theory were Fernando H. Cardoso, Enzo Faletto, Ruy Mauro Marini, Celso Furtado, Vania Bambirra. Fernando H. Cardoso and Enzo Faletto. See *Dependencia y desarrollo en América Latina* (Mexico: Siglo XXI, 1969); Ruy Mauro Marini, *Dialéctica de*

la dependencia (Mexico: Era, 1973); Celso Furtado, *Desarrollo y subdesarrollo* (Mexico, Eudeba, 1964); Fernando. H. Cardoso, *Problemas del subdesarrollo latinoamericano* (Mexico: Nuestro Tiempo, 1973); Teotonio Dos Santos, *Dependencia y cambio social* (Santiago: Cuadernos de Estudios Socio Económicos, Universidad De Chile, 1970). To understand the shift from dependency theory to decolonial thought see Ramón Grosfoguel, "Developmentalism, Modernity, and Dependency Theory in Latin America," eds., Mabel Moraña, Enrique Dussel, and Carlos A. Jaúregui, *Coloniality at Large: Latin American and the Postcolonial Debate* (Durham: Duke Press, 2008), 307. The fact that the Peruvian-Mexican critic invited Pedrosa to participate in a series of lectures at the Museo de Arte Moderno de México between 1973 and 1974 is evidence of the common ground they shared. Pedrosa was also asked to write for the MAM's magazine *Artes Visuales*, for which he wrote: Mário Pedrosa, "Arte hoy, ¿Hacia dónde vamos? Manifiesto para los Tupininquis o Nambás," *Artes Visuales*, Museo de Arte Moderno, Mexico, no. 10 (April–June,1976): 31–35.

15   These proposals were exhibited in 1970, based on a proposed manifesto and exhibit entitled *Do Corpo à Terra* and the show *Objeto e Participação*, both presented in Belo Horizonte, Brazil. See also Frederico Morais, *Artes Plásticas, A crise da hora atual* (Rio de Janeiro: Paz e Terra, 1975).

16   This state of affairs led Brest, Pedrosa, Acha, Bayón, and Traba to study and analyze the substantial changes in artistic production from a national point of view, on a stage that included geometric abstraction and informalism, until eventually Pop art made its appearance.

17   Greg Grandin, *Empire's Workshop. Latin America, the United States, and the Rise of the New Imperialism* (New York: Metropolitan Books/Henry Holt and Company, 2010).

18   This process began through Pan-Americanism, which emerged from policies related to the New Deal. It was consolidated through the postwar welfare state and reorganized based on the neoliberal project.

19   Toni Negri, *Revolution Retrieved: Writings on Marx, Keynes, Capitalist Crisis and New Social Subjects* (London: Red Notes, 1988). Negri explains that in 1944, Karl Polanyi, in his work entitled *The Great Transformation*, described the beginning of the protectionist policy of the postwar welfare state, an economic process described as Keynesianism, which implied a rejection of laissez-faire liberalism, necessary to a balance that became known as the socialization of capitalist production. In these writings, a consequence of the Great Depression, Keynes claimed that political intervention was needed to mediate all economic activity.

20   At the center of these two moments are the political upheavals that took place throughout the world in 1968, as well as what is known as the self-assertion of the Third World, decisively affected by the Cuban Revolution and the Vietnam War. The civil rights movement and the rise of feminism are clear examples, which led to a restructuring and reconfiguration of the economic or-

der through what we now call neoliberalism. See Brian Holmes, "Investigaciones extradisciplinares. Hacia una nueva crítica de las instituciones.," trans. Marcelo Expósito (European Institute for Progressive Cultural Policies, 2007), accessed May 4, 2017, http://eipcp.net/transversal/0106/holmes/es.

21   Barbara and John Ehrenreich, "The Professional-Managerial Class," in *Between Labor and Capital*, ed. Pat Walker (New York: South End Press, 1979), 213–278.

22   Bayón's taxonomy includes: *crítico-jefe de clan* (critic-clan chief), *crítico-teórico* (critic-theorist), *crítico-sociólogo* (critic sociologist), *crítico-artista* (critic-artist). See Ana Longoni, *Oscar Masotta. La teoría como acción/Theory as Action* (Mexico City: Museo Universitario de Arte Contemporáneo, UNAM, 2017).

23   Certain exhibitions that took place during the developmentalist period had the support of the Organization of American States (OAS), the Pan American Union, and José Gómez Sicre. Also, several salons and biennials were created, often sponsored by corporations in partnership with Washington, such as the ESSO Salon between 1964–1965, which was held in Colombia, Mexico, and Peru. Biennials were also important, especially the São Paulo Biennial, as well as counter biennials, such as the one held in Córdoba and the Latin American Biennial of São Paulo. Claire F. Fox, *Making Art Panamerican: Cultural Policy and the Cold War* (Minneapolis: University of Minnesota Press, 2013). The antecedent to these symposiums was a meeting organized by Damián Bayón in Ecuador, "América Latina y sus artes." See Damián Bayón, in *América Latina y sus artes* (Mexico: Siglo XXI, 1974). After that, the symposium "La dicotomía entre arte culto y el arte popular" was held in Zacatecas, organized by the UNAM's Instituto de Investigaciones Estéticas in 1975, followed by "El artista latinoamericano y su identidad" in Austin, Texas, in collaboration with The University of Texas, the Blanton Museum, Acha, Kasuya Sakai, and Bayón. See Rita Eder, "Juan Acha: pensar el arte desde América Latina," *Post: Notes on Modern & Contemporary Art Around the Globe*, The Museum of Modern Art, posted September 27, 2016, accessed May 2, 2017, http://post.at.moma.org/ content_items/752-juan-acha-pensar-el-arte-desde-america-latina.

24   This was the case of Mário Pedrosa, who moved from Brazil to Chile, and Oscar Masotta and Damián Bayón, who left Argentina and moved to Spain and the United States, respectively. Marta Traba left Colombia for Puerto Rico, and Juan Acha moved from Peru to Mexico.

25   Frederico Morais, *Las artes plásticas en América Latina. Del trance a los trasitorio* (La Habana: Casa de las Américas, 1990).

26   Juan Acha, "Hacia una crítica como productora de teorías," *Artes Visuales* (Spring, 1977): 29. Acha describes this concept in: *El arte y su distribución* (1984); *Arte y Sociedad en Latinoamérica. El producto artístico y su estructura* (1979); and *Arte y Sociedad en Latinoamérica. El sistema de producción* (1979). For many artists from the continent, this concept paved

the way for practices similar to Conceptualism but that, at the same time, differed from this international tendency. See also Alberto Sierra Maya, Víctor Manuel Manrique, and Augusto del Valle, *Memorias del Primer Coloquio Latinoamericano sobre Arte No-objetual y Arte Urbano* (Medellin: Museo de Antioquia, Museo de Arte Moderno de Medellín, 2011).

27   Juan Acha, "Teoría y práctica no-objetualistas en América Latina." See also Alberto Sierra Maya et al., *Memorias del Primer Coloquio Latinoamericano sobre Arte No-objetual y Arte Urbano*, 75–88.

28   Octavio Paz, the leading figure in Mexico in the development of art criticism and the internationalist impulse, in opposition to local nationalism, could be added to this pair. In fact, a text by Paz served as the introduction to one of the most important Latin Americanist symposiums, organized by Damián Bayón at the University of Texas at Austin in 1975. See Damián Bayón, *El artista latinoamericano y su identidad* (Caracas: Monte Ávila Editores, 1977).

29   Morais, *Las artes plásticas en América Latina. Del trance a lo transitorio*, 17.

30   Frederico Morais, "Arte brasileira, anos 70: o fim da vanguarda?," *Módulo*, Brazil, no. 55 (September 1979): 50–60.

31   Giunta, *Vanguardia, internacionalismo y política*, 116. See also Mário Pedrosa, "*Vicissitudes do arte sovietico*" in *Mário Pedrosa. Arte e Ensaios* (São Paulo: Cosac Naify, 2015), 359–364. For example, for Pedrosa, this response had to distance itself as much from commercialization as from ideology, that is, from the capitalist system itself, and also from the image-illustration of Soviet art. The magazine *Artes Visuales*, edited by Carla Stellweg, was one of the publications that addressed the social role of the critic mentioned by Frederico Morais. Contributors to this magazine included: Juan Acha, as guest editor, Mário Pedrosa, Néstor García Caclini, Rita Eder, Jorge Alberto Manrique, Alaíde Foppa, Clemente Padín, Damián Bayón, Jorge Romero Brest, Aracy Amaral, Juan Downey, Jorge Glusberg, M.A. Rojas Mix, Marta Traba, and Adelaida de Juan. Translations of texts by Les Levine, Lucy R. Lippard, and Marshall McLuhan were also included.

32   Juan Acha, "El arte del video tape contra la TV," *Diorama de la Cultura*, supplement, *Excélsior*, July 15, 1973.

33   Ferreira Gullar, *Vanguarda e subdesenvolvimento* (Rio de Janeiro: Editora Civilização Brasileira S.A., 1978), 24.

34   Juan Acha, "Vanguardismo y subdesarrollo," in *Ensayos y ponencias latinoamericanistas* (Caracas: Galería de Arte Nacional, 1984), 11–26.

35   Jorge Romero Brest, "La pintura pop" in *El arte en la Argentina. Últimas décadas* (Buenos Aires: Paidós, 1969), 69. See also López, "Cosmopolitan F(r)ictions," 29–30.

36   Soledad García and Daniela Berger, *La emergencia del pop. Irreverencia y calle en Chile* (Santiago: Museo de la Solidaridad Salvador Allende, 2016), 33. See also

http://mssa.cl/mssa3/wp-content/uploads/2016/05/CATALOGOPOPpp.pdf.

37   Pierre Restany, *Uriburu: Utopia from the South* (Buenos Aires: Electa, Nicolás García Uriburu Foundation, 2001), 16. Restany points out that this taste for what was happening in New York led to a "transformist adaptation." He states that "between 1963 and 1964 the awareness of a *lunfardo* reality is affirmed and consolidated: a modern, industrial, urban, and media-related, both a source of poetic self-expression and multimedia language," developed also by Rubén Santantonín, Dalila Puzzovio, and Delia Cancela. See Marta Minujín, Rubén Santantonín, and Jorge Romero Brest, "*La Menesunda*," *Listen, Here, Now!*, 107–110.

38   Gustavo Buntinx, "El poder y la ilusión. Pérdida y restauración del aura en la 'República de Weimar peruana' (1980–1992)" in *Arte contemporáneo. Colección Museo de Arte de Lima* (Lima: Museo de Arte de Lima, 2013), 73. The term *achorado* is an adjective derived from popular slang, referring to that which is uninhibited, wild, and insolent. The term *Pop achorado* was coined by Ruiz Durán in 1984 when describing his own posters.

39   Ibid., 73.

40   James Metcalf, "Dom-Art: El espejo ahumado de Tezcatlipoca," *Dom-Art* file (archiving in process), Fundación Juan José Gurrola archives. Thanks to Daniel Escoto for his help with the sound research into *Dom-Art*.

41   López, "Cosmopolitan F(r)ictions," 30–34. In this regard, Juan Acha and Oscar Masotta coincide in offering political action based on art, as opposed to the orthodox left that considered political militancy to be the only valid revolutionary act. Ana Longoni has, in various texts, pointed out that this was Masotta's stance.

42   Olivier Debroise, "Looking at the Sky in Buenos Aires," *Oscar Masotta. La teoría como acción*, 68.

43   Roberto Jacoby, Eduardo Costa and Raúl Escari, "Media Art," *Listen, Here, Now!*, 223–225.

44   Acha, "Vanguardismo y subdesarrollo," 26.

45   Juan Acha, "Felipe Ehrenberg y la subversión conceptualista," *Diorama de la Cultura*, supplement, *Excélsior*, March 4, 1973, 2.

46   Acha, "Felipe Ehrenberg y la subversión conceptualista," 2. See also *Ehrenberg* (Mexico: Instituto Nacional de Bellas Artes, 1973).

47   Oscar Masotta, "Yo cometí un happening," *Oscar Masotta, Revolución en el arte*, 35.

NATALIA DE LA ROSA

LOS ESCRITOS SOBRE EL ARTE POP EN AMÉRICA: ENTRE LA CRÍTICA Y LA TEORÍA

En 1965, el crítico cubano-americano Mario Amaya planteó una problemática inherente a la corriente denominada "arte pop" al mostrar las complicaciones implícitas en su definición.[1] Las obras estudiadas por Amaya se habían realizado bajo el método de producción en masa y los referentes de un "folk" urbano, y mostraban un nuevo ímpetu por unir las esferas de la vida y el arte en un solo ámbito. La condición vanguardista del pop, que Amaya vinculó al *ready-made*, salía directamente de las líneas de ensamblaje y los medios de comunicación masiva de Londres y Nueva York, medios que presentaban un lenguaje conectado al cine, la televisión, el cómic, los periódicos, las revistas de moda, los espectáculos y la publicidad.[2]

Mientras Amaya, quien entonces vivía en Nueva York, elaboraba este recuento temprano del pop e identificaba a los críticos que definieron este nuevo momento de las artes, como Pierre Restany, Lucy Lippard, Max Kozloff, Lawrence Alloway, Harold Rosenberg e incluso Clement Greenberg, diversas voces en Argentina, Perú, Brasil, Colombia y México también comenzaron a analizar los cambios drásticos en las artes de esos países.[3] Con ello se daba evidencia de una vertiente insólita en las artes del sur del continente y el inicio de otro momento

en la escritura crítica. Diversas posturas se manifestaron ante estas primeras referencias al arte pop, desde un efusivo ataque hasta un constante apoyo y, en algunos casos, una radical reapropiación. Este texto no intenta establecer una definición del arte pop en América, siguiendo la línea planteada por Amaya, sino que reflexiona sobre su impacto en la escritura crítica y estudia el diálogo entre agentes específicos que acompañaron su concepción y, en muchos casos, su presentación pública. Los ejemplos corresponden a algunas de las primeras exhibiciones que implicaron el despliegue de instalaciones, *happenings* y experimentos mediáticos e interdisciplinares que fueron determinantes para el desarrollo del arte contemporáneo en este contexto.[4]

Jorge Romero Brest, Damián Bayón, Juan Acha, Marta Traba, Mário Pedrosa, Aracy Amaral, Frederico Morais y Oscar Masotta fueron todos críticos que probaron, en sus propios desplazamientos, la necesidad de una acción política por medio de la escritura.[5] Los debates sobre el pop surgieron en un momento de irrupción política que significó en muchas de estas figuras una transición desde una práctica crítica hacia una teoría concreta que acompañó el desarrollo del papel del teórico-artista junto al del artista-teórico.[6] Son casos de escritura en los que el crítico no fue observador de la producción artística, dados los momentos de irrupción política, sino partícipe activo.[7]

Un claro ejemplo es el caso del argentino Jorge Romero Brest, quien confesó que debió anular su juicio crítico por un momento al ver los "objetos" de Claes Oldenburg en 1963 y repensar el arte clásico frente al pop para, posteriormente, modificar y apoyar este tipo de expresiones capaces de responder a un "ser en el mundo", como sucedió con *Revuélquese y viva* (1964) de Marta Minujín.[8] Desde Brasil, Mário Pedrosa evitó tratar al arte pop como dadá y prefirió analizar estas obras como un cambio de época.[9] Marta Traba, crítica argentina que radicó y consolidó su trabajo en Colombia, mostró desconfianza y acusó a estas imágenes de ser imitaciones, proponiendo poco después la nacionalización del pop por vía de la artista colombiana Beatriz González.[10] En el caso del Perú, Juan Acha, aunque dudoso en un primer momento, apoyó las primeras exhibiciones pop que estuvieron acompañadas por acciones y ambientaciones (ver página 160, figura 5.1).[11] En el ámbito argentino, Oscar Masotta analizó reproducciones impresas de Andy Warhol, Claes Oldenburg y Robert Rauschenberg para profundizar sus acercamientos estructuralistas y dedicó un texto al movimiento, proponiendo el concepto de "imagineros" seguido por el de "desmaterialización" en una obra posterior referente a los *happenings*.[12] Masotta reaccionó claramente a una serie de imágenes, objetos y prácticas que, a pesar de su diálogo con el arte pop norteamericano, también se diferenciaban de él, como lo demuestran las expresiones del *antihappening* que compartió con Roberto Jacoby.[13]

Cabe aclarar que no todas las escrituras fueron homogéneas, y todas ellas expresan un estatuto distinto: mientras Traba cae en un extremismo con pocos matices, Masotta se mantiene al margen de los grupos de críticos preocupados por descifrar la identidad latinoamericana, a fin de construir una alternativa teórica desde la interdisciplinaridad y la relación directa con los artistas. Por otra parte, Acha adaptó los presupuestos económicos dependentistas y encontró variantes heterodoxas al recuperar las particularidades de su formación como ingeniero químico y traducirlas a una teoría afín a la fisiología de la visión, en este punto muy cercano a Mário Pedrosa.[14] El brasileño Frederico Morais descifró en la nueva crítica una forma de creación artística y se preocupó por desarrollar una vanguardia cercana a la participación colectiva y a la activación de objetos.[15] Más allá de estos puntos, el panorama trazado nos permite entender cómo se pensó el arte pop desde una variedad de acercamientos que destacan la complejidad de su desarrollo en un contexto que abrió las fronteras de lo que se conocía como lo "latinoamericano" y redefinió lo "americano".

DE LA CRÍTICA A LA TEORÍA

Este texto propone pensar el arte pop desde una serie de diálogos generados en el hemisferio. El proceso se asume como una expansión de redes creadas a partir de una especie de vinculación dialéctica y mediante un dinamismo que discutió las vías de una intervención tecnológica y de consumo entre diversos puntos de la región, mostrando algunas respuestas desde lo que se denominó en la época como Tercer Mundo. Si en algo coinciden estos autores es en que el arte pop funcionó como punto de quiebre y como un nuevo estadio para la revaloración vanguardista y el reposicionamiento político-estético.[16] Cabe destacar que esta tendencia artística "urbana", por lo menos en Estados Unidos, partió de un programa económico que buscó incidir directamente en varios puntos del continente americano.[17] Por tanto, el arte pop no puede pensarse como un producto aislado, sino que su condición de posibilidad recayó en la relación de esta nación con el resto del continente.[18] En términos de la reacción crítico-teórica, el camino marcado por la crítica se inició con el análisis del desarrollismo, seguido por la denuncia dependendista y hasta un incipiente señalamiento descolonial ante la crisis mundial generada a inicios de 1970, que tuvo consecuencias directas en todo el continente.[19] De forma paralela, existieron cuestionamientos en el interior de Estados Unidos que mostraron las contradicciones de las condiciones socioeconómicas globales.[20] Este ensayo, en cierta forma, destaca esa presión ejercida por el Tercer Mundo durante una década concreta, la cual intentó alterar el orden económico mundial en los albores del giro financiero.[21] La escritura surgida en este proceso evidencia la disolución de una promesa de modernización y una toma de conciencia sobre nuevas formas de colonialidad, siendo el pop una vía clara de presentación de esta problemática.

Más allá de la taxonomía que Damián Bayón presentó sobre los distintos críticos de la región, lo que podemos asegurar es que esta práctica fue la esfera de una reformulación de la postura activa del intelectual y, en algunos casos, una respuesta a los presupuestos tradicionales marxistas al ofrecer una alternativa de izquierda en forma de posicionamientos radicales y heterodoxos.[22]

A inicios de la década de 1970 se publicaron diversos estudios que tomaron la categoría "América Latina" como objeto de estudio a partir de cuestionamientos sobre el ser latinoamericano y sus artes, teniendo como herramienta libros previos sobre las artes de cada país, revistas con una mirada transnacional, exhibiciones, instituciones y coloquios internacionales que sustentaron la creación de un tejido crítico dirigido a dicha problemática.[23] Esta red creció a raíz de los propios desplazamientos que tuvo cada uno de estos autores, quienes salieron de sus países tras la imposición de dictaduras y golpes de estado, e incluso la vivencia de represiones directas.[24] La salida del contexto nacional de muchas de estas figuras permitió una expansión y radicalización de las propuestas críticas y teóricas.

El crítico brasileño Frederico Morais presentó en el libro *Del trance a lo transitorio* (1977) un listado de ediciones regionales con el fin de promover la "sociabilización de la crítica".[25] Morais respondió así al artículo de Juan Acha "Hacia una crítica de arte como productora de teorías" (1976), en el cual el crítico peruano-mexicano exigió la creación de conceptos surgidos desde la realidad local, como sería el no-objetualismo desarrollado por este autor en esos años.[26] Valiéndose de esta categoría, Acha estudió el arte y la cultura popular y el diseño gráfico e industrial con el fin de denunciar la fetichización del arte, esto es, la comercialización y distribución de las obras y su impacto en la sociedad. Las prácticas no-objetuales designan un arte de ideas, intervenciones urbanas, objetos efímeros y artesanales, acciones corporales y ejercicios mediáticos (ver página 161, figura 5.2).[27]

En su respuesta, Frederico Morais presentó las distintas vertientes críticas desarrolladas entre 1950 y 1970. Como antecedentes, el crítico se refirió a los trabajos de Jorge Romero Brest y Mário Pedrosa.[28] En una siguiente generación señaló a Juan Acha, Marta Traba y Damián Bayón, y luego nombró a los jóvenes críticos que presentaban nuevos aportes en la década de 1970: Jorge Alberto Manrique, Rita Eder, Mirko Lauer, Jorge Glusberg, Néstor García Canclini, Aracy Amaral y el propio Morais. La conclusión fue que todas estas voces exigían la necesidad de una unidad crítica y una pluralidad artística. Para él, debían dejarse las preguntas sobre la existencia, características y necesidades del arte latinoamericano a favor de una acción (praxis) de esa teoría —y del arte mismo— ante una crisis de la vanguardia.[29] Para Morais, la vanguardia era una actitud y postura artística que implicaba un comportamiento radical, político o contra-artístico, y una forma de impacto directo en la realidad.[30]

Superada la tendencia internacionalista del arte y con el peligro de un regreso a la retórica nacional impulsada por las dictaduras, la producción artística y crítica desarrolló una opción de respuesta activa y de transformación política desde un arte que, en lugar de resistir, debía liberar, siendo señalado como una "necesidad vital" y un "impulso individual libre".[31] Para alcanzar esta tentativa de liberación debían radicalizarse las estrategias artísticas. Una opción era la reapropiación de los medios de comunicación externos para crear una mediación alternativa que orientara de otra forma las condiciones sensitivo-visuales del espectador, como lo expuso Juan Acha en el texto "El arte del video-tape contra la TV".[32] También existía la posibilidad de recuperar formas de expresión locales, donde el pop y lo popular se enfrentaban para generar la síntesis de una imagen u objeto nuevo que exponía las condiciones de la realidad económica y social.

POP Y SUBDESARROLLO: ARTE, DISEÑO Y ARTESANÍA

El texto *Vanguardia y subdesarrollo* (1969) del poeta Ferreira Gullar, escrito en los años de consolidación del régimen militar en Brasil, marcó un aspecto fundamental para el cambio en las teorías sobre el arte. Mediante un estudio basado en el radicalismo revolucionario de la vanguardia, Gullar subrayó la expansión de los temas políticos y la inclusión popular en el arte. En este escrito expresó la necesidad de una vanguardia radical, consciente del juego de espejos entre los países desarrollados y subdesarrollados. El poeta analizó las economías de la posguerra con estructuras sociales opuestas, en las que subyacía la promesa de la "novedad", y generó una paradoja casi insoluble: "Necesitamos la industria y el *know-how* que ellos tienen, pero con esa industria y ese *know-how*, que necesitamos para liberarnos, viene la dominación".[33] El choque entre los modelos económicos de los países industrializados y los no industrializados fue determinante para repensar la producción artística, ya que se asumiría como evidencia de una nueva dependencia cultural y económica.

En 1968, el año del golpe de Juan Velasco Alvarado en Perú, Juan Acha presentó un texto de título similar al de Gullar, articulado como un desglose de distintos presupuestos desarrollistas confrontados por el Tercer Mundo.[34] En esa primera tentativa de programa, Acha señaló un punto intermedio existente entre las sociedades subdesarrolladas y las sociedades industrializadas, dando cabida a un nuevo modelo cultural, que debía unir dos polos.

Aunque generalmente se había acusado, como lo hizo Traba, a las imágenes del arte pop de expresar sumisión hacia el proyecto modernizador, en realidad las obras realizadas en América Latina siempre mantuvieron una ambivalencia con el término "popular". Parece que ese "folk" urbano que señaló Amaya aquí no podía ser solo brillante y alegre, sino que desde un principio, amén de los ímpetus cosmopolitas de algunos artistas como Delia Cancela o Emilio Hernández Saavedra ante Bob Dylan, Twiggy y las camisas de flores, existieron obras que pusieron en tensión dos modelos de producción, en versiones satíricas y violentas.[35] Un ejemplo son las obras de Guillermo Núñez, que en respuesta al contexto de la guerra de Vietnam remiten a "la muerte o vulnerabilidad de los soldados."[36]

Existen otros casos divergentes de pop regional. Uno de ellos es el "pop lunfardo" argentino (término propuesto por Pierre Restany), surgido a partir de las series de "colectivos" de Nicolás García Uriburu en 1964 y del proyecto grupal *La Menesunda* (1965) (lámina 98), cuyo manifiesto fue firmado por Rubén Santantonín, Marta Minujín y Jorge Romero Brest, evidencia de la complicidad entre artistas y críticos.[37] Otro caso es el de las *caixas* (1966, lámina 106) de Rubens Gerchman, quien en obras como *Lindonéia, a Gioconda do subúrbio* (Lindonéia, la Gioconda del suburbio) (1966–1968, lámina 105) señalaba la propagación de las imágenes en los medios al mismo tiempo que aludía al ámbito popular-urbano. Asimismo en Perú, Jesús Ruiz Durand realizó entre 1968 y 1973 una serie de carteles para el velasquismo (ver página 14, figura 1.6) que combinaban fórmulas op y pop con la técnica de la "solarización" y la temática campesina, inaugurando así el "pop achorado".[38] Estas soluciones pasan de la imitación a la apropiación, donde lo popular se actualiza y lo cosmopolita se subvierte.[39] En México, Juan José Gurrola presentó el *dom art*, o arte doméstico (1966–1967, láminas 24–30). Se trata de una serie de obras consistentes en *collages*, pinturas efímeras, acciones mediáticas y *happenings* sonoros (ver página 162; figuras 5.3, 5.4). Como parte de estos ejercicios produjo un *collage* donde la lata de sopa Campbell's estaba abierta y funcionó como dualidad, ese reflejo frente a Estados Unidos que describió Ferreira Gullar. Dicha estrategia fue comparada con el "espejo humeante de Tezcatlipoca" de la cosmogonía prehispánica, en este caso para mostrar la introducción del *American way of life* en la cultura mexicana.[40] Al mismo tiempo, Gurrola elaboró un montaje sonoro poético-publicitario que unía interpretaciones de *The Moon Was Yellow* (1958) en versión del dúo Ferrante & Teicher, canciones en el estilo operístico de la estadounidense Mrs. Miller y anuncios de radio falsos en clave humorística mezclados con otros oficiales del programa *La hora nacional*. Este acercamiento experimental, en el que la arquitectura también se piensa como elemento de consumo, condujo al *happening* titulado *Museo Dinámico Dom*, presentado en la inauguración de la casa diseñada por el arquitecto Manuel Larrosa para la familia Michel en Ciudad de México en 1967.

Juan Acha también refirió en "Vanguardismo y subdesarrollo" a la pertinencia de una revolución cultural en la que el artista fuera capaz de crear una alternativa a la fórmula de consumo generada por los países industrializados.[41] No se trataba solamente de revelar las contradicciones de la cultura de masas y el furor tecnológico expuestas en los presupuestos de Marshall McLuhan, sino de generar tentativas para que esta intervención fuera más allá del ámbito artístico.[42] Ese tipo de intervención la habían insinuado en su manifiesto (*Un arte de los medios de comunicación*) y en sus acciones Roberto Jacoby, Eduardo Costa y Raúl Escari, quienes terminaron por separarse del arte pop.[43] Son momentos de fusión entre el arte y la vida cotidiana por medio de intervenciones concretas (mediáticas), como sucedió también con el *Fashion Fiction I* de Eduardo Costa para la revista *Vogue* (1966–1969, lámina 94) y con el proyecto musical *2+8 en Pop* de Pixie Hopkin y Nacho Méndez producido por Juan José Gurrola en 1964 (ver página 163; figuras 5.5, 5.6).

La utopía vanguardista presentada por Acha y radicalizada durante la siguiente década fue un llamado a exponer el funcionamiento de los medios de producción, consumo y distribución del capitalismo tardío con el fin de "denunciar los errores de la sociedad de consumo y proponer ciertas correcciones por medio del vanguardismo".[44] Estas obras y prácticas, que Acha designó como no-objetuales, se inscriben como imágenes de televisión en forma de videoarte, prácticas efímeras y arte de fotocopias, pero también en artesanías locales. Estas yuxtaposiciones fueron evidentes en la muestra *Chicles, chocolates y cacahuates: Obras y conceptos* (1973) de Felipe Ehrenberg, en la que el artista, editor y neólogo combinó piezas relativas a su trabajo realizado en Inglaterra con la Beau Geste Press entre 1968 y 1974 y otras expresiones "cercanas al pop,"[45] llevándolas al contexto de la colonia Peralvillo de la capital mexicana: documentos en proceso, proyectos imposibles, *mail art*, denuncias icónico-verbales, recetas de cocina, poesía, *collages*, *slogans* y hasta elementos de la cultura popular mexicana y "nuestra sensibilidad diaria", como la lucha libre.[46] Pueden trazarse también esos momentos en que la teoría se mezcló con la práctica y la acción se tradujo como manifiesto activo: Masotta realizando un *happening* (1967) para manifestar las condiciones de significación ambivalente en la comunicación;[47] la incitación de Morais a los residentes de Belo Horizonte en *Do Corpo à Terra* (1970) al organizar un conjunto de intervenciones, situaciones y acciones en el espacio público; o Acha anunciando que la crítica, al igual que el arte, solo era posible en la acción pública (1978).

Podemos concluir que el arte pop descrito por estos autores, aunque solo hayamos examinado brevemente algunos de ellos, no es un arte que solo muestra o fragmenta objetos salidos de la línea de montaje. Son obras que exponen y reaccionan a una condición extrema del capitalismo al reclamar una alternativa en que la teoría, así como el arte, buscan fundirse con la vida. El objetivo fue modificar las condiciones de dicho modelo económico instauradas en este continente. Además de escritos y acciones, estas reflexiones son preguntas reiteradas que se hicieron en una época, las cuales quedan todavía abiertas y como diálogo necesario para todo el hemisferio.

NOTAS

1   Mario Amaya, *Pop Art ...and After* (Nueva York: The Viking Press, 1965), 9. La cita de Amaya es: "Es casi imposible definir el arte pop en el sentido estricto, como se puede definir, digamos, el cubismo o el surrealismo". En este apartado, Amaya señala también que los propios artistas se sentían incómodos y se negaban a ser señalados como "pop", resistiéndose a ser agrupados en un solo movimiento. El término *pop art* surge en Inglaterra y es propuesto por Lawrence Alloway. Ver Lawrence Alloway, "The Arts and the Mass Media", *Architectural Design & Construction*, no. 28 (febrero de 1958): 84–85.

2   Amaya, *Pop Art ...and After*, 15.

3   Los textos aludidos por Amaya son: Lawrence Alloway, "Pop Art since 1949", *The Listener* (Londres: 27 de diciembre de 1962); Lucy R. Lippard, "New York Letter," *Art International* IX, no. 3 (abril de 1965): 48–64; Lucy R. Lippard, "New York Letter", *Art International* IX, no. 4 (mayo de 1965): 52–59; Max Kozloff, "'Pop' Culture and the New Vulgarians", *Art International* VI, no. 2 (marzo de 1962): 34–37; The Museum of Modern Art, "Pop Art Symposium at the Museum of Modern Art", diciembre de 1962. Reimpreso en *Arts Magazine*, vol. 37, no. 7, (abril de 1963).

4   Todas estas personas escribían textos críticos y teóricos sobre las producciones pop, mientras colaboraban en espacios específicos de exhibición. Jorge Romero Brest y Oscar Masotta lo hicieron en el Instituto Torcuato Di Tella, hasta la desaparición del Centro de Artes Visuales en 1970; Damián Bayón desde la Universidad de Austin organizó coloquios y exhibiciones; Juan Acha, tras el exilio, fue subdirector del Museo de Arte Moderno de México, recinto que de ser un proyecto dedicado al arte nacional se convirtió en eje de la crítica regional, y la colección dio un giro hacia el latinoamericanismo; Marta Traba fue directora del Museo de Arte Moderno de Bogotá y Aracy Amaral fue directora de la Pinacoteca de São Paulo, donde impulsó la incorporación de las obras al recinto de lo que llamó la "generación pop".

5   También es importante recalcar el papel de personajes como Adelaida de Juan en Cuba, Ida Rodríguez Prampolini en México o Alaíde Foppa en Guatemala, quienes, sin pertenecer al grupo "latinoamericanista", representaron otro tipo de agrupación que pensó la crítica como una opción de acción política.

6   Uno de los estudios que analizan el papel del intelectual como personaje activo y promotor de una transformación política desde las artes es el realizado por Ana Longoni a partir de la figura de Oscar Masotta. Ver Ana Longoni, ed., "Oscar Masotta: Vanguardia y revolución en los años sesenta", en *Oscar Masotta, Revolución en el arte* (Buenos Aires: Editorial Mansalva, 2017), 7–67. Entre los artistas que pensaron la práctica artística y la escritura de forma conjunta están Roberto Jacoby, Eduardo Costa, Felipe Ehrenberg, Juan José Gurrola, Beatriz González y Hélio Oiticica.

7   Estos críticos realizaron interpretaciones de autores ligados al estructuralismo, la teoría crítica, la teoría de la comunicación y el postestructuralismo. También tuvieron un diálogo con corrientes como la filosofía de la liberación y con otros exponentes de la teoría local, como es el caso de Aníbal Quijano, consultado por Mirko Lauer y Juan Acha, o Paulo Freire, por Frederico Morais. Ver Aníbal Quijano, *Dominación y cultura. Notas sobre problemas de la participación cultural* (Buenos Aires: CLACSO, 2014); Mirko Lauer, *Introducción a la pintura peruana* (Lima: Mosca Azul Editores, 1976); Juan Acha, "El geometrismo reciente en Latinoamérica", en *El geometrismo mexicano* (México, IIE-UNAM, 1977), 29–50; Paulo Freire, *Pedagogy of the Oppressed*, trad. Myra Bergman (Londres: Penguin Books, 2017).

8   Jorge Romero Brest, "Report and Reflection on Pop Art", en *Listen, Here, Now!: Argentine Art of the 1960s. Writings of the Avant-Garde*, ed. Inés Katzenstein (Nueva York: The Museum of Modern Art, 2004), 119–129. Este pasaje también es recuperado en: Andrea Giunta, *Vanguardia e internacionalismo. Arte argentino de los sesenta* (Buenos Aires, México y Barcelona: Paidós, 2001). Rodrigo Alonso marca el inicio del "pop vernáculo" en Argentina, todavía con resabios existencialistas y cercano al nuevo realismo indicial francés, a través de las muestras del Premio Braque y el Premio Ver y Estimar de 1962. Se llega a una consolidación en 1964, con la presencia de los máximos representantes internacionales del movimiento, entre ellos Robert Rauschenberg en el Premio Di Tella, y a la institucionalización en 1966, con los premios a Susana Salgado, Dalila Puzzovio y Juan Stoppani en el mismo Instituto Torcuato Di Tella. Rodrigo Alonso, *El Espíritu Pop* (Mar del Plata, Argentina: Museo de Arte Contemporáneo de Mar del Plata, 2014).

9   Lorenzo Mammì, "prefacio" en Mário Pedrosa, *Arte e ensaios* (São Paulo: Cosac Naify, 2015), 16.

10   Marta Traba, "Beatriz González", *Revista Eco*, no. 169 (noviembre de 1974): 65–73. Ver también Marta Traba, *Dos décadas vulnerables en las artes plásticas latinoamericanas, 1950-1970* (Buenos Aires: Siglo Veintiuno Editores, 2005).

11   Juan Acha, "Arte Pop: Procedimientos y finalidades", *El Comercio*, suplemento, *El Dominical*, 25 de mayo de 1969, 38–39. Ver también Juan Acha, "Ambientes expresionistas de Teresa Burga", *El Comercio*, 27 de julio de 1967, 23. Este período es analizado en Miguel A. López, "F(r)icciones cosmopolitas. Redefiniciones estéticas y políticas de una idea de vanguardia en los años 60", en *Arte contemporáneo. Colección Museo de Arte de Lima*, ed. Sharon Lerner (Lima: Museo de Arte de Lima, 2013), 17–39.

12   Oscar Masotta, "El 'Pop-Art' y 'Happenings'", en *Oscar Masotta. Revolución en el arte*, 69–130 y 131–206.

13   Roberto Jacoby, "Against the Happening", *Listen, Here, Now!*, 229.

14   La teoría de la dependencia es un modelo de explicación económica que tuvo gran auge entre las décadas de 1960 y 1970. Surgió como respuesta al programa desarrollista de la Comisión Económica para América Latina y planteó una lectura dialéctica entre la región con otros centros. Los autores que desarrollaron esta teoría fueron Fernando H. Cardoso, Enzo Faletto, Ruy Mauro Marini, Celso Furtado, Vania Bambirra, Fernando H. Cardoso y Enzo Faletto. Ver *Dependencia y desarrollo en América Latina* (México: Siglo XXI, 1969); Ruy Mauro Marini, *Dialéctica de la dependencia* (México: Era, 1973); Celso Furtado, *Desarrollo y subdesarrollo* (México: Eudeba, 1964); Fernando. H. Cardoso, *Problemas del subdesarrollo latinoamericano* (México: Nuestro Tiempo, 1973); Teotonio Dos Santos, *Dependencia y cambio social* (Santiago: Cuadernos de Estudios Socioeconómicos, Universidad De Chile, 1970). Para entender este cambio de la teoría de la dependencia al pensamiento descolonial: Ramón Grosfoguel, "Developmentalism, Modernity, and the Dependency Theory in Latin America"; Mabel Moraña, Enrique Dussel y Carlos A. Jáuregui, eds., *Coloniality at Large: Latin America and the Postcolonial Debate* (Durham: Duke Press, 2008), 307. La cercanía entre Juan Acha y Mário Pedrosa es evidente en las invitaciones que el crítico peruano-mexicano hizo a Pedrosa para dar una serie de pláticas en el Museo de Arte Moderno de México entre 1973 y 1974. También fue invitado a publicar en la revista *Artes Visuales* del MAM, donde presentó "Arte hoy, ¿hacia dónde? Manifiesto para los Tupininquis o Nambás", *Artes Visuales*, Museo de Arte Moderno, México, no. 10 (abril–junio de 1976): 31–35.

15   Estas propuestas fueron se expusieron en 1970, a partir del proyecto de manifiesto y exposición "Do Corpo à Terra" y de la muestra "Objeto e Participação", ambas presentadas en Belo Horizonte, Brasil. Ver también Frederico Morais, *Artes plásticas. A crise da hora atual* (Río de Janeiro: Paz e Terra, 1975).

16   Ante este escenario, Brest, Pedrosa, Acha, Bayón y Traba estudiaron y problematizaron desde ámbitos nacionales los cambios sustanciales en la producción artística, en una balanza que enfrentó el geometrismo o el informalismo, hasta el momento en que hizo su aparición el arte pop.

17   Greg Grandin, *Empire's Workshop. Latin America, the United States, and the Rise of the New Imperialism* (Nueva York: Metropolitan Books/Henry Holt and Company, 2010).

18   Este proceso se inició a través del proyecto panamericanista surgido a partir de las políticas del New Deal, se consolidó mediante la instauración del Estado benefactor de la posguerra y se reorganizó a partir del planteamiento del proyecto neoliberal.

19   Toni Negri, *Revolution Retrieved: Writings on Marx, Keynes, Capitalist Crisis and New Social Subjects* (Londres: Red Notes, 1988). Negri explica que en 1944 Karl Polanyi describió en su obra *La gran transformación* el inicio de la política proteccionista del Estado benefactor de la posguerra, proceso económico denominado keynesianismo, el cual implicaba un cierto rechazo al liberalismo del *laissez-faire*, necesario como forma de equilibrio y definido como socialización de la producción capitalista. En estos escritos, consecuencia de la Gran Depresión, Keynes insistió en la intervención política para mediar en toda actividad económica.

20   En el centro de estos dos momentos se insertan las revueltas mundiales de 1968, y también lo que se conoce como la autoafirmación del Tercer Mundo, procesos en los que la Revolución cubana o la guerra de Vietnam fueron determinantes. Esto fue evidente

en el movimiento de lucha por los derechos civiles y el feminismo, los cuales llevaron a reestructurar y reconfigurar el orden económico a través de lo que ahora conocemos como neoliberalismo. Ver Brian Holmes, "Investigaciones extradisciplinares. Hacia una nueva crítica de las instituciones", trad. Marcelo Expósito (European Institute for Progressive Cultural Policies, 2007), consultado 4 de mayo de 2017, http://eipcp.net/transversal/0106/holmes/es.

21 Barbara y John Ehrenreich, "The Professional-Managerial Class", en *Between Labor and Capital*, ed. Pat Walker (Nueva York: South End Press, 1979), 213–278.

22 La taxonomía de Bayón incluye: crítico-jefe de clan, crítico-teórico, crítico sociólogo, crítico-artista. Ver Ana Longoni, *Oscar Masotta. La teoría como acción* (Ciudad de México: Museo Universitario de Arte Contemporáneo, UNAM, 2017).

23 Algunas de las exhibiciones durante la época desarrollista fueron apoyadas por la Organización de Estados Americanos (OEA), la Pan American Union y José Gómez Sicre. Además, se crearon salones y bienales muchas veces patrocinados por corporaciones en alianza con Washington, como es el caso del Salón ESSO de 1964–1965, celebrado en Colombia, México y Perú. También fueron importantes las bienales, sobre todo la de São Paulo, así como las contrabienales, como la de Córdoba y la Bienal Latinoamericana de São Paulo. Ver Claire F. Fox, *Making Art Panamerican: Cultural Policy and the Cold War* (Minneapolis: University of Minnesota Press, 2013). El antecedente de esos coloquios fue el encuentro organizado por Damián Bayón en Ecuador, "América Latina y sus artes". Ver Damián Bayón, *América Latina y sus artes* (México: Siglo XXI, 1974). Después se presentó el coloquio de Zacatecas, "La dicotomía entre arte culto y arte popular", organizado por el Instituto de Investigaciones Estéticas de la UNAM en 1975, continuado por el de "El artista latinoamericano y su identidad", realizado en Austin, Texas, en colaboración con la Universidad de Texas, el Blanton Museum, Juan Acha, Kasuya Sakai y Bayón. Ver Rita Eder, "Juan Acha: Pensar desde América Latina", *Post: Notes on Modern & Contemporary Art Around the Globe*, The Museum of Modern Art, publicado el 27 de septiembre de 2016, consultado el 2 de mayo de 2017, http://post.at.moma.org/content_items/752-juan-acha-pensar-el-arte-desde-america-latina.

24 Este fue el caso de Mário Pedrosa, que viaja de Brasil a Chile; Oscar Masotta y Damián Bayón, que salen de Argentina hacia España y Estados Unidos, respectivamente; Marta Traba, que parte de Colombia a Puerto Rico; y Juan Acha, que llega a México desde Perú.

25 Frederico Morais, *Las artes plásticas en América Latina. Del trance a lo transitorio* (La Habana: Casa de las Américas, 1990).

26 Juan Acha, "Hacia una crítica como productora de teorías", *Artes Visuales* (primavera de 1977): 29. Este concepto fue expuesto por Acha en: *El arte y su distribución* (1984), *Arte y sociedad en Latinoamérica. El producto artístico y su estructura* (1979); y *Arte y sociedad en Latinoamérica. El sistema de producción* (1979). Para

muchos artistas del continente, este concepto abrió el camino para pensar prácticas cercanas al conceptualismo, pero que, su vez, también se diferenciaban de esta tendencia internacional. Ver también Alberto Sierra Maya, Víctor Manuel Manrique y Augusto del Valle, *Memorias del Primer Coloquio Latinoamericano sobre Arte No-objetual y Arte Urbano* (Medellín: Museo de Antioquia, Museo de Arte Moderno de Medellín, 2011).

27 Juan Acha, "Teoría y práctica no-objetualistas en América Latina". Ver también Alberto Sierra Maya et al., *Memorias del Primer Coloquio Latinoamericano sobre Arte No-objetual y Arte Urbano*, 75–88.

28 Podría sumarse a este par la figura de Octavio Paz, quien en México fue el protagonista del desarrollo de la crítica de arte y del impulso internacionalista, en oposición al nacionalismo local. De hecho, un texto de Paz sirvió como introducción a uno de los simposios latinoamericanistas más importantes, organizado por Damián Bayón en la Universidad de Austin en 1975. Damián Bayón, *El artista latinoamericano y su identidad* (Caracas: Monte Ávila Editores, 1977).

29 Morais, *Las artes plásticas en América Latina. Del trance a lo transitorio*, 17.

30 Frederico Morais, "Arte brasileira, anos 70: O fim da vanguarda?", *Módulo*, Brasil, no. 55 (septiembre de 1979): 50–60.

31 Giunta, *Vanguardia, internacionalismo y política*, 116. Ver también Mário Pedrosa, "Vicissitudes do artista sovietico", *Arte e ensaios*, 359–364. Por ejemplo, para Pedrosa, esta respuesta debía separarse tanto de la mercantilización como de la ideologización, es decir, tanto de la reproducción del sistema capitalista como de la imagen-ilustración del arte soviético. La revista *Artes Visuales*, dirigida por Carla Stellweg, fue uno de los espacios donde se habló de este tema relacionado a la sociabilización de la crítica que menciona Frederico Morais. En ella colaboraron: Juan Acha como editor invitado, Mário Pedrosa, Néstor García Canclini, Rita Eder, Jorge Alberto Manrique, Alaíde Foppa, Clemente Padín, Damián Bayón, Jorge Romero Brest, Aracy Amaral, Juan Downey, Jorge Glusberg, M.A. Rojas Mix, Marta Traba y Adelaida de Juan. También se tradujeron textos de Les Levine, Lucy R. Lippard y Marshall McLuhan.

32 Juan Acha, "El arte del video-tape contra la TV", *Diorama de la cultura*, suplemento, *Excélsior*, 15 de julio de 1973.

33 Ferreira Gullar, *Vanguarda e subdesenvolvimento* (Río de Janeiro: Editora Civilização Brasileira S.A., 1978), 24.

34 Juan Acha, "Vanguardismo y subdesarrollo", en *Ensayos y ponencias latinoamericanistas* (Caracas: Galería de Arte Nacional, 1984), 11–26.

35 Jorge Romero Brest, "La pintura pop", en *El arte en la Argentina. Últimas décadas* (Buenos Aires: Paidós, 1969), 69. Ver también López, "F(r)icciones cosmopolitas", 29–30.

36 Soledad García y Daniela Berger, *La emergencia del pop. Irreverencia y calle en Chile* (Santiago: Museo de la Solidaridad Salvador Allende, 2016), 33. http://mssa.cl/mssa3/wp-content/uploads/2016/05/CATALOGOPOPpp.pdf.

37 Pierre Restany, *Uriburu: Utopia from the South* (Buenos Aires: Electa, Nicolás García Uriburu Foundation, 2001), 16. Restany distingue que ese gusto por lo que acontecía en Nueva York desencadenó una "adaptación transformista". Menciona Restany que "entre 1963 y 1964 se afirma y se consolida la concientización de una realidad lunfarda: una naturaleza moderna, industrial, urbana, mediática, en tanto fuente de autoexpresión poética y de lenguaje multimedia", desarrollada también por Rubén Santantonín, Dalila Puzzovio y Delia Cancela. Marta Minujín, Rubén Santantonín y Jorge Romero Brest, "La Menesunda", *Listen, Here, Now!*, 107–110.

38 Gustavo Buntinx, "El poder y la ilusión. Pérdida y restauración del aura en la 'República de Weimar peruana' (1980–1992)", en *Arte contemporáneo. Colección Museo de Arte de Lima* (Lima: Museo de Arte de Lima, 2013), 73. Achorado es un adjetivo derivado del lenguaje popular que alude a lo desinhibido, lo salvaje e insolente. El pop achorado fue propuesto por el propio Ruiz Durand en 1984 al referirse a sus propios carteles.

39 Ibíd., 73.

40 James Metcalf, "Dom-Art: El espejo ahumado de Tezcatlipoca", Archivo Fundación Juan José Gurrola, expediente *Dom-Art* (archivo en proceso de clasificación). Agradezco a Daniel Escoto su ayuda en la investigacion sonora sobre el *Dom-Art*.

41 López, "F(r)icciones cosmopolitas", 30–34. En este aspecto, Juan Acha y Oscar Masotta coinciden en ofrecer a partir de las artes una acción política contraria a la alternativa de la izquierda ortodoxa, que veía solo en la militancia política una actitud válida de revolución. Ana Longoni ha señalado esta actitud de Masotta en diversos textos.

42 Olivier Debroise, "Mirando al cielo en Buenos Aires", *Oscar Masotta. La teoría como acción*, 68.

43 Roberto Jacoby, Eduardo Costa y Raúl Escari, "*Media Art*", *Listen, Here, Now!*, 223–225.

44 Acha, "Vanguardismo y subdesarrollo", 26.

45 Juan Acha, "Felipe Ehrenberg y la subversión conceptualista", *Diorama de la cultura*, suplemento, *Excélsior*, 4 de marzo de 1973, 2.

46 Acha, "Felipe Ehrenberg y la subversión conceptualista", 2. Ver también *Ehrenberg* (México: Instituto Nacional de Bellas Artes, 1973).

47 Oscar Masotta, "Yo cometí un happening", *Oscar Masotta, Revolución en el arte*, 35.

SERGIO DELGADO MOYA

DEFILEMENT, DEFACEMENT, AND DISFIGURATION

A return to figurative art after a period dominated by various forms of abstraction is among the defining features of Pop art.[1] It is an aspect powerfully on display in the works brought together in this exhibition, and one I wish to engage by grappling with the traces of defilement, defacement, and disfigurement evident in Pop depictions of historical figures. Figuration in the sense that I mean here resonates with the more playful sense of the disfigured visible in Rupert García's *Decay Dance* (1969, plate 20). It anticipates the kind of political commentary Juan Dávila put forward with *El libertador Simón Bolívar* (The Liberator Simón Bolívar) (see page 174, figure 6.1), a colorful, finger-flipping, half-naked, and (trans)sexualized version of the founding father of South American independence, which drew the ire of government officials across the region.[2]

Borrowing generously from the found images and clichés of popular and commercial culture, the artists studied over the course of the next few pages record faces and facts from history. Their work thus points to an irreverent return of history painting in Pop art, a return grounded on the material and historical specificities (emergent consumer societies, war, revolutionary strife) of life in América in the 1960s and 1970s.[3]

Jointly considered, the work of the artists studied constitutes a corpus of Pop art that conjugates a sense of conceptual and compositional innovation with an intense and sustained engagement with politically inflected subject matter. This in turn forces us to revisit, in reference to Pop art in particular and art more generally, the kind of reductionist divisions of labor that locates a disaffected concern with Pop and consumer culture in the global north, and a politicized and subversive approach to this same culture in the global south.[4]

Figuration as dismemberment and disfigurement, and disfigurement as an approach to history painting, feature prominently in some of the earliest examples of Pop art. We see them materialized in Andy Warhol's Death and Disaster series from the early 1960s.[5] These silkscreens, though relatively underplayed in mainstream accounts of the history of Pop, stand out from the rest of Warhol's work for the way in which they capture what Thomas Crow describes as "the open sores in American political life."[6] As Crow argues, Warhol's images of death and disaster can be defined to include his early portraits of female celebrities, portraits that seem darker and more somber than they have been made out to be. They reference disease (Elizabeth Taylor and the illness that afflicted her on the set of *Cleopatra*) and death (Marilyn Monroe a few weeks after dying, Jackie Kennedy mourning the assassination of her husband) as much as they pay homage to celebrity (see page 175, figure 6.2).[7] Warhol sourced many of the images for these portraits from tabloids and other sensationalist publications, as well as from photographs shot for print that were too grim to be publicly distributed.[8] The source of these images is telling, inasmuch as it points not to photography at large, but to a specific kind of photograph—the tabloid photograph—as an important, perhaps crucial register of the human figure in mid-twentieth-century visual culture.

Tabloids specializing in crime reporting and publications generally categorized as sensationalist proliferated across América in the years Warhol made his Disaster works, with crime tabloids becoming among the most popular publications in countries like Mexico, Chile, and Colombia. Though sourced from one of the more reputable Colombian newspapers, the image in Beatriz González's breakthrough series of paintings, titled *Los suicidas del Sisga (I–III)* (The Suicides of the Sisga) (see page 176, figure 6.3), signals this context almost immediately. It is the kind of image (a suicide image) featured often, and loudly, in the popular tabloids that bourgeoned around the time that González completed her paintings. The paintings feature a tidily-dressed couple posing for a formal portrait, a bouquet of flowers held lovingly between them. The couple commissioned the portrait, originally a photograph, as a memento of their love and of their death: they posed for the picture shortly before committing suicide. When this photograph and the story behind it appeared in leading newspapers of Bogotá (*El espectador*, *El tiempo*), González was captivated by the flatness of the photograph, by the smoothness of the couple's faces (the photo had been heavily retouched), and by the way all the textures and surfaces in the picture appeared flattened to the same level, having gone through multiple newspaper reproductions.[9] González heightened this flatness (which is often thought to make the human face more attractive, but which takes away all contrast and shadings) using a bright and characteristically Pop method of color blocking. As a result, González's painting of the dead couple looks like a cartoon or an advertisement.[10] The overall effect was scandalous. The painting gave visibility to a kind of event usually relegated to the pages of the tabloids, but it did so with colors and a compositional style too irreverent to match the subject matter. In the process, and largely thanks to the bright colors and flat composition of her painting, González undermined the sentimental and melodramatic overtones that the story of the couple had assumed in tabloid coverage of their suicide.

Painting as a field of visibility and portraiture in particular remained, for centuries, accessible only to a select repertoire of persons, composed mostly of historical and mythological figures as well as wealthy and prominent members of society. Since the nineteenth century, painting and portraiture expanded this repertoire of persons to include the more popular sectors of society. González's approach to portraiture is part of a larger tendency in the history of painting, but it is also, and perhaps more importantly, an expansion of this tendency. The subjects she portrays are sourced from a segment of visual culture—the tabloid press—that manages to be both wildly popular and largely discredited,

even cheapened, on account of its popularity and on account of the defilement tabloid journalism usually performs on its subject matter.

For González and for artists like the Chilean Francisco Smythe, who spent the better part of the 1970s mining tabloids for his collages and paintings (see page 178, figure 6.6), the world of tabloid journalism and the visual and print culture to which this type of journalism belongs is more than an object of scorn, and more than a window onto the margins of society. It is a field of visibility united by its pervasiveness, by its widespread circulation, by its seemingly ubiquitous presence in public spaces and in the intimacy of the home. Calendars, product packaging, popular print publications, and other cheap print platforms are the vessels of this visual culture, a culture capacious (or rather, voracious) enough to include a vast expanse of images: from celebrity photographs to religious imagery, to photographs of grizzly accidents and horrible deaths, to reproductions of artworks of every conceivable kind and quality. For González and for many of her contemporaries, artwork reproductions as they appeared on the packaging of products and as featured on the pages of calendars constituted an ironic point of entry to a register of references and images all but denied to artists in Latin America. Local art institutions rarely hold collections of "great" Western art, except, of course, as reproductions.

The paradox of this access to high culture—access through copies, through reproductions, through the cheapest and most ubiquitous forms of printed matter—did not escape González. She assumed this paradox and transformed it into one of the most generative aspects of her artworks. Witness one of her earliest series of portraits, her variations on Johannes Vermeer's *Woman with a Pearl Necklace* (c. 1662–1665). There is a tension in her compulsive return to the masterpiece by Vermeer, a tension González attributes to "the transformations that the work of art endures in underdeveloped countries."[11] "The way in which images arrive; such exquisite icons as Vermeer's *Woman with a Pearl Necklace*," González writes, "are represented here [in Colombia] in a bulletin on sexual education; reproductions of Leonardo's *The Last Supper* (1495–1498) are placed in houses as a protection against thieves."[12] Calendars, printed plates, product packaging, and cheap reproductions defile and desacralize the works of the masters, but they also give them unexpected meanings, and are all the more generative for it.

Soon after completing her variations on Vermeer's painting, González moved to renderings of tabloid press subjects like the ones she portrayed in *Los suicidas del Sisga*, and then to history painting and to portraits of national heroes. The semblances of the founding fathers, already trivialized by their reproduction in currency bills, calendars, lottery tickets, and the like, is pressed close to the world of furnishings, advertisements, and domestic space in paintings including *Apuntes para la historia extensa, Tomo I* (Notes for the Extensive History, Volume I) (see page 177, figure 6.4) and *Tomo II* (Volume II) (see page 177, figure 6.5), both from 1967. Tin ovals, shower curtains, and the flat surfaces of furniture entered into González's work as material support for her paintings. The popular, commercial, and domestic provenances of these supports stand in sharp contrast to the subject matter: portraits of historical figures.[13] The style of these portraits—like the portraits in *Lesa majestad* (High Treason) (1974,

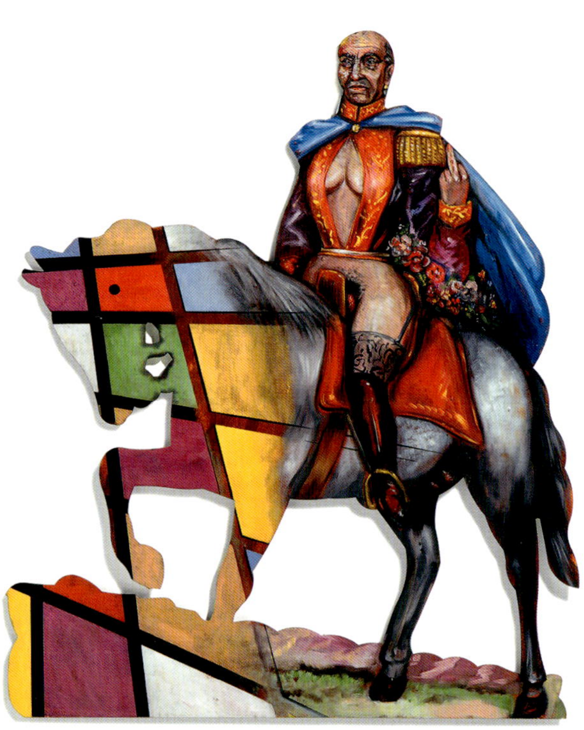

plate 84), visibly modeled on postal stamps—is too bright, too vivacious; their support is too cheap to match the solemnity with which these figures are invested. Colombian audiences and critics, shocked with the apparent defilement of national heroes, met González's early incursions into this genre with resistance.

González achieves the ambivalent desecration of national heroes—brightly celebrated and memorialized, brightly disfigured and defiled—even more powerfully in *Mutis por el foro (cama)* (Exit Stage Rear [Bed]) (1973), in which a postcard version of Pedro Alcántara Quijano Montero's *El libertador muerto* (The Dead Liberator) (1930) serves as the basis for another Pop-inflected history painting. The artist keeps the scene of the original canvas—the deathbed of Simón Bolívar, the nineteenth-century leader in the wars of independence—more or less intact, except for a few key omissions.[14] The support used for González's painting adds another layer of meaning to *Mutis por el foro*, as well as to *La muerte del justo* (Death of the Just) (1973, plate 76), where a religious deathbed scene is painted on an actual bed frame and displayed on the floor, horizontally, on the same level as furniture. The image as remade by González rests undignified on the ground, instead of vertically on the wall as befitting a religious image or, in the case of *Mutis por el foro*, a history painting.[15] In these and other paintings, González displays the semblance of reverential figures horizontally, defacing religious images as well as images of national heroes, revealing these images in their routine commonality, in their commercial reality, in their reality as clichés.[16]

In the 1960s and 1970s, at a time when the faces of (mostly male) revolutionary heroes populated the pages of the press and the airwaves of a rising television culture, there was something repulsive about Pop renderings of men like José Martí, Emiliano Zapata, and Che Guevara, historical figures revered, to this day, with a solemnity that borders on the hagiographical. Quickly and fiercely, thanks in large part to the thriving commercial culture to which Pop art responds and to which it contributes, revolutionary heroes were cast as favorite subjects for pins, posters, and other such objects of trade and propaganda. Argentine Roberto Jacoby denounced this fact of figuration in *Un guerrillero no muere para que se lo cuelgue en la pared* (A Guerrilla Doesn't Die to Be Hung on a Wall) (1968, plate 65), a potent though not unambiguous response to the trivialization and commercialization of revolutionary heroes.[17] Posters, though, for all their banality and despite their (usually) meretricious purpose, memorialize and enshrine the semblance of heroes, inscribing this semblance in the popular imagination in powerful and compact ways. We see this take place in the work of Diego Arango and Nirma Zárate for the Colombian art collective Taller 4 Rojo, particularly in the triptych of posters featuring female Vietcong combatants titled *Agresión del imperialismo* (Aggression of Imperialism) (1972, plate 34). Using color blocking and photomontage, the triptych presents viewers with a succession of images suggesting a story of capitalist invasion signaled by dollar bills and fighter jets defeated at the hands of a female soldier. The transformation of a peasant woman from victim of the US invasion to vanquisher of fighter aircraft, and the expansion of the category of the hero to include her, are perhaps the most consequent aspects of this triptych.[18] They speak

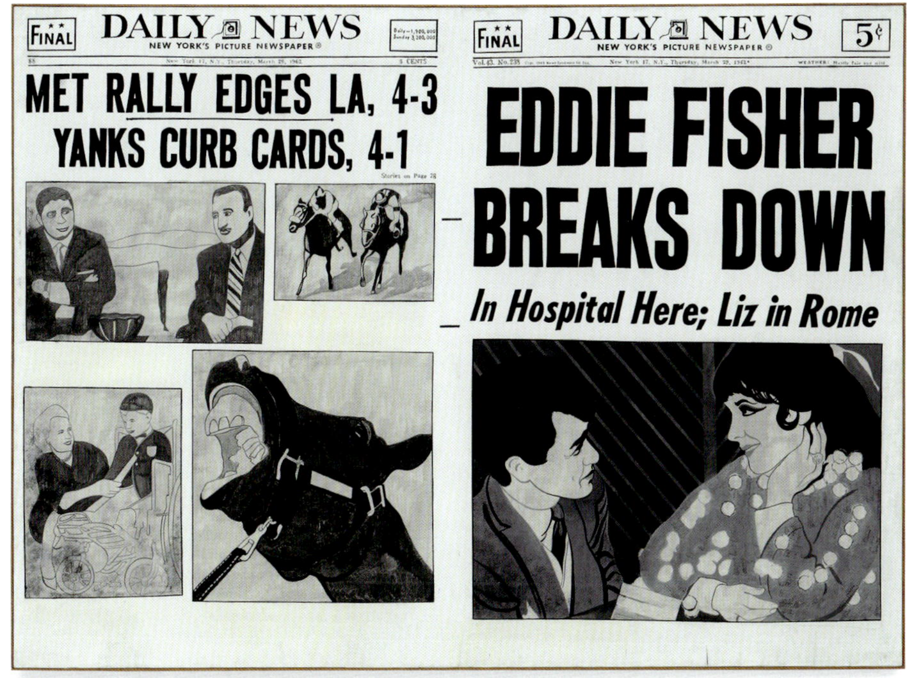

of the powerful and potentially radical function posters can play in the promotion of unhailed heroes, of the kind systemically excluded from the annals of history.

In paintings that look like posters, Cuban Raúl Martínez committed fully to the portraiture of national heroes in a style that registers as too bright, too commercial, too attractive to match the solemnity of historical figures. A popular and eminently market-friendly form of visibility is referenced in, and populated by, the paintings of Martínez, the prolific artist, photographer, and graphic designer. Martínez's vast and richly varied body of work includes advertising, book design, and the posters he produced for the Instituto Cubano del Arte e Industria Cinematográficos (ICAIC).[19] As early as 1964, when Martínez was still practicing the decisively abstract style that characterized the early stages of his career, photographs and popular iconography began to make their way into his canvases. He includes three images, all of popular provenance (the first a photograph of Fidel Castro against the Cuban flag; the second a calendar page; the third the cover page of the Second Declaration of Havana) in his expressionistic 1964 commemoration of the beginning of the revolution, *26 de Julio* (July 26). Photographs and images from popular publications are also visible in one of his early renditions of José Martí (1966).

Already in 1966, in works like *15 repeticiones de Martí* (15 Repetitions of Martí) (see page 75, figure 3.2) and *24 repeticiones de Martí con números y flechas* (24 Repetitions of Martí with Numbers and Arrows), Martínez foregrounded what is perhaps the most significant gesture in

his portraits of national heroes: a very distinctive approach to repetition, one that had less to do with mechanical serialization than with a careful and almost loving reworking of the same image. There is something both tender and analytical about Martínez's serialized variations of the same revered face. Painted oval frames within the frame give these portraits a grid-like order, and variations in everything from color scheme to orientation (some portraits of Martí face slightly to the left, others slightly to the right) infuse the grid with a sense of dynamism. A careful mapping of the national hero's face into broad and distinct areas, combined with the simple but marvelous variations that each one of these areas receives within each individual portrait, add up to produce an extraordinarily rich set of versions of Martí. Some are earnest and some more playful, some are whimsical and some more somber. The sum of these variations belies the monolithic image of the revolutionary hero, gesturing instead to the complexities of Martí's legacy, and to the domestication and the commercialization of his political myth.

Martínez's later portraits of national heroes lose the grid-like order and embrace a composition style closer to collage. In *Repeticiones de Martí* (1968), a looser structure anchored by four larger portraits of Martí includes three smaller versions of the hero's face. A lily on the left side of the frame adds a sense of whimsy. In *Rosas y Estrellas* (Roses and Stars) (1972), the founding fathers and heroes center around the large bouquet of roses Martí holds, which honor the men portrayed, but also upset the usual reverence reserved for these paragons of masculine achievement. Remarkably, given their usual pose of manliness, the heroes seem tinged with a sense of ecstasy, of eroticism and jubilation. A

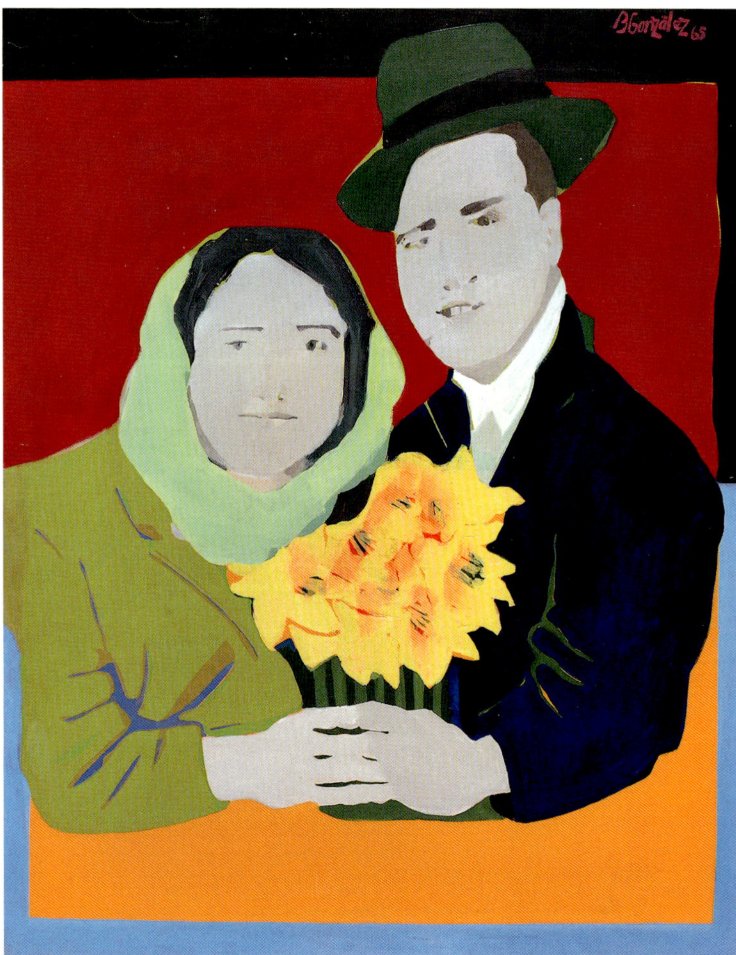

Fig. 6.3. Beatriz González, *Los suicidas del Sisga III* (The Suicides of the Sisga III), 1965. Oil on canvas, 39 x 31.2 inches (100 x 80 cm). Collection of the Museo Nacional de Colombia, Bogotá. © Beatriz González. Image courtesy of the artist and Casas Riegner Gallery, Bogotá, Colombia.

round frame of green leaves surrounds them and adds to their exuberance, inserting the heroes in the kind of idyllic, Edenic, and eroticized setting Martínez portrayed more explicitly in *Adán y Julieta* (Adam and Juliet) (1973, plate 15).

Martínez extends his reworking of religious and fatherland myths to popular figures and everyday Cubans in intervened photographs such as *Sin título (Tres amigos)* (Untitled [Three Friends]) (1969) and *El vaquero* (Cowboy) (c. 1969, plate 104). The features of the young cowboy in *El vaquero*, like Martí in the repetition portraits, are carefully intervened to add shadows and contour, his arm painted in a tone of fleshy pink that highlights the pose of his body. The cigarette in the young cowboy's mouth and the patterned shirt he wears are brightly painted by Martínez, his swagger leaving behind a trail of vibrant, stellar colors. This theme is repeated in *Che* (1968, plate 63), where Guevara's iconic beret extends upwards and beyond the confines of the hero's contour. Like the speech balloons used in comic strips, the stars draw the eye of the viewer beyond the figure, to the transatlantic world that floats above him like an idea or a dreamlike dialogue globe.

If Martínez achieves Pop defilement by "softening" the semblance of founding fathers, Mexican artist Alberto Gironella proceeds by "dismemberment or deconstruction."[20] His method of cutting, framing, reinterpreting, and dissecting historical figures in assemblages made with an eccentric and carefully calibrated array of textures and objects manages to be grizzly, darkly humorous, iconoclastic, and profoundly reverent all at the same time.[21] A significant portion of the historical figures in Gironella's portraits belong to the seventeenth-century Spanish royal court, as painted by the Golden Age master Diego Velázquez, whose paintings of Spanish royals provide the most consistent source of figurative materials for Gironella.[22] Assemblages populated by odd objects and by images drawn from a wide spectrum of sources—photographs, advertisements, packaging, and taxidermy, as in *Homenaje a Pablo Picasso* (Tribute to Pablo Picasso) (1971), make up a significant portion of Gironella's work. Most of these assemblages look like altars, and include objects drawn from the world of consumer goods, of the kind found in grocery stores in mid-twentieth-century Mexico (canned goods, bottle caps, advertisements, and the like).[23] Gironella's father, a Catalan immigrant to Mexico, owned one such store, specializing in *ultramarinos*, canned and preserved goods referred to as such since they were brought from overseas.[24]

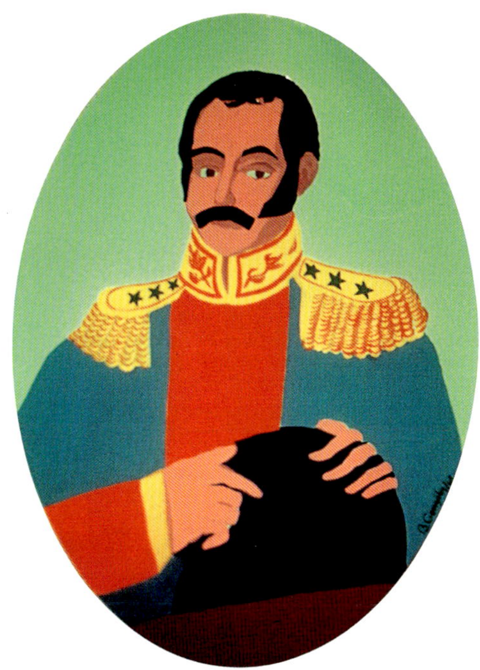

Fig. 6.4. Beatriz González, *Apuntes para la historia extensa, Tomo I* (Notes for the Extensive History, Volume I), 1967. Enamel on tin plate, 39.37 × 31.5 inches (100 × 80 cm). Private collection. © Beatriz González. Image courtesy of the artist and Casas Riegner Gallery, Bogotá, Colombia.

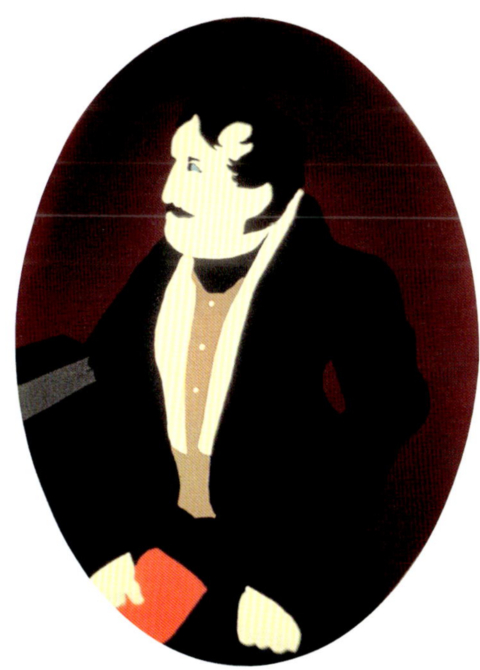

Fig. 6.5. Beatriz González, *Apuntes para la historia extensa, Tomo II* (Notes for the Extensive History, Volume II), 1967. Enamel on tin plate, 39.37 × 31.5 inches (100 × 80 cm). Propal Collection, Cali, Colombia. © Beatriz González. Image courtesy of the artist and Casas Riegner Gallery, Bogotá, Colombia.

In Mexico City, these *tiendas de ultramarinos* were located in the popular La Merced marketplace and owned mostly by Spanish immigrants.[25] There are manifest transatlantic overtones in Gironella's decades-long reworking of Spanish Golden Age painting, and the inclusion of *ultramarinos* in his assemblages is one of the vast array of materials and symbolic artifacts the Mexican artist used to signal, abstrusely but unequivocally, the history of domination and exchange between Spain and its New World colonies.[26]

Though most of Gironella's work with historical figures happens by way of his ongoing dialogue with Velázquez and thus entails the figures of the Spanish royal court, there is one protagonist of modern Mexican history whom he engages repeatedly and to great effect: Emiliano Zapata, icon of the Mexican revolution and of insurgency in Mexico more generally. Gironella's series of works featuring Zapata was widely celebrated in the 1972 exhibition *Gironella: El entierro de Zapata y otros enterramientos* (Gironella: The Burial of Zapata and Other Burials) at the Palacio de Bellas Artes in Mexico City.[27] The homage to the *caudillo* (strongman) and Gironella's characteristic inclusion of emblems of history and art history were clear from the title of the exhibition, which referenced the revolutionary hero as well as the sixteenth-century painting by El Greco, *El entierro del Conde Orgaz* (The Burial of the Count of Orgaz) (1586–1588). Some critics have highlighted the hagiographical turn in Gironella's take on Zapata, as if in his paintings and assemblages the agrarian leader was descending back to earth, saintly but concretely material, embodied in his relics.[28] Gironella's assemblages, though, work as altars and relic holders as much as they work as window displays, fusing the commercial and the sacred.

A striking parallelism exists between Gironella's Zapata assemblages and a historical object directly related to Zapata's death. A photograph dated 1919 shows a display box with the personal effects Zapata was wearing at the time of his assassination. The box is a reliquary of sorts for the national hero, a cabinet for the objects that prove the hero's life as well as his death. But Zapata's effects as gathered in the box and as shown in the photograph are more than the relics of a dead hero. They are also, and principally, pieces of evidence gathered by Pablo González, the general responsible for killing Zapata, mailed to the Mexico City newspaper, *El Pueblo*, where they were displayed as proof of the *caudillo's* death, and where they also functioned, deliberately or not, as indirect evidence of the gruesomeness of revolutionary violence.

Gironella plays up the grimness of Zapata's death graphically by peppering his assemblages with bottle caps that look like bullet holes, as in *Zapata con marca de ganado* (Zapata with Cattle Brand) (1972, plate 75), or by staining the shirt of the revolutionary hero with patches of blood-red paint, as in *Objeto Zapata 666* (Zapata Object 666) (1972). The "number of the beast" as included in the title of this last work, together with the repurposed and partially covered sign for the Mexican ointment brand "666" included in the assemblage, add a sense of apocalyptic undoing to the work as a whole. The apocalypse is also alluded to, though much more cryptically, in *Zapata con marca de ganado*, the title of which points to the six livestock brandings surrounding the image of Zapata, while also referencing *la marca de la bestia*, the Spanish translation of "the number of the beast." An earlier

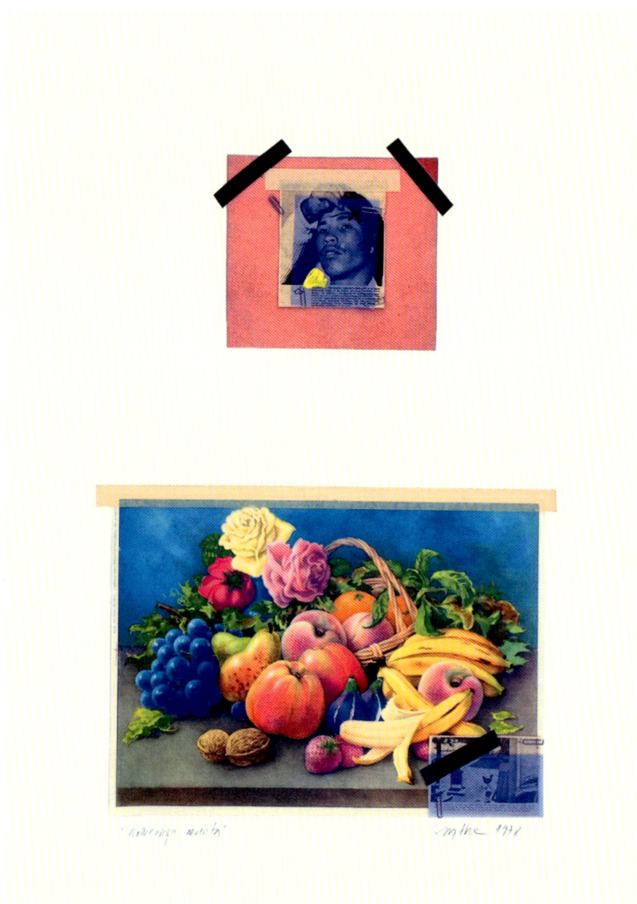

Fig. 6.6. Francisco Smythe, *Naturaleza muerta* (Still Life), 1978. Acrylic and tape on printed plate, newspaper clippings, acetate, and fabric on paper; 31.2 x 42.9 inches (80 x 110 cm). Image courtesy of the Francisco Smythe Estate, Santiago, Chile.

portrait, *Zapata tradicional* (Traditional Zapata) (1957), a painting without the profusion of objects that would characterize much of Gironella's later work, shows the hero against a blood red landscape, a sash with the colors of the Mexican flag proudly draped over his shoulder, skulls scattered around the floor where he stands. Violence, death, and grim undoing seem to emanate from Zapata in this earlier picture, in much the same way as they victimize him in the later assemblages. Defilement and defacement in Gironella's images of Zapata derail any one of the single, unifying, idealized visions of the revolutionary hero's place in history, the kind of visions we might be tempted to project onto reverential figures more generally.

Disfigurement in Pop art of América is both an affront to and an embrace of the found image, of *fait divers*, and of the cliché. Disfiguration in the works here discussed keeps the figures these works appropriate—religious and historical figures, figures of popular and commercial culture—recognizable, taking them for what they have become: clichés. The way in which disfigurement works over popular and iconic images, the order in which it appropriates them and intervenes in them, is that of a wider spectrum of visual culture that includes the high arts, but only as a segment, and not necessarily the most interesting one. Disfigurement operates at the level of the standardized image, at the level of the cliché. It dissects, by means of meticulous dismemberment, the figuration that sustains and is sustained by the cliché.[29]

1   Robert Indiana, the US Pop artist, colorfully described this feature in his response to the question "What is Pop?" Indiana's response is as follows: "It is basically a U-turn back to a representational visual communication, moving at a break-away speed in several sharp late models. It is an abrupt return to Father after an abstract 15-year exploration of the Womb. Pop is a re-enlistment in the world." See G. R. Swenson, "What is Pop Art? Answers from 8 Painters, Part I," *ARTnews* 62 (November 1963): 27.

2   For the significance of Dávila's irreverent intervention on Martí as founding father, see Francine Masiello, *The Art of Transition: Latin American Culture and Neoliberal Crisis* (Durham: Duke University Press, 2001), 54: "Dávila calls attention to the role that sexuality plays in defining Latin American subjects; he interrogates fixed notions of identity passed on from founding fathers as he obliges us to rethink our understanding of *lo popular*. If he asks about the corporeal grammar that organizes memory and history, he also inquires about the authorized voices that name national longings."

3   Both Thomas Crow and Ana María Reyes have suggested just such a return in US and Colombian Pop art respectively. See Thomas Crow, "Saturday Disasters: Trace and Reference in Early Warhol," in *Reconstructing Modernism: Art in New York, Paris, and Montreal 1945-1964*, ed. Serge Guilbaut (Cambrigde: MIT Press, 1990), 320: "In his particular dramatization of medium, Warhol found room for a dramatization of feeling and even a kind of history painting." See also Ana María Reyes, "In Bed with Dead Bolívar: Beatriz González's Case for Critical History Painting," in *Simón Bolívar: Travels and Transformations of a Cultural Icon*, eds., Maureen G. Shanahan and Ana María Reyes (Gainesville: University Press of Florida, 2016), 148: "In two works by Beatriz González the artist repurposed well-known representations of Bolívar: *Apuntes para la historia extensa* (1967) and *Mutis por el foro* (1973). These works revitalized contemporary history painting, being neither the falsified and decorous official versions nor the complete disavowal of the genre through abstraction—which has served as evidence of Latin American modernity in the international art circuit—but rather a critical re-vision."

4   See for instance what Robert Rauschenberg has to say on the occasion of the opening of the Rauschenberg Overseas Culture Interchange in Mexico: "The Rauschenberg Overseas Culture Exchange (R.O.C.I.)—that is presented in Mexico with the title *The Dream World of Rauschenberg*... is a private project that for four years will bring, create, and exchange art and deeds through the entire world. Special emphasis will be placed on sharing experiences with societies that rarely express ideas that are not related to politics, and in which the possibility of communicating with the world through art has not been presented." See Robert Rauschenberg, "Manifesto," in *El soñado mundo de Rauschenberg* (Mexico City: Museo Rufuno Tamayo, 1985), n.p.

5   Swenson, "What Is Pop Art? Part I," 26: *Death in America* was the title of a projected show in Paris of "the electric-chair pictures and the dogs in Birmingham and car wreck and some suicide pictures." See also Crow, "Saturday Disasters," 324.

6   Hal Foster points out that the Death and Disaster images inaugurate a certain, perhaps central, genealogy of Pop art. See Hal Foster, *The Return of the Real: The Avant-Garde at the End of the Century* (Cambridge: MIT Press, 1996), 128. See also Crow, "Saturday Disasters," 324.

7   This reading of Warhol's female celebrity portraits goes against the grain of persistent interpretations of them as mechanized pictures of beauty, surface, and glamour. For a rehearsal of this argument, see Rodrigo Alonso, "Un arte de contradicciones," in *Arte de contradicciones: Pop, realismos y política. Brasil-Argentina 1960* (Buenos Aires: Fundación Proa, 2012), 27.

8   Crow, "Saturday Disasters," 322: "In his selection of these photographs, Warhol was as little as ever the passive receptor of commonly available imagery. Rather than relying upon newspaper reproductions that might have come to hand randomly, he sought out glossy press-agency prints normally seen only by professional journalists. (Some of these were apparently regarded as too bizarre or gruesome ever to see print; that is, they were barred from public reproduction precisely because of their capacity to disturb.)." Newspaper matter features often, and often prominently, in the history of crossings between modernist art and mass media. Before Warhol, Marcel Duchamp had been at work for two decades on his "givens," *Étant donnés: 1. La chute d'eau, 2. Le gaz d'éclairage* (1946–1966), the deeply disturbing assemblage-qua-peep show permanently installed at the Philadelphia Museum of Art and principally based, in Jean-Michel Rabaté's reading, on the widely disseminated photographs of the Black Dahlia murder in Los Angeles in 1947.

9   Carolina Ponce de León, "Beatriz González: The Extended History of Colombia," in *Beatriz González, What an Honor to be with You at this Historic Moment* (New York: El Museo del Barrio, 1998), 20.

10   On the link between flatness, advertising, and Pop art, see Luis Camnitzer, *On Art, Artists, Latin America, and Other Utopias* (Austin: University of Texas Press, 2009), 32: "From outside of American consumer society, Pop's most evident and understandable contribution was the change of the rules of composition. The work of art is now 'laid out' like a piece of advertising instead of having the traditional 'composition' expected in art."

11   Beatriz González, "Other People and Their Ideas," *ArtReview* (January–February 2016): 57. The Colombian artist Álvaro Barrios also assumes the commercialized field of visibility of 1960s print culture as the context of his work. He describes it as follows: "I made some collages about an imaginary world where The Beatles, the Vietnam War, Batman and Robin, Che Guevara, Dick Tracy, the warrior priest Camilo Torres and Tarzan lived in harmony" in Beatriz González, "Andy Warhol y la recepción del arte pop en Colombia." Augusto de Campos, the Brazilian Concrete poet, gives a fuller but strikingly similar account of this flattened field of visibility when he writes: "The new media of mass communication, journals and magazines, radio and television, have their major headquarters in metropolises, whose 'centers' irradiate information to thousands of people in regions more numerous each day. Universal intercommunication is more intense and more difficult to contain every day, to such a degree that it is literally impossible for any citizen to live his daily life without confronting Vietnam, the Beatles, strikes, 007, the Moon, Mao or the Pope at every step." See Augusto de Campos, *Balanço da bossa e outras bossas* (São Paulo: Editora Perspectiva, 1974): 59–60.

12   Ibid., "Other People and Their Ideas," 57.

13   For more on the material support of these paintings, see Reyes, "In Bed with Dead Bolívar," 152.

14   Ibid., 161.

15   For comparison, consider Robert Rauschenberg's *Bed* (1955), an oil and pencil work made on a pillow, quilt, and sheet set resting on wood supports. Rauschenberg's *Bed* is displayed hanging from a wall, on the vertical axis of traditional painting. In Rauschenberg's work, the bed, in all its routine materiality, rises to the dignity of the vertical wall. In González's work, the national heroes come down from the wall. Rauschenberg's influence on Latin American artists associated with Pop was significant, although it is unclear whether he had any influence at all on González. He did seem to have a strong effect on Alberto Gironella, who kept catalogues of the American painter's work as well as magazine clippings of reports on the artist. For the reception of

Pop in Colombia and its place in the work of González, see González, "Andy Warhol y la recepción del arte Pop en Colombia." See also González, "Actitudes de una década," in *Sin título 1966–1968. Luis Caballero* (Bogotá: Museo Nacional de Colombia, 1997), 33, 39. For González's view on the impact of Pop on her own work, see González "Other People and Their Ideas," 57.

16   A year before González's *Mutis por el foro* was completed, Quijano Moreno's 1930 painting was reproduced on lottery tickets in Colombia. See Reyes, "In Bed with Dead Bolívar," 160. The theme of "the death of the sinner" as well its counterpart, the theme of "good death," were also available as popular prints in Colombia at the time González completed her painting. See Ana María Reyes, "Incorporated Vision: Artistic Critiques of the Development Discourse in Latin America," *Revista Letral* 13 (2014): 107. González's work with the cliché predates her adoption of a Pop aesthetic: her breakthrough series of paintings titled *Encajera* (1963–64) is based on a plate of Jan Vermeer's *The Lacemaker* (1665) reproduced in popular calendars. See Ponce de León, "Beatriz González: The Extended History of Colombia," 18.

17   Jacoby later denounces the puritan limits of the leftist, progressive imagination in his theorization of what he calls "the strategy of joy." See Roberto Jacoby, *El deseo nace del derrumbe: acciones, conceptos, escritos* (Barcelona: Ediciones de la Central, 2011), 411: "Skin was considered a territory of pleasure and not of torment. The 'surface' was also the opposite of a prison cell and clandestineness. It is easy to see that the moralizing tone of these critiques turned toward traditional revolutionary puritanism, a mixture of Stalinism with Christian and military asceticism, which was hegemonic as much within progressive as reactionary forces."

18   María Sol Barón and Camilo Ordoñez Robayo, "Literatura," Paper presented at the "Coloquio Revista ERRATA. El lugar del arte en lo político," Bogotá, Colombia, July 2010: "The first time that I saw a work by Taller 4 Rojo was in an art class at school. The exercise consisted in freely examining art publications in the bookshelves of the library. I was about 16 years old then and preferred to page through something random like a volume of the Salvat Art Encyclopedia of Colombia until those Vietnamese women appeared. On television, the Vietnam War was represented with Asian troops that seemed more like a group of identical actors, poorly armed, and barefoot, that spoke in monosyllables and monotones in the face of North American soldiers."

19   For more on Martínez's work in advertising and graphic design, see Jennifer Josten's essay in this catalogue and Corina Matamoros, *Raúl Martínez: la gran familia* (Spain: Ediciones Vanguardia Cubana, 2012), 124.

20   Holliday T. Qay and Hollister Sturges, *Art of the Fantastic: Latin America, 1920–1987* (Indianapolis: Indianapolis Museum of Art, 1987), 138: "Alberto Gironella is most famous for his dismemberment or deconstruction of the great paintings of the seventeenth-century Spanish Golden Age into fantastic, macabre creations that explore the role of Spanish tradition in Mexican mestizo culture."

21   Valerie Fraser, "Surrealising the Baroque: Mexico's Spanish Heritage and the Work of Alberto Gironella," *Oxford Art Journal* 14.1 (1991): 35: "For him [Gironella] the reworking of familiar images is not simply a matter of drawing attention to the way in which mass-reproduction numbs the optic nerves, by shocking the spectator with a moustached Mona Lisa, but rather, using a peculiar blend of both iconoclasm and a sort of wry homage, of investigating the power of certain images, particularly those which have national resonance. In this sense, his Habsburg and Bourbon portraits are not dissimilar to Jasper Johns's American flag series, except of course that the flag, whatever individuals may think of it, is unquestionably American, the lineage is clear."

22   Ibid., 34: "It is worth emphasizing that the period spanned by the lives of El Greco and Velázquez saw in Latin America the consolidation of colonial government and of the Christian church, the establishment of the Spanish language and of European culture, the introduction of new methods of exploitation of people and resources."

23   Ibid., 39: "The origins of Gironella's peculiar assemblages lie in his childhood. His earliest memories are of stacks of colorful imported tins, boxes, bottles, and packets of the family grocery business, and of the paraphernalia of popular Catholicism, which would have included reliquaries and tabernacles, retables combining paintings and sculpture, altars decorated with damask cloth, candles, flowers, and *ex votos* of an often intensely personal nature. He recalls building himself private altars of chocolate wrappers and tin cans."

24   Ibid.: "The packaging of imported products has continued to fascinate [Gironella], for intrinsic qualities—the names, the colors and the designs—but also no doubt because of the way products from far away have been integrated into the domestic Mexican environment. Such products are known by the general term *ultramarinos*, 'from across the ocean.'"

25   Rosa Casanova and Adriana Konzevik, *Luces sobre México: catálogo selectivo de la Fototeca Nacional del INAH* (Mexico City: Editorial RM, 2006), 53.

26   For an extended discussion of the traces of a colonial past in Gironella's paintings, see Orianna Baddeley and Valerie Fraser, *Drawing the Line: Art and Cultural Identity in Contemporary Latin America* (New York: Verso, 1989), 50–60.

27   Juan Acha, "Gironella, lo mejor: balance de un buen año artístico," *Diorama de la Cultura*, supplement, *Excélsior*, December 30, 1972, 3: "1972 was witness to a notable work: *The Burial of Zapata and Other Burials*, an installation by Gironella, in which the exhibition in itself constituted the work; that is, it had nothing to do with a typical exhibition of paintings and objects. As a work, it was the best and most modern of the second half of the year, if we go by the commentaries in the press."

28   Jorge Hernández Campos, "Gironella y la transfiguración de Zapata," in *Gironella: El entierro de Zapata y otros enterramientos* (Mexico City: 1972), n.p.: "The fact that Gironella now centers his meditations on Emiliano Zapata must demand reflection. It means, in the connection with El Greco and *The Burial of Count Ordaz*, the transfiguration of the southern *caudillo* (strongman), the battle for the land and the Mexican Revolution toward the order of our transnational culture, and through that, to universal values. Thereafter, it means the re-descent of Zapata toward us, with the smell of the filth of his countryside and all the outrage of his necessary bullets."

29   Olivier Debroise, "Alberto Gironella también pinta," *La Cultura en México* (August 1, 1979): "Gironella respects the composition and the chromatic density of the deep *chiaroscuro* of Velázquez: only he includes—as in a collage—elements foreign to the work: a minimal subversion that does not affect the context. Gironella just pays homage to the Master and, in doing so, recuperates and over-mythologizes works already mythologized from their reproduction (with educational aims) in millions of packages of Corn Flakes."

SERGIO DELGADO MOYA

PROFANACIÓN, DEFORMACIÓN, Y DESFIGURACIÓN

El regreso al arte figurativo, tras un período definido en gran parte por diversas formas de abstracción, es uno de los rasgos distintivos del arte pop.[1] Este aspecto queda plasmado contundentemente en las obras reunidas en esta exposición, y quisiera abordarlo analizando las huellas de profanación, deformación y desfiguración que evidencian las imágenes pop de los personajes históricos. La figuración, en el sentido al que me refiero aquí, resuena con un tono más lúdico, por ejemplo, en la desfiguración que vemos en *Decay Dance* (Danza de la decadencia) (1969, lámina 20) de Rupert García. Es una estrategia artística que anticipa el tipo de comentario político que hace Juan Dávila en *El libertador Simón Bolívar* (1994), una versión colorida, insolente, semidesnuda y (tran)sexualizada del padre de la independencia latinoamericana, que provocó la ira de las autoridades gubernamentales en toda la región (ver página 174, figura 6.1).[2]

Apropiándose ampliamente de imágenes encontradas y clichés de la cultura popular y comercial, los artistas examinados en las próximas páginas crearon un registro de rostros y hechos históricos. Es así que su obra señala un regreso irreverente de la pintura histórica en el arte pop,[3] un regreso fundamentado en las especificidades materiales e históricas (las emergentes sociedades de consumo, las guerras y las luchas revolucionarias) de la vida en América durante las décadas de 1960 y 1970. En su conjunto, las obras de estos artistas constituyen un corpus de arte pop que conjuga un sentido de innovación conceptual y compositiva con un tratamiento intenso y sostenido de temas de índole política. Esto a su vez nos obliga a revisitar, en el contexto del arte pop en particular y del arte en general, el tipo de distinción esquemática

que ubica un enfoque desafecto del pop y la cultura del consumo en el norte y un enfoque subversivo y politizado de esa misma cultura en el sur del hemisferio.[4]

En algunos de los primeros ejemplos de arte pop aparece con prominencia la figuración como desmembramiento y desfiguración, y la desfiguración como acercamiento a la pintura histórica. Vemos materializados estos aspectos en la serie *Death* and *Disaster* (Muerte y Desastre) de Andy Warhol a principios de los años sesenta.[5] Estas serigrafías, aunque relativamente minimizadas en la narrativa convencional de la historia del pop,[6] sobresalen del resto de la obra de Warhol por la manera en que captan lo que Thomas Crow describe como "las llagas abiertas en la vida política de Estados Unidos". Sostiene Crow que al definir las imágenes de muerte y desastre de Warhol podrían incluirse también sus primeros retratos de celebridades femeninas, retratos que parecen más oscuros y sombríos de lo que se ha pretendido hasta ahora. Éstos aluden a la enfermedad (Elizabeth Taylor y sus padecimientos mientras filmaba *Cleopatra*) y a la muerte (Marilyn Monroe a pocas semanas de su fallecimiento, Jackie Kennedy en duelo por el asesinato de su marido) en la misma medida que rinden tributo a la celebridad (ver página 175, figura 6.2).[7] Muchas de las imágenes que Warhol utilizó para estos retratos provenían de tabloides y otras publicaciones sensacionalistas, además de fotos tomadas en un principio para publicarse pero que luego resultaron demasiado lúgubres y no se difundieron al público.[8] La fuente de estas imágenes es reveladora, en el sentido de que no apunta a la fotografía en general, sino a un tipo específico de fotografía —la de tabloide— como documento importante, quizás crucial, de la figura humana en la cultura visual de mediados del siglo XX.

La prensa amarillista especializada en crímenes, y en general las publicaciones clasificadas como sensacionalistas, proliferaron en Estados Unidos hacia los años en que Warhol creó sus obras de la serie *Disaster*, a la vez que en países como México, Chile y Colombia los tabloides de crímenes se situaron entre las publicaciones más populares. Aunque tomada de uno de los periódicos colombianos de mejor reputación, la imagen que aparece en la exitosa serie de pinturas de Beatriz González titulada *Los suicidas del Sisga (I–III)* (ver página 176, figura 6.3) apunta a este contexto casi de inmediato. Es el tipo de imagen (la de un suicidio) que se publicaba frecuente y llamativamente en los tabloides que abundaban hacia la época en que González completó sus pinturas. En ellas aparece una pareja muy bien vestida que posa para un retrato formal sosteniendo amorosamente un ramo de flores entre ambos. La pareja encargó el retrato fotográfico como recuerdo de su amor y de su muerte: posaron para la cámara poco antes de suicidarse. Cuando la foto y su historia aparecieron en los principales periódicos de Bogotá (*El Espectador*, *El Tiempo*), González quedó cautivada por la planitud de la imagen, la tersura de los rostros (había bastantes retoques) y el hecho de que todas las texturas y superficies parecían aplanadas al mismo nivel, habiendo pasado por múltiples reproducciones en los periódicos.[9] La artista resaltó este efecto plano (que muchos consideran un buen recurso para embellecer el rostro humano, pero que en realidad le quita todo contraste y sombreado) utilizando un método de bloques de color que produce una imagen vívida muy característica del pop. El resultado es que, en la pintura de González, la pareja fallecida parece una caricatura o un anuncio publicitario.[10] El efecto general causó un escándalo. La pintura daba visibilidad a un tipo de suceso que solía relegarse a las páginas de los tabloides, y además lo hacía con unos colores y un estilo de composición demasiado irreverentes para el tema. En todo este proceso, y gracias sobre todo a los colores brillantes y la composición plana de su obra, González atenuó el matiz sentimental y melodramático que había tomado la cobertura del suicidio de la pareja en los tabloides.

La pintura como campo de visibilidad, y en particular el retrato, por siglos solo fue accesible para un selecto grupo, en su mayoría figuras históricas y mitológicas además de personas prominentes y adineradas de la sociedad. No fue hasta el siglo XIX que la pintura y el retrato expandieron su repertorio de temas para incluir a sectores sociales más populares. Es así que el acercamiento de González al retrato forma parte de una tendencia más amplia en la historia de la pintura, pero además, y quizás sea esto lo más importante, es una expansión de esa tendencia, en cuanto los sujetos que retrata provienen de un segmento de la cultura visual —la prensa amarillista— que es sumamente popular pero a la vez está muy desacreditado, incluso desvalorizado, a causa de su misma popularidad y del acto profanador que ese tipo de periodismo suele ejercer sobre su contenido.

Para González —y para artistas como el chileno Francisco Smythe, quien pasó gran parte de los años setenta buscando en los tabloides imágenes para sus collages y pinturas (ver página 178, figuras 6.6)— el mundo de la prensa amarillista, y la cultura de lo visual y lo impreso a la cual pertenece este tipo de prensa, es más que un objeto de desprecio y más que una ventana hacia los márgenes de la sociedad. Es un campo de visibilidad unificado por su penetración, su amplia circulación y su presencia aparentemente ubicua en los espacios públicos y

en la intimidad de los hogares. Los calendarios, empaques de productos, publicaciones populares y otras plataformas de impresos baratos son los vehículos de esta cultura visual, una cultura con suficiente capacidad (o más bien voracidad) como para incluir una enorme gama de imágenes: desde fotos de celebridades, imágenes religiosas y vistas morbosas de accidentes y muertes horribles hasta reproducciones de obras de arte de todo tipo y calidad posible. Para González y muchos de sus colegas contemporáneos, las reproducciones de obras de arte que aparecían en los empaques de productos y páginas de calendarios constituyeron un irónico punto de entrada a un registro de referencias e imágenes a las que apenas tenían acceso los artistas latinoamericanos. Las instituciones locales de arte no suelen poseer colecciones con "obras maestras" del arte occidental, excepto, por supuesto, en reproducciones.

González no pasó por alto la paradoja de este acceso a la alta cultura —acceso a través de copias y reproducciones, el tipo de impreso más barato y ubicuo—. La artista asumió esta paradoja y la transformó en uno de los aspectos más generativos de su obra, como se puede apreciar en una de sus primeras series de retratos, sus variaciones sobre *La joven de la perla* (c. 1662–1665) de Johannes Vermeer. Existe una cierta tensión en su regreso compulsivo a la obra maestra de Vermeer, una tensión que González atribuye a "las transformaciones que sufren las obras de arte en los países subdesarrollados".[11] "La forma en que llegan las imágenes; íconos tan exquisitos como *La joven de la perla* de Vermeer", escribe González, "aquí [en Colombia] aparecen en folletos de educación sexual; la gente coloca reproducciones de *La última cena* de Da Vinci (1495–1498) en las casas para que los proteja de robos".[12] Los calendarios, platos decorados, empaques de productos y reproducciones baratas profanan y desacralizan las obras de los grandes maestros, pero también les otorgan significados inesperados, y por ello son aún más generativos.

Al poco tiempo de completar sus variaciones sobre el cuadro de Vermeer, González empezó a trabajar con imágenes publicadas en los tabloides, como la pareja que presenta en *Los suicidas del Sisga*, y luego pasó a pinturas históricas y retratos de héroes nacionales. Las efigies de los padres de la patria, ya trivializadas en billetes de divisa, calendarios, billetes de lotería y otros, son ubicadas por la artista en el mundo del mobiliario, la publicidad y el espacio doméstico en obras como *Apuntes para la historia extensa, Tomo I y Tomo II* (ver página 177; figuras 6.4, 6.5), ambas de 1967. Es aquí que los óvalos de latón, las cortinas de baño y las superficies planas de los muebles entran en la obra de González como soporte material para las pinturas. La procedencia popular, comercial y doméstica de estos soportes crea un fuerte contraste con el tema: retratos de figuras históricas.[13] El estilo de estos retratos —como en *Lesa majestad* (1974, lámina 84), claramente inspirado en un timbre postal— es demasiado brillante, demasiado vivo; lo barato del soporte no corresponde a la solemnidad de las figuras. El público y los críticos colombianos, impactados por la aparente profanación de los héroes nacionales, recibieron las primeras incursiones de González en este género con reticencia.

González logra con mayor fuerza la ambivalente profanación de los héroes nacionales (celebrados y conmemorados brillantemente, desfigurados y profanados brillantemente) en *Mutis por el foro (cama)*.

Aquí se basa en una tarjeta postal con la imagen de *El libertador muerto* (1930), de Pedro Alcántara Quijano Montero, para crear otra pintura histórica en vertiente pop. La artista conserva más o menos intacta la escena del cuadro original —el lecho de muerte de Simón Bolívar, líder de las guerras de independencia en el siglo XIX—, pero omite algunos elementos clave.[14] El soporte utilizado agrega otro estrato de significado tanto a *Mutis por el foro* como a *La muerte del justo* (1973, lámina 76), escena religiosa de un lecho de muerte pintada en el armazón de una cama y expuesta en el suelo, horizontalmente, al mismo nivel que cualquier mueble. La imagen, según la rehace González, yace sin dignidad en el piso en vez de ir colocada verticalmente en la pared, como correspondería a una imagen religiosa o, en el caso de *Mutis por el foro*, a una pintura histórica.[15] En éstas y otras obras, al presentar horizontalmente las efigies de figuras reverenciadas, deformando lo mismo imágenes religiosas que retratos de héroes nacionales, González los revela en lo común de su cotidianidad, en su realidad comercial, en su realidad como clichés.[16]

Durante las décadas de 1960 y 1970, época en que los rostros de los héroes revolucionarios nacionales (en su mayoría hombres) poblaban las páginas de la prensa y los espacios de una creciente cultura televisiva, había algo de repulsivo en las representaciones pop de personajes como José Martí, Emiliano Zapata y el Che Guevara, figuras históricas que hasta el día de hoy son veneradas con una solemnidad que raya en lo hagiográfico. Rápida y ferozmente, en gran medida gracias a la próspera cultura comercial a que responde y contribuye el arte pop, las imágenes de los héroes revolucionarios se convirtieron en *pins*, carteles y otros objetos comerciales y propagandísticos. El argentino Roberto Jacoby denunció este hecho en *Un guerrillero no muere para que se lo cuelgue en la pared* (1968, lámina 65), respuesta potente aunque un tanto ambigua a la trivialización y comercialización de los héroes revolucionarios. No obstante, los carteles, por más banales y (en general) aparatosos que sean, conmemoran y consagran las imágenes de los héroes, grabándolas en la imaginación popular de forma intensa y compacta.[17] Este hecho lo vemos en la obra de Diego Arango y Nirma Zárate para el colectivo artístico colombiano Taller 4 Rojo, sobre todo en el tríptico de carteles que presenta a mujeres combatientes del Vietcong, titulado *Agresión del imperialismo* (1972, lámina 34). Con bloques de color y fotomontajes, el tríptico presenta al espectador una sucesión de imágenes que sugieren la narrativa de una invasión capitalista (simbolizada por billetes de dólares y aviones de combate) que es derrotada por una mujer soldado. Tal vez los aspectos más consecuentes del tríptico sean el hecho de que una campesina se transforme de víctima de la invasión estadounidense en vencedora de aviones de guerra, y la consiguiente expansión de la categoría de héroe para ahora incluirla a ella.[18] Esto habla del poder y el potencial radical de los carteles en la promoción de los héroes desconocidos, los que quedan sistemáticamente excluidos de los anales de la historia.

En pinturas que parecen carteles, el cubano Raúl Martínez se dedicó al retrato de héroes nacionales con un estilo que se registra como demasiado vívido, comercial y atractivo para la solemnidad de las figuras históricas. Las obras de Martínez, prolífico artista, fotógrafo y diseñador gráfico, toman como referencia, y a la vez habitan, un tipo de visibilidad popular y sumamente mercadeable. Su extensa y variada producción incluye trabajos publicitarios, diseño de libros y

los carteles que produjo para el Instituto Cubano del Arte e Industria Cinematográficos (ICAIC).[19] Desde 1964, cuando Martínez todavía empleaba el estilo decididamente abstracto que caracterizó sus primeras obras, las fotografías y la iconografía popular empezaron a abrirse paso en sus lienzos. El artista incluye tres imágenes, todas de procedencia popular (una foto de Fidel Castro con la bandera cubana de fondo; una página de calendario; la portada de la Segunda Declaración de La Habana), en su expresionista conmemoración del inicio de la revolución, titulada *26 de julio* (1964). En uno de sus primeros retratos de José Martí (1966) también pueden apreciarse fotos e imágenes provenientes de publicaciones populares.

Ya en 1966, en obras como *15 repeticiones de Martí* (ver página 75, figura 3.2) y *24 repeticiones de Martí con números y flechas*, Martínez estaba destacando lo que tal vez sea el gesto más significativo de sus retratos de héroes nacionales: un acercamiento muy distintivo a la repetición, que tiene menos que ver con la serialización mecánica y más con el acto de retrabajar la misma imagen con cuidado, casi con amor. Hay algo de tierno y a la vez analítico en las variaciones seriadas que hace Martínez del venerado rostro martiano. Los marcos ovalados pintados dentro del marco de estos retratos les dan un orden casi de cuadrícula, y las variaciones que van desde el esquema de colores hasta la orientación (algunos retratos Martí están levemente hacia la izquierda y otros hacia la derecha) otorgan a la cuadrícula una sensación de dinamismo. El cuidadoso mapeo del rostro del héroe en áreas amplias y definidas, combinado con las sencillas pero maravillosas variaciones que cada una de estas áreas recibe dentro de cada retrato individual, producen un conjunto de versiones de Martí extraordinariamente rico. Algunas son serias y otras más bien lúdicas, algunas fantasiosas y otras más sombrías. La suma de ellas desmiente la imagen monolítica del héroe revolucionario, señalando no solo las complejidades del legado de Martí sino la domesticación y comercialización de su mito político.

Los posteriores retratos de héroes nacionales de Martínez pierden el orden de la cuadrícula y adoptan un estilo de composición más cercano al collage. *Repeticiones de Martí* (1968) presenta una estructura más suelta, anclada por cuatro retratos grandes de Martí acompañados de tres versiones más pequeñas. Una flor al lado izquierdo del marco añade un toque fantasioso. En *Rosas y estrellas* (1972), los padres y héroes de la patria aparecen reunidos en torno al gran ramo de rosas que sostiene Martí y que, a pesar de ser un homenaje a los retratados, altera el tono reverencial que suele reservase para estos arquetipos de proeza masculina. Dadas las típicas poses viriles, sorprende que los héroes tengan un cierto aire de éxtasis, erotismo y júbilo. Un marco de hojas verdes los rodea, realzando su exuberancia e insertándolos en el tipo de entorno idílico, edénico y erotizado que Martínez representa de forma más explícita en *Adán y Julieta* (1973, lámina 15).

Martínez extiende su reformulación de mitos religiosos y patrióticos a figuras populares y cubanos comunes y corrientes en fotografías intervenidas como *Sin título (Tres amigos)* (1969) y *El vaquero* (c. 1969, lámina 104). En esta última, las facciones del joven vaquero, al igual que las de Martí en los retratos repetidos, están cuidadosamente intervenidas con sombras y contornos, y el brazo está pintado de un rosa carnoso que hace resaltar su pose. El cigarrillo en la boca del joven y su camisa estampada están pintados con viveza, y a su paso parece ir dejando una estela de vibrantes colores. Este mismo tema se repite en *Che* (1968, lámina 63), donde la icónica boina de Guevara se extiende hacia arriba, rebasando los confines de su silueta. Al igual que los globos de diálogo en las tiras cómicas, las estrellas dirigen la mirada del espectador más allá de la figura, al mundo trasatlántico que flota sobre él como una idea o un onírico globo de diálogo.

Mientras Martínez ejecuta su profanación pop "suavizando" las imágenes de los padres de la patria, el mexicano Alberto Gironella procede a utilizar "desmembramiento o deconstrucción".[20] Su método de recortar, encuadrar, reinterpretar y diseccionar figuras históricas en ensamblajes elaborados con una excéntrica y muy calibrada gama de texturas y objetos logra un efecto siniestro, de humor negro, iconoclasta y al mismo tiempo profundamente reverente.[21] La mayoría de estas figuras históricas que incluye en sus retratos proviene de la corte española del siglo XVII según la pintó Diego Velázquez, maestro del Siglo de Oro cuyos cuadros de la realeza española son la fuente más constante de material figurativo para Gironella.[22] Estos ensamblajes poblados de objetos extraños e imágenes de variadísimas fuentes —fotografías, anuncios publicitarios, embalajes y taxidermia, como en *Homenaje a Pablo Picasso*— constituyen una gran parte de la obra de Gironella. La mayoría parecen altares y contienen objetos tomados del mundo del consumo, como los que se podrían encontrar en las tiendas de alimentos mexicanas de mediados del siglo XX (productos enlatados, tapas de botellas, anuncios publicitarios, etc.).[23] El padre de Gironella, un catalán que emigró a México, tenía una de esas tiendas y se especializaba en ultramarinos,[24] productos enlatados y conservas denominados así porque provenían de ultramar. En Ciudad de México, estas tiendas de ultramarinos se encontraban en el mercado popular de La Merced, y los propietarios eran en su mayoría inmigrantes españoles.[25] Existen obvias alusiones trasatlánticas en las obras que durante décadas Gironella creó retrabajando la pintura del Siglo de Oro español, y los productos ultramarinos que incluye en sus ensamblajes son tan solo una parte de la gran variedad de materiales y objetos simbólicos que el artista mexicano empleó para denunciar, de forma abstrusa pero inequívoca, la historia de dominación e intercambio entre España y sus colonias en el Nuevo Mundo.[26]

Aunque casi toda la obra de Gironella con figuras históricas se materializa a través de su continuo diálogo con Velázquez, y por lo tanto implica a las figuras de la corte española, hay un protagonista de la historia mexicana moderna que el artista presenta repetidamente y con impactantes resultados: Emiliano Zapata, ícono de la revolución mexicana y en general de la insurgencia en el país. Las obras de Gironella sobre Zapata fueron muy celebradas en la exposición de 1972 titulada *Gironella: El entierro de Zapata y otros enterramientos* en el Palacio de Bellas Artes en Ciudad de México.[27] El homenaje de Gironella al caudillo y su gesto típico de incluir emblemas de la historia, y de la historia del arte en particular, quedan claros ya desde el título de la exposición, alusivo al héroe revolucionario y también a una pintura del siglo XVI, obra del Greco: *El entierro del Conde Orgaz* (1586–1588). Ciertos críticos han recalcado el giro hagiográfico en la versión de Zapata que construye Gironella,[28] como si en sus pinturas y ensamblajes el líder agrario redescendiera a la tierra, santo y a la vez

materializado, encarnado en sus reliquias. Aun así, los ensamblajes de Gironella funcionan como altares y relicarios en la misma medida que como escaparates de tiendas, fusionando lo comercial con lo sagrado.

Hay un paralelismo sorprendente entre estos ensamblajes de Zapata y un objeto histórico que guarda relación directa con la muerte del líder. Una fotografía de 1919 muestra una vitrina con los efectos personales que Zapata llevaba consigo cuando fue asesinado. La vitrina es una especie de relicario del héroe nacional, un gabinete para los objetos que testimonian la vida del héroe, así como de su muerte. Pero esos efectos reunidos en la vitrina y registrados la fotografía son más que reliquias de un héroe fallecido. Son también, y más que nada, piezas de evidencia reunidas por Pablo González, el general responsable del asesinato de Zapata, que se enviaron por correo al periódico capitalino *El Pueblo*, donde fueron exhibidas para confirmar la muerte del caudillo, y donde también sirvieron, intencionalmente o no, como evidencia indirecta de la espantosa violencia de la revolución.

Gironella exagera gráficamente el lado sombrío de la muerte de Zapata colocando tapas de botella que parecen agujeros de balas, como en *Zapata con marca de ganado* (1972, lámina 75), o manchando la camisa del héroe con pintura rojo sangre, como en *Objeto Zapata 666* (1972). La "marca de la bestia" que se incluye en el título de esta última obra, junto con la etiqueta semioculta del ungüento mexicano marca "666" que Gironella reutiliza en el ensamblaje, dan a la obra un tono apocalíptico. Al apocalipsis se alude también, aunque de forma más críptica, en *Zapata con marca de ganado*, título que apunta a las seis marcas de ganado que rodean la imagen de Zapata así como a "la marca de la bestia". Un retrato anterior, *Zapata tradicional* (1957), pintura carente de la profusión de objetos que caracterizaría gran parte de las obras posteriores de Gironella, muestra al héroe llevando orgulloso en bandolera los colores de la bandera mexicana con un paisaje rojo sangre de fondo y calaveras en el suelo donde está parado. Violencia, muerte y fatídica desgracia parecen emanar de Zapata en esta imagen temprana, del mismo modo que parecen martirizarlo en ensamblajes posteriores. La profanación y la deformación efectuadas en las imágenes de Zapata por Gironella malogran todas y cada una de las visiones unificadoras e idealizadas que se tengan del lugar del héroe revolucionario en la historia, el tipo de visión que tenderíamos a proyectar de manera más general en cualquier figura venerada.

La desfiguración en el arte pop de América es un acto de afrenta y a la vez de acogida a la imagen encontrada, a las páginas de sucesos de los diarios y al cliché. En las obras que aquí se han examinado, el acto de desfiguración no implica que las figuras de las cuales se apropian las obras (figuras históricas y religiosas, figuras de la cultura popular y comercial) dejen de ser reconocibles, sino que las presenta por aquello en que se han convertido: clichés. La manera en que la desfiguración afecta las imágenes populares e icónicas, el orden en que se apropia de ellas y las interviene, pertenece a un espectro más amplio de la cultura visual que incluye a la alta cultura, pero solo como un segmento, y no necesariamente el más interesante. La desfiguración opera al nivel de la imagen estandarizada, al nivel del cliché. Disecciona, mediante un cuidadoso desmembramiento, la figuración que sustenta y es sustentada por el cliché.[29]

NOTAS

1   El artista pop estadounidense Robert Indiana describió este aspecto de manera pintoresca en su respuesta a la pregunta "¿Qué es el pop?". Indiana respondió lo siguiente: "Es básicamente un viraje en U hacia una comunicación visual figurativa a velocidad de vértigo en autos elegantes último modelo. Es un regreso abrupto al Padre tras 15 años de exploración abstracta del Útero. El pop es inscribirse de nuevo en el mundo". Ver G. R. Swenson, "What is Pop Art? Answers from 8 Painters, Part I", *ARTnews* 62 (noviembre de 1963): 27.

2   Para obtener información sobre la importancia de la irreverente intervención de Dávila en la figura de Martí como padre de la patria, ver Francine Masiello, *The Art of Transition: Latin American Culture and Neoliberal Crisis* (Durham: Duke University Press, 2001), 54: "Dávila señala el papel que juega la sexualidad a la hora de definir temas latinoamericanos; cuestiona las nociones establecidas de identidad heredadas de los padres de la patria al tiempo que nos obliga a repensar lo que entendemos por *lo popular*. Si bien cuestiona la gramática corpórea que organiza la memoria y la historia, también indaga en las voces autorizadas que definen las aspiraciones nacionales".

3   Tanto Thomas Crow como Ana María Reyes han sugerido este tipo de regreso en el arte pop estadounidense y colombiano, respectivamente. Ver Thomas Crow, "Saturday Disasters: Trace and Reference in Early Warhol", en *Reconstructing Modernism: Art in New York, Paris, and Montreal 1945–1964*, ed. Serge Guilbaut (Cambridge: MIT Press, 1990), 320: "En su forma particular de dramatizar el medio, Warhol encontró lugar para la dramatización del sentimiento y hasta una especie de pintura histórica". Ver también Ana María Reyes, "In Bed with Dead Bolívar: Beatriz González's Case for Critical History Painting", en *Simón Bolívar: Travels and Transformations of a Cultural Icon*, eds., Maureen G. Shanahan y Ana María Reyes (Gainesville: University Press of Florida, 2016), 148: "En dos de sus obras, Beatriz González reutilizó conocidas representaciones de Bolívar: *Apuntes para la historia extensa* (1967) y *Mutis por el foro* (1973). Estas obras revitalizaron la pintura histórica contemporánea porque no son ni versiones oficiales —falsificadas y decorosas— ni la negación absoluta del género mediante la abstracción —que ha servido como prueba de la modernidad latinoamericana en el circuito internacional de arte—, sino re-visiones críticas".

4   Ver, por ejemplo, lo que dice Robert Rauschenberg en la inauguración del Rauschenberg Overseas Culture Interchange en México: "El proyecto Rauschenberg Overseas Culture Interchange (R.O.C.I.), que se presenta en México con el título de *El soñado mundo de Rauschenberg* [...] es un proyecto privado que durante cuatro años llevará, creará e intercambiará arte y hechos por el mundo entero. Se pondrá especial énfasis en compartir experiencias con sociedades en las que rara vez se expresan ideas no políticas y en las que no se ha planteado la posibilidad de comunicarse con el mundo mediante el arte". Ver Robert Rauschenberg, "Manifiesto", *El soñado mundo de Rauschenberg* (Ciudad de México: Museo Rufino Tamayo, 1985), s.p.

5   Swenson, "What Is Pop Art? Part I", 26: *Death in America* era el título de una exposición prevista para París de "fotografías de sillas eléctricas y los perros en Birmingham y accidentes automovilísticos y algunos suicidios". Ver también Crow, "Saturday Disasters", 324.

6   Hal Foster señala que las imágenes de Death y Disaster inauguran una cierta genealogía, tal vez central, del arte pop. Ver Hal Foster, *The Return of the Real: The Avant-Garde at the End of the Century* (Cambridge: MIT Press, 1996), 128. Ver también Crow, "Saturday Disasters", 324.

7   Esta lectura de los retratos de celebridades femeninas de Warhol va en contra de la interpretación persistente que las considera imágenes mecanizadas de belleza, superficialidad y glamur. También perturba la distinción esquemática que ubica un enfoque desafecto del pop y la cultura del consumo en el norte y un enfoque subversivo y politizado de esa misma cultura en el sur del hemisferio. Para ver un ensayo de este argumento, ver Rodrigo Alonso, "Un arte de contradicciones", en *Arte de contradicciones: Pop, realismos y política. Brasil-Argentina 1960* (Buenos Aires: Fundación Proa, 2012), 27.

8   Crow, "Saturday Disasters", 322: "A la hora de seleccionar estas fotografías, Warhol no solía ser un receptor pasivo de imágenes disponibles comúnmente. En vez de usar reproducciones de periódicos que pudieran haber caído en sus manos por casualidad, buscaba fotos de calidad que iban destinadas a las agencias de prensa y que normalmente solo veían los periodistas profesionales. (Parece que algunas de éstas se consideraban demasiado extrañas o morbosas para publicarse; es decir, se restringía su publicación para el público general precisamente por su carácter perturbador)". El material periodístico figura a menudo, y con prominencia, en la historia del cruce entre el arte moderno y los medios masivos de comunicación. Antes de Warhol, Marcel Duchamp ya había trabajado durante dos décadas en su obra *Étant donnés: 1. La chute d'eau, 2. Le gaz d'éclairage* (Dado que: 1. La cascada, 2. La farola) (1946–1966), un perturbador montaje tipo *peepshow* instalado de forma permanente en el Philadelphia Museum of Art y basado principalmente, según Jean-Michel Rabaté, en fotografías ampliamente difundidas del asesinato de la Dalia Negra en Los Ángeles en 1947.

9   Carolina Ponce de León, "Beatriz González: The Extended History of Colombia", en *Beatriz González, What an Honor to be with You at this Historic Moment* (Nueva York: El Museo del Barrio, 1998), 20.

10 Para obtener mayor información sobre el vínculo entre lo plano, la publicidad y el arte pop, ver Luis Camnitzer, *On Art, Artists, Latin America, and Other Utopias* (Austin: University of Texas Press, 2009), 32: "Desde fuera de la sociedad de consumo estadounidense, la contribución más evidente y comprensible del pop fue el cambio en las reglas de composición. La obra de arte ahora es 'diagramada' como un anuncio publicitario, en vez de tener la 'composición' tradicional que se espera del arte".

11 Beatriz González, "Other People and Their Ideas," *ArtReview* (enero-febrero 2016): 57. El artista colombiano Álvaro Barrios también asume el campo de visibilidad comercializado de la cultura de imprenta de la década de 1960 como contexto de su obra. Lo describe de esta manera: "Yo hacía unos collages acerca de un mundo imaginario donde convivían armónicamente Los Beatles, la guerra de Vietnam, Batman y Robin, el Che Guevara, Dick Tracy, el cura guerrillero Camilo Torres y Tarzán." En Beatriz González, "Andy Warhol y la recepción del arte pop en Colombia". Augusto de Campos, el poeta concreto brasileño, hace un recuento más amplio, aunque sorprendentemente similar, de su campo aplanado de visibilidad: "Los nuevos medios de comunicación masiva, periódicos y revistas, radio y televisión, tienen sus grandes matrices en las metrópolis, de cuyas 'centrales' se emiten las informaciones a millares de personas en regiones cada vez más numerosas. La intercomunicación universal es cada vez intensa y más difícil de contener, de modo que resulta literalmente imposible para un ciudadano cualquiera vivir su vida diaria sin enfrentarse a cada paso con Vietnam, los Beatles, las huelgas, el 007, la Luna, Mao o el Papa". Ver Augusto de Campos, *Balanço da bossa e outras bossas* (São Paulo: Editora Perspectiva, 1974): 59–60.

12 Ibíd., "Other People and Their Ideas", 57.

13 Para obtener mayor información acerca del soporte material de estas pinturas, ver Reyes, "In Bed with Dead Bolívar", 152.

14 Ibíd., 161.

15 A manera de comparación, ver *Bed* (1955) de Robert Rauschenberg, obra hecha en óleo y lápiz sobre una almohada, una colcha y un juego de sábanas con soportes de madera. La obra *Bed* de Rauschenberg se expone colgada de la pared, en el eje vertical de la pintura tradicional. En ella, la cama, en toda su materialidad cotidiana, se eleva a la dignidad de la pared vertical. En la obra de González, los héroes nacionales descienden de la pared. Rauschenberg influenció mucho a los artistas latinoamericanos asociados con el pop, aunque no queda claro si tuvo alguna influencia en González. Ciertamente impactó a Alberto Gironella, quien guardaba catálogos de la obra del pintor estadounidense, así como recortes de revistas sobre el artista. Para obtener mayor información sobre la acogida del pop en Colombia y su lugar en la obra de González, ver González, "Andy Warhol y la recepción del arte Pop en Colombia". Ver también González, "Actitudes de una década", en *Sin título 1966–1968. Luis Caballero* (Bogotá: Museo Nacional de Colombia, 1997), 33, 39. Para conocer el punto de vista de González sobre el impacto que tuvo el pop en su obra, ver González, "Other People and Their Ideas", 57.

16 Un año antes de que González completara *Mutis por el foro*, la pintura de 1930 de Quijano Moreno fue reproducida en los billetes de lotería en Colombia. Ver Reyes, "In Bed with Dead Bolívar", 160. El tema de "la muerte del pecador" así como su contraparte, el

tema de "la muerte del justo", también se difundieron como impresos populares en Colombia para la época en que González terminó su pintura. Ver Ana María Reyes, "Incorporated Vision: Artistic Critiques of the Development Discourse in Latin America", *Revista Letral* 13 (2014): 107. El trabajo de González con el cliché es anterior a su adopción de la estética pop: su innovadora serie de pinturas titulada *Encajera* (1963–64) está basada en una ilustración la obra *La encajera* de Jan Vermeer (1665) que se reprodujo en calendarios populares. Ver Ponce de León, "Beatriz González: The Extended History of Colombia," 18.

17   Jacoby luego denuncia los límites puritanos de la imaginación progresista de izquierda al teorizar lo que él denomina "la estrategia de la alegría". Ver Roberto Jacoby, *El deseo nace del derrumbe: acciones, conceptos, escritos* (Barcelona: Ediciones de la Central, 2011), 411: "La piel era considerada como territorio de placer y no de tormento. La 'superficie' también era lo opuesto al calabozo y la clandestinidad. Es fácil de ver que en el tono moralizante de esas críticas se vertía el puritanismo revolucionario tradicional, mezcla del estalinismo con el ascetismo cristiano y militar, hegemónico tanto dentro de las fuerzas progresistas como de las reaccionarias".

18   María Sol Barón y Camilo Ordóñez Robayo, "Literatura", ponencia presentada en el "Coloquio Revista ERRATA. El lugar del arte en lo político", Bogotá, Colombia, julio de 2010: "La primera vez que vi una obra del Taller 4 Rojo fue en medio de una clase de arte en el colegio. El ejercicio consistía en revisar libremente publicaciones sobre arte en la estantería de la biblioteca. Entonces tenía 16 años y preferí hojear aleatoriamente algún tomo de la Enciclopedia Salvat del Arte Colombiano hasta que aparecieron esas mujeres vietnamitas. En televisión, la guerra del Vietnam era representada con combatientes asiáticos que parecían más bien un grupo de actores idénticos, mal armados, y descalzos que expresaban monosílabos y sonsonetes torpes ante soldados norteamericanos".

19   Para obtener mayor información sobre el trabajo publicitario y de diseño gráfico de Martínez, ver el ensayo de Jennifer Josten en este catálogo y Corina Matamoros, *Raúl Martínez: La gran familia* (España: Ediciones Vanguardia Cubana, 2012), 124.

20   Holliday T. Qay y Hollister Sturges, *Art of the Fantastic: Latin America, 1920–1987* (Indianápolis: Indianapolis Museum of Art, 1987), 138: "Alberto Gironella es mejor conocido por su desmembramiento o desconstrucción de las grandes pinturas del Siglo de Oro español (siglo XVI) para crear obras fantásticas y macabras que exploran el papel de la tradición española en la cultura mestiza mexicana".

21   Valerie Fraser, "Surrealising the Baroque: Mexico's Spanish Heritage and the Work of Alberto Gironella", *Oxford Art Journal* 14.1 (1991): 35: "Para él [Gironella], retrabajar las imágenes conocidas no es simplemente cuestión de llamar la atención al hecho de que la reproducción en masa insensibiliza el nervio óptico impactando al espectador con una Mona Lisa con bigote, sino que implica utilizar una mezcla peculiar de iconoclasia y homenaje irónico, de investigar el poder que tienen ciertas imágenes, sobre todo las que son relevantes al país. En ese sentido, sus retratos de Habsburgos y Borbones se asemejan a la serie de banderas estadounidenses de Jasper Johns, salvo que la bandera, por supuesto, sea cual sea la opinión de cada quien, es indiscutiblemente estadounidense, el linaje es evidente".

22   Ibíd., 34: "Cabe recalcar que el período que abarca las vidas del Greco y Velázquez fue una época en que en América Latina se consolidaron el gobierno colonial y la Iglesia católica, se estableció la lengua española y la cultura europea, y se introdujeron nuevos métodos de explotación de personas y recursos naturales".

23   Ibíd., 39: "Los orígenes de los peculiares ensamblajes de Gironella se remontan a su infancia. Sus primeros recuerdos son de coloridas pilas de latas importadas, cajas, botellas y paquetes de la tienda de alimentos que era el negocio de la familia y de la parafernalia del catolicismo popular, que seguramente incluía relicarios y tabernáculos, retablos que combinaban escultura y pintura, altares decorados con damascos, velas, flores y exvotos, objetos a menudo de carácter muy personal. Gironella recuerda haberse construido sus propios altares con latas y envoltorios de chocolates".

24   Ibíd.: "El empaque de los productos importados sigue fascinando [a Gironella] por sus cualidades intrínsecas —los nombres, colores y diseños— pero sin duda también por la manera en que los productos de lejana procedencia han sido integrados al entorno mexicano. Estos productos llevan el nombre general de ultramarinos, por venir 'del otro lado del mar'".

25   Rosa Casanova y Adriana Konzevik, *Luces sobre México: Catálogo selectivo de la Fototeca Nacional del INAH* (Ciudad de México: Editorial RM, 2006), 59.

26   Con respecto a una discusión más amplia de las huellas del pasado colonial en las pinturas de Gironella, ver Orianna Baddeley y Valerie Fraser, *Drawing the Line: Art and Cultural Identity in Contemporary Latin America* (Nueva York: Verso, 1989), 50–60.

27   Juan Acha, "Gironella, lo mejor: Balance de un buen año artístico", *Diorama en la Cultura*, suplemento, *Excélsior*, 30 de diciembre de 1972, 3: "1972 fue testigo de una obra notable: *El entierro de Zapata y otros enterramientos*, una ambientación de Gironella, en la cual la exhibición en sí constituye la obra, o sea no se trata de una de las usuales exposiciones de cuadros u objetos. Como obra, fue la mejor y más moderna del segundo semestre y del año si nos atenemos a los comentarios de la prensa".

28   Jorge Hernández Campos, "Gironella y la transfiguración de Zapata", en *Gironella: El entierro de Zapata y otros enterramientos* (Ciudad de México: 1972), s.p.: "El hecho de que Gironella centró ahora sus meditaciones en Emiliano Zapata debería imponernos reflexión. Significa, por el enlace con el Greco y el entierro del conde de Orgaz, la trasfiguración del caudillo suriano, de la lucha por la tierra y de la revolución mexicana hacia los órdenes de nuestra cultura supranacional y, a través de ésta, de los valores universales. En seguida, quiere decir el re-descendimiento de Zapata hacia nosotros, con todo el olor intacto de su mugre campestre y todo el ultraje de sus balazos necesarios".

29   Olivier Debroise, "Alberto Gironella también pinta", *La Cultura en México* (1 de agosto de 1979): "Gironella respeta la composición y la densidad cromática del profundo claroscuro de Velázquez: únicamente incluye –como en un collage– elementos ajenos a la obra: mínima subversión que no afecta al contexto. Gironella solo rinde un homenaje al Maestro y, con ello, recupera y sobremitifica obras de por sí mitificadas desde su reproducción (con fines didácticos) en millones de empaques de corn-flakes".

FACING

AMÉRICA

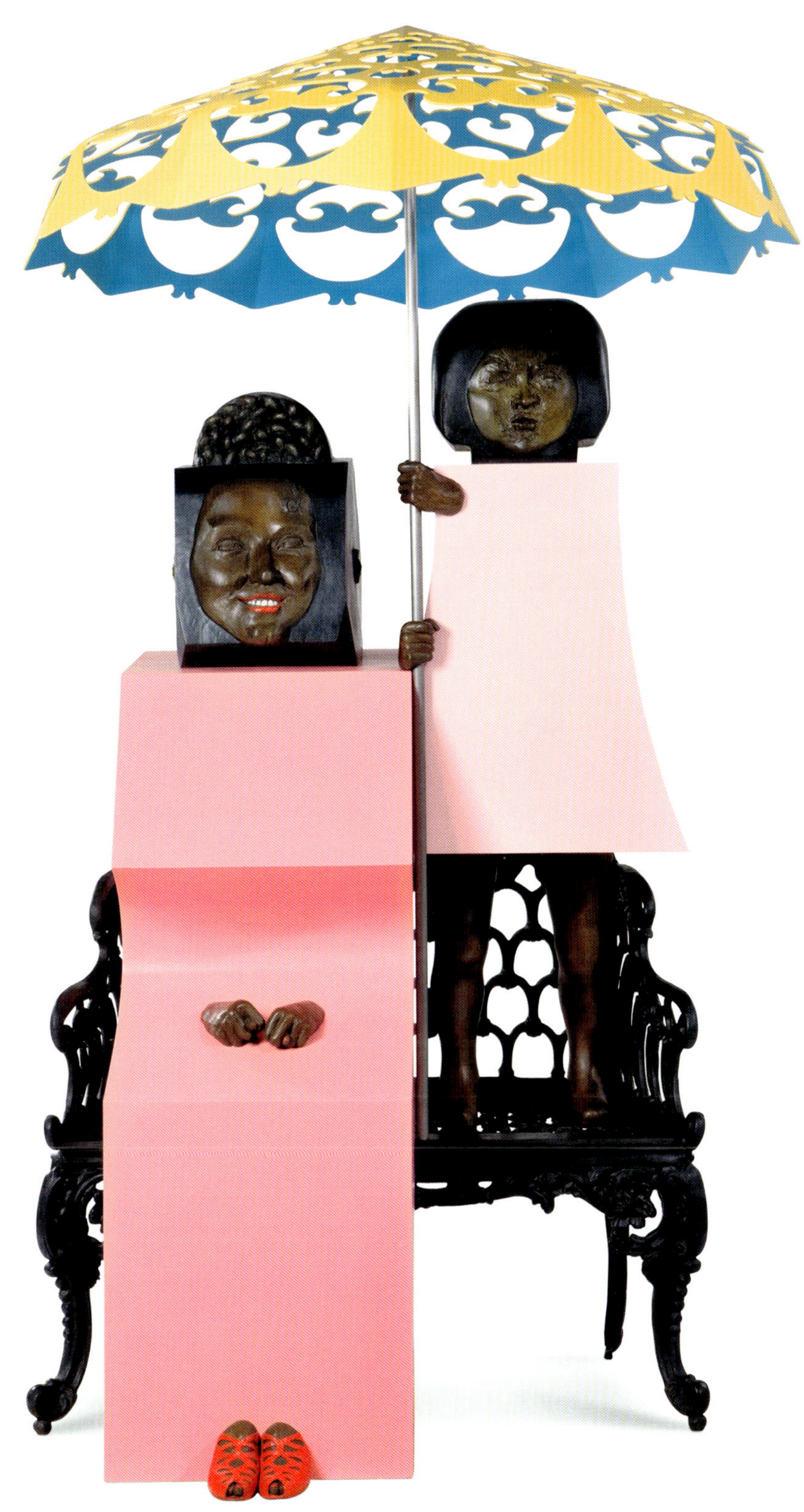

Pl. 99. Marisol Escobar (known as Marisol), *Mi mamá y yo* (My Mother and I), 1968. Steel and aluminum, 79.75 x 56.5 x 55.75 inches (202.56 x 143.51 x 141.6 cm). Collection of Albright-Knox Art Gallery, Buffalo, New York. Bequest of Marisol, 2016. © 2018 Estate of Marisol. Licensed by Artists Rights Society (ARS), New York, New York.

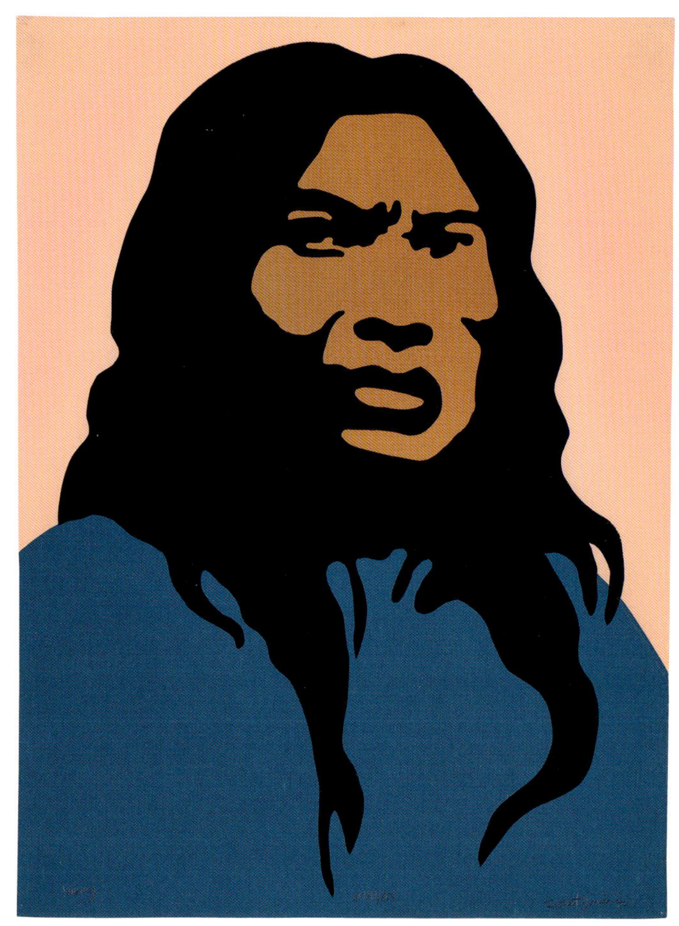

Pl. 100. Rupert García, *Maya*, 1970. Screenprint on wove paper, 24.05 x 17.95 inches (61.1 x 45.6 cm). Collection of the Fine Arts Museums of San Francisco, De Young, Legion of Honor Museum, California. Gift of Mr. and Mrs. Robert Marcus. © Rupert García. Courtesy of the artist and Rena Bransten Gallery, San Francisco, California.

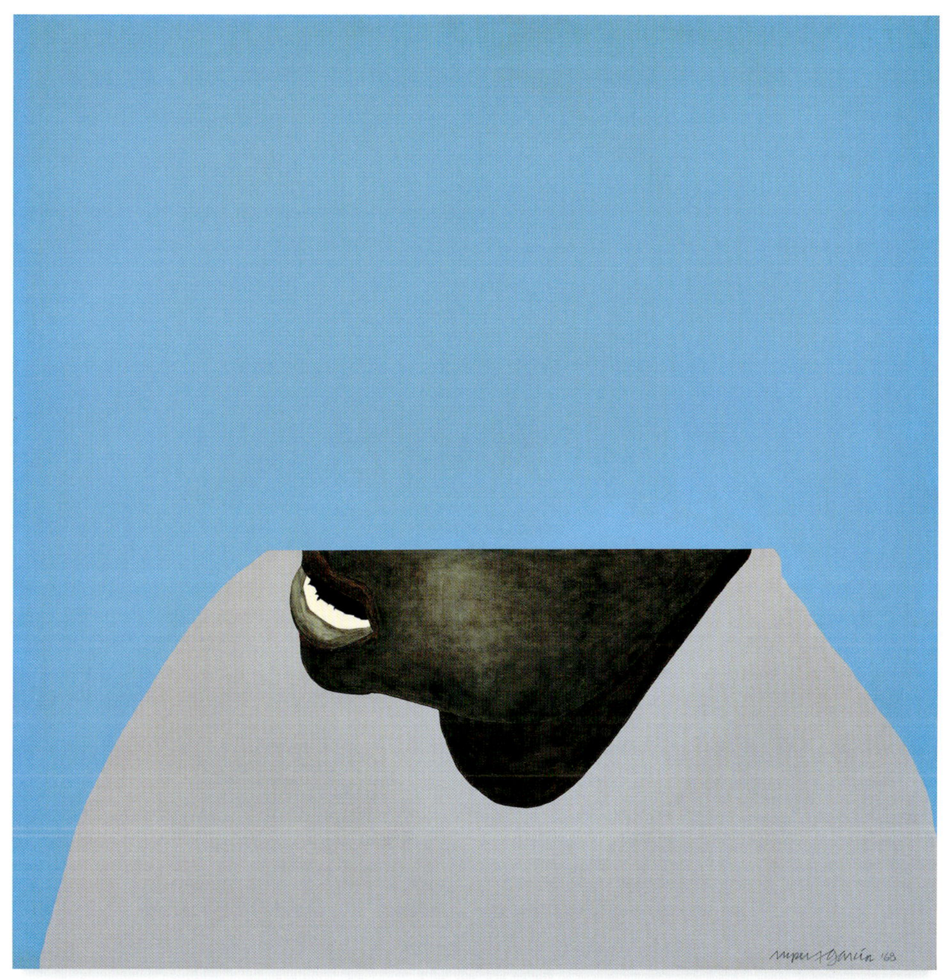

Pl. 101. Rupert García, *Unfinished Man*, 1968. Acrylic on canvas, 48.03 x 48.03 inches (122 x 122 cm). Courtesy of the artist and Rena Bransten Gallery, San Francisco, California. © Rupert García. Photo by John Janca.

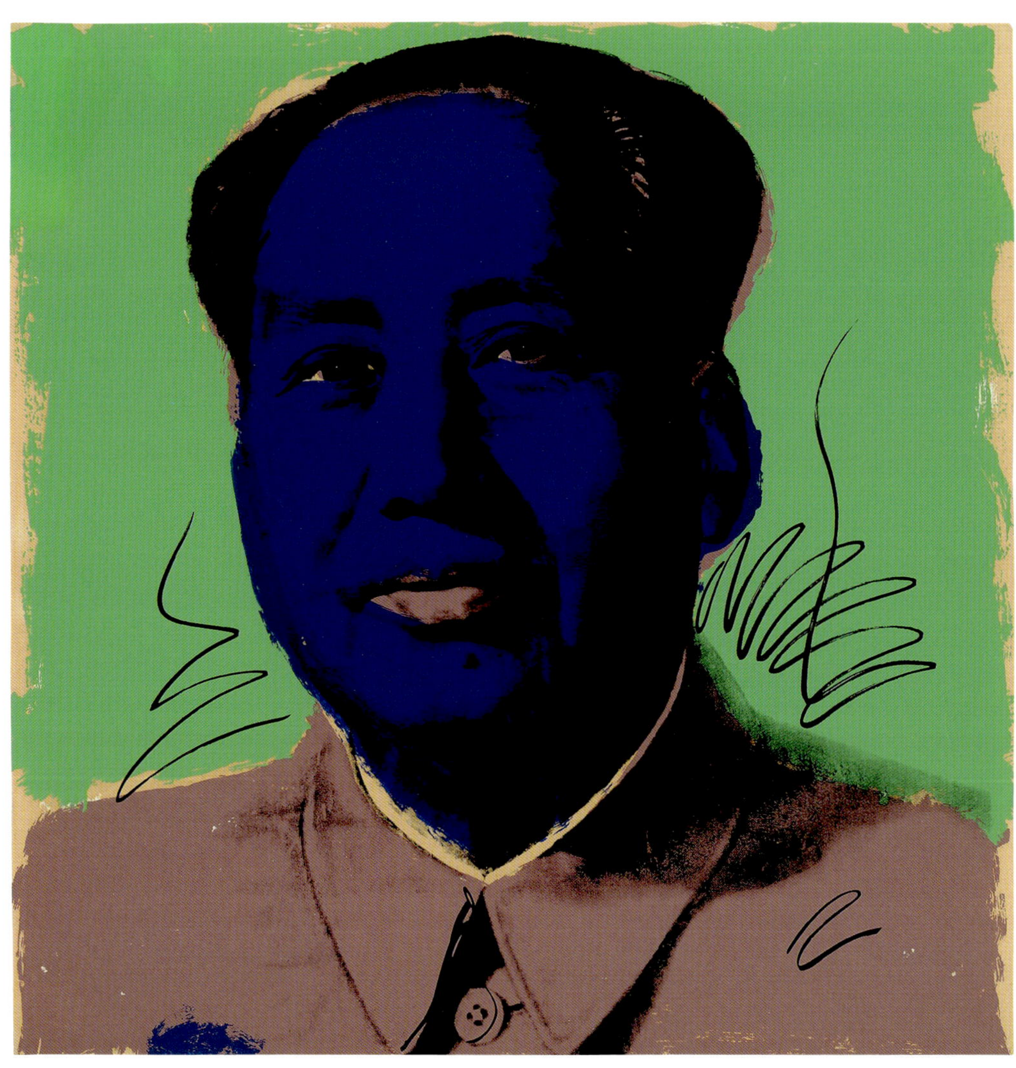

Pl. 102. Andy Warhol, *Mao*, 1972. Screenprint on paper, 36 x 36 inches (91.44 x 91.44 cm). Collection of the Nasher Museum of Art at Duke University, Durham, North Carolina. Museum purchase. © 2018 The Andy Warhol Foundation for the Visual Arts, Inc. Licensed by Artists Rights Society (ARS), New York, New York. Photo by Peter Paul Geoffrion.

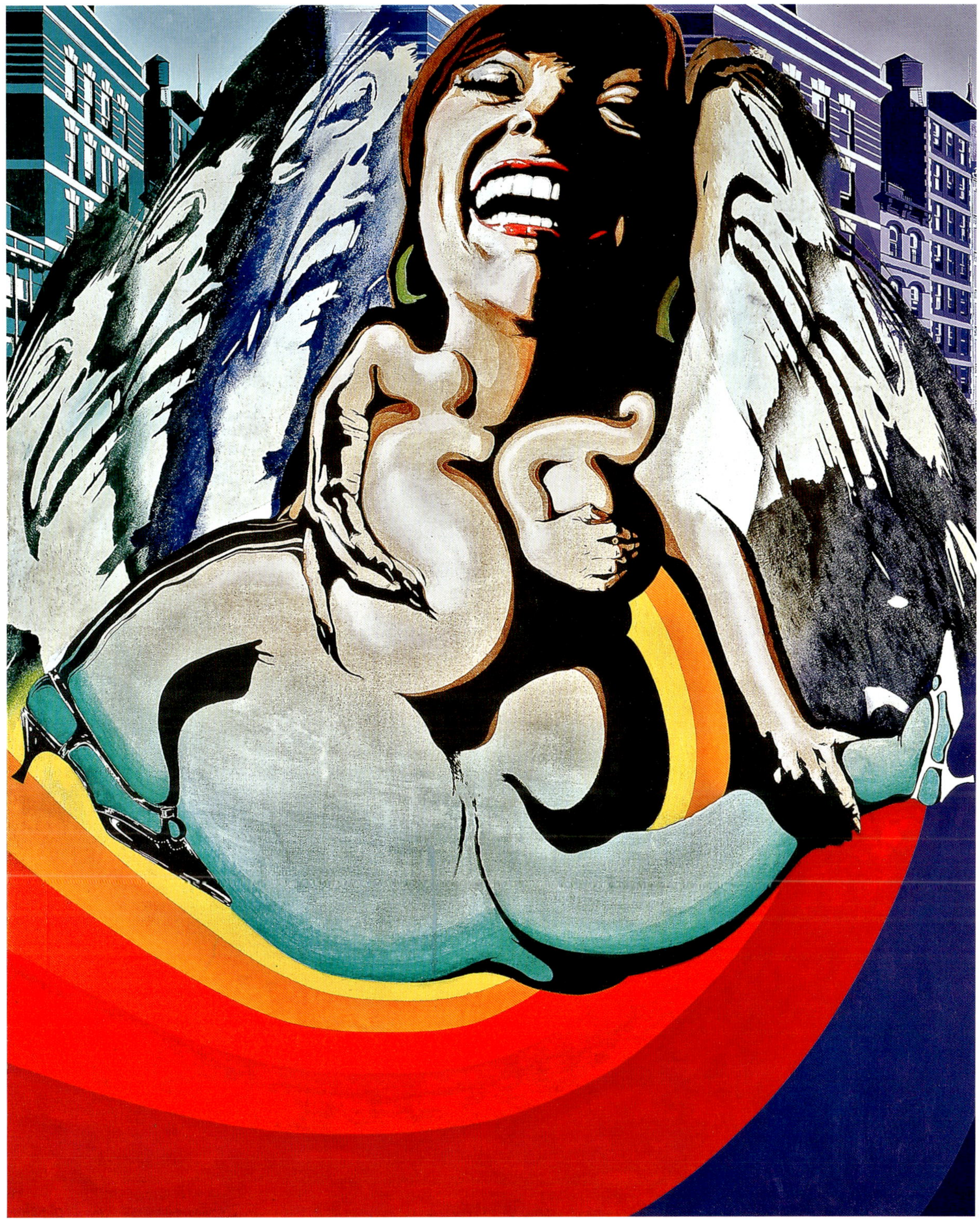

Pl. 103. Jorge de la Vega, *Go, Go, Go*, 1967. Acrylic and collage on canvas, 77 x 64.17 inches (195.6 x 163 cm). Collection of the Blanton Museum of Art, the University of Texas at Austin. Gift of Gunther Oppenheim. © Estate of Jorge de la Vega.

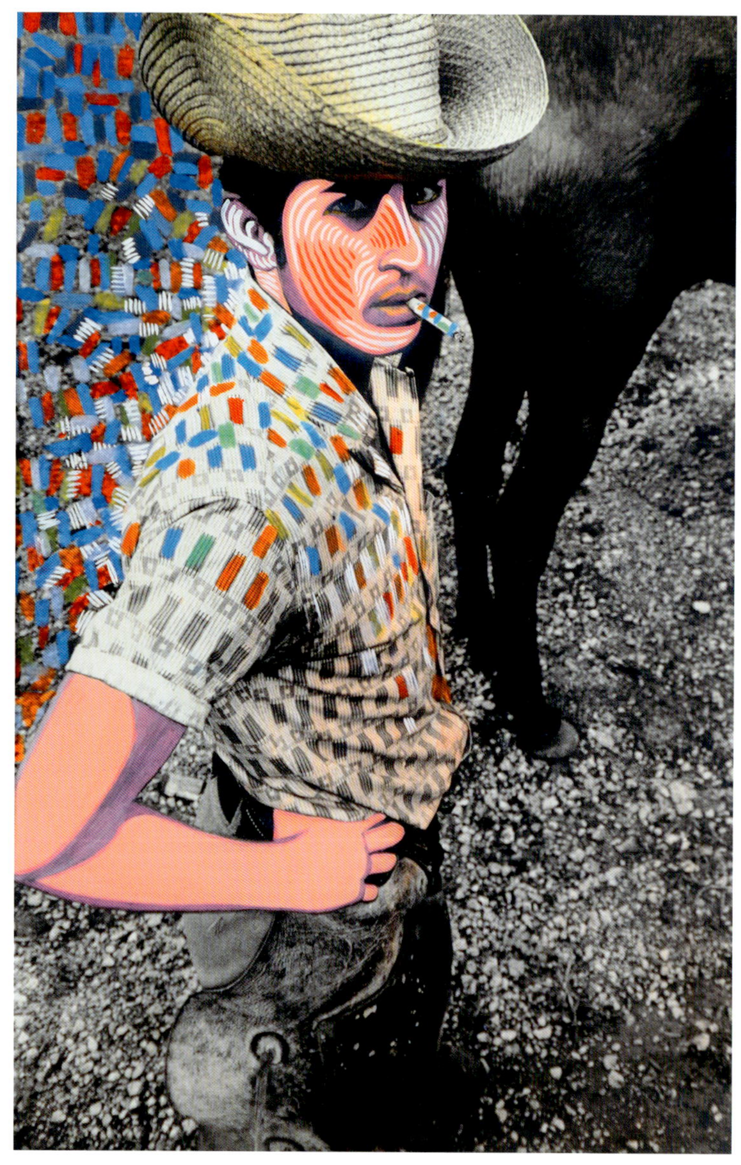

Pl. 104. Raúl Martínez, *El vaquero* (Cowboy), c. 1969. Acrylic on black-and-white photograph, 21.5 x 16.75 inches (54.61 x 42.54 cm). The Shelley and Donald Rubin Private Collection. © Raúl Martínez Estate, Ciego de Ávila, Cuba. Image courtesy of the Raúl Martínez Estate and Corina Matamoros.

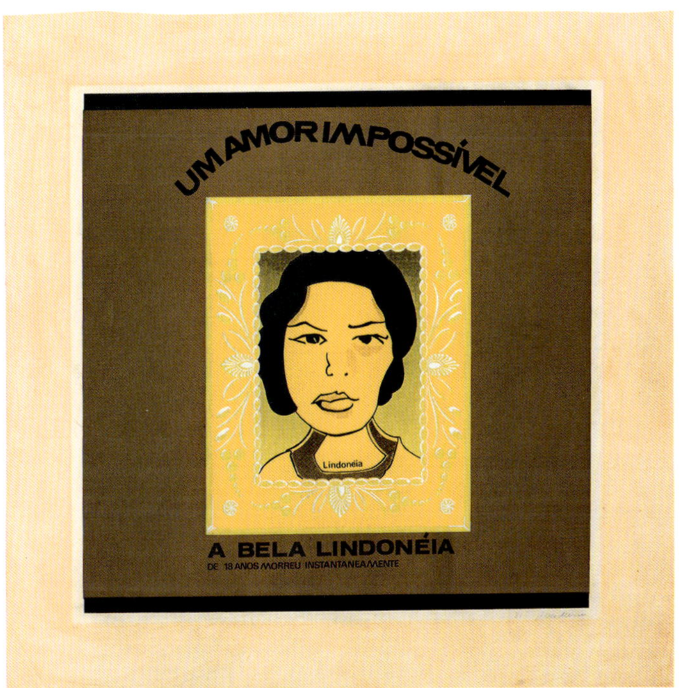

Pl. 105. Rubens Gerchman, *Lindonéia, a Gioconda do subúrbio* (Lindonéia: The Mona Lisa of the Slum), 1966–1968. Screenprint on paper, 19.68 x 19.72 inches (50 x 50.1 cm). Collection of Roger Wright on long-term loan to the Pinacoteca do Estado de São Paulo, Brazil. © Rubens Gerchman Institute, Rio de Janeiro, Brazil. Photo by Isabella Matheus.

Pl. 106. Rubens Gerchman, *Caixa de origem* (Origin Box), 1966. Acrylic, canvas, wood, and sandblasted mirrored glass on particle board, 66.92 x 66.92 x 0.98 inches (170 x 170 x 2.5 cm). Collection of Roger Wright on long-term loan to the Pinacoteca do Estado de São Paulo, Brazil. © Rubens Gerchman Institute, Rio de Janeiro, Brazil. Photo by Edouard Fraipont.

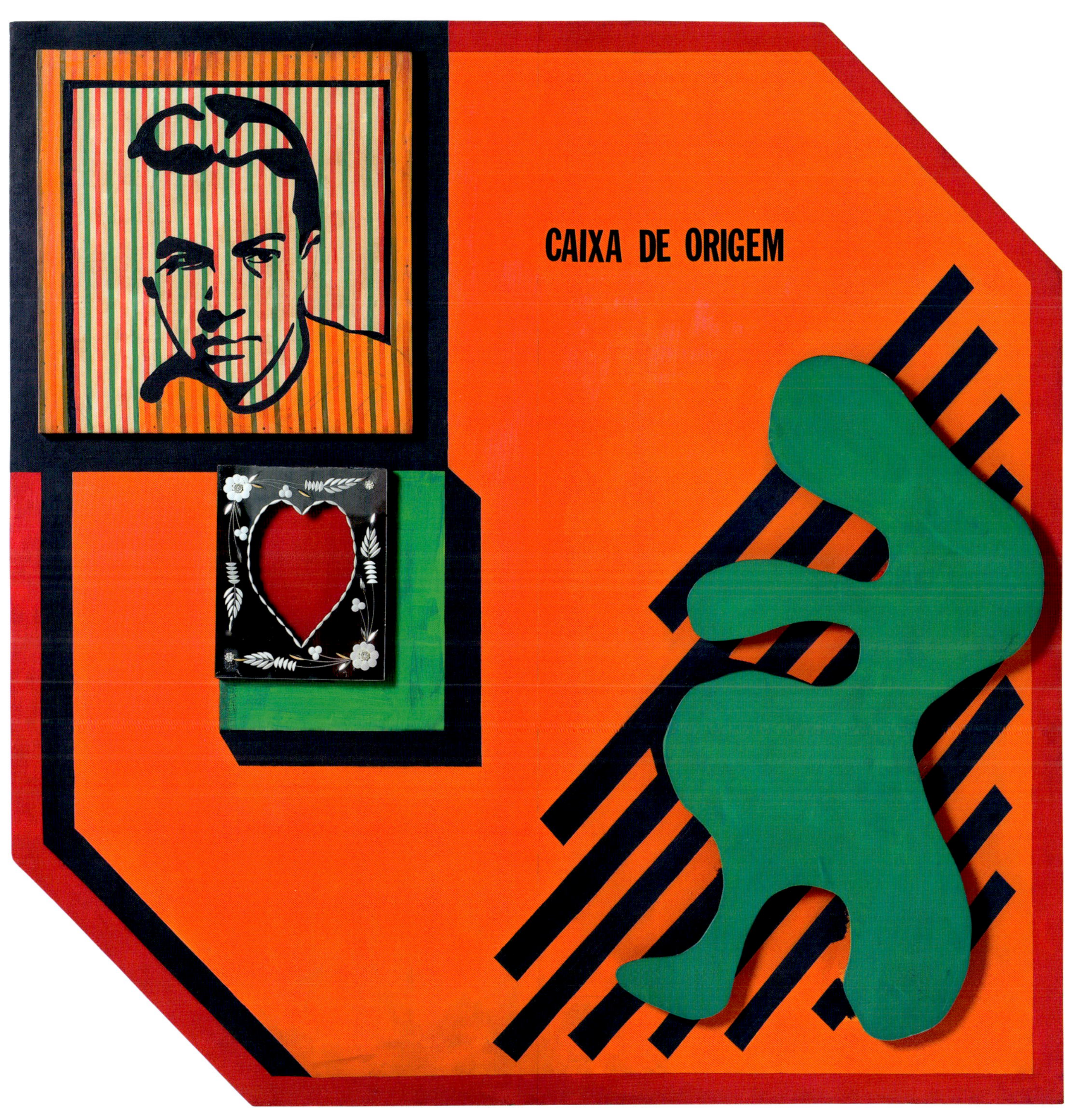
CAIXA DE ORIGEM

RODRIGO ALONSO

THE ART OF PROVOCATION/
EL ARTE DE LA PROVOCACIÓN

Pop is a social art. Its intention—sometimes conscious, unconscious at others—is to "ironize" social structures. It is democratic art par excellence, since only societies that have freedom as the basis of their values . . . permit their foundations to be "ironized." In this sense, it is the art of anti-power. It represents the highest form of the socialization process to which contemporary man has subjected himself. It is in no way an art exclusive to the United States. In places where Power has not been completely corrupted, and therefore allows man to challenge it through artistic creation, it will appear as a warning and possibility.—Luis Pazos, 1966[1]

In the early 1960s, much of Argentine art went through the same transformations that were occurring in other latitudes. Abstraction was losing its seductive power over young creators, and neo-figurative proposals seemed unable to account for a society that, thanks to the advent of mass media and consumerism, was changing at a frenetic pace. A new sensibility was born; one that proposed celebrating life by exhausting all its possibilities, one which left behind the fears of the distant but threatening armed conflict in Europe and joined the optimism of a world longing to recapture its joy.

The social conditions in Argentina were ideal for this type of artistic transformation. Historically a purely agrarian country, Argentina enjoyed enormous economic benefits from exporting food to Europe during postwar reconstruction efforts. During the same period, the country launched a process of rapid industrialization that made it one of the most prosperous countries in the global postwar economy.

In this context, the Argentine manufacturing company Siam Di Tella—which produced household appliances and automobiles—created the Instituto Torcuato Di Tella, a foundation dedicated to promoting the arts. In 1963, the Di Tella opened an exhibition space, musical research laboratory, and venue for experimental stage performance. Although the first manifestations of local Pop art did not take place in the institution, the Di Tella would become the main sounding board for artists involved in this new trend.[2] The Di Tella exhibited the work of Marta Minujín, Edgardo Giménez, Dalila Puzzovio, Delia Cancela, Pablo Mesejean, Charlie Squirru, Susana Salgado, Alfredo Rodríguez

El pop es un arte social. Su objetivo —consciente en algunos casos, inconsciente en otros— es "ironizar" las estructuras sociales. Es el arte por excelencia de la democracia, ya que solo una sociedad que tiene a la libertad como base de sus valores […] permite que se "ironice" sobre sus fundamentos. En este sentido es el arte del antipoder. Constituye la máxima expresión del proceso de sociabilización al que se halla sometido el hombre contemporáneo. De ninguna manera es un arte exclusivamente norteamericano. Allí donde el Poder no se ha corrompido absolutamente y, por consiguiente, permite que el hombre lo enfrente a través de la creación artística, allí surgirá como advertencia y posibilidad. —Luis Pazos, 1966[1]

Hacia los inicios de la década de 1960, una buena parte del arte argentino sufre una mutación similar a la que se observa en otras latitudes del planeta. La abstracción pierde su poder de seducción sobre los jóvenes creadores y las propuestas neofigurativas no parecen adecuadas para dar cuenta de una sociedad que crece al ritmo frenético de los medios de comunicación y los objetos de consumo. Nace una nueva sensibilidad que se propone celebrar la vida agotando todas sus posibilidades, que deja atrás los temores de un conflicto bélico lejano pero amenazador, y que se suma al optimismo de un mundo que anhela recuperar su alegría.

Las condiciones sociales son por demás propicias. La Argentina, un país netamente agroproductor, se beneficia económicamente de la reconstrucción europea proveyendo los alimentos que aceitan ese proceso. Al mismo tiempo, emprende una modernización industrial que la ubica entre las naciones más prósperas de la posguerra.

En este contexto, la empresa Siam Di Tella —productora de electrodomésticos y automóviles— crea una fundación para la promoción artística, el Instituto Torcuato Di Tella, que en 1963 inaugura un espacio de exposiciones, un laboratorio de investigación musical y otro de experimentación escénica. Si bien las primeras manifestaciones del pop art local no tienen lugar en ella,[2] esta institución será la principal caja de resonancia de los artistas enrolados en la nueva tendencia. Aquí exponen Marta Minujín, Edgardo Giménez, Dalila Puzzovio, Delia Cancela, Pablo Mesejean, Charlie Squirru, Susana Salgado, Alfredo Rodríguez Arias y Juan Stoppani, junto a otros artistas con

Arias, and Juan Stoppani, as well as other artists sporadically linked to Pop art, such as Jorge de la Vega, Eduardo Costa, Oscar Bony, and Roberto Jacoby. The coexistence of Di Tella's diverse centers for the arts promoted interdisciplinary creation and sustained intellectual thought, which stood out particularly in the work of Oscar Masotta.[3]

There was also a group of noteworthy Pop artists whose work was not exhibited in the Instituto Torcuato Di Tella's galleries. Nicolás García Uriburu, Antonio Seguí, and Martha Peluffo were among the artists who showed their work in the many alternative spaces that thrived in Buenos Aires at the time. Around 1964, Pop artists reigned supreme in the city's most prominent galleries and received the most prestigious awards, although not without resistance. Their works caused scandals and indignation. In addition, continuous happenings, parties, and urban interventions disturbed art critics and a generally conservative society.

One of the most reiterated controversies about Pop art in América is that it was an "imported aesthetic" with no connection to local traditions. However, Luis Pazos presents a compelling argument: Pop is an art form rooted in its historical and political context, and therefore an ideal instrument for social critique through which artists question authority. His words appear in 1966, the year the military coup d'état in Argentina curtailed individual, social, and artistic freedoms.[4]

Reactions to the changed political scene were extremely varied. Certain artists shifted their practice toward the sphere of everyday life, abandoning galleries and institutions and instead focusing on the production of clothing, design, and everyday utilitarian objects.[5] Others abandoned artistic production altogether and turned to radical activism against the political establishment.[6] Some found a way to continue their work by producing intensely critical pieces veiled by the ambiguities of aesthetic language. Pop, broached ironically, was in fact the ideal tool for these artists. Its schematic and mocking tone allowed them to dodge censorship and open a path to freedom and expression during a dark time when little could be said. Even under dictatorship, artists in Argentina reinvented and reaffirmed Pop as "the art of democracy."

vínculos esporádicos con el pop, como Jorge de la Vega, Eduardo Costa, Oscar Bony o Roberto Jacoby. La coexistencia de sus distintos centros de arte promueve la creación interdisciplinaria y alienta el pensamiento intelectual, que brilla en la figura de Oscar Masotta.[3] Pero también hay un conjunto de artistas pop destacados que no llegan a las salas del Instituto Torcuato Di Tella, como Nicolás García Uriburu, Antonio Seguí o Martha Peluffo, y que circulan por los numerosos espacios alternativos del nutrido circuito artístico porteño de estos años.

Hacia 1964, los artistas pop conquistan las principales galerías y los premios más destacados, aunque no sin resistencia. Sus obras generan escándalos e indignación. A esto se suma su continua producción de happenings, fiestas e intervenciones urbanas, que incomodan a una crítica y una sociedad todavía conservadoras.

Una de las controversias más reiteradas sostiene que el pop es una "estética importada", sin lazos con las tradiciones locales. Sin embargo, Luis Pazos esgrime un argumento por demás contundente: como arte enraizado en su momento histórico y político, el pop es un instrumento ideal para la crítica social allí donde los artistas se proponen cuestionar al poder. Sus palabras ven la luz en 1966, el mismo año en que un golpe de estado[4] cercena las libertades individuales, sociales y artísticas.

Las reacciones al nuevo escenario político son de lo más variadas. Algunos artistas abandonan las galerías e instituciones consagratorias y se vuelcan en la producción de ropa, objetos de diseño y artículos de uso, con la intención de desplazar su práctica hacia los ámbitos de la vida cotidiana.[5] Otros reniegan por completo de la producción artística, algunos de ellos para embarcarse en un activismo de enfrentamiento radical con el poder político.[6] Incluso otros encuentran una vía para continuar su trabajo mediante obras de un intenso tenor crítico, disimulado en las ambigüedades que muchas veces habilitan los lenguajes estéticos. El pop, abordado en clave irónica, resulta una herramienta ideal para ellos. Su tono esquemático y burlón, les permite sortear la censura y abrir un camino hacia la expresión y la libertad en un oscuro tiempo en que muy pocas cosas podían ser dichas. Así, el "arte de la democracia" se reinventa y reafirma, incluso en épocas de dictadura.

NOTES

1   Luis Pazos, "El advenimiento del objeto," *Diagonal Cero*, 17 (March 1966): 24.

2   Argentine Pop art emerged around 1962 in exhibits and in art galleries and came to the fore particularly through awards granted to artists associated with the movement.

3   Masotta published a book on Pop art in 1965 and another on happenings in 1967.

4   In June 1966, a military coup d'état ended the presidency of Arturo Umberto Illia. Democracy was momentarily reestablished in 1973, only to succumb once more to the military between 1976 and 1983 (the last military government).

5   While Pop art became institutionalized and commercially successful in Europe and the United States, the opposite happened in Argentina: artists distanced themselves from spaces that could limit their vitality and creative freedom and instead immersed themselves in everyday life.

6   Some of these artists are on the list of the 30,000 *desaparecidos*, people who "disappeared" during the rule of Argentina's last military government.

NOTAS

1   Luis Pazos, "El advenimiento del objeto", *Diagonal Cero*, 17 (marzo de 1966): 24.

2   El pop art argentino nace hacia 1962 en exposiciones llevadas a cabo en galerías de arte, y principalmente en los premios que comienzan a destacar las obras de los artistas identificados con esta línea de producción.

3   Masotta publica un libro sobre el *pop art* en 1965 y otro sobre los *happenings* en 1967.

4   En junio de 1966, un golpe militar termina con la presidencia de Arturo Umberto Illia. La democracia se restablece momentáneamente en 1973, para volver a sucumbir en manos de los militares entre 1976 y 1983 (último gobierno militar).

5   Mientras en Europa y Estados Unidos el *pop art* se institucionaliza y triunfa en el mercado, en la Argentina sucede lo contrario: los artistas se alejan de los espacios que podrían limitar su vitalidad y libertad creativa para integrarse de lleno en la vida cotidiana.

6   Algunos de estos artistas conforman la lista de los 30,000 desaparecidos que dejó el último gobierno militar en la Argentina.

LYLE W. WILLIAMS

ROBERT INDIANA'S STUDY FOR VIVA HEMISFAIR/EL ESTUDIO PARA VIVA HEMISFAIR DE ROBERT INDIANA

San Antonio's geography has long influenced its history, culture, and economy. Once a frontier outpost of New Spain, the city was at the intersection of the vast eighteenth-century network of roads and trails, some laid out by Native Americans, that made up the El Camino Real de los Tejas. This network linked New Spain's capital in Mexico City with the Catholic missions scattered throughout Texas and Louisiana. The sense of being at the crossroads of different places and cultures became even stronger in San Antonio after the Pan-American Highway system was proposed in the 1920s. Though the Pan-American Highway remains more an idea than a reality, if one were to trace the highway from its northern terminus at Prudhoe Bay in Alaska to Buenos Aires, Argentina, one of its South American destinations, San Antonio would be about halfway along the route.[1] It is not surprising, therefore, that when city leaders wanted to celebrate the 250th anniversary of the founding of the city with a World's Fair, they hit upon a theme that would commemorate the "cultural heritage shared by San Antonio and the nations of Latin America."[2] The resulting HemisFair '68 was a milestone for the city.

The fair, ambitious for a city with a population of just over half a million in 1960, had as its central theme the Confluence of Civilizations in the Americas. Art, and in particular Robert Indiana's *Viva HemisFair* poster (1967, plate 5), was to play an outsized role in making the event a success. San Antonio art collector and philanthropist Robert L. B. Tobin was a good friend and patron of Robert Indiana's and approached him about designing a poster for HemisFair. That such a small city could attract the talents of an internationally renowned artist like Indiana was a key factor in securing approval for the fair from the Bureau International des Expositions (BIE) in 1965.[3]

Indiana used a cut paper collage to work out his design for the poster, which was meant to be eventually printed as a lithograph.[4] The bits of highly saturated colored papers he used in the study were perfectly suited to the poster's bold design. The composition is comprised of carefully constructed geometries with a large light orange inverted triangle providing the main structure. Within the top center of the triangle is a circle, the diameter of which is determined by the points of a large yellow star. Within this star is a blue silhouette of the state of Texas, with a smaller star marking San Antonio's location within the state. Four arrows point to the smaller star, emphasizing not only

La posición geográfica de San Antonio ha influenciado su historia, cultura y economía desde hace mucho tiempo. Fue puesto fronterizo de la Nueva España, ubicado entonces en la intersección de la vasta red de caminos y senderos —algunos trazados por los indígenas americanos— que en el siglo XVIII conformaban El Camino Real de los Tejas. Esta red unía a la capital de la Nueva España, situada en Ciudad de México, con las misiones católicas diseminadas a lo largo de Texas y Luisiana. La sensación de estar en el punto de cruce entre diversos lugares y culturas se acentuó en San Antonio tras la propuesta de construir una Carretera Panamericana en la década de 1920. Aunque la Panamericana sigue siendo una idea más que una realidad, si uno trazara la carretera desde su extremo norte en Prudhoe Bay, Alaska, hasta Buenos Aires, Argentina, uno de sus destinos sudamericanos, San Antonio quedaría más o menos en el punto medio de la ruta.[1] Entonces no es de sorprender que cuando los líderes de la ciudad quisieron celebrar los 250 años de su fundación con una Feria Mundial, concibieron un tema que conmemoraría la "herencia cultural que San Antonio comparte con las naciones de América Latina".[2] El HemisFair 68 fue un hito para la ciudad.

Proyecto ambicioso para una ciudad que contaba con poco más de medio millón de habitantes en 1960, la feria llevaba como tema central La confluencia de civilizaciones en las Américas. El arte, y en particular el cartel de Robert Indiana *Viva HemisFair* (1967, lámina 5), tendrían un papel preponderante en el éxito del evento. El coleccionista de arte y filántropo de San Antonio Robert L. B. Tobin era muy amigo y mecenas de Robert Indiana, y le propuso diseñar un cartel para HemisFair. El hecho de que una ciudad tan pequeña pudiera atraer a un artista de renombre internacional como Indiana fue un factor clave para lograr que el Bureau International des Expositions (BIE) aprobara en 1965 que la feria se efectuara allí.[3]

Indiana empleó un collage con papel cortado para proyectar el diseño de su cartel, que al final debía imprimirse en litografía.[4] Los pedazos de papel que utilizó para este estudio, con colores muy saturados, iban a la perfección con el audaz diseño del cartel. La composición consiste de geometrías cuidadosamente construidas con un gran triángulo invertido de color naranja claro a manera de estructura principal. En la parte superior central del triángulo hay un círculo cuyo diámetro está determinado por las puntas de una estrella amarilla grande. Dentro de

the location of the fair, but also symbolizing the crowds of people that would come from all over América to attend.

When the poster's design was unveiled at Robert L. B. Tobin's San Antonio home in the spring of 1968, the reviews were overwhelmingly positive. The *San Antonio Express-News* noted that the warm colors captured the "feeling of southern Texas where [Indiana] was stationed in the U.S. Air Force." The prominently placed Spanish word "*VIVA*" was seen as epitomizing the "gaiety of the fair as well as the Latin American orientation of its theme."[5]

There is, of course, an unavoidable paradox of the optimism of Indiana's poster and of the fair itself. In the United States and around the world, 1968 was a tumultuous year. Just days before HemisFair opened, Martin Luther King, Jr. was assassinated in Memphis. In the middle of the fair's run, Robert F. Kennedy was assassinated, and later that summer, riots broke out at the Democratic National Convention in Chicago.[6] Shortly before HemisFair closed, government forces in Mexico cracked down on a student uprising in Mexico City, killing at least 300 people. What would be called the Tlatelolco massacre occurred ten days before the opening ceremonies of the Mexico City Summer Olympics. The graphics of the Olympics, designed by a team led by the architect Pedro Ramírez Vázquez, have an optimistic feel similar to that of Indiana's HemisFair poster. These programs celebrated a vision of design in the service of the very concepts of "progress" and "modernity" that were being debated in the struggles for political and cultural change in 1968.

la estrella está la silueta del estado de Texas en azul, con una estrella más pequeña que señala la ubicación de San Antonio dentro del estado. Cuatro flechas apuntan hacia la estrella pequeña, no solo para enfatizar la ubicación de la feria, sino también para simbolizar las multitudes que asistirían desde todas partes de las Américas.

Cuando se presentó el diseño del cartel en la casa de Robert L. B. Tobin en San Antonio en la primavera de 1968, las críticas fueron abrumadoramente positivas. El *San Antonio Express-News* observó que los colores cálidos captaban "la atmósfera del sur de Texas, donde [Indiana] estuvo destacado con la Fuerza Aérea de Estados Unidos". La prominente palabra "VIVA" en español se interpretó como epítome de la "alegría de la feria y de la orientación latinoamericana de su tema".[5]

Por supuesto, existe una paradoja insoslayable entre el optimismo del cartel de Indiana y la feria misma. En Estados Unidos, como en muchas partes del mundo, 1968 fue un año tumultuoso. Pocos días antes de inaugurarse HemisFair, Martin Luther King, Jr. fue asesinado en Memphis. Ya durante el transcurso de la feria asesinaron a Robert F. Kennedy, y al final de ese mismo verano estallaron disturbios en la Convención Nacional Demócrata en Chicago.[6] Poco antes de terminar HemisFair, las fuerzas del gobierno mexicano sofocaron una revuelta estudiantil en Ciudad de México, matando a por lo menos 300 personas. Lo que luego se conocería como la Masacre de Tlatelolco ocurrió diez días antes de la inauguración de los Juegos Olímpicos de Verano en Ciudad de México. El arte gráfico de los Juegos Olímpicos, a cargo de un equipo encabezado por el arquitecto Pedro Ramírez Vázquez, proyecta una sensación de optimismo similar a la del cartel de Indiana. En última instancia, estos programas celebraban una visión del diseño al servicio de los mismos conceptos de "progreso" y "modernidad" que se estaban debatiendo en las luchas por cambios políticos y culturales en 1968.

NOTES

1   San Antonio is roughly 4,500 miles from Prudhoe Bay and just over 5,000 miles from Buenos Aires.

2   Frank Duane, "HemisFair '68," *Handbook of Texas Online*, accessed July 31, 2017, http://tshaonline.org/handbook/online/article/kh01.

3   Patsy Steves, interview by Lyle W. Williams, August 8, 2017. Mrs. Steves was the wife of Marshall Steves who served as president of the fair's Executive Committee at the time of the BIE approval in 1965.

4   Indiana would use the same process for his designs for the Santa Fe Opera's production of Virgil Thomson's *The Mother of Us All*, an opera about the life of suffragist Susan B. Anthony presented in celebration of the United States Bicentennial in 1976.

5   Mavis Bryant, "Official HemisFair Poster Unveiled," *San Antonio Express-News*, March 8, 1968, 8F.

6   Despite receiving death threats in the days following King's assassination, Lady Bird Johnson attended the opening ceremonies under heavy security, as did Texas Governor John Connally.

NOTAS

1   San Antonio queda a unas 4,500 millas de Prudhoe Bay y a un poco más de 5,000 millas de Buenos Aires.

2   Frank Duane, "HemisFair '68," *Handbook of Texas Online*, consultado el 31 de julio de 2017, http://tshaonline.org/handbook/online/article/kh01.

3   Patsy Steves en entrevista con Lyle W. William, 8 de agosto de 2017. Patsy Stevens fue esposa de Marshall Steves, quien era presidente del Comité Ejecutivo de la feria en 1965, cuando la BIE aprobó que San Antonio fuese la sede.

4   Indiana utilizó el mismo proceso en sus diseños para la producción de *The Mother of Us All*, de Virgil Thomson, en la Ópera de Santa Fe. La ópera trata sobre la vida de la sufragista Susan B. Anthony y fue presentada como parte de las celebraciones del bicentenario de Estados Unidos en 1976.

5   Mavis Bryant, "Official HemisFair Poster Unveiled", *San Antonio Express-News*, 8 de marzo de 1968, 8F.

6   A pesar de recibir amenazas de muerte en los días posteriores al asesinato de King, Lady Bird Johnson asistió a las ceremonias de inauguración de la feria, si bien con fuerzas de seguridad, como también lo hizo el gobernador de Texas, John Connally.

PILAR GARCÍA

NOTES ON POP ART IN MEXICO/NOTAS SOBRE EL ARTE POP EN MÉXICO

Mexico City underwent a great transformation in the late 1960s, as the country's economy exploded in response to a period of unprecedented development. For the city's residents, advertising and mass media became an increasingly prominent part of everyday life. The escalating quotidian presence of advertising created new ways of life for Mexico City residents, and inspired artistic sensibilities related to Pop art and the Beatnik movement. Two artists in particular exemplify the radical social changes that took place and paved the way for artistic practices that continue to this day: José Luis Cuevas (1934–2017) and Felipe Ehrenberg (1943–2017). Employing new visual languages and experimenting with industrial materials, these artists called into question the prevailing social order, idealizing or rejecting new patterns of consumerism.

The urban setting was central: the Zona Rosa neighborhood in Mexico City represented a place of tolerance and change. In its streets, fashion posed a challenge to the dominant moral code, as did the behavior of the younger generations. The appearance of cafés, galleries, and nightclubs made possible intense exchanges among artists, filmmakers, and writers, who began to subvert the habits of art consumption and made it possible for people to imagine the transformation of prevailing social structures. There, on the rooftop of a building at the corner of Génova and Londres streets in the summer of 1967, José Luis Cuevas created one of the most paradigmatic works of art of the period, relevant as much for its intention as for its appropriation of modern advertising techniques. The *Mural efímero* (Ephemeral Mural) incorporated urban space by using a billboard as its supporting structure. While he supervised the process, Cuevas sent the work to be fabricated by the advertising company Calafell. The artist's hand was no longer necessary to execute the piece. Cuevas made full use of the media; he created and inaugurated the *Mural efímero* in front of photographers and television cameras in order to turn his artistic act into an urban cultural happening. He thereby upset the dominant categories of art in Mexico at the time. Art became spectacle and a consumer good.

Following this advertising device that blurred the line between art and life—a hypothesis that later would be central to Conceptual art—in 1970, Vicente Rojo produced a poster for a political campaign Cuevas ran titled *Vote por José Luis Cuevas como candidato independiente a Diputado del Primer Distrito* (Vote for Independent Candidate José Luis Cuevas to Serve as Representative of the First District). In protest against and as a challenge to the system, Cuevas appears smiling in

A fines de la década de los sesenta, la ciudad de México experimentó un crecimiento urbano y una importante transformación como resultado del desarrollo económico del país. La creciente incorporación de la publicidad en la cotidianidad propició nuevos estilos de vida, y una producción artística ligada a distintas vertientes de la sensibilidad del arte pop y a la afiliación al movimiento *beatnik*. Dos artistas ejemplifican estos cambios radicales y señalan el camino hacia prácticas que siguen vigentes hoy: José Luis Cuevas y Felipe Ehrenberg. Emplearon nuevos lenguajes visuales y comenzaron a experimentar con materiales industriales, así como a cuestionar el orden social, idealizando o rechazando los nuevos medios de consumo.

A nivel urbano, la Zona Rosa de México representó un lugar de tolerancia y cambio en la manera de actuar de las jóvenes generaciones. En sus calles, la moda marcó un reto al código moral dominante. La aparición de cafés, galerías y clubs nocturnos hizo posible un intenso intercambio entre artistas, cineastas y escritores, quienes comenzaron a trastocar los hábitos de consumo del arte y permitieron imaginar una posible transformación de las estructuras sociales. Allí, sobre la azotea de un edificio en la esquina de Génova y Londres, en junio de 1967, José Luis Cuevas realizó una de las piezas paradigmáticas de este período, tanto por la intención como por la apropiación de las técnicas publicitarias modernas. El *Mural efímero* se incorporó al espacio citadino utilizando como soporte un anuncio espectacular (un *billboard*). Bajo su supervisión, Cuevas mandó a hacer su obra a la empresa de anuncios comerciales Calafell. La mano creativa del artista no era ya indispensable para ejecutar la pieza. Cuevas se valió del apoyo mediático; trabajó e inauguró la pieza frente al lente de fotógrafos y cámaras de televisión para convertir el acto artístico en un acontecimiento cultural urbano que trastocó las categorías del arte entonces prevalecientes en el contexto mexicano —el arte como espectáculo y producto de consumo.

Siguiendo este dispositivo publicitario en el que los linderos entre arte y vida comienzan a desdibujarse —postulado que después será central en el arte conceptual—, en 1970 Vicente Rojo realizó un cartel para la campaña política de Cuevas titulado *Vote por José Luis Cuevas como candidato independiente a Diputado del Primer Distrito*. Como protesta y desafío al sistema, Cuevas aparece sonriendo en primer plano, como una estrella de rock, de manera similar a las celebridades representadas por Andy Warhol, haciendo con su

the foreground, like a rock star, in the style of Andy Warhol's celebrity portraits. He is shown making the sign for victory with his right hand, a gesture that characterized the students' movement of 1968.[1] The poster clearly shows Vicente Rojo's mark as a designer, and his interest in Pop formulas is evident in the creation of a powerful image surrounded by a series of faces that visually defied the old order. That same year, Cuevas had a show at the University Museum of Sciences and Art (MUCA) titled *Cuevas: Estatura, peso y color* (Cuevas: Height, Weight, and Color). The exhibition's graphic identity and installation reflected the same Pop strategy that helped project Cuevas's image as a rebellious artist, only this time in dialogue with work including drawings, graphics, and letters.

Without a doubt, Felipe Ehrenberg is one of the artists most closely associated with Pop. He contributed many drawings to the magazine *El Corno Emplumado* (The Plumed Horn) (see page 127; figures 4.6, 4.7) that revisit iconic images—mainly codified female bodies as they were represented in advertising—and are accompanied by texts and numbers with typographies common to graphic publications. Two exhibitions in particular show the artist's propensity for Pop art. In a gallery in Mexico City's Alameda Park, he produced a show called *Kinekaligráfica* that included drawings, one of which appropriated a Kodak advertising character into a life-sized figure that "greeted" visitors. In 1968, at Jack Mizrahi's gallery, Ehrenberg presented a series of "wood constructions," painted with glossy acrylic paint on which he subversively drew flat female silhouettes in bright colors and with defined edges surrounded by recognizable signs, such as arrows. Similar works were exhibited at the Salón Independiente (Independent Salon) of 1969. But his most iconic work is the piece made up of 200 postcards that he sent to Mexico from England—one of the first works of mail art in the country—exhibited at the Tercer Salon Independiente (Third Independent Salon) entitled *Obra secretamente titulada arriba y adelante . . . y si no pues también* (Work Secretly Titled Upwards and Onwards . . . whether you like it or not) (1970). The piece uses Pop iconography and is depicted like a puzzle, in black and white ink, representing the figure of a naked woman in three-quarter profile, holding her breast in her right hand and a soccer ball in her left, in reference to the 1970 World Cup held in Mexico. As a criticism of the government, Ehrenberg associates the title with the presidential campaign slogan of Luis Echeverría and with a figure that references pornographic calendars and comic books.

By the end of the 1970s, many other artists in Mexico had taken up Pop language in a variety of ways, making use of media images as poignant signs and symbols and as a basis for artistic proposals that later became associated exclusively with Conceptual art. These powerful interventions by Ehrenberg and Cuevas demonstrate the fundamental role of Pop in Mexican art and politics of the decade, and in the emergence of modes of contemporary art since.

mano derecha la señal de la victoria que caracterizó al movimiento estudiantil de 1968.[1] En este cartel, la impronta de Vicente Rojo como diseñador y su interés en la fórmula pop quedan evidenciados con la creación de una imagen de impacto rodeada de rostros en serie que visualmente también desafiaban el viejo orden. Ese mismo año, Cuevas tuvo una exposición en el Museo Universitario de Ciencias y Arte (MUCA) titulada *Cuevas: Estatura, peso y color*. La identidad gráfica del montaje museográfico reflejó esa misma estrategia gráfica pop que coadyuvaba a proyectar la actitud de Cuevas como artista rebelde, esta vez en diálogo con los dibujos, obras gráficas y cartas presentados en la exposición.

Sin duda, Felipe Ehrenberg es uno de los artistas más ligados a la vertiente pop. Desde la revista *El Corno Emplumado*, aportó numerosos dibujos que retoman imágenes icónicas —principalmente cuerpos femeninos precodificados por los medios publicitarios— y que conviven con textos y números provenientes de tipografías vinculadas a otras ediciones gráficas. Dos exposiciones muestran la cercanía del artista con el arte pop. En las Galerías de la Ciudad de México, ubicadas en la Alameda, realizó la muestra titulada *Kinekaligráfica*, cuyos dibujos se apropiaron de un figurín publicitario de Kodak, tamaño natural, que recibía a los visitantes. En la Galería de Jack Mizrahi, en 1968, presentó una serie de "construcciones de madera" pintadas con pintura acrílica brillante en las que con intención subversiva dibujaba siluetas femeninas planas, de colores vivos y bordes definidos, rodeadas de signos de reconocimiento inmediato como flechas. Obras similares expuso en el Salón Independiente de 1969, pero, sin duda, la obra más icónica es la compuesta por 200 tarjetas postales que envió de Inglaterra a México —uno de los primeros trabajos de arte correo en el país— para mostrarse en el Tercer Salón Independiente, titulada *Obra secretamente titulada arriba y adelante . . . y si no pues también* (1970). La obra recurre a la iconografía pop y perfila a manera de rompecabezas en tinta en blanco y negro la figura de una mujer desnuda de tres cuartos de perfil, sosteniendo en su mano derecha sus pechos y con la izquierda un balón de fútbol alusivo a la Copa Mundial de 1970. Como crítica al sistema de gobierno, Ehrenberg relaciona el título con el eslogan de la campaña a la presidencia de Luis Echeverría y con una figura que remite a la cultura porno de calendarios y cómics.

A fines de los años sesenta, no pocos son los artistas en el entorno mexicano que desde diferentes flancos recuperan el lenguaje del arte pop y se valen de las imágenes de los medios como signos de impacto y como soporte para diversas propuestas artísticas que, poco tiempo después, comenzarán a dar cabida a propuestas de corte conceptual.

NOTES

1   José Luis Cuevas, "Por qué lancé mi candidatura como diputado" (Why I Ran for Representative), in *Cuevario* (Mexico: Grijalbo, 1973), 123.

NOTAS

1   José Luis Cuevas, "Por qué lancé mi candidatura como diputado", en *Cuevario* (México: Grijalbo, 1973), 123.

CONTRIBUTOR BIOGRAPHIES

RODRIGO ALONSO (M.A., University of Buenos Aires) is a researcher and theoretician in the field of technology-based arts and performance. As an independent curator, he has organized exhibitions worldwide, including *Seeing Is Not Believing* (2016), *Transitio MX* (2014), *Pop, Realisms, and Politics: Brazil/Argentina 1960s* (2012), *Untimely Archaeologies* (2012), *Situating No-Land* (2011), and *Tales of Resistance and Change* (2010). In 2011, Alonso was the curator of the Argentine Pavilion at the 54th Venice Biennale. He has taught at both graduate and postgraduate levels at the University of Buenos Aires, University of Salvador, and the National University of Arts, Buenos Aires. Alonso also serves as an advisor for international art foundations.

NATALIA DE LA ROSA (Ph.D., National Autonomous University of Mexico) is a postdoctoral associate in the Franklin Humanities Institute at Duke University (2016–2018). Her areas of expertise include modern art and visual culture in Latin America; Mexican muralism and public art; and cinema, architecture, and theory of the avant-garde in Latin America, highlighting networks among artists, institutions, and groups in countries including Mexico and Brazil. De la Rosa has published on David Alfaro Siqueiros, painting, cinema, poetry, and Pop art in Mexico with the National Autonomous University of Mexico (UNAM), the National Institute of Fine Arts (INBA), the Ministry of Education (SEP), and *Artl@s Bulletin*. She was an associate curator at the Museum of Modern Art, Mexico City (2014–2016), where she coordinated and curated the exhibition *Cineplastic. Film about Art in Mexico, 1960–1975* (2015–2016) and co-curated the exhibitions *Paul Westheim: Sense of Form* (2016) and *Juan Acha: For a New Artistic Problem* (2016–2017).

ESTHER GABARA (Ph.D., Stanford University) is the E. Blake Byrne Associate Professor of Romance Studies and an associate professor in the Department of Art, Art History & Visual Studies at Duke University. A specialist in modern and contemporary Latin American literature and visual culture, she co-directed the Global Brazil Lab at Duke University's Franklin Humanities Institute, supported by a Mellon Foundation grant (2014–2017). She contributed to two exhibitions included in the Pacific Standard Time: Los Angeles/Latin America (LA/LA) 2017 program supported by the Getty Foundation: *La Raza* at the Autry Museum of the American West and *Revolution and Ritual: The Photographs of Sara Castrejón, Graciela Iturbide,*

and Tatiana Parcero at the Ruth Chandler Williamson Gallery at Scripps College. Gabara has worked on several exhibitions including *Brazil: Body and Soul* (2000–2001) curated by Edward Sullivan at the Solomon R. Guggenheim Museum and *The American Century, 1950–2000* (1999–2000) curated by Lisa Phillips at the Whitney Museum of American Art. She has written numerous exhibition catalogue essays and scholarly articles, as well as the monograph *Errant Modernism: The Ethos of Photography in Mexico and Brazil* (2008, Duke University Press). Forthcoming texts will be included in *Independent Salons, 1968–1971* (2018, Contemporary Art University Museum, UNAM) and *Estudios de Cultura Visual en América Latina* (2018, Institute of Aesthetic Research, UNAM).

PILAR GARCÍA (M.A., Ibero-American University, Mexico City) is the curator of the artistic collection of the University Museum of Contemporary Art (MUAC) at the National Autonomous University of Mexico. Five years prior, she led the creation of Arkheia, the documentation center of MUAC, where she started a program of archival exhibitions. She has also contributed to exhibitions fundamental to the understanding of the emergence of contemporary art in Mexico, including *The Age of Discrepancies: Art and Visual Culture in Mexico, 1968–1997* (2007) and *Defying Stability: Artistic Processes in Mexico, 1952–1967* (2014). Other projects include the exhibition *Pentagon Process Group: The Politics of Intervention, 1969–1976–2015* (2015–2016); *Risk Zone: Carlos Aguirre Retrospective* (2015); *Coming & Going – Lance Wyman – Urban Icons* (2014); and the retrospective *Brian Nissen: In the Crosshairs* (2012). She has also published essays in catalogues and specialized magazines in Mexico and abroad.

JENNIFER JOSTEN (Ph.D., Yale University) is assistant professor of modern and contemporary art in the Department of History of Art and Architecture at the University of Pittsburgh. Her research on twentieth-century artistic exchanges across the Americas and Europe has been supported by fellowships from the Getty Research Institute and Fulbright-Hays Program. Josten's book, *Mathias Goeritz: Modernist Art and Architecture in Cold War Mexico*, is forthcoming from Yale University Press. She has also contributed essays to *Found in Translation: Design in California and Mexico, 1915–1985* (2017, Los Angeles County Museum of Art); *Lucio Fontana: Ambienti/ Environments* (2017, Pirelli HangarBicocca); *Ida Rodríguez*

Prampolini: Art Criticism in the 20th Century (2017, Institute of Aesthetic Research, UNAM); *Defying Stability: Artistic Processes in Mexico, 1952–1967* (2014, Contemporary Art University Museum, UNAM); and *The Return of the Snake: Mathias Goeritz and the Invention of Emotional Architecture* (2014, Queen Sofia National Center of Art Museum).

CAMILA MAROJA (Ph.D., Duke University) is assistant professor of Contemporary Art in the Global World at McGill University. Previously, she was the Kindler Distinguished Historian of Global Contemporary Art and assistant professor of art and art history at Colgate University and a postdoctoral fellow in international humanities at Brown University. She is currently working on a book manuscript, *Framing Latin American Art*, which examines how artists and critics in Brazil have mobilized the tropes of earlier generations. Her additional research interests include exhibition histories, cultural interchanges between South and North America, the ways in which artists negotiate and localize production in a globalized world, and Conceptual and Performance art. She has published essays in *ArtMargins*, *Art & Documentation*, *Artl@s Bulletin*, and *Carte Semiotiche*.

SERGIO DELGADO MOYA (Ph.D., Princeton University) is associate professor of romance languages and literatures at Harvard University. He is the author of *Delirious Consumption: Aesthetics and Consumer Capitalism in Mexico and Brazil* (2017, University of Texas Press) and co-editor, with Tom Cummins and José Falconi, of *Conceptual Stumblings*, a volume on experimental art in Chile (forthcoming 2018). His articles, reviews, and short-form essays are published in *Film Criticism*, *Revista Hispánica Moderna*, *Revista de Estudios Hispánicos*, *Review: Literature and Arts of the Americas*, *Frieze Magazine*, *HemiPress*, and *Online Activism in Latin América* (2017, Routledge), with forthcoming contributions to *Cuadernos de Literatura* and *Handbook of International Futurism* (2018, De Gruyter). He is active in the ARTS@DRCLAS program at Harvard and is curator of *The Hunger of My Heart* (2016–2017), an installation of Raúl Zurita's monumental poetry, which was on view in the offices of the David Rockefeller Center for Latin American Studies.

ROBERTO TEJADA (Ph.D., University at Buffalo, State University of New York) is the Hugh Roy and Lillie Cranz Cullen Distinguished Professor at the University of Houston, Texas. His multifaceted cultural studies and creative activities have been recognized with numerous fellowships and grants including awards from the National Endowment for the Arts, the Fulbright Foundation, The Creative Capital | Andy Warhol Foundation Arts Writers Grant Program, Armando Alvares Penteado Foundation, as well as the Clark Art Institute and the Oakley Center for the Humanities and Social Sciences, Williams College. He has taught at the National Autonomous University of Mexico (UNAM), Dartmouth College, University of California San Diego, University of Texas at Austin, Southern Methodist University Meadows School of the Arts, and the Milton Avery Graduate School of the Arts at Bard College. Tejada's research and creative interests involve the language arts and image worlds of Latin America, especially Mexico and Brazil, the US-Mexico borderlands, and other sites of US Latino cultural production. His scholarly books include *National Camera: Photography and Mexico's Image Environment* (2009, University of Minnesota Press) and *Modern Art in Africa, Asia, and Latin America: An Introduction to Global Modernisms* (2012, Wiley-Blackwell).

LYLE W. WILLIAMS (M.A., University of Texas at Austin) became the first dedicated curator of prints and drawings at the McNay Art Museum in San Antonio, Texas, in 1992. Prior to joining the McNay, he studied at the Yale University Art Gallery with Richard S. Field, curator emeritus of prints and drawings. Two of Williams's publications, *Estampas de la Raza: Contemporary Prints from the Romo Collection* (2012, University of Texas Press) and *Mexico and Modern Printmaking: A Revolution in the Graphic Arts 1920–1950* (2006, Yale University Press), have won the International Fine Print Dealers Association's book of the year award. He is the founding curator of the annual McNay Print Fair established in 1996.

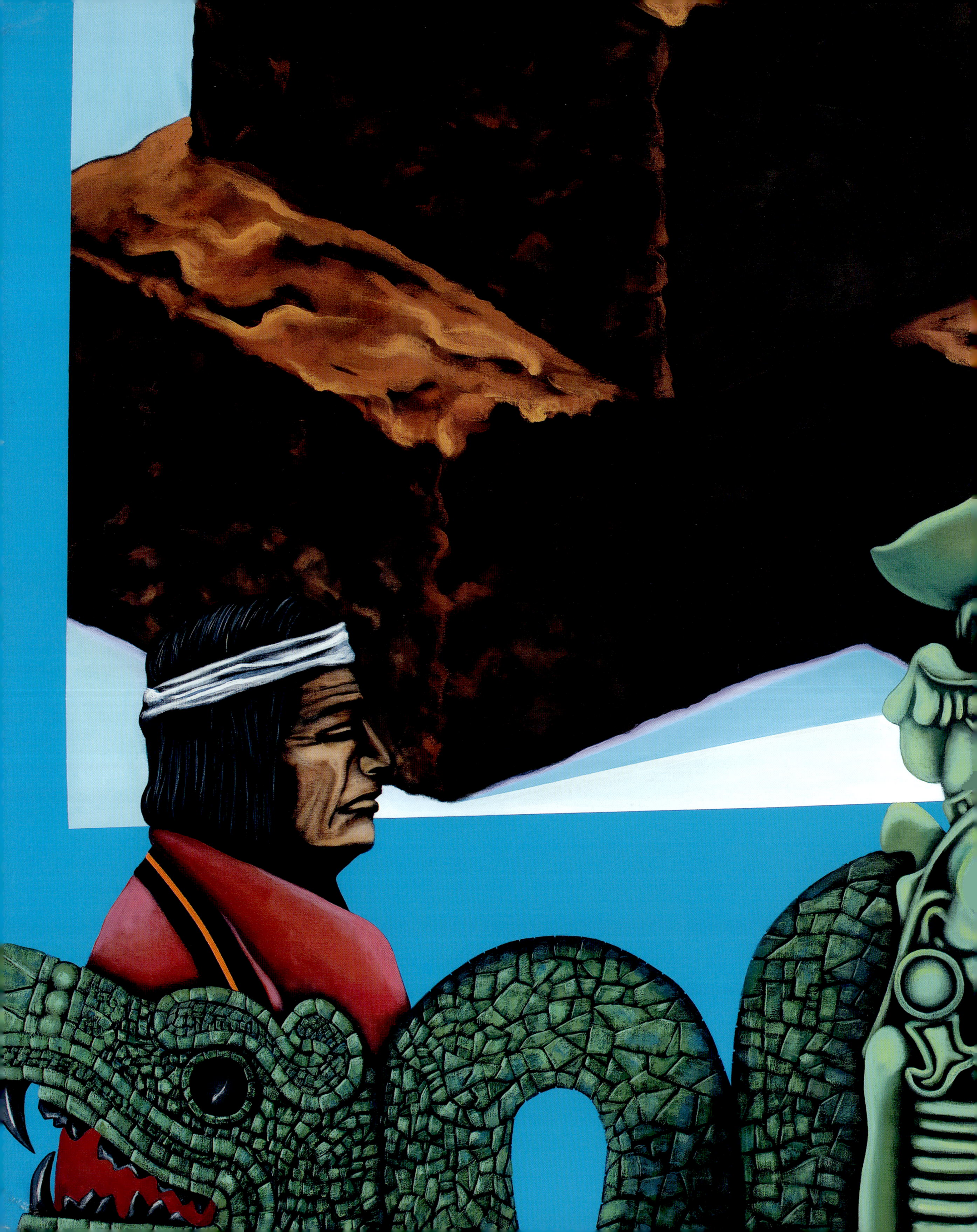

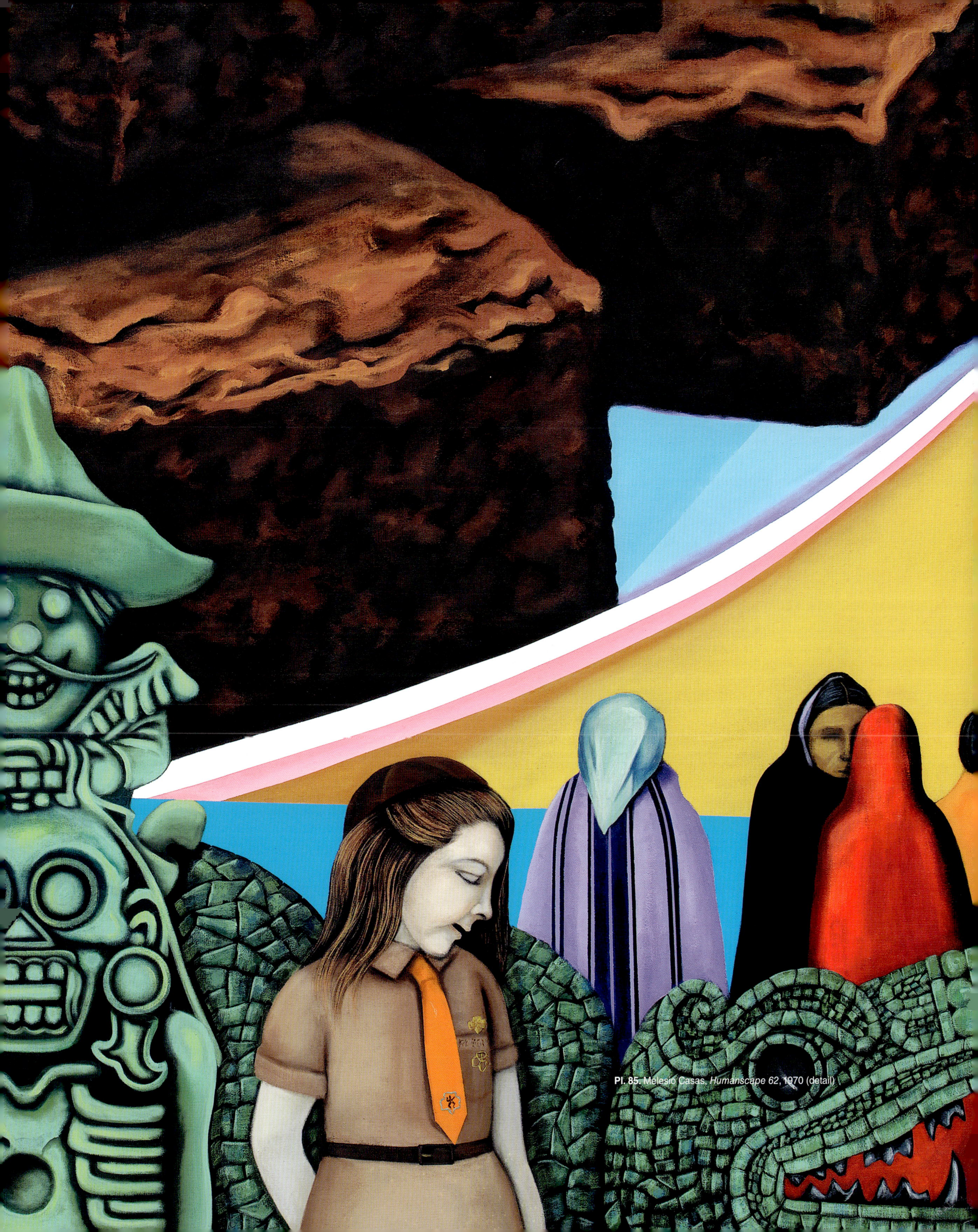

Pl. 85. Melesio Casas, *Humanscape 62*, 1970 (detail)

LÁZARO ABREU PADRÓN (DESIGNER), EMORY DOUGLAS (ARTIST), OSPAAAL (PUBLISHER)
Born in Havana, Cuba, 1940–2017
Born in Grand Rapids, Michigan, 1943–
Publisher in Havana, Cuba, active 1966–present

Solidarity with the African American People
(Solidaridad con el pueblo afro-norteamericano), 1968
Offset lithograph on paper
21.31 x 14 inches (54.1 x 35.6 cm)
Collection of the Prints and Photographs
Division, Library of Congress, Washington, DC
Gift of Gary Yanker, 1975–1983
PL. 72, P. 117

ANTÔNIO HENRIQUE AMARAL
Born in São Paulo, Brazil, 1935–2015

From the portfolio *O meu e o seu: impressões
de nosso tempo* (Mine and Yours: Impressions
of Our Time/Lo mío y lo tuyo: impresiones de
nuestros tiempos), 1967
Collection of Clayton C. Kirking and Edward
J. Sullivan

Bocas (Mouths)
Woodcut on paper, edition 238/300
27.56 x 23.62 inches (70 x 60 cm)
PL. 86, P. 148

Madona (Madonna)
Woodcut on paper, edition 238/300
27.56 x 23.62 inches (70 x 60 cm)
PL. 87, P. 148

o idolatrado (the idolized/el idolatrado)
Woodcut on paper, edition 238/300
27.56 x 23.62 inches (70 x 60 cm)
PL. 88, P. 149

Passatempo Séc. XX (20th-Century Hobby/
Pasatiempo siglo XX)
Woodcut on paper, edition 238/300
27.56 x 23.62 inches (70 x 60 cm)
PL. 89, P. 149

Personagem contemporâneo (Contemporary
Character/Personaje contemporáneo)
Woodcut on paper, edition 238/300
23.62 x 27.56 inches (60 x 70 cm)
PL. 90, P. 150

Realidades, culpas? (Realities, Remorses?)
Woodcut on paper, edition 238/300
23.62 x 27.56 inches (60 x 70 cm)
PL. 91, P. 150

Sem saída (No Way Out/Sin salida)
Woodcut on paper, edition 238/300
23.62 x 27.56 inches (60 x 70 cm)
PL. 92, P. 151

Um + um = dois? (One + One = Two?/
¿Uno + uno = dos?)
Woodcut on paper, edition 238/300
23.62 x 27.56 inches (60 x 70 cm)
PL. 93, P. 151

Battlefield 31 (Campo de batalla 31), 1974
Oil on canvas
36.02 x 48.03 inches (91.5 cm x 122 cm)
Collection of the Blanton Museum of Art,
the University of Texas at Austin
Archer M. Huntington Museum Fund, P1975.21.1
PL. 32, P. 69

ARTIST UNKNOWN/ARTISTA DESCONOCIDO
Mexico City, Mexico

From the series *Gráfica del '68* (Prints of '68), 1968
Collection of the Museo Universitario Arte
Contemporáneo (MUAC) de la Universidad
Nacional Autónoma de México (UNAM),
Mexico City, Mexico.

Todo es posible en la paz. Prensa vendida
(Everything is Possible in Peace. Sell-Out Press)
Linocut on paper
12 x 11.22 inches (30.5 x 28.5 cm)
Donated by Arnulfo Aquino, 2002; 08-780182
PL.60, P. 104

Caricatura, granadero a color (Caricature,
Grenadier in Color)
Screenprint on paper
13.18 x 8.46 inches (33.5 x 21.5 cm)
Donated by Arnulfo Aquino, 2002; 08-780242
PL. 59, P. 104

México '68 (ENAP, Cueto abajo) (Mexico '68
[ENAP, Down with Cueto])
Linocut on paper
5.11 x 27.55 inches (13 x 70 cm)
Donated by Arnulfo Aquino, 2002; 08-780088
PL. 58, P. 103

México '68 (granadero) (Mexico '68 [Grenadier])
Linocut on paper
4.72 x 27.55 inches (12 x 70 cm)
Donated by Arnulfo Aquino, 2002; 08-780089
PL. 57, P. 103

ASCO (HARRY GAMBOA, JR., GRONK, WILLIE F. HERRÓN III, PATSSI VALDEZ)
Art collective in Los Angeles, California, active
1972–1987

No Movie Award (Premio a la No-Película), 1975
Plaster with gold spray paint
17 x 10 x 10 inches (45.1 x 25.4 x 25.4 cm)
Collection of the UCLA Chicano Studies
Research Center, Los Angeles, California
The Gronk Papers
PL. 96, P. 155

JUDITH F. BACA
Born in Los Angeles, California, 1946–

Las tres Marías (The Three Marias), 1976
Colored pencil on paper mounted on panel
with upholstery backing and mirror
68.25 x 50.25 x 2.25 inches (173.36 x 127.64 x
5.72 cm), overall
Collection of the Smithsonian American Art
Museum, Washington, DC. Museum purchase
made possible by William T. Evans, 1998.162A–C
PL. 1, P. 29

GERALDO DE BARROS

Born in Chavantes, Brazil, 1923–1998

Diálogo (Dialogue), 1964
Acrylic, enamel, oil pastel, oil, and
newspaper on particle board
30.9 x 45.03 inches (78.5 x 114.4 cm)
Collection of Roger Wright on long-term
loan to the Pinacoteca do Estado de São
Paulo, Brazil, COM_CRW_031
PL. 79, P. 141

ANTONIO BERNI

Born in Rosario, Argentina, 1905–1981

Mediodía (Noontime), 1976
Acrylic and collage on canvas
78.22 x 78.34 inches (198.7 cm x 199 cm)
Collection of the Blanton Museum of Art,
the University of Texas at Austin
Barbara Duncan Fund, 1977.97
PL. 21, P. 63

ANTONIO CARO

Born in Bogota, Colombia, 1950–

Colombia Coca-Cola, 1976 (fabricated 2010)
Enamel on sheet metal, edition 11/25
19.5 x 27.5 x 1.13 inches (49.53 x 69.85 x 2.86 cm)
Collection of the MIT List Visual Arts Center,
Cambridge, Massachusetts. Purchased with funds
from the Alan May Endowment, CNS.2011.006
PL. 19, P. 61

MELESIO CASAS

Born in El Paso, Texas, 1929–2014

Humanscape 62 (Paisaje humano 62), 1970
Acrylic on canvas
73 x 97 inches (185.42 x 246.38 cm)
Collection of the Smithsonian American Art
Museum, Washington, DC. Museum purchase
through the Luisita L. and Franz H. Denghausen
Endowment, 2012.37
PL. 85, P. 147

EDUARDO COSTA

Born in Buenos Aires, Argentina, 1940–

Fashion Fiction I (Ficción de moda I), 1966–1970
24-karat gold wearable sculpture and photograph
(first published in *Vogue*, February 1, 1968; photo
by Richard Avedon and modeled by Maria Berenson)
2.55 x 1.57 x 0.59 inches (6.5 x 4 x 1.5 cm), ear
12 x 5 inches (30.5 x 24 cm), magazine
Courtesy of the artist (ear) and private
collection (magazine)
PL. 94, PP. 152-153

LUIS CRUZ AZACETA

Born in Havana, Cuba, 1942–

Ji Ji Ji Express, 1974–1975
Oil, canvas cutouts, and cardboard on canvas
70 x 45 inches (177.8 x 114.3 cm)
Courtesy of the artist and Arthur Rogers Gallery,
New Orleans, Louisiana
PL. 31, P. 68

ANTONIO DIAS

Born in Campina Grande, Brazil, 1944–

The Illustration of Art I (La ilustración
del arte I), 1971
Super 8mm transferred to video (color, silent)
4:12 minutes
Courtesy of the artist and Galeria Nara Roesler,
New York, New York, and Rio de Janeiro, Brazil
PL. 81, P. 143

*The Illustration of Art/Uncovering the
Cover-Up* (La ilustración del arte/Descubriendo
el encubrimiento), 1973
Screenprint and acrylic on canvas
35.82 x 53.54 inches (91 x 136 cm)
Courtesy of the artist and Galeria Nara Roesler,
New York, New York, and Rio de Janeiro, Brazil
PL. 80, P. 142

MARCOS DIMAS

Born in Cabo Rojo, Puerto Rico, 1943–

Lolita Lebrón, Puerto Rican Freedom Fighter (Lolita
Lebrón, luchadora por la libertad de Puerto Rico), 1971
Screenprint on paper
28.5 x 22.62 inches (72.4 x 57.46 cm)
Collection of El Museo del Barrio, New
York, New York, W91.1460
PL. 70, P. 115

FELIPE EHRENBERG

Born in Mexico City, Mexico, 1943–2017

Caja no. 25495 (Box no. 25495), 1968
Acrylic on wooden box with marbles
39.37 x 31.49 x 4.33 inches (100 x 80 x 11 cm)
Collection of the Museo Universitario Arte
Contemporáneo (MUAC) de la Universidad
Nacional Autónoma de México (UNAM),
Mexico City, Mexico, 08.851303
PL. 77, P. 139

No podemos ponerla (We Cannot Raise It), 1969
Acrylic on wooden box
23.42 x 31.49 x 2.16 inches (59.5 x 80 x 5.5 cm)
Collection of the Museo Universitario Arte
Contemporáneo (MUAC) de la Universidad
Nacional Autónoma de México (UNAM),
Mexico City, Mexico, 08.851301
PL. 78, P. 140

MARISOL ESCOBAR
(KNOWN AS MARISOL)

Born in Paris, France, 1930–2016

Saca la lengua (Stick Out Your Tongue) from the
portfolio *La paz* (Peace), 1972
Lithograph on paper, edition 24/150
41.25 x 29.25 inches (104.77 x 74.29 cm)
Collection of the McNay Art Museum, San Antonio,
Texas. Gift of Don and Lynn Watt, 1983.15.7
PL. 23, P. 65

Mi mamá y yo (My Mother and I), 1968
Steel and aluminum
79.75 x 56.5 x 55.75 inches
(202.56 x 143.51 x 141.6 cm)
Collection of Albright-Knox Art Gallery,
Buffalo, New York. Bequest of Marisol, 2016
PL. 99, P. 187

Hand and Purse (Mano y bolsa), 1965
Lithograph on paper, artist's proof
41.5 x 29.5 inches (105.4 x 74.9 cm)
Collection of the North Carolina Museum of Art,
Raleigh. Purchased with funds from the National
Endowment for the Arts and the North Carolina
State Art Society (Robert F. Phifer Bequest), G.73.7.5
PL. 43, P. 94

RUPERT GARCÍA
Born in French Camp, California, 1941–

Black Man and Flag (Hombre negro y bandera), 1967
Etching and collagraph on paper
21.65 x 23.18 inches (55.4 x 58.9 cm)
Collection of the Fine Arts Museums of San
Francisco, De Young, Legion of Honor Museum,
California. Gift of Mr. and Mrs. Robert Marcus,
1990.1.56
PL. 6, P. 34

Unfinished Man (Hombre inacabado), 1968
Acrylic on canvas
48.03 x 48.03 inches (122 x 122 cm)
Courtesy of the artist and Rena Bransten
Gallery, San Francisco, California
PL. 101, P. 189

Decay Dance (Danza de la decadencia), 1969
Screenprint on paper, artist's print
26.12 x 20.87 inches (66.4 x 50.9 cm)
Collection of the Fine Arts Museums of San
Francisco, De Young, Legion of Honor Museum,
California. Gift of Mr. and Mrs. Robert Marcus,
1990.1.67
PL. 20, P. 62

Maya, 1970
Screenprint on wove paper
24.05 x 17.95 inches (61.1 x 45.6 cm)
Collection of the Fine Arts Museums of San
Francisco, De Young, Legion of Honor Museum,
California. Gift of Mr. and Mrs. Robert Marcus,
1990.1.78
PL. 100, P. 188

RUBENS GERCHMAN
Born in Rio de Janeiro, Brazil, 1942–2008

Os superhomens (The Supermen/Los
superhombres), 1965
Acrylic on canvas
43.18 x 63 inches (109.7 x 160 cm)
Collection of Roger Wright on long-term
loan to the Pinacoteca do Estado de São
Paulo, Brazil, COM_CRW_134
PL. 83, P. 145

Caixa de origem (Origin Box/Caja de origen), 1966
Acrylic, canvas, wood, and sandblasted mirrored
glass on particle board
66.92 x 66.92 x 0.98 inches (170 x 170 x 2.5 cm)
Collection of Roger Wright on long-term loan
to the Pinacoteca do Estado de São Paulo, Brazil,
COM_CRW_132
PL. 106, P. 195

Lindonéia, a Gioconda do subúrbio (Lindonéia:
The Mona Lisa of the Slum/Lindonéia: La
Gioconda del suburbio), 1966–1968
Screenprint on paper
19.68 x 19.72 inches (50 x 50.1 cm)
Collection of Roger Wright on long-term loan
to the Pinacoteca do Estado de São Paulo,
Brazil, COM_CRW_137
PL. 105, P. 193

LUTE (FIGHT/LUCHA) from the series *Cartilha
no superlativo* (Primer in the Superlative/Cartilla
en superlativo), 1967 (fabricated 2018)
Formica on fiber board
68.89 x 220.47 x 27.55 inches (175 x 560 x 70 cm)
Courtesy of the Rubens Gerchman Institute,
Rio de Janeiro, Brazil
PL. 73, PP. 118-119

Tropicália ou panis et circencis (Tropicalia or Bread
and Circuses)/Tropicalia o pan y circos), 1968
Album cover, original pressing
12.59 x 12.59 inches (32 x 32 cm)
Collection of Marcelo Noah and Marina Bedran
PL. 82, P. 144

AR (AIR/AIRE) from the series *Cartilha no
superlativo* (Primer in the Superlative/
Cartilla en superlativo), c. 1972
Screenprint on paper, edition AP/68
24.37 x 18.25 inches (61.91 x 46.35 cm)
Collection of the Weatherspoon Art Museum,
the University of North Carolina at Greensboro
Museum purchase with funds from the Benefactors
Fund, 1973.1910.
PL. 74, P. 120

Triunfo hermético (Hermetic Triumph), 1972
35mm film transferred to video (color, sound)
12:00 minutes
Courtesy of the Rubens Gerchman Institute,
Rio de Janeiro, Brazil
PL. 16, PP. 40-41

EDGARDO GIMÉNEZ
Born in Santa Fe, Argentina, 1942–

Sin título (Fuera de caja) (Untitled [Out of
the Box]), 1970
Offset print on paper
14.75 x 22 inches (37.46 x 55.88 cm)
Private collection
PL. 47, P. 97

Las panteras, objetos (The Panthers,
Objects), 1966
Offset print on paper
13.75 x 23 inches (34.92 x 58.42 cm)
Private collection

PL. 48, P. 97

ALBERTO GIRONELLA
Born in Mexico City, Mexico, 1929–1999

Zapata con marca de ganado (Zapata
with Cattle Brand), 1972
Assemblage
39.37 x 31.49 inches (100 x 80 cm)
Collection of Emiliano Gironella Parra

PL. 75, P. 121

JOSÉ GÓMEZ FRESQUET
(KNOWN AS FRÉMEZ)
Born in Havana, Cuba, 1939–2007

Vietnam (La modela y la vietnamita)
(Vietnam [The Model and the Vietnamese
Woman]) from the series *Canción Americana*
(American Song), 1969
Lithograph on paper
18.06 x 23.37 inches (45.8 x 59.3 cm)
Collection of the Center for Cuban Studies,
New York, New York

PL. 42, P. 93

BEATRIZ GONZÁLEZ
Born in Bucaramanga, Colombia, 1938–

La muerte del justo (Death of the Just), 1973
Enamel on metal sheet mounted on metal furniture
47.24 x 70.86 x 35.43 inches (120 x 180 x 90 cm)
Collection of Diane and Bruce Halle

PL. 76, PP. 122-123

Lesa majestad (High Treason), 1974
Screenprint on BFK Rives paper, artist's proof
30.11 x 22.24 inches (76.5 x 56.5 cm)
Collection of the Blanton Museum of Art,
the University of Texas at Austin. Archer M.
Huntington Museum Fund, P.1976.13.2

PL. 84, P. 146

GRONK
Born in Los Angeles, California, 1954–

*Patssi Valdez Receiving No Movie Award for
Best Actress* (Patssi Valdez recibe el Premio a
la No-Película por mejor actriz), 1976
Chromogenic print
20 x 13 inches (50.8 x 33.02 cm)
Collection of the UCLA Chicano Studies Research
Center, Los Angeles, California
The Gronk Papers

PL. 97, P. 155

JUAN JOSÉ GURROLA
Born in Mexico City, Mexico, 1935–2007

From the series *Dom-Art*, 1966–1967
(fabricated 2018)
Courtesy of the Fundación Gurrola A.C. and
House of Gaga, Mexico City, Mexico, and
Los Angeles, California.

No tocar (Do Not Play)
Photographic slide
2 x 2 inches (5.08 x 5.08 cm)

PL. 30, P. 67

Familia Kool Aid (Kool Aid Family)
Photographic slide
2 x 2 inches (5.08 x 5.08 cm)

PL. 24, P. 66

Familia Sandwich (Sandwich Family)
Photographic slide
2 x 2 inches (5.08 x 5.08 cm)

PL. 25, P. 66

Familia Sandwich (Sandwich Family)
Photographic slide
2 x 2 inches (5.08 x 5.08 cm)

PL. 26, P. 66

Plano y anillo (Plan and Ring)
Photographic slide
2 x 2 inches (5.08 x 5.08 cm)

PL. 29, P. 67

Sin título (Untitled)
Photographic slide
2 x 2 inches (5.08 x 5.08 cm)

PL. 27, P. 67

Sin título (Untitled)
Photographic slide
2 x 2 inches (5.08 x 5.08 cm)

PL. 28, P. 67

2+8 en Pop (2+8 in Pop), c. 1965
Audio tape recording transferred to MP3
4:00 minutes
Courtesy of the Fundación Gurrola A.C. and
the Fonoteca Nacional, Mexico City, Mexico

PL. 107 (NOT PICTURED)

Museo Dinámico Dom (Dom Dynamic
Museum), 1967
Audio tape recording and sampling
transferred to MP3
5:55 minutes
Courtesy of the Fundación Gurrola A.C. and
the Fonoteca Nacional, Mexico City, Mexico

PL. 108 (NOT PICTURED)

EMILIO HERNÁNDEZ SAAVEDRA
Born in Huancayo, Peru, 1940–

Bang Bang, 1967
Latex paint on fabric
78.62 x 55 inches (200 x 140 cm)
Courtesy of the Private Archives of Emilio Hernández
Saavedra and Henrique Faria Fine Art, New York,
New York, and Buenos Aires, Argentina

PL. 35, P. 89

El museo de arte borrado (The Erased
Museum of Art), 1970 (printed 2016)
Inkjet printing on cotton Hahnemühle paper
(photo by Rag Baryta)
21.06 x 19.68 inches (53.5 x 50 cm)
Courtesy of the Private Archives of Emilio Hernández
Saavedra and Henrique Faria Fine Art, New York,
New York, and Buenos Aires, Argentina

PL. 41, P. 93

ROBERT INDIANA

Born in New Castle, Indiana, 1928–2018

Route 66 (Ruta 66), 1962
Oil on canvas
12.25 x 11.5 inches (31.11 x 29.21 cm)
Collection of the Weatherspoon Art Museum,
the University of North Carolina at Greensboro
Museum purchase with funds from the
Benefactors Fund, 1987.3913

PL. 4, P. 32

Study for *Viva HemisFair* poster (Estudio
para el cartel Viva HemisFair), 1967
Collage and graphite on board
60 x 40 inches (152.4 x 101.6 cm)
Collection of the Tobin Theatre Arts Fund, San
Antonio, Texas; 84.2007. Courtesy of the McNay
Art Museum, San Antonio, Texas

PL. 5, P. 33

CARLOS IRIZARRY

Born in Santa Isabel, Puerto Rico, 1938–

Moratorium (Moratoria), 1969
Screenprints on paper; edition 20/100, left
panel, and 18/100, right panel
22 x 30 inches (55.9 x 76.2 cm), left panel;
22.25 x 30 inches (56.5 x 76.2 cm), right panel
Collection of El Museo del Barrio, New York,
New York, W91.111, W91.432.15

PL. 66, P. 112

ROBERTO JACOBY

Born in Buenos Aires, Argentina, 1944–

*Un guerrillero no muere para que se lo
cuelgue en la pared* (A Guerrilla Doesn't
Die to Be Hung on a Wall), 1968
Screenprint on paper
14.96 x 10.43 inches (38 x 26.5 cm)
Private collection

PL. 65, P. 111

NELSON LEIRNER

Born in São Paulo, Brazil, 1932–

Stripencores (Stripincolors/Stripencolores), 1968
Fabric and zippers
62 x 26 inches (157 x 65 cm), 50 x 24 inches
(128 x 60 cm), 39 x 21.5 inches (100 x 54 cm),
and 31.5 x 20.5 inches (80 x 52 cm)
Courtesy of the artist and Silvia Cintra + Box 4
Gallery, Rio de Janeiro, Brazil

PL. 62, PP. 106-107

ROY LICHTENSTEIN

Born in New York City, New York, 1923–1997

Explosion (Explosión) from *Portfolio 9*, 1967
Lithograph on Rives paper, edition XII/XX
22.15 x 17.12 inches (56.2 x 43.5 cm)
Collection of Jonathan J. Prinz

PL. 2, P. 30

ANNA MARIA MAIOLINO

Born in Scalea, Italy, 1942–

Glu... Glu... Glu... (Gulp... Gulp... Gulp...), 1967
Woodcut on paper
24.48 x 16.88 inches (62.2 x 42.9 cm)
Collection of the Pinacoteca do Estado
de São Paulo, Brazil. Donated by the artist,
2007; PINA06807

PL. 22, P. 64

RAÚL MARTÍNEZ

Born in Ciego de Ávila, Cuba, 1927–1995

Che, 1968
Screenprint on paper
29.93 x 20.06 inches (76 x 51 cm)
Collection of the Ackland Art Museum, the
University of North Carolina at Chapel Hill
Gift of Dr. David L. Craven, 2008.43.4

PL. 63, P. 109

El Che y Camilo (Che [Guevara] and
Camilo [Cienfuegos]), 1968
Screenprint on paper
31 x 23 inches (79 x 58.5 cm)
Collection of the David M. Rubenstein Rare
Book & Manuscript Library, Duke University,
Durham, North Carolina. Bobbye S. Ortiz Papers;
1919–1993, folder 14 oversize

PL. 64, P. 110

Lucía, 1968
Screenprint on paper
29.87 x 20 inches (75.9 x 50.8 cm)
Collection of the Ackland Art Museum, the
University of North Carolina at Chapel Hill
Gift of Dr. David L. Craven, 2007.21.4

PL. 46, P. 96

El vaquero (Cowboy), c. 1969
Acrylic on black-and-white photograph
21.5 x 16.75 inches (54.61 x 42.54 cm)
Courtesy of the Shelley and Donald Rubin
Private collection

PL. 104, P. 192

Adán y Julieta (Adam and Juliet), 1973
Acrylic on canvas
84.37 x 60.25 inches (214.32 x 153.03 cm), overall
Pizzuti Collection, Columbus, Ohio

PL. 15, P. 39

CILDO MEIRELES
Born in Rio de Janeiro, Brazil, 1948–

Inserções em circuitos ideológicos: Projeto Coca-Cola (Insertions into Ideological Circuits: Coca-Cola Project/Inserciones en circuitos ideológicos: Proyecto Coca-Cola), 1970
Three glass Coca-Cola bottles, three metal caps, liquid, and vinyl-transfer text
9.25 x 2.33 x 2.33 inches (23.49 x 5.92 x 5.92 cm), each bottle
Private collection
PL. 17, P. 59

Zero cruzeiro (Cero cruceiro), 1974–1978
Photolithograph on paper
2.79 x 6.1 inches (7.1 x 15.5 cm)
Collection of the Blanton Museum of Art, the University of Texas at Austin
Gift of Paulo Figueiredo, 1982.180.1–2
PL. 33, P. 70

MARTA MINUJÍN
Born in Buenos Aires, Argentina, 1943–

Frac-asado (Grilled-Tuxedo), 1975
Mixed-media dress on stand and metal crown of thorns
62.5 inches (158.75 cm), overall
Estrellita B. Brodsky Collection
PL. 37, P. 91

El fracaso como mancha (Failure as a Stain), 1975
Archival document
9 x 8.7 inches (23 x 22 cm)
Estrellita B. Brodsky Collection
PL. 39, P. 92

Máximo galardón (Top Prize), 1975
Pencil on paper
20 x 17.5 inches (50.8 x 44.5 cm)
Estrellita B. Brodsky Collection
PL. 38, P. 92

Test ("A Son of Yours Fails Regularly in Something He Believe[s] In") (Un hijo tuyo fracasa regularmente en algo en lo que cree), 1975
Archival document
14 x 8.5 inches (35.5 x 21.5 cm)
Estrellita B. Brodsky Collection
PL. 40, P. 92

Test para situarse en el fracaso (Test to Situate Yourself in the Face of Failure), 1975
Archival documents
8.5 x 11 inches (21.59 x 27.94 cm)
Estrellita B. Brodsky Collection
PL. 36, P. 90

MARTA MINUJÍN AND RUBÉN SANTANTONÍN
Born in Buenos Aires, Argentina, 1943–
Born in Buenos Aires, Argentina, 1919– 1969

La Menesunda (Mayhem), 1965
16mm film transferred to video (black-and-white, sound); documented by Leopoldo Maler in collaboration with David Lamelas, Floreal Amor, Rodolfo Prayon, and Pablo Suárez
8.09 minutes
Courtesy of Marta Minujín Archives, Buenos Aires, Argentina
PL. 98, PP. 156-157

SERGIO MONDRAGÓN AND MARGARET RANDALL (EDITORS)
Born in Cuernavaca, Mexico, 1935
Born in New York City, New York, 1936

El Corno Emplumado (The Plumed Horn), April 1968 (issue no. 26)
Printed quarterly journal
7.68 x 5.5 inches (19.52 x 13.97 cm)
Private collection
PL. 68, P. 114

HÉLIO OITICICA
Born in Rio de Janeiro, Brazil, 1937–1980

Bandera-poema (Seja marginal, seja herói) (Flag Poem [Be an Outlaw, Be a Hero]/Bandera-poema [Sé marginal, sé un héroe]), 1968
Screenprint on fabric
44 x 32.06 inches (111.76 x 81.44 cm)
Private collection
PL. 67, P. 113

CLAES OLDENBURG
Born in Stockholm, Sweden, 1929–

Miniature Soft Drum Set (Juego de tambores suaves en miniatura), 1969 (completed 1970)
Screenprints on canvas with wood and rope, edition 58/200
9.75 x 19 x 13.75 inches (24.8 x 48.3 x 34.9 cm), dimensions variable
Collection of the McNay Art Museum, San Antonio, Texas
Gift of Robert L. B. Tobin, 1969.49
PL. 95, P. 154

DALILA PUZZOVIO
Born in Buenos Aires, Argentina, 1942–

Dalila doble plataforma (Dalila Double Platform), 1967
Ink and crayon on Fabriano paper with PVC additions and acetate paper on top
18.25 x 12 inches (46.35 x 30.48 cm)
Private collection
PL. 44, P. 95

Dalila doble plataforma (Dalila Double Platform), 1967
Pencil and crayon on paper
14.12 x 11.18 inches (35.87 x 28.41 cm)
Private collection
PL. 45, P. 95

HUGO RIVERA-SCOTT
Born in Viña del Mar, Chile, 1943–

Pop América, 1968
Collage on cardboard
30 x 21.5 inches (76.5 x 54.5 cm)
Courtesy of the artist
PL. 3, P. 31

ELENA SERRANO (ARTIST) AND OSPAAAL (PUBLISHER)
Born in Havana, Cuba, 1933–
Publisher in Havana, Cuba, active 1966–present

Día del guerrillero heroico (Day of the Heroic
Guerrilla), 1968
Offset lithograph on paper
19.5 x 13.56 inches (49.4 x 34.5 cm)
Collection of the Prints & Photographs Division,
Library of Congress, Washington, DC
Gift of Gary Yanker; 1975–1983, POS – Cuba,
no. 3 (C size) [P&P]
PL. 7, P. 35

DUGALD STERMER (EDITOR) AND MCGRAW-HILL BOOK COMPANY (PUBLISHER)
Born in Los Angeles, California, 1936–2011
Publisher in New York, New York, active
1909–present

The Art of Revolution: Castro's Cuba, 1959–1970
(El arte en la revolución: Cuba y Castro, 1959–
1970), 1970
Paperback book
17.5 x 13.25 inches (44.45 x 33.65 cm)
Collection of Duke University Libraries,
Durham, North Carolina, F1788 .S7 1970
PL. 69, P. 114

TALLER 4 ROJO (DIEGO ARANGO AND NIRMA ZÁRATE, FOUNDING MEMBERS)
Art collective in Colombia, active 1971–1974

Agresión del imperialismo (Aggression
of Imperialism), 1972
Screenprints on photographic paper
39.76 x 28.15 inches (101 x 71.5 cm), each panel
Collection of the Museo de Arte de la Universidad
Nacional de Colombia, Bogotá, OG.239–241
PL.34, P. 71

NICOLÁS GARCÍA URIBURU
Born in Buenos Aires, Argentina, 1937–2016

La pantera roja (The Red Panther), 1969
Oil on canvas
39.5 x 50.75 inches (100 x 129 cm)
Private collection
PL. 14, P. 38

From the portfolio *Manifiesto* (Manifesto), 1973
Portfolio of six screenprints on paper, edition 96/111
30 x 22.25 inches (76.2 x 56.5 cm)
Collection of El Museo del Barrio, New York,
New York

1970: Intercontinental Environment of the Waters
(1970: Ambiente intercontinental de las aguas)
Gift of Margarita J. Aguilar, 2008.40.1.4
PL. 10, P. 37

Artist's Statement (Declaración del artista)
Gift of Margarita J. Aguilar, 2008.40.1.2
PL. 8, P. 36

June 19, 1968, First Green Venice (19 de
junio de 1968, primera Venecia verde)
Gift of Margarita J. Aguilar, 2008.40.1.3
PL. 9, P. 36

*Latinoamérica: Reservas naturales del futuro,
unida o sometida* (Latin America: Natural
Resources of the Future, United or Repressed)
Gift of Margarita J. Aguilar, 2008.40.1.7
PL. 13, P. 37

Sex Coloration, New York, October 1971 (Coloración
de sexo, Nueva York, Octubre de 1971)
Gift of Margarita J. Aguilar, 2008.40.1.5
PL. 11, P. 37

*Vertical Project: Green Coloration, Iguazú
Falls, Argentina* (Proyecto vertical: Coloración
verde, cataratas del Iguazú, Argentina)
Gift of Margarita J. Aguilar, 2008.40.1.6
PL. 12, P. 37

JORGE DE LA VEGA
Born in Buenos Aires, Argentina, 1930–1971

Go, Go, Go (Ve, ve, ve), 1967
Acrylic and collage on canvas
77 x 64.17 inches (195.6 x 163 cm)
Collection of the Blanton Museum of Art, the
University of Texas at Austin. Gift of Gunther
Oppenheim, G1975.36.1
PL. 103, P. 191

ANDY WARHOL
Born in Pittsburgh, Pennsylvania, 1928–1987

Birmingham Race Riot (Disturbio racial en
Birmingham) from the portfolio *X+X (Ten
Works by Ten Painters)* (X+X [Diez obras
de diez pintores]), 1964
Screenprint on wove paper
20 x 24 inches (50.8 x 60.96 cm)
Collection of the Amon Carter Museum of
American Art, Fort Worth, Texas. Gift of Edith
G. Halpert, 1967.49.4
PL. 71, P. 116

Campbell's Soup I (Tomato)
(Sopa Campbell's I [Tomate]), 1968
Screenprint on paper
35.06 x 23.18 inches (89.1 x 58.9 cm)
Collection of the Nasher Museum of Art
at Duke University, Durham, North Carolina
Gift of the Andy Warhol Foundation for the
Visual Arts, Inc.; 2013.9.3
PL. 18, P. 60

Mao, 1972
Screenprint on paper
36 x 36 inches (91.44 x 91.44 cm)
Collection of the Nasher Museum of Art at
Duke University, Durham, North Carolina
Museum purchase, 2000.9.1
PL. 102, P. 190

LANCE WYMAN
Born in Newark, New Jersey, 1937–

Logotype color proof for Olympic newsletter
masthead (Prueba de color para logotipo de la
cabecera del boletín olímpico), 1967
Offset print on paper
8 x 11.87 inches (20.32 x 30.16 cm)
Courtesy of the artist
PL. 56, P. 102

LANCE WYMAN, EDUARDO TERRAZAS, PEDRO RAMÍREZ VÁZQUEZ, AND THE DEPARTMENT OF PUBLICATIONS AND URBAN DESIGN OF THE ORGANIZING COMMITTEE OF THE XIX OLYMPIAD
Born in Newark, New Jersey, 1937–
Born in Guadalajara, Mexico, 1936–
Born in Mexico City, Mexico, 1919–2013

MEXICO '68, 1967
Offset lithograph on paper
33.87 x 34.12 inches (86.04 x 86.67 cm)
Private collection
PL. 50, P. 99

LANCE WYMAN
Born in Newark, New Jersey, 1937–

Third pre-Olympic postal issue (Tercera emisión
de sellos postales pre-Olimpiadas), 1967
Courtesy of the artist

Basketball (Baloncesto), 1967
Postage stamps
10.25 x 8.68 inches (26.03 x 22.06 cm)
PL. 51, P. 100

Cycling (Ciclismo), 1967
Postage stamps
10.25 x 8.68 inches (26.03 x 22.06 cm)
PL. 52, P. 101

Diving (Clavado), 1967
Postage stamps
10.25 x 8.68 inches (26.03 x 22.06 cm)
PL. 53, P. 101

Field hockey (Hockey sobre hierba), 1967
Postage stamps
10.25 x 8.68 inches (26.03 x 22.06 cm)
PL. 54, P. 101

Rowing (Remo), 1967
Postage stamps
10.25 x 8.68 inches (26.03 x 22.06 cm)
PL. 55, P. 101

LANCE WYMAN AND JULIA JOHNSON-MARSHALL
Born in Newark, New Jersey, 1937–
Born in England, 1943–

Hostess dress and cape from the XIX Olympics
(Vestido y capa de edecán para los XIX Juegos
Olímpicos), 1968
Screenprinted polyester knit (jersey) and cotton twill
31.25 inches (79.38 cm) center back length, dress;
24.5 inches (62.23 cm) center back length, cape
Collection of the Los Angeles County Museum
of Art, California
Purchased with funds provided by the Bernard
and Edith Lewin Deaccession Fund, M.2015.123a–b
PL. 61, P. 105

LANCE WYMAN AND JAN STORNFELT
Born in Newark, New Jersey, 1937–
Born in unknown location, 1944–

Image of an Aztec calendar made from
Olympic sport and cultural event icons
(Imagen de un calendario azteca hecho con
íconos de eventos deportivos y culturales
de los Juegos Olímpicos), 1968
Offset lithograph on paper
23.5 x 23.5 inches (59.69 x 59.69 cm)
Courtesy of Lance Wyman
PL. 49, P. 98

LENDERS TO THE EXHIBITION

Ackland Art Museum, the University of North Carolina at Chapel Hill
Albright-Knox Art Gallery
Amon Carter Museum of American Art
Arthur Rogers Gallery
The Artists
Blanton Museum of Art, the University of Texas at Austin
Center for Cuban Studies
David M. Rubenstein Rare Book & Manuscript Library, Duke University
Duke University Libraries
Fine Arts Museums of San Francisco, De Young, Legion of Honor Museum
Fonoteca Nacional
Fundación Gurrola A.C.
Galeria Nara Roesler
Emiliano Gironella Parra
Estrellita B. Brodsky Collection
Diane and Bruce Halle
Henrique Faria Fine Art
House of Gaga
Clayton C. Kirking and Edward J. Sullivan
Los Angeles County Museum of Art
Marta Minujín Archives
McNay Art Museum
MIT List Visual Arts Center
Museo de Arte de la Universidad Nacional de Colombia
El Museo del Barrio
Museo Universitario Arte Contemporáneo (MUAC) de la Universidad
Nacional Autónoma de México (UNAM)
Nasher Museum of Art at Duke University
Marcelo Noah and Marina Bedran
North Carolina Museum of Art
Pinacoteca do Estado de São Paulo
Pizzuti Collection
Prints and Photographs Division, Library of Congress
Jonathan J. Prinz
Private Collections
Rena Bransten Gallery
Rubens Gerchman Institute
Shelley and Donald Rubin Private Collection
Silvia Cintra + Box 4 Gallery
Smithsonian American Art Museum
Tobin Theatre Arts Fund
UCLA Chicano Studies Research Center
Weatherspoon Art Museum, the University of North Carolina at Greensboro
Roger Wright

POP AMÉRICA

1965-1975